KARL MARX
FREDERICK ENGELS

Volume 40

MARX AND ENGELS: 1856-59

INTERNATIONAL PUBLISHERS
NEW YORK

This volume has been prepared jointly by Lawrence & Wishart Ltd., London, International Publishers Co. Inc., New York, and Progress Publishers, Moscow, in collaboration with the Institute of Marxism-Leninism, Moscow.

Library of Congress Cataloging in Publication Data

Marx, Karl, 1818-1883.

Karl Marx, Frederick Engels: collected works.

1. Socialism—Collected works. 2. Economics—Collected works. I. Engels, Friedrich, 1820-1895. Works. English. 1975. II. Title.
HX39.5.A 16 1975 335.4 73-84671
ISBN 0-7178-0540-9 (v. 40)

Printed in the Union of Soviet Socialist Republics

Contents

KARL MARX AND FREDERICK ENGELS

LETTERS

January 1856-December 1859

1856

1858

APPENDIX

NOTES AND INDEXES

ILLUSTRATIONS

Translated by

PETER and BETTY ROSS

Preface

Volume 40 of this edition contains the correspondence of Marx and Engels from 1856 to 1859. The latter half of the 1850s rounded off the period of political reaction that had set in in Europe after the Revolution of 1848-49. The first capitalist world economic crisis (1857-58) heralded a new rise of the democratic and working-class movements.

During these years, Marx and Engels continued to develop their revolutionary teaching. They set out to arm the proletarian party, then in the process of formation, with the theory for the forthcoming battles. 'I hope to win a scientific victory for our party,' Marx wrote to his friend Joseph Weydemeyer on 1 February 1859 concerning the main goal he had set himself in his economic research (this volume, p. 377).

The letters in this volume reflect the further development of Marxist theory, of its three component parts—political economy, philosophy and the theory of the communist transformation of society—and the advance of Marxist thought in various other fields. They give an idea of the progress Marx was making in his economic studies. In 1857, he began to collate and sum up the vast material on political economy he had accumulated over many years. In 1857 and 1858, he wrote a series of economic manuscripts which form the first rough draft of *Capital.* In these manuscripts Marx worked out the theory of money in general terms and outlined his theory of surplus value, which Engels called Marx's second great discovery, the first being the materialist conception of history. These two discoveries turned socialism into a science.

The letters show what titanic labours these manuscripts cost him. The economic crisis, and the certainty that it would be followed by profound revolutionary upheavals, made him hasten the work in every way. 'I am working like mad all night and every night collating my economic studies so that I at least get the outlines clear before the *déluge*,' he wrote to Engels on 8 December 1857 (p. 217). The correspondence shows that Marx made very great demands on himself as a scholar. Grudging in his judgments of his own achievements, he wrote to Engels with satisfaction on 16 January 1858: 'I had been overdoing very much my nocturnal labours.... I am, by the way, discovering some nice arguments. E.g. I have completely demolished the theory of profit' (p. 249).

The Economic Manuscripts of 1857-58, also known as the *Grundrisse der Kritik der Politischen Ökonomie* (they will be found, together with *A Contribution to the Critique of Political Economy. Part One,* 1859, in Vols. 29 and 30), testify that in his economic works too Marx was enriching other areas of social science, especially philosophy, and was also perfecting his method of research into social phenomena. Marx attached great importance to dialectics, reinterpreted in the materialist spirit on the basis of a critical understanding of Hegel's philosophy. Marx even had the intention, which he unfortunately never carried out, of writing a book on this subject. 'If ever the time comes when such work is again possible, I should very much like to write 2 or 3 sheets making accessible to the common reader the *rational* aspect of the method which Hegel not only discovered but also mystified' (p. 249).

As Marx built up his new economic theory, he was also developing the structure of his future economic work. The letters give us an idea of the scope and comprehensive nature of the work he planned, which was to cover the economic foundations and political superstructure of the capitalist system. His letters to Ferdinand Lassalle of 22 February and to Engels of 2 April 1858, and also the letter to Joseph Weydemeyer of 1 February 1859, show that Marx intended to publish the work in six books: 1) On Capital, 2) On Landed Property, 3) On Wage Labour, 4) On the State, 5) International Trade, 6) World Market (p. 270). Even while the first book was being written, some changes had to be made in this plan. Marx was unable to fit in all the material, so he decided to divide it into two parts, the first on the commodity and money, the second specifically on capital (the production of surplus value, etc.).

A Contribution to the Critique of Political Economy. Part One, which came off the press on 11 June 1859, was a major event in the history of economic thought. Although, because of its limited range, the book could not include Marx's fundamental work on the theory of surplus value, it did contain the scientific prerequisites for it in the shape of a new theory of money and value. As can be seen from the letters, Marx considered it extremely important to popularise this work. The first successful attempt in this direction was undertaken by Engels, whose review is mentioned in the correspondence.

Marx began work on the second part shortly after sending the manuscript of the first to the publishers (Marx to Engels, 21 February 1859). However, he soon realised that he would need to do more research on a number of important aspects of surplus value and its transmuted forms (profit, interest and rent). The work dragged on and grew beyond the limits initially marked out for it. Furthermore, as the letters of 1859 show, Marx repeatedly had to break off in order to attend to urgent practical matters (the publication of the newspaper *Das Volk*, etc.). Subsequent letters give an idea of the further stages in his work.

Marx kept Engels constantly informed of the progress and results of his economic research. Engels readily helped him with advice, gave freely of the knowledge and experience he had acquired in long commercial practice, and supplied Marx with valuable material.

The correspondence published in this volume also gives some idea of Marx's and Engels' work in other fields of knowledge during this period, and of the variety and scope of their interests. They exchanged opinions on world history, the history of diplomacy, the history of various countries and peoples (among them Russia, Prussia and Poland), philology (especially in connection with Engels' study of the Slavonic languages), world literature, the natural sciences, and so on.

Prominent in Engels' work of the 1850s and early 1860s were studies in military history and the theory of warfare, for he was aware of the importance to proletarian revolutionaries of mastering military knowledge for the expected new outburst of revolutionary struggle. On 15 November 1857, Engels wrote to Marx that, should another revolution break out in Europe following the economic crisis, this would at once give 'a more practical slant' to his military studies (pp. 203-04).

Engels continued to publish reviews of current military events in periodicals, and also wrote a series of articles on the art of war and military history for *The New American Cyclopaedia* (see present edition, Vol. 18). The letters in this volume show that he did this in close cooperation with Marx. The two friends helped one another in finding sources and selecting material, and some of the articles for the *Cyclopaedia* were, in effect, written by them jointly. Besides doing all the articles on specifically military problems, Engels constantly helped Marx by handling the military questions in the articles that Marx wrote for the *Cyclopaedia*, especially in the biographical essays on military and political leaders (Barclay de Tolly, Bem, Blücher and others). Marx used some of Engels' letters (pp. 163-64, 166-68, 178-80) as preliminary drafts of articles. For his part, Marx looked up references for Engels in the British Museum Library and copied out extracts from various sources.

Engels' articles for *The New American Cyclopaedia*, especially on general subjects, such as 'Army', 'Artillery', 'Cavalry', 'Fortification' and 'Infantry', were an important contribution to Marxist military science. Marx believed that in them Engels had given further proof of the universal relevance of the materialist conception of history. 'Your "Army" is capital,' he wrote to Engels on 25 September 1857. 'More graphically than anything else the history of the *army* demonstrates the rightness of our views as to the connection between the productive forces and social relations' (p. 186). He also praised Engels' other articles (see, for example, his letters to Engels of 10 June and 10 October 1859).

Marx valued his friend's ability to discuss questions of military history in the context of the political tasks that faced the proletarian revolutionaries, and to substantiate revolutionary tactics militarily. A case in point is Engels' pamphlet *Po and Rhine* (1859), in which military analysis serves to prove the need for a proletarian approach to the problem of Italy's unification, as well as to denounce the policies of the French Bonapartists and the Prussian and Austrian ruling circles. 'Have read it all; exceedingly clever; the political side is also splendidly done and that was damned difficult,' Marx wrote to Engels after he had gone over the pamphlet (p. 400).

Observing the spectacular development of the natural sciences in the mid-19th century, Marx and Engels considered it essential to interpret the latest scientific achievements in the light of their revolutionary world outlook. They regarded progress in these fields as expanding the scientific basis of their theories.

Engels' letter to Marx of 14 July 1858, containing an extensive programme for the study of the latest findings of science, shows that Engels had already conceived the idea of giving a philosophical generalisation, from a dialectical materialist position, of the development of physics, chemistry, biology and the other sciences, which he eventually realised in his *Dialectics of Nature.*

Engels was one of the first to grasp the enormous significance of Darwin's theory of evolution. He read *On the Origin of Species by Means of Natural Selection* in 1859, when the book was published, and wrote to Marx as follows: 'Darwin ... whom I'm reading just now, is absolutely splendid. There was one aspect of teleology that had yet to be demolished, and that has now been done. Never before has so grandiose an attempt been made to demonstrate historical evolution in Nature, and certainly never to such good effect' (p. 551).

In the years covered by this volume, political journalism remained for Marx and Engels their most important means of disseminating revolutionary ideas, and substantiating proletarian revolutionary tactics on crucial social and political problems. The correspondence reflects their intensive journalistic activities during this period. In many letters they discuss the contents of articles for the *New-York Daily Tribune* and other periodicals. Economic processes in the capitalist world were increasingly attracting their attention. Observing the rapid growth of capitalist production, Marx compared the 1850s with the dawn of the capitalist era, which was marked by abrupt changes in economic and social relations. 'There is no denying that bourgeois society has for the second time experienced its 16th century,' he wrote to Engels on 8 October 1858 (p. 346). Marx and Engels also saw the reverse side of the rise of the capitalist economy: the deepening of its inherent contradictions and the inevitability of periodic economic crises. In many letters they pointed to the world-wide scale of the 1857 crisis and noted the gradual involvement of different countries in it, its spread to various spheres of the economy, and the grave effect it had on the position of the masses. Apart from the series of articles on the crisis published in the *New-York Daily Tribune,* Marx intended to write, jointly with Engels, a pamphlet on the subject (Marx to Engels, 18 December 1857). However, the plan did not materialise.

Marx and Engels followed current events very closely, especially the social and political shifts caused by the 1857 crisis. Although it did not lead directly to revolutionary upheavals, its revolutionising effect on society was very considerable. 'Taken all in all, the crisis has been burrowing away like the good old mole it is,' Marx wrote to Engels on 22 February 1858 (p. 274).

Marx and Engels considered it highly important that the 1857 crisis should have hit industry and finance in England, the most economically developed country in the capitalist world of that time. In a letter to Engels dated 8 December 1857 Marx pointed out that despite all the attempts by bourgeois economists and political writers to represent England's economy as stable and invulnerable, catastrophe had descended on this citadel of capitalism (p. 215). The economic upheaval in England was aggravating its internal situation and intensifying the dissatisfaction of the masses with the obsolete oligarchic system. As can be seen from the letters, Marx and Engels did not rule out the possibility that the economic crisis might give rise to violent political conflicts and demonstrations against the ruling class by broad social sections, especially the proletariat. As a result, England might be drawn into revolutionary events should they occur again in Continental Europe. As early as 31 March 1857, when the first symptoms of the economic difficulties appeared, Marx wrote to Engels: 'England is entering upon a *sérieuse* crisis ... and if the move is resumed on the Continent, John Bull will not maintain the stance of supercilious detachment he adopted in 1848' (p. 113).

The economic crisis had an even greater effect on France. The entrepreneurial fever prevalent in the Second Empire, the unbridled Stock Exchange speculation, the corruption at all levels of the state machinery, and the predatory policy of the banks, such as the Crédit mobilier, resulted in the economic crisis being particularly destructive. Marx wrote to Engels on 18 December 1857 about 'the general rottenness of the bankrupt State' (p. 225). Marx and Engels held that during the economic crisis Napoleon III's empire had taken yet another step towards its inevitable collapse, as was manifest, particularly, in the growing anti-Bonapartist mood everywhere. In a letter to Marx on 17 March 1858, Engels pointed to the ferment among the Paris workers, who openly displayed their republican convictions and their sympathies for Orsini, the Italian patriot executed for an attempt to assassinate Louis Napoleon. Deportations and arrests, he wrote, had borne as little fruit as the workers' settlements and the national workshops. The government's police measures and attempts to pose as a patron of the working class were unable to arrest the growing movement against the Bonapartist dictatorship (p. 289).

Developments in Germany, which were also considerably influenced by the crisis, seemed to give an indication of the changes that were in the offing. Marx and Engels were particularly interested in the position of Prussia. In their opinion, the virtual restoration of absolutism there after the Revolution of 1848-49, an absolutism only scantily veiled by pseudo-constitutional institutions, had been a consequence of the German bourgeoisie's cowardly half-measures. In the 1850s, too, the bourgeoisie, with its constitutional-monarchy illusions and its fear of the masses, continued to display a timid circumspection. 'The bourgeois and philistines have, at any rate, got even worse since 1848,' Engels wrote to Marx on 17 March 1858. '...Plainly your good, honest German has not yet emerged from the hibernation that followed the strenuous exertions of 1848' (p. 292). However, the rapid growth of industry and trade, which Marx and Engels noted in their letters more than once, was deepening the conflict between the demands of economic and social development and the semi-feudal political system and making the fragmentation of the country more and more intolerable. In Prussia and the other German states all this was sowing the seeds of further conflict between the forces of progress and reaction.

In their letters of 1858 and subsequent years, Marx and Engels noted that Russia was becoming one of the hotbeds of revolutionary ferment in Europe. The crisis of the feudal serf system, aggravated by defeat in the 1853-56 Crimean War, and growing peasant unrest which drove the ruling circles to look for a solution in peasant reform, were seen by Marx and Engels as evidence that major revolutionary events were imminent in Russia. In a letter to Engels on 29 April 1858, Marx expressed the hope that should such events take place, the Tsarist autocracy's position would be undermined both within the country and internationally. 'The movement for the emancipation of the serfs in Russia strikes me as important in so far as it indicates the beginning of an internal development that might run counter to the country's traditional foreign policy' (p. 310).

The ideologists of the working class were coming round to the idea that a revolutionary Russia was arising in opposition to the Tsarist autocracy—the revolutionary movement's worst enemy—and they welcomed it as a powerful force for social progress and as a major factor in the struggle for the revolutionary renewal of the whole of Europe.

Events in the colonies were a further important topic of the correspondence. In the 1850s, Marx and Engels repeatedly denounced the capitalist colonial system in the press. Aware of the importance of working out a programme on the national and colonial question, and of the need to define the attitude of the working class to the national liberation movement of the oppressed peoples, Marx and Engels unmasked the policy of colonial expansion, to which more and more Asian and African countries were falling victim, and the savage rule of the capitalist 'mother countries' in the colonies.

Engels' letter to Marx of 23 May 1856 in which, from personal knowledge, he describes the consequences of the English landlords' and bourgeoisie's domination in Ireland is a powerful expression of his views. He wrote that the country had been utterly ruined by wars of conquest, by punitive police measures and by the ruthless exploitation of the working people. '...Through systematic oppression,' Engels wrote, the Irish 'have come to be a completely wretched nation...' (p. 50). The famine of 1845-47, the mass emigration which completely depopulated the country, and the landowners' transition to large-scale sheep-breeding, accompanied by the expulsion of small tenant farmers (the 'clearances'), were an appalling tragedy for the Irish masses. Ireland had been reduced to an agrarian adjunct of capitalist England. Engels wrote that 'Ireland may be regarded as the earliest English colony and one which, by reason of her proximity, is still governed in exactly the same old way; here one cannot fail to notice that the English citizen's so-called freedom is based on the oppression of the colonies' (p. 49).

Marx and Engels witnessed a series of new colonial wars unleashed by the ruling classes of West European countries: the Anglo-Persian war of 1856-57, the Anglo-Franco-Chinese war of 1856-60, the Spanish-Moroccan war of 1859-60. In their letters they characterised these as wars of annexation and plunder. Engels called the British government's colonial actions 'military ventures' (p. 115). Marx gives similar descriptions (see his letters to Engels of 24 March and 22 May 1857).

The correspondence gives an idea of the sympathy with which Marx and Engels followed the development of the mass struggle against foreign oppression in the colonies and dependent countries. They showed particular interest in the great popular uprising of 1857-59 in India, which shook English rule there, and made references to it in many of their letters (Marx to Engels, 6 and 14 July, 23 September, 20 October 1857 and 14 January 1858; Engels to Marx, 24 September and 29 October 1857). In the uprising, started by the sepoys in the Bengal army, Marx and Engels saw indications of a true national liberation struggle, a sign of mounting resistance to the colonialists by the oppressed peoples. Although the insurgents were defeated, Marx and Engels regarded their action as a portent of the future collapse of colonialism under the blows of the anti-colonial movement.

The Indian uprising convinced Marx of the correctness of his earlier conclusion that the national liberation movement and the proletariat's struggle against the capitalist system were closely interlinked. The blows dealt to capitalism in the colonies were shaking its position at home and making it more difficult for capitalism to use colonial resources for strengthening its domination, and facilitating the triumph of the proletarian revolution. 'In view of the drain of men and bullion which she will cost the English, India is now our best ally,' Marx wrote to Engels on 16 January 1858 (p. 249).

As in the preceding years, Marx and Engels devoted much attention in their letters to a wide range of problems concerning the foreign policies pursued by the ruling classes of the European powers and the history of diplomacy. In assessing the international situation after the Crimean War of 1853-56, Marx and Engels found it fraught with new complications and wars. They saw the Bonapartist Second Empire as the main source of military danger. Its rulers combined adventurism and ambitions for conquest with blatant demagogy in the national question, their purpose being to exploit the national movements in the interests of Bonapartist France. The proletarian revolutionaries regarded the denunciation of this 'most repulsive combination of Bonapartism and drivel about nationalities' (Marx to Lassalle, 22 November 1859) as one of their main tasks (p. 537).

This became particularly urgent in view of the war of France and Piedmont against Austria, which broke out in April 1859. The interference of Napoleon III in Italian affairs was motivated by the desire to avert a revolutionary explosion on the Apennine Peninsula, to strengthen the Second Empire's hegemony in Europe and, by external successes, to consolidate the shaky Bonapartist regime in France itself. The Piedmontese liberal-monarchist circles were acting in alliance with the Bonapartists, with whose aid they were trying to unify Italy under the House of Savoy, which ruled Piedmont (see Marx's letter to Lassalle of 4 February 1859). At the same time, the war against the Austrian monarchy, Italy's age-old oppressor, was welcomed by patriotic forces as a signal for the liberation struggle. Popular uprisings occurred in a number of Italian states. This drove Napoleon III to conclude a hasty peace with the Austrians, which Marx and Engels described as discreditable (see Engels' letter to Marx of 15 July 1859). As a result, Italy remained fragmented.

As can be seen from their letters, Marx and Engels considered it essential to show that French Bonapartism was as big a barrier to the national liberation and unification of Italy as the Austrian Empire, that the Bonapartist regime was a threat to all progressive forces in Europe, and that it was, in particular, an obstacle to a united Germany.

During the Italian crisis, when even democrats in Europe had fallen for Bonapartist propaganda and 'the confusion presently reigning in men's minds has reached a curious peak' (p. 436), Marx and Engels worked out clear-cut tactics to turn what was on both sides a dynastic war of annexation into a revolutionary war of liberation by the Italian and German peoples. They elaborated their views on the war in a number of writings published at the time (see, for example, Engels' *Po and Rhine* and Marx's 'On Italian Unity' in Vol. 16 of the present edition). The main points were also elucidated in the letters included in this volume.

Marx and Engels held that both Italy and Germany should be united 'from below', by revolutionary action on the part of the masses, and regarded the defeat of Bonapartism—the main opponent of a democratic solution to the Italian and German national problems—as the most urgent task. Hence the states in the German Confederation should not remain neutral; they should come out against Bonapartist France. According to Marx and Engels, this was in no way tantamount to supporting Austria. In their opinion, a war for the German people's national interests was bound to assume a revolutionary character and therefore contribute to the liberation of Italy, and rouse the revolutionary forces in other European countries, including France. Disclosing the essence of this tactic, Marx wrote to Engels on 6 May 1859 that it was absolutely essential that the proletarian revolutionaries 'do not identify' their cause 'with that of the present German governments' (p. 431). They should strive for a development of events that would lead to an all-European revolution, and it was particularly important that things should 'come to a head in Paris' (p. 430). The ideas on the 1859 Italian crisis contained in the letters of Marx and Engels hold an important place in the tactical arsenal of proletarian parties.

This volume also throws light on the efforts of Marx and Engels to create a proletarian party. They were above all concerned with the ideological education of their followers and comrades-in-arms, the proletarian revolutionaries who had been members of the

Communist League and who were to form the nucleus of the future party. Without predetermining its organisational structure, for they believed that this must depend on the actual conditions in which the working-class movement developed, Marx and Engels were working both to rally the proletarian forces internationally and, wherever possible, to unite the working class on a national scale. They thought it vital to strengthen the ties among the working-class leaders of various countries and, as can be seen from their correspondence, did everything to this end.

German workers and intellectuals wrote to Marx, seeking his advice on tactical matters. Thus, in the spring of 1856, he was approached from Germany by Johannes Miquel, a former member of the Communist League (Marx to Engels, 26 April and 7 May 1856). At the end of February that year, Gustav Levy visited Marx with a message from the workers of Düsseldorf, and Marx explained the need for meticulous organisation and propaganda, warning him of the danger of premature local uprisings in the midst of a general lull in the revolutionary movement (Marx to Engels, 5 March 1856).

Information on the state of the working-class movement in the USA was supplied to Marx and Engels by Joseph Weydemeyer. The organisers of the Communist Club in New York also kept in touch with Marx (Marx to Engels, 13 August 1858 and 9 February 1859, and Engels to Marx, 18 July 1859).

Marx and Engels pinned great hopes on the revolutionary wing of the English working-class movement, as represented by the Left Chartists led by Ernest Jones. Their activities opened up prospects for establishing a mass working-class party in England. It was with this in mind that Marx advised Jones to transfer the centre of agitation directly into the midst of the industrial proletariat. Jones 'should begin by *forming* a party, for which purpose he must go to the manufacturing districts,' Marx wrote to Engels on 24 November 1857 (p. 210).

However, these hopes were not justified. By then, the Chartist movement was steadily losing support among the masses. Jones' ideological vacillations, especially his tendency to follow the lead of the radical bourgeoisie, were a disturbing symptom. Marx repeatedly warned the Chartist leader about his mistakes (Marx to Engels, 24 November and 22 December 1857 and 14 January 1858). At one point, Marx and Engels even temporarily broke with Jones.

Jones' political vacillations reflected the rise of a reformist trend within the English working-class movement. Marx and Engels saw it as the result of a privileged section forming in the English working class. On 7 October 1858, Engels wrote to Marx: '...The English proletariat is actually becoming more and more bourgeois, so that the ultimate aim of this most bourgeois of all nations would appear to be the possession, *alongside* the bourgeoisie, of a bourgeois aristocracy and a bourgeois proletariat. In the case of a nation which exploits the entire world this is, of course, justified to some extent' (p. 344). This development of a labour aristocracy, a new phenomenon detected by Engels and, at the time, characteristic only of England, was made possible by England's industrial and colonial monopoly, which enabled the English bourgeoisie to use part of its super-profits to buy off a section of the working class. 'In both respects,' Lenin wrote, referring to England's vast colonies and monopoly profit in the context of this passage in Engels' letter, 'England at that time was an exception among capitalist countries, and Engels and Marx, analysing this exception, quite clearly and definitely indicated its *connection* with the (temporary) victory of opportunism in the English labour movement' (*Collected Works*, Vol. 23, p. 112).

However, despite the decline of Chartism, Marx and Engels were convinced that the revolutionary trend in the English working-class movement would in some form be reborn and carry on Chartism's finest traditions. They therefore considered it essential to help to awaken the revolutionary energy of the British working class in every possible way.

The new development in the working-class movement in the late 1850s—the spread of strikes, the emergence of new professional and other organisations, and the workers' participation in political campaigns—stimulated Marx and Engels to step up their efforts to strengthen the nucleus of the future proletarian party. The situation demanded vigorous action, the intensified propagation of revolutionary theory and closer contact with the masses. Marx in particular resumed his participation in the London German Workers' Educational Society, in which sectarian and adventurist elements had prevailed for a period. By this time, however, Marx's comrades had regained their influence in the society.

Marx was seeking new ways of popularising the principles of the proletarian party then being formed. He thought it possible also to use Europe's progressive bourgeois press to this end. 'Times have changed,' he wrote to Lassalle on 28 March 1859, 'and I now consider it essential that our party should secure positions wherever possible, even if only for a time, so that others should not gain possession of the terrain' (p. 409). The long negotiations

Marx held with the editors of the Viennese liberal newspaper *Die Presse* on work as a correspondent reflect this attitude, as do the ideas he expressed on the terms under which a journalist committed to the cause of the proletariat could contribute to a bourgeois press organ (Marx to Engels, 16 April and 16 and 18 May 1859; to Lassalle, 22 February 1858, 28 March and 5 May 1859, and to Friedländer, 16 May 1859). Marx's main stipulation was the right to express his own views on political issues, without adapting to editorial policies.

It was at this time that Marx endeavoured to start a proletarian paper. From the letters published in this volume it can be seen how much energy he spent on converting the newspaper *Das Volk*, which had been published by the German Workers' Educational Society and other German workers' organisations in London from May 1859, into a mouthpiece of the proletarian party (see, in particular, his letters to Engels of 18 May and 10 June 1859).

From the beginning of July, Marx was its *de facto* editor, handling all administrative and business matters, whose management until then had left 'a great deal to be desired', as he had earlier written to Engels (p. 457). Under Marx's management, and thanks also to Engels' cooperation, the paper became a real communist propaganda organ, a medium for explaining the principles of the theory and tactics of the proletarian revolutionaries. However, it proved impossible to regularise its finances, and, after the sixteenth issue on 10 August 1859, the paper ceased publication.

The process of forming a working-class party inevitably involved the dissociation of the proletarian revolutionaries from the proponents of sectarian and reformist ideologies alien to them. Marx's and Engels' relationship with Ferdinand Lassalle, the father of a special brand of petty-bourgeois socialism and of an opportunist trend in the German working-class movement, provides a good illustration of this, and their correspondence with him is most revealing in this respect.

Lassalle first met Marx and Engels in Germany during the Revolution of 1848-49 and kept in touch with them in the years that followed. In his letters to Marx he called himself the latter's pupil. For some time, Marx and Engels considered him a man close to their own circle, though they had been hearing about the dissatisfaction of workers in the Rhine Province with Lassalle's arrogance and overweening behaviour (Marx to Engels, 5 March and 10 April 1856). However, they valued his energy and his talent as a propagandist and orator, and hoped that he would overcome these failings.

Early in 1858, after reading Lassalle's two-volume work, *Die Philosophie Herakleitos des Dunklen von Ephesos*, Marx came to the conclusion that Lassalle's views were far removed from the revolutionary materialist world outlook. '*Heraclitus, the Dark Philosopher* by Lassalle the Luminous One is, *au fond*, a very silly concoction,' he wrote to Engels on 1 February, stressing that essentially Lassalle confined himself to restating some of the propositions of Hegel's idealistic philosophy, of which, moreover, he only had a superficial understanding (p. 259). In a letter to Lassalle, on 31 May 1858, Marx tried to explain the need for a critical mastery of Hegel's dialectics, for a review of its idealistic basis, for divesting it of the 'mystical aura' given it by Hegel (p. 316).

It soon turned out that Lassalle also had differences with Marx and Engels on politics and tactics. In March 1859, he sent them his historical drama, *Franz von Sickingen*, which dealt with the uprising of the Swabian and Rhenish knights against their feudal lords in 1522-23, on the eve of the great Peasant War (1525). In analysing the drama Marx and Engels formulated some cardinal propositions of Marxist aesthetics. The letters to Lassalle from Marx on 19 April and from Engels on 18 May 1859 disclosed the essence of realism as the most progressive method of portraying life in art. Discussing the faults and merits of Lassalle's work, Marx and Engels reproached him above all for his departure from realism, for using abstract rhetoric in place of a truthful and visual portrayal of the characters, thus turning them into 'mere mouthpieces for the spirit of the times' (p. 420). The main character, Sickingen, has none of the traits of a rebellious knight. He epitomises the insoluble and therefore tragic contradiction between the leaders and the masses, a contradiction which Lassalle held to be a feature of any revolution. Lassalle's drama, in Engels' words, was 'too abstract, not realistic enough' (p. 444). Marx and Engels also held that Lassalle's inability to give a true picture of the historical situation betrayed itself in the way he virtually ignored the social background of the events he depicted—the peasants and the plebs in the grip of revolutionary ferment.

According to Marx and Engels, the characters in realistic works should be both individual and typical, and should reflect the nature of the class to which they belong. Moreover, realist authors should not express their ideas as reasoned arguments, but through full-blooded characters and lively action. In Marx's and Engels' view, Lassalle shared, in an exaggerated form, a weakness of the great poet and dramatist Schiller—his inclination to abstract didacticism. A realist writer, however, should, as Engels pointed out, try for 'the complete fusion of greater intellectual profundity, of a consciously historical content', typical of Schiller's dramas, 'with Shakespearean vivacity and wealth of action', with Shakespeare's ability to portray true human passion and suffering, the complexity and contradictory aspects of human nature (p. 442).

In their letters, Marx and Engels touch on the problem of the writer's political position, and on the connection of literature and art with life. Believing that a definite ideological and political orientation is inherent in any work of art, the founders of Marxism always deplored attempts to separate art and politics—the theory of 'art for art's sake'. It was at that time that they condemned the tendency of the poet Ferdinand Freiligrath to oppose literary interests to party obligations (Engels to Marx, 28 November 1859, Marx to Engels, 10 December 1859). In the opinion of Marx and Engels, it was the organic combination of ideology and artistic mastery which made art and literature such a powerful lever of social progress.

Marx and Engels regarded as quite legitimate Lassalle's endeavour to make his drama topical, to link it with the vital task of uniting Germany, but they held that its political tendency was profoundly wrong. It was obvious to them that Sickingen, the knight, was in effect a reactionary whose movement aimed at a return to the era of feudal injustice and club-law, and that Lassalle was aggrandising the historical predecessor of the German Junkers, representing him as the true champion of national unification. Marx pointed this out to Lassalle: 'Have not you yourself—like your Franz von Sickingen—succumbed, to some extent, to the diplomatic error of regarding the Lutheran-knightly opposition as superior to the plebeian-Münzerian?' (p. 420).

The preference for chivalry and the burgher opposition Lassalle showed in his drama reflected his view of the part played by their historical successors—the Junkers and the bourgeoisie—in the cause of German unity. He underestimated the role of the masses in this process and had a nihilistic attitude to the peasants, whom he attributed to the reactionary mass. In contrast, Marx and Engels considered that only vigorous action by the working class and its ally, the peasantry, could give the struggle for national unity a truly democratic revolutionary character, and that the consolidation of this alliance would open up prospects for a transition to the socialist stage of revolution. 'The whole thing in

Germany will depend on whether it is possible to back the Proletarian revolution by some second edition of the Peasants' War' (p. 41).

Lassalle's position on the unification of Germany was laid wide open when in May 1859 he published the pamphlet *Der italienische Krieg und die Aufgabe Preußens.* By aligning himself with the Prussophile bourgeoisie and the Junkers, Lassalle was virtually urging Prussia to avail itself of Austria's defeat to carry out its plans for unification, plans which envisaged no changes in the political or social system. Meanwhile, Lassalle depicted Napoleon III's Italian policy as objectively progressive.

These views were completely at odds with those of Marx and Engels. Characterising the essence of their political differences, Lenin wrote: 'Lassalle was adapting himself to the victory of Prussia and Bismarck, to the lack of sufficient strength in the democratic national movements of Italy and Germany. Thus Lassalle deviated towards a national-liberal labour policy, whereas Marx encouraged and developed an independent, consistently democratic policy hostile to national-liberal cowardice' (*Collected Works,* Vol. 21, p. 141).

'Lassalle's pamphlet is an enormous blunder,' Marx wrote to Engels on 18 May 1859 (p. 435). In a letter of 10 June that year, he told Lassalle that the pamphlet 'in no way corresponds with my own view or that of my party friends in England' (p. 460). Marx was particularly angered by Lassalle's posing as the spokesman of the party. He regarded it as a breach of party discipline to make statements in the press on behalf of the party without ascertaining the views of other members (p. 435).

Marx saw that Lassalle's position was very close to that of the liberal bourgeoisie, and also of pro-Bonaparte and Prussophile vulgar democrats such as Karl Vogt. Lassalle 'in point of fact was piping the same tune as Vogt', he wrote to Engels on 26 November 1859 (p. 542). Marx considered that Lassalle attempted to obstruct the public denunciation of Vogt as a Bonapartist agent and a slanderer of the proletarian revolutionaries because Vogt and Lassalle held identical views. In his work *Herr Vogt,* published in 1860 (this edition, Vol. 17), he therefore not only dealt a crushing blow at the political concepts of Vogt but, without mentioning Lassalle by name, attacked his views too.

Lassalle's literary and political activities were making his unreliability as a comrade-in-arms increasingly clear to Marx and Engels. Nevertheless, they had not yet finally lost hope of setting him on the right road, of stimulating him to act at least as a fellow-traveller of the proletarian revolutionaries. Subsequent events, however, widened the rift and led to a final rupture.

The letters in this volume contain valuable biographical material on the life of Marx and his family and of Engels in these years.

The second half of the 1850s were hard years for Marx. As before, he was in serious financial difficulties and fighting for his very existence. 'I would not wish my worst enemy to have to wade through the quagmire in which I've been trapped for the past two months, fuming the while over the innumerable vexations that are ruining my intellect and destroying my capacity for work,' he wrote to Engels at a moment of extreme distress (p. 331). The moral and political atmosphere that surrounded the revolutionary refugees was also oppressive. After Orsini's assassination attempt, refugees in England were put under political surveillance and their letters were opened (see the letters of Marx to Engels of 2 and 5 March and Engels' letter to Marx of 4 March 1858). They had to face repeated insinuations in the bourgeois press, slanderous allegations by their enemies among the vulgar democrats (Kinkel, Heinzen, Vogt), the cowardly apostasy of their allies (Blind) and the withdrawal from politics of former friends (Dronke, Cluss and Freiligrath).

Marx, however, bore all his trials with courage and remarkable fortitude. The letters in this volume are permeated with optimism and the expectation of new revolutionary events.

The letters show vividly how the unique friendship between Marx and Engels strengthened with the years and how great was their mutual attachment. In Engels this manifested itself in his selfless willingness time and again to come to the aid of Marx and his family, to spend his energies on 'accursed commerce' (Engels to Marx, 17 November 1856) in order to be able to give Marx material support, and to take upon himself a considerable part of Marx's journalistic work so as to free him for economic research; while on Marx's part, it expressed itself in infinite gratitude, respect and trust. Whenever anything went amiss with Engels, Marx would be seriously alarmed. His friend's illness in the summer of 1857 caused him a great deal of worry. 'Nothing could please me more than to hear that your health is progressing,' he wrote to Engels on 21 September that year, having heard that there were signs of an improvement (p. 173).

Marx and Engels treated their comrades-in-arms with touching attention and great sensitivity. They grieved over the losses unavoidable under the harsh conditions of life in emigration, and especially over the death of the proletarian poet Georg Weerth (see, in particular, the letter from Engels to Marx, written not before 27 September 1856, and the letters from Marx to Lassalle, 21 December 1857 and 22 February 1858). On the death of Conrad Schramm, an eminent member of the working-class movement, Engels wrote in sorrow to Marx on 25 January 1858: 'Our old guard is rapidly dwindling away during this long spell of peace' (p. 253). Marx and Engels showed unfailing concern for their old comrades in the Communist League, and kept up friendly relations with Wilhelm Wolff (Lupus), Friedrich Lessner, Georg Eccarius, Joseph Weydemeyer, Wilhelm Liebknecht, Peter Imandt and others.

The outstanding quality of Marx's relationship with his wife is illustrated by his remarkable love letter to Jenny Marx (21 June 1856) in Trier, where she had gone to visit her dying mother.

* * *

Volume 40 contains 317 letters by Marx and Engels, of which 307 were written in German and 10 in English. The great majority of the letters are being published in English for the first time. Only 73 appeared in English before (53 of these in incomplete form). These publications are indicated in the notes. The 11 letters by Jenny Marx included in the Appendix are given in English translation for the first time. The two letters by Karl Marx to Collet Dobson Collet written in June 1857 and Jenny Marx's letter to Engels of 31 July 1857 have never been published in any language before.

The dating of some of the letters was ascertained in the course of the preparation of this volume. Information on undiscovered letters mentioned in the text will be found in the notes. If a fact or event is referred to in several letters, the same note number is used each time.

Obvious slips in the text are corrected without comment. The authors' contractions of proper and geographical names and individual words are given in full. Defects in the manuscripts, where the text is missing or illegible, are indicated by three dots in square brackets. If the text allows a reconstruction of the missing or illegible passages, this is also given in square brackets. Anything crossed out by the authors is reproduced in the footnotes only where the disparity in meaning is considerable. If a letter is a rough copy, an extract quoted elsewhere, etc., this is marked either in the text itself or in the notes.

Foreign words and phrases in the letters are given in italics. If they were underlined by the authors they are in spaced italics. Words written in English in the original are given in small caps. Longer passages written in English in the original are placed in asterisks.

The volume was compiled, the text prepared and the notes written by Stanislav Nikonenko (letters from January 1856 to mid-February 1858), Natalia Martynova (letters from mid-February 1858 to early February 1859) and Tatyana Andrushchenko (letters from early February to December 1859 and the Appendix). Tatyana Andrushchenko also wrote the Preface. The volume was edited by Lev Golman and Tatyana Yeremeyeva (Institute of Marxism-Leninism of the CC CPSU). The name index and the index of periodicals were prepared by Yelena Vashchenko, the index of quoted and mentioned literature by Natalia Martynova, and the subject index by Tatyana Andrushchenko (Institute of Marxism-Leninism of the CC CPSU).

The translations were made by Peter and Betty Ross and edited by E. J. Hobsbawm, Nicholas Jacobs (Lawrence & Wishart), Richard Dixon, Lydia Belyakova and Victor Schnittke (Progress Publishers), and Larisa Miskievich, scientific editor (Institute of Marxism-Leninism of the CC CPSU).

The volume was prepared for the press by the editor Mzia Pitskhelauri.

Note: The name of the late Margaret Mynatt was unfortunately omitted from the list of editors who worked on Volume 38, the first of the thirteen volumes devoted to the correspondence of Marx and Engels.

KARL MARX
and
FREDERICK ENGELS

LETTERS

January 1856-December 1859

1856

1

MARX TO ENGELS[1]

IN MANCHESTER

[London,] 18 January 1856
28 Dean Street, Soho

Dear Frederic,

Today I emptied the 6th and last medicine-BOTTLE. Pretty well again on the whole, save for persistent and highly perfidious piles.

I haven't touched on Cobden's pamphlet[2] in my ARTICLES, because I have devoted many tedious columns exclusively to the HISTORY of the DANUBIAN PROVINCES and Sweden.[3] I should be very glad if you would take on Cobden.

I shall add a short piece to your article[a] as soon as I have seen the 2nd edition of *The Times.* Its ANNOUNCEMENT yesterday AS TO THE '*UNCONDITIONAL* ACCEPTANCE'[4] was a sheer Stock Exchange swindle which brought it in a great deal of money. As early as 1772, at the Congress of Focşani,[5] Catherine II had already proposed to the Turks 'THE INDEPENDENCE OF THE PRINCIPALITIES UNDER THE COMMON PROTECTION OF THE PRINCIPAL POWERS OF EUROPE'. At the Library[b] I discovered a work of Herrmann's which appeared in Germany in 1841.[c] He got hold of a manuscript of Field Marshal Münnich's on the Crimean campaign under Anna[6] in one of the German libraries and published it with a foreword. I shall make excerpts from it for you if you are interested.

You may, perhaps, have seen in the *Augsburger* the high praise Fallmerayer accords to Muralt for his history of Byzantium from the 6th to the 16th century, which won a Petersburg Academy prize.[d]

---

[a] F. Engels, 'The European War'. - [b] of the British Museum - [c] E. Herrmann, *Beiträge zur Geschichte des russischen Reiches,* Leipzig, 1843 (wrong date in the original). - [d] E. de Muralt, *Essai de chronographie Byzantine pour servir à l'examen des annales du Bas-Empire et particulièrement des chronographes slavons de 395 à 1057.* Fallmerayer's review of this book was published in the Augsburg *Allgemeine Zeitung,* Nos. 11 and 12 (supplement), 11 and 12 January 1856.

Have seen Bruno[a] again on various occasions. Romanticism increasingly turns out to be a 'prerequisite' for the critical criticism. In economics expresses enthusiasm for the Physiocrats, whom he misconstrues, and believes in the specifically beneficial effects of landed property. Moreover he rates very high the economic fantasies of Adam Müller, the German romantic.[7] In military science his *summus princeps*[b] is the 'genius' Bülow. I told him that these latest disclosures of his had fully enlightened me regarding his arduous work of ratiocination. AS TO RUSSIA he says that the old state of affairs in the West must be swept away and that this could only be done from the East, since the Easterner alone feels real hatred—for the Westerner, that is—and Russia is the only close-knit power in the East, BESIDES being the only country in Europe where there is still 'cohesion'. As to our illusions about internal class struggles, he maintains that 1. the workers feel no 'hatred'; 2. if they did feel hatred, they would never have achieved anything by it; 3. they are a 'rabble' (who have no interest in the Synoptics[8]) and ought to be curbed and directed solely by force and cunning; 4. with them one silver groschen rise in pay is enough to settle 'the whole caboodle'. In any case, no one who was not a 'descendant of the conquerors' could play an historical role, except in the field of theory. And there something had doubtless been done during the past 16 years, though only in Germany and, indeed, by Bruno alone. It was thanks to him that 'scientific' theology had ceased to exist in Germany, the only place where it had existed, and that 'Tholuck was writing no longer'. *Voilà un résultat immense.*[c] In other respects, a pleasant old gentleman. Proposes to stay a year in England. I believe he is planning to *introduce into England* the 'scientific theology' which has ceased to exist in Germany. He declares Humboldt to be a complete ass because he has fraudulently arrogated to himself abroad the fame due to Bruno.

You should write to old Harvey about your ears. He is also treating Lina[d] from afar and, having heard that she is merely a GOVERNESS *in spe*,[e] has not even charged her a centime. Herewith Lina's first report, which you should return.

I am sending you a scrawl of Urquhart's[f] which they sent me before the paper came out.[9] The 'revelations' about the HISTORY OF CHARTISM [are] INDEED highly naive, since Urquhart turns out to be

---

[a] Bruno Bauer - [b] great exemplar - [c] That's tremendous result. - [d] Caroline Schöler - [e] prospective - [f] 'The Chartist Correspondence', *The Free Press*, No. 15, 19 January 1856.

an English police spy while deluding himself that he played Cicero to Catiline. I see in the Berlin *National-Zeitung* that Bucher, Prussian minister *in spe,* has even adopted Urquhart's 'philosophy' which he repeats parrot-fashion. That's *très fort*[a] for a GERMAN.

Salut.

Your
K. M.

First published in *Der Briefwechsel zwischen F. Engels und K. Marx,* Bd. 2, Stuttgart, 1913

Printed according to the original
Published in English in full for the first time

2

ENGELS TO MARX

IN LONDON

Manchester, 7 February 1856

Dear Marx,

You will be most annoyed with me for not having written for so long. But until I've coped with a number of jobs at the office which will keep me busy for the next fortnight or so, I shall hardly be in a position to turn my mind to anything else. On top of that my old man[b] keeps pestering me frightfully over purchases of yarn, etc., on his behalf, and I have to send him a confidential report at least twice a week.[10]

Enclosed Pan-Slavism No. II, in which want of substance is at least partially offset by verbosity.[11] With No. III I shall at last get *in medias res.*[c]

You should now read the *Guardian*'s Paris correspondent regularly; very odd things are happening there.[12] Over the past few days the correspondent of the *Examiner & Times* has provided even fuller and better particulars. I have just tried to buy the latest issues for you but they had all been sold out. Perhaps I can get them from Belfield.

---

[a] very good - [b] Friedrich Engels Sr., father of Frederick Engels - [c] really into the thing

Bonaparte is VERY FAST ON THE DECLINE. That Drouyn de Lhuys is missing from the official list of senators for this year you will have seen, but not, I imagine, that recently, apropos a sensational act of opposition, he left his card on an Orleanist (Rémusat, if I'm not mistaken) with a bold line drawn through the title: *vice-président du Sénat.* Recently, the infantry were called out against the students escorting Monsieur Nisard home. At the cry: *Vive la ligne!*[a] the troops ordered arms and had to be speedily withdrawn lest fraternisation should become a *fait accompli.* The recent conspiracy in the south-west, on account of which *5,000* arrests (according to a *Bonapartist* statement) were made, had wide ramifications in the army; the NCO school at La Flèche was completely disbanded. Almost all the students were implicated and had to be returned to their regiments; IN FACT, it is said to have been very difficult to find *reliable* regiments to which they could be posted. When Bonaparte was at the Odéon recently with his spouse,[b] the university students who filled the pit sang the *Sire de Franc Boissy*[13] throughout the evening, carefully intoning some of the more embarrassing bits. In Paris the workers are singing a little ditty, having the refrain:

Voilà qu'il part, voilà qu'il part,
Le petit marchand de moutarde,
Voilà qu'il part pour son pays
Avec tous ses outils.[c]

In order that there should be no doubt about the identity of the *petit marchand de moutarde,* the police have banned the song.[d]

All these impudent manifestations of oppositional and positively anti-Bonapartist impulses, and Mr. Bonaparte's corresponding feebleness are proof that a great change is under way. The measures adopted during the coup d'état[14] will no longer do, and the courage to apply them is no longer there. You will have seen that even *The Times,* on two successive days, first described Napoleon personally as a mere stopgap so far as France was concerned—BECAUSE NOT ONE SINGLE MAN WAS TO BE FOUND IN WHICH THE NATION COULD PLACE ITS CONFIDENCE AND ESTEEM—and then characterised his entire general staff of ministers, etc., as swindlers and scoundrels.[e] In today's *Guardian* there is another nice story about

---

[a] Long live the troops of the line! - [b] Eugénie - [c] He is leaving, he is leaving, / The little mustard-vendor./ He is leaving for his country / With all his belongings. [d] 'From Our Paris Correspondent. Paris, Monday Evening', *Manchester Daily Examiner & Times,* No. 305, 6 February 1856. - [e] A reference to the leading articles in *The Times,* Nos. 22278, 22279 and 22280, 31 January, 1 and 2 February 1856.

Frederick Engels. 1856. Manchester

that rascal Fiorentino, Bonapartist court feuilletonist and Knight of the Legion of Honour. Mr Espinasse, too, had to decamp from Paris; he has been involved in scandals, concerning which I shall probably hear more in a day or two. Something is also afoot with de Morny; the fellow has more or less fallen out with his worthy brother[a] and is once more intriguing on his own account.

This Bonaparte, for whom in the past everything, however stupid, craven and infamous, turned out so well, will now discover that henceforward everything will go badly for him. This he is already discovering in the war and peace question; everyone blamed him for the war, no one thanks him for the peaceful turn of events. Incidentally, the matter of the peace is far from being settled. The preliminaries to the preliminaries contain, *au fond,*[b] nothing but the Bessarabian clause, and that is offset by a total disregard for Kars.[15] All the rest consists of nothing but bogus concessions. Moreover Bonaparte no longer cares a rap about the conditions upon which he makes peace. For him it is now his bread and butter that is at stake, as once with old Dolleschall,[c] and I'm convinced that the Russians know this better than he does himself. Never before have the French been so wholly indifferent to their *gloire*; since 1848 the fellows have been concerned with other things than the traditional *gloire* and parliamentary swindling.

So it seems as though we have safely weathered the Aliens Bill[16]—*au train que les choses vont en France,*[d] there will soon be no further need to worry one's head about the aspirations of Palmerston and Co. The Bonapartist house of cards will most likely collapse this summer just as did Louis Philippe's in the year of scandal 1847, and exactly when the gust of wind comes that completely demolishes the walls is a matter of mere chance. I now lead a very sober life, but on that day I shall get drunk in Manchester, probably for the last time.

Don't be long in telling me something more about old Bruno[e]; the fellow's new romantic turn is too amusing. Kindest regards to your wife and children.

Your

F. E.

First published abridged in *Der Briefwechsel zwischen F. Engels und K. Marx,* Bd. 2, Stuttgart, 1913 and in full in: Marx and Engels, *Works,* First Russian Edition, Vol. XXII, Moscow, 1929

Printed according to the original

Published in English for the first time

---

[a] Napoleon III - [b] at bottom - [c] Laurenz Dolleschall, censor of the *Rheinische Zeitung* in 1842, claimed that he was forced to do this work because he had to support his family. - [d] the way things are going in France - [e] Bruno Bauer

3

MARX TO ENGELS[1]

IN MANCHESTER

[London,] 12 February 1856
28 Dean Street, Soho

Dear Frederic,

I am still being *plus ou moins*[a] persecuted by State haemorrhoids and consequent DULLNESS of spirits. On top of which Pieper has just been playing me some music of the future.[17] *C'est affreux*[b] and makes one afraid of the 'future', including its poetical music.

At the Museum[c] I have made a number of historical discoveries about the end of the 17th and the early decades of the 18th centuries concerning the struggle between Peter I and Charles XII and the decisive role played in that drama by *England.* At that time the foreign policy of the Tories and Whigs differed quite simply in that the former sold themselves to France, the latter to Russia. This venality was taken for granted and is discussed and declared 'a matter of course' by contemporary writers. From the start, William III harboured MISGIVINGS about *Sa Majesté Czarienne,*[d] as is proved by his offensive and defensive treaty with Charles XII. Under him the ministers acted *contrary* to his inclination. From George I onwards things were easy for the Whigs since the ELECTORS of Hanover were already pursuing a foolish dynastic policy and regarded Verden and Bremen as the focal points of European interest. That mainly England contributed to turning Russia into a BALTIC POWER is, perhaps, less interesting than the fact that, as early as the beginning of the 18th century, this policy was already being denounced, and the future growth of the MUSCOVITE EMPIRE predicted with remarkable accuracy. Despite the unexampled indulgence of the official British and the direct aid they accorded Peter, the latter was at the same time engaging in underhand dealings with the Pretender.[e] In this his personal physician (Erskine), a relation of the Comte de Mar, acted as go-between. The main sources for the whole of this mysterious story are:

a) *Truth is Truth, as it is timed, or Our Ministry's present Measures against the Muscovite vindicated by Plain and Obvious reasons, tending*

---

[a] more or less - [b] It's horrible - [c] the British Museum Library - [d] His Imperial Majesty (Peter I) - [e] James Edward Stuart

to prove that it is no less the interest of Our British trade, than that of Our State, that the Czar be not suffered to retain a Fleet, if needs must that he should [have] a Sea Port in the Baltick etc. London 1719.

The author[a] was ambassador in Petersburg from 1710-1715 and, as he says, was

'dismissed the service because the Czar desired it; for that he had learnt, that I had given Our Court such Light into his affairs as is contain'd in this Paper', etc.

b) *Mémoire présenté à Sa Maj. Britannique par M. Wesselowsky, Ministre de Sa Maj. Czar.* London 1717.

An apologia by the Russians respecting their underhand dealings with the Pretender, especially remarkable for being altogether in the style (although not yet with quite the polish) of Pozzo di Borgo and Co.,[18] hence evidence that qualitatively Russian diplomacy has made no progress since Pierre I.

c) *The defensive treaty concluded in the year 1700 between His late M. King William of Glorious Memory and His Present Swedish Maj. King Charles XII,* etc., to which some queries are appended (1716).

d) *The Northern Crisis, or Impartial Reflections on the Policies of the Czar.... 'Parvo motu primo mox se attollit in auras'.*[b] London 1716.

One of the most extraordinary pamphlets ever written. Might, with minor MODIFICATIONS, have appeared in the year 1853. Contains, as do also a) and c), evidence of English treachery. In a *postscript* the anonymous author[c] says:

*'I flatter myself, that this little History is of that curious Nature, and on Matters hitherto so unobserved, that I consider it with Pride, as a valuable New-Year's Gift to the present world; and that posterity will accept it, as the like, for many years after, and read it over on the Anniversary, and call it their *Warning-Piece.* I must have my Exegi Monumentum[d] as well as others.'*

e) *An Inquiry into the Reasons of the Conduct of Great Britain with Relation to the Present State of Affairs in Europe.* London 1727.[e]

Interesting only because it reveals that Ripperda, the Spanish diplomatic *chevalier d'industrie,* subsequently a minister, 'HAD A VERY PARTICULAR INTIMACY WITH THE RUSSIAN MINISTER', etc. Likewise the other leading double-dealer in the diplomatic world of the time, Baron Görtz.

f) *Tagebuch Peters des Grossen vom Jahre 1698 bis zum Schlusse des Neustädter Friedens, aus dem russischen Original übersetzt, so nach denen im Archive befindlichen und von Seiner Kaiserlichen Majestät eigenhändigen ergänzenden Handschriften gedruckt worden.* With a

---

[a] George Mackenzie - [b] 'Having at first little impulsion, he presently rose into the air' (Virgil, *Aeneid,* IV, 176). - [c] Carl Gyllenborg - [d] 'I have raised a monument' (Horace, *Odes,* III,XXX, 1). - [e] by B. Hoadley

prefatory note by the Russian editor, Prince Mikhail Shcherbatov (Щербатовъ) (Petersburg, 2 August 1770), in German, Berlin and Leipzig 1773.

Although Catherine II naturally had this diary censored before publication, it nevertheless contains much that confirms the FACTS given in the above-mentioned pamphlets.

g) *Copies and Extracts of several letters written by the King of Sweden and his Ministers relating to the Negociations of Baron Görtz etc., published at Copenhagen by order of the King of Denmark.* London 1717.

h) *Letters which passed between Count Gyllenborg, the Baron Görtz, Sparre etc.*, published by authority. London 1717.

g) and h) are, of course, well known to all historians who, however, lack the key to the proper understanding of the same. Both publications turn more especially on Charles XII's plan, conceived as an act of vengeance upon England, to land a Swedish army on the English coast and proclaim the Pretender.

Besides these pamphlets there are a number of other writings which occasionally refer to the Swedish-English-Russian business, or English pamphlets obviously inspired by the Swedish ambassador Gyllenborg, as, for instance, *Remarks on Mr Jackson's Memorial etc.*

You can see what kind of means the Whigs resorted to from their having put it about

> *'that the King of Sweden was a Roman Catholic and that the Czar was a good Protestant'*.

No one can fail to notice that, at the very time the English were making such a ridiculous hullaballoo about Austria setting up the Compagnie des Indes at Ostend, they formally placed their fleet at Peter's disposal and helped him found his ports in the Baltic. Yet from the *complaints of the English BALTIC MERCHANTS* of that time it transpires that Monsieur Peter was very far from gentle with them. England was, moreover, the first great European power to recognize his *imperial* title, etc. What the above-mentioned pamphlets prove above all is that she was acting neither under an illusion nor out of ignorance.

The following anecdotes about Peter from the *Memoirs of Frederick the Great's Sister*[a] will amuse you. Peter and the Czarina[b] were paying them a visit at Potsdam.

---

[a] *Mémoires de Frédérique Sophie Wilhelmine, Margrave de Bareith, soeur de Frédéric le Grand....* Here and below Marx quotes from Volume I of *Mémoires*, pp. 41 and 44. (Later, historians questioned the authenticity of the *Mémoires.*) - [b] Catherine I

'La Czarine débuta par baiser la main à la reine[a] qu'il voulut embrasser, mais elle le repoussa. Elle lui présenta ensuite le duc et la duchesse de Mecklenbourg[b] qui les avaient accompagnés et 400 soi-disant dames qui étaient à sa suite. C'était pour la plupart, des servantes allemandes, qui faisaient les fonctions de dames, de femmes de chambre, de cuisinières et de blanchisseuses. Presque toutes ces créatures portaient chacune sur les bras un enfant richement vêtu; et lorsqu'on leur demandait, si c'étaient les leurs, elles répondaient en faisant des salamalecs à la Russienne: *Le Czar m'a fait l'honneur de me faire cet enfant.* La reine ne voulut pas saluer ces créatures' etc.[c]

In one of the rooms at Potsdam there stood a Priapus

'dans une posture très indécente. Le Czar admira cette statue beaucoup et ordonna à la Czarine de la baiser. Elle voulut s'en défendre, il se fâcha et lui dit en allemand corrompu: *Kop ab....* La Czarine eût si peur qu'elle fit tout ce qu'il voulut. Il demanda sans façon cette statue et plusieurs autres au roi[d] qui ne put les lui refuser' etc.[e]

I should like to put to some use the curious items I have discovered at the Museum. They are too retrospective for a newspaper. So I shall try *'Putnam'. But first* you must let me *know when* the 'IMPROVEMENTS IN MODERN WARFARE' can be ready, since Putnam will, of course, insist on having the goods he ordered first[19] before he considers any fresh offers.

I was most interested in the French business and would ask you to send me the *Examiner* whenever it contains similar stuff. Here the *Guardian* may be seen at Wylde's. Writing for the papers is at present very onerous, since *nothing* is happening in England and the turn economic affairs are taking is still far from clear. Crucial in this respect just now are the stock market swindles, concerning which the necessary material is wanting.

Have since seen Bruno[f] once or twice. The fellow clearly has

---

[a] Sophie Dorothea - [b] Karl Leopold and Catherine - [c] 'The Czarina began by kissing the hand of the Queen, whom he sought to embrace, but was repulsed. Next she presented to her the Duke and Duchess of Mecklenburg who had accompanied them and 400 self-styled ladies belonging to her suite. These were, for the most part, German servants fulfilling the duties of ladies-in-waiting, chamber-maids, cooks and laundresses. Practically every one of these creatures carried a richly clad child in her arms; and, when asked if it was hers, would reply, making salaams Russian-fashion: *"The Czar did me the honour of presenting me with this child."* The Queen refused to greet these creatures' etc. - [d] Frederick William I - [e] 'in a most indecent posture. The Czar greatly admired this statue and commanded the Czarina to kiss it. When she demurred, he grew angry and said in bad German: *"Kop ab...."* ["Head off".] The Czarina was so frightened that she did all that he wished. He made no bones about asking for this statue and a number of others which the King was unable to refuse him' etc. - [f] Bruno Bauer

something in mind, having come *sans le sou*[a] to his *cher frère*.[b] He's a thorough-going old bachelor, anxiously concerned for his own conservation and preservation, and not without secret MISGIVINGS about his attitude to the present. Little by little he is discovering that London is a remarkable place, that in it there are 'contrasts between poor and rich' and other suchlike 'discoveries'. His would-be gentility and repudiation of the world on the one hand, and his childish curiosity and rustic astonishment at EVERYTHING and ANYTHING on the other, provide a far from edifying contrast. At present he is engaged mainly in mugging up English. As soon as I have another encounter with him I shall tell you about it.

Salut.

Your

K. M.

First published abridged in *Der Briefwechsel zwischen F. Engels und K. Marx*, Bd. 2, Stuttgart, 1913 and in full in: Marx and Engels, *Works*, First Russian Edition, Vol. XXII, Moscow, 1929

Printed according to the original

Published in English in full for the first time

4

MARX TO ENGELS[20]

IN MANCHESTER

London, 13 February 1856
28 Dean Street, Soho

DEAR Fred,

According to a letter I've had from Imandt, Heise is gradually approaching extinction as a result of the undue amount of 'oil' he has been pouring on the lamp of life.[c] Imandt himself grumbles a great deal about the Scots, with whom it is impossible to have more than 12 lessons to teach them German, whatever

[a] penniless - [b] dear brother (Edgar Bauer) - [c] In his letter to Marx of 6 February 1856 Imandt wrote that Heise, ill with tuberculosis, was drinking too much whisky.

ruses he adopts. The fellows are keen on "grasping" out of avarice.

But the great event, the event which has caused me to send this second epistle following hard on the heels of the first, is the *Seiler event.* You will recall what the auspices for this Sebastian Sheetanchor[a] looked like when last you were here. The old GREENGROCER proved RATHER adamant, and Seiler himself, with the happy instinct characteristic of the man, soon discovered that it would be altogether foolish to lay out some £200 on amortising the past rather than greasing the wheels of the future. So he takes the heroic decision to advise his father-in-law not to pay *one single creditor,* but rather look on unconcernedly should he be locked up. His intention, then, was to pass through the COURT OF INSOLVENCY and, thus purged, start a new career with the old man's help. This seemed very practical to the old man. Seiler for his part was tempted by the prospect—once initiated into the *crapuleuse*[b] company of the Queen's Bench[21]—of keeping open board thanks to generous supplies from wife and mother-in-law and, incidentally, of completing his immortal work on Alexander II—consisting of extracts from the Augsburg *Allgemeine Zeitung,* upon which he has spread an equivocal syrup. The matter was AT ONCE put in hand. There began a golden era of *farniente*[c] and 'business errands' into town. But what was particularly embarrassing was that, despite the WARRANTS taken out against him and despite the OSTENTATIOUS EXHIBITION of his worthy person in the streets of London, not a single creditor took steps to have Sebastian arrested. The old GREENGROCER, whose faith in the 'personality' of his son-in-law was in no way reinforced by the latter's inviolability, told him the time had come to vacate the house and withdraw with his wife to a distant COTTAGE. During the actual removal some of the effects were confiscated by vigilant creditors, among them 7 pairs of boots belonging to Sebastian. Sebastian himself took care that there should be no secret about the COTTAGE either, since a quiet and secluded existence with his cabbage of a wife had no place whatsoever in his plans. In short, to such good effect did he intrigue with the cabbage, the mother-in-law and the GREENGROCER, that it has been decided to despatch him to the 'New World'—New York, OF COURSE—whither his spouse is to follow him once he has secured a 'position'. The matter now turns—he is expected to

[a] An ironical allusion to Sebaldus Nothanker (literally: Sheetanchor), the hero of Ch. Fr. Nicolai's novel *Das Leben und die Meinungen des Herrn Magister Sebaldus Nothanker.* - [b] lewd - [c] doing nothing

leave this week—on the number of £s he is to take with him for his travelling expenses. He is asking for £60. The GREENGROCER reckons that half as much will suffice. Sebastian plans, once in America, to extract one 5 pound note after the other from his dear spouse, to pamper his belly, to publish his *Kaspar Hauser* and Alexander II, and, as a grass widower, never to forego the sweet melancholy of separation from his cabbage. It would be interesting if a creditor did catch him after all. At all events he has succeeded in leaving England too as a 'financial' fugitive, only in more respectable CIRCUMSTANCES than those attending his departure from Germany, Belgium and Switzerland. His plan was that Pieper should go with him as companion. Pieper had only pretended to fall in with this plan so as to get a share of the 7 pairs of boots, but in the event he was forestalled by the BROKERS.

Pieper was here one evening not long ago giving lessons to the children when the POSTMAN knocked at the door downstairs. A letter for Pieper in a female hand. Invitation to a rendezvous. Since he was unfamiliar with the hand and equally with the signature, he gave himself over to great expectations and passed the letter to my wife to read. From the signature she at once recognised our ex-nurse, the fat old Irish slattern, who cannot write herself and therefore had the letter written by a third hand. You can imagine how we teased Fridolin[a] with our laughter. But he kept his rendezvous with the COW. Such, then, are his ADVENTURES. O King Visvamitra, what an ox you are![b]

Don't forget the Pan-Slavism.[11]

Salut.

Your

K. M.

First published in: Marx and Engels, *Works*, First Russian Edition, Vol. XXII, Moscow, 1929

Printed according to the original

Published in English in full for the first time

---

[a] Marx ironically compares Wilhelm Pieper with Fridolin, a character from Schiller's ballad *Der Gang nach dem Eisenhammer*. - [b] H. Heine, 'Den König Wiswamitra...' (from *Buch der Lieder,* 'Die Heimkehr').

5

MARX TO ENGELS

IN MANCHESTER

[London,] 29 February 1856
28 Dean Street, Soho

Dear Engels,

For the whole of this week I've had a visitor in the person of G. Levy from Düsseldorf, sent over as their delegate by the workers there. He only left yesterday and took up all my spare time, so that despite the best of intentions I did not succeed in writing to you. Further on I shall give you an account of the news, some of it important, of which he was the CARRIER.[a]

Not one of the 3 books you asked for was available at Norgate and Williams. I have *ordered* the *Lay of Igor*[22] but wanted to let you know about the other two first.

Dobrowsky's *'Slavin', Hanka* edition, is very far from fulfilling the expectations aroused by its title. The book falls into 2 parts as regards the contents, if not the arrangement, viz.:

1. Short ESSAYS on Slavonic linguistic studies which, in view of more recent studies, could at most be of antiquarian interest (e.g. sample from the Wendish New Testament, Slavonic declension, on the Slavonic translation of the Old Testament, etc.).

2. An attempt, *wholly* devoid of polemic bite, to reconstitute the character of the Slav peoples *in integrum*.[b] This is done by taking excerpts from sundry works, mostly *German* writings. Here is a list of these essays, which make up the bulk of the book[c]:

'Slawische Völker'. (From Herder's *Ideen*[d] etc.)

'Sitten der Croaten'. (From von Engels' *Geschichte* von Dalmatien, Croatien, Slavonien. Halle 1798.)

'Sitten und Gebräuche der Illyrier, der Morlaken etc.' (From *ditto.*)

'Charakter der Illyrier'. (From Taube's *Beschreibung des Königreichs Slavonien.* Leipzig 1777.)

'Die Tracht der Illyrier'. (From Hacquet's *Beobachtungen auf einer Reise nach Semlin.*[e])

---

[a] See this volume, pp. 23-25. - [b] as a whole - [c] Here Marx gives the titles of a number of chapters from Dobrowsky's book and some excerpts from it. - [d] J. G. Herder, *Ideen zur Philosophie der Geschichte der Menschheit,* Theil 4. - [e] Serbian name: Zemun.

'Prokops Schilderung der Slawen und Anten'. (From Stritter's 'Geschichte der Slawen nach den Byzantinern' in Schlözer's *Allgemeine Nordische Geschichte.*)

'Auszüge aus des Herrn Professor B. Hacquet's *Abbildung und Beschreibung der südwest- und östlichen Slawen'.*

'Volkstümliches der Russen'. (From Dupré de St. Maure, *Observations sur les moeurs et les usages russes.* Paris 1829. 3 vols.)

'Charakter und Kultur der Slawen im Allgemeinen'. (From Schaffarik, *Geschichte der slawischen Sprache,* etc. Ofen[a] 1826.)

That's about all. Appended is 'Der böhmische Cato' in Czech, 'from an old manuscript described by the late Voigt in *Acta litteraria'.*[23]

Dobrowsky writes in a bumbling, good-natured, naive style, with the greatest cordiality towards his German colleagues, whether 'late' or still living. All that seemed of interest to me in the *Slavin* were a few passages in which he directly recognises the Germans as the fathers of Slavonic historical and linguistic studies.

As regards linguistic studies, he cites among others 'Schlözer, *Vorschlag zu einer allgemeinen vergleichenden slawischen Sprachlehre und Wörterbuch'.*[24] Further, 'Schlözer, *Vorschlag, das Russische vollkommen richtig und genau mit lateinischer Schrift auszudrücken'.* In general 'Herr Hofrat Schlözer' would appear to be the patriarch of whom the others profess to be the disciples.

'Schlözer's *Nestor*: A work indispensable to anyone wishing to acquaint himself with the critical approach to Slavonic history in general and the Russian annals in particular.'

Of Voigt's *Geschichte Preussens*:

'Was *the first* to acquaint the *Bohemians* with the monuments of Antiquity.'[25]

Also cited:

'Johann Leonhard Frischen's *Programmen von der slawischen Literatur',* 1727-1736,

'which has elucidated the history of several Slavonic dialects'.

'Slawischer Bücherdruck in Würtenberg im 16ten Jahrhundert. Ein literarischer Bericht von Chr. Friedr. Schnurrer, Prof. in Tübingen, 1799'—

'a very valuable book which contains the finest and most important contributions to the history of Wendish and Croat bibliography'.

Others cited are: Schlözer, *Allgemeine Nordische Geschichte.* Joh. Christoph de Jordan, *De originibus Slavicis opus* etc., Vienna 1745,

---

a Hungarian name: Buda.

fol. 2. Father Gelasius Dobner, *ad* Hajek, *Annales Bohemorum,* Prague 1761 and '63. (Of this Schlözer remarks: *primus delirare desiit.*[a]) Stritter, *Memoriae populorum ad Danubium e Script. Byzantinis,* Petersburg 1774. Gercken, *Versuch in der ältesten Geschichte der Slaven,* Leipzig 1771. Gatterer's *Einleitung in die synchronistische Universalhistorie,* Göttingen 1771, and Gebhardi, *Allgemeine Welthistorie,* 1789.

Of all these works *only* the titles are given, with the exception of the opinions extracted above. *Voilà le 'Slavin'.*[b]

As regards the 3rd work, the title is: Dr. M. W. Heffter, *Der Weltkampf der Deutschen und Slaven seit dem Ende des 5ten Jahrhunderts,* 1847 (costs 7/-). Even in his preface the author admits that he only has a detailed and first-hand knowledge of Slavonic history in so far as it refers to the Prussian 'Fatherland'. More than $^3/_4$ of his book of 481 pages is devoted to the period between the end of the 5th century and 1147. Only here and there does the remainder go beyond the 13th, or at latest the 14th, century, and then quite cursorily.

Having given you an opinion on these two works, I await your instructions whether or not to order them. Another book by Heffter has been published: *Das Slawentum,* Leipzig 1852 (45 pages or so). Constitutes the 10th booklet in the Brockhaus series *Unterhaltungen, Belehrungen etc.*[c] A popular compendium of Slavonic history. It was from this little book I learned that in 1849 Nicholas issued a ukase by which

> 'all his subjects were strictly forbidden to take part in Pan-Slavism'.

At the Museum I discovered, and made extracts from, 5 *manuscript* folio volumes on Russia (18th century only). They are part of the literary legacy of ARCHDEACON Coxe, known for his zeal as a collector.[26] They contain many original (hitherto unpublished) letters from English ambassadors in Petersburg to the Cabinet here, some of them VERY COMPROMISING INDEED. Amongst the papers dated 1768 there is a manuscript by one of the Embassy attachés on 'the character of the Russian nation'.[d] I shall send you some extracts from it. There is also interesting information on the Russian 'artels' by the Embassy chaplain, a cousin of Pitt's.[e]

---

[a] the first to have ceased to rave - [b] There you have the *Slavin.* - [c] *Unterhaltende Belehrungen zur Förderung allgemeiner Bildung.* 1-27 Bändchen, Leipzig 1851-1856. - [d] *Various Papers on the Genius and Character of the Russians,* 1768 (MS). - [e] L. K. Pitt, *Ueber den russischen Handel* (MS).

Although anti-Russian, recent French writings are, with few exceptions, almost all tinged with Pan-Slavism. Thus Desprez,[a] but more particularly Cyprien Robert who, in Paris in 1848, published the journal, *La Pologne. Annales contemporaines des peuples de l'Europe orientale,* etc. The same man has published, among other things, *Les Slaves de la Turquie, édition de 1844, précédée d'une introduction,* etc., 8°, Paris 1852. Further, *Le Monde slave, son passé, son état présent et son avenir,* Paris 1852. A Parisian author,[b] whose *nom de guerre* is *Edmond,* but who is said to be a Pole, is exceptional in having published an exceedingly venomous attack on Russian pretensions to socialism, and comments on their communes, etc. I haven't yet been able to trace this, but shall have a look at the *Revue des deux Mondes* which apparently contains extracts from it.

I began this letter today with the intention of sending you masses of gossip. But, having strayed off in another direction and time being short, I shall leave that till tomorrow and confine myself for today to telling you that Heise, under the influence of strong liquor (so Imandt writes), is rapidly approaching his end[c]; that Oswald—of tobacco and refugee fame—who doesn't speak a word of French, has been appointed Professor of the French Language at UNIVERSITY COLLEGE, London; that Ruge's friends are putting it around that he's suffering from 'dropsy' though it's probably nothing but water on the brain; that a number of German worthies (Faucher, Meyen, Franck, Tausenau, etc.) will be meeting tomorrow *chez* mine host Kerb, in order to achieve an *entente cordiale* as to the Fatherland's requirements, and that 'Meyen' has expressed the 'hope' that he can persuade Bucher to 'take part' in this confabulation; finally, that Proudhon has become a director of the royal imperial French railways.

Salut.

Your

K. M.

First published abridged in *Der Briefwechsel zwischen F. Engels und K. Marx,* Bd. 2, Stuttgart, 1913 and in full in: Marx and Engels, *Works,* First Russian Edition, Vol. XXII, Moscow, 1929

Printed according to the original

Published in English for the first time

---

[a] H. Desprez, *Les peuples de l'Autriche et de la Turquie.* - [b] Charles Edmond Chojecki - [c] See this volume, p. 12.

6

MARX TO ENGELS[1]

IN MANCHESTER

[London,] 5 March 1856
28 Dean Street, Soho

Dear Frederic,

Next week I shall take a closer look at the Heffter.[a] If there's anything to it, I shall order it. Eichhoff's *Histoire de la langue et de la littérature des Slaves,* Paris 1839, is very poor indeed. Apart from the grammatical section, which I'm unable to assess (but I notice that the Lithuanians and Letts are said to be Slavs. Isn't that NONSENSE?), the rest is mostly plagiarisms from Schaffarik.[b] The fellow also gives samples of the Slavs' vernacular poetry in the original, together with a French translation. Indeed, it was amongst these that I found Igor's expedition.[22] In essence, the poem is a call for unity on the part of the Russian princes just before the invasion by the Mongol hordes proper. The poem contains a curious passage, 'Voici les jolies filles des Gothes entonnent leurs chants au bord de la Mer noire'.[c] From this it would seem that the Getae or Goths celebrated the victory of the Turkish Polovtsians[27] over the Russians. The whole poem is epic-Christian, although heathen elements are still strongly in evidence. The Bohemian epic *Zaboi* (Samo?), in the anthology of Bohemian epic poetry in a German translation published by *Hanka and Swoboda,*[28] is, on the other hand, fairly polemical and fanatically anti-German. Appears to be directed against a German *capitano* of Dagobert's who was beaten by the Bohemians. But it is a call for vengeance as much upon Christianity as upon the Germans, who are reproached in the most naively poetical terms with having, amongst other things, sought to compel the worthy Bohemians to be satisfied with only one wife. Other folk poetry I discovered (the Poles have none save for *Adalbert's Prayer* to the Mother of God[29]) are:

---

[a] M. W. Heffter, *Der Weltkampf der Deutschen und Slaven seit dem Ende des fünften Jahrhunderts....* - [b] P. J. Schaffarik, *Geschichte der slawischen Sprache und Literatur nach allen Mundarten.* - [c] Here are the pretty daughters of the Goths singing their songs on the shore of the Black Sea.

Götze, *Fürst Vladimir und seine Tafelrunde,*[a] 1819. *Stimmen des russischen Volkes,* 1828.

Kapper (Siegfried), *Slavische Melodien,* Leipzig 1844. By the same, *Die Gesänge der Serben,* 1852. (More comprehensive than [those] of Jakob.[b] Lastly, by Vuk Stephanovitsch, *Serbische Hochzeitslieder.* German by E. Wesely. Pest 1826.

Works which I have noted and shall be looking through for you next week are, besides the Cyprien and the Desprez[c]: *Südslavische Wanderungen im Sommer 1850,* 2 vols, Leipzig 1851.[d] (Has also been translated into English.) *Betrachtungen über das Fürstenthum Serbien,* Vienna 1851. *Die serbische Bewegung in Südungarn,* 1851 Berlin. *Slawismus und Pseudomagyarismus. Von aller Menschen Freunde, nur der Pseudomagyaren Feinde,* Leipzig 1842. *Die Beschwerden und Klagen der Slaven in Ungarn,* Leipzig 1843.

I don't remember whether the *Neue Preussische Zeitung* is to be had in Manchester. At present it is very interesting. The Prussian government has now, as once Louis XVIII, got its *chambre introuvable,* and the bureaucratic government is beginning to be afraid of the backwoods squires, who are taking their victory *au sérieux.*[30] During debates on rural parish, rural court, and land tenure relations, when, as old Dolleschall said, 'it's his bread and butter that is at stake'[e]—the clashes in the Prussian Chamber are becoming serious. You will have seen, among other things, that Count Pfeil claimed for landowners the privilege of flogging their people, and boasted of having himself performed heroic deeds in this line. Now the Left has dug up posters of 1848, signed by this same Pfeil in 1848, and altogether in the style of the 'crazy year'.[31] There have even been duels between the two sides, and today the *Neue Preussische Zeitung* carries a LEADER[f] roundly declaring that there are 'depraved scoundrels' in its party just as there are very 'noble' people in the Liberal Party. It preaches 'moderation', 'conciliation', 'a battle of principles, but no personalities'. The Left is adjured to reflect that 'the Mountain will always swallow the

---

[a] The name of the publisher or translator is not indicated on the title-page of this book. It is probable, however, that it was not P. O. Götze but von Busse who translated it. - [b] A reference to *Volkslieder der Serben* by Therese Albertine Luise von Jakob-Robinson (she wrote under the pen-name of Talvj). - [c] Cyprien Robert, *Les slaves de Turquie*; H. Desprez, *Les peuples de l'Autriche et de la Turquie.* - [d] The author was S. Kapper. In English the book appeared under the title *A Visit to Belgrade.* - [e] Laurenz Dolleschall, censor of the *Rheinische Zeitung* in 1842, claimed that he was forced to do this work because he had to support his family. - [f] 'Den Streitenden', *Neue Preußische Zeitung,* No. 54, 4 March 1856.

Gironde'[32] and to consider that 'peace or no peace, for Prussia there lies ahead a time of very great confusion, at home or abroad' and that at this moment a 'party split' means 'suicide'. Capital, is it not? And withal no one in Prussia cares a rap about the Chamber and its splits. All the more significant, then, this admission of fear. Father Leo delivered a lecture before the King[a] on *Münzer* (part of which was printed in the *Neue Preussische*[b]). One might almost think it was a direct riposte to your essay in the *Revue der Neuen Rheinischen Zeitung*.[c] Essential, of course, that the Reformation be absolved of the responsibility of having given birth to the Revolution. Münzer was a 'fanatic' who said: *'intelligo ut credam'*.[d] Luther said: *'credo ut intelligam'*.[e] The *Spenersche*'s[f] reply was that in his later years Luther repented, etc., of the abject role he had played in politics. As you see, the ferment is at work even in official circles.

Apropos the Reformation, it was Austria who, from the start, laid the foundations of the Slav peril at a time when all races save the Russian were inclined to support the Reformation. With the Reformation came the translation of the Bible into all the popular Slav dialects. And thereby of course awakening national consciousness. On the other hand, deep-rooted alliance with the German Protestant North. Had Austria not suppressed this movement, Protestantism would have provided not only the foundations for the dominance of the German spirit, but also and equally, bulwarks against Greek-Orthodox Russia. Not a pitfall but Austria has driven the Germans into it and, in Germany as in the East, she paved the way for the Russians.

Did you read about last Friday's parliamentary sitting,[g] at which Evans reproached Palmerston for feigning incredulity when, 3 1/2 months ago, he warned him about Kars[15]; at which he said that Panmure in the despatch informing Simpson, 'YOU ARE NOMINATED SUCCESSOR OF RAGLAN', added 'TAKE CARE OF DOWB'. The unfortunate Simpson replied: 'REPEAT YOUR DESPATCH', whereat Panmure (*'Lord Carnot'* as Evans calls him), 'TAKE CARE OF DOWBIGGIN', a cousin of his[33]; at which, finally, Lord Hamilton slated *Evans* for having, after the battle of Inkerman,[34] advised Raglan to abandon cannon and TRENCHES and to embark the British army. The day before

[a] Frederick William IV - [b] 'Leo über Thomas Münzer', *Neue Preußische Zeitung*, No. 51, 29 February 1856. - [c] F. Engels, *The Peasant War in Germany* (published in the *Neue Rheinische Zeitung. Politisch-ökonomische Revue*). - [d] I understand in order to believe. - [e] I believe in order to understand. - [f] *Berlinische Nachrichten von Staats- und gelehrten Sachen*, 27 February 1856. - [g] A reference to the parliamentary sitting on 29 February 1856, reported on in *The Times*, No. 22304, 1 March 1856.

yesterday, poor Evans made *amende honorable.*[a] That there was a betrayal at Kars would seem to be pretty clear from the written account of a certain Swan,[b] recently returned from the East—a betrayal which took place not during the last few days but earlier, in order to bring the situation about.

Now for *Seiler.* Threatened with prosecution by the SHERIFF, he set off for America some 3 weeks ago by the Southampton STEAMER, fully intending on arrival in Halifax to telegraph the *New-Yorker Staatszeitung* (for which he once wrote) as follows: 'Sebastian Seiler, the famous author of *Kaspar Hauser,* has landed safely on the west coast of the Atlantic Ocean.' The great man left behind his Alexander II, 55 pages, mostly extracts from the Augsburg *Allgemeine Zeitung,* one copy of which was to be sent on immediately in his wake. For it is to appear on both sides of the Atlantic. This gossipy rubbish he surrounded with a great deal of humbug, having parts of it copied out by his wife, sister-in-law, etc., so that one and all they were astounded by POOR Sebastian's untiring industry. Negotiations with the London booksellers over this Alexander II served to give a veneer of erudition to his 'business errands' to town where every day he carefully investigated the quality of the LOBSTER and suchlike, not forgetting the French 'omelette'. Besides this Alexander, he has left other unpleasant surprises behind. You will remember that Liebknecht signed a bill for him, lured on by the foolish hope that Seiler would deduct a few pounds in his favour from the amount discounted. The bill fell due but was not presented. Seiler made out that he had paid it. He had only renewed it. Two days after he left, Liebknecht got a letter from a lawyer in the City requiring him to pay the bill. Pieper, whom Seiler's green-bespectacled sister-in-law loves for the sake of his glassy eyes, was despatched to the GREENGROCER. Consternation in the FAMILY. For Sebastian had already received the money to pay the bill, but had poured it down his gullet. Love, however, overcomes all obstacles, and his wife is convinced that she can lay claim to love *only once,* and then only from Sebastian. Hence she is trying to arrange matters. But the GREENGROCER is grave and glum, becoming daily more enlightened as to the WHEREABOUTS OF HIS DEAR SON-IN-LAW. The thing is still pending. Meanwhile fresh bills, allegedly honoured, keep arriving every day.

Levy. Sent here by the Düsseldorf workers with a *twofold* mission.

---

[a] Marx refers to Evans' speech in the House of Commons on 3 March 1856, published in *The Times,* No. 22306, 4 March 1856. - [b] This refers to *A Narrative of the Siege of Kars...* by H. Sandwith.

1. *Denunciation of Lassalle.* And, having considered the matter *very carefully,* I think *they are right.* Since the countess[a] got her 300,000 talers,[35] Lassalle has changed completely; deliberately repulsing the workers, a sybarite, coquetting with the Blues.[b] He is further accused of having constantly exploited the party for his filthy *personal ends* and wanting to make use of the workers themselves for *personal crimes* in the interests of the law-suit. The law-suit ended as follows: Count Hatzfeldt's head clerk, Stockum who, as you know, was subsequently sentenced at the Assizes to 5 years' penal servitude, had quarrelled with the count. He gave Lassalle to understand that he had in his possession documents which could have the count put in chains for perjury, forgery, etc. Lassalle promises him 10,000 talers. On the other hand, Lassalle persuades Kösteritz, the Chief Public Prosecutor (who has been compelled to resign as a result of this affair), to let Count Hatzfeldt know that there's a bill of indictment hanging over his head. Hatzfeldt is making a bolt for Paris when Lassalle hands him the incriminating documents *in return for his signing the settlement* with the countess, and withdraws the bill of indictment. (Kösteritz, of course, was acting purely as his INSTRUMENT.) Hence it was not his *legal* acumen that brought the law-suit to a sudden close, but a quite vulgar intrigue. Lassalle did not pay Stockum the 10,000 talers, and the workers are right in saying that such a breach of faith would be excusable only if he had handed over the money to the party instead of fraudulently keeping it for the countess. They report a host of personal dirty tricks which I cannot repeat because too many to remember. For instance, Lassalle gambled in foreign government paper with Scheuer of Düsseldorf, who advanced him the money for the purpose. They lost. Meanwhile Scheuer went bankrupt. Lassalle wins the law-suit. Scheuer demands the money he advanced Lassalle. The latter contemptuously draws his attention to §6 of the Code, which forbids gambling on foreign Exchanges. The workers say they turned a blind eye to everything done by Lassalle because of his plea that he was involved in the law-suit for reasons of honour. Now, having won, instead of getting the countess to pay him for his work and achieving independence, he is, they say, living shamefully under her thumb as *homme entretenu,*[c] WITHOUT ANY PRETEXT WHATEVER. He had always boasted about what he would do as soon as the law-suit had been won and now he was casting them aside, deliberately and defiantly, as redundant instruments of no further use. He had

---

[a] Sophie von Hatzfeldt - [b] the aristocracy - [c] kept man

attended one more (private) meeting on New Year's Day because a French colonel was present. To everyone's astonishment, he addressed 60 working-men exclusively on the subject of 'the struggle of civilisation against barbarism', the Western Powers versus Russia. Apparently he had planned to go to Berlin, play the grand gentleman there and open a salon. On his return, he promised the countess in Levy's presence to set up 'a court of literati' for her. Likewise in Levy's presence, he was constantly reiterating his 'dictatorial aspirations', etc., etc. (he seems to see himself quite differently from the way we see him, regarding himself as able to subdue the world because of his ruthlessness in a private intrigue, as though a man of real worth would sacrifice 10 years to such a bagatelle). An instance, by the by, of how dangerous he can be: in order to smuggle a labour party man into the police, ostensibly as a spy, he *gave* him *one of my letters* with instructions to say he had stolen it from Lassalle to establish his credibility. The workers further say that, being the diplomat he is, he would not have behaved so brusquely towards them had it not been his direct intention to go over to the bourgeois party. At the same time, he believes his influence is such that if he climbed onto a table at a moment of insurrection and harangued the masses, etc., he could talk them round. According to Levy, he is so much hated that, whatever we might decide, the workers would massacre him should he be in Düsseldorf at the moment of action. They are, by the by, convinced that he would lose no time in placing himself at the disposal of the other side should he hear of anything suspicious.

These are nothing but isolated points, deduced from what I heard, and only partially retained. The *whole* thing made a *distinct* impression on myself and Freiligrath, however prejudiced in Lassalle's favour and mistrustful of workers' tittle-tattle I may have been. I told Levy that it was, of course, impossible to reach any conclusion on the strength of a report from one side only; suspicion was in place whatever the circumstances; they should continue to keep an eye on the man but for the time being avoid any public row; we might perhaps find some opportunity of forcing Lassalle to make his position clear, etc., etc.

Qu'en pensez-vous?[a] I should like to have Lupus' opinion too.

2. The second purpose of Levy's mission was to give me information on how things stand with the workers in the Rhine Province. The Düsseldorf workers are still in contact with the

---

[a] What do you think of it?

Cologne people, amongst whom there are no longer any 'gentlemen'. But those chiefly concerned with propaganda are now the *factory workers in Solingen, Iserlohn and district, Elberfeld* and the ducal-Westphalia area. In the iron districts the fellows are all for force, and are held back only by the prospect of a French revolution and the fact that 'the Londoners think the time is not yet ripe'.[36] If the thing drags on much longer Levy believes that a rising will be difficult to prevent. But whatever the circumstances, an insurrection in Paris would be the signal. These people seem to be firmly convinced that *we and our friends would instantly hasten to join them.* They naturally feel the need for political and military leaders. Not that one can in any way blame the chaps for that. But I fear that, with their exceedingly artless plans, they would be smashed to smithereens before we had so much as a chance of leaving England. At all events, we owe it them to point out exactly what is and what isn't feasible from the military point of view. I have, OF COURSE, declared that, *circumstances permitting,* we would range ourselves with the Rhenish workers; that any uprising, undertaken off their own bat, without prior initiatives in Paris or Vienna or Berlin, would be idiotic; that, should Paris give the signal, it would be advisable, whatever the circumstances, to risk all, since then even the ill-effects of a momentary defeat could themselves be no more than momentary; that I and my friends would seriously consider what direct action might be taken by the working population of the Rhine Province, and that in due course they should again send someone to London, but do *nothing* without prior agreement.

The tanners of Elberfeld (or Barmen?) who were pretty reactionary in 1848 and '49, are now particularly eager for revolution. Levy assures me that the workers in the Wupper valley regard you, personally, as 'their' man. It would seem, by the way, that on the Rhine the belief in a revolution in France is fairly widespread, and even the philistines are saying: 'This time it will be different from 1848. This time there'll be people like Robespierre, etc., instead of the chatter-boxes of 1848.' On the Rhine at least, democracy's reputation has sunk very LOW.

Salut.

Your

K. M.

First published abridged in *Der Briefwechsel zwischen F. Engels und K. Marx,* Bd. 2, Stuttgart, 1913 and in full in: Marx and Engels, *Works,* First Russian Edition, Vol. XXII, Moscow, 1929

Printed according to the original

Published in English in full for the first time

7

ENGELS TO MARX

IN LONDON

Manchester, 7 March 1856

Dear Marx,

Much obliged to you for your exhaustive letter *ad Slavica*.[a] Eichhoff is already known to me as a philological quack who has actually out-quacked Klaproth (who did know something). I shall look into the business of the Goths in *Igor*[22] as soon as I have got the book. However, it has been established that a number of Goths remained in the Crimea until the 10th, and possibly the 11th, century; at least they figure as Goths in Byzantine [sources]. Could you let me know the title and price of Hanka and Swoboda's Bohemian anthology?[28] It is sure to be highly uncritical, for they are both complete asses.—Polish folk songs were published somewhere or other during the 40s.—I have found quotations from Götze, *Wladimir*,[b] etc., in Grimm's translation of Wuk's *Serbische Grammatik* with the comment 'unfortunately without the Russian text'. Kapper is a Prague Jew who published his *Südslavische Wanderungen* in the Bohemian constitutionalist paper[c] in 1848/49. He's a writer of *belles lettres*, but whether his translations are any good I couldn't say—*j'en doute cependant*.[d] All the Serbian wedding songs have been translated by the Jakob woman.[e] The political works you mention on the Hungarian and Turkish Serbs might be worth looking at if they are in the Museum.[f]

The *Neue Preussische Zeitung* isn't available in Manchester, but I followed the Pfeil business in the *Kölner* and the *Augsburger*[g] and derived much joy from it. However the penitent LEADER in the *N. Pr.*[h] was, of course, new to me; really too delightful, the sudden discovery that despite all the feudal gewgaws, nobility and bourgeoisie are today *au fond*[i] one.

What you say about Austria in regard to the Slavs and Protestantism is perfectly right. Fortunately a very strong form of

---

[a] on things Slavonic - [b] See this volume, p. 20. - [c] probably the *Constitutionelles Blatt aus Böhmen* - [d] I doubt it, however. - [e] Therese Albertine Luise von Jakob-Robinson (pen-name: Talvj), who published the collection *Volkslieder der Serben*. - [f] the British Museum Library - [g] The *Kölnische Zeitung* and the *Allgemeine Zeitung* - [h] 'Den Streitenden', *Neue Preußische Zeitung*, No. 54, 4 March 1856. - [i] basically

Protestantism has survived in Slovakia, and has greatly contributed to the inaction of the Slovaks against the Hungarians,[a] while in Bohemia every serious national movement other than the proletarian will in addition receive a strong admixture of Hussite historical memories which in turn will weaken the specifically national element. Pity about the Slovenian peasants who fought so splendidly in the 15th century.

I shall read about the Kars affair. What is Swan's piece called?[b]

The course taken by the Seileriad will assuredly please everyone except Liebknecht and the GREENGROCER. An unpleasant whiff of the cesspit.

Lassalle. It would be a pity about the fellow because of his great ability, but these goings-on are really too bad. He was always a man one had to keep a devilish sharp eye on and as a real Jew from the Slav border was always to exploit anyone for his own private ends on party pretexts. And then his urge to push his way into polite society, *de parvenir,*[c] if only for appearance's sake, to disguise the greasy Breslau Jew with all kinds of pomade and paint was always repulsive. However all these were simply things which made it necessary to keep a sharp eye on him. But if he gets up to the kind of tricks that will actually result in his changing parties, I can't blame the Düsseldorf workers for the hatred they have conceived against him. I shall go and see Lupus this evening and put the matter to him. None of us ever trusted Lassalle but we did, of course, protect him against stupidities emanating from H. Bürgers. To my mind, everything should be allowed to proceed in the manner you prescribed for the Düsseldorfers. If he can be induced to commit a direct and OVERT ACT against the party, then we shall have him. But as yet there would seem to be none of that and in any case a row would be quite out of place.

The business of the Hatzfeldt woman and the 300,000 talers[35] was quite new to me. I imagined she was simply receiving something monthly or yearly. He can never be forgiven for having saved Hatzfeldt from the black and yellow jacket.[d] I shall come back to the other matters.

Your

F. E.

First published abridged in *Der Briefwechsel zwischen F. Engels und K. Marx*, Bd. 2, Stuttgart, 1913 and in full in: Marx and Engels, *Works,* First Russian Edition, Vol. XXII, Moscow, 1929

Printed according to the original

Published in English for the first time

---

[a] i.e. against the Hungarian Revolution of 1848-49 - [b] A reference to *A Narrative of the Siege of Kars...* by H. Sandwith. - [c] come up in the world - [d] See this volume, p. 23.

8

MARX TO ENGELS

IN MANCHESTER

[London,] Tuesday [25 March 1856][37]

Dear Engels,

In one of my next letters I shall reply to your last. Today simply an inquiry, to which I should like, if possible, an answer *by return*. I did *not* send any article to the *Tribune* today because I hadn't finished reading the *Blue Book*[38] *on Kars*[a]—I only got hold of it late yesterday evening. I have to send off my article[b] on Friday, at the same time as the one I am expecting from you. Well, *ad rem*[c]:

A large part of the Blue Book is of a purely military nature; you will be able to see later whether anything can be done with it. But there's one point on which I want your critical opinion, since it is also material to the political-diplomatic aspect of the matter and I have got to discuss it in *this* Friday's article. At the end of June the Turks proposed to send reinforcements to Redoute-Kaleh[d] in order to operate from there in the direction of Kutais,[e] etc. The British government, on the other hand, wanted to send a relief force to Erzerum via Trebizond and, it seems, to abandon Kars as a place of little importance, regarding Erzerum as the centre of resistance. At all events this dispute meant that the moment propitious for action was irretrievably lost. So that you may be fully informed on the question I append here the crucial extracts.

Stratford de Redcliffe to Clarendon. 28th June, 1855.

'The Turkish ministers, who had talked of sending 10,000 men from Batoum[f] to Erzeroum, now, in their embarrassment, incline to another plan. They propose to form an entrenched camp at Redoute-Kaleh, and to concentrate there the corps of General Vivian—completed by a draft of 10,000 men from the Bulgarian army—that of General Beatson, and the detachment from Batoum, reduced to 7,000 men. The total of these combined forces would be about 30,000 of all arms. Stationary they might operate as a diversion in favour of the army at Kars or Erzeroum; advancing by Kutais or Georgia they might either attack the Russians in the rear or force them to retreat.'

---

[a] *Papers Relative to Military Affairs in Asiatic Turkey, and the Defence and Capitulation of Kars* (below Marx quotes in English from this collection). - [b] K. Marx, 'The Fall of Kars'. - [c] to the point - [d] Kulevi - [e] Kutaisi - [f] Batumi

Id to id., 30th June, 1855.

'The meeting which I had previously announced, took place this morning at the Grand Vizier's[a] house on the Bosphorus. In addition to his Highness, the Seraskier[b] and Fuad Effendi were present. I was accompanied by Brigadier-General Mansfield.... It appears, that the Russians advancing from Gumri[c] with an amount of force varying from 20-30,000, had presented themselves before Kars; that a partial engagement of Cavalry had taken place, followed two days later by an attack, which had been repulsed, on the part of the enemy, and that the town was threatened with a siege.... It was clear, to all present, that whether the Russians besieged or turned Kars, the Turkish army required an effort to be made for its relief with all practicable despatch, and that of 3 possible modes of acting for that purpose, the only one likely to prove effective was an expedition by Kutais into Georgia. To send reinforcements by Trebizond would be at best a palliative. To establish an entrenched camp at Redoute-Kaleh, would, at this unhealthy season, be equivalent to consigning the troops to destruction. The real question was, whether a force numerically sufficient, and in all respects effective, could be collected in time at Kutais to make an excursion into Georgia and threaten the communications of the Russian army.... The Turkish ministers proposed that the expeditionary force should be composed of 12,000 men from Batoum and the neighbouring stations; of the troops made over to General Vivian, and estimated at 10,000 of all arms; of General Beatson's Irregular Cavalry, of 10,000 men to be detracted from the army in Bulgaria as the complement of the Turkish contingent; of 5,000 more derived from the same source; of an Egyptian regiment of horse now here, and of another regiment expected from Tunis. To these the Seraskier proposed to add 2,000 Albanians by way of riflemen. These several forces ... would present a total of 44,000 men, not perhaps to be reckoned with prudence at more than 36,000 effectives.'

Id. to id., 1st July, 1855

* '...the proposed diversion at Redoute-Kaleh originated with the Porte.'*

Clarendon to Stratford de Redcliffe. July 13th, 1855.

*'...Her Majesty's[d] government are of opinion, that the wiser course would be to send reinforcements *to the rear of the Turkish army,* instead of sending an expedition to the rear of the Russian army. The reinforcements might go to Trebizond, and be directed from thence upon Erzeroum. The distance from Trebizond to Erzeroum is less than that from Redoute-Kaleh to Tiflis,[e] and the march is through a friendly instead of through a hostile country; and at Erzeroum the army would meet supporting friends instead of opposing enemies, and supplies instead of famine. If the army at Kars cannot maintain that position against the Russians, [...] it will be easier to defeat them by the whole force collected, than by divided portions of that force; and a defeat would be the more decisive, the further it took place within the Turkish frontier. Trebizond is a place where supplies of all kinds might be landed etc.'*

Id. to id., 14th July, 1855 (telegraphic).

* 'The plan for reinforcing the army at Kars contained in your despatch of the 30th June and lst inst., is disapproved. [...] Trebizond ought to be the base of

[a] Ali Mehemet Pasha - [b] Rushdi Pasha, Turkish War Minister - [c] now Leninakan - [d] Victoria - [e] Tbilisi

operations, and if the Turkish army of Kars and Erzeroum cannot hold out at the latter place against the Russians, *it might fall back on Trebizond*, where it would easily be reinforced.'*

Id. to id., 16th July, 1855.

'If, indeed, Omer Pasha ... should determine to take any part of his own army, with Tunisians and Albanians to Redoute-Kaleh, Her Majesty's government would have nothing to say to that proceeding, but as regards the contingent under General Vivian and General Beatson's Horse, Her Majesty's government abide by their opinion that they should be directed through Trebizond or Erzeroum.'

Lord Panmure to General Vivian, 14th July, 1855.

*'...I place such full reliance on your professional ability, that I feel no anxiety lest you should undertake any expedition of a nature so wild and ill-digested as that contemplated by the Porte.... *A coup de main* by means of suddenly throwing an army on the coast to threaten, or even to attack an enemy's stronghold, is one thing, but a deliberate expedition to invade an enemy's country, and on his own territory to make war upon him, is quite another.'*

I must confess that Clarendon's strategy strikes me as curious in the extreme, as does also the fine distinction drawn by Lord Panmure Carnot favouring the Sevastopol '*coup de main*' against the Turkish plan for a strategic move in Georgia.

If possible, then, an answer to these points *by return*.

Salut.

Your

K. M.

First published in *Der Briefwechsel zwischen F. Engels und K. Marx*, Bd. 2, Stuttgart, 1913

Printed according to the original

Published in English for the first time

9

MARX TO ENGELS[20]

IN MANCHESTER

[London,] 10 April 1856

Dear Frederic,

It is high time I wrote again. I've been prevented from doing so by all kinds of domesticities.

Enclosed 1 letter from Levy to me, from Düsseldorf. The Touroute mentioned in the letter is a French ex-colonel. He called yesterday while I was out and so I shall not be seeing him for several days as he has gone to Liverpool. He had a longish conversation with my wife, the quintessence of which is contained in *enclosure 2*,[39] composed by *Madame* herself. The M. mentioned in Levy's letter is Miquel.

In a few days' time you will receive *Igor*,[22] which has now arrived; Russian-German; the BLUE BOOK[a]; Destrilhes, *Confidences sur la Turquie* and a cutting from *L'Homme*, which I have mislaid and hence cannot send today, viz. a letter from a *déporté* in Cayenne, Tassilier by name, to M. le Ministre de la Marine,[b] in which the frightful abominations to which Boustrapa[40] subjects the deportees are revealed.[41] You would have had the BLUE BOOK long ago but *d'abord*[c] the PRESSURE of daily events has several times compelled me to suspend work on my articles[d] on this subject and write about other themes, so that I was unable to do without the book. Then the friends whom you know arrived. They wanted to have the NOVELTY just for *one* day, and had not yet returned it a week later.

AS TO THESE KARS PAPERS, *The Times*, in three fulminating LEADERS,[e] gave a rehash of the section covering August 1854 to ABOUT February 1855, i.e. *did not so much as touch on* the really interesting and crucial period. The object of this is, of course, to shift all RESPONSIBILITY from the Ministry onto Redcliffe and the Turkish pashas in Asia. The best of it is that the English government, as you will see from Destrilhes, forcibly kept at the helm Redcliffe's rotten Turkish ministry, thus partly condoning and partly bringing about the abominations of which Williams complains. That, however, is only a minor matter. By a procedure similar to the one used in Stieber's case[f]—namely, by producing proof of FALSIFIED DATES AND FORGED PASSAGES—I have, in my view, proved irrefutably that the responsibility for planning the fall of Kars and for the systematic execution of that plan, lay with the British GOVERNMENT, which furthermore had the good fortune this time to figure in Bonaparte's eyes as zealous 'in the cause'. I have not, OF COURSE, gone into the military aspect proper, i.e. the DEFENCE OF KARS; I have some MISGIVINGS, however, about the 'stature' of Williams.

---

[a] *Papers Relative to Military Affairs in Asiatic Turkey, and the Defence and Capitulation of Kars* - [b] F. A. Hamelin - [c] first of all - [d] A series of articles entitled *The Fall of Kars* which Marx was writing for *The People's Paper*. It was based on his article of the same title written for the *New-York Daily Tribune*. - [e] 'The Capitulation of Kars', *The Times*, Nos. 22320, 22322 and 22323, 20, 22 and 24 March 1856. - [f] Marx refers to his pamphlet *Revelations Concerning the Communist Trial in Cologne*.

Jones, to whom I have shown my manuscript, intends IF POSSIBLE—i.e. if he can get together enough money to take St. Martin's Hall[a]—to LECTURE on the FALL OF KARS at the said venue before the debate on it in Parliament begins.

There is now going on a bitter controversy between the Chartists and the Urquhartites at Newcastle upon Tyne, London, Birmingham, and several other places.[42] As you will have heard, Jones, with Finlen for shadow, has proclaimed himself dictator of Chartism and set up a new organisation which, INDEED, is in process of growing but has, on the other hand, evoked a great storm of indignation against him.[43]

The 'speculation upon speculation'—not in ideas but in shares—which has invaded the Rhine Province and Berlin from France would appear to be proliferating as viciously there as on the other side of the Rhine. Jeremiads about this social MISCHIEF, this infatuation, are appearing in the Ministry's *Preussische Correspondenz*, in which the imminence of an 'inevitable' and general financial crisis IS SERIOUSLY AND EMPHATICALLY hinted at.

You will know about Heine's death, but not about Ludwig Simon of Trier pissing—passing water, I mean—on his grave in the New York *Neue Zeit* run by Löwe, quondam lion[b] of the Parliament of the 'Cherman' Nation[44] after its retreat to Stuckert.[c] This poet or minnesinger of the female Yid, Madame Hohenscheisse-esche or-linden of Frankfurt am Main, is naturally of the opinion that Heine was no poet; he had 'no sensibility', was full of 'malevolence' and calumniated not only Kobes I,[d] but even Berne's[e] lady friend, the great Berne's 'mouse', muse or moose—the Strauss woman.[f]

Down here there is A SOCIETY FOR THE PROTECTION OF SMALL TRADESMEN. This SOCIETY publishes a weekly rag[g] for the said protection. In that weekly our friend Seiler 'along with his wife' is pilloried as a 'SWINDLER'.

BUT greater things are afoot. Pieper, thanks to his genius, has again been living a freebooter's existence since January and, despite the not inconsiderable SUBSIDIES provided by me, has been daily on the *qui vive* vis-à-vis his LANDLADY. Now it has suddenly occurred to him that all he requires to become a great man is a

[a] a venue of public gatherings in London. The inaugural meeting of the International Working Men's Association was held there in September 1864. - [b] Löwe von Calbe - [c] Stuttgart (Marx deliberately uses this word and a number of others in this paragraph in their South German dialectal form). - [d] Nickname of Jakob Venedey under which he was ridiculed by Heine in his poem 'Kobes I' (*Kobes* means Jakob in the Cologne dialect). - [e] Ludwig Börne - [f] Jeanette Wohl-Straus. Heine described Börne's relations with her in his 'Ludwig Börne'. - [g] *Protection for Trade*

little capital. Seiler's SISTER-IN-LAW, the GREENGROCER'S 2nd daughter, a tallow-candle in green spectacles, has long been mortally in love with the said Pieper. Her entire person green like verdigris rather than veg., and GREENS to boot without ANY MEAT OT FLESH WHATEVER. While declaring her to be ugly as the day, Pieper has nevertheless discovered that she is not without intelligence, of which she gives incontrovertible proof by regarding our Hanoverian lambkin as a German Byron *manqué*. So, the day before yesterday, therefore, Pieper, to whom this person clings, not simply like a burr but like a CATERPILLAR, resolved to pour out his heart to Seiler's father-in-law. He did not wish to do so in front of his 'beloved' for fear he might have to kiss her, which indeed is HARD WORK for an occidental unaccustomed TO FEED UPON TALLOW. But in true Pieper-fashion, the declaration of love was combined with—a touch for a loan. Pieper could not disburden his heart to the GREENGROCER without inviting the GREENGROCER to disburden his POCKETS, not to say his till. On the grounds, that is, of his needing a little capital, SAY 20-40 POUNDS, TO CREATE HIMSELF A POSITION as a FASHIONABLE tutor. Meanwhile he intends to let his 'beloved' enjoy the pleasures of widowhood while still betrothed, nor will his compassion *ever* permit him to marry her. GREENS or no GREENS, the whole business is most unsavoury, but Pieper imagines he will come out of it as a man of honour, i.e. AT A CERTAIN EPOCH LOOMING IN THE FUTURE repay down to the last farthing the advances he 'hopes' to obtain from his would-be father-in-law, generously leaving him his daughter into the bargain. Since that fateful day he has been back to my house only once, for a minute, while I was out. Called himself a 'happy man'. Little Jenny called him 'BENEDICK THE MARRIED MAN',[a] but little Laura said: 'BENEDICK WAS A WIT, HE IS BUT "A' CLOWN", AND "A CHEAP CLOWN" TOO.' The children are constantly reading Shakespeare.

Liebknecht has at last achieved something, to wit, a little Liebknecht.

By 'His Majesty's supreme and special command' my wife has received a passport from Berlin. In May she will travel to Trier with the whole FAMILY for *3-4 months*.

Salut. Regards to Lupus.

K. M.

First published abridged in *Der Briefwechsel zwischen F. Engels und K. Marx*, Bd. 2, Stuttgart, 1913 and in full in: Marx and Engels, *Works*, First Russian Edition, Vol. XXII, Moscow, 1929

Printed according to the original

Published in English in full for the first time

---

[a] Shakespeare, *Much Ado about Nothing*, Act V, Scene 4.

10

ENGELS TO MARX[1]

IN LONDON

Manchester, 14 April 1856

Dear Marx,

I eagerly look forward to the Blue Book.[a] But since I shall not have time for the process of chronological comparison to which you subjected it, you might give me a few hints some time as to the main snags; I shall have to confine myself solely to the military side, which I shall go through carefully, comparing it with Sandwith's book[b] when possible. Up here we've heard absolutely nothing about Jones' coup d'état[43] and the consequent pother; I must certainly start getting *The People's Paper* again.

Never before has the speculation shown such sparkling form in Germany. Mevissen is king of the Rhine Province, has bought the *Indépendance* jointly with Morny, and is setting up an international (hurrah!) bank in Luxembourg (!). I have seen the jeremiad in the *Preussische Correspondenz.* However, steps have been taken to ensure that neither Manteuffel nor von der Heydt suppresses the swindle; Crédits mobiliers[45] are being set up in Hanover, Leipzig *et al.* and what these fail to accomplish is sure to be made good by unofficial crookery. The final phase of the gamble is now beginning: Russia is importing capital and speculation and, given these distances, these hundreds of miles of railways, the gamble may well develop in such a way as to come to an early and sticky end. Once we hear of the Grand Irkutsk Trunk Line with branches to Pekin, etc., etc., that will be the moment for us to pack up. This time the crash will be quite unprecedented; all the ingredients are there: intensity, universal scope, and the involvement of all propertied and ruling social elements. What I find funniest is your worthy Englishman's unshakable conviction, that, in view of the 'sound' state of trade, nothing like that could possibly happen here. It is clear enough that no one is speculating heavily in industrial *production,* it being common knowledge that a modest amount of investment in direct production could bring about saturation in all markets within a year, and this particularly so long as the colossal calls on capital for communications persist. But

---

[a] *Papers Relative to Military Affairs in Asiatic Turkey, and the Defence and Capitulation of Kars* - [b] H. Sandwith, *A Narrative of the Siege of Kars....*

as a result of speculation in communications, even industrial production is increasing out of all proportion, though more slowly than e.g. in 1833-36 or 1842-45. This year cotton prices are rising rapidly despite a hitherto unprecedented crop of 3,500,000 bales, which looks no larger this year than e.g. $2^1/_2$ million bales would have looked in 1850. Moreover, relative to England, the Continent is taking almost 3 times as much as 5 years ago, as is proved by the following table of exports from America between 1 September and 1 April each year (in thousands of bales):

	1856	1855	1854	1853
Export to England over 7 months	1,131	963	840	1,100
to France over 7 months	354	249	229	255
to other European ports over 7 months	346	167	179	204[a]

So the Continent which, in 1853, took $\frac{45}{110} = \frac{1}{3}$ of the English figure, took $\frac{70}{113} = \frac{5}{8}$ in 1856. And to this must be added what was obtained by the Continent from England. As you can see, the growth of the industry on the Continent is out of all proportion to that in England, and the worthy British, BEING RATHER ON THE DECLINE, have every reason not to OVERTRADE in their cotton industry; 1853 and 1856, however, provide the best comparison, since in both years the crop was a very large one—3,300,000 and 3,500,000 bales. The substantial exports to France are purely fictitious, for a portion goes from Le Havre to Switzerland, Baden, Frankfurt and Antwerp. But it is in this enormous leap forward of industry on the Continent that the most viable embryo of English revolution lies.

While I see the rag *Protection for Trade* from time to time, I didn't, alas, have a chance to admire *amicum*[b] Sebastian[c] therein.

The Pieperiad is becoming distinctly distasteful. This little tale has some very amusing aspects, but also some nasty twists, and the thread of vanity running through it creates a disagreeable impression. Only let the fellow out of your sight for the space of 2 minutes and he'll go and do something idiotic on the assumption, shared by no one else, that he's a genius. I hope that he'll have to

[a] In the manuscript Marx added three noughts to all the figures in this table. - [b] friend - [c] Seiler

marry his tallow candle and that he *doesn't* get that little sum; it would serve him right.

Should the case arise, we must demonstrate our gratitude for the gallantry shown to your wife by supreme and special command.[a] Whatever happens he[b] must be given his ALLOWANCE of champagne in his *cachot*.[c]

I found the Lassalliads[39] most entertaining; the ringleted Jewish noddle must look charming indeed above the red nightshirt and the 'marquisian' drapery, while his every movement betrays the Polish Izzy. All things considered, the fellow must produce a most sordid and repulsive impression.

I am keeping Levy's letter here[d] and shall write to you, tomorrow if possible, about sundry matters concerning the workers' business. It would, by the way, be advisable to secure letters containing this sort of stuff with sealing wax. At the same time I shall return you Levy's letter.

I have already told you that I can hear again; three abscesses burst in my ear one after the other, and that did the trick.

Warm regards to your wife and children.

Your

F. E.

First published abridged in *Der Briefwechsel zwischen F. Engels und K. Marx*, Bd. 2, Stuttgart, 1913 and in full in: Marx and Engels, *Works*, Second Russian Edition, Vol. 29, Moscow, 1962

Printed according to the original

Published in English in full for the first time

11

ENGELS TO WILHELM STEFFEN

IN BRIGHTON

Manchester, 15 April 1856

Dear Steffen,

Can you recommend a good map of Germany suitable for military studies and not too expensive—scale about 1:100,000 or, better still, 1:80,000, 1:60,000, etc. In addition a map, in rather

---

[a] See this volume, p. 33. - [b] Frederick William IV - [c] cell - [d] See this volume, pp. 30-31.

more detail (1:60,000 to 1:40,000 would, of course, do), of the Rhine Province and Westphalia—a good one, however, and not too dear; the Prussian General Staff maps are, I believe, fearfully expensive and as yet incomplete. Even 1:150-200,000 might do for the map of Germany, that is not so important as that it should be good and really suitable. Provided it enables one to distinguish the *general features* of a battlefield, e.g. at Jena or Austerlitz,[46] even without an auxiliary plan, I shall be satisfied. The one for the Rhine Province and Westphalia should, of course, show what is shown on the 1 inch to the mile (about 1:60,000) English ORDNANCE MAP.

Little that's new up here. Lupus has a great deal to do at the moment, but for him, too, the lean holiday period is approaching. Is there a chance of your coming up to these parts in the summer?

Your

F. Engels

Add. as before:
Care of Mchr. Ermen & Engels

First published in: Marx and Engels, *Works*, First Russian Edition, Vol. XXV, Moscow, 1934

Printed according to the original

Published in English for the first time

12

MARX TO ENGELS[1]

IN MANCHESTER

London, 16 April 1856

DEAR Frederic,

A packet went off to you today through the usual PARCELS company. It contains: 1. Kars PAPERS.[a] 2. *Igor.*[22] 3. Destrilhes, *Confidences sur la Turquie.* 4. 2 issues of *L'Homme*; in one, the letter from Cayenne, in the other, Pyat's litany to Marianne,[47] which he read aloud on 25 February of this year at a Chartist

[a] *Papers Relative to Military Affairs in Asiatic Turkey, and the Defence and Capitulation of Kars*

meeting in honour of the French Revolution. The good fellow was, of course, hoping to see a repetition of the row caused by his 'lettre à la reine'.[16] Was disappointed, however. From this you will also gather how subordinate is the attitude adopted by the French would-be revolutionaries here vis-à-vis 'Marianne'. 5. 2 cuttings from *The People's Paper,* my first 2 articles on the Kars PAPERS.[a] Shall also send you third and final instalments. Since the original of Article I had gone astray, and time, not to mention Ernest Jones, was pressing, I had to do a hasty rehash of the *Tribune* article out of my head, so that sundry bits of nonsense have crept in which will certainly not elude your keen nose. BUT NEVER MIND THAT! I mention it simply to let you know why I didn't send you the thing straight away.

The day before yesterday a little banquet took place to celebrate the anniversary of *The People's Paper.* On this occasion, the times seeming to require it, I accepted the invitation, the more so since (AS ANNOUNCED IN THE *PAPER*) I *alone* of the whole emigration was invited, and the first toast also fell to me, i.e. I was asked to propose one to the *souveraineté du prolétariat dans tous les pays.*[b] So I made a short SPEECH in English, which, however, I shall not allow to appear in print.[48] The end I sought has been achieved. Mr Talandier—who had to pay 2/6d for his TICKET—is now convinced, like the rest of the French and other émigré crews, that we are the Chartists' only 'intimate' allies and that, though we may hold aloof from public demonstrations and leave it to the FRENCHMEN to flirt openly with Chartism, it is always in our power to resume the position already allotted to us by history. This had become all the more necessary because, at the above-mentioned meeting of 25 February presided over by Pyat, the German lout *Scherzer* (OLD BOY) spoke and, in truly dreadful Straubingerian style,[49] denounced the German 'scholars', the 'intellectual workers', for having left them (the louts) in the lurch, thus forcing them to make fools of themselves in the eyes of the other nationalities. You will remember Scherzer from Paris days. I have met friend *Schapper* again several times and have found him very much the repentant sinner. The retirement in which he has been living for the past 2 years would seem RATHER to have sharpened his wits than otherwise. As you will realise, there are all sorts of contingencies in

---

a The first two articles from Marx's series *The Fall of Kars* published in *The People's Paper* on 5 and 12 April 1856 and based on Marx's article of the same title for the *New-York Daily Tribune* mentioned further in the text. - b the sovereignty of the proletariat in all countries (see K. Marx, 'Speech at the Anniversary of *The People's Paper.* Delivered in London, April 14, 1856').

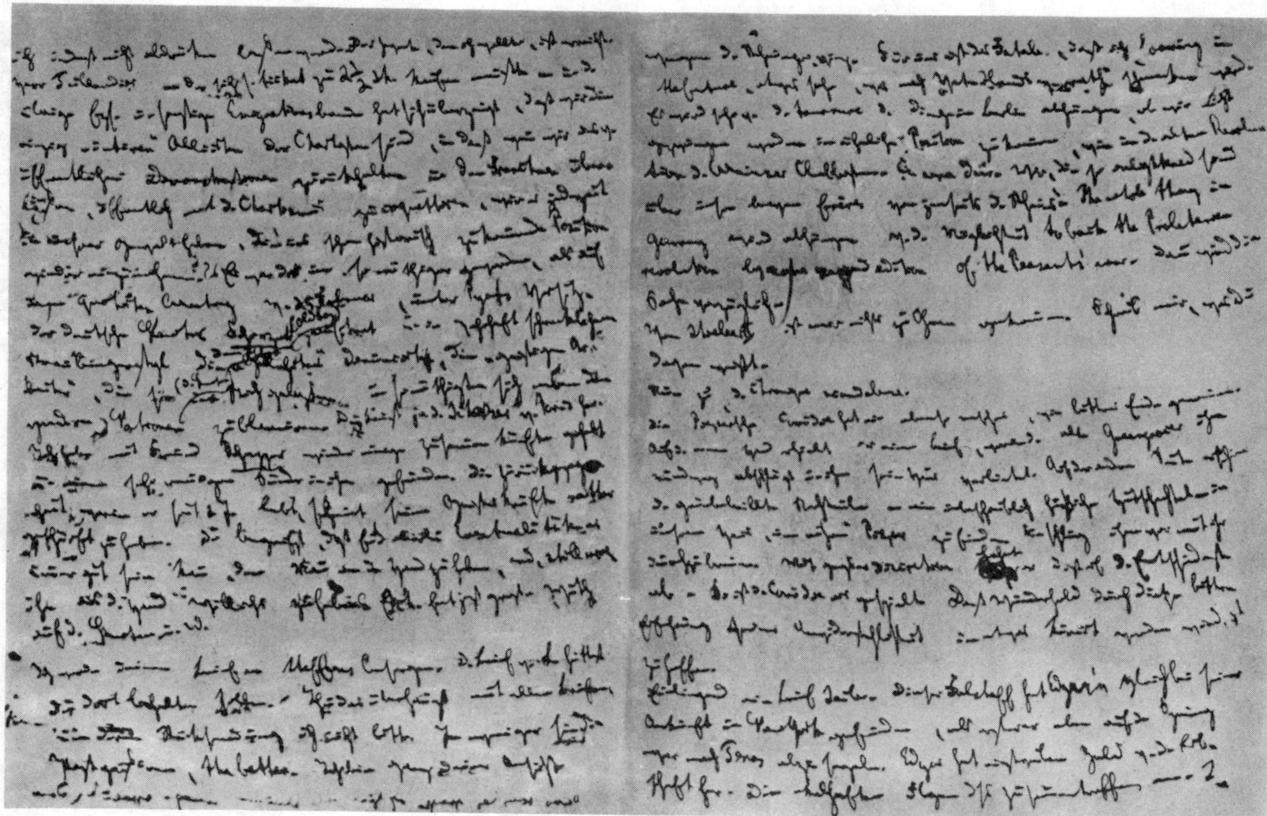

The second and third pages of Marx's letter to Engels of 16 April 1856

which it might be advantageous to have the man to hand AND, STILL MORE, to have him out of the hands of Willich. Schapper is now furiously angry with the Windmill[50] louts.

I shall forward your letter to Steffen. You ought to have kept Levy's letter[a] there. Do so in general with all letters I don't ask you to return. The less they go through the post THE BETTER. I fully agree with you about the Rhine Province. As for us, the worst of it is that, LOOMING IN THE FUTURE, I see something that looks like 'high treason'. Whether we are forced into the same kind of position as the Mainz Clubbists[51] in the old revolution will largely depend on the *tournure*[b] things take in Berlin. *Ça sera dur.*[c] We, who are so ENLIGHTENED about our good *frères* from across the Rhine! THE WHOLE THING IN GERMANY will depend on whether it is possible TO BACK THE PROLETARIAN REVOLUTION BY SOME SECOND EDITION OF THE PEASANTS' WAR. In which case the affair should go swimmingly.

I have heard nothing whatever about Stieber II. Write and tell me what you know on this score.

Now for the *chronique scandaleuse.*[d]

The Pieper comedy came to an end as abrupt as it was bitter. On the one hand, he got a letter in which the old GREENGROCER turned him down out of hand and forbade him the house. On the other, the green-bespectacled screech-owl—an indescribably hideous piece of baggage—turned up at our house in search of 'her' Pieper. She proposed that they should elope together. With great tact he refused quite unequivocally. So the comedy is over. It is to be hoped that this bitter experience, the result of his irresistibleness, will have some salutory effect upon Prince Charming.

Enclosed a letter from Seiler. As soon as this Falstaff arrived in New York he caught Edgar[e] just as the latter was about to set out for Texas. Edgar has in the meantime come into some money from the inheritance. The nasty consequences of this meeting with Seiler will be apparent to you from the letter.

A fine pair, Seiler and Conrad Schramm!

Salut.

Your

K. M.

First published abridged in *Der Briefwechsel zwischen F. Engels und K. Marx*, Bd. 2, Stuttgart, 1913 and in full in: Marx and Engels, *Works*, First Russian Edition, Vol. XXII, Moscow, 1929

Printed according to the original

Published in English in full for the first time

---

[a] See this volume, pp. 30-31. - [b] turn - [c] It will be tough. - [d] gossip column - [e] Edgar von Westphalen

13

MARX TO ENGELS

IN MANCHESTER

London, 26 April 1856
28 Dean Street, Soho

DEAR Frederic,

Enclosed you will find

1. 2 Kars PAPERS, third and final instalments.[a]

2. An article on the Duke of York[b] which I gave Jones, and in which I imitate OLD Cobbett's manner *tant bien que mal*.[c] Sent especially for Lupus' information.

3. The SPEECH made by Frost, the old Chartist, in New York.[d]

4. A letter from Miquel. This last *to be returned*. For I have not yet replied, as I should like to have your detailed 'OPINION' before doing so. It's a somewhat ticklish matter. 'Questions, sometimes insidious',[e] and when replying it is difficult to know how far one can properly go.[52]

Que dites-vous du discours de M. de Walewski?[f 53] Everyone in London is furious with the GOVERNMENT and even the SHOPKEEPERS are mouthing revolutionary slogans.

If you can, send Pieper something. It is now possible that he will get a job as CORRECTOR on *The People's Paper*. All I can do now is keep him in commons. I have taken him seriously to task for his silly antics, which have landed him on the streets again. I could tell you a thing or two about politics down here, but to do so by post might be risky.

The news from Paris in today's *Advertiser* contains a brief but interesting report on an action brought against some members of Marianne[47]; they're conducting themselves splendidly.

In the *Presse* (Paris) some edifying aspersions on Bonaparte's

---

[a] K. Marx, *The Fall of Kars*, Articles III and IV - [b] K. Marx, 'The House of Lords and the Duke of York's Monument'. - [c] after a fashion - [d] *The People's Paper*, No. 208, 26 April 1856 - [e] H. Heine, *Deutschland. Ein Wintermärchen*, Chapter 20. - [f] What do you say to M. de Walewski's speech? (The speech was reported in *The Times*, No. 22352, 26 April 1856.)

législateur poète—Belmontet—by Pelletan, in which the latter has so insulted the 'empereur'[a] that he will probably be expelled.

Salut.

Your

K. M.

First published abridged in *Der Briefwechsel zwischen F. Engels und K. Marx*, Bd. 2, Stuttgart, 1913 and in full in: Marx and Engels, *Works*, First Russian Edition, Vol. XXII, Moscow, 1929

Printed according to the original

Published in English for the first time

14

MARX TO ENGELS

IN MANCHESTER

[London,] 7 May 1856
28 Dean Street, Soho

Dear Frederic,

I have another letter from Germany to send on to you. But since you haven't yet acknowledged *receipt* either of the PARCEL or of the *letter* enclosing Miquel's,[b] I don't know whether these things have reached you. Let me know by return. In the case of compromising letters, it's essential to be sure they are delivered.

Salut.

Your

K. M.

First published in: Marx and Engels, *Works*, First Russian Edition, Vol. XXII, Moscow, 1929

Printed according to the original

Published in English for the first time

15

MARX TO ENGELS[54]

IN MANCHESTER

[London,] 8 May[c] 1856
28 Dean Street, Soho

DEAR Frederic,

Received your letter.[55] My PRESSURE upon you in YESTERDAY'S LETTER explicable *d'abord*[d] by the fact that an earlier parcel of my wife's

---

[a] Napoleon III - [b] See previous letter. - [c] April in the original - [d] first of all

did *not* arrive in Manchester, although sent by post. Secondly, however, you know how a man feels when he's kept on the hop by piles. *And such a man am I.*

I am glad to hear that you and Lupus are entirely of my opinion with regard to Miquel's letter[52]—the attempt to digest this 'wisdom' fairly 'turned my stomach'.

Unless something goes wrong with the pecuniary arrangements I have made, my family will be leaving in 10 to 14 days at the latest.[a] A pity you are so overworked, otherwise we might have done *un petit tour*[b] to Scotland.

I shall carry out your commissions at the Museum[c] as soon as I go there again.

Enclosed:

2 letters, 1. from Imandt; 2. from Cologne.[56] Would it not be best if I replied to the Cologne people through my wife? THERE EXISTS SOME JEALOUSY between Cologne and Düsseldorf AS TO THE LEADING OF THE PROLETARIAN MOVEMENT. BESIDES, I don't know whether the Cologne people are aware that the Düsseldorfers have completely broken with Lassalle who has fallen into general disrepute among them.

Yesterday the following comical missive arrived from Sheffield:

*Council Hall, Sheffield,
May 6th, '56.

Doctor,

The Sheffield Foreign Affairs Committee[57] instructs me to convey to you an expression of their warm thanks for the great public service you have rendered by your admirable *exposé* of the Kars Papers published in *The People's Paper*.[d] I have the Honour etc.

Cyples, Secretary.*

That is magnanimous, there being war to the death between *The People's Paper* and *The Free Press,* as between Chartism and Urquhartism generally.[42] The great Ironside went one step further and decreed THAT THE 'THANKS OF THE COUNTRY' WERE DUE TO DR. M.[e] ETC. It would have been much better had the chaps sent me the money they made out by reprinting the Palmerston articles under the title *Story of the Life etc.* (in pamphlet form).[58]

From New York Seiler has sent me—came today—'Das Recht deutscher vereinigter Staatenbürger in Europa' in the *Democrat.*[f] Will never be read, not in this world at any rate.

Since handing over your £2 to Pieper I haven't set eyes on him. Moreover, Jones has sent word that, up till *yesterday evening,* he had not delivered the work he had accepted for *The People's Paper.*

---

[a] See this volume, p. 33. - [b] short trip - [c] the British Museum Library - [d] K. Marx, *The Fall of Kars.* - [e] Marx - [f] *New-Yorker Demokrat*

Nous verrons.[a] If he wilfully throws away this opportunity as well, let him go to the devil. Now's his chance, the silly ass.

Salut.

Your

K. M.

Apropos! Have seen Heine's will[59]! A return to the 'living God', and a 'Recantation before God and man' if ever he wrote anything 'immoral'!

Didn't see Colonel Touroute again before he left for Germany.

Enclosed letters *not* to be returned. Regards to Lupus.

First published in *Der Briefwechsel zwischen F. Engels und K. Marx,* Bd. 2, Stuttgart, 1913

Printed according to the original

Published in English in full for the first time

16

MARX TO ENGELS[20]

IN MANCHESTER

[London,] 23 May 1856
28 Dean Street, Soho

Dear Engels,

The family went off yesterday.[b] I have been incapable of work this week, partly because of the TROUBLE in the house, partly because of a rheumaticky back such as I have never experienced before.

Herewith Bazancourt—the 'Napoleonic' account of the Crimean business.[c] Might not something be made of it for *Putnam's*?[60] It's urgent that I obtain the services of this firm since the money and gear needed for the journey have compelled me to accept through Zitschke a sole bill for £30 on myself, payable in 3 months' time. A man from *Putnam's* has been to see Freiligrath, and they are willing to take articles.

I have only read the excerpts from Bazancourt that were published in the French papers. To judge by them, it would appear to provide much amusing matter. The thing cannot, I

---

[a] We shall see. - [b] See this volume, p. 33. - [c] Bazancourt, *L'expédition de Crimée jusqu' à la prise de Sébastopol.*

think, be treated other than flippantly. If done, it should not be made too short, but solely with the idea of filling up space.

Trübner, who looked like accepting my Swedish stuff two months ago but then gave no further sign of life, wrote yesterday and arranged an *entrevue*[a] on Tuesday to discuss the matter. That would provide 20 sheets of work.[61]

I am in a SERIOUS DILEMMA as to whether or not I should now go on a TRIP. On the one hand I've got to slog away at making money. On the other the doctor[b] has told me—and I believe he's right—that I should travel a bit and have a change of air, as my liver is again functioning irregularly. I AM NOT YET DECIDED what I should do. It's not as though staying here were especially economical, since I also have Pieper round my neck. But the main thing is my work.

AS TO Bazancourt, let me know whether you need the first part as well. If nothing can be made of the thing it would be better not to buy it.

I am incapable of writing today, but must nevertheless ask you to clear up a philological doubt. In *Henry IV*, Shakespeare used the word 'hiren' for 'siren' and, according to a note made by that pedant, Johnson,[c] the form 'hiren' also occurs in other early English writers.[d] The substitution of h for s is QUITE in order, but might there not be some connection between 'hiren' and 'Hure',[e] and hence also 'siren'? Or with 'hoeren', *auris*,[f] etc.? You can see TO WHICH LOW STATE OF SPIRIT I am DEPRESSED today from the great interest I show in this matter.

I have received some very curious information about Ruge's tragedy, the *Neue Welt*, in which 'the tragedy of love turns into a farce'. Shall tell you about it in my next.

Herzen is going to Switzerland. I await your COMMUNICATIONS on Ireland.

Salut.

Your

K. M.

First published abridged in *Der Briefwechsel zwischen F. Engels und K. Marx*, Bd. 2, Stuttgart, 1913 and in full in: Marx and Engels, *Works*, First Russian Edition, Vol. XXII, Moscow, 1929

Printed according to the original

Published in English in full for the first time

---

[a] interview - [b] Freund - [c] Marx means Johnson's notes in *Plays of W. Shakespeare. With Notes of Samuel Johnson. King Henry IV* is in Vol. 4 of this edition. - [d] Notably in George Peele's play *The Turkish Mahomet and Hyrin in the Fair Greek* [Trans.]. - [e] whore - [f] to hear, hearing

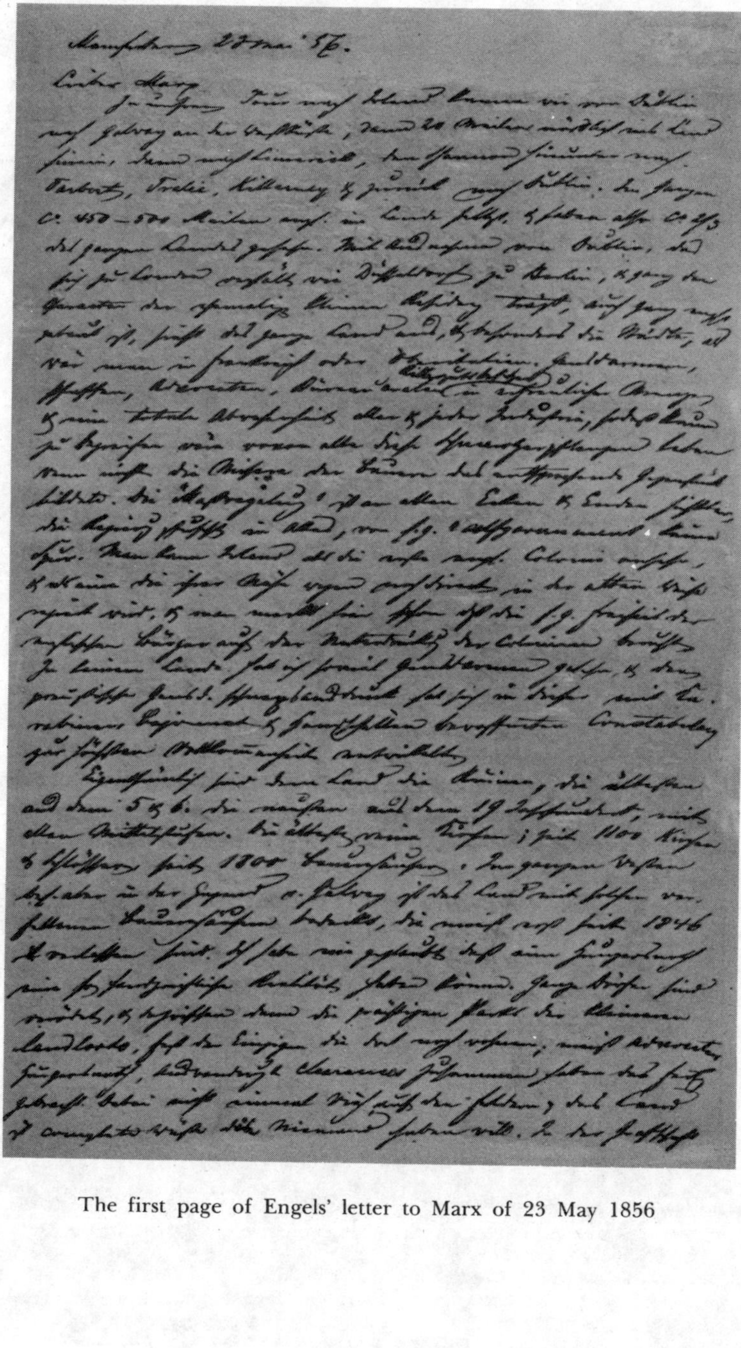
Manchester 23 Mai 56.

Lieber Marx

The first page of Engels' letter to Marx of 23 May 1856

17

ENGELS TO MARX [62]

IN LONDON

Manchester, 23 May 1856

Dear Marx,

During our trip to Ireland [63] we travelled from Dublin to Galway on the West Coast, then 20 miles north and inland, on to Limerick, down the Shannon to Tarbert, Tralee and Killarney, and back to Dublin. In all approx. 450-500 English miles within the country itself, so we have seen approx. $^2/_3$ of the entire country. With the exception of Dublin, which is to London what Düsseldorf is to Berlin, bears altogether the stamp of having been a small royal seat and is, moreover, built entirely in the English style, the whole country and particularly the towns give one the impression of being in France or Northern Italy. Gendarmes, priests, lawyers, bureaucrats, lords of the manor in cheerful profusion and a total absence of any and every industry, so that one could barely conceive what all these parasitic plants live on, were there no counterpart in the wretchedness of the peasants. The 'iron hand' is visible in every nook and cranny; the government meddles in everything, not a trace of so-called SELF-GOVERNMENT. Ireland may be regarded as the earliest English colony and one which, by reason of her proximity, is still governed in exactly the same old way; here one cannot fail to notice that the English citizen's so-called freedom is based on the oppression of the colonies. In no other country have I seen so many gendarmes, and it is in the CONSTABULARY, which is armed with carbine, bayonet and handcuffs, that the bibulous expression of your Prussian gendarme reaches its ultimate state of perfection.

Peculiar to the country are its ruins, the oldest 5th and 6th century, the most recent 19th, and every stage in between. The earliest, all churches; from 1100, churches and castles; from 1800, farmhouses. Throughout the west, but particularly the Galway region, the countryside is strewn with these derelict farmhouses, most of which have only been abandoned since 1846. I had never imagined that famine could be so tangibly real.[64] Whole villages are deserted; in between the splendid parks of the smaller LANDLORDS, virtually the only people still living there, lawyers mostly.

Famine, emigration and CLEARANCES[65] between them have brought this about. The fields are empty even of cattle; the countryside is a complete wilderness unwanted by anybody. In County Clare, south of Galway, things improve a bit, for there's some cattle at least and, towards Limerick, the hills are excellently cultivated, mostly by Scottish FARMERS, the ruins have been cleared away, and the country has a domesticated air. In the south-west, numerous mountains and bogs but also marvellously luxuriant woodland; further on, fine pastures again, especially in Tipperary and, approaching Dublin, increasing signs that the land is occupied by big farmers.

The English wars of conquest from 1100[a] to 1850 (*au fond*[b] they lasted as long as this, as did also martial law) utterly ruined the country. With regard to most of the ruins, it has been established that the destruction took place during these wars. Thus the very people have acquired their unusual character and, for all their fanatical Irish nationalism, the fellows no longer feel at home in their own country. IRELAND FOR THE SAXON! That is now becoming a reality. The Irishman knows that he cannot compete with the Englishman, who comes armed with resources in every respect superior to his own; emigration will continue until the predominantly, indeed almost exclusively, Celtic nature of the population has gone to pot. How often have the Irish set out to achieve something and each time been crushed, politically and industrially! In this artificial manner, through systematic oppression, they have come to be a completely wretched nation and now, as everyone knows, they have the job of providing England, America, Australia, etc., with whores, day labourers, *maquereaux*,[c] pickpockets, swindlers, beggars and other wretches. Even the aristocracy are infected by this wretchedness. The landowners, wholly bourgeoisified everywhere else, are here completely down-at-heel. Their country seats are surrounded by huge and lovely parks but all around there is desolation and where the money is supposed to come from heaven only knows. These fellows are too funny for words: of mixed blood, for the most part tall, strong, handsome types, all with enormous moustaches under a vast Roman nose, they give themselves the bogus martial airs of a *colonel en retraite*,[d] travel the country in search of every imaginable diversion and, on inquiry, prove to be as poor as church mice, up to their eyes

[a] More precisely, from 1169, when the English feudal lords first invaded Ireland. - [b] in the main - [c] pimps - [d] retired colonel

in debt, and living in constant fear of the ENCUMBERED ESTATES COURT.[66]

About England's method of governing this country—repression and corruption (long before Bonaparte tried them)—more very shortly if you don't come up soon. What are the prospects?

Your

F. E.

First published in *Der Briefwechsel zwischen F. Engels und K. Marx,* Bd. 2, Stuttgart, 1913

Printed according to the original

18

ENGELS TO MARX

IN LONDON

Manchester, 26 May 1856

Dear Marx,

Herewith the article,[11] but you should read it over first. Today the office again prevented me from doing so myself.

Bazancourt[a] will be of some use—Bonaparte's *Batrachomyomachia.*[67] But Vol. I absolutely essential. I shall send you 6/- worth of stamps for it tomorrow, or rather, they are enclosed herewith.

I would advise you to pack your bags at once, taking such papers as are absolutely necessary. Then you can work here as well as in Scotland, at least on certain subjects. We could do Bazancourt ±[b] together.[60] Admittedly, you would have to do most of the work for, with business expanding rapidly, commerce is making such demands on me that there can be no thought of regular and sustained work. If you finished this thing here (1 article would of course suffice), you could always either do parliamentary articles here, or else take a trip to Scotland and get down to some hard work here on your return. Until the Pan-Slavism is finished I should be reluctant to saddle myself with

---

[a] Bazancourt, *L'expédition de Crimée jusqu' à la prise de Sébastopol.* - [b] more or less

any other promises which I might eventually be unable to fulfil; but after all, your health is also a consideration and, as to that, I think I have something good for you—viz. light Bavarian beer and another dozen or so bottles of Bordeaux. Better, at all events—with a change of air—than HALF AND HALF, etc.

I may drop you another line tomorrow. Let me know what you decide to do.

Your
F. E.

First published in: Marx and Engels, *Works*, First Russian Edition, Vol. XXII, Moscow, 1929

Printed according to the original

Published in English for the first time

19

MARX TO ENGELS

IN MANCHESTER

[London,] 29 May 1856[a]
28 Dean Street, Soho

Dear Engels,

I shall hardly be able to leave here before the end of *next* week, since the business with Trübner[b] will not have been decided before then and I must, besides, have a word with Zitschke, who is unlikely to be back in London until then. At all events I shall let you know beforehand when I shall be leaving.

Salut.

Your
K. M.

First published in: Marx and Engels, *Works*, First Russian Edition, Vol. XXII, Moscow, 1929

Printed according to the original

Published in English for the first time

[a] Year added by Engels. - [b] See this volume, p. 46.

20

MARX TO ENGELS

IN MANCHESTER

[London,] 5 June 1856
28 Dean Street, Soho

Dear Frederic,

I leave for Scotland at the end of this week, and shall come on to you from there after an interval of 6 days, but will of course give you prior notice. Should you write to me during this week, address the letters 'C. Marx, CARE OF P. Imandt, 29 Cowgate, Dundee'. There was a twofold reason for my decision to come to you *via* Scotland:

1. *Medical*, because I know that the sea-voyage will put me to rights and it was only the day before yesterday that I got rid of my rheumatism. Moreover, there have been other unpleasantnesses, including excessive bleeding at stool. I have, of course, also consulted my SURGEON.

2. *Pieper*. He will accompany me to Scotland and then return to London. Had I not agreed to this arrangement, the lad—he obtained the money for the trip from his former pupil, A. Rothschild—was fully determined to make his way to Paris on a false passport, allegedly with the intention of proceeding from there to Geneva on foot. You will realise what a strange and compromising end SUCH AN EXPEDITION LIKELY WAS TO ARRIVE AT.

Salut.

Your
K. M.

First published in *Der Briefwechsel zwischen F. Engels und K. Marx*, Bd. 2, Stuttgart, 1913

Printed according to the original

Published in English for the first time

21

MARX TO ENGELS

IN MANCHESTER

[London,] 6 June 1856

Dear Engels,

PLAN AGAIN CHANGED. Why, when we meet. Pieper will accompany me to Hull, then return to London. I shall come on to you from Hull.[68]

Your

K. M.

First published in: Marx and Engels, *Works*, First Russian Edition, Vol. XXII, Moscow, 1929

Printed according to the original

Published in English for the first time

22

MARX TO JENNY MARX[20]

IN TRIER[69]

Manchester, 21 June 1856
34 Butler Street, Greenheys

My darling Sweetheart,

I am writing to you again because I am alone and because it is irksome to converse with you all the time in my head without you knowing or hearing or being able to answer me. Bad as your portrait is, it serves its end well enough, and I now understand how it is that even the least flattering portraits of the mother of God, the 'Black Madonnas',[70] could have their inveterate admirers—more admirers, indeed, than the good portraits. At any rate, none of these 'Black Madonna' portraits has ever been so much kissed and ogled and adored as your photograph which, while admittedly not black, has a crabbed expression and in no way reflects your dear, lovely, kissable, *dolce*[a] countenance. But I put

[a] sweet

right what the sun's rays have wrongly depicted, discovering that my eyes, spoiled though they are by lamplight and tobacco smoke, can nevertheless paint not only in the dreaming but also in the waking state. There you are before me, large as life, and I lift you up in my arms and I kiss you all over from top to toe, and I fall on my knees before you and cry: 'Madame, I love you.'[a] And love you I do, with a love greater than was ever felt by the Moor of Venice.[b] Falsely and foully doth the false and foul world all characters construe. Who of my many calumniators and venomous-tongued enemies has ever reproached me with being called upon to play the romantic lead in a second-rate theatre? And yet it is true. Had the scoundrels possessed the wit, they would have depicted 'the productive and social relations' on one side and, on the other, myself at your feet. Beneath it they would have written: LOOK TO THIS PICTURE AND TO THAT.[c] But stupid the scoundrels are and stupid they will remain, *in seculum seculorum*.[d]

Temporary absence is good, for in a person's presence things look too much alike for them to be distinguished. At close quarters even towers appear dwarfed, whereas what is petty and commonplace, seen close at hand, assumes undue proportions. So, too, with the passions. Little habits which, by their very proximity, obtrude upon one, and thus assume the form of passions, vanish as soon as their immediate object is out of sight. Great passions which, by the proximity of their object, take on the form of little habits, wax large and resume their natural proportions under the magical effect of distance. So it is with my love. Mere spatial separation from you suffices to make me instantly aware that time has done for my love just what the sun and the rain do for plants—made it grow. My love for you, as soon as you are away from me, appears for what it is, a giant, and into it all the vigour of my mind and all the ardour of my heart are compressed. I feel myself once more a man because I feel intense passion, and the multifariousness in which we are involved by study and modern education, no less than the scepticism which inevitably leads us to cavil at every subjective and objective impression, is calculated to render each one of us petty and weak and fretful and vacillating. But love, not for Feuerbachian Man, not for Moleschottian metabolism, not for the proletariat, but love for a sweetheart and notably for yourself, turns a man back into a man again.

---

[a] H. Heine, 'Die Jahre kommen und gehen...' (*Buch der Lieder. Die Heimkehr*). - [b] Shakespeare, *Othello*. - [c] Shakespeare, *Hamlet*, Act III, Scene 4. - [d] for ever and ever

You will smile, my dear heart, and wonder 'why this rhetoric all of a sudden?' But if I could press your sweet white bosom to mine, I would be silent and say not a word. Since I cannot kiss with my lips I must kiss with my tongue and frame words. I could, indeed, even frame verse, German *Books of Sorrow* after the manner of Ovid's *Libri Tristium*. He, however, had merely been banished by the Emperor Augustus; I have been banished from you,[a] and that is something Ovid could not understand.

There are, indeed, many women in the world, and a few of them are beautiful. But where else shall I find a face of which every lineament, every line even, reawakens the greatest and sweetest memories of my life? In your sweet countenance I can read even my infinite sorrows, my irreplaceable losses,[b] and when I kiss your sweet face I kiss away my sorrow. 'Buried in her arms, revived by her kisses'—in your arms, that is, and by your kisses—and let the Brahmins and Pythagoras keep their doctrine of re-birth, and Christianity its doctrine of resurrection.

To conclude with SOME FACTS. I have today sent Isaac Ironside the FIRST PAPER OF THE SERIES[61] and have, in addition, made notes (i.e. on the text of the despatches) in my own hand and in my own English.[c] I must say I felt a bit anxious when Frederic,[d] with that little quizzical look he has, calmly read through the stuff[e] before it was sent off. *Mais pour la première fois*[f] *he was quite astonished and exclaimed that this important work ought to be published in another form and, above all things, to be published in German.* I shall send the first issue to you and to old Schlosser, the historian, in Germany.

Apropos. I see from the *Augsburger*,[g] which refers directly to our circular letters[h] discussed at the communist trial in Cologne,[71] that another circular letter, 'reputedly' from the same source, has been sent out from London. It is a forgery, a miserable gallimaufry of our things, put together by Mr Stieber who, not having been accorded due honour in Prussia of late, now seeks to set himself up as a great man in Hanover. Engels and I intend to publish a counter-statement in the Augsburg *Allgemeine Zeitung*.[72]

---

[a] There is a pun here in German, the word *von* meaning either *by* or *from*. - [b] the death of his children Guido, Franziska and Edgar - [c] See this volume, pp. 57-58. - [d] Frederick Engels - [e] K. Marx, *Revelations of the Diplomatic History of the 18th Century*. - [f] But for the first time - [g] *Allgemeine Zeitung*. Marx refers to a report from Hanover published in issue No. 169, 16 June 1856. - [h] K. Marx and F. Engels, 'Address of the Central Authority to the League', March 1850, and 'Address of the Central Authority to the League', June 1850.

Farewell my dear heart. A thousand kisses to you, and the children too, from

Your
Karl

First published in *Annali,* an. I, Milano, 1958

Printed according to the original

Published in English in full for the first time

23

MARX TO ISAAC IRONSIDE [73]

IN SHEFFIELD

[Draft]

Manchester, [21 June 1856]
34 Butler St., Greenheys

Dear Sir,

I received your letter d.d. June 14 this morning only, as it had to be sent to me here to Manchester where I shall stay for some weeks.

I have duly considered your proposal, and, on the whole, accede to it.[74] In a matter like this, it is impossible to mention expressly every small particular, to agree upon the size of type pp., neither can I anticipate that any difficulties may arise therefrom, nor from the reservations to make as to 'copy *used*'.

I shall therefore provide you in time for next Saturday's but one's publication with fully 2 columns of matter and keep you amply supplied every week to that extent.

It would be most convenient to me (if your arrangements admit of it) to receive a remittance say after every fresh weekly publication.

As to your reprinting the papers in your serials, I have no objection, reserving to myself, of course, the right of using the materials, later on, in any way I may see it fit to use them.

As I am sure that you will not suppress historical truth out of prejudice or party-consideration [...][a]

As to the latter point you will think it only just, that should any points be suppressed, which in my conviction are of decisive

[a] The sentence is unfinished in the original.

historical importance, I shall consider myself obliged to stop the publication.

In thanking you for the serials you were so kind to send me, I cannot but regret that you did not think fit to communicate to me the proof-sheets of the 'Story of the life of Lord Palmerston'.[58] Sentences, historical data, quotations from Palmerston's speeches—everything is so disfigured by *errata* that, in my opinion, the pamphlet, in its present form, is not only useless but positively mischievous.

A few words on the plan of the whole publication[a] will suffice. I do not adopt the usual manner of opening the whole theme by general considerations, but on the contrary commence with facts.[b]

In contradistinction to the usual manner of historical writers, I shall not commence this publication with general considerations, but with facts. The first chapter will be composed of despatches belonging to different epochs of that century, in order to show up the Russian spirit of English diplomacy during the 18th.[c]

I hope I need not tell you that I am no 'commercial' writer and that no [...][d]

First published in: Marx and Engels, *Works*, Second Russian Edition, Vol. 29, Moscow, 1962

Reproduced from the original

Published in English for the first time

24

MARX TO WILLIAM CYPLES[75]

IN SHEFFIELD

[Draft]

[London,] 22 July 1856

Dear Sir,

I write again myself to show that I bear not the least ill will against you for which, indeed, there would be no cause. In your

---

[a] K. Marx, *Revelations of the Diplomatic History of the 18th Century*. - [b] This paragraph is crossed out in the original. - [c] Here the following passage is crossed out in the manuscript: 'There are to follow some English pamphlets belonging to the epoch of Peter I; having thus made the reader familiar 1) [with] the infamies of English diplomacy, 2) with the protest [...]. From one of these despatches you will see how England conspired with Russia to crush [...]. These despatches will form a more eloquent introduction to [...].' - [d] The manuscript breaks off here.

letter d.d. July 19,[a] you say: 'It could not be satisfactory etc.' Now as to my own satisfaction please to leave it altogether out of the question. As to Mr Ironside's 'satisfaction' I'll quote you the exact words of his 'note'.[b] Having told you, that already the first article had *'overdosed'* him, he continues as follows:

'They' (Dr Marx's articles) 'are entombing the paper. This must not be. *They must be brought to a close forthwith.* You must not have more than two more doses—this week and the next. You had better write him at once *to that effect.*'

I *positively* decline making myself guilty of manslaughter by administering another 'dose' to Mr Isaac Ironside and 'entombing' him in the sheets of his own paper.

Yours etc.

Dr K. M.

First published in *Der Briefwechsel zwischen F. Engels und K. Marx,* Bd. 2, Stuttgart, 1913

Reproduced from the original

25

MARX TO ENGELS

IN MANCHESTER

London, 28 July 1856
28 Dean Street, Soho

Dear Frederic,

A letter from my wife received today via Manchester brings news of her mother's[c] death on July 23. This will hasten her return to London.

At the same time a letter from Miquel, who is thinking of coming over here in a week or 10 days' time. Highly inconvenient just now.

Pieper lost his job a fortnight ago. Not his fault this time. He kept the thing secret so long as Lupus was here. The compositors conspired together to bring in a chap who belongs to their FRIENDLY SOCIETY.[76]

---

[a] See this volume, p. 60. - [b] Below Marx quotes from a non-extant letter by Ironside to Cyples. - [c] Caroline von Westphalen

As regards Sheffield, the matter stands as follows:

In the last issue the fellows made some disgraceful cuts, whereupon Pieper wrote to Cyples: *'I am directed by Dr Marx to inform you that he cannot congratulate you upon the emendations, etc.'*[77]

Then the following letter arrived from Ironside[a]:

*Free Press Office, Sheffield,
July 19, 1856

Dear Doctor,

It could not be satisfactory either to us or to yourself to close your article in the abrupt way which you on the instant proposed. I am sorry that I was so unsuccessful in cutting down last week's contributions, and should have hesitated in doing so had it not unfortunately happened that there was really no other alternative. As to Mr Ironside's note, permit me to say that in another letter since received from him, he expresses regret that you should have construed his scrap as he did not intend it, and intimates a doubt that *I* have in some way offended you? I see no reason why our professional intercourse may not continue and be pleasant; and I venture to hope to receive the usual packet of copy for next week's issue. You will be so good as to excuse my tardiness in writing. I have been so busy. Your etc. *Cyples.**

Reply

*'July 22, 1856

'Dear Sir, I write again myself to show that I bear not the least ill will against you for which, indeed, there would be no cause. In your letter d.d. July 19, you say: "It could not be satisfactory etc." Now as to my own satisfaction please to leave it altogether out of the question. As to Mr Ironside's "satisfaction" I'll quote you the exact words of his "note". Having told you, that already the first article had "*overdosed*" him, he continues as follows:

"They" (Dr Marx's articles) "are entombing the paper. This must not be. *They must be brought to a close forthwith.* You must not have more than two more doses—this week and the next. You had better write him at once *to that effect.*"

'I *positively* decline making myself guilty of manslaughter by administering another "dose" to Mr Isaac Ironside and "entombing" him in the sheets of his own paper. Yours etc.

Dr K. M.'*

Since then the correspondence has lapsed. But still no sign of any *money.* Jones tells me I could have taken the fellows to court over the whole affair AT THE OUTSET.

---

[a] Marx means Cyples.

As you can imagine, I am like a cat on hot bricks. I shall have to do something about lodgings when the FAMILY arrives, but have no idea how to get out of the old ones or move into new, having neither the MEANS nor any immediate prospects. My electric brush strives vainly to make my hair darker, for *atra cura*[a] is making it whiter than ever. Zitschke has decamped, so at least I am excused *sine die* from paying him.

Espartero and Pucheta in the Spanish farce—never before has history so nicely confronted the hero of the liberal bourgeoisie with the hero of the 'mob'.[78]

Salut.

Your

K. M.

Freiligrath has no one above him now apart from the BOARD OF DIRECTORS, which meets every Saturday.

First published in *Der Briefwechsel zwischen F. Engels und K. Marx,* Bd. 2, Stuttgart, 1913

Printed according to the original

Published in English for the first time

26

MARX TO ENGELS[20]

IN MANCHESTER

[London,] 1 August 1856
28 Dean Street, Soho

Dear E.,

The £5 note most gratefully received but not as yet the letter you promised me. Herewith a letter from the crazy Mirbach, which I have received—via Berlin!

No money from Sheffield yet. Today I got Pieper to send a dunning letter. Meanwhile there has been the following incident: Yesterday *Urquhart's* bulldog—THE CELEBRATED Collet—appeared at my house. He had come, he said, at the behest of the Grand Cophta[79] himself. Urquhart was *very sorry, regretted, indeed, very

[a] black care

much that Mr Ironside had interfered at all with my articles etc., which he thought of extraordinary value etc.* Then he asked me to tell him how the matter had come about. *Mr Urquhart imagined that the principal cause of the quarrel was the suppression of some parts of the copy etc.* I then told him what had happened[75] and showed him the written *corpora delicti*.[a] Next, he asked me *whether I was willing to enter upon any compromise, which question I flatly denied, telling him that I was no penny-a-liner and not to be treated like the London literary vagabonds.* It seemed he was only awaiting this statement in order to tell me with EXTRAORDINARY SOLEMNITY that Urquhart thought *The Free Press* 'inadequate'. *Mr Ironside was placed on the horns of a dilemma because *The Free Press* was, indeed, but an extract from the *Sheffield Free Press*—a paper, by the bye, twice the dimensions of the *F. P.*—and what was suited to the wants of the readers of the *Sh. F. P.* was not all palatable to the readers of the *F. P.* and vice versa. Mr Urquhart had, therefore, resolved upon starting in about a month a diplomatic journal at London.* He hoped that I would let him have the whole of the *Revelations*[80] and not bear him a GRUDGE. I returned a vague answer capable of being construed in the affirmative but leaving me free—if the conditions should prove too poor or the paper too crazy—to refuse. It will all depend on the nature of the paper. In London things are rather different from Sheffield, and, should Urquhart come out with his counter-revolutionary nonsense in such a way that collaboration with him would discredit me in the eyes of the revolutionaries here, I would be obliged, *of course, hard as it would be under the present miserable circumstances,* to decide against it. However, *nous verrons*.[b] At all events I have now received adequate satisfaction as regards my LITERARY POINT OF HONOUR, in as much as the chief has all but disowned his LIEUTENANT. This is a satisfactory dénouement, if only on account of Bucher and the democratic riff-raff.

There will now be much wrangling within the Urquhartite camp itself. It seemed to me that they evinced a bad TENDENCY to make a SCAPEGOAT of poor Cyples. E.g., Collet said he wasn't sure whether it was with Ironside's knowledge that Cyples had sent me the former's letter. To this I replied that Cyples seemed to be an honest fellow who had heard 'SECRET DIPLOMACY' so greatly decried that he naturally assumed 'PUBLIC DIPLOMACY' to be the rule at the *F. P.* OFFICE.

---

a pieces of evidence - b we shall see

Received a letter today from my wife. She seems greatly affected by the old lady's[a] death. She will have to spend a week or 10 days in Trier in order to put up for auction what little in the way of effects her mother has left and to share the PROCEEDS with Edgar.[b] She has proposed the following scheme: After spending a few days more in the vicinity of Trier with a woman friend of hers, she will travel to Paris and thence direct to *Jersey*, having decided that we ought to spend September and October there. First, so that she herself can recuperate; secondly, because it's cheaper and pleasanter than London and, finally, so that the children should learn French, etc. She doesn't, of course, know anything about what has been taking place here. For the present I have written to say that it's a splendid scheme, although I cannot in fact see how it can be put into effect. Yesterday I again saw the *New-York Tribune* (WEEKLY). The whole paper is filled with nothing but the ELECTORAL DODGE and so it will be for months to come. We cannot hope seriously to tackle the *N.-Y. T.* until the presidential business is over.

Salut.

Your

K. M.

P.S. At Blind's, saw 2 volumes of Simon of Trier's émigré jeremiad.[c] Watered-down twaddle, every other word a solecism, callow botchery, weak-kneed affectation, foppish naive pretension, a mess of Grünian Jew's ears in beggar's broth, one long platitude—nothing of the kind has ever before appeared in print. All that was needed to give the 'German Parliament'[44] the final kick in the arse was this self-exposure on the part of one of its heroes. Needless to say, I did no more than leaf through it. I'd sooner swill soap-suds or hobnob with Zoroaster over mulled cow's piss than read through all that stuff. He and Co. are perpetually haunted by our ghost. L. Blanc, Blanqui, Marx and Engels are his Unholy Quadrinity which he never forgets. We two—the propounders of 'equal economic rights'—are said *inter alia* to have advocated '*Armed* (!) appropriation of capital'. Even the jokes we cracked about Switzerland in the *Revue* 'fill him with indignation'. 'No Civil List, no standing army, no millionaires, no beggars'[d]—

[a] Caroline von Westphalen - [b] Edgar von Westphalen, Jenny Marx's brother - [c] L. Simon, *Aus dem Exil*, Bd. 1-2. - [d] Paraphrased quotation from Engels' 'The Campaign for the German Imperial Constitution' published in the *Neue Rheinische Zeitung. Politisch-ökonomische Revue* (see present edition, Vol. 10, p. 177).

'Marx and Engels hope that Germany will never sink to such depths of degradation'. It's exceedingly odd, the way he speaks of us in the *singular*—'Marx and Engels *says*', etc.

First published abridged in *Der Briefwechsel zwischen F. Engels und K. Marx*, Bd. 2, Stuttgart, 1913 and in full in: Marx and Engels, *Works,* First Russian Edition, Vol. XXII, Moscow, 1929

Printed according to the original

Published in English in full for the first time

27

ENGELS TO MARX

IN LONDON

Manchester, 4 August 1856

Dear Marx,

The letter that didn't arrive must have melted in the heat. I don't know whether you down there too have suddenly been assailed by this tropical heat which has brought everything to a standstill, apart from the continuous sluicing and bathing of the outer man with water and the inner man with a variety of other fluids. Yesterday I was totally incapable of anything and barely in a condition to go out. I haven't stopped sweating since Thursday, even in my bath; and the sordid work at the office is so exhausting that afterwards one feels utterly down. Moreover the nights are equally stifling.

It's most satisfactory that the Urquhart business should have turned out as it did.[a] There's no doubt that what most impresses the rabble is our resolute manner. I hope it will be possible for the pieces[b] to appear in Urquhart's thing, *nous verrons.*[c]

I'm daily awaiting a letter from my mater summoning me to London. I am arranging matters in such a way as to be able to leave on Saturday, should the summons come. I shall be moving out of here on Saturday though I haven't yet taken new lodgings,

---

[a] See previous letter. - [b] K. Marx, *Revelations of the Diplomatic History of the 18th Century.* - [c] we shall see

and still don't know whether I shall do so or spend a week knocking about, since I intend on my return to engage in all kinds of mad escapades.

My brother-in-law[a] has been here—a good chap, communist out of principle, bourgeois out of interest, as he himself most naively puts it, but he always uses '*we*' when referring to communist matters; tried to talk me into making tentative approaches to the Prussians about an amnesty, whereupon I, of course, gave a very determined answer and finally he, too, saw that 1. I couldn't do so, and 2. that the Prussians would tell me to shove it, etc.—The man seemed to have few illusions about my frame of mind and certainly had even fewer when he left. However, he was very surprised to find me so cheerful.

I shall write to Mirbach as soon as it gets a little cooler; it's too much to expect just now. 24 degrees Réaumur is no joke when one has to traipse round in clothes proper to the Exchange.

If the Jersey scheme can be carried out—it certainly has its good points and is not entirely impossible—make sure that while in Paris, your wife finds out exactly how things stand regarding route and communications, for otherwise she might get into serious difficulties. I believe that Saint-Malo is the only place in France to which steamers go from Jersey. Get one or two of the *crapauds*[81] to tell you what the position is. After all, you know several who have been there.

You can give the great Pieper my assurance that I read his great 'filtered' article on Spain in *The People's Paper*[b] before the original appeared in the *Tribune*,[c] 'HANG IT!' *C'est beau*.[d] By the way, the *P. P.* deserves to be relegated to the W.C. Just consider this stinker: WE REGRET TO LEARN THAT LORD SO AND SO HAS CUT HIS FINGER, etc. You really must get Jones to give his SUB-EDITOR a damned good dressing-down for permitting such drivel.

On no account let the rabble in Sheffield sit on the money—they'll have to shell out in any case.

Your

F. E.

First published abridged in *Der Briefwechsel zwischen F. Engels und K. Marx*, Bd. 2, Stuttgart, 1913 and in full in: Marx and Engels, *Works*, First Russian Edition, Vol. XXII, Moscow, 1929

Printed according to the original

Published in English for the first time

---

[a] Karl Emil Blank - [b] W. Pieper, 'The Coup d'État in Spain', *The People's Paper*, No. 221, 26 July 1856. - [c] K. Marx, 'The Spanish Coup d'État', *New-York Daily Tribune*, No. 4775, 8 August 1856 (an allusion to the fact that Marx helped Pieper in writing his article for *The People's Paper*). - [d] It's fine.

28

MARX TO JENNY MARX[82]

IN TRIER

[London,] 8 August 1856
28 Dean Street, Soho

My one and only Sweetheart,

This morning, at the same time as your letter, I received a note from Frederic[a] containing 15 talers for Lenchen.[b] *Acknowledge it*, as he is *most meticulous* in such matters. More tomorrow; today I have the 'IMMORTAL COLLET' here in the room with me and am keeping him in check by saying *'I am obliged to write some lines to Mrs Marx'*.

LILY-WHITE SANDY is settled *IN REALITY*, not *IN FANCY*.

Much though I hanker after you and the children—and this *QUITE indescribably*—I should like you to stay on *in Trier for another week*. It would do you and the children no end of good. More tomorrow.

Your
K. M.

P.S. The Urquhartites are being damned importunate.[c] A good thing financially. But I don't know whether, *POLITICALLY*, I ought to get too involved with the fellows. A thousand kisses, my beloved sweetheart.

P.S.II. Lina[d] has got the famous post. Won't be taking it up *for weeks* yet.

It's ghastly for me, having to play the man of fashion *chez* Liebknecht now. HANG IT! On top of that, I have Pieper sleeping with me in your stead. HORRIBLE. In the same room, at any rate. *Engels is coming next week*.[83] That's a relief. For 3 weeks I've been as hypochondriacal as the devil.

First published in *Annali*, an. I, Milano, 1958

Printed according to the original

---

[a] Frederick Engels - [b] Helene Demuth - [c] See this volume, pp. 61-62. - [d] Caroline Schöler

29

MARX TO COLLET DOBSON COLLET

IN LONDON

[Draft]

London, 11 August 1856
28 Dean St., Soho

Dear Sir,

I approve, of course, of the suggestions of your letter of the 8th inst. regarding the headings per 'chapters' and the cyphering of the notes at the bottom of the text.[a] As to the cutting of chapters into parts, you must of course use your discretion as called for by the exigences of space etc. The alterations considered necessary in Chapter II will be forwarded in the course of the week.

Y. f.

K. M.

C. D. Collet, Esq.

First published in: Marx and Engels, *Works*, First Russian Edition, Vol. XXV, Moscow, 1934

Reproduced from the original

Published in English for the first time

30

MARX TO ENGELS[20]

IN MANCHESTER

[London,] 22 September 1856
28 Dean Street, Soho

Dear Engels,

I would have ACKNOWLEDGED your last letter before this, but for ABOUT a fortnight past the whole day from morn till night has been spent in search of lodgings. In no circumstances could we remain

[a] K. Marx, *Revelations of the Diplomatic History of the 18th Century.*

in the old hole. At last we found a place—a whole house which we have to FURNISH ourselves. It is 9 Grafton Terrace, Maitland Park, Haverstock Hill, Hampstead Road. Rent £36. We are to move in on 29 September; this week we have to furnish it. We are in something of a quandary, as we have ABOUT £26 to pay out in town, and a great deal more for the new set-up. I.e. we are short of £10-£15—if only for the time being, since there is still a sizeable sum due to my wife from her brother[a] in Berlin as a result of the Trier legacy.[84] Yesterday he wrote to say that he couldn't send the money because the Lower Silesian Railway Bonds in which the capital due to my wife is invested could be sold *dans ce moment*[b] only at a considerable loss. As *M. le Ministre* sadly remarks:

'It is, to be sure, an unfavourable moment just now, since all genuine securities such as these have fallen sharply as a result of frenzied speculation in Crédit mobilier[45] and limited liability companies.'

If you can supply part of what is wanted, I think I can manage the remainder with the help of the pawnshop until the money arrives from Berlin. The worst of it is that there's no time to be lost.

I was terribly affected by the news of Weerth's death,[85] which I found hard to believe. Freiligrath, too, has already written to me about an obituary. But I must confess that I can't think of a likely paper in Germany. The only possibility might be an obituary in the *Tribune* until the times permit us to do something bigger and better. WHAT IS YOUR OPINION?

Today I have been invited to dine with the *Putnam's* chap[c] who is over here again. I don't know whether I shall go. My poor spoken English might put me to shame.

The *Tribune* has returned me the *unpublished* articles. These are, ALL IN ALL, Pan-Slavism[11] and my articles on the DANUBIAN PRINCIPALITIES.[3] Mr Dana says in his letter that, if I cannot place the things elsewhere, they will be legally responsible for any 'LOSS' incurred, since they failed to register their objections soon enough. In the opposite case, they expect to get PART of their EXPENSES back. *Nous verrons.*[d]

Bruno Bauer is bringing out 2 volumes of England.[86] No doubt he will write at length about his *cher frère*'s[e] PIGSTY. I don't know what else he has seen in England.

---

[a] Ferdinand von Westphalen - [b] at present - [c] Frederick Olmsted of *Putnam's Monthly Magazine* - [d] We shall see. - [e] dear brother (Edgar Bauer)

Pieper, whom I threw out on my wife's return, found his way back and settled in again 2 days later which, just now, is far from pleasant. When I move into our new home, I shall leave him behind, safely installed on my surety in the little hole you know in Dean Street.

A Prussian amnesty is expected on 15 October. Otto's mother died leaving 2,000 talers; these were confiscated by the Prussian government to pay the 'costs of the Cologne trial'.[71]

Strohn was here last Friday. The fellow has put on an enormous amount of weight, in consequence of which his spirits seem to have improved SOMEWHAT at the expense of his wits. Nor is his expression now so wry—benevolent, RATHER.

I have heard all sorts of details concerning Heine, recounted to my wife in Paris by Reinhardt. Shall write about these at length some other time. For the present only that

'Eight had barely struck, yet she
Was quaffing wine with laughter free'[a]

came true LITERALLY in his case. While his corpse was still in the mortuary—on the day of the funeral—the *maquereau*[b] of Mathilde the mild, angelic child, did in fact appear on the doorstep and fetch her away. The worthy 'Meissner', who doled out such sloppy rubbish about Heine to the German public,[c] was paid in cash by 'Mathilde' to sing the praises of this trollop who had tormented POOR Heine to death.

But now for another story about Moses Hess. That lad's fame WAS DUE TO A GREAT PART—TO Sazonov. When Hess and the Moses woman[d] arrived in Paris, this Russian was in very sore straits, very down at heel, without money or credit and consequently very plebeian and revolutionary and receptive to ideas of world subversion. Sazonov heard that Moses was not without 'ducats'. He therefore took his stand behind Moses and in front of the Moses woman. The latter he bedded, the former he extolled AS A GREAT LITERARY LUMEN, putting him in touch with the editorial boards of reviews and newspapers. Vladimir,[e] OF COURSE, had a finger in every pie and a foot in every door. Thus he extracted enough ducats from the tight-fisted Moses to enable him to 'shine' again and to put out decoys for further credit. And with these Sazonov enticed a rich old Jewess with whom he entered into kosher WEDLOCK. From then on, however, he became a man of fashion again and turned

---

[a] H. Heine, 'Ein Weib' (from *Romanzen*). - [b] pimp - [c] A. Meissner, *Heinrich Heine. Erinnerungen*. - [d] Sibylle Hess - [e] Nikolai Sazonov

his back on Moses, declaring him to be A VERY COMMON AND SUBORDINATE FELLOW. The Moses woman, however, was heartlessly abandoned and she is now running round Paris, scolding and cursing and telling anyone who will listen about the perfidious Muscovite's betrayal. Such, in a manner of speaking, is the story of the *Grandeur et Décadence de la Maison Moses.*[a]

Have you seen Golovin's paper, *Russia* etc., now appearing in London?

Faute de moyens,[b] *L'Homme* has temporarily ceased publication. *La Nation* has ceased to exist. The only thing still in the same LINE, though much poorer, is *Le National.*

Kindest regards to Lupus.

Your

K. M.

First published abridged in *Der Briefwechsel zwischen F. Engels und K. Marx,* Bd. 2, Stuttgart, 1913 and in full in: Marx and Engels, *Works,* First Russian Edition, Vol. XXII, Moscow, 1929

Printed according to the original

Published in English in full for the first time

31

MARX TO ENGELS[20]

IN MANCHESTER

London, 26 September 1856
28 Dean Street, Soho

Dear Frederick,

FIRST, I must ACKNOWLEDGE with THANKS RECEIPT of the money. I would have done so yesterday had we not been in a veritable HURLY-BURLY with our removal. It remains doubtful, moreover, whether we shall be out of here before Monday since, even with your money and what the pawnshop has yielded, we still haven't QUITE got the requisite amount. The present crisis on the European stock exchanges has come at an awkward time for us personally.

No news apart from what you may already know, namely that *Stirner* has died. A letter has also reached London, or so

a The Grandeur and Decline of the House of Moses (an ironical allusion to Balzac's *L'Histoire de la grandeur et de la décadence de Cézar Birotteau*). - b For want of means

Freiligrath tells me, from his 'ex-sweetheart'[a] in Australia, in which she says that she has married again but has at the same time turned religious and, by harping on the 'better life to come', has contrived to drive her *novum hominem*[b] into the 'madhouse'. This last is meant *verbatim*.

Well, I went to *souper* with the *Putnam's* man.[c] Besides myself, the only people present were Freiligrath and an old Yankee. The *Putnam's* man was a quiet, genial soul, the other Yankee a jaunty, witty chap. Putnam wants us if possible, after the Bazancourt,[60] to revert to the 'SHIPS AGAINST WALLS' question, as being of special interest to Americans in connection with the recent war.[d] Then again, something on floating batteries and gunboats; light or heavy guns, etc. All this seems to be with an eye to an American war, at a closer or more distant time, against England. Besides these *militaribus* I am then to write on Heine. In short, we can now engage in REGULAR INTERCOURSE with this very 'good' house.

Considering the rent, the house I have taken is very nice and could hardly have been let so cheaply were not the immediate neighbourhood, roads, etc., SOMEWHAT UNFINISHED. When you come up to London you'll find a complete HOME.

WHAT DO *YOU* THINK OF THE ASPECT OF THE MONEY MARKET? There is no doubt that the increases in the discount rate on the Continent are partly associated with the appreciation of silver against gold due to the Californian and Australian gold (the Belgian Bank is now giving only 19 frs. 40 c.—silver—for one *napoléon d'or*[e]) and hence bullion dealers everywhere where gold and silver are the legal STANDARD are withdrawing the latter from the banks. But whatever the reason for the increases in the discount rate, these are at least precipitating the DOWNFALL of the vast speculative transactions and, more specifically, of the GRAND PAWNINGSHOP AT PARIS.[f] I don't believe that the great monetary crisis will outlast the winter of 1857. Those stupid asses, the BRITISHERS, imagine that this time all is SOUND over here, as opposed to the Continent. Apart from the intimate connection between the OLD LADY OF THREADNEEDLE STREET and the Paris concern,[87] the asses overlook the fact that a large part of English capital is tied up in continental credits and that their 'SOUND' OVERTRADING (exports this year are expected to reach £110 million) is based on the Continent's 'UNSOUND' SPECULATION, just as their civilisational propaganda of 1854-56 was on the coup d'état of

---

[a] Marie Wilhelmine Dähnhardt - [b] new man - [c] Frederick Olmsted - [d] the Crimean war, 1853-56 - [e] *napoléon d'or*—a twenty-franc gold coin issued by Napoleon I - [f] probably the Bank of France

1851. This time, however, as opposed to earlier crises, France has discovered the form in which speculation could be and has been propagated throughout the whole of Europe. In contrast to the Gallic *raffinement* of St. Simonism,[88] STOCKJOBBERY and imperialism, your English speculator at home appears to have reverted to the primitive form of simple and UNMITIGATED *FRAUD*. Witness Strahan, Paul and Bates, the TIPPERARY BANK OF SADLEIR MEMORY, the GREAT CITY FRAUDS OF Davidson, Cole and Co., now the ROYAL BRITISH BANK and, finally, the Crystal Palace affair[89] (4,000 bogus shares put into circulation). The BRITISHERS abroad speculate under continental COLOURS, those at home revert to *fraude simple*, and that's what the chaps call a 'SOUND STATE OF COMMERCE'.[90]

This time, by the by, the thing has assumed European dimensions such as have never been seen before, and I don't suppose we'll be able to spend much longer here merely as spectators. The very fact that I've at last got round to setting up house again and sending for my books[91] seems to me to prove that the 'mobilisation' of our persons is AT HAND.

Salut.

Your

K. M.

First published in *Der Briefwechsel zwischen F. Engels und K. Marx*, Bd. 2, Stuttgart, 1913

Printed according to the original

Published in English in full for the first time

32

ENGELS TO MARX[92]

IN LONDON

[Manchester, not before 27 September 1856]

[....] As regards Weerth[85] I shall write to [....] in Berlin, who might perhaps get something into a paper, *n'importe*[a] which, so long as it appears. For 10 days and more after my return from London[83] Lupus did not breathe a word of the news and not until quite late, just before 11 o'clock on the eve of my old man's

[a] no matter

arrival, did he come out with it. You can imagine how staggered and annoyed I was at this idiotic conduct. For the next 8-14 days I hardly had a moment to myself and couldn't even go and see Steinthal to find out more, let alone turn my thoughts to an obituary or the like. He has probably left some written work and I shall make sure I get a sight of it.

You might send me the Pan-Slavism[11] when you have an opportunity. As soon as I have the time I shall revise the thing and knock it into reasonable shape—for *Putnam's* (?) or anything else that might turn up in the meantime. *Now*, while the mischief is still in progress, I would offer the 'PRINCIPALITIES'[3] to an English paper or MONTHLY. How are things going on with Urquhart [....][61] very doubtful about it [....] I can see no possibility so far. In any case, we shall not be affected by the amnesty.

The stories about Moses[a] and the Moses woman[b] made us laugh a great deal.[c] So, just like Ewerbeck, *il s'est acheté une place au Père-Lachaise de la littérature française.*[d 93]

Have not seen Golovin's *Russia*. You might send one or 2 issues so that I can see what it's like; it's quite unknown up here.

Bazancourt still on the stocks.[60] I think I shall finish it in about 10 days or a fortnight. It's not going so quickly after all, you see, I had no time to do any preparatory work. If only I had my *Tribune* articles on the war[94]! Now all the material has to be got together again. After this, we can offer them SHIPS AGAINST WALLS and then we should manage to keep the ball rolling all right.

That gold has depreciated against silver is no longer in any doubt. However it is also a fact that silver has *vanished*, but where to, I cannot quite make out. Such is the state of confusion that a great deal must have been buried or tucked away in China. Again, the BALANCE OF TRADE has recently been extremely favourable to India and China *vis-à-vis* England, the Continent and America taken together. At all events it must be highly gratifying for John Bull to find that he is already worth 6d IN THE POUND less.

The clouds gathering over the money market are sombre indeed, and the *Constitutionnel*'s old 'HORIZON POLITIQUE' may well come into its own again.[95] Last Tuesday's affair at the Bank, when 1 million in gold was withdrawn, is significant. It almost looks as though the storm is about to break, but this might, of course, be no more than a prelude. In theory, the crash cannot come until Russia is right up to the neck in speculation, but this is hardly to

---

[a] Moses Hess - [b] Sibylle Hess - [c] See this volume, pp. 69-70. - [d] He has bought himself a place in the Père-Lachaise of French literature.

be expected and perhaps it is better so. Another thing which considerably restrains speculators over here is the high price of all raw materials, particularly silk, cotton and wool, where it is far from SAFE to do anything at all. When the CRASH comes, however, there'll be a rude awakening for the English. I should like to know how many of the Continent's speculative shares have found their way to England—vast numbers, I imagine. This time there'll be a *dies irae*[a] such as has never been seen before; the whole of Europe's industry in ruins, all markets over-stocked (already nothing more is being shipped to India), all the propertied classes in the soup, complete bankruptcy of the bourgeoisie, war and profligacy to the nth degree. I, too, believe that it will all come to pass in 1857, and when I heard that you were again buying furniture, I promptly declared the thing to be a dead certainty and offered to take bets on it.

Adieu for today; cordial regards to your wife and children.

Your

F. E.

First published abridged in *Der Briefwechsel zwischen F. Engels und K. Marx*, Bd. 2, Stuttgart, 1913 and in full in: Marx and Engels, *Works*, First Russian Edition, Vol. XXII, Moscow, 1929

Printed according to the original

Published in English for the first time

33

MARX TO ENGELS

IN MANCHESTER

London, 16 October 1856
9 Grafton Terrace, Maitland Park,
Haverstock Hill

Dear Engels,

After receipt of the POST OFFICE order we moved out[96] and, for the first 2 weeks, had to do a frightful lot of running to and fro between here and town in order to put things more or less straight in the house. Hence my silence.

---

[a] day of wrath

Herewith an excerpt from a book by Mieroslawski.[a] As you know he's not without *esprit*.[b] But there's also much *esprit de mauvais aloi*[c] in his writing, in particular a great deal of the *style amphigourique*[d] which the French have been at such tremendous pains to acquire since they became 'profound' and ceased being superficial Voltairians. Also much of that enthusiastic unguent used by 'unappreciated' nationalities to glorify their *passé*.[e] Hatred of Russia and even more of Germany; anti-Pan-Slavism but, on the other hand, free CONFEDERATION of Slav *nations* with the Poles as the *peuple Archimède*.[97] Distinct emphasis on social revolution in Poland as the basic condition of the political one; but seeks to show by means of historical deduction, which proves exactly the *reverse*, that orthodoxy lies in restoring the old agrarian communes (*gmina*=the Russian commune *latinised*).

In the past few weeks I have been studying the question of silver in greater detail and shall in due course give you an account thereof.

In my view Bonaparte will hardly be able to avoid the SUSPENSION OF CASH PAYMENTS and then, *va la Galère!*[f]

Guardian received. More very soon. Otto has been pardoned.

Your

K. M.

As regards the Urquhartites (who, until the week before last, with intervals, were reprinting my old stuff revised by me[98]) have made no progress at all as yet. However the matter must be decided before the week is out. Urquhart has been playing the oracle in *The Morning Herald* by disgorging these things, which are wholly new to him, as though they were long-cherished secrets of his. In the *National-Zeitung* the great Bucher—appropriating my very words—spoke of 'interesting revelations', but suppresses my name, giving the impression that they came from the *English* side. You can see how envious and irritating these scoundrels are.

First published abridged in *Der Briefwechsel zwischen F. Engels und K. Marx*, Bd. 2, Stuttgart, 1913 and in full in: Marx and Engels, *Works*, First Russian Edition, Vol. XXII, Moscow, 1929

Printed according to the original

Published in English for the first time

---

[a] L. Mieroslawski, *De la nationalité polonaise dans l'équilibre européen*. - [b] wit - [c] wit of base quality - [d] tortuous style - [e] past - [f] (Here)—come what may!

34

MARX TO COLLET DOBSON COLLET[a]

IN LONDON

[Draft]

[London,] 23 October 1856

Dear Sir,

Having been absent from London during the last month, and seeing that your paper professed to be wanting space, I have deferred the continuation of my articles until to day. In transmitting the inclosed new manuscript it occurs to me that, from the difference in size between the old and new *Free Press*,[99] it would be desirable to come to a new understanding as to the terms on which my contributions to your paper are to take place.

In answer to your last letter I have to state that it is indifferent to me whether you reprint the old *pamphlets* in large or small type, but as to documents never before published I consider it would be spoiling the case to put them in small type. Concerning the alleged desirability of my own comments not taking the form of notes, you will see that this is being done only where really expedient, and that under the form of introductions to the different chapters they occupy already the space of the text. Lastly as to the suggestion of drawing parallelisms between the epoch I treat upon and the present time, it has been anticipated to a certain extent in the chapters you published. To trace systematically these parallelisms more would be altering my plan, which is rather to give new materials for a new history, than new reflections on well-known materials. To satisfy the wants of his readers in that respect I hold to be rather the duty of the editor.

First published in: Marx and Engels, *Works*, First Russian Edition, Vol. XXV, Moscow, 1934

Reproduced from the original

Published in English for the first time

[a] This draft is written in Wilhelm Pieper's hand, the date in Marx's.

9 Grafton Terrace, Maitland Park, Haverstock Hill, London, where Marx lived from October 1856 to 1868

35

MARX TO ENGELS

IN MANCHESTER

[London,] 30 October 1856
9 Grafton Terrace, Maitland Park,
Haverstock Hill

DEAR Frederic,

I am at this moment dictating an article on Persia.[a] Hence no more than a line or two. Your £5 received. Could you possibly send me *some military stuff on Switzerland* before the week is out, for that is what's holding me up and preventing me from getting on with my articles. Will write at greater length very shortly.

Your
K. M.

Ruge is publishing:

1. *Stories of the Chase for Children.*[b]
2. Philosophical considerations on the religion of Ancient Egypt. He told this to Blind, who on the same occasion discovered that Papa Ruge hadn't so much as heard of Röth's book.[c]

First published in: Marx and Engels, *Works*, First Russian Edition, Vol. XXII, Moscow, 1929

Printed according to the original
Published in English for the first time

---

[a] K. Marx, 'The Anglo-Persian War'. - [b] A. Ruge, *Jagden und Tiergeschichte für Kinder.* - [c] E. Röth, *Geschichte unserer abendländischen Philosophie.* Bd. 1: *Die ägyptische und zoroastrische Glaubenslehre als die ältesten Quellen unserer speculativen Ideen.*

36

MARX TO ENGELS[100]

IN MANCHESTER

[London,] 30 October 1856
9 Grafton Terrace, Maitland Park,
Haverstock Hill

Dear Engels,

The article on Bazancourt[60] is splendid. Enclosed the last bit of the Mieroslawski.[a] If I have seemed lazy about writing it is largely because my wife has been ill these past few months.

As you will yourself observe in the Mieroslawski, 1. the very man who holds *un royaume diplomatique*[b] in Poland to be impossible, wanted to bring about *une révolution diplomatique* there, i.e. under the AUSPICES OF Louis Bonaparte and Palmerston; 2. the fate of the 'democratic' *gmina* of the Lechites[c] in Poland is an inevitable one; the actual *dominium*[d] is usurped by the Crown, aristocracy, etc.; the patriarchal relations between *dominium* and peasant communities lead to serfdom; optional land-division creates a kind of *peasant middle estate*, the *ordre équestre*,[101] to which the peasant can rise only so long as wars of conquest and colonisation are still in progress, though both these necessarily tend to accelerate his DOWNFALL. As soon as the borderline is reached, this *ordre équestre*, incapable of sustaining the role of a true middle estate, turns into the lumpenproletariat of the aristocracy. A similar fate overtakes *dominium* and peasant among the Romanic population of Moldavia, Wallachia, etc. This type of development is interesting in that it shows how serfdom comes into being as a result of purely economic factors, without the intermediate link of conquest or racial dualism.

Your *Manchester Guardian* has the singular distinction of being regarded as the immediate cause of Bonaparte's statement against the English press. Please send me X[e] from time to time. Having discovered that Bonaparte's 1847 is approaching, Palmerston is

---

[a] Excerpts from L. Mieroslawski's book *De la nationalité polonaise dans l'équilibre européen*. - [b] diplomatic kingdom - [c] See this volume, p. 75. - [d] landed property - [e] Presumably the sign of the correspondent who wrote the anti-Bonapartist articles in *The Manchester Guardian*.

bending every effort to jockey him into precisely the same position as he jockeyed Louis Philippe during the Sonderbund War[102]—into an alliance with Russia against England. Whereas on the one hand he takes him in tow against Austria in the filthy Neapolitan affair, in Turkey he sides against him with Austria.[103] Once again the French newspapers are full of MISGIVINGS about the machinations of perfidious Albion. The commercial crisis would certainly seem to have reached its consummation in the Russian railways. The bankruptcy of the CONTRACTORS to the 'palace of international industry'[104] affords a GLIMPSE into the participation of English capitalists in continental enterprises. In Germany the setting-up of industrial and banking undertakings goes on briskly. The Berlin *National-Zeitung* contains whole columns devoted solely to enumerating the names of these CONCERNS.

I learnt from Putnam's man, Olmsted, and an American travelling companion who was with him that Gurowski (the Pole) had acquired much influence with Dana. At the same time these gentlemen told me that the said worthy fellow received regular cash grants direct from the Russian *ambassade*[a] in Washington. This Gurowski advocated Pan-Slavism in opposition to ourselves, which was the only reason why your article[11] was rejected. When returning my manuscript on the Danubian Principalities,[3] Mr Dana forgot TO BLOT OUT a comment written in French by this self-same Gurowski, who remarks on my statistical data relating to the Romanian population:

> 'Tous ces chiffres sont exagérés pour faire mousser l'idée de nationalité Roumaine. Ils sont démentis par les faits, l'histoire et la logique.'[b]

So we can boast of having, or rather of having *had*, our articles inspected and censored directly by the Russian embassy. In the end Dana appears also to have seen through Gurowski.

Today a letter from Collet to whom I had sent some new stuff.[61] The fellow agrees to everything, except that he doesn't say anything about MONETARY TERMS although I expressly asked him about this point in my last letter. So I shall have to PUT ON THE SCREW all over again, since this is the only point of interest to me in my INTERCOURSE WITH THOSE CALIBANS.[c]

---

[a] embassy - [b] 'All these figures are exaggerated for the purpose of inflating the idea of Romanian nationality. They are contradicted by the facts, by history and by logic.' - [c] Caliban is a character in Shakespeare's *The Tempest.*

Write to me soon concerning yourself and those about you. With kindest regards from my wife and children.

Children very well.

Your

K. M.

First published abridged in *Der Briefwechsel zwischen F. Engels und K. Marx*, Bd. 2, Stuttgart, 1913 and in full in: Marx and Engels, *Works*, First Russian Edition, Vol. XXII, Moscow, 1929

Printed according to the original

Published in English in full for the first time

37

ENGELS TO MARX

IN LONDON

Manchester, 17 November 1856

Dear Marx,

Day after day this accursed COMMERCE has prevented me from writing. I now have three lads to keep in control and am forever checking, correcting, telling off and giving orders. Add to this the running battle with manufacturers over bad yarn or late delivery, and my own work. I wish it might occur to Mr Bonaparte to rid France of his own person and me of all this turmoil.

Come to that, the said Bonaparte is in damned hot water. The spate of stories about placards and the unrest among the workers sent in by the *Times* correspondent, after the *Moniteur* article[a] had led to his being ordered *de parler plus haut*,[b] have made an enormous impression on the English philistines here.[105] Everyone believes in his SPEEDY DOWNFALL. The explanation for the sudden discovery that, *au fond*,[c] the fellow is after all an ass and indeed of a very ordinary kind, is as follows: he used to be a genius but has now so ruined himself by his profligate way of life that it has affected his brain. While there may, of course, be something in this, the fellow's behaviour has on the whole been quite

[a] 'Paris, le 23 octobre', *Le Moniteur universel*, No. 298, 24 October 1856. - [b] to talk louder - [c] at bottom

consistent, and only the English philistines can see any qualitative difference between the man he used to be and the man he is now.

Today's *Guardian* contains some interesting statistics about bankruptcies in France; I am sending it to you.

It looks as though the financial crisis will linger on through the winter, becoming gradually more acute though with occasional ups and downs. This means that in the spring it will be considerably worse than if it had broken out in acute form now. The greater the capital paid in to companies hitherto existing largely on paper and the greater the extent to which floating capital becomes fixed, the better. So long as the discount rate doesn't fall below 7 per cent—and the recent rise shows that it will have to be raised yet further—there is no prospect that even half the speculative companies will be able to obtain payment for their third or fourth calls. The Austrian Crédit mobilier [106] can't even collect the money for its second call, and yet the government enters into agreements in Austria, by which the Bank is compelled to resume CASH PAYMENTS!—I'd like to have the money Bonaparte has probably spent over the past 6 weeks to keep government stocks above 66 per cent; precisely because of the great efforts made towards that end, I shall account the day a turning-point when government stocks first drop *below* 66.[107]

The longer this chronic PRESSURE goes on, the more numerous will be the revelations concerning the dirty work of the Bonapartist clique and the greater the rage of the working-men who could not previously have been aware of the details. This chap Morny is really a prime example of a *suitier*,[a] nor would he seem to have any wish to return to Paris; *for him*, certainly, there could be no more appropriate way to invest his money than in Russian railways and government paper.

Never again, perhaps, will the revolution find such a fine *tabula rasa* as now. All socialist DODGES exhausted, the compulsory employment of labour anticipated and EXPLODED 6 years since, no opportunity for new experiments or slogans. On the other hand, however, the difficulties will be starkly in evidence; the bull will have to be taken literally by the horns, and I'd dearly like to see how the next French provisional government will set about cutting its teeth. Nothing, luckily, can be done this time except by dint of the most reckless courage, for we no longer have any reason to fear as swift an ebb as in 1848.

---

[a] wastrel

Strohn has been here recently; had heard sundry things about the little man[a]; *entre nous*, the fellow is thinking seriously about setting up in business on his own! He imagines his patter will serve to entice customers away from his present principal.

I have in front of me at this moment James' *Naval History of England,* 1792-1820, mainly for the sake of SHIPS AGAINST WALLS.[b] It shows that the English had to fight very hard to gain NAVAL SUPERIORITY over the French and, more especially, the Spanish. Given parity of strength, the French and Spanish, during the early years of the war, were a match for the English on almost every occasion, and a mass of vessels was captured from the latter.[108] Though I haven't yet got beyond 1796, I can already see that under Napoleon the French fleet reached an absolute *nadir,* for which he was probably partly to blame.—The superiority of the English at sea lies chiefly in their better *gunnery*; the French always fired too high, though the Spanish were much better. The story about the *Vengeur,* said to have gone down on 1 June 1794 *au cri de vive la république*[c] is, by the way, a myth. The *Vengeur surrendered* to the English but, before she was actually seized, several French vessels again began to close; she rehoisted the French flag, the rescuers were beaten off and the English approached, but the ship went down, most of her crew being saved. She sank 4-6 hours after the end of the battle.

Kindest regards to your wife and children.

Your

F. E.

First published abridged in *Der Briefwechsel zwischen F. Engels und K. Marx,* Bd. 2, Stuttgart, 1913 and in full in: Marx and Engels, *Works,* First Russian Edition, Vol. XXII, Moscow, 1929

Printed according to the original

Published in English for the first time

---

[a] Ernst Dronke - [b] See this volume, p. 71. - [c] to cries of 'Long live the Republic!'

38

MARX TO ENGELS[1]

IN MANCHESTER

[London,] 2 December 1856
9 Grafton Terrace, Maitland Park,
Haverstock Hill

Dear Frederic,

My wife is still dosing herself continually and hence the house is always in such a disarray that it is difficult for me to settle down and write.

As regards the Mieroslawski,[a] a providential 'apportionment' would appear to have taken place, most of the excerpts intended for you (there were ABOUT two sheets) having been torn out of the middle of the manuscript, probably for spills. However, you haven't lost much. I afterwards read Lelewel's *Considérations*—not to be confused with his popular history.[b] He, together with Maciejowski (?) (I cite the name from memory), provides most of the material upon which Mieroslawski exercises his mind. By the by, in my recent studies of Polish history, what led me *décidément* to plump for Poland was the historical fact that the intensity and the viability of all revolutions since 1789 may be gauged with fair accuracy by their attitude towards Poland. Poland is their 'external' thermometer. This is demonstrable *en détail* from French history. It is conspicuous in our brief German revolutionary period, likewise in the Hungarian. Of all the revolutionary governments, including that of Napoleon I, the Comité du salut public[109] is an exception only in as much as it refused to intervene, not out of weakness, but out of 'mistrust'. In 1794 it sent for the *employé*[c] of the Polish insurgents[d] and asked this *citoyen*[e] the following questions:

'How is it that your Kosciusko, a popular dictator, tolerates the existence alongside himself of a king[f] of whom, moreover, he cannot but know that he was put on the throne by Russia? How is it that your dictator does not dare effect the

---

[a] L. Mieroslawski, *De la nationalité polonaise dans l'équilibre européen*. - [b] A reference to *Considérations sur l'état politique de l'ancienne Pologne et sur l'histoire de son peuple* (further in the text Marx quotes a passage from it in free translation), which constitutes Part 2 of Volume 2 of Joachim Lelevel's *Histoire de Pologne*. Part 1 of Volume 1 is entitled *L'Histoire de la Pologne racontée par un oncle à ses neveux*. - [c] representative - [d] Franciszek Barss - [e] citizen - [f] Stanislaus II Augustus

levée en masse of the peasants for fear of the aristocrats, who do not wish to be deprived of any of their "hands"? How is it that the revolutionary complexion of his proclamations pales in proportion to the distance his march removes him from Cracow? How is it that he *immediately* punished with the gallows the popular insurgents in Warsaw, whereas the aristocratic *"traîtres de la patrie"*[a] are allowed to remain at large, or are given refuge in the lengthy formalities of a trial? Answer!'

Whereat the Polish '*citoyen*' could only remain silent.

Que dites-vous de Neuchâtel et Valangin?[b][110] This CASE has led me to try and remedy my highly inadequate knowledge of Prussian history. INDEED AND INDEED, never has the history of the world produced anything so sordid. How the nominal kings of France came to be real kings is also one long recital of petty struggle, betrayal and intrigue, but it is the history of the birth of a nation. Austrian history—the founding of a dynasty by a vassal of the German Empire—acquires interest from the circumstance that the vassal defrauds himself in his capacity as Emperor, from involvement in the East, Bohemia, Italy, Hungary, etc., and finally, too, from the circumstance that dynasty assumes such dimensions as to arouse fears in Europe of its becoming a universal monarchy. Nothing of all this in Prussia. She failed to subdue so much as one powerful Slav nation, and took 500 years to acquire Pomerania, and then only by 'barter'.[111] Come to that, the Margraviate of Brandenburg—as it was when taken over by the Hohenzollerns—hasn't been able to boast a single *conquest*, with the exception of *Silesia*. Perhaps it is because this was her *one and only* conquest that Frederick II's sobriquet is 'the One and Only'.[112] Petty theft, BRIBERY, outright purchase, succession intrigue, and such like shabby dealings is all that Prussian history really boils down to. What is interesting in feudal history elsewhere—the struggle of the monarch against his vassals, double-dealing with the towns, etc.—is all of it here dwarfed to a caricature because the towns are boringly small-minded, the feudal lords boorishly insignificant and the monarch himself a nonentity. During the Reformation, as during the French Revolution, she oscillated between perfidy, neutrality, separate peace treaties and snatching at scraps tossed to her by Russia in the course of partitions organised by the latter—*vide* Sweden, Poland, Saxony. Withal, a dramatis personae of rulers with only 3 masks—the Pietist,[113] the non-commissioned officer, the clown—succeeding one another as surely as night follows day, the only irregularity consisting not in the introduction of fresh characters but in the varying order of their appearance.

---

[a] traitors to the country - [b] What do you make of Neuchâtel and Valangin?

What has kept the State on its legs nonetheless is *mediocrity—aurea mediocritas*[a]—meticulous book-keeping, an avoidance of extremes, the preciseness of the drill book, a kind of homespun vulgarity and 'ecclesial institutionalism'.[114] *C'est dégoûtant!*[b]

How is trade in Manchester just now? Can you let me have some particulars about the state of BUSINESS in the MANUFACTURING DISTRICTS?

I haven't yet informed you that papa Heise passed through on his way from Utrecht. Has now rejoined Imandt. He has filled out and looks better than ever.

Götz, too, suddenly turned up here again. Disappeared with equal suddenness. Freiligrath very satisfied with his business and with himself. Valdenaire—the 'agreer'[115] *manqué*—is over here on a visit from Trier. For what purpose, more in my next.

Finally, I have a ticklish matter to put to you. At the *end of December* I have some fairly substantial sums to pay out. Could you possibly let me have something before then? My wife's money has largely gone on setting up house and making up for very substantial losses in income.

When are you coming down here? What is Lupus doing?

Your

K. M.

First published abridged in *Der Briefwechsel zwischen F. Engels und K. Marx*, Bd. 2, Stuttgart, 1913 and in full in: Marx and Engels, *Works*, First Russian Edition, Vol. XXII, Moscow, 1929

Printed according to the original

Published in English in full for the first time

39

MARX TO ENGELS

IN MANCHESTER

[London,] 22 December 1856

Dear Engels,

You would oblige me greatly if you could send me the money before the week is out. I have just been to see Freiligrath and asked him whether he could advance me anything against my bill

---

[a] golden mean - [b] It's disgusting!

on America, which is drawable only in 2 or 3 weeks' time, *mais impossible*! I was expecting the money from *Putnam's* today; hasn't arrived. The TRANSACTIONS with Urquhart's wretched rabble—on whom I have claims—are still in suspense.[a] If I'm late with the first payment to my LANDLORD, I shall be *entièrement discrédité*.

In great haste.

Salut.

Your

K. M.

P.S. Can you send me any *bon mots* on the military aspects of the Prussia-Neuchâtel conflict? [110] They would be very timely. I have dealt with the diplomatic part myself.[b]

Red Wolff[c] is in Blackburn, Lancashire,[d] with his family. Schoolmaster at a salary of £60.

First published in: Marx and Engels, *Works*, First Russian Edition, Vol. XXII, Moscow, 1929

Printed according to the original

Published in English for the first time

---

[a] See this volume, p. 76. - [b] A reference to Marx's article 'The Right Divine of the Hohenzollerns'. - [c] Ferdinand Wolff - [d] Yorkshire in the original.

1857

40

MARX TO ENGELS

IN MANCHESTER

[London,] 10 January 1857
9 Grafton Terrace, Maitland Park,
Haverstock Hill

Dear Frederic,

D'abord[a] my best wishes for the New Year, albeit retrospective. As a result of watery ink and several nights' writing, one of my eyes is so inflamed that writing is irksome to me.

Both the £5 (the second) and the Mountain Warfare [b] received. For both of them my best thanks.

Is it true that Lupus has again been attacked and robbed by Manchester highwaymen? Or is the rumour circulating here simply an indiscriminate rehash of the old story?

The best thing old Hill can do is retire, either to paradise or to some idyllic Swiss hill, so that he has to be replaced once and for all in your office and can no longer saddle you with double the work under the false pretence of his 'temporary' illnesses.

The Neuchâtel question [110] isn't quite so close to settlement as some papers make out. Both sides may already have gone too far with their braggadocio. Both have already brought discredit upon themselves: our Hohenzollern[c] with his *déférence* for Bonaparte, the Swiss with their 'dignified' attitude. Thus the rascals have deported several hundred factory workers to Piedmont because of their propagandist demonstrations. In this way the 'lenders'[d] hope to secure the esteem of Bonaparte and of Austria, too. What do you make of Lamoricière and Bedeau offering their *épées*[e] to the Swiss burghers? Obviously just an anti-Bonaparte gesture, since the

---

[a] First - [b] F. Engels, 'Mountain Warfare in the Past and Present'. - [c] Frederick William IV - [d] Here and further in the text Marx puns on the words *Borger* (lenders) and *Bürger* (citizens, also burghers). The allusion is to the Swiss bankers who extended loans to French manufacturers. - [e] swords

fellows could be sure the lenders of Switzerland would not take them at their word.

There is great excitement in the *petite démocratie.* Just the kind of clash they want. On top of that, of course, your South German patriot regards the Swiss as kinsmen and in fact sees in the present clash nothing but a sequel to the 1849 campaign for the Constitution.[116] In addition, risings are expected in the Black Forest, etc. The Prussian, for his part, is certainly doing everything in his power to prevent A 'BREACH OF THE PEACE'. That is why Fatty[a] wrote to his brother-in-law[b] in Petersburg in terms reminiscent of the man who bade his wife stay him lest he jump out of the window. 'Stay me!' is a call our hereditary monarch has addressed to each of the great powers in turn. The question is whether they want to 'hold him back' and whether East and West, delighting equally in his discomfiture, will not add fuel to the flames. Whichever way the thing turns out, there will be no lack of red faces.

Proudhon is in process of bringing out an 'economic bible'[c] in Paris. *Destruam et aedificabo.*[d] The first part, or so he says, was set forth in the *Philosophie de la misère.*[e] The second he is about to 'reveal'. The scribble is appearing in German, translated by Ludwig Simon now duly installed as clerk with Königswärter (or some such name, the well-known banker to the *National*) in Paris. I have here a recent piece by one of Proudhon's disciples: *De la Réforme des Banques* par Alfred Darimon, 1856. Same old tale. The *démonétisation de l'or et de l'argent,* or rather *que toutes les marchandises* should be transformed into *instruments d'échange au même titre que l'or et l'argent.*[f] The piece has an introduction by Emil Girardin and betrays evident admiration for Isaac Péreire. Hence it enables one to get some idea of the kind of socialist coups d'état Bonaparte thinks himself capable of resorting to, even at the eleventh hour.

I have a whole LOT [OF] PAMPHLETS written by Bruno Bauer during the Russian war.[117] Feeble and pretentious. In company with his brother Egbert the worthy fellow has now rented from the Berlin municipality 50 acres of land outside Berlin. The intention is that the London Edgar's[g] mother-in-law—an old washerwoman or

---

[a] Frederick William IV - [b] Alexander II - [c] This presumably refers to P. J. Proudhon's *Manuel du spéculateur à la bourse.* - [d] I shall destroy and I shall build. - [e] P. J. Proudhon, *Système des contradictions économiques, ou Philosophie de la misère,* Tomes I-II. - [f] The demonetisation of gold and silver, or rather that all merchandise should be transformed into instruments of exchange in the same way as gold and silver. - [g] Edgar Bauer

SOMETHING OF THE SORT—should look after the 'market side'. Bruno has written to Edgar telling him that this is the way to 'independence'. He is paying a rent of 5 reichstalers PER ACRE, i.e. 250 reichstalers a year. It's old fallow land. Bruno hopes that the profit and the produce from this land will enable him to write at leisure his *Geschichte des Urchristentums*,[118] intended as an 'historical' test-piece for his critique of the Gospels.[a] Nice critical fantasies these, and to some extent Bruno may have been influenced by the recollection that in Part 2 Faust becomes a land-owner.[b] Only he forgets that Faust obtained the money for that transformation from the Devil.

Lallerstedt, *La Scandinavie, ses craintes et ses espérances*, Swedish pendant to Mieroslawski's book.[c] Contains one or two FACTS of interest. In particular Lallerstedt recognises that, during the last century, England was constantly playing Russian tricks on Sweden. Recounts how Admiral Norris, sent by England on an ostensibly *anti*-Russian mission after the death of Charles XII, was bribed by Peter I with a precious stone of great value. Also has new material that throws light on the behaviour of Bernadotte.

Nothing new here. I go out little and hear little.

Salut.

Your

K. M.

Mr Faucher from Berlin is one of the PRINCIPAL SUB-EDITORS of *The Morning Star*. In a diatribe against Lupus in the *London Illustrated News*, Horace Mayhew writes inter alia:

* 'Symptoms of being a confirmed old Bachelor: When a man cannot go anywhere without his umbrella, that's a symptom. When a man thinks every one is cheating him, that's a symptom. When a man does all the shopping himself etc.' *[d]

First published abridged in *Der Briefwechsel zwischen F. Engels und K. Marx*, Bd. 2, Stuttgart, 1913 and in full in: Marx and Engels, *Works*, First Russian Edition, Vol. XXII, Moscow, 1929

Printed according to the original

Published in English for the first time

[a] A reference to B. Bauer's *Kritik der Evangelien und Geschichte ihres Ursprungs*, Bd. I-IV. - [b] J. W. von Goethe, *Faust. Der Tragödie zweiter Teil*, Act V. - [c] L. Mieroslawski, *De la nationalité polonaise dans l'équilibre européen*. - [d] *The Illustrated London News*, No. 836 (supplement), 20 December 1856.

41

MARX TO ENGELS

IN MANCHESTER

[London,] 14 January 1857
9 Grafton Terrace, Maitland Park,
Haverstock Hill

Dear Engels,

Edgar von Westphalen has sent over a man—address enclosed—with two letters, one for me, and one for you. This man Erich wishes to establish connections with London business men and then return to New York. He has recommendations from New York, but none from England. With regard to Edgar's letter, he has given you and myself as references, you as an English merchant, me as correspondent of the *New-York Tribune.* I told him that we couldn't possibly provide information about his financial circumstances, since we knew nothing of them. REPLY: neither were we required to do so, but only to confirm, if asked, that he was 'Erich' of New York and had been 'recommended' to us from that quarter. IT IS ALTOGETHER A SILLY BUSINESS of the kind often initiated by Edgar. The fellow seems to be a decent sort of chap and I couldn't, of course, tell him that a recommendation from my brother-in-law was likely to be more of a hindrance than a help, even in our case. As regards yourself, I naturally made no promises but merely undertook to send you Edgar's letter, at the same time informing you that the 'recommendation', if requested, should *au fond*[a] be restricted to confirming the man's identity.

Cornelius will shortly be leaving London. Is to be manager of a joint stock mining company in Nassau. He has offered Roesgen's cousin what is said to be a good position (in an emigration agency) in Le Havre. *Guardians* received. The FACT concerning the floods is INTERESTING.[119]

Salut.

Your
K. M.

First published in: Marx and Engels, *Works,* First Russian Edition, Vol. XXII, Moscow, 1929

Printed according to the original
Published in English for the first time

[a] by and large

42

MARX TO ENGELS[20]

IN MANCHESTER

[London,] 20 January 1857
9 Grafton Terrace, Maitland Park,
Haverstock Hill

Dear Engels,

I really have monumentally bad luck! For the past 3 weeks or so Mr Dana has been sending me the daily *Tribune*—obviously with the sole intention of showing me that they aren't publishing *any more* of my stuff. Except for some 40 lines on the MOVES of the Banque de France,[a] not a single line of mine has been included. Week after week I have put off drawing anything on the *Tribune* in the belief that the articles would sooner or later appear. BUT NOTHING OF THE SORT. My articles on Prussia, Persia, Austria all regularly REJECTED.[b] Having for some 4 years printed all my things (and yours TOO) under their own name, the curs have succeeded in eclipsing the name I was making for myself among the Yankees and which would have enabled me to find another paper, or to hold over their heads the threat of transferring to one. *Que faire?*[c] Good advice is valuable IN THESE CIRCUMSTANCES. As soon as I draw something they will make it a pretext to get rid of me once and for all; and writing two articles a week in the hope of having *perhaps* one in ten published and paid for is a procedure too ruinous to carry on. And how can I draw anything unless something is published?

And then another piece of bad luck. I've had a look at the November, December and January numbers of *Putnam's.* No sign of the article on[d] Bazancourt.[60] Either it has got lost (although I took it to the main POST OFFICE myself) or it will not be coming out until later. I can't believe that the fellows had got the thing, don't want to publish it and fail to notify me out of sheer bad manners!

I have not yet succeeded in arranging any definite terms with

[a] 'The Crisis in Europe' - [b] A reference to Marx's articles 'The Right Divine of the Hohenzollerns', 'The Anglo-Persian War' and 'The Maritime Commerce of Austria' (two articles) all of which were published in the *Tribune* later. - [c] What is to be done? - [d] In the original *von* (by)

the Urquhartites,[a] and besides, theirs is a tiny little sheet which may bring out short fragments of an article over a month and often not finish it off for 5 to 6 weeks.[61] At best they can serve only as a small, secondary source of income. The *Tribune*, in exceedingly poor and insipid LEADERS, is moreover adopting a view almost diametrically opposed to all that I write. RUSSIAN INFLUENCE is unmistakable.[b]

So here I am, without any prospects and with growing domestic liabilities, completely stranded in a house into which I have put what little cash I possessed and where it is impossible to scrape along from day to day as we did in DEAN STREET.[120] I am utterly at a loss what to do, being, indeed, in a more desperate situation than 5 years ago. I thought I had tasted the bitterest dregs of life. *Mais non!* And the worst of it is that this is no mere passing crisis. I cannot see how I am to extricate myself.

The miserable collapse of Switzerland's braggadocio[121] was only to be anticipated. In no way were the fellows driven TO EAT DIRT by *force supérieure*. For, as Cornelius saw with his own eyes in Paris, the discontent, not only among Parisians, but in the army as well, was so great that in no circumstances could Bonaparte have permitted the Prussians to carry out serious military operations—on the French frontier least of all. Hence his EFFORTS to settle the affair. The discredit of the Swiss is only matched by that of Bonaparte, who first offered to stand surety for Switzerland vis-à-vis the Prussians and vented his spleen in the *Moniteur* when Switzerland repudiated his authority; then offered to stand surety for Prussia vis-à-vis Switzerland, and now finds himself compelled to admit, in little semi-official articles, that Prussia refuses to enter into any obligation towards himself. He has virtually endorsed the démenti he received from the *Neue Preussische Zeitung*.[122] So low has the fellow sunk. In the meantime his half-brother, Morny, has had the foresight to secure for himself a post in the Russian service.

I don't know whether you've seen that Mr Ledru-Rollin has publicly invited the French 'Republicans' to take part in the elections of Boustrapa's[40] Corps législatif[123]? So he has descended to the naïveté of legal opposition. While this shows on the one hand that he has relinquished the grandiloquent title of pretender, it shows beyond a doubt on the other that opposition is again

---

a See this volume, p. 76. - b An allusion to A. Gurowski's influence (see this volume, p. 81).

considered feasible actually inside France, and that the bourgeois Republicans are hastening to resume, along with the Orleanists,[124] a position in parliament that will enable them to shuffle the next revolution under the carpet.

I think I have already told you that the Brussels *Nation* has gone under, being now replaced by its rival the *National*, an inane, uninteresting Belgian gossip sheet. The noble *L'Homme*, too, has breathed its last. In its stead there appeared a *Journal des Proscrits* which proved incapable of surviving for more than a fortnight. In addition, diminutive pamphlets after the manner of Pyat's *Ave Maria* are published from time to time by the French *réfugiés*—inflated, hollow verbiage—printed crinoline save that they cost less to produce and are harder to sell.

The *Tribune* has discovered that, during the past 30 years (up till 1851), France has enriched herself far more than England and thus is *now* also her superior politically.[a] *The proof*: In France, the value (i.e. *nominal*) of landed property has increased twofold, in England not so much. True, the French estimate included houses while the English one did not; but since the English population increased by only 33 per cent in the area concerned, the same could be assumed of the *number* of houses (which the *Tribune* appears to equate with their value).

Erich has achieved his purpose here without any need for further references.

Your

K. M.

Your military exposé[125] WAS BEAUTIFUL. The *Augsburger* contained an article in which the passage at Constance is described as very difficult.[b] I have only skimmed over it.

First published abridged in *Der Briefwechsel zwischen F. Engels und K. Marx*, Bd. 2, Stuttgart, 1913 and in full in: Marx and Engels, *Works*, First Russian Edition, Vol. XXII, Moscow, 1929

Printed according to the original

Published in English in full for the first time

[a] 'That France is rapidly taking the leadership...', *New-York Daily Tribune*, No. 4903, 6 January 1857. - [b] 'Die örtliche Vertheidigung des Bodensees', *Allgemeine Zeitung*, No. 13, 13 January 1857.

43

ENGELS TO MARX

IN LONDON

[Manchester, about 22 January 1857][126]

Dear Marx,

Your letter arrived like a bolt from the blue. I had believed that everything was going splendidly at last—you in a decent house and the whole BUSINESS settled; and now it turns out that everything's in doubt. What damned stingy fellows these Yankees are; the people on the *Tribune* seem to imagine that, having squeezed you like a lemon, they must now proceed to squeeze another one. But the manner in which they are trying to break things off is particularly mean and cowardly. They want to force you to take the initiative. Furthermore, ever since Cluss fell so strangely silent, we've not had one reliable man in the whole of America.

Que faire cependant?[a] Since the *Tribune* is definitely intent on breaking with you this time, I think the best thing would be to establish connections with another New York paper. Might not something be arranged with the *Herald* or the *Times?*[b] In your place I would at once make a move and keep the chaps on the *Tribune* dangling until everything is arranged. In view of the fellows' shabby behaviour you need only consult your own interests and show no consideration for them. If you think that an *indirect* move would be better, let me know. I will gladly carry out the negotiations in *my* name, so that you shan't be compromised; I could write saying I have reason to believe that you don't get on as well as you used to with the *Tribune* people and that some arrangement might perhaps be made, etc., etc. *Enfin,*[c] anything you want, *pourvu que quelque chose soit faite.*[d]

I wouldn't put it beyond the *Tribune* fellows to have stirred up trouble with Putnam too. I should write at once to Putnam to clear the matter up. One doesn't even know whether to write the article on coastal fortifications or not.[e] At all events it would be advisable to keep this source of income open as well.

I shall send you £5 early in February and for the time being you can count on getting this every month. Even if it means my

---

[a] But what's to be done? - [b] *The New-York Herald* and *The New-York Times* - [c] In short - [d] provided that something is done - [e] See this volume, p. 81.

facing the new financial year with a load of debts, *c'est égal.*[a] I only wish you had told me about the business a fortnight earlier. For my Christmas present my old man gave me the money to buy a horse and, as there was a good one going, I bought it last week. If I'd known about this business of yours I would have waited a month or two and saved the cost of its keep. But NEVER MIND, that doesn't have to be paid for straight away. But I'm exceedingly vexed that I should be keeping a horse here while you and your family are down on your luck in London. It goes without saying, by the way, that you shouldn't let the promise of £5 a month deter you from approaching me again in case of hardships, for if anything can be done I shall do it. Anyhow, I've got to turn over a new leaf; I've been leading far too frivolous an existence of late.

Warm regards to your wife and children and let me know soon what you propose to do and how things stand.

Your
F. E.

First published abridged in *Der Briefwechsel zwischen F. Engels und K. Marx,* Bd. 2, Stuttgart, 1913 and in full in: Marx and Engels, *Works,* First Russian Edition, Vol. XXII, Moscow, 1929

Printed according to the original

Published in English for the first time

44

MARX TO ENGELS[82]

IN MANCHESTER

[London,] 23 January 1857
9 Grafton Terrace, Maitland Park, Haverstock Hill

Dear Engels,

D'abord,[b] very many thanks for your kind letter.

I wrote to Olmsted about 10 days ago; am therefore awaiting his reply. It strikes me that Dana's annoyance over Freiligrath's blabbing his secret has something to do with the *Tribune*'s

---

[a] no matter - [b] First

behaviour, or rather with the fact that Dana has not brought his influence to bear.[127]

To work for *The New-York Herald* is out of the question; *The New-York Times* is the one to go for. I am thinking of approaching them unobtrusively through Dr Abraham Jacobi, who is at least discreet and whose quiet manner seems to impress the Yankees GENERALLY. I intend to write to him next Tuesday, and at the same time to Dana in such a manner as will at any rate involve him in a contretemps more disagreeable than he had bargained for. I should be grateful if you could let me have by Tuesday—after Tuesday I shall probably discontinue the articles for the *Tribune* pending further news from New York—a military article on *Persia*.[a] No need for much detail this time. Just a few general strategic VIEWS. The *Tribune* probably imagines that, now they have turned me out, I shall resign myself to abandoning the American camp altogether. The prospect of their 'military' and 'financial' monopoly going over to another paper is hardly likely to please them. Accordingly, I have *today* sent them a 'financial' piece.[128] An introduction to the *Persian war*,[129] however cursory, would be important because it would give them to understand that we still have a 'WAR' up our sleeves with which other papers could be helped to make a splash. The (military) prospects of the Russians and English need only be hinted at, of course.

So I shall postpone any outright rupture until I find out whether I can fix anything up elsewhere in New York. If I cannot and the *Tribune*, for its part, does not change its attitude, then the break will have to be made, of course. But in a sordid contest like this I believe it important to gain time. It seems to me the *Tribune* has come to believe that, since the 'great turn' taken by events in America,[130] it can dispense with all special editions (European ones, at least). It's truly nauseating that one should be condemned to count it a blessing when taken aboard by a blotting-paper vendor such as this. To crush up bones, grind them and make them into soup like PAUPERS in the WORKHOUSE—that's what the political work to which one is condemned in such large measure in a CONCERN like this boils down to. I am aware I have been an ass in giving these laddies more than their money's worth—not just recently but for years past.

Pieper is taking a schoolmaster's post SOMEWHERE between Portsmouth and Brighton; has been chasing after something of the kind for months.

---

[a] F. Engels, 'Prospects of the Anglo-Persian War'.

What about that ADVENTURE of Lupus'? You forgot to say anything about it.

Your
K. M.

P.S. I envy fellows who can turn somersaults. It must be a splendid way of ridding the mind of vexation and bourgeois ordure.

I saw in *The Morning Advertiser* an excerpt, strategic in content, from the *Grenzboten* concerning the Persian business.

First published abridged in *Der Briefwechsel zwischen F. Engels und K. Marx*, Bd. 2, Stuttgart, 1913 and in full in: Marx and Engels, *Works*, First Russian Edition, Vol. XXII, Moscow, 1929

Printed according to the original

45

MARX TO ENGELS

IN MANCHESTER

[London,] 6 February 1857

Dear Engels,

An ACKNOWLEDGMENT, in great haste, of the pounds that arrived today.

Enclosed a letter from Miquel. I wrote to him at once. The situation as regards the *Tribune* is as I foresaw. Once again not a word. So today I wrote the fellows a forthright letter as I had originally intended but did *not* tell them that meanwhile—until their answer arrives—I shall discontinue my articles entirely.

Salut.

Your
K. M.

First published in *Der Briefwechsel zwischen F. Engels und K. Marx*, Bd. 2, Stuttgart, 1913

Printed according to the original

Published in English for the first time

46

MARX TO ENGELS

IN MANCHESTER

[London,] 16 February 1857
9 Grafton Terrace, Maitland Park,
Haverstock Hill, N. W.

Dear Engels,

Enclosed a letter from Olmsted in reply to my inquiry. So this particular ARTICLE wasn't accepted.[131] However, even after this letter I believe that they will be glad to publish 'SHIPS AGAINST WALLS'.[a] The question is, have you got the time to write it? No doubt we ought to try Putnam again before giving up altogether. At any rate it was exceedingly impertinent of that gentleman not to let me know what the position was until after 4 months. Since I shall in any case have to write to Olmsted, see if you can make out his *Christian name* from this letter.

You will probably have had Miquel's letter. Freiligrath tells me that, besides Ruge and Hess, Oppenheim and other disreputable good-for-nothings write for the *Jahrhundert*.

Freiligrath requests you not to let the matter of Weerth remain dormant. Assuming that that Jew Steinthal has got his hands on Weerth's diaries (about which the noble Campe has already written to Weerth's brother[b]), there is the additional danger that, should Weerth's relations get hold of them, they might *in usum delphini*[c] publish them amended and censored. It is to be hoped that Weerth's brother will approach you direct. If the diaries eventually turn up, this would also mean that you could appeal to the philistines' consciences. Incidentally, it is exceedingly mean of Steinthal to have no more than bluntly notified the old woman[d] of Weerth's death, without any details and without either preamble or postscript. That haggler with his saccharine smirk!

I have been rereading (but haven't quite finished) your essays on Pan-Slavism,[11] partly for my own edification, partly in order to note the passages which, in the event of a German version, would necessitate your referring to sources not readily available in

---

[a] See this volume, p. 96. - [b] Karl Weerth - [c] Literally: for the use of the dauphin (the phrase was used in the second half of the 17th century to mark 'expurgated' editions of Latin authors intended for the French crown prince). - [d] Wilhelmine Weerth

England save at the British Museum. While thus engaged I discovered that the same unknown hand (provisionally I make so bold as to ascribe it to the Polish renegade Gurowski) which wrote above my rejected DANUBIAN PRINCIPALITIES articles,[a] 'Tout ces chiffrés sont éxagérés',[b] etc., etc. (nice French), has also adorned the Pan-Slavism articles with marginal glosses, viz.:

ad[c] *article I.* At the end: Σ. *C'est ni bon.*[d] (What the Σ is supposed to be (German C?) is beyond me.) (Nice French sentence! *C'est ni bon.* Period.)

ad article IX. Written at the top: *Changéz l'introduction*[e] and, as heading: '*Southern Slavi*'.

Again, re the sentence, 'BY THIS LOGIC ETC. IT WOULD FOLLOW THAT THE HINDOOS ARE THE MOST YOUTHFUL PEOPLE ETC.' he comments, 'THIS DEDUCTION IS ILLOGICAL'.

On the statistical survey of the Serbian race: 'GERMAN (instead of GERMAN) INFLUENCES DESTROYED THEM IN OTHER BRANCHES UNDER AUSTRIAN DOMINION.' (Nice English!) Again, on your censure of Montenegrin BRIGANDAGE, 'THIS (instead of 'TIS) NOT TRUE'.

Again, on 'CROATIA ETC. HAVE FOR CENTURIES PAST BEEN ANNEXED TO HUNGARY', he comments, 'BUT HUNGARY IS A COMPOUND OF THOSE VARIOUS LANDS'.

The passage about the Mohammedan Bosnians, 'THEY WILL HAVE TO BE EXTERMINATED, NO DOUBT ABOUT THAT' is distorted in true Russian fashion by striking out the next passage: 'THESE ARE, HOWEVER, BUT THE INTERNAL DIFFICULTIES OPPOSING THE ERECTION OF A SOUTH SLAVONIC EMPIRE ETC.'

That these notes are all of Russian inspiration is obvious. Likewise, that no Frenchman could have written French with this kind of ACCENTUATION and such mistakes; likewise and no less, that a Yankee would never talk about 'Southern Slav*i*' and would express himself altogether differently. Hence I should say that the provenance of these notes is beyond doubt. And if, as Olmsted's (Yankee) travelling companion maintained in front of myself, Freiligrath and Olmsted, Gurowski is in the direct pay of the Russian Embassy in Washington, the whole crisis with the *Tribune* becomes perfectly explicable. By the by, from the notes and deletions it transpires that originally it was still intended to publish a modified version of the articles on Pan-Slavism (up to and perhaps including No. 9), and that the idea was not completely abandoned until the fellow realised what we were driving at. Hence, too, Dana's belated decision.

---

[a] See this volume, pp. 68, 81. - [b] All these figures are exaggerated. - [c] re - [d] It's neither good. - [e] Change the introduction

Since, in the midst of my own crisis, it is very edifying for me to hear about crises, drop me a few lines telling me how things are in the industrial districts. Not at all well, according to the reports in the London papers.

The two final volumes of Tooke's *History of Prices*—from 1849 onwards—have come out. It is, of course, a pity that in his unrelenting battle with the CURRENCY chaps and Peel's Acts,[132] the old gentleman is too exclusively concerned with the question of circulation. Still, it's interesting at this particular juncture.

Salut.

Your
K. M.

First published abridged in *Der Briefwechsel zwischen F. Engels und K. Marx*, Bd. 2, Stuttgart, 1913 and in full in: Marx and Engels, *Works*, First Russian Edition, Vol. XXII, Moscow, 1929

Printed according to the original

Published in English for the first time

47

MARX TO ENGELS

IN MANCHESTER

[London,] 24 February [1857]
9 Grafton Terrace, Maitland Park,
Haverstock Hill

Dear Engels,

Are you laughing, are you weeping, are you waking, are you sleeping?[a] Have had no reply to the various letters I have sent to Manchester over the past 3 weeks. However, I assume they have arrived. Send me back what I enclosed in my last—Olmsted's letter—since I *must* answer it ONE WAY OR THE OTHER.

Salut.

Your
K. M.

First published in: Marx and Engels, *Works*, First Russian Edition, Vol. XXII, Moscow, 1929

Printed according to the original

Published in English for the first time

[a] G. A. Bürger, 'Lenore'.

48

ENGELS TO FERDINAND FREILIGRATH[133]

IN LONDON

[Manchester, not later than 25 February 1857]

...The only literary piece of Weerth's that has arrived here so far is a humoristic history of trade (a fragment from the Brussels-Bradford period, 1845-47),[a] but Steinthal is expecting a further packing case of papers. I shall most willingly do all I can to get the things, but it is important that Weerth's brother[b] should write a letter for me, so that I shall have some kind of authorisation. There should hardly be much difficulty; Steinthal is perfectly willing to help. But as regards details probably more than one point of disagreement will crop up.

The diaries, as far as my knowledge of them from Weerth's last stay here goes, contain only matter-of-fact notes.

Meanwhile, as I have already said, as soon as I am authorised to collect the things, I shall certainly make sure that I get everything....

First published in: M. Häckel, *Freiligraths Briefwechsel mit Marx und Engels*, Teil I, Berlin, 1968

Printed according to the manuscript of Freiligrath's letter

Published in English for the first time

49

ENGELS TO MARX

IN LONDON

Manchester, 11 March 1857

Dear Marx,

It's rather as though God and the universe had conspired to stop me writing to you. Whenever I think I have caught up to

[a] G. Weerth, 'Humoristische Skizzen aus dem deutschen Handelsleben', *Kölnische Zeitung*, No. 318, 14 November 1847; No. 337, 3 December 1847; No. 348, 14 December 1847; No. 33, 2 February 1848 (the middle part is extant in manuscript, the ending was published in the *Neue Rheinische Zeitung*, Nos. 1-4, 1-4 June 1848; No. 16, 16 June 1848; No. 18, 18 June 1848; No. 28, 28 June 1848; No. 36, 6 July 1848). - [b] Karl Weerth

some extent with my commercial rubbish, I discover a whole pile of unsuspected arrears, am overrun by chaps, have to reply to hundreds of business queries on behalf of my old man and pander to fresh whims of Mr Gottfr.'s.[a] Just to make sure that I am sitting really fast, Freiligrath saddles me with Prussian ex-lieutenants, dabblers in bonds, who spend the entire day trying to borrow money (something he, Freiligrath, himself thought fit to warn me against) and who, after their departure, send me pawn tickets so that I can redeem their watches at my own expense. I am not in the least obliged to Freiligrath for landing me with the importunate fellow.[b] What is more I wrote to him today about my adventure with the brute. Let him clear the business up himself.

Last Friday[c] Mr Ernst Dronke turned up at the office all of a sudden from Glasgow. He was here for only an hour or two on business. I saw him almost exclusively in the presence of Charles,[d] when it wouldn't have done to argue with him or treat him roughly. On top of that his arrival was so sudden that I was unable to recall all of his intrigues. I treated him with reserve, just as I would treat an ordinary commercial traveller with whom I was only superficially acquainted and confined my remarks to trifling matters, and he was extremely careful to avoid any subject relating to the party. He shoved off during the afternoon and intends to come back in May, at which time I shall probably be in London. I hope he will remain a *commerçant* all his days; he certainly looks the part and the carefree existence seems greatly to his liking.

I presume you got the £5 note I sent you last Friday (or was it Thursday?).

The TORIES, FREETRADERS and Peelites could have done Pam no greater favour than put him in a minority over *this* question.[134] What luck the fellow has and how stupid are his opponents! There is a great deal of agitation up here just now, but since 4,000 new VOTERS are on the register, all small SHOPKEEPERS and CLERKS and OVERLOOKERS, and therefore predominantly pro-Bright, it is unlikely that there will be any change. Bob Lowe and Sir J. Potter (A BORN ALDERMAN[135] and once a mighty wencher) are to be nominated here. WILL NOT DO. You could probably let me have some details about Bob Lowe's early exploits in Australia and elsewhere. These would be very useful just now.[136]

---

[a] Gottfried Ermen - [b] Hugo von Selmnitz - [c] 6 March - [d] Charles Roesgen

What is the price of Mieroslawski's thick book on Poland?[a] It's really essential to have a compendium of this kind—and what is the price of Lelewel's work on which it is based,[b] if you can find this out?

I shall, by the way, send you a few more *Guardians*; they contain some really capital witticisms. I suppose you got the six copies I sent you recently (IN 2 LOTS)? Morny has already smelt a rat good and proper; these purchases the fellow is making in Russia must worry Bonaparte to death. That was also a fine to-do over the Docks Napoléon, Berryer *jeune*[c] and Fox, Henderson & Co.[137]—you must have read about it in *The Times*.[d]

I'm most anxious to hear how the *Tribune* affair is progressing and likewise what you wrote to Olmsted. I think that I shall shortly be able to start work again and will see whether anything can be made out of China. The affair is bound to yield some interesting military aspect.[e] But no hope of that so long as I have to slave away in the office until 8 o'clock each evening and can't start work till 10 o'clock, after SUPPER, etc., etc., is over. At present I have to be at the office by 10 o'clock in the morning at the very latest and ACCORDINGLY go to bed at about one. *C'est embêtant!*[f] Just when one has really got into one's stride, one has to go to bed; *cela ne va pas. Enfin, nous verrons.*[g] This summer things have got to be reorganised, otherwise there'll be a rumpus at the office. I intend to organise myself in such a way that I work from 10 to 5 or 6 and then leave and be damned to the business.

Warm regards to your wife and children. You are all well, I hope?

Tout à toi.[h]

F. E.

First published abridged in *Der Briefwechsel zwischen F. Engels und K. Marx*, Bd. 2, Stuttgart, 1913 and in full in: Marx and Engels, *Works*, First Russian Edition, Vol. XXII, Moscow, 1929

Printed according to the original
Published in English for the first time

---

[a] L. Mieroslawski, *De la nationalité polonaise dans l'équilibre européen*. - [b] J. Lelevel, *Histoire de Pologne*, Tomes I-II. - [c] junior - [d] This probably refers to a report from Paris in *The Times*, No. 22624. 10 March 1857. - [e] F. Engels, 'The New English Expedition in China'. - [f] It's a nuisance! - [g] that won't do. Well, we shall see. - [h] All yours.

50

MARX TO ENGELS

IN MANCHESTER

London, 18 March [1857]
9 Grafton Terrace, Maitland Park,
Haverstock Hill

Dear Engels,

You must excuse me for not having acknowledged receipt of the £5 or of your letter before now. My wife is very unwell and our domestic arrangements generally are in such a state of crisis that I am quite bemused and cannot write.

Guardians received today. No answer yet from the *New-York Tribune.* The only thing I could say to Olmsted, of course, was that if he had failed to place the article[60] with Harper, he should send it back.

Proudhon's new book on economics, not yet to hand, has already run into 7 editions.[a]

How Miquel could believe I could write for the *Jahrhundert* is beyond my comprehension—a weekly rag whose contributors are Ruge, L. Simon, Meyen, B. Oppenheim, M. Hess, etc. I haven't read any of it but have seen the cover of No. 1, Vol. 2, on which is printed the following *list of contents*: 'Nach dem Kriege, vor der Entscheidung. IV. Von Arnold Ruge'. 'Briefe aus Paris, der Schweiz und London' (i.e., L. Simon, Kolatschek, Meyen). 'Der Geist unserer Zeit; zum Neujahrsgruss. Von Arnold Ruge'. 'Naturwissenschaft und Gesellschaftslehre. V. Von M. Hess'. 'Erziehung zum Glauben und Erziehung zur Humanität'. 'Notiz'.

Edgar Bauer is putting out a book, *Englische Eindrücke.*[b] Should be splendid.

I shall find out the price of Mieroslawski's and Lelewel's books (the latter's first volume nothing but a children's history).[c]

Concerning the blackguard—Bob Lowe—I have no information at present, but might find out something this week. He's the kind

---

[a] P. J. Proudhon, *Manuel du spéculateur à la bourse.* - [b] E. Bauer, *Englische Freiheit.* - [c] L. Mieroslawski, *De la nationalité polonaise dans l'équilibre européen*; J. Lelevel, *Histoire de Pologne.* Tome I: 1. *L'Histoire de la Pologne racontée par un oncle à ses neveux.*

of fellow who would have been at home in the Société du dix Décembre.[138]

Every day brings fresh revelations about Pam's 'liberal' foreign policy. First, the 'SECRET TREATY' with Austria.[139] Now, the fact that he has given Bonaparte his word to suppress any kind of revolution in Naples. The latter, however, wanted this done only in so far as a 'Murat' restoration[140] was not subsumed under the heading 'revolution'. It was this 'MISUNDERSTANDING' which scuppered the Naples expedition.[103] In the COMMONS yesterday Pam denied the charge in a very 'AMBIGUOUS MANNER'.[a] But this week is likely to see the appearance of further documents which will give him the lie.

The Russians haven't acted with quite their usual circumspection this time. The first Continental paper since the crisis in Parliament[134] to defend Pam as a 'TRULY BRITISH MINISTER'[141] is the *Nord*, which usually affects a fanatical hatred of Pam. Even the *Neue Preussische Zeitung* speaks of 'UNPRINCIPLED COALITION'.

The *Persian* affair has fizzled out as I supposed: England has gained *nothing*, apart from a few nominal concessions; rather she has given way to the Persian court on the main issue.[129] Russia, on the other hand, has obtained a small piece of territory, as Layard yesterday confided to the gaping COCKNEYS. Needless to say, he did not have the courage to place these two FACTS in their correct causal nexus. He also repeated the assertion (already made by Disraeli in the Lower House without eliciting a word from Pam in reply) that, during the war with Russia, Pam *forbade* the Persians to take an offensive stand against the Russians as had been their intention. For at the time the fellows had hopes of recapturing the provinces that had been wrested from them. He had had the same admonition conveyed to them at the time of the Polish revolution (1830).

In order to assess correctly the Persian, as also the Chinese fracas, both should be compared with Pam's earlier doings in these REGIONS, since both are merely repetitions.[142] So long as he was at the helm, the first Chinese war was conducted in such a way that it could have gone on for 100 years without any result save an increase in the RUSSIAN OVERLAND TEA-TRADE and a growth of Russian influence in Pekin. It was only under Sir Robert Peel that this war was given an 'English' twist by Ellenborough.

---

[a] An account of Palmerston's speech in the House of Commons was published in *The Times*, No. 22631, 18 March 1857.

It is to be hoped—and is indeed probable—that this time a parliament will be returned which will pledge itself to nothing save passive obedience to Pam. The dissolution of the former parties expressed as a *coalition ministry*, like that of Aberdeen,[143] seemed rather to make the MIDDLE CLASS feel able to rest on its laurels than to alarm it. This same dissolution expressed as *Pam's dictatorship* is bound to lead, not only to the most gratifying fiascos and complications abroad, but also to the most violent agitation if not to revolution at home. The old boy, who was partly responsible for the Manchester '*massacre en miniature*' and helped to draw up the 6 'GAGGING ACTS',[144] won't so much as turn a hair. *Mutatis mutandis*, Pam's DICTATORSHIP will be to the coalition ministry what the rule of the Royalists, who coalesced in the last French *Assemblée*, was to the rule of Bonaparte.[145] In England, things will at last be brought to a head.

Apropos *Bangya*. Since 1855 this same Bangya has been Sefer Pasha's *adlatus*.[a] He has married the daughter of a Circassian chief (which must be equally gratifying to his lawful wife in Pest and his unlawful one in Paris), and is now himself a Circassian chief. Through his connections in London he has recruited 300 Poles and shipped them to the BLACK SEA together with supplies of ammunition, etc. According to the news in the papers, they have run the gauntlet of the Russian CRUISERS and safely reached Sefer Pasha. WHAT DO YOU THINK OF THAT? The fellow, realising that his role was played out in the West, has embarked on a new one in the Orient. Whether again as a democratic *mouchard*[b] or in good faith is another question.

Write soon, as your letters are now essential TO [help me] PLUCK UP. The SITUATION is horrible.

Salut (to Lupus as well).

Your

K. M.

First published abridged in *Der Briefwechsel zwischen F. Engels und K. Marx*, Bd. 2, Stuttgart, 1913 and in full in: Marx and Engels, *Works*, First Russian Edition, Vol. XXII, Moscow, 1929

Printed according to the original

Published in English for the first time

[a] aide - [b] informer

51

ENGELS TO MARX

IN LONDON

Manchester, 20 March 1857

Dear Marx,

It had already occurred to me that you might once again be in something of a hole. Whatever can be done by me, will be done. If at all possible I'll send you another five-pound note next week or, if I can't get hold of one, a POST OFFICE ORDER. In the latter case, be sure to let me know at what POST OFFICE I should make it payable. I've had very heavy debts to pay this month, with people tracking me down to the office, so that there was no option but to stump up. Otherwise you'd have had the five pounds straight away. It's lucky, by the way, that this parliament business has begun, with China thrown in for good measure [134]; at this juncture the *Tribune* will need help again and will be forced to come to TERMS.

I've been sounding the *Guardian* chap about the possibility of making contact with REVIEWS and MAGAZINES up here. But this chap, too, seems to be hunting round in the hope of fixing up something for himself and there's not much to be got out of him. However, I shall see. Since he knows my opinion of Palmerston and declares it to be PREPOSTEROUS he is all the less likely to give us a recommendation *in politicis.*[a] All the same, I have a certain HOLD ON THE FELLOW but as yet haven't devised any way of exploiting it.

I share your view of Palmerston's intentions and prospects in the new parliament. Bonapartist despotism wielded by Pam together with a Corps législatif. [123] We shall see what that leads to.

According to the Augsburg *Allgemeine Zeitung,*[b] the Circassians (which, not specified) have actually appointed Bangya 'head of the house'; he was selected for this snug berth precisely because he is a foreigner, so that none of the native chiefs could complain of having been slighted. What has become of Sefer Pasha (a man of quite a different stamp to Kościelski) is far from clear. I regard the whole thing as a stroke of genius on the part of the Russians, and we shall probably hear no more of the 300 Polish Spartans. [146]

The *Nord* must have changed its mind again. The *Guardian's* Brussels correspondent quotes passages that are violently anti-

[a] as far as politics are concerned - [b] 'Pera. 20 Febr.', *Allgemeine Zeitung,* No. 63, 4 March 1857.

Palmerston. Can you let me have the most relevant bit? That sort of thing never comes my way here and in any controversy I must always have CHAPTER AND VERSE immediately to hand.

While putting my old newspapers in order recently, I discovered the loss of one of the main bundles of *English* papers and cuttings from the *Guardian, Free Press,* etc., etc. Nothing, luckily, connected with our party archives—they are safely stored away. But *everything,* with a few exceptions, *relating to Palmerston*—Tucker's pamphlets,[147] the cuttings containing your articles you had sent me (many of these are also being sat on by Lupus, etc.). I needed and was looking for them precisely in order to refresh my memory as to detail. Have you got any duplicates you could send me, likewise the full text of your articles which appeared in Urquhart's *London* paper[61]? These should be fairly easy to get hold of. I would find the things particularly handy just now.

Bob Lowe's prospects up here are poor. Some of the philistines have come out against Bright; however I believe he will scrape through this time. Lowe will make an ass of himself as soon as he arrives here. But it would be splendid were he to get in.[136]

Warm regards to your wife and children. Write again soon and tell me how your wife is.

Your

F. E.

First published abridged in *Der Briefwechsel zwischen F. Engels und K. Marx,* Bd. 2, Stuttgart, 1913 and in full in: Marx and Engels, *Works,* First Russian Edition, Vol. XXII, Moscow, 1929

Printed according to the original

Published in English for the first time

52

MARX TO ENGELS[20]

IN MANCHESTER

London, 24 March 1857
9 Grafton Terrace, Maitland Park,
Haverstock Hill

Dear Engels,

Herewith some anti-Palmerstoniana, viz.: 1. *Betrayal of England,* 2 COPIES. (*NB.* The self-same Coningham who here reproduces excerpts from Anstey's speech[a] is now an ultra-PALMERSTONIAN candidate in Brighton.) 2. *TUCKER-PAMPHLETS,*[147] 8 COPIES. 3. *Anstey's speech.*[b] 4. *Palmerston for Premier.* 5. *Palmerston in Three Epochs.*[c] (With the exception of the *Hungarian* affair, cribbed from Urquhart, the remainder has been lifted by Mr Wilks—just like him, of course—from my articles in the *Tribune.*[148]) No need for you to preserve numbers 1 and 2; but possibly numbers 3, 4 and 5. Tomorrow, if I can find them, I shall send a few other pamphlets. AS TO THE *Nord,* note that the *Post* itself (in one of the numbers appearing between 4 and 9 March) carried the article I have mentioned.[d] Later, however, it changed its tune.

Now for PRIVATE AFFAIRS. *D'abord*[e] a letter has arrived from the *Tribune,* which I shall send you as soon as I have answered it. My threat to write to another paper has worked after all, at least up to a point. Despite its *very friendly* tone, the letter shows that I was not mistaken about these gentlemen. For what they propose is to pay for *one article* a week, whether or not they print it; the *second* I send at my own risk, and draw on it *if* printed. Thus they are *au fait*[f] cutting me down by one half. However I shall *agree* to it and *must agree to it.* Also, if things in England take the course I think they will, it won't be long before my income reaches its former level again.

I'm very sorry that, in the meantime, I must continue to depend on you, having so greatly fallen into arrears that everything that could be pawned has been pawned and the drop in income cannot be made up until I have found some new resource. On top of that, and since I cannot after all withhold the FACT from you, my wife is IN HIGHLY INTERESTING CIRCUMSTANCES. However, all I intended in my last was to explain why I hadn't answered for so long—*certainly not* ANYTHING ELSE. You will understand that even the most equable of men—and in a mess such as this I do INDEED possess a great deal of equanimity—will sometimes lose patience and let himself go, especially vis à vis his friends.

I should be most grateful if you could let me have a few *'humorous'* LINES, SAY 50 OR 100 ONES, on the Orlandian bravery[g] evinced by the English in Persia and before Canton.[134] The Bushire expedition,[149] as you will have seen, pivoted mainly on the

---

[a] Coningham made use of Th. Anstey's speeches delivered during the debates in the House of Commons from 8 February to 1 March 1848. - [b] in the House of Commons on 23 February 1848 - [c] by W. Wilks - [d] 'From Our Own Correspondent. Brussels, March 6', *The Morning Post,* No. 25955, 9 March 1857 (see also this volume, p. 107). - [e] First - [f] in effect - [g] L. Ariosto, *L'Orlando furioso.*

espionage of one Captain Jones, who was sent to Bushire under FALSE PRETENCES as POLITICAL AGENT. Probably more tomorrow, as I want to send you the pamphlets today.

Salut.

Your

K. M.

NB. It does after all make a difference whether one stages a coup d'état first and elections afterwards, or elections first with a subsequent coup d'état in view. Without doubt Palmerston, or at least his PAPERS, have OVERDONE THEIR PART. Take the *Advertiser*, for instance, wallowing in filth up to its eyebrows. This has, OF COURSE, evoked a measure of reaction.

First published in *Der Briefwechsel zwischen F. Engels und K. Marx*, Bd. 2, Stuttgart, 1913

Printed according to the original

Published in English in full for the first time

53

MARX TO COLLET DOBSON COLLET
IN LONDON

[Draft]

[London,] 25 March 1857

Dear Sir,

Enclosed Chapter V of the diplomatic relations.[61] The forwarding of the gratification due for the printed contributions would oblige me. Should your time permit, you would oblige me by calling at my house any day except Friday. I have to communicate you some highly important information.[a]

The illness of Mrs Marx does not allow me seeing you at Ampton-place.

Yours truly

etc.

Mr D. Collet

First published in: Marx and Engels, *Works*, First Russian Edition, Vol. XXV, Moscow, 1929

Reproduced from the original

Published in English for the first time

[a] Here Marx crossed out the words 'respecting Circassia' (a reference to the revealing material on J. Bangya which Marx included in his article 'A Traitor in Circassia').

54

MARX TO ENGELS
IN MANCHESTER

London, 31 March 1857
9 Grafton Terrace, Maitland Park,
Haverstock Hill

Dear Engels,

Received the £5.

I should like you to send me some *Manchester Examiners* if convenient. The BRIGHT PARTY'S EXPLANATIONS are of interest to me just now. It is only through their defeat that the election has acquired any historical POINT.[134] Palmerston's position will become dangerous only now, when he has a commanding majority inside Parliament, whereas outside Parliament there is a recrudescence—for the first time since the Anti-Corn Law League[150]—of SERIOUS ANTI-MINISTERIAL AGITATION. England is entering upon a *sérieuse* crisis—as *The Times* already intimates, with its reference to the CLOUD WHICH IT SEES GATHERING[a]—and if the MOVE is resumed on the Continent, John Bull will not maintain the stance of supercilious detachment he adopted in 1848. Pam's victory marks the culmination of events which began in June 1848.[151] Amongst the more intelligent members of the London PUBLIC the news from Manchester, accompanied as it was by a commentary in the shape of Pam's brazen address and speech,[b] was greeted with a kind of stupefaction. Seen from here—and all are unanimous on this point—Manchester has brought disgrace, serious disgrace, upon itself. Had *Punch* not been bought by Pam—*Taylor*, a chief editor thereof, has been given a post at the General Board of Health at a salary of £1,000—Potter, Turner, and Garnett, at any rate, would have figured in it next Wednesday. Send me some particulars about these laddies and their WHEREABOUTS.

Mr Dronke has written to Freiligrath telling him that he 'will break with his Jew and set up as an independent agent'.

I have provided Urquhart with some notes on Bangya[c]—in view of the latter's connections with Constantinople and Circassia.

---

[a] 'Sir De Lacy Evans is the first-born...', *The Times*, No. 22641, 30 March 1857 (leader). - [b] Palmerston's speech before the electors of Tiverton published in *The Times*, No. 22641, 30 March 1857. - [c] K. Marx, 'A Traitor in Circassia'.

Enclosed a cutting from *Reynolds* about the editor of *The Morning Advertiser*—Mr Grant. Every word of it true.

Also Dana's letter. Let me have it back. In his enumeration of the articles published he mentions only the last ones,[a] and even some of these he didn't publish until 5 or 6 weeks after their arrival in New York when he saw that things were taking a new turn.[152] His proposal *re* money is the best possible indication that I was not mistaken about the gentleman's intentions. His remark about the length of the articles suits me well. I shall have all the less to send. What strikes me, though, is that for months past he has been able to find 2 or 3 columns for the most insipid London GOSSIP.

In Prussia too there is a minor parliamentary crisis. Once AGAIN the dictum 'Geniality leaves off where money matters begin'[153] would seem to be proving true there.

It seems highly probable that the Swiss will agree to expel all the refugees.

Salut.

Your
K. M.

Did you take note of the bubbles that burst last week—the Australian Agricultural Company, the London and Eastern Bank, and the North of Europe Steam Company, one of the directors being Mr Peto?

First published abridged in *Der Briefwechsel zwischen F. Engels und K. Marx,* Bd. 2, Stuttgart, 1913 and in full in: Marx and Engels, *Works,* First Russian Edition, Vol. XXII, Moscow, 1929

Printed according to the original

Published in English for the first time

55

ENGELS TO MARX

IN LONDON

Manchester, 31 March 1857

Dear Marx,

You will have received the £5 note, K/S 84562, this morning. As regards 'depending on' me, don't give it another thought. I should

[a] K. Marx, 'The Anglo-Persian War', 'The Maritime Commerce of Austria'.

take umbrage if you were *not* to inform me when the SOVEREIGNS' armed intervention is required. I shall see how my finances go in April; I think I shall be able to manage a bit more during the second half, at any rate.

The *Tribune*'s proposal is most cunning and, since the chaps are practically *certain* to print only one article a week, I shouldn't send two save on special occasions such as the present elections, etc., etc. However, circumstances will come to your aid, and in all probability the good Yankees will have no reason to complain about the DULLNESS OF EUROPEAN POLITICS this summer and autumn, while their own merry-go-round will gradually come to a halt.

I have hardly followed the Persian and Chinese military ventures[a] at all, indeed there has been a great dearth of detail. About Captain Jones I know nothing. It would now be utterly impossible to get together the necessary material, but when we get fuller news about the last big cavalry attack in Persia I shall see what can be done.

The pamphlets have arrived.[b] If only I could get hold of your old *Tribune* articles![148] Most of the stuff is in them. Washington Wilks[c] and *Palmerston for Premier* contain only generalities, and Chisholm Anstey's speech[d] is fearfully *décousu*[e] though very important, more especially by reason of the personal matters relating to the *Portfolio*[154] but also, here and there, by reason of its contents. The only really cogent pamphlets are your two Tucker pamphlets, especially *Unkiar Skelessi.*[147] If you can supply me with any more material, *tant mieux.*[f] I have taken steps to improve the storage arrangements.

The eight thousand philistines who voted for the fattest man in Manchester (Potter) because he makes up for his lack of brains by the size of his bottom, are already ashamed of their victory. All the same, the elections have made an enormous impression here, and the 'Manchester' Party[134] is beginning to take stock of its performance over the past 6 years and to discover in what it has failed. I don't think we shall hear very much more of PEACE-PARTY TALK[155] for the time being, while on the other hand Bright (*if* he rallies) will, with one or two others, undoubtedly advocate a more far-reaching electoral reform and, before long, Jones may well receive some propositions from these bourgeois. For Pam the most gratifying thing must be his triumph over Bright, Gibson, Cobden,

---

[a] A reference to the Anglo-Persian war of 1856-57 and the second Opium War, 1856-60. - [b] See this volume, pp. 110-11. - [c] W. Wilks, *Palmerston in Three Epochs*. - [d] in the House of Commons on 23 February 1848 - [e] disjointed - [f] so much the better

Miall and Fox (Oldham); I am inclined to believe that the fellow will get a WORKING MAJORITY of 60-100. But be that as it may, *nous aurons du Palmerston tout pur,*[a] and WITH A VENGEANCE

I've found one of the passages from the *Nord* in *The Morning Post,* but only eulogising his abilities.[b] The one in which he appears as a 'TRULY BRITISH MINISTER'[141] is not to be found.

Our local Palmerstonians and bourgeois offered Bob Lowe, should he be defeated here, the sum of *£2,000* to cover his election expenses in some other wretched hole. The ass refused, preferring the safety of Kidderminster, only to be trounced there. But never again will he be able to come to Manchester; he has behaved like a real blackguard—first he allows the philistines to compromise themselves on his behalf, then cries off and, *at the same time,* writes an article for *The Times* in which he says it would be scandalous if Manchester were *not* to return Bright.[c]

This time Philistia was tremendously divided. The vast majority of the bourgeoisie, a small majority of the lower-middle class, against Bright and Gibson. Quakers[156] and Catholics for Bright to a man; the Greeks likewise; the *established* Germans against him. A drunken anti-Bright man shouted: 'WE WON'T HAVE HOME POLICY, WE WANT FOREIGN POLICY.' What the rationale of the local elections more or less amounts to is: To hell with all questions of reform and class matters. After all, we philistines form the majority of voters, *cela suffit.*[d] The clamour against the aristocracy, etc., is tedious and produces no tangible result. WE DEARLY LOVE A LORD FOR ALL THAT. We've got FREE TRADE and as much *bourgeois* social reform as we require. We're flourishing like mad, especially since Pam reduced war INCOME TAX. So let's all foregather on territory where we are all equal, and let's be ENGLISHMEN, John Bulls, under the leadership of that TRULY BRITISH MINISTER Pam. Such is the present mood of the majority of philistines.

What is piquant about the business up here is the burial of the Anti-Corn Law League[150]; Smith P. Robinson (HON. SEC.) and George Wilson, 'THAT RESPECTABLE FIXTURE' are being thrown out of Newalls Buildings[157] and the GREAT LIBERAL PARTY is casting about for a new organisation. G. Wilson loses his snug berth and his status on the strength of which he rose to be CHAIRMAN of the Lancashire and Yorkshire railways at a salary of £1,000 per annum—another snug berth that will soon go west, permitting

---

[a] we shall have unadulterated Palmerston - [b] 'From Our Own Correspondent. Brussels, March 6', *The Morning Post,* No. 25955, 9 March 1857. - [c] 'One of the greatest advantages...', *The Times,* No. 22634, 21 March 1857. - [d] that suffices

Wilson to go back to starch manufacturing as in the days of PROTECTION. But your Manchester philistine—even if a partisan of Bright—heaves a sigh of relief at the long-awaited demise of that old incubus, THE LEAGUE [136]!

Apropos, I believe that the Ch. Anstey pamphlet contains only a small part of Pam's reply[a]—the debate lasted 4 days. Couldn't you get hold of the rest? And could you send me a copy of Urquhart's new rag, *The Free Press*[99] or whatever it's called? What is there in it by you?

NB. You might also, *s'il y a lieu*,[b] send me the titles of anything else *of any use* concerning the Pam affair; I could then get them myself up here.

Hearty congratulations on your family prospects. What are the girls doing? They must be quite big by now. I look forward very much to seeing them at Whitsun. Warm regards to them and your wife.

Your

F. E.

First published abridged in *Der Briefwechsel zwischen F. Engels und K. Marx*, Bd. 2, Stuttgart, 1913 and in full in: Marx and Engels, *Works*, First Russian Edition, Vol. XXII, Moscow, 1929

Printed according to the original

Published in English for the first time

56

ENGELS TO MARX

IN LONDON

Manchester, 2 April 1857

D. M.,

Potter is a great big, enormously fat fellow, aged about 46 years, red haired and red faced, has been mayor of Manchester 3 times, VERY JOLLY, HAS NO BRAINS, but plenty of belly and bottom, introduced robes into the corporation here on the occasion OF THE QUEEN'S VISIT, for which he was dubbed a knight, is a lifelong whoremonger (a

[a] Engels presumably refers to the pamphlet *The Betrayal of England*, compiled of Anstey's speeches in the House of Commons debate lasting from 8 February to 1 March 1848. - [b] if called for

BACHELOR still), on particularly intimate terms with the celebrated Miss Chester (*alias* Polly Evans) whose brothel he has twice fitted out and towards whose LAW EXPENSES he allegedly contributed £50 when she appeared before the Liverpool Assizes on a charge of abortion and was acquitted. A man who will greatly please the COUNTRY SQUIRES and whose reputation rests solely on the fact that his father, Sir Thomas Potter, KNIGHT, was once leader of the local liberal movement and introduced Milner Gibson here. He himself is popular with whores, CAB-DRIVERS, PUBLICANS, street urchins and the less respectable variety of philistine GENERALLY. While he was MAYOR the police left the whores in peace. Views—moderate liberal.

J. A. Turner is a respectable philistine who has never forgotten that he once went bankrupt and who, within his restricted circle, makes himself *plus ou moins*[a] useful as chairman of the COMMERCIAL ASSOCIATION (the rival of the more liberal CHAMBER OF COMMERCE). Might also gain some influence in the House of Commons by his detailed knowledge of commercial questions. Is a Tory (moderate) and very rich. His elder son, Jack Turner, COMMONLY CALLED THE FAT BOY, is a great toper and a good billiards player. His second, an impudent lad, is a FOXHUNTER with considerable pretensions to good horsemanship, an ugly mug and red moustache. To the horror of his family, he married the ballet dancer Annie Payne.[158]

Your

F. E.

First published in: Marx and Engels, *Works*, First Russian Edition, Vol. XXII, Moscow, 1929

Printed according to the original

Published in English for the first time

57

MARX TO ENGELS

IN MANCHESTER

London, 9 April 1857
9 Grafton Terrace, Maitland Park,
Haverstock Hill

Dear Engels,

You must excuse me for being so late in answering. For a fortnight my wife has been in worse health than for many months

---
[a] more or less

past, and there has been great TROUBLE in the house. Be so good as to let me have Dana's letter back.

I am sending you through the parcels company a small bottle of eye lotion. Cornelius brought me a bottle of it from Paris, where he had had trouble with his eyes. For several weeks I had myself been suffering from inflammation of the eyes due to intensive work at night. The lotion put me right within a few days and will do you a similar service. All you have to do is put a few drops into the bad eye on getting up and on going to bed.

Conrad Schramm has died in Philadelphia of a chest complaint. I hear that in New York the *Neue Zeit* announcing his death has published an obituary of sorts. I haven't yet seen it.[159]

The apparent improvement on the Stock Exchanges is again petering out. Bank rate is rising again. Crédit mobilier[45] and French *rentes* are again going DOWN, while revelations of commercial sharp practice by joint stock companies in London and Paris are becoming increasingly frequent. In the latter place, I'm glad to say, the government is directly involved. You have, I suppose, read about the row between Péreire and Féline? I'd have copied it out for you had I not assumed that *The Manchester Guardian*'s [woman] correspondent CHRONICLES everything of that nature. I now see the Paris *Figaro* from time to time, the only *real* journal of the Empire; it has cast off all semblance of respectability.

I don't know whether I have already drawn your attention to the two new pieces of evidence against Pam. First, Herbert told his CONSTITUENTS in *South Wilts*[a] that he had given orders for the bombardment of Odessa[160]; upon his resigning, Pam sent an order written with his own hand to SPARE it. Secondly, Russell told the City electorate[b] that Palmerston had given him written instructions on how to conduct himself at the Congress of Vienna,[161] instructions which Clarendon forbade him to make public and in the execution of which LITTLE JOHN so splendidly BROKE DOWN. It's typical of old Pam to keep harping in *his* newspapers on Herbert's Odessa TREASON (it was Pam's popular rag, the *Advertiser*, that first drew attention to Herbert's family ties with Vorontsov[c]) and on Russell's Vienna TREASON.[162]

---

[a] An account of S. Herbert's speech, delivered on 19 March, was published in *The Times*, No. 22633, 20 March 1857. - [b] An account of Russell's speech, delivered on 27 March, was published in *The Times*, No. 22640, 28 March 1857. - [c] 'The Sham Blockade of Russia', *The Morning Advertiser*, No. 19832, 12 January 1855.

I shall search out more anti-Palmerstoniana for you. Pam's speech against Anstey (a fat pamphlet) ought to be in my possession if Pieper hasn't pinched it from me. Lengthier works are Parish, *Diplomatic History of Greece* and Urquhart, *Central Asia.*[a] On the first topic you might also read the EXPOSITIONS by Thiersch[b] and Maurenbrecher[c] which came out in 1836 (?). (It's a long time since I set eyes on them.) Of all the *Blue Books,*[38] the one that has impressed me most strongly is that on the second Syro-Turkish War.[d]

I've only had 5 articles in *The Free Press.*[61] Liebknecht, etc., have filched them from me. However I'll get them together for you. In the last one I used the text of one of your articles, in which you speak of Peter I.[163] I've only just completed the introduction. But at first the chaps dragged their feet for months. Later, they brought it out rather more quickly. But now, when the first payment is due, I dun them in vain. If they don't do better on this POINT than hitherto, I shall have to sever the CONNECTION ALTOGETHER. They have given me a new contract, but what good is a contract to me if they don't abide by it *in puncto puncti*[e]?

Salut.

Your

K. M.

Regards to Lupus. Tell him that in Grimm[f] I have found the scientific derivation of Farina, the Eau de Cologne manufacturer, viz. Sanscrit: *vâri*[g]—Gen. *vârinas.*

First published abridged in *Der Briefwechsel zwischen F. Engels und K. Marx,* Bd. 2, Stuttgart, 1913 and in full in: Marx and Engels, *Works,* First Russian Edition, Vol. XXII, Moscow, 1929

Printed according to the original

Published in English for the first time

[a] *Diplomatic Transactions in Central Asia...* - [b] Fr. Thiersch, *De l'état actuel de la Grèce...* - [c] It has not been established which work by Maurenbrecher Marx had in mind. - [d] *Correspondence 1839-1841, Relative to the Affairs of the East, and the Conflict Between Egypt and Turkey* - [e] to the letter - [f] J. Grimm, *Geschichte der deutschen Sprache.* - [g] water

58

ENGELS TO JENNY MARX[164]

IN LONDON

[Manchester, about 16 April 1857]

Dear Mrs Marx,

Herewith the article,[a] and at the same time 4 *Guardians*. A new map of London has now at last enabled me to locate your Grafton Terrace. You really are right out in the country, at the foot of Hampstead Hills and, if the hachures on the map are correct, in a highly romantic district. But if the result is nothing but ill-health, toothaches, swellings of the head and digestive upsets, it doesn't say much for country air and romanticism. At all events, I hope that both you and the Moor are by now feeling very much better.

Lupus suggests that the Moor's etymology of Farina is quite wrong and that the Sanscrit *vârinas* is, rather, the root of Varina shag.[b] This answer will certainly come as no surprise to the Moor and should therefore not be withheld from him. A new chapter is about to open in old Lupus' life. Don't be alarmed—it isn't marriage. On the contrary, it's divorce, for he's leaving the LANDLADY he's been with for 3 years, and moving closer to where I live. The old gent is now very popular with a group of German clerks who come to the Chatsworth from time to time, and over whom he presides with great dignity every Sunday night. They simply couldn't live without Lupus, any more than the English philistines who patronise the pub.

All eyes up here are fixed on fat Potter in anticipation of the day when he seconds the address in Parliament; a fine spectacle that will be!

Again, best wishes for your recovery. Warm regards to the girls—the air out there will undoubtedly suit them better. How they must have grown!

With warm regards,

Your

F. Engels

First published in *Der Briefwechsel zwischen F. Engels und K. Marx*, Bd. 2, Stuttgart, 1913

Printed according to the original

Published in English for the first time

---

[a] F. Engels, 'Changes in the Russian Army'. - [b] See previous letter.

59

MARX TO ENGELS[82]

IN MANCHESTER

[London,] 21 April 1857

Dear Engels,

Be so kind as to write *by return*, telling me how to reply to the enclosed letter from Dana.[165] I must send off an answer by Friday's post.

By following Christ's precept 'if thy tooth offend thee, pluck it out',[a] I have at last found relief, at the same time discovering that this wretched tooth was the source of all the other ailments that have been plaguing me for months. You have located our house correctly. The title of Mr Edgar's[b] book is not *Englische Eindrücke* but *Englische Freiheit*.[c] $^1/_4$ of it is said to be about Mormonism. The whole claims to provide the physiognomy OR, IF YOU LIKE, physiology of the national character. I haven't read any of it. Will write to you IN SOME DAYS.

Salut.

Your

K. M.

First published in: Marx and Engels, *Works*, First Russian Edition, Vol. XXII, Moscow, 1929

Printed according to the original

60

ENGELS TO MARX

IN LONDON

[Manchester, 22 April 1857][166]

Dear Moor,

This business of the Cyclopaedia[165] has come as a real boon to me, and to you too, no doubt. *Voilà enfin*[d] a prospect of making good your loss of earnings and, for me, a prospect of a regular

---

[a] Cf. Matthew 5:29, 30 - [b] Edgar Bauer's - [c] See this volume, p. 106. - [d] At last there's

occupation in the evenings. *La paix allait me démoraliser*[a]; ever since there have been no more articles to write for the *Tribune* I have been doing far too much loafing, for which there is every inducement up here. As to the *militaria*, Dana must provide an immediate answer to the following questions:

1. How many volumes, roughly, will the whole amount to and how far does he propose to get in Vol. 1 or Vols. 1 and 2?

2. Are the military articles to be confined primarily to defining technical terms, e.g. ARTILLERY, CASTRAMETATION, COLUMN, with historical notes and a brief synopsis of the individual branches of military science—thus e.g. artillery: 1. Definition. 2. History and present state. 3. Résumé of the branches of the modern science of artillery (gunnery, personnel, transport, use in the field and before fortresses, etc., etc.)?

3. Or is the intention to have additional articles on military history, e.g. under the HEAD Austerlitz, Arbela, etc., etc., brief *comptes rendus*[b] of the actual battles, and under Alexander, Caesar, Carnot, etc., etc., military biographies together with particulars in each case of any epoch-making progress?

Next, you must write to Steffen *at once* and ask him for the title or author of an encyclopaedia of military science, as short and complete as possible; one that has the most but also the shortest articles would be best, since all I want is to know at once what articles to do and to have the alphabetical material as complete and HANDY as possible. As soon as I have this I can start work on Letters A and B—perhaps even sooner, since I can do a lot of articles from *Brockhaus*[c] alone and a few more without it.

The PAY is quite profitable, even at $2 per large page; a lot of the stuff will only have to be copied or translated and the longer articles won't involve a great deal of work. I shall take a look at one or two English encyclopaedias straight away to see *what* military articles they contain, but then concentrate on *Brockhaus* which, after all, not only provides a better basis but is also more complete and is evidently looked upon by Dana as a model.

Should there be any philological sections for the taking, e.g. the Germanic languages, Middle High German, Old High German, etc., etc., literature (likewise in the Romance languages, especially Provençal), no harm would be done. Either the Jakob woman or Mr Gurowski will have taken on the Slav things; the former knows more about those languages than I do.

---

[a] I was becoming demoralised by inactivity. - [b] accounts - [c] *Brockhaus' Konversations-Lexikon*

Which articles shall you be taking on? German philosophy, at any rate—biographies of modern English and French statesmen? Some financial pieces? Chartism? Communism? Socialism? Aristotle—Epicurus—Code Napoléon—and the like. Themes certainly harder to handle without any PARTY TENDENCY WHATEVER than the good old military stuff, where needless to say one always sides with the victor.

Take as many articles as you can and set up an office by degrees. Mr Pieper can toil away, too; he will do well enough for biographical pieces and will, at the same time, get some plain wholesome information into his genius' noddle. Lupus might also be prepared to do something in the early classical field; *je verrai!*[a]

Even though the work won't be very interesting (most of it, at any rate), I'm immensely tickled by the whole thing since it will mean an enormous LIFT for you. I was really hellish anxious this time about how the *Tribune* business would turn out, particularly when Dana tried to put you on half-pay. But now everything is going to be all right again and even though there's no immediate prospect of payment, it's still a very secure berth and one need have no qualms about doing one or two letters of the alphabet in advance; the money will arrive in its own good time.

Haven't you heard anything from Olmsted about *Putnam's*? I should very much like to have the article on Bazancourt[60]; maybe I can do something with it here through Acton. Apart from that there may be a possibility of doing something further with *Putnam's*—PROGRESS IN THE ART OF WAR, IMPROVEMENTS IN ARTILLERY, SMALL ARMS, etc., etc., SHIPS AGAINST STONE WALLS; I'm willing to do anything so long as the fellows undertake *to publish it*. Dana would certainly arrange it to make you less dependent on the *Tribune*. By the way, get the EDITOR of *Putnam's* to *write in person, cela vaut mieux*.[b]

You must also find out from Dana whether the articles should in general take up more or less space than e.g. in *Brockhaus*, and whether the whole is intended to be bigger or smaller than *Brockhaus*. Then we shall know what we are about. Also *when* they will pay—and by when the job must be completed. It's as well to know all this.

In your place I should offer to do the whole encyclopaedia alone; we could manage it all right. At all events, take whatever you can get. If we have 100 to 200 pages in each volume it won't be too much. We can easily supply that amount of 'unalloyed'

---

a I shall see! - b that would be better

erudition so long as unalloyed Californian gold is substituted for it.

But now, warm regards to your wife and children; let me hear from you again soon.

Your

F. Engels

Most obliged for the eye lotion. I'm still having some trouble but think it's because I've recently been drinking more port than usual—DROP THAT!

First published abridged in *Der Briefwechsel zwischen F. Engels und K. Marx*, Bd. 2, Stuttgart, 1913 and in full in: Marx and Engels, *Works*, First Russian Edition, Vol. XXII, Moscow, 1929

Printed according to the original

Published in English for the first time

61

MARX TO ENGELS

IN MANCHESTER

London, 23 April 1857
9 Grafton Terrace, Maitland Park,
Haverstock Hill

Dear Fred,

I shall write to Dana not later than tomorrow. For me, the thing has come as a godsend, as you can imagine. It has also reassured my wife, which is important in her present SITUATION. I shall write to Steffen straight away (the fellow has changed his lodgings without notifying me, but is still in Brighton). Pieper, as you will remember from one of my previous letters,[a] has been a schoolmaster in Bognor since Christmas, AND I SHALL CERTAINLY LEAVE HIM THERE. He was becoming daily more vacuous, idle, useless and expensive. Under the iron rod of the parson in whose service he now is, he will again come to his senses. Moreover, the laddie left me just at a time when, because of my wife's condition, he thought himself indispensable and did not seem averse to the idea of my

[a] See this volume, p. 98.

pressing him to remain on more favourable terms. I DID NOTHING OF THE SORT but merely expressed my satisfaction at his having at long last found a post. In the event, it transpired that his 'indispensability' was merely a figment of his own imagination. My wife fulfils the function of secretary without all the BOTHER created by the noble youth. As tutor to the girls he was quite unsuitable. So both parties have benefited from the change and, if the fellow again becomes serviceable, as I am convinced he will, he'll be much fortified by the realisation that I do *not need* him in any way.

Hence there can be no question of setting up an office in London. There is no one here who is any good. It's possible—and this I shall know within a day or two—that Dana has approached Freiligrath direct. Our Freiligrath is again MALCONTENT with his post though it enables him to earn £300 very comfortably with little or nothing to do. What he finds tedious is, for one thing, the moaning and groaning of the shareholders, who vent their displeasure on him, and, for another, his admittedly ambiguous position, which places a great deal of responsibility on him while allowing him barely a semblance of autonomy. That, AT LEAST, is the interpretation he himself puts on his FEELINGS. What in fact LURKS beneath all this is, or so it seems to me, a general distaste for RESPONSIBILITY. A clerical post which would relieve him of it, as at Hood's, is and always will be his dream. Then, too, he is tormented by the conflict between his renown as a poet and the rate of exchange. So far as I can gather from his occasional CONFESSIONS, all these Crédits mobiliers[45] are privily assailed by considerable MISGIVINGS. He was assured by an old hand on the Stock Exchange that never, in a practice of 40 YEARS' STANDING, had he experienced a chronic state of crisis such as now prevails. I haven't yet got round to it, but some time I must really investigate the relationship between the rate of exchange and BULLION. The role played by money as such in determining the bank rate and the MONEY MARKET IS SOMETHING STRIKING AND QUITE ANTAGONISTIC TO ALL LAWS OF POLITICAL ECONOMY. Worthy of note are the 2 newly published volumes of Tooke's *History of Prices*. A pity the old man's head-on collision with the CURRENCY PRINCIPLE chaps[132] should lead him to give such a one-sided TURN to all his disquisitions.

I wrote to Dana as much as a fortnight ago asking for the return of your Bazancourt.[60]

The Urquhartites—who have asked me to send them a detailed BILL—have paid me £10 on account[a]; this was most welcome, since

---

[a] See this volume, p. 120.

I owed that much to baker and butcher alone. The girls are growing up very quickly and their education, too, is becoming expensive. At the LADIES SEMINARY they frequent, they are having PRIVATE LESSONS with an Italian, a Frenchman and a DRAWING MASTER. Now I have also got to find a chap for music. They learn extraordinarily fast. The youngest one—the BABY[a]—is an astonishingly witty little thing and claims that SHE HAS GOT TWO BRAINS.

For my own part I would much prefer to supply Dana with articles on, say, Ricardo, Sismondi, etc. That sort of thing does at least admit of objective treatment from the Yankee point of view. German philosophy is difficult to write about in English. However, I shall suggest various things to Dana and leave the choice to him.

For the past six months I've been constantly having to call in the doctor for my wife. She is, indeed, very much run down.

Apropos. *Dr Freund has passed through the court of bankruptcy—assets £200, debts £3,000.*

The Bright and Cobden party cannot help but thrive now that Faucher is the foreign editor of their London paper, *The Morning Star.* I'm now on speaking terms with the chap since I can't help encountering him sometimes at Edgar Bauer's. The man considers himself the finest fellow in the world. 'Bruno Bauer has lost his self-confidence. He feels that it is I, not he, who will conquer Prussia.' He is A CURIOUS FREETRADER TOO, who doesn't even know what the MIDDLE CLASSES are. Prussia is, and ought to be, ruled by 'the officer and the student', 'I bowl over any English meeting at which I speak', 'I have made history. It was I who drew up Cobden's Canton MOTION',[167] to cite only a few of his tropes. The chap's a veritable Munchausen of mendacity, a veritable Ancient Pistol[b] of braggadocio, and once in 6 months it's amusing to listen to his boasting.

Have you—or Lupus—heard anything about a *Römische Geschichte* published somewhere near Heidelberg, which is said to contain much that is new[c]?

How goes it with the landlord of the Golden LION?

Salut.

Your

K. M.

First published abridged in *Der Briefwechsel zwischen F. Engels und K. Marx,* Bd. 2, Stuttgart, 1913 and in full in: Marx and Engels, *Works,* First Russian Edition, Vol. XXII, Moscow, 1929

Printed according to the original

Published in English for the first time

---

[a] Eleanor Marx - [b] See W. Shakespeare, *King Henry IV, King Henry V* and *The Merry Wives of Windsor.* - [c] Th. Mommsen, *Römische Geschichte,* Bd. 1-3.

62

MARX TO ENGELS[20]

IN MANCHESTER

[London,] 8 May 1857

Dear Frederick,

The £5 received.

Herewith a letter from Lassalle[a] which, when Lupus has seen it, you should return to me at the beginning of next week. What should I do about fellow? Reply or not reply? You'll be amused by the comical vanity of the laddie, who will do anything to become famous and, entirely without provocation, writes 75 sheets on Greek philosophy.[b]

I have written to Dana in exactly the terms you suggested. As regards your Bazancourt,[60] I had already urged him to return it. Steffen doesn't know of any book such as you require; he himself appears to be engaged on an English translation of Rüstow's *Cäsars Heerwesen.*

Pieper is on the point of falling back into his former foolishness. Has written me a 'genius's' letter. The enthusiasm—not the enthusiasm inspired in him by his new post, but that which he inspired in his new post *cum* attendant principal—appears AS USUALLY to have waned. He wishes to go to Switzerland as a 'courier', *or else* sever connections with his principal at midsummer and once again cut a dash in London with £20 in his pocket. When I next write I shall pour cold water on the genius. If he is ever to become 'serviceable' again this young man must endure the parson's lash for some while yet.

Have you read the Crédit mobilier's[45] last report? It was in *The Times.*[c] Indicates a DECLINE.

Pam AS REFORMER! He'll reform those boys WITH A VENGEANCE.

If you possibly can, write a military piece on Persia or China next week. My wife is drawing ever closer to the catastrophe and is finding her secretarial duties increasingly onerous.

As regards your toothache, I would advise you to have recourse to the same means as I did after eighteen months' hesitation. Pull

---

[a] Lassalle's letter to Marx of 26 April 1857 - [b] Lassalle's *Die Philosophie Herakleitos des Dunklen von Ephesos,* published later. - [c] 'The Crédit Mobilier of France', *The Times,* No. 22670, 2 May 1857.

the bugger out! I, too, always supposed my toothache to be rheumatic. Yet in the end a *corpus delicti* was discovered after all. When are you coming down here?

Salut.

Your

K. M.

With the coming of spring the children always go down with various ailments. So it has been again, first the youngest[a] and Laura and now it's little Jenny's turn.

First published abridged in *Der Briefwechsel zwischen F. Engels und K. Marx*, Bd. 2, Stuttgart, 1913 and in full in: Marx and Engels, *Works,* First Russian Edition, Vol. XXII, Moscow, 1929

Printed according to the original
Published in English in full for the first time

63

ENGELS TO MARX

IN LONDON

[Manchester,] Monday, 11 May 1857

My dear Moor,

I return Lassalle's letter herewith. Effery eench the puerile Jew. What a pretty compilation it must be, likewise the thing that is going to 'set things alight' and about which he is so mysterious.[168]

We know, of course, that there is nothing to the fellow but it is difficult to find any positive reason for breaking with him, particularly as we have heard nothing further from the Düsseldorf workers.[b] From this letter he would appear to have ceased all intercourse with them, or rather they with him, since he finds nothing positive to say about how things are going with the workers in Germany. But whether he wouldn't again make use of a letter from you to regain some kudos in their eyes is another matter. In your place I should write to him—you can't very well do otherwise—but ask him outright how things stand with the workers' movement on the Rhine and especially in Düsseldorf, so

---

[a] Eleanor Marx - [b] See this volume, pp. 24-25.

working your letter that he will keep his mouth shut about it and must either *plus ou moins*[a] declare himself or be deterred from corresponding with you. Lupus was much amused by the letter but our discussion on the subject was interrupted. I should, by the way, also make a point of asking him how he comes to slip your letters into the hands of the police.

There is absolutely nothing to say about Persia; the campaign itself was rotten and the accounts are even more so. There was, of course, something to be said about China on the arrival of the last MAIL as there still is, but *now*, ten days after the last MAIL, it's too late to do anything. So I shall wait until the next MAIL arrives, when I shall at once set to work so that the article[b] will reach you in time for Friday or the following Tuesday. As far as possible, then, make your arrangements accordingly. I think the MAIL arrives at the end of this week.

WHAT'S THE MATTER WITH THE CHILDREN? I trust little Jenny is ALL RIGHT again. Warm regards to them all and also to your wife.

Your

F. E.

First published abridged in *Der Briefwechsel zwischen F. Engels und K. Marx*, Bd. 2, Stuttgart, 1913 and in full in: Marx and Engels, *Works*, First Russian Edition, Vol. XXII, Moscow, 1929

Printed according to the original

Published in English for the first time

64

ENGELS TO MARX

IN LONDON

Manchester, 20 May 1857

Dear Marx,

As you will no doubt see from the enclosed article,[b] it was written UNDER DIFFICULTIES. Each time I propose to do a *Tribune* article, it seems to bring out all the evil humours latent in my frame. On this occasion I'm sitting at home with linseed poultices on the left-hand side of my face in the hope of getting the better

---

[a] more or less - [b] F. Engels, 'Persia—China'.

of a nasty abscess; I've been put on a frugal diet and forbidden beer, but by good fortune ordered to take a glass of wine. It's alleged that I've been eating too much roast beef; at all events I have had continual trouble with my face for the past month—first toothache, then a swollen cheek, then more toothache and now the whole thing has blossomed out into a furuncle, as little Heckscher calls it. In addition, I have to drink mineral water and—great fun, this—go out at 7 o'clock each morning.

Everyone up here is an art lover just now and the talk is all of the pictures at the exhibition. The thing is proving *plus ou moins*[a] a FAILURE, financially, at any rate. Admittedly there are some very fine pictures, though most of those by the better or very best artists are no more than SECOND-RATE. Among the finest is a magnificent portrait of Ariosto by Titian. The later German and French schools very poor, hardly represented at all. Three-quarters consists of English trash. Best represented are the Spanish and Flemish and, after them, the Italians. *S'il y a moyen,*[b] you and your wife ought to come up this summer and see the thing. It wouldn't do to write about it for the *Tribune*; and I wouldn't know where to begin—the *Tribune* can find the usual chit-chat in any paper.

Lupus, as I believe I told you, has moved out and is again fighting the good fight with his LANDLADY. To make matters worse, his new LANDLADY was brought to bed a week after he moved in. Next door there's a chap who not only has a fiddle which he plays badly but also a French horn which he plays completely out of tune. Hence the study of the pedagogic sciences is attended by enormous difficulties, so that the old chap is spending more time than usual at the Chatsworth.

I shall be in London in a fortnight or 3 weeks' time, either during Whitsuntide or the week after.[169]

Warm regards to your wife and children.

Your

F. E.

First published abridged in *Der Briefwechsel zwischen F Engels und K. Marx*, Bd. 2, Stuttgart, 1913 and in full in: Marx and Engels, *Works,* First Russian Edition, Vol. XXII, Moscow, 1929

Printed according to the original

Published in English for the first time

---

[a] more or less - [b] If possible

65

MARX TO ENGELS[20]

IN MANCHESTER

[London,] 22 May 1857
9 Grafton Terrace, Maitland Park,
Haverstock Hill

Dear Engels,

It may be some consolation to you to learn that for the past 3 weeks right up to this very day, I have been submerged in pills and potions as a result of my old and, as I believe, hereditary LIVER COMPLAINTS. Only by dint of the utmost exertions have I been able to supply the 'goods'—for the *Tribune* I mean—being otherwise QUITE DISABLED. In order that my time should not be entirely wasted I have, *faute de mieux*,[a] been mastering the *dansk sprog*[b] and am presently applying myself to *Af mit Livs og min Tids Historie*, a colossal state haemorrhoid, *af*[c] (ex-minister) Ørsted. Opening oysters would be an altogether more amusing proposition. However, if the doctor's promises are anything to go by, I have prospects of becoming a human being again next week. Meanwhile I'm still as yellow as a quince, and vastly more crabbed.

As regards your own tribulations, I am firmly convinced that they all stem from a hollow tooth which ought to come out and which, by a series of concatenations, underlies all the other unpleasant symptoms. Heckscher will deny this, OF COURSE. However, when you come down here—which I greatly look forward to—it can do you no harm at least to accompany me to a really first-rate dentist and get him to examine your teeth. My view is based on the fact that two years ago, when I was suffering from very much the same trouble, Dr Freund also declared I had been eating too much meat, yet a few months ago a courageous visit to the dentist at last uncovered the source of the trouble. Your intermittent toothache is, of course, the main factor in my argument.

My wife expects to be confined at the end of the month, this time in not altogether agreeable CIRCUMSTANCES. It will be a long time now—another 3 weeks at very best—before I have accumulated enough to be able to draw on the *Tribune*. I tried to draw a bill on myself to cover the interim period, but failed with éclat. The

[a] for want of anything better - [b] Danish language - [c] by

actual HOUSEHOLD debts I can put off paying, but in the case of the rates this is possible only up to a certain point, and besides, the afore-mentioned circumstances call for certain preparations which have to be paid for on the nail.

As you will have seen in the papers, a second director of the Crédit mobilier[45]—the first was Place—viz. the BANKER Thurneyssen, has decamped leaving massive debts of ABOUT 30-40 million frs. This splendid institution's latest report[170]—that of 28 April ultimo[a]—reveals that, although the NET PROFIT still amounts to 23%, it has nevertheless fallen by about a half compared with 1855. According to Mr Péreire, the fall is due 1. to the *ordre* in the *Moniteur* of March 1856 by which Bonaparte forbade the Crédit to skim the cream off the excessive speculation then going on in France; 2. to the fact that, by an oversight, this *'ordre de la sagesse suprême'*[b] extended only to *sociétés anonymes*,[c] thus laying the Crédit open to highly improper competition in the shape of *sociétés de commandite*[d]; 3. to the crisis during the last 3 months of 1856. True, the Crédit sought to exploit that crisis to bring off a few financial *coups de main*, but was obstructed in this 'patriotic' work by the NARROW SELFISHNESS of the Banque de France and the syndicate of Paris BANKERS headed by Rothschild; 4. Bonaparte has still not permitted them to make the statutory ISSUE of 600 millions in paper money of their own devising. *That issue is still looming in the future.* Péreire seems to be exerting severe pressure on Bonaparte. Should the latter shrink from giving his authorisation, a MIDDLE COURSE would seem to be envisaged, namely to turn the Banque de France into the instrument of the Crédit by loftier means, i. e. new draft legislation. From this report it further transpires that the Crédit's business is still vastly disproportionate to its capital and that it has used the capital loaned by the public exclusively to further its gambles on the Bourse. As a quasi-state institution of Bonaparte's on the one hand, the Crédit mobilier declares that it is called upon to maintain the prices of FUNDS, SHARES, BONDS, in short, of all securities on the national Bourse, by advancing the money borrowed from the public to COMPANIES or INDIVIDUAL STOCK-JOBBERS for their operations on the Bourse. As a 'private institution', on the other hand, its main business consists in speculating on the rises *and* falls in the stock-market. Péreire reconciles this contradiction by something Moses Hess might well call 'social philosophy'.[171]

---

[a] Published in *Le Moniteur universel*, No. 120, 30 April 1857 and *The Times*, No. 22670, 2 May 1857 (see this volume, p. 128). - [b] order of the supreme wisdom - [c] joint-stock companies - [d] joint-stock companies with limited liability

I have omitted only one or two small items from your China-Persia article,[a] and altered an expression here and there. I agree with the whole thing, only I don't think that the troops stationed in Persia will be sent to China so soon. The treaty expressly stipulates that they will not leave Persia until the Persians evacuate Herat.[129] Pam won't spare them the hot season. That his instructions in this respect were again highly 'incomprehensible' would seem to follow from the fact that the Governor-General of India—Canning—tendered his resignation at the same time as the British general and the British admiral[b] committed suicide. Meanwhile, as announced in the *Vienna* newspapers, the main object has been attained. Persia has ceded two STRIPS OF LAND to Russia.

I have heard from Mickel[c] and shall send you his letter one of these days. Trusting I shall soon hear that you are fit and well again.

Salut.

Your

K. M.

First published abridged in *Der Briefwechsel zwischen F. Engels und K. Marx*, Bd. 2, Stuttgart, 1913 and in full in: Marx and Engels, *Works*, First Russian Edition, Vol. XXII, Moscow, 1929

Printed according to the original

Published in English in full for the first time

66

MARX TO ENGELS

IN MANCHESTER

[London,] 23 May 1857

Dear Engels,

The enclosed arrived from Dana this morning. It puzzles me how the Yankee can expect the stuff for Vol. I[165] to be in New York by the beginning of July if he doesn't let us know what he wants until the end of May.

---

[a] F. Engels, 'Persia—China'. - [b] Stalker and Etheridge - [c] Johannes Miquel

You might reconsider which articles one should offer to do, apart from the military. Philosophical stuff is, in fact, too badly paid and also difficult when it has TO BE DONE IN ENGLISH. Do you know if there happens to be any German or French book on the biographies of big industrialists?

I'm equally puzzled as to how aesthetics is to be dealt with in 1 PAGE, FUNDAMENTALLY, and on a Hegelian basis.

Does Lupus feel inclined to take something on?

Enclosed also a letter from Miquel. I do not, in fact, understand his theory of 'non-overproduction' and yet of 'lack of the wherewith to pay for production', unless it be that the utterly superficial blather of the utterly wretched CURRENCY chaps[132] has taken root in Germany.

Salut.

Your
K. M.

First published in *Der Briefwechsel zwischen F. Engels und K. Marx*, Bd. 2, Stuttgart, 1913

Printed according to the original

Published in English for the first time

67

ENGELS TO MARX

IN LONDON

Manchester, 28 May 1857

Dear Marx,

Dana must be out of his mind to stipulate 1 page for aesthetics. Nor has the chap any inkling of military matters. See list of articles overleaf, occurring to me exclusively from *Brockhaus* and from memory. But since I must first check it against an *English* military encyclopaedia it can't be final; how could anyone remember all the technical expressions which in English begin with A? Apropos, there is an encyclopaedia of this kind by a hack of the most wretched variety, one J. H. Stocqueler.[a] Could you make inquiries about price, scope, etc., etc.?

---

[a] J. H. Stocqueler, *The Military Encyclopaedia.*

And then, if you please, he wants to have the articles—of the desired thoroughness and brevity—over there by 1 July. Once again, typical Yankee. Anyway, it proves that they are counting more on SHOW than on real substance, as is already evident from the $2 per page.

Send Dana the list—*as a provisional one*—and point out that since it's impossible to work ON SPECULATION at this PAY, he must say what he wants. (It's precisely these patched together articles, being the easiest, that make the PAY acceptable.) A 2nd list of *technical* expressions for A will follow very shortly. Once this is SETTLED he might just as well let us have the list up to D, E or G so that we can get on with it.

I know nothing about Airey's (General) former career. You might look it up in an ARMY LIST, which will at least provide the bare bones.

I know nothing about the *Spanish Armada* either, but this could be found—likewise *Ayacucho*.

I'm not yet in sufficiently good shape to be able to come up tomorrow, and propose to leave on Saturday.[169] Can one take a CAB from Camden STATION (to which one books the TICKETS) to your place? And how far is it?

I shall bring Miquel's letter with me; because of my illness I haven't seen Lupus for a whole week.

More when we meet. As you can imagine, I have my hands really full, what with arrears, etc., etc.

Your

F. E.

* Abensberg (battle of 1809)	1/4 p.
Abukir ditto	1/4 p.
Axle (artillery)	1/8 ditto
Acre (St. Jean-d'-Sièges of)	1/4 ditto à 1/2
Actium (battle of)	1/8-1/4
Adjutant	1/4-1/2
Afghanistan (invasion by English)	2
Åland Isles see Bomarsund	
Albuera (battle)	1/4
Aldenhoven ditto 1797	1/4
Alessandria (fortress and sieges)	1/4
Algeria (French conquest of and English bombardment of)	2-3
Almeida (siege of in Peninsular War)	1/4
Amusette (artillery)	1/10

Anglesey (Marquis of)	1/2
Attack (in battle and siege)	1/2
Antwerp (fortress & sieges)	1
Approaches	1/2 fully
Arbela (battle of)	1/4
Arquebusier	1/8
Aspern and Essling (battle 1809)	3/4
Augereau (Marshal)	1/2
Advanced guard	1/2 * [172]

First published abridged in *Der Briefwechsel zwischen F. Engels und K. Marx*, Bd. 2, Stuttgart, 1913 and in full in: *Marx-Engels Gesamtausgabe*, Abt. III, Bd. 2, Berlin, 1930

Printed according to the original
Published in English for the first time

68

ENGELS TO MARX [173]

IN LONDON

[London,] Friday morning
[5 June 1857]

Dear Moor,

Instead of coming to see you I am once more condemned to no less than four days of hot poultices. My face is again very bad and the whole business has begun all over again. But this time I intend to get rid of it for good. This will, of course, postpone my departure for Manchester *ad infinitum*. If the thing clears up quickly I might be able to go out for a bit on Monday.

In case you have any news for me in the meantime, drop me a line. The address you know: 7 Grove Hill, Camberwell.

I am RATHER annoyed by this business, as you can imagine, but *que faire* [a]?

Warm regards to your wife and children.

Your
F. E.

First published in: Marx and Engels, *Works*, First Russian Edition, Vol. XXII, Moscow, 1929

Printed according to the original
Published in English for the first time

---

[a] what can be done?

69

MARX TO COLLET DOBSON COLLET

IN LONDON

[Draft]

[London, about 10 June 1857][174]

Dear Sir,

According to your wish I send you the account for my contributions to *The Free Press*.[a] They fill somewhat more than 27 columns. You will excuse me for having interrupted. Since I had the pleasure to see you last, I was constantly labouring under serious liver complaints, and thus forced to interrupt my contributions to *The Free Press* which, however, I hope to be able to resume next week.

Yours truly

D. K. M.

Contributed to the London *Free Press* 26 columns; the column at 1/2 Guinea; makes 13 Guineas. Received on them 10£. St.; remains due to me 3£. St. 13sh.

Published for the first time — Reproduced from the original

70

MARX TO COLLET DOBSON COLLET[175]

IN LONDON

[Draft]

[London, after 10 June 1857]

Dear Sir,

Having myself not made up, but only copied the account forwarded to you, I felt, on receiving your note, very anxious, indeed, lest my claims should have been overstated. Consequently,

[a] K. Marx, *Revelations of the Diplomatic History of the 18th Century.*

I reexamined the reckonings. The case is simply this, that you make $22^1/_3$ columns, that you have omitted No. 34,[a] and that the only mistake on my part consists in having put down 4 columns for No. 34, which really amounts to $5^1/_2$ columns.

Yours truly
K. Marx

D. Collet, Esq.

Published for the first time

Reproduced from the original

71

MARX TO ENGELS

[IN LONDON]

[London,] 15 June 1857

Dear Engels,

Are you laughing or are you weeping,
Are you waking or are you sleeping?[b] We here are seriously concerned about you. So write and tell us how you are. I hope you aren't being given any more hot poultices which, as a method of treatment, is *quite out-of-date* and has now more or less fallen into *disrepute.* But assuming you are using internal remedies only—as is rational and up-to-date—I fail to see why you have to keep yourself so anxiously secluded.

My wife very unwell. But she sounded the bugle too soon and as yet nothing has happened.

Salut.

Your
K. M.

First published in: Marx and Engels, *Works,* First Russian Edition, Vol. XXII, Moscow, 1929

Printed according to the original

Published in English for the first time

---

[a] Issue No. 34 of *The Free Press,* 1 April 1857, containing a section of Marx's *Revelations of the Diplomatic History of the 18th Century.* - [b] G. A. Bürger, 'Lenore'.

72

MARX TO ENGELS[176]

IN MANCHESTER

[London,] 29 June 1857

Dear Engels,

From the enclosed letter you will see that Dana is expecting the manuscript soon.[a] What am I to tell him? I can't plead sickness, since I am continuing to send ARTICLES to the *Tribune*. It's a very awkward CASE.

My wife is still in the *status quo*. On top of that, a nasty cough and domestic worries, serious ones. I hope you are recovering. Steffen was here yesterday.

Your
K. M.

First published in *Der Briefwechsel zwischen F. Engels und K. Marx*, Bd. 2, Stuttgart, 1913

Printed according to the original

Published in English for the first time

73

MARX TO ENGELS

IN MANCHESTER

[London,] Friday, 3 July [1857]
9 Grafton Terrace, Maitland Park,
Haverstock Hill

Dear Engels,

Shall be writing tomorrow. This is just to inform you that the second half of the note had still not arrived by this evening. Considering the bad luck which has been dogging me of late, it

[a] The reference is presumably to the article 'Army' requested by Dana for *The New American Cyclopaedia*.

may well have got lost. I couldn't go to Williams' since my wife's condition has meant—pretty well ever since you left[169]—that I can't leave her on her own.

Your
K. M.

First published in: Marx and Engels, *Works*, First Russian Edition, Vol. XXII, Moscow, 1929

Printed according to the original
Published in English for the first time

74

MARX TO ENGELS

IN MANCHESTER

[London,] 3 July [1857]

DEAR Frederic,

I am writing again TO GAINSAY my earlier note. No. II arrived on the stroke of 6. No letter has ever arrived so late before, and hence I wrote in order to avert possible MISCHIEF.

Salut.

Your
K. M.

First published in: Marx and Engels, *Works*, First Russian Edition, Vol. XXII, Moscow, 1929

Printed according to the original
Published in English for the first time

75

MARX TO ENGELS

IN MANCHESTER

[London,] 6 July 1857
9 Grafton Terrace, Maitland Park, Haverstock Hill

Dear Engels,

Rüstow[a] is not to be had at Williams'. And I wouldn't care to write to Steffen on this score for, being himself engaged on an

[a] W. Rüstow, *Heerwesen und Kriegführung C. Julius Cäsars.*

English rendering of the book, he tends to be mistrustful. So far as the ancient world is concerned, I believe you could restrict yourself to a few generalities and simply say—in the article itself[a]—that these themes are to be discussed under the headings 'Greek Army' and 'Roman Army'. This will save time, during which it will be possible not only to procure Rüstow but also to send you a mass of other data, for I have now discovered at the Museum,[b] after prolonged searching, a complete list of sources on the military history of Antiquity. But at the moment speed is the main consideration. As you know, I took your advice and sent Dana a second list.[177] So what excuse can I offer the man? I cannot plead illness, for if I do I shall have to interrupt my writing for the *Tribune* altogether and so reduce to nothing my already exiguous income. At a pinch Dana could have recourse to the man who already provides him with some of the military articles. In which case I would be elbowed out. To obviate this I shall have to write on Friday. But the difficulty is, what?

As you will understand, nothing could be more distasteful to me than TO PRESS UPON YOU while you are ill; nor, indeed, when you left here did I have any inkling that, in the state you are in, you would at once resume—and so SERIOUSLY at that—your work in the office.

My own situation is such that everything depends on whether I can persuade little Bamberger to discount a bill on myself this week. The end of the quarter has come, and all hell will now be let loose.

Freiligrath has written me a note from which I can see the Crédit mobilier's scare.[45] The constant fall in securities on the Paris Bourse, despite the prospect of a good harvest, has given rise to a veritable PANIC amongst the financiers.

The Indian affair is delicious.[178] Mazzini's putsch quite in the old official style.[179] The ass might at least have avoided dragging in Genoa!

Salut.

Your
K. M.

There is a cheap *Dictionary of Military Science* by Campbell.

First published abridged in *Der Briefwechsel zwischen F. Engels und K. Marx*, Bd. 2, Stuttgart, 1913 and in full in: Marx and Engels, *Works*, First Russian Edition, Vol. XXII, Moscow, 1929

Printed according to the original

Published in English for the first time

---

[a] A reference to the article 'Army' for *The New American Cyclopaedia*. - [b] the British Museum Library

76

MARX TO ENGELS[82]

IN MANCHESTER

[London,] 8 July 1857

Dear Frederic,

My wife has at last been brought to bed. The CHILD, however, not being viable, died immediately. In itself, this was no disaster. Yet partly because of the circumstances immediately attendant on it, which have branded themselves on my mind, and partly because of the circumstances responsible for this result, it is agonizing to look back upon. Nor is it possible to go into such matters in a letter.

Salut. Give my regards to Lupus and pass on the news to him.

Your
K. M.

First published in *Der Briefwechsel zwischen F. Engels und K. Marx,* Bd. 2, Stuttgart, 1913

Printed according to the original

77

ENGELS TO MARX

IN LONDON

Manchester, Saturday, [11] July 1857[a]

Dear Marx,

It was only this morning that your short note was brought to me from the office. The WAREHOUSEMAN who generally brings me my mail thought it more convenient to run his errand the next morning instead of the previous night. I was deeply affected by the contents of your letter, cryptic though it was, knowing how

[a] Engels dated the letter 10 July, which is a mistake, for 10 July 1857 was a Friday, not a Saturday.

painful it must be for you to write like that. You yourself may be taking the child's death stoically, but hardly your wife. How *she* is, you don't say, and hence I assume that all is well, but let me know *for certain* or I shan't have a moment's peace of mind. In this respect, your mysterious insinuations leave too much room for conjecture. Providing she herself is well it is perhaps better that it should now all be over.

Today I can *definitely* promise you the manuscripts for Dana for Friday, i.e. the articles 'Alma', 'Abensberg', 'Adjutant', 'Ammunition' and more such small stuff, thus pretty well finishing off the whole of A (except 'Algeria' and 'Afghanistan') up to Ap and Aq.[a] I have got together the material for all this and should be able to work without interruption since, as a result of my breathing fresh air again, my illness has suddenly taken a turn for the better, which in all likelihood will finally put paid to the thing. This turn took place *last night* and, since I've been ordered to take exercise in the open air outside the town, I shall not be going to the office until Thursday. As soon as I've finished these first articles, I'll tackle 'Army' (modern times, 1300 to 1850) and 'Artillery'; the first part of 'Army' I shall do last and, at the same time, let you have the list of B's. 'Artillery' will be ready to go off on Friday week, 'Army' as well perhaps. I may send you some of the shorter things tomorrow for Tuesday's post.

A couple of days ago Lupus left for France and Switzerland. The French vice-consul here, a businessman, gave him a passport without further ado. On his return he will probably pay you a visit (in approx. 3 weeks).

I dare not show my face at the office, but as soon as I can put in an appearance there I shall send you some more money.

Give my warm regards to your wife and assure her of my sincerest sympathy. Love to the girls, and see that they keep in good health.

Your old friend,
F. E.

First published in *Der Briefwechsel zwischen F. Engels und K. Marx,* Bd. 2, Stuttgart, 1913

Printed according to the original

Published in English for the first time

---

[a] This refers to the following items by Engels for *The New American Cyclopaedia*: 'Abensberg', 'Acre', 'Actium', 'Åland Islands', 'Albuera', 'Aldenhoven', 'Alessandria', 'Amusette' and 'Antwerp' (see this volume, pp. 136-37).

78

MARX TO ENGELS

IN MANCHESTER

[London,] 11 July 1857

Dear Frederic,

The chief thing for you at present is naturally to recover your health. I shall have to see how I can put Dana off again. Don't worry your head about it. Next week I'll send you something on the military systems of Antiquity.

Hastings, or so I hear, is the *only* resort in England that is of real benefit to complaints like yours. So *that's* where you must go, the time having come to tackle your illness seriously.—The *use of iron* to inhibit further development of the malady is at any rate rational, WHATEVER MR HECKSCHER MAY THINK OF IT. You ought to consult yet a third doctor about this too. Assuming that none of the chaps knows more than half of his job, it's advisable to check one against the other.

My wife is getting better. However, her condition still makes it difficult for me to leave the house.

The revolution marches on apace AS SHOWN BY THE MARCH OF THE Crédit mobilier[45] and Bonaparte's FINANCES IN GENERAL.

With best wishes for your recovery,

Your

K. M.

First published in *Der Briefwechsel zwischen F. Engels und K. Marx,* Bd. 2, Stuttgart, 1913

Printed according to the original

Published in English for the first time

79

MARX TO ENGELS

IN MANCHESTER

[London,] 14 July 1857

Dear Engels,

You may be certain that despite all mishaps I and my wife (who, by the by, is well on the way to recovery) found our own AFFAIRS less disquieting than your latest report on the state of your health. While delighted beyond measure that you should be improving, I am thoroughly alarmed to learn that you intend to return to the office—and to do so this very week. If nothing else, the whole course of your illness should have shown you that what you needed physically was to rest, recuperate and temporarily shake off the dust of the office. You must go to the seaside AS SOON AS POSSIBLE. If, at this crucial moment, you should be so childish (pardon the expression) as to shut yourself up in the office again, you will suffer further relapses, and your resistance to the disease will at the same time be progressively impaired. Such relapses might ultimately lead to an infection of the lungs, in which case all attempts at a cure would be fruitless. Surely it is not your ambition to go down to posterity as one who sacrificed himself on the altar of Ermen & Engels' office? One would feel sorry for a person with your complaint if he were compelled by circumstances to chain himself anew to his business rather than restore his health. In your case, however, all that is needed is a vigorous decision to do what is medically necessary. Only consider how long the trouble has been dragging on already, and how many relapses you've had, and you will see how necessary it is FOR SOME TIME TO LET MR ERMEN SHIFT FOR HIMSELF and to restore your health by breathing the sea air and enjoying relative leisure. I hope you will take the thing seriously and abandon your former mistaken system of alternating between medicine bottle and office. It would be unpardonable for you to persist in it.

I can only relate verbally the circumstances that attended my wife's confinement and UNNERVED ME FOR SOME DAYS. I cannot write about such things.

I have received your articles.[a] MY BEST THANKS FOR THEM.

The Indian revolt[178] has placed me in something of a quandary. As far as the *Tribune* is concerned, I am EXPECTED TO HAVE SOME SUPERIOR VIEW OF MILITARY AFFAIRS. If you can supply me with a few general axioms, I can easily combine them with the stuff I've already got together to make a readable article.[b] The situation of the insurgents in Delhi and the MOVES of the British army are the only points on which a few military generalities are needed. All the rest is MATTER OF FACT.

Mr Bamberger has kept me dangling for the past fortnight by

---

[a] for *The New American Cyclopaedia* (see this volume, p. 144). - [b] Marx's article 'The Revolt in India' appeared in the *New-York Daily Tribune*, No. 5082, on 4 August 1857.

making bogus rendezvous at which he never appears. I shall now give the laddie up, of course.

Jones' wife died last April; he seems to be keeping relatively well.

A letter received from Imandt today. He has the EXPECTATION of a post which he puts at £300 a year. Regarding Dronke he tells me that he is said to be living *en famille* with a woman who is pregnant by him. It isn't Miss Smith, however.

Salut.

Your
K. M.

First published abridged in *Der Briefwechsel zwischen F. Engels und K. Marx*, Bd. 2, Stuttgart, 1913 and in full in: Marx and Engels, *Works*, First Russian Edition, Vol. XXII, Moscow, 1929

Printed according to the original

Published in English for the first time

80

MARX TO ENGELS

IN MANCHESTER

[London,] 16 July 1857

Dear Frederic,

I have today sent you the Rüstow,[a] which you should return as soon as possible, since Steffen is working on it just now. I told him I wanted it *for myself.*

The enclosed notes are of little value, EXCEPT PERHAPS for a quotation or two.[180] I did, in fact, take a look at the *Encyclopaedia Britannica* but there was no time to read it properly. I fear that the notes will contain little that is new to you. Were taken from: Ersch and Gruber: *Encyclopédie universelle*[b]; Pauly: *Realencyclopädie der classischen Alterthumswissenschaft* (1844-52). Impossible for me to read the works themselves just now. Pity I didn't apply myself to them sooner. The *Encyclopaedia Britannica* seems to have been

---

[a] W. Rüstow, *Heerwesen und Kriegführung C. Julius Cäsars.* - [b] This probably refers to the French translation of *Allgemeine Encyclopädie der Wissenschaften und Künste...* herausgegeben von J. S. Ersch und J. G. Gruber.

copied pretty well word for word from the German and French works and hence is difficult to get away from unless one reads the specialised writings.

My wife better physically; however still in bed; also extraordinarily out of temper for which, *au fond de coeur*[a] and UNDER PRESENT AUSPICES, I don't blame her though I find it wearisome.

Salut.

Your
K. M.

I trust your health keeps improving.

First published in *Der Briefwechsel zwischen F. Engels und K. Marx,* Bd. 2, Stuttgart, 1913

Printed according to the original
Published in English for the first time

81

MARX TO ENGELS

IN MANCHESTER

[London,] 24 July 1857

Dear Engels,

Received the *Cyclopaedia* stuff TO-DAY.[b] [181]

If at all possible will you send me some money? On Monday I'm threatened with the BROKER on account of rates and LANDLORD. Besides this the total WANT OF CASH during the past fortnight has made it impossible to obtain the small COMFORTS the doctor has prescribed for my wife, whose RECOVERY is very slow—indeed, she would seem to be getting weaker every day.

During this time I have been trying with conspicuous lack of success either to discount a bill or, as is quite customary in London, to raise a LOAN from a LOAN SOCIETY.[182] The latter operation calls for two respectable guarantors and my attempts to find them have been a total failure.

The money outstanding to me from the *Tribune* is so insignificant that I cannot think of drawing a bill on them for

a at the bottom of my heart - b Engels' articles 'Arbela', 'Arquebuse', 'Aspern', 'Airey' and 'Attack'.

another 2 weeks. It would have been more if, on the one hand, I hadn't been previously compelled to overdraw and, on the other, the troubles at home had not caused some loss of earnings.

Nothing could be more distasteful to me than to burden you with my woes during your illness, but I'm so completely isolated that there is nothing else I can do.

I trust that, at the seaside, you will soon recuperate. Don't forget to let me have your address straight away.

Salut.

Your

K. M.

Have attended to the enclosed letter for Imandt.

First published in: Marx and Engels, *Works*, First Russian Edition, Vol. XXII, Moscow, 1929

Printed according to the original

Published in English for the first time

82

ENGELS TO MARX

IN LONDON

Waterloo near Liverpool,
29 July[a] (Wednesday) 1857

Dear Marx,

Here I am at last at the seaside, where I have been since the evening of the day before yesterday.[183] It's 3 miles beyond New Brighton, but to the north of the Mersey. Unfortunately I arrived with a raging cold which has temporarily aggravated the glandular trouble, caused me a great deal of pain and spoilt my sleep. The worst of it is that for a day or two I shall be pretty well incapable of work, my daily report for Heckscher and other such unavoidable notes being as much as I can manage. In the evening I'm in such intense pain and so enervated that up till now I haven't even been able to read. That this damned thing should have had to happen now! Thus, since Friday evening or Saturday morning all my time has been wasted first by interruptions, then

[a] wrong date in the original: 30 July

by my illness. I'm one of your really miserable figures, stooped, lame and weak and—e.g. as at present—beside myself with pain.

I had a hamper of wine sent to you from Manchester which will do your wife good: 6 bottles of Bordeaux, 3 of port, 3 of sherry. It should be there by now if the thing was properly attended to. Let me know the colour of the seals on the port and sherry so that I can keep a check on my wine merchant. Sherry ought to be *yellow,* port, I think, green. The Bordeaux bears the label Co. Destournel; I have just imported it.

You will have the *militaria*[a] as soon as at all possible. Unfortunately I don't know whether the post reaches London in 1 day; I shall only discover that from experience within the next few days.

I hope that the sea air will soon make me fit again for the usual drudgery. As things are now, I'm bored to death.

Warmest regards to your wife and daughters.

Your

F. E.

You'll have received the £5 note.

Address: F. E., care of Mr Swingwood,
Bath St., Waterloo near Liverpool

First published abridged in *Der Briefwechsel zwischen F. Engels und K. Marx,* Bd. 2, Stuttgart, 1913 and in full in: Marx and Engels, *Works,* First Russian Edition, Vol. XXII, Moscow, 1929

Printed according to the original

Published in English for the first time

83

MARX TO ENGELS

IN WATERLOO NEAR LIVERPOOL

[London,] 9 August 1857

Dear Engels,

Today I am prevented from writing more than a few lines—just my best wishes for your recovery. My ANXIETY for your

[a] Articles on military matters for *The American Cyclopaedia*

BODILY welfare is as great as if I myself were ill—greater, perhaps.

How are things in regard to 'coughing'? So far as I can judge from your letters, at least you're not much troubled with it.

My doctor, who has treated a great many CASES such as yours, says that if a patient's condition does not permit of his bathing in the sea, he has successfully prescribed washing all over in heated (TEPID) sea water, the temperature being gradually reduced.

Let me know whether you are taking iron. In cases such as yours, as in many others, iron has proved stronger than the affliction.[a]

Salut.

Your

K. M.

First published in: Marx and Engels, *Works*, First Russian Edition, Vol. XXII, Moscow, 1929

Printed according to the original

Published in English for the first time

84

MARX TO ENGELS[184]

IN WATERLOO NEAR LIVERPOOL

[London,] 15 August 1857

Dear Frederick,

I am delighted to hear that the sea is doing you good, as was to be expected. As soon as you are fit enough to bathe, it will take effect even more quickly.

The sea itself is, of course, the principal remedy. However, some medicaments ought to be taken internally, partly preventive, partly curative, so as to introduce into the blood those substances it lacks. As opposed to your assumptions in your letter to my wife[185] and basing myself on the most recent French, English and German literature, which I have been reading on the subject of your illness, I put forward the following, which you may submit to the scrutiny of any college of physicians or pharmacists:

---

[a] Marx uses an inversion of the German saying 'Not bricht Eisen', literally 'Necessity breaks iron', making a pun on the word 'Not', which also means 'affliction'.

1. Whereas cod-liver oil requires 3 months to take effect, iron does so in 3 weeks.

2. Cod-liver oil and iron are not mutually exclusive but complement each other during treatment.

3. A temporary *iron shortage in the blood* is the primary characteristic of your disease. Besides bathing in the sea, you must take iron, even should there no longer be any outward sign of the disease.

4. In your case the therapeutic element in cod-liver oil is iodine, since the oil's fattening properties are of no moment to you. Hence IODIDE OF IRON combines both the elements you need, one of which you would obtain from cod-liver oil. At the same time, it would spare your stomach the extra ballast inevitable in the case of cod-liver oil.

Voilà mes thèses,[a] and I hope you will give them your serious consideration so that, once cured, you do not suffer subsequent relapses which are said to be EXCEEDINGLY disagreeable.

As to the Delhi affair, it seems to me that the English ought to begin their retreat as soon as the RAINY SEASON HAS SET IN in real earnest. Being obliged for the present to hold the fort for you as the *Tribune*'s military correspondent,[b] I have taken it upon myself to put this forward.[186] NB, ON THE SUPPOSITION that the REPORTS to date have been true. It's possible that I shall make an ass of myself. But in that case one can always get out of it with a little dialectic. I have, of course, so worded my proposition as to be right either way. The persistent rumours about the fall of Delhi are being circulated throughout India by the government in Calcutta, no less, and are intended, as I see from the Indian papers, as the chief means of preventing unrest in the Madras and Bombay PRESIDENCIES. For your diversion I enclose herewith a plan of Delhi *which, however, you must let me have back.*

From most of the reports of the Banque de France[c] it is already apparent that, in place of d'Argout, there is a Bonapartist[d] at the helm who makes little difficulty about discounting operations and note issues. The financial *débâcle* in France must inevitably assume vast proportions, since a frenzied activity is contributing to it on every hand.

Imandt's presence has seriously disrupted my work. The POT is

---

[a] Such are my theses - [b] See Marx's articles 'State of the Indian Insurrection' and 'The Indian Insurrection'. - [c] 'Situation de la banque de France et de ses succursales', *Le Moniteur universel,* Nos. 163 and 191, 12 June and 10 July 1857. - [d] Charles Gabriel Germiny

in effect the only medium through which one can establish any rapport with these SPIRIT-RAPPERS.

With best wishes for your health from myself and wife.

Your

K. M.

First published abridged in *Der Briefwechsel zwischen F. Engels und K. Marx*, Bd. 2, Stuttgart, 1913 and in full in: Marx and Engels, *Works*, First Russian Edition, Vol. XXII, Moscow, 1929

Printed according to the original

Published in English in full for the first time

85

ENGELS TO MARX

IN LONDON

Waterloo, 21 August 1857

Dear Moor,

You will have received the articles this morning.[187]

I do, indeed, regard your theses as OPEN TO SOME OBSERVATIONS. That iron takes effect in 3 weeks as compared with 3 months for cod-liver oil is surely not to be taken literally. There could be absolutely no question of a disease of this kind being cured in 3 weeks; on the contrary, I should say that, iron or no iron, cases have more often been known to take 3 years rather than 3 weeks to cure.

That lack of iron in the blood is a *primary characteristic* of scrofula is certainly news to me. But whatever the literature on the subject, there is no doubt that, for some time past, it has become increasingly the fashion to reduce all diseases to lack of iron in the blood, a fashion which is already beginning to evoke a reaction; as to the disease of which, *more than any other*, this is known to be the primary characteristic—anaemia—some Frenchmen have latterly declared that iron has nothing at all to do with it. Exactly what the *primary characteristic* of scrofula is would seem to be still far from clear.

That iodine is one *amongst others* of the principal elements responsible for the effect of cod-liver oil is not in doubt. But it is by no means the only one. If one takes iodine in other forms one doesn't make such good progress. Besides, cod-liver oil contains chlorine and bromine, both of which have a direct or indirect effect on the disorder, and to what extent that effect is helped by the gall constituents and volatile fatty acids has not yet been established. All I know is that Norwegian cod-liver oil, which has the bitter taste of gall, has done me more good than the Newfoundland or English product, which does not taste of it.

I took *iron iodide* all the time I was in Manchester (in between London[169] and Waterloo[183]) along with cod-liver oil, and the inflammation grew steadily worse until finally it became chronic. Since I have been here I haven't taken *any more* iron iodide and Heckscher and I agreed long ago that either iron iodide or Quévenne's iron should be used in *after-treatment.*

The fat in cod-liver oil is, *pour le moment*,[a] by no means useless ballast so far as I am concerned. Since regaining my strength, I am again accumulating fat. Needless to say, my diet may contain only a small proportion of ready-formed animal fats. Consequently I have to eat more starch flour and, in fact, I sometimes feel a positive craving for bread; I am eating twice as much meat, but four times as much bread as I usually do. The fat in cod-liver oil is an invaluable aid to this battening process, being taken in an exceedingly innocuous form and less of an irritant than animal fat or things cooked in fat.

So you see, iron has never been completely out of our view and, even after I had been taking it for more than 3 weeks without any result (and it may, indeed, in the then circumstances, have made matters worse), we have nevertheless already reserved it for my after-treatment. Heckscher, to whom I spoke about iron last Sunday, was definitely against my taking it again at this juncture, in view of previous experience, and I must agree with him. Later, of course. I repeat that, despite the unanimity of the literature on the subject, I shall continue to entertain grave doubts about the reduction of all diseases to iron shortage until we know more than we now do about the condition and the normal level of iron in the blood. At all events, *I* had sufficient iron in my blood at the start of this business, as any of the doctors who saw me at the time can testify. I am perfectly willing to believe that people of definitely scrofular habit—pallor, transparent skin, etc.—may be suffering from a shortage of iron.

---

[a] at the moment

But *admis*[a] that this is the basic character, the INDISCRIMINATE and immediate use of iron is by no means indicated. It is extremely difficult to introduce iron into the blood otherwise than in the small amounts contained in ordinary food. Assuming, then, that the nature of my disease was the inability of the blood to assimilate the iron in food, how much less would it assimilate the iron in medicine? Sea air and sea bathing so invigorate the system as to restore the blood's ability in this respect. Thus it again assimilates the iron in meat and bread and, since I am eating more than formerly, concomitantly more iron. It is now, when this ability has been restored, that iron taken medicinally can help, although I believe that $^{9}/_{10}$ of it passes through the body unused and, even if one accepts the iron theory, the use of iron during *every* phase of the disease has been shown to be incorrect. On top of which one has to consider the wide variety of individual cases and constitutions. I myself, for instance, appear to be particularly sensitive to all metals; even the external application of quicksilver to prevent the local spread of the inflammation took effect very rapidly in my case, and it is quite possible that iron iodide, taken at a time when my blood was too disorganised to assimilate it, helped aggravate the inflammation.

At all events, and even admitting the iron theory, I don't see how your theses materially confute the assumptions in my previous letter,[b] in which I was, by the way, considering only the immediate use of iron, not in any specific form, and ruling out cod-liver oil.

Today I bathed in the sea for the first time. It did me no end of good and made me ravenously hungry. For the time being I am to bathe only every other day.

But now it's time for the post. Am working on 'Army'.

Many regards to your wife and children.

Your

F. E.

First published abridged in *Der Briefwechsel zwischen F. Engels und K. Marx*, Bd. 2, Stuttgart, 1913 and in full in: Marx and Engels, *Works*, First Russian Edition, Vol. XXII, Moscow, 1929

Printed according to the original

Published in English for the first time

[a] even granted - [b] See this volume, pp. 151-53.

86

ENGELS TO MARX

IN LONDON

Waterloo, 25 August 1857

Dear Marx,

My last letter was abruptly broken off because the post was leaving. I had meant to tell you about Lupus' adventures in France. He had neither time nor money enough to stop in London and therefore travelled straight through to Manchester, arriving with 2/- in his pocket. At Lille he was spotted by the French police and from then on they harried him. With his usual luck he arrived slap in the middle of the elections and a nice little assassination plot. He went to a small hotel near the Louvre, intending to visit Versailles. On this trip 2 *mouchards*[a] took possession of him, pushed their way into his carriage both on the way there and on the way back, and never let him out of their sight. Back at the hotel two *mouchards*, one an Alsatian Jew, sat at his table while he ate supper, and passed remarks about him in German, French and broken English. *'That chap eats with much appetite and his head is not worth a farthing. The telegraphic despatch has just arrived',*[b] etc. Lupus kept mum—compelled, of course, by his bad political conscience, else he'd have been dragged off to clink and made to establish in the Préfecture what kind of a wolf he was—and drowned his anger in drink, after which he went up to his room and stationed himself by the window—*au premier*.[c] From there he caught sight of his Versailles friends in the gateway. The gang, growing ever larger, shouted loud remarks to him while their chief parleyed with the landlady. Subsequently the fellows took over the whole house and roistered and caroused half the night through. They occupied the rooms above and to the left and right of Lupus who, as you can imagine, was in a fine STEW—on top of which it was stiflingly hot. The fellows woke him early in the morning, banging on the walls on either side and dragging tables, beds, etc., etc., across the floor

---

[a] police spies - [b] In the original this sentence occurs twice: in English, as given here, and, prior to this, in the Alsatian dialect: 'Un was der Kerl noch mit einem Appetit fresse kann, un sei Kopp is doch nit e Pfennig wert.' - [c] on the first floor

above so that he almost took leave of his senses. Presently Lupus plucked up sufficient courage to visit the w.c. The Jew and his mate were sitting on the stairs and in a loud voice the Jew said 'The fellow's going for a shit now'. He ordered breakfast in his room and inquired when the train left for Strasbourg. One by one the fellows disappeared, for it was the day of the by-elections and they had achieved their aim of hounding Lupus out of Paris. Once again his Versailles friend was on the train and accompanied him in the same carriage as far as the fourth or fifth station, where another man took over. So conspicuously did the fellows push their way into the packed carriage that a French philistine jocularly remarked: *'Il y a donc un criminel parmi nous?'*[a] In this way he was escorted to Lyons, the Versailles chap having reappeared on the steamer from Châlons on the Saône. At Lyons Lupus went to the first hotel but discovered that waiters and all were on the pay-roll, pointed him out and notified the chaps by telegraph when he was arriving. Whenever he left the room the waiter gave a whistle while the man in the office shouted out: *'Le voilà!'*[b], whereupon he was compelled to pass in review before the *mouchard* élite. They continued to harry him on the train to Seyssel as far as the point at which a line branches off in the direction of Plombières, where Mr Bonaparte happened to be. From then on, as soon as they saw that he was not going to Plombières, Lupus was free. On the return journey he wasn't harried at all.

One can see what Mr Bonaparte has set in train with the Société du dix Décembre.[138] There is no mistaking the types, particularly as regards their roistering and the playful manner in which they make life a misery for suspects visiting Paris. Had Lupus not left, one of them would probably have started a brawl so as to have a pretext for taking him to the Préfecture. Just imagine how many chaps must be on the pay-roll if an entire cohort can be set on to Lupus, who is COMPARATIVELY unknown to them. And then the roping in of landlords, waiters, BOOTS, etc., etc., as collaborators.

I have just been bathing again which, while generally most invigorating and refreshing, seems at first rather to aggravate the inflammation. But that was only to be expected. On the whole I feel very well and the sores don't trouble me much. My old man is probably in Manchester by now; I shall know definitely tomorrow,

---

[a] Is there a criminal among us then? - [b] There he is!

in which case I shall at once go to Manchester and then, within a few days, to a more bracing seaside resort, possibly the Isle of Man. So write to Manchester in the meantime. As soon as I'm completely recovered and no longer require such regular sea-bathing I intend to take a sea trip, probably by STEAMER via Dublin to Portsmouth and the Isle of Wight, where we could hold a council of war together. But that will depend on circumstances.

'Army' is making progress; Antiquity is done, Middle Ages will be short and then modern times. However, Antiquity alone will run to 6 or 7 pages; I shall have to see what further deletions can be made. But we can't be bound too strictly by Mr Dana's conditions. It won't be possible to let you have the thing by Friday because of the disruption caused by my old man—but by Tuesday, I hope. Apropos, hasn't Dana said anything at all about the manuscripts or the list for B? Why, I wonder? It would certainly be curious if one were not to hear anything at all from him. Kindest regards.

Your

F. E.

First published in *Der Briefwechsel zwischen F. Engels und K. Marx,* Bd. 2, Stuttgart, 1913

Printed according to the original

Published in English for the first time

87

MARX TO ENGELS

IN MANCHESTER

[London,] 26 August 1857

Dear Engels,

Herewith a note for you from Schramm. Drop him a line or two. I don't suppose there's much hope for him now.[188]

Lupus' adventure most amusing.

Why not go to Hastings, which is famed for its efficacy in cases like yours. It's the only specific watering-place of the kind in England. The Isle of Man, in so far as I had the pleasure of seeing it in your company—not much of it, to be sure—is remarkable chiefly for its stench.

The situation in regard to Dana is a little awkward. During the acute phase of your illness I thought it inopportune to keep you informed of the details of the affair. It was quite some time ago that Dana sent me the enclosed B list (in which there are only two non-military articles, 'Blum' and 'Bourrienne'). On the same occasion he said that the sooner they got the contributions to the ensuing volumes, the better they would be pleased, while I, for my part, could always receive my fee immediately after sending in the articles. But what was I to do, at a time when the contributions to A could not be sent off, and any failure to respond to so urgent a request—on terms so favourable to myself—would inevitably have aroused suspicion? My only recourse was to refrain for a time from writing to New York, and then do so only at longish intervals—SAY, EVERY FORTNIGHT—so that later on it would still be open to me to tell them with some plausibility that domestic TROUBLES and my own indisposition had made any sort of writing very difficult for me, as the paucity of my contributions to the paper[a] also went to show. To send your B list to Dana in such circumstances would have been QUITE inexpedient and would have placed me in an even more invidious position. In the meantime I had also learned that Major Ripley[b] had become co-editor of the *Tribune*, so that in case of need Dana had a *pis aller*[c] for the *Cyclopaedia.*

WELL, on 24 July I despatched your first pieces.[181] August was nearly upon us and your condition seemed to have deteriorated again. On 11 August another package arrived from you.[d] Instinct warned me that a letter from New York was now imminent and would place me in something of a quandary since your illness meant that it was OUT OF [THE] QUESTION to speed up the work. So in order to leave a loophole for myself, I sent the package off to Dana together with a letter[189] in which I 1. informed him that the BULK of the contributions had gone off on 7 August (to make him think the manuscript had gone astray), at the same time telling him that the tardiness and delay were due to an indisposition which had not yet quite SUBSIDED. I took this step because it covered any eventuality. Thus, when Dana protests (probably at the beginning of September) the manuscript for A either will or will not be ready. In the first case, he either will or will not still be

---

[a] *New-York Daily Tribune* - [b] Marx seems mistakenly to identify George Ripley, editor of *The New American Cyclopaedia,* with the military writer Roswell Sabine Ripley. - [c] stop-gap - [d] the articles 'Abatis' and 'Afghanistan'

able to use it. If the former, nothing will have been lost. If the latter, the blame will be seen to attach to the post office. If not READY at all, then all the more need for him to be hoodwinked.

On 17 August[a] I received the enclosed letter from Dana.

As regards B, there can now be no question of adding to the list; rather, it must be polished off as quickly as possible. Otherwise we'll have to abandon the whole thing.

As a result my economic position has become completely untenable and even my position on the *Tribune* has grown precarious.

Be so good as to return the plan of Delhi and write and let me know what you think of the INDIAN AFFAIR.[b]

Your

K. M.

First published in *Der Briefwechsel zwischen F. Engels und K. Marx,* Bd. 2, Stuttgart, 1913

Printed according to the original

Published in English for the first time

88

ENGELS TO MARX

IN LONDON

Ryde, Isle of Wight, 8 September 1857
Kelston Cottage, Trinity St.

Dear Marx,

I finally arrived today at my new lodgings[183] in the middle of a frightful downpour and tomorrow shall at once get down to the army again. Yesterday in Portsmouth I noted what was worth seeing on the military side, so all that now remains is the navy, which at this moment looks distinctly sparse. My health continues good and if the weather improves I hope I shall soon be completely cured. It takes half an hour to get here from Portsmouth and it's a

---

[a] April in the original - [b] See this volume, p. 152.

very aristocratic little spot, though lodgings are not as dear as in Waterloo. At the end of the week I shall doubtless know what the situation is as regards food. However the hotels, etc., etc., are scandalously expensive.

In Portsmouth one might almost be at home in Germany. One is barely aware of the NAVY in the town, which, by contrast, is lorded over by the subaltern—the false dignity, the affectation of reserve and the strangulated English that go to make up your OFFICER AND GENTLEMAN. Moreover, almost everyone goes around in uniform. I watched the 47th Regiment drilling, all of them bemedalled veterans of the Crimea,[a] newly arrived from the Mediterranean. The more simple evolutions were passable but the intricate 'model' manoeuvres, of which there are so many in the English manual, were carried out very shakily. Square formation from marching in open order, each file proceeding diagonally, thus /////, was botched completely and the most hellish confusion arose. By contrast the march past in line, with the entire battalion deployed, was very well done. The commanding officer was very calm but as with us there was cursing and swearing within the companies. All movements were executed at the same gait as ours, somewhat longer paces perhaps, but performed rapidly though with great nonchalance on the part of individual men. A Prussian lieutenant's comment would be: The chaps lack drill. Still very poor at the double. Shoot as though half-asleep. Conclusion: Manual rotten, men better than manual. So far little learnt from the French in the Crimea. The modern stuff either not introduced at all or else rottenly done.

I shall send you 'Army' as soon as it is finished. Warmest regards to your wife and children.

Your

F. E.

First published in *Der Briefwechsel zwischen F. Engels und K. Marx,* Bd. 2, Stuttgart, 1913

Printed according to the original

Published in English for the first time

[a] i.e. of the Crimean war of 1853-56 waged by Britain, France, Sardinia and Turkey against Russia

89

ENGELS TO MARX[190]

IN LONDON

[Ryde,] 10 September [1857,] Thursday

Dear Marx,

Herewith 'Bennigsen' and 'Barclay'.[a] I am taking a closer look at the Napoleonic generals, who will follow tomorrow or the day after. 'Army' ready shortly.

Your

F. E.

All that I know about Bennigsen is that in 1807, at the beginning of the campaign under Kamenski, he commanded the First Army (there were 2 of them, the 2nd under Buxhövden); on 26 December 1806, he was attacked by Lannes near Pultusk and, having the superiority in numbers, he held out (because Napoleon attacked the other army with the main force) and then, assuming himself to be the victor, wanted to attack in strength. He was soon given the supreme command and attacked Napoleon's winter quarters at the end of January 1807; was soon pressed hard and by mere chance evaded the trap which Napoleon had set for him; he fought at Eylau on 7 and 8 February.[191] On the 7th Napoleon captured Eylau (*Barclay de Tolly*, who directed the defence, *distinguishing himself*), and on the 8th the main engagement took place, Bennigsen being obliged to give battle in order to evade hot pursuit by Napoleon, and being saved from total defeat only by the toughness of his troops, the arrival of the Prussians under Lestock and the slowness with which Napoleon's individual corps appeared on the battlefield. In the spring Bennigsen entrenched himself at Heilsberg, because he was the weaker; he did not attack Napoleon while part of the French army was absent, engaged in the siege of Danzig[192]; but when Danzig had fallen and the French army was united, he attacked (!), let himself be held up by Napoleon's vanguard, which had only $^1/_3$ the strength he had, and then be manoeuvred back into his entrenched camp by Napoleon. This Napoleon attacked without success on 10 [June]

---

[a] The material that follows was used by Marx and Engels in their articles 'Bennigsen' and 'Barclay de Tolly'.

with only 2 corps and several battalions of the Guard, but on the very next day he forced Bennigsen out of his camp and caused him to beat a hasty retreat; however, Bennigsen suddenly went over to the offensive *without* waiting for a corps of 28,000 men, which was already in Tilsit, occupied Friedland and established himself there, with his *back to the river* and therefore with only *one* line of retreat, the Friedland bridge (always wrong to give battle *before* a defile). Instead of advancing rapidly before Napoleon could concentrate his corps, he let himself be held up for 5-6 hours by Lannes and Mortier ('coupe-gorge dans lequel Bennigsen s'était engagé',[a] says Jomini of this position) until at about 5 o'clock[b] Napoleon was ready and gave the order for the attack. The Russians were thrown back to the river, Friedland was captured, the bridge having been destroyed by the Russians themselves while their whole right wing was still on the other side and escaped only over fords and with the loss of its artillery. 20,000 men lost. Bennigsen

> 'avait fait fautes sur fautes dans cette journée ... il y eut dans sa conduite un mélange d'imprudence téméraire et d'irrésolution'.[c]

In 1812 he followed Russian headquarters around inveighing against Barclay in order to get his place, intriguing against him until Alexander relieved Bennigsen of his post. In 1813 he was ordered to lead the reserve army out of Russia into Bohemia, and when it arrived it was disbanded and Bennigsen disappeared.

Barclay de Tolly commanded a brigade at Eylau, etc. (see above); in 1812 commanded the First West Army and was War Minister; after Alexander's departure until Kutuzov's arrival was General-in-Chief, directed the retreat of the Russian army skilfully and had the great merit of resisting the clamourous demands of the Russians and of the whole headquarters to give battle. When he *had to* fight, as at Smolensk, he took up such a position that he could not be involved in a decisive battle,[193] and when this could no longer be avoided—shortly before Moscow—he selected a position by Gzhatsk which was almost impregnable from the front and could be bypassed only by a very big detour. The army had already occupied this position when Kutuzov arrived, and naturally he would not agree to it because it was not *he* who had chosen it, and so the Russians had to fight in the unfavourable position at

---

[a] 'A robbers' den into which Bennigsen has ventured' (A. H. Jomini, *Vie politique et militaire de Napoléon,* t. 2, p. 414). - [b] 14 June 1807 - [c] 'committed mistake after mistake on that day ... his conduct was a mixture of rash imprudence and irresolution' (A. H. Jomini, op. cit., t. 2, p. 421).

Borodino.[194] In 1813 and 1814 Barclay commanded not an independent corps, but all the Russians in the Allied Army under Schwarzenberg, and as these were in separate corps and often split up, it was an administrative and diplomatic rather than a combatant position,[195] and he proved himself, as earlier, to be one of the better of the average generals—having *bon sens*[a] and staying power—and at any rate the best of the older generals that the Russians had.

First published: the first paragraph in: Marx and Engels, *Works*, First Russian Edition, Vol. XXII, Moscow, 1929; the rest of the text in: Marx and Engels, *Works*, Second Russian Edition, Vol. 44, Moscow, 1977

Printed according to the original

Published in English for the first time

90

ENGELS TO MARX[196]

IN LONDON

[Ryde, 11 or 12 September 1857]

[...] Berthier was a mere CLERK without an idea in his head, but frightfully zealous in the service and punctilious; when Napoleon sent him to Bavaria in 1809 to organise the troops before his own arrival, his *ordres et contreordres*[b] split the army into three. Half of it was with Davout at Regensburg, the remainder with Masséna at Augsburg, and the Bavarians in between at Abensberg, so that a rapid advance by Archduke Charles would have enabled him to defeat the various corps one by one. It was only Napoleon's arrival and the slowness of the Austrians that saved the French.

In 1813 Bernadotte was not a general at all but a diplomat. He prevented the generals under him from attacking and when, in contravention of this order, Bülow won his two victories at Grossbeeren and Dennewitz,[197] Bernadotte stopped the pursuit. He was in constant touch with the French. When Blücher marched to the Elbe to join up with him and to force him at last to act, he continued to prevaricate until Sir Ch. Stewart (the English commissary in his camp) told him that if he didn't march immediately, he wouldn't pay out another penny. This helped—

---

a common sense - b An allusion to Napoleon's words 'ordre, contreordre, désordre'.

nevertheless it was purely *honoris causa* that the Swedes appeared in the firing-line at Leipzig,[198] and during the whole campaign they lost less than 200 men in battle.—In 1798 Bernadotte was French ambassador in Vienna; to celebrate the anniversary of a victory over the Austrians he hoisted the tricolor, whereupon the populace stormed his residence and burned the flag. He left, but Napoleon decided against him and persuaded the Directory[199] TO LET THE MATTER DROP.[a] [...]

[...] Jomini, *Vie politique et militaire de Napoléon*, t. II, p. 60 qq. (Napoleon says)[b]

'*Bernadotte* ... un homme fin, d'un extérieur brillant; les plans d'opération qu'il avait faits comme ministre de la guerre, prouvaient qu'il était meilleur lieutenant, que général en chef'[c] [p. 60].

'*Marmont*, jadis mon aide de camp et officier d'artillerie' [pp. 60-61].

'*Davout*, qui avait reçu une bonne éducation, avait la tête fortement organisée et des idées de guerre très justes. Ses manières rudes et un caractère à la fois soupçonneux et dur lui ont fait beaucoup d'ennemis, et dans les graves circonstances où il s'est trouvé, l'esprit de parti s'est déchaîné contre lui avec une grande injustice. Sévère, mais juste envers ses subordonnés, mieux qu'aucun autre il sut maintenir la discipline parmi ses soldats; aucun de mes maréchaux n'exigeait plus de ses subordonnés, et aucun ne les fit servir avec tant d'exactitude' [p. 61].

'*Soult*, d'un physique mâle, d'un esprit étendu, laborieux, actif, infatigable, avait fait preuve de talents supérieurs' [p. 61].

'*Lannes*; couvert de gloire et de blessures, ce brave manquait de principes faits sur la guerre; mais il y suppléait par un jugement admirable et sur le champ de bataille il ne le cédait à aucun de ses collègues' [p. 61].

'*Ney*. Lannes fut peut être aussi brillant que lui dans maintes attaques; mais la force d'âme que Ney déploya dans le grand désastre de 1812 où il commanda successivement tous les corps de l'armée, lui assigne le premier rang parmi les braves de tous les jours. *De même que plusieurs de ses collègues il n'entendait point la guerre en grand sur la carte*[d]; mais sur le terrain, rien n'égalait son assurance, son coup d'oeil et son aplomb' [p. 62].

'*Murat*, qui avait dû à sa bonne mine, à son courage et à son activité l'honneur d'être mon aide de camp et mon beau-frère, *n'a jamais été à la hauteur de la réputation colossale que je lui avais faite*. Du reste, il avait de l'esprit naturel, un courage brillant et une grande activité' [p. 63].

'*Masséna* reçut de la nature tout ce qui fait un excellent homme de guerre, doué d'un grand caractère, d'un courage éprouvé et d'un coup d'oeil qui inspirait les résolutions les plus promptes et les plus heureuses, on ne peut lui refuser une place distinguée parmi les capitaines modernes. Cependant il faut avouer qu'il brillait plus dans les combats que dans le conseil' [p. 63].

'*Brune* ne manquait pas de certain mérite, c'était pourtant pour tout prendre un général de tribune bien plus qu'un militaire redoutable'[e] [p. 64].

---

[a] The relevant passages were used by Marx in his articles 'Berthier' and 'Bernadotte'. The facts connected with Bernadotte's diplomatic mission in Vienna are here distorted (see also this volume, pp. 169-70). - [b] Engels condenses some of the quotations from Jomini's book. - [c] Used by Marx in his article 'Bernadotte'. - [d] Here and below Engels' italics. - [e] Used by Marx in his article 'Brune'.

'*Mortier,* moins brillant, était pourtant plus solide, son calme et son sang-froid, passés en proverbe parmi les soldats, lui avaient valu plus d'un succès et il était du nombre de ceux qui pouvaient conduire un corps sous ma direction' [p. 64].

'*Bessières* avait fait ses preuves près de moi à l'armée d'Italie où il commandait mes guides à cheval. Il n'avait pour lui qu'un grand esprit d'ordre et une valeur reconnue. Il était méthodique et d'une timidité exessive dans le conseil' [p. 64].

'*Lefebvre,* duc de Dantzic, était un vrai grenadier. Enfant de la nature, il ne devait rien qu'à son esprit naturel, à une grande bravoure, et à un caractère simple et naif. Il savait se faire aimer du soldat et le mener droit à une position; c'était tout son mérite' [p. 64].

'*Jourdan* avait dû à la fortune une grande partie de sa réputation. Bon administrateur, laborieux, homme d'ordre et intègre. Et ayant de l'instruction, il eût été fort bon chef d'état major d'une grande armée sous un chef qui l'eut bien dirigé' [p. 64].

'*Macdonald* ... avait fort mal manoeuvré à la Trebbia' [...][a] [p. 65].

Berthier is not mentioned in this collection.

Apropos: what about your material on Bem? Of him it must be said that he excelled in command of smaller corps of 5-10,000 men and could inspire younger troops with self-assurance by good

---

[a] '*Bernadotte* ... a man of refinement, of brilliant appearance; the plans of operations which he drew up in his capacity as War Minister proved him to be better as a subaltern than as a general-in-chief' (p. 60).

'*Marmont,* formerly my ADC and artillery officer' (pp. 60-61).

'*Davout,* who had a good education, possessed a well-organised brain and very correct ideas about war. His rough ways and a disposition at once suspicious and harsh earned him many enemies, and in the grave circumstances in which he found himself the spirit of prejudice broke loose against him with great injustice. Severe but fair towards his subordinates, he knew better than anyone else how to maintain discipline among his men; not one of my marshals demanded so much of his subordinates, and not one of them induced them to serve with such punctiliousness' (p. 61).

'*Soult,* with his manly build, his broad, hard-working, active and untiring mind, had demonstrated superior talents' (p. 61).

'*Lannes;* covered with glory and with wounds, this brave man lacked set principles concerning war; but he made up for this with his admirable judgment, and on the battlefield he was second to none of his colleagues' (p. 61).

'*Ney.* Lannes was perhaps as brilliant as he in many an attack; but the fortitude which Ney displayed in the great disaster of 1812, when he commanded all the corps of the army in succession, ranks him first among the brave men of all times. *Like many of his colleagues, he understood nothing about war on a large scale on the map;* but on the ground his assurance, his sharpsightedness and his poise were unequalled' (p. 62).

'*Murat,* who was indebted to his good looks, his courage and his activity for the honour of being my ADC and my brother-in-law, *never lived up to the colossal reputation which I had made for him.* For the rest, he had a natural wit, brilliant courage and great energy' (p. 63).

'*Masséna* received from nature all that goes to make an excellent soldier, endowed with a splendid character, a courage which stood the test and a sharpsightedness which inspired the most prompt and most felicitous decisions; he cannot be denied a distinguished place among the captains of our time. But it must be admitted that he shone more in battle than at the council table' (p. 63).

use of natural cover and [artillery] support; that he particularly distinguished himself in the small [mountain] warfare into which the whole of the first Transylvanian campaign[200] developed, but that he had A CONSIDERABLE DASH OF THE PARTISAN, which made him incapable of commanding bigger armies. In the second Transylvanian campaign, when masses of Russians invaded, he operated again with rash raids after the manner of partisans without any consideration for the relative strength of the opposing forces and thus lost not only Transylvania but the whole of his army too. His march into the Banat (before the second Transylvanian campaign) achieved nothing[201]; he seems to have been unable to cope with the greater masses he was in command of. Praise is due to his great fortitude and his art of arousing the men's confidence in his otherwise unmartial-looking person. He could quickly achieve superficial organisation and discipline, but was satisfied at that. He neglected to build up a body of picked troops, for which the first Transylvanian campaign provided time enough and which was the *greatest necessity*, and hence all the outward organisation—and relative discipline—disappeared at the first setback. His bigger campaign plans all bear a heavy *empreinte*[a] of partisan warfare; the basic features are mostly correct but presuppose far different means from those available, and even supposing that they were available they could be put to better use. E.g. his plan to abandon Hungary and break through to Italy via Trieste. Had the means for this been at his disposal and capable of being concentrated, the forces would thus have been provided with which to defeat Haynau,

---

'*Brune* was not without a certain merit, but all considered, he was a tribune general rather than a formidable soldier' (p. 64).

'*Mortier*, less brilliant, was however more reliable; his calm and sangfroid, which became proverbial among his soldiers, won him success more than once, and he was one of those who could lead a corps under my direction' (p. 64).

'*Bessières* had proved his worth with me in the army of Italy, in which he commanded my mounted guides. All he had to distinguish him was a great spirit of order and a recognised valour. He was methodical and excessively timid at the council table' (p. 64).

'*Lefebvre*, Duke of Danzig, was a true grenadier. A child of nature, he owed everything to his natural wit, to his great bravery and his straightforward, naive character. He knew how to win the soldiers' love and lead them straight into action; that was where his merit lay' (p. 64).

'*Jourdan* owed much of his reputation to fortune. A good administrator, hard-working, a man of order and integrity. And had he had training, he would have made a very good chief of staff of a great army under a commander who directed him well' (p. 64).

'*Macdonald* ... manoeuvred very badly at La Trebbia' (p. 65).

[a] stamp

whereupon the Russians, instead of concentrating, would *have been obliged* to split up in order to hold what they had captured, and hence could have been defeated piecemeal. It must not be forgotten, however, that in an insurrectionary war these partisan methods are partially justified precisely because of the uncertainty concerning the means really available; the bigger the scale of the war, however, the less appropriate they become.[a]

[...] Can you find out what *Bockbrücken* (*ponts à chevalets*[b]) are in English? I should also like to have a description of the Austrian Birago pontoons and a brief excerpt—merely an outline—on the design of pontoons in the various armies (SEE Sir Howard Douglas, *Military Bridges*), also whether the Russians and Prussians still have canvas pontoons. I have no material here, and such as I have in Manchester is very old. I have something on English pontoons [...].

First published abridged in: Marx and Engels, *Works*, Second Russian Edition, Vol. 29, Moscow, 1962

Published in this form for the first time

Printed according to the original

Published in English for the first time

91

MARX TO ENGELS

IN RYDE

[London,] 15 September [1857]

Dear Engels,

You must excuse my silence and non-ACKNOWLEDGMENT of your various packages, due firstly to a great deal of work and secondly to numerous time-consuming errands in which 'inner compulsion' played no part whatever. I trust *your health continues to improve* despite the bad weather, and have still not abandoned the NOTION that you will be taking iron in the end. Only I'm afraid all this writing may be harmful to you.

I expect a letter from Dana on Friday. Today I sent him 'Barclay', 'Berthier', 'Blum', 'Bourrienne'[202] and your contributions.[c] It is important that I should send off the 2nd lot of B's next week. I have certain queries to put to you in my next about the

[a] Engels' description of Bem was partly reproduced in the article 'Bem' by Marx and Engels. - [b] trestle-bridges - [c] 'Barbette', 'Bastion' and 'Bayonet'

French generals who are next on my list. As to Bem's Polish DEEDS have found the following[a]:

'Distinguished himself at the battle of Iganin, when he engaged 40 Russian heavy calibre cannon with 12 light and 4 heavy guns, and subsequently at the battle of Ostrolenka.[203] Here he galloped his battery up to the line of Russian skirmishers, subjected the detachments which had crossed the Narev to devastating fire, withstood a hail of shot from 80 guns, and forced the enemy to withdraw. After this engagement promoted to colonel, shortly afterwards to command of the entire artillery and, when the Polish forces were concentrating at Warsaw, to general. During 5 and 6 September Bem committed all his guns to battle, siting his field pieces between the separate defensive works of the outer line. On the 6th, he advanced with 40 guns until he was just below Wola, already in Russian hands, but, having neither infantry nor cavalry in support, was compelled to retire. When the Polish army fell back on Praga during the night of the 7th, he occupied the bridge with 40 guns. On the morning of the 8th, however, he was informed of the agreement made with the Russians and of Malachowski's order to proceed with the artillery to Modlin. Cf. his memoir, *Allgemeine Augsburger Zeitung*, 1831, in which he discusses recent developments and attacks Krukowiecki.'[b]

I don't trust the above authority an inch and would therefore ask you to investigate and to do me a short, amended version of the passage concerned, if possible putting it straight into English.

I shall look up the information you ask for at the Museum tomorrow.[c]

Your

K. M.

First published in: Marx and Engels, *Works*, First Russian Edition, Vol. XXII, Moscow, 1929

Printed according to the original

Published in English for the first time

92

MARX TO ENGELS

IN RYDE

[London,] 17 September[d] [1857]

Dear Engels,

'Bernadotte' is a difficult subject. The French generals who wrote under Louis Philippe are mostly his unqualified PARTISANS, just as

---

[a] The source quoted below has not been found. - [b] See J. Bem, 'Ueber die Vertheidigung Warschau's am 6 und 7 Sept. 1831', *Allgemeine Zeitung*, Nos. 470-75, 3-6 December 1831. - [c] A reference to the material for Engels' article 'Bridge, Military' which Marx promised to look up for him in the British Museum Library. - [d] April in the original

the present writers under Boustrapa[40] are his unqualified opponents. The main points at issue upon which I should appreciate information from you are:

1. His part in the battle of Austerlitz[204] as a consequence of the manoeuvres he executed before the same.

2. His conduct at the battle of Jena[46]; and *before* the battle of Eylau.[191]

3. His conduct at the battle of Wagram.[206]

As regards his embassy in Vienna, things were not quite as you present them.[a] It has been *shown* (by *inter alia* Schlosser, *Zur Beurtheilung Napoleons*) that the Bonapartist journals in Paris denounced Bernadotte as a royalist because he did *not* hang out the French flag. They drove him into taking the step which Bonaparte subsequently disavowed.

All in all, Bonaparte sensed that Bernadotte was the 'statesman' amongst his generals and one intent on pursuing his 'own plans'. He, and more notably his brothers, by their base and petty intrigues against Bernadotte, gave him greater prominence than he could otherwise have laid claim to.

Napoleon was, in general, beastly to anyone he suspected of 'self-seeking'.

Your

K. M.

Blücher. I'd like you to write something about his principal battles, his military qualities generally and, finally, the tactical merits upon which Griesheim lays so much stress.[b]

Bessières, Brune, Brown, Bugeaud, ditto.

Bosquet in the Crimean campaign.

Let me have Dana's list of B's as I have lost my copy.

Your

K. M.

First published in *Der Briefwechsel zwischen F. Engels und K. Marx,* Bd. 2, Stuttgart, 1913

Printed according to the original

Published in English for the first time

---

[a] See this volume, p. 165. - [b] G. von Griesheim, *Vorlesungen über die Taktik.*

93

ENGELS TO MARX

IN LONDON

Ryde, Friday, 18 September 1857

Dear Marx,

Your letter arrived yesterday afternoon, too late for me to get anything done for B. Moreover, I was in Portsmouth when the letter got here, so that more time was lost, otherwise I'd have been able to translate the Bem thing for you.[a] You seem to be having bad weather; here it's persistently fine, only too hot; last week there was an occasional heavy shower, but apart from that it was fine and warm all the time. The climate here is really marvellous and the vegetation, except for things needing very hot sunshine, is so southern one might almost be in Naples. The hedges are laurel. I'm improving rapidly, the actual complaint is quite *over*, there's no longer a sign of inflamed glands and my one concern now is the process—admittedly a lengthy one—of patching up, getting the sores to heal, and putting on flesh and fat. Bathing does me a great deal of good and I find I can swim like a fish again—proof of how well my treatment is going. I've been to see Pieper at Bognor; quite a nice little place, but not a patch on Ryde; I wonder how long he'll stay there—he's lucky, but for that very reason his 'yeenius' is again reasserting itself; he attributes his luck to personal merit and already half fancies himself king of Bognor. He's coming over on Sunday and Steffen too, perhaps. I am going to Brighton SOMETIME NEXT WEEK and sailing from there to Jersey; Schramm is also going there,[188] or so he writes. Why don't you slip down to Brighton and, if it can be fitted in with the work, come to Jersey too? Anyhow the sea-trip would do you good. What do you think? I shall stay here until Tuesday at any rate, perhaps even longer: *je verrai*.[b]

As to Bem, all I should say is this:

*At the battle of Iganin, where he commanded the artillery, he was noticed for the skill and perseverance with which he fought it against the superior Russian batteries. At Ostrolenka, he again commanded the artillery in this capacity[c]; when the Polish army

---

[a] See this volume, pp. 166-68. - [b] I shall see - [c] as an artillery major

had been finally repulsed in its attacks against the Russians who had passed the Narev, he covered the retreat by a bold advance with the whole of his guns.[203] He was now created colonel, soon after general and called to the command in chief of the whole Polish artillery. When the Russians assaulted the entrenchments of Warsaw and took Wola, Bem advanced with forty guns against this, the principal work of the whole line, but the superior force of Russian artillery opposed to him prevented the Polish infantry from returning to the assault and compelled Bem to retire.*[a]

The other matters are quite trivial. I have no material to hand about Iganin; it was a quite unimportant engagement, the defence of a dam, rendered fruitless as usual by an outflanking movement—the 40 cannon of *heavy* calibre are certainly a figment, likewise the Russian *retreat* at Ostrolenka, which can only have referred to *tirailleurs*[b] and *soutiens*,[c] or a couple of exposed battalions. What I have said above puts the thing in the most favourable light, for Diebitsch *forbade* any pursuit.

Many thanks for the thing on bridges.[d] Wholly adequate. On Sunday or Monday I shall be sending you 'Battle', 'Battery' and any other B's I have finished, and then get on smartly with the remainder. I shall also let you have something on Blücher one of these days, as soon as I've read through Müffling.[e]

Which French generals and which of their exploits do you wish me to investigate more particularly? Allow me as much time as possible since I can't work very well for more than 2 hours at a stretch.

Your

F. E.

First published abridged in *Der Briefwechsel zwischen F. Engels und K. Marx*, Bd. 2, Stuttgart, 1913 and in full in: Marx and Engels, *Works*, First Russian Edition, Vol. XXII, Moscow, 1929

Printed according to the original

Published in English for the first time

[a] Part of this passage was used by Marx and Engels in their article 'Bem'. - [b] skirmishers - [c] second-line troops - [d] excerpts from various sources made by Marx for the article 'Bridge, Military', on which Engels was working - [e] [F.K.F.] Müffling, *Passages from My Life*.

94

MARX TO ENGELS

IN RYDE

[London,] 21 September 1857
9 Grafton Terrace, Maitland Park,
Haverstock Hill

Dear Engels,

Nothing could please me more than to hear that your health is progressing.

Last Friday, a letter arrived from Dana, cool and curt. I replied that I would complain to the POST OFFICE at once. Further, having *'Algeria'* and *'Ammunition'* to hand, I sent them off[207] with the comment that I had ***copies*** of them; also that I had *'Army'* in the *original,* and would send it off immediately a fresh copy had been made (I did this because in recent letters you have several times mentioned that 'Army' was almost finished); also, that *'Artillery'* would for the most part come under the HISTORY OF CANNON and that I *no longer* had the manuscript. The *only A's now remaining*—and these I would send on the off-chance, although it is probably by now too late—were, all told, 'Army', 'Armada' and 'Ayacucho'. I mentioned the last 2 because you can keep them *quite short,* while the material I have sent you will provide some original stuff on the Armada and Ayacucho (about Espartero). That's how matters stand.

Tomorrow I shall send off 3 more biographies.[a]

My circumstances won't permit me to come to Brighton, still less accompany you to Jersey.

On closer examination I find that all I want from you on the generals under B is an answer to my question about Bernadotte together with the essentials concerning Blücher, Bugeaud, Bosquet (in the Crimean War). I have enough on the other Frenchmen. Finally, Sir *G. Brown,* about whom I know nothing. Not much needed on the man.

I have sent Dana your B and C lists.

Salut.

Your

K. M.

First published in *Der Briefwechsel zwischen F. Engels und K. Marx,* Bd. 2, Stuttgart, 1913

Printed according to the original

Published in English for the first time

[a] 'Bennigsen' by Marx and Engels and 'Blum' and 'Bourrienne' by Marx

95

ENGELS TO MARX

IN LONDON

Ryde, 21 September 1857

Dear Marx,

Steffen and Pieper have been here in company with a friend of Pieper's and, as the two last have only just left, I've hardly any time before the post goes to take a look at the enclosed article[a] or write to you about 'Bernadotte'.

Austerlitz.[204] He was sent to Iglau[b] by Napoleon in order to keep an eye on the Archduke Ferdinand in Bohemia. Having received in good time Napoleon's order to come to Brünn,[c] which he did, he was placed with his corps between Soult and Lannes (in the centre) where he helped repulse the outflanking movement of the allied right wing. I don't recall any particularly important action of Bernadotte's on this occasion, nor can I find anything in Jomini.[d]

Jena.[205] Here it is a fact that Bernadotte did indeed receive orders from Napoleon to march from Naumburg to Dornburg while Davout, who was also in Naumburg, was to march to Apolda. The order received by Davout stated that, if Bernadotte had already joined him, they might *both* march to Apolda together. Davout was in favour of the latter, having reconnoitred the Prussian lines of advance in person and satisfied himself that Bernadotte wouldn't meet the enemy in the Dornburg direction. He even offered *to place himself under Bernadotte's command.* The latter, however, insisted that, in the orders *he* had received, the passage relating to Apolda did not appear, and he moved off. The result was that on the 14th he spent the whole day marching round without meeting the enemy, while Davout was compelled to fight alone at Auerstedt. Had Bernadotte been there, or had he simply marched towards the thunder of the cannon on the 14th, this *au fond*[e] indecisive victory could have been every bit as decisive as the one at Jena. Only because of the meeting of the Auerstedt Prussian army with the fugitives from Jena and also

---

[a] F. Engels, 'Battle'. - [b] Czech name: Jihlava. - [c] Czech name: Brno. - [d] A. H. Jomini, *Vie politique et militaire de Napoléon,* t. 2. - [e] basically

because of the strategic preparations Napoleon had made for the battle, did the affair prove decisive after all in its consequences. *Why* Bernadotte did this nobody has ever found out. Jomini calls it *une exactitude trop scrupuleuse.*[a] Probably Bernadotte was glad to discredit Napoleon by sticking rigidly to his instructions, for in this instance the latter had undoubtedly acted on false premises.

Eylau.[191] When Bennigsen moved off to engage Ney's troops, who had ventured too far forward, Bernadotte being to their left rear, Napoleon laid a trap for him. Ney withdrew to the south and Bernadotte to the south-west with orders to lure Bennigsen towards the Vistula, while Napoleon marched north from Poland towards Bennigsen's communications. An orderly officer carrying written orders for Bernadotte was captured by the Cossacks and in this way Bennigsen learnt of the impending danger, which he just managed to elude. Bernadotte, on the other hand, remained without instructions as a result of the same incident and accordingly stayed to the rear of the line. I don't see that there is anything to reproach him with on this score.

Wagram.[206] On the first day of the battle

> 'Eugène[b] déboucha près de Wagram; mais, donnant ici au milieu des réserves ennemies, et n'étant pas soutenu par Bernadotte qui ne s'était engagé ni assez tôt ni assez franchement, il fut attaqué de front et en flanc, et ramené vertement jusqu'à ma garde.'[c]

I can discover nothing of special moment about Bernadotte on the 2nd day of the battle.

At all events Monsieur Bernadotte was not a great general; nowhere did he distinguish himself and even as a politician there was much of the Gascon in him—what an idea, wanting to become Emperor after Napoleon![d]

I have absolutely nothing to say about Bessières save that for the most part he was in command of the Guard, in particular the cavalry, a post that hardly demanded a superfluity of intelligence. He was brave, *voilà tout.*[e]

I intend to finish B this week if possible, or at any rate break

---

[a] undue punctiliousness (A. H. Jomini, op. cit., p. 290) - [b] Beauharnais - [c] 'Eugène debouched near Wagram, but having arrived in the midst of the enemy reserves and not being supported by Bernadotte, who had not joined battle either early enough or resolutely enough, he was attacked on his front and flanks and was smartly driven back as far as my Guard' (A. H. Jomini, op. cit., t. 3, p. 266. Here Jomini quotes Napoleon). - [d] Engels' notes on Bernadotte were used by Marx in his article 'Bernadotte'. - [e] that's all

the back of the letter, after which I shall send you what is needed on Blücher. It's time for the post now.

Warm regards to your wife and children.

Your

F. E.

What's the position as regards your trip?

Havelock seems to be the best chap in India, and it is a really tremendous feat to have marched 126 miles in a week in that climate, not to mention fighting 5 or 6 engagements. That it would end in a general outbreak of cholera might have been predicted.

I hardly see *The Times* at all here, otherwise I could write to you at greater length about India, but getting hold of newspapers to read here is altogether too difficult.

First published in *Der Briefwechsel zwischen F. Engels und K. Marx*, Bd. 2, Stuttgart, 1913

Printed according to the original

Published in English for the first time

96

ENGELS TO MARX

IN LONDON

Ryde, 22 September 1857

Dear Marx,

Here is a bit more about Bernadotte at Wagram[206]: On 5 July, when the French attack had been halted—largely as a result of his irresolute conduct—Bernadotte was occupying the village of Aderklaa in the centre, and slightly in advance of the French line. On the morning of the 6th, when the Austrians moved up for a concentric attack, he was out in the open plain *in front of* Aderklaa instead of occupying the village in strength and positioning his front to the rear of it. When the Austrians arrived on the scene he thought this position too hazardous (on the previous day his troops had ultimately suffered severe losses owing to his irresolute conduct) and withdrew to a plateau *behind* Aderklaa, yet left the village *unoccupied*, whereupon Bellegarde's Austrians promptly occupied it in strength.

This endangered the French centre, and Masséna, who commanded it, sent forward a division which recaptured the place only to be thrown out by d'Aspre's grenadiers. Then Napoleon himself arrived, assumed command and devised a new battle plan, thereby foiling the manoeuvres of the Austrians. If Jomini's account is at all accurate,[a] there can be absolutely no dispute about Bernadotte's blunders on this occasion.

'Army' is finished, so far as the historical side is concerned, up to the French Revolution. I shall now get on with the modern period and questions of organisation generally, with which I conclude, and then, as soon as possible, go back to doing B's so that you can keep on sending stuff, thus putting Mr Dana into a better humour. Meanwhile I have received a little more money and enclose a £5 note. Perhaps you will manage to spend one or two days in Brighton after all; I shall stay here a day or two longer and let you know when I am going there.

Bugeaud. Most of this is already implicit in the article 'Algeria'. He was a mediocre general whose victories in Algeria and Morocco are of no great significance. That he conquered Algeria with 100,000 men, adapted his conduct of the war there to the terrain and the enemy, and broke, or rather suppressed, the resistance of the Arabs (not the Kabyles), does not, to my mind, earn him a very high rating, for I don't believe he was responsible for the plans. He was something of a *sabreur*[b] and, on the Tafna,[208] showed not only that he was venal but also that he was irresolute when in a tight corner. With 100,000 men and subordinates such as Lamoricière, Changarnier, Cavaignac, Négrier and Duvivier, who had ten years of warfare behind them, he would not need very much natural ability to achieve something—especially since the French General Staff is *very good;* furthermore, his activity was largely confined to making dispositions (where there's no knowing how much was done *for him* by the staff) and to commanding the reserve, since only individual divisions and brigades were operating at any one spot.

Bosquet. On the Alma[209] he led the French right wing in an outflanking movement against the Russian left wing with a determination and speed which earned the recognition of the Russians; he even succeeded in getting the artillery onto the plateau up trackless defiles regarded as impassable. For this he would deserve high praise had he not been facing a numerically very much inferior opponent.—At Balaklava he was immediate-

---

[a] A. H. Jomini, *Vie politique et militaire de Napoléon,* t. 3. Engels' notes on Bernadotte (see this volume, pp. 164-65) were used by Marx in his article 'Bernadotte'. - [b] swashbuckler

ly at hand to help disengage the English right wing, thus enabling the rest of the English light cavalry to withdraw under cover of his troops and discouraging the Russians from advancing any further. At Inkerman,[34] in the early hours of the morning, he was ready to intervene with 3 battalions and 2 batteries, but, his help having been refused, he placed 3 brigades in reserve behind the English right wing (on the Chernaya slope) and at 11 o'clock moved up with 2 of them into the firing line, whereupon the Russians began to withdraw. The English had committed all their troops whereas the Russians still had 16 battalions at their disposal and, but for Bosquet, the English would have been lost. The 16 intact Russian battalions covered the retreat. There could be little question of pursuit in this case, there being no more than 3,000 paces between the battle field and the edge of the plateau. On each occasion, then, Bosquet showed himself quick off the mark, alert, active, in short, an exemplary corps commander—as he did also throughout the time he led the covering corps on the Chernaya slope.[a] Whether he's up to much as a *général en chef* is hard to say; he has a number of qualities and if, as in his case, a man is a first-rate vanguard general, all that remains is for him to prove his *strategic* ability, but for this there was not much opportunity throughout the whole of the Sebastopol campaign.[210]

Blücher. During the 1794 campaign in the Palatinate[211] he distinguished himself as an outpost general and light cavalry commander. The best proof of this is to be found in his published diary, still regarded as a classic despite the bad German.[b] He kept the French constantly on the *qui vive,* while providing his headquarters with first-rate intelligence on the movements of the enemy, and he was continually carrying out *coups de main* and surprise attacks, for the most part successfully. At Auerstedt in 1806,[205] when his cavalry charge miscarried, his advice that it be repeated using all available reinforcements was rejected (*this from memory*). His withdrawal to Lübeck and the stubborn stand he put up is one of the few honourable episodes in this affair, though during the course of it his strategic moves were often of the Hussar type. Nor was it his fault that he was finally captured for, like the whole of the Prussian army, he was cut off and had, moreover, the longest detour to make round the rearguard. During the period up to 1813 he was regarded by Scharnhorst and the Tugendbund[212] (being one of its known leaders,

---

a Almost the whole of this passage is reproduced in the article 'Bosquet' by Marx and Engels. - b G. L. Blücher, *Kampagne-Journal der Jahre 1793 und 1794.*

Gneisenau remained throughout his life SUSPECT in the King's[a] eyes) as the only possible and suitable leader and was dubbed a hero by them, as Hecker was by Blind and Co.[213] Nor could they have picked on a better man. He was, as Müffling says,[b] THE MODEL OF A SOLDIER while at the same time sharing to the full the intense popular antipathy to Napoleon and the French. Plebeian in his appetites, dialect, turns of phrase and manners, he had a tremendous gift for inspiring the common soldier with enthusiasm. As a soldier he possessed reckless courage, a keen eye for terrain, quickness of decision and enough intelligence to discover for *himself* what was best in more simple situations, and to rely on Gneisenau and Müffling in more complex ones. Of strategy, he had no inkling.

'It was no secret to Europe, that Prince Blücher who had now, 1815, passed his 70th year, understood nothing whatever of the conduct of a war; so little, indeed, that when a plan was laid before him for approval, even relating to some unimportant operation, he could not form any clear idea of it or judge whether it was good or bad.'

For he was quite incapable of reading a map, a strategical disability he shared with almost half of Napoleon's marshals. On the other hand he had Gneisenau, whom he trusted implicitly. Without Blücher, the campaign of 1813 and 1814 would have ended very differently; no other general of that time could have done what he did—namely, by means of a victory and a skilfully conducted pursuit (Katzbach[c]) weld the most refractory elements (Langeron and York in open rebellion against him) into a homogeneous army[214] capable of anything and with which, on his own responsibility, he could risk marching on Wartenburg and the Saale—militarily a most audacious but politically (because of Bernadotte) an essential move, thereby abandoning all his communications and compelling the sluggish large army (which he had saved in Silesia after the battle of Dresden,[215] by pursuing the French as far as Bautzen so that Napoleon had to turn against him) to chance its arm too at Leipzig.[198] Altogether it was a somewhat rebellious time, and Blücher had agreed with $^{3}/_{4}$ of the Army of the North (Bülow, Tauentzien, Wintzingerode) that if Bernadotte made no move they would, on their own responsibility, join up with Blücher. After the battle of Leipzig, Blücher was the only one who applied himself in any way to the pursuit, though

---

[a] Frederick William III - [b] [F. K. F.] Müffling, *Passages from My Life* (below Engels quotes from p. 225 of this book). - [c] Polish name: Kaczawa.

even this wasn't what it should have been—he was hampered by the presence of the princes. The strategic blunders that were so severely punished in the Montmirail region in 1814 must be laid at the door of Gneisenau and Müffling,[216] while the decision to march on Paris, *coûte que coûte*,[a] which resolved the campaign, must be credited to Blücher. The march on Waterloo in 1815 after the battle of Ligny[217] is another considerable feather in Blücher's cap; here he is almost without equal and no general except Blücher could have spurred his troops on to such EFFORTS—namely, to embark forthwith on the exemplary pursuit to Paris which ranks equally with that from Jena[46] to Stettin[b] as a classic prototype. That Blücher was able to overawe even abler generals is evident from his attitude to Langeron (who had commanded a large army against the Turks and was a cultivated French émigré) and to York, both of whom, for all their initial refractoriness, not only soon submitted to him, but actually went right over onto his side, becoming his best subordinates. *Au fond*[c] Blücher was a cavalry general; that was his speciality and in it he excelled because this is a purely tactical role which does not presuppose any strategic knowledge. He asked a great deal of his troops but they did it, and willingly, and I don't suppose any other 19th-century general save Napoleon and, more latterly, Radetzky, could have exacted from them what Blücher did. It should further be recognised that nowhere and at no time did he lose head or heart, that he was as dogged in defence as he was resolute in attack and that in difficult situations he was quick to make up his mind. *Enfin*,[d] in the 1813-15 war, which was half way to being an insurrectionary war, he was quite the right man and was well complemented by his staff; and such being the case he was a *very dangerous* adversary.[e]

Your

F. E.

Note O/H *06012*, Manchester, *15 Jan. 1857*

First published in *Der Briefwechsel zwischen F. Engels und K. Marx*, Bd. 2, Stuttgart, 1913

Printed according to the original

Published in English for the first time

---

[a] at whatever cost - [b] Szczecin - [c] Basically - [d] Finally - [e] Engels' description of Blücher here was used in the article 'Blücher' by Marx and Engels.

97

MARX TO ENGELS

IN RYDE

[London,] 23 September [1857]

Dear Engels,

Very many thanks for the letter and enclosure.

I would, of course, very much like to see you before you leave. *If at all feasible* I shall come down to Brighton. The trouble is that the end of the quarter brings an accumulation of all the DIFFICULTIES one has been staving off throughout the summer. The main thing—and the only way out of my quandary—is to get on quickly with the *Cyclopaedia*. The coming of autumn also means redeeming this and that from the pawnshops.

I hope to have done with the biographies (all of them) by next week.[218] (Is there anything to be said about that jackass, *Sir G. Brown?*)

I have begun a SERIES in the *Tribune* on the Bonaparte régime's deeds of financial derring-do.[219] To this I devote the days when there is no Indian news. I should like also to have a personal discussion with you about India, MAP IN HAND. Up till now I have always managed instinctively to hit the nail on the head. But soon it will be time for me to provide a kind of *general military summary* of the affair.

A few days ago, on my way to the Museum,[a] I came such a purler that my forehead is still complaining.

I trust you are taking iron. A day or two ago I was talking to Dr Lichtenberg at the German hospital, a very knowledgable little chap. He said that it was indispensable in after-treatment.

Your

K. M.

First published in *Der Briefwechsel zwischen F. Engels und K. Marx,* Bd. 2, Stuttgart, 1913

Printed according to the original

Published in English for the first time

---

[a] the British Museum

98

ENGELS TO MARX[220]

IN LONDON

Ryde, 24 September 1857

Dear Marx,

Depicted above is the castle where Cromwell incarcerated Charles I for a while. I shall inspect it more closely on Sunday.

Your wishes concerning India coincided with an idea I had that you might perhaps like to have my views on the business. At the same time I took the opportunity of going over the contents of the latest MAIL map in hand and *voici ce qui en résulte.*[a]

The situation of the English in the middle and upper reaches of the Ganges is so incongruous that militarily speaking the only right course would be to effect a junction between Havelock's column and the one from Delhi, if possible at Agra, after each had done everything possible to evacuate the detached or invested

---

[a] here is the result

garrisons in the area; to man, besides Agra, only the neighbouring stations *south* of the Ganges, especially Gwalior (on account of the Central Indian princes) and to hold the stations lower down the Ganges—Allahabad, Benares, Dinapur—with the existing garrisons and reinforcements from Calcutta; meanwhile to escort women and non-combatants down river, so that the troops again become mobile; and to employ mobile columns to instil respect in the region and to obtain supplies. If Agra cannot be held, there must be a withdrawal to Cawnpore or Allahabad; the latter *to be held at all costs* since it is the key to the territory between the Ganges and the Jumna.

If *Agra* can be held and the Bombay army remains available, the armies of Bombay and Madras must hold the peninsula proper up to the latitude of Ahmedabad and Calcutta and send out columns to establish communications with the north—the Bombay army via Indor and Gwalior to Agra, the Madras army via Saugor and Gwalior to Agra, and via Jubbulpore to Allahabad. The other lines of communication would then run to Agra from the Punjab, assuming it is held, and from Calcutta via Dinapur and Allahabad, so that there would be 4 lines of communication and, excluding the Punjab, 3 lines of withdrawal, to Calcutta, Bombay and Madras. Concentrating the troops arriving from the south at Agra would, therefore, serve the dual purpose of keeping the Central Indian princes in check and subduing the insurgent districts astride the line of march.

If Agra cannot be held, the Madras army must first establish communications with Allahabad and then make for Agra with the Allahabad troops, while the Bombay army makes for Gwalior.

The Madras army would seem to have been recruited exclusively from the ragtag and bobtail and to that extent is reliable. In Bombay they have 150 or more Hindus to a battalion and these are dangerous in that they may disaffect the rest. If the Bombay army revolts, all military calculations will temporarily cease to apply, and then nothing is more certain than that there'll be one colossal MASSACRE from Kashmir to Cape Comorin. If the situation in Bombay is such that in future also the army cannot be used against the insurgents, then at least the Madras columns, which will by now have pushed on beyond Nagpur, will have to be reinforced and communications established as speedily as possible with Allahabad or Benares.

The absurdity of the position in which the English have now been placed by the total absence of any real supreme command is demonstrated mainly by 2 complementary circumstances, namely, 1. that they permit themselves to be invested when dispersed over a host of small, far flung stations while 2. they tie down their one and only mobile column in front of Delhi where not only can it do nothing but is actually going to pot. The English general who ordered the march on Delhi[a] deserves to be cashiered and hanged, for he must have known what we have only just learned, viz. that the British had strengthened the old fortifications to the point where the place could only be taken by a systematic siege, for which a minimum of 15-20,000 men would be required, and far more if it was *well* defended. Now that they are there they will have *to stick it out for political reasons*; a withdrawal would be a defeat and will nevertheless be difficult to avoid.[b]

Havelock's troops have worked wonders. 126 miles in 8 days including 6 to 8[c] engagements in that climate and at this time of year is truly superhuman. But they're also quite played out; he, too, will probably have to let himself be invested after exhausting himself still further by excursions over a narrow radius round Cawnpore. Or he will have to return to Allahabad.

The actual route of reconquest will run up the valley of the Ganges. Bengal proper will be easier to hold since the population has so greatly degenerated; the really dangerous region begins at Dinapur. Hence the positions at Dinapur, Benares, Mirzapur and particularly Allahabad are of the utmost importance; from Allahabad, it would first be necessary to take the Doab (between the Ganges and the Jumna) and the cities on these two rivers, then Oudh, then the rest. The lines from Madras and Bombay to Agra and Allahabad can only be secondary lines of operations.

The main thing, as always, is concentration. The reinforcements sent up the Ganges are scattered all over the place and so far not one man has reached Allahabad. Unavoidable, perhaps, if these stations were to be made secure and then again, perhaps not.[d] At all events, the number of stations to be held must be reduced to a minimum and forces must be concentrated for the field. If C. Campbell, about whom we know nothing save that he is a brave man, wants to distinguish himself as a general, he must create a mobile army, *coûte que coûte*,[e] whether or not Delhi is abandoned.

---

[a] George Anson - [b] In the original Marx marked this paragraph with a vertical line in the margin (the italics are also his). - [c] The figures were inserted by Marx. - [d] In the original the first three sentences of this paragraph were marked with a vertical line by Marx. - [e] cost what it may

And where, *summa summarum,* there are 25-30,000 European soldiers, no situation is so desperate that 5,000 at least cannot be mustered for a campaign, their losses being made good by the garrisons withdrawn from the stations. Only *then* will Campbell be able to see how he stands and what kind of enemy is actually confronting him. THE ODDS ARE, HOWEVER, that LIKE A FOOL he will *se blottir devant*[a] Delhi and watch his men go to pot AT THE RATE OF 100 A DAY, in which case it will be all the more 'brave' simply to stay there until everyone has cheerfully met his doom. Now as in the past brave stupidity is the order of the day.[b]

Concentration of forces for the fighting in the north, vigorous support from Madras and, if possible, from Bombay, that's all. Even if the Mahratta princes[221] on the Nerbudda defect it can do little harm save by way of an example, for their troops are already with the insurgents. Certainly the very most that can be done is to hold out until the first reinforcements arrive from Europe at the end of October. But if a few more Bombay regiments revolt, that will be the end of strategy and tactics; it's there that the decision lies.[222]

I leave for Brighton on Tuesday at the latest and set out from there for Jersey at 10 o'clock on Wednesday night, but will let you have further details, and hope that you will come. Tomorrow shall start on 'Battery', etc.[223] Today I drove round the island and, as I again slogged away until 3 o'clock yesterday, now propose to have a good long sleep.

Your

F. E.

First published slightly abridged in *Der Briefwechsel zwischen F. Engels und K. Marx,* Bd. 2, Stuttgart, 1913 and in full in: Marx and Engels, *Works,* First Russian Edition, Vol. XXII, Moscow, 1929

Printed according to the original
Published in English in full for the first time

---

[a] squat down before - [b] Marx marked the last two sentences with a vertical line in the original.

99

MARX TO ENGELS[224]

IN RYDE

[London,] 25 September 1857

Dear Engels,

I presume you will have received today my letter of the day before yesterday acknowledging the £5. I cannot understand the delay, having myself taken it to the post on time.

Your *'Army'* is capital; except that I was thunderstruck by the sheer bulk of it—so much work can't possibly be good for you. And if I'd known that you would work late into the night I would rather have let the whole thing go to the devil.

More graphically than anything else the history of the ARMY demonstrates the rightness of our views as to the connection between the productive forces and social relations. Altogether, the ARMY is of importance in economic development. E.g. it was in the army of Antiquity that the *salaire*[a] was first fully developed. Likewise the *peculium castrense* in Rome, the first legal form according recognition to the movable property of others than fathers of families. Likewise the guild system in the corporation of the *fabri*.[225] Here too the first use of machinery on a large scale. Even the special value of metals and their USE as money would seem to have been based originally—as soon as Grimm's Stone Age was over—on their significance in war. Again, the division of labour *within* a branch was first put into practice by armies. All this, moreover, a very striking epitome of the whole history of civil societies. If you ever have the time, you might work the thing out from that point of view.

The only points I think you have overlooked in your account are: 1. the earliest manifestation of a ready-made mercenary system on a large scale AND AT ONCE among the Carthaginians (for our own PRIVATE USE I shall take a look at a work—previously unknown to me—by a Berlin man on the Carthaginian armies[b]); 2. the development of the army system in the 15th and early 16th centuries in Italy, where tactical ruses, at any rate, were perfected. Likewise an extremely humorous description of Machiavelli's

---

[a] wages - [b] Presumably W. Bötticher's *Geschichte der Carthager.*

(which I shall extract for you) in his *History of Florence*[a] of how the *condottieri*[226] fought. (But if I come and meet you in Brighton (when?),[227] perhaps I had better bring you the Machiavelli. The *History of Florence* is a masterpiece.) Lastly, 3. the Asiatic military system as it first appeared in Persia and subsequently in various much modified forms among, *inter alia,* the Mongols and Turks.

In writing my biographies, etc., I naturally had to consult all sorts of encyclopaedias, including German ones. In so doing I discovered that, under the headings 'Labour', 'Classes', 'Production', etc., much had been systematically if stupidly cribbed from us. On the other hand, everyone had eschewed all mention of ourselves, even when devoting whole columns to Mr Edgar Bauer and other such panjandrums. *Tant mieux pour nous.*[b] The biographies in the German encyclopaedias are written for children under 8 years of age. The French, if biased, are at least urbane. The English encyclopaedias crib systematically from the French and German. In the latter, the same fellows appear to unload the same twaddle onto different publishers. Ersch and Gruber[c] not much good except in the later volumes, wherein many learned articles.

Salut.

Your

K. M.

Pauly's *Realencyclopädie des Alterthums* is reliable.

First published in *Der Briefwechsel zwischen F. Engels und K. Marx,* Bd. 2, Stuttgart, 1913

Printed according to the original

100

ENGELS TO MARX[228]

IN LONDON

St. Hélier, Jersey, 6 October 1857
3 Edward Place

Dear Marx,

L'affaire Harney resolved itself when the noble fellow called on Schramm yesterday evening while I was there. He has grown a

---

[a] N. Machiavelli, *Le Istorie Fiorentine* (in *Tutte le opere di Niccolò Machiavelli...,* t. 1). - [b] So much the better for us. - [c] *Allgemeine Encyclopädie der Wissenschaften und Künste*

big, jet-black beard thereby giving himself a strange appearance in some ways not unlike that of the greasy Jew in the boat that brought us ashore from the STEAMER; CERTAINLY an IMPROVEMENT. He made rather light of his Jersey POLITICS, saying he got A GREAT DEAL OF FUN out of them, etc.[229]; the more serious view he certainly takes of them will no doubt emerge later on. Afterwards he and I went on a mild spree and I got him to tell me about the constitution, etc., etc., here; not a word was said about the old days. For the time being he seems DAM'D GLAD to have withdrawn from high politics into his little *royaume des aveugles.* As a *borgne*[a] he's king of the opposition here, on his right THE FIRST GROCER, on his left THE FIRST TALLOW-CHANDLER IN THE TOWN. The battles are fought out in Royal Square and it was here that the GROCER knocked DOWN the *rédacteur en chef* of the *Impartial de Jersey,* a Bonapartist spy called Lemoine, the upshot of which was a lawsuit that has gone on for the past year and is to be decided on Monday. The *Impartial* has been suspended since the beginning of the monetary crisis in Paris and, so long as this lasts, will remain so. In Harney's view the whole history of Jersey may be divided into 2 periods: before and after the Hejira, or the expulsion of the *crapauds.*[230] They are noteworthy for the fact that nothing happened during either of them.

Schramm is busy with plans for new lodgings but will probably stay where he is after all. I urged him to move further south but, like most people in his condition, he tends to be contrary and also says that it is a question of money and that his relatives were already doing what they could. From Harney's description it's often downright cold here in winter when there's an east wind, and Schramm lives on the side of the town most exposed to the north-west winds. If, as he says, his difficulty in walking is no greater than it was three years ago, the disease may of course drag on for some time yet. Proof that here, too, people can contract consumption and die of it is provided by a case in this very house, for the daughter of my fat landlady succumbed to it. I hardly like to speak to him any more about moving south; it rubs him up the wrong way and he is after all very tetchy, as is only natural. As things stand I have not yet got down to work and there is also a mass of letters to be written; but tomorrow I shall make a start.

---

a Engels alludes to the French saying, 'Au royaume des aveugles les borgnes sont rois' ('In the kingdom of the blind the one-eyed man is king').

Yesterday I walked to the north coast—5 or 6 miles from here, very good roads, a pretty avenue here and there, magnificent blackberries *en masse* and a few very lovely small inlets on the coast. The island forms a plateau and once you're on top, it rises very gently almost as far as the north coast, and the beds of the streams are quite shallow. From the northern end you can see a long stretch of France (west coast of the Département de la Manche) and the island of Sark. I couldn't see Guernsey.

Schramm's brother[a] has informed him that a friend of his, a (probably Prussian) lawyer by the name of Berger,[b] about 50 years old, will be arriving in a few days and will spend the winter here. Do you know this individual? Presumably the fellow lives in London, and it is always as well to be informed to some extent about Mr Rudolf Schramm's acquaintances. I have a vague recollection that a fellow of this description bumped into us once in London.

I have also tracked down Steffen's guerrilla warfare in respect of Berg and the Mark: Holleben, *Militairische Betrachtungen aus den Erfahrungen eines preussischen Offiziers.* This book is his chief authority and maintains that the hedge and ditch country in parts of the Mark and Cleves recalls La Vendée,[231] and is admirably suited to a people's war. Not so the people who live there, unfortunately—this being the flat, agricultural part of the Mark. For the rest the book is a good one, but just the thing to encourage Steffen's predilection for skirmishes and guerrilla warfare; it leans too far in this direction.

Enclosed the list for C with comments.[232]

Kindest regards to your wife and children.

Your

F. E.

First published abridged in *Der Briefwechsel zwischen F. Engels und K. Marx,* Bd. 2, Stuttgart, 1913 and in full in: Marx and Engels, *Works,* First Russian Edition, Vol. XXII, Moscow, 1929

Printed according to the original

Published in English for the first time

[a] Rudolf Schramm - [b] Engels means Hermann Buck.

101

ENGELS TO MARX[233]

IN LONDON

[St. Hélier,] Jersey, 19 October 1857
3 Edward Place

Dear Marx,

Herewith the BALANCE of the old sins of omission, also the original notes on the Armada. I couldn't quite decipher some of the names, which you will have to try and fill in.[234] I am now going on to the HISTORY OF CANNON.[235]

Schramm seems to me to be getting rather worse, though his condition changes from day to day. At present he has Berger[a] with him, a philistine sent by his brother,[b] who has taken lodgings in the same house and to whom he is giving English lessons. He's a dirty-minded old Prussian who tells lewd jokes devoid of wit about all the court rabble in Berlin, *que le diable l'emporte!*[c] I haven't seen FRIEND Harney for a week. He's awfully stupid and feels very COMFORTABLE indeed in his philistine role here, although even on his PAPER[d] he is clearly subject to the owner's censorship. He anticipates, of course, that sooner or later the English workers will do something or other, but that it won't be at all in the Chartist line, and anyway what he says is so much theoretical hot air and he would undoubtedly detest being jolted out of his petty philistine agitation here. HE IS VERY BUSY, BUT BUSY DOING NOTHING. His friend the GROCER, who thrashed the French spy,[e] has been fined £5.

Besides the HISTORY OF CANNON, I intend to do a few of the shorter things and send them to you from time to time so that Dana may see that we're keeping the ball rolling. But do send me those notes about which I wrote to you, and the list of military articles for *D.* I presume you got the letter containing the copy of the C list,[232] and also the article 'Military Bridges'[f] sent off later.

I have firmly resolved to return to Manchester in a fortnight's time. Business has taken a very nasty turn and it's important for

---

[a] Engels means Hermann Buck. - [b] Rudolf Schramm - [c] the devil take him! - [d] *The Jersey Independent* - [e] Lemoine - [f] F. Engels, 'Bridge, Military'.

me to be there. Moreover, my health is now good; yesterday, I spent 7 hours in the saddle, and I have also bidden farewell to virtue.

Your
F. E.

First published abridged in *Der Briefwechsel zwischen F. Engels und K. Marx,* Bd. 2, Stuttgart, 1913 and in full in: Marx and Engels, *Works,* First Russian Edition, Vol. XXII, Moscow, 1929

Printed according to the original

Published in English for the first time

102

MARX TO ENGELS

IN ST. HÉLIER IN JERSEY

[London,] 20 October 1857

Dear Frederick,

You must excuse my long silence. In the first place, we've had a visitor for the past week, to wit Imandt junior (aged 13), who has arrived here from Trier en route to his uncle,[a] and I have had to show the lad round. In the second, much work.

Now *d'abord,*[b] your plan to return to Manchester. You must know whether or not your presence is necessary. It certainly won't do your health any good, for the weather over here is ABOMINABLE. Allen thinks that you owe it to yourself to spend far more time recuperating in a better climate than the Manchester ONE, since any relapse might be fatal. But it must be supposed that you consult your doctor[c] before coming to a decision.

The American crisis—its outbreak in New York was forecast by us in the November 1850 *Revue*[d]—is BEAUTIFUL and has had IMMEDIATE repercussions on French industry, since silk goods are now being sold in New York more cheaply than they are produced in Lyons. The lamentations of the English MONEY ARTICLE WRITERS, who complain that, while their English TRADE is SOUND, their customers abroad are UNHEALTHY, are as original as they are diverting. How are the Manchester manufacturers getting on? Those in Glasgow have, it now transpires, sent off a great deal on consignment.

---

[a] probably Peter Imandt - [b] first - [c] Martin Heckscher - [d] K. Marx and F. Engels, 'Review. May to October [1850]'.

What do you think of the English in India? As usual the chaps are lucky even in adversity. I now have a pretty detailed list of their troop shipments since 18 June, along with the dates on which, by the government's reckoning, they *ought* to arrive and the *locus*[a] of arrival. The following is a resumé:

Day of	Arrival	Total	Calcutta	Ceylon	Bombay	Karachi	Madras
September	20	214	214				
October	2	300	300				
	15	1,906	124	1,782			
	17	288	288				
	20	4,235	3,845	390			
	30	2,028	479	1,549			
October		8,757	5,036	3,721			
November	1	3,495	1,234	1,629		632	
	5	879	879				
	10	2,700	904	340	400	1,056	
	12	1,633	1,633				
	15	2,610	2,132	478			
	19	234				234	
	20	1,216		278	938		
	24	406		406			
	25	1,276					1,276
	30	666		462	204		
November		15,115	6,782	3,593	1,542	1,922	1,276
December	1	354			354		
	5	459			201		258
	10	1,758		607		1,151	
	14	1,057			1,057		
	15	948			647	301	
	20	693	185		300	208	
	25	624				624	
December		5,893	185	607	2,559	2,284	258
January	1	340			340		
	5	220					220
	15	140					140
	20	220					220
January		920			340		580
Sept.-Jan.		30,899	12,217	7,921	4,431	4,206	2,114

[a] place

Day of	Arrival	Total	Calcutta	Ceylon	Bombay	Karachi	Madras
			Troops despatched by Overland Mail				
October	2	235	Engineers	117		118	
	12	221	Artillerymen				
	14	244	Engineers	122		122	
October		700		460		240	

The 30,899 men are composed of:

Infantry:	24,739
Artillery:	2,334
Cavalry:	3,826

Of the ARTILLERY, only 100 men arrive at Calcutta in October. The actual ARRIVALS commence on 15 November. The first cavalry arrives on 10 November.[a]

Now that I'm onto figures, here are a few more particulars about Bonaparte's economy. The *FUNDED DEBT* authentic. The *FLOATED* for 1856 and 1857 based on an AVERAGE estimate; for the other years, the *Moniteur.* (The French maintain that this FLOATED DEBT is 2,000 mill., which is what it seems to work out at.)

Funded Debt

Louis Philippe (18 years)

Year	Mill. frs
1831	162$^1/_2$
1832	150
1841	187$^1/_2$
1844	325
1847	87$^1/_2$
Total	912$^1/_2$
AVERAGE for 18 years:	50

Bonaparte (6 years 1852-57)

Year	Mill. frs
DECREE OF APRIL 1852	100
MARCH 1853	250
DECEMBER 1854	500
JULY 1855	750
August 1855 (Filiated from EXCESS of the SUBSCRIPTION)	31$^1/_4$
1857 (BANK OF FRANCE COIN)	100
Total	1,731,250,000
AVERAGE for 6 years: NEAR	300

[a] This table, slightly abridged, was appended to Marx's article 'The Revolt in India' published in the *New-York Daily Tribune,* 14 November 1857.

Floating Debt

	Mill. frs
Louis Philippe ABOUT	1,000
Republic end of 1851 no more than	700

Increases under Bonaparte

	Mill. frs
1852	50
53	262 1/4
54	205 3/4
55	152 1/4
56, 57	335 1/8
Total	1,005 and FRACTION
Increases since the time of the Republic	700
	1,705 mill.

In addition, all MUNICIPAL and DEPARTMENTAL treasuries also up to their eyes in debt, *par ordre de Muphti*.[a]

If one reflects that, at the fellow's accession, the FUNDED DEBT was ABOUT 4,000 mill. frs—i.e. from the time of the First Republic's *Tiers consolidé*[b] onwards—and that in 6 years he increased the FUNDED and FLOATING DEBT by ABOUT 2,700 millions, there can be no contesting that his stay in London was a fruitful one. Moreover, in *his* estimate of the *dette flottante* such curious tricks are played with the *SINKING FUND*, etc., that the AUDITING is exceedingly equivocal. But the fellow is not without a certain gambler's humour. By his reckoning there was no deficit *whatever* and no FLOATING DEBT in 1852—the 1st year of the imperial millennium. For he placed 50 million frs to the ACCOUNT of 1851 (in accordance with the absurd French practice, the 1851 budget was FIXED in August 1850, but not CLOSED until 1854), and debited 1853 with the balance. Unlike Louis Philippe, he ushered in his régime with a *NO DEFICIT*, but in 1853, the very next year, unblushingly presented the biggest FLOATING DEBT France had known since 1800. When in 1849 the Finance Minister, Passy, proposed that he limit and fund the FLOATING DEBT, he dismissed him forthwith and appointed Achille Fould. Come to that, his financial system is the same as Louis Philippe's save that it is *sans gêne*,[c] is taken to extremes, and SLEIGHTS OF HAND are the rule.

I shall send you what you require for the *Cyclopaedia* as soon as I have a moment to spare.

Your

K. M.

---

[a] by order of the Mufti (i.e. of Napoleon III) - [b] *Tiers consolidé*—the French national debt after its reduction by two-thirds in 1797. - [c] brazen

Thank you for sending the articles.[a] The one name you failed to decipher was Lord Burleigh.

Best regards to Schramm.

First published abridged in *Der Briefwechsel zwischen F. Engels und K. Marx*, Bd. 2, Stuttgart, 1913 and in full in: Marx and Engels, *Works*, First Russian Edition, Vol. XXII, Moscow, 1929

Printed according to the original

Published in English for the first time

103

ENGELS TO MARX[236]

IN LONDON

[St. Hélier,] Jersey, 29 October 1857
3 Edward Place

Dear Marx,

I shall be returning to Manchester a week from today,[183] but don't yet know what route I shall take. Your letter induced me to question Heckscher again (I had, of course, already consulted him concerning my return) about the possibility of a fatal relapse. From his reply I can only conclude that he believes a relapse might be fatal only if the lungs were affected, and is willing to guarantee that this will not be so in my case. At all events, he doesn't think Jersey is of much benefit to me any more; either the thing's over, or I must go much further south, and should anyhow return to Manchester, if only as an experiment, since I can always go away again. Now I'm simply waiting for some money and then I'll be off. By that time the HISTORY OF CANNON[235] will be finished and I'd rather do the other things—with possibly a few small exceptions—in Manchester where my books are. I should like to have the D list soon, otherwise Mr Dana will steal a march on us. What else does the noble fellow have to say, or haven't you heard from him?

So drastically has the iron acted on my blood that my pulse has begun racing madly and the blood is always rising to my head; it's

[a] A reference to the articles 'Armada' and 'Ayacucho' by Marx and Engels (see this volume, p. 173).

as though I'd been drinking—I feel quite fuddled and my excitation is such that I can't sleep at night. So for the time being I've had to stop taking it again. When I go back onto it in Manchester I shall have to reduce the dose considerably.

The advancing season is having a most debilitating effect on Schramm. Needless to say, he can only go out very little now and seldom comes into the town and only at the cost of considerable effort. The old philistine[a] sent to him by his brother[b] is a very bawdy fellow, who knows all the Berlin gossip, but in other ways stupid and boring. However, he'll be able to pester Konrad's worthy brother on Konrad's behalf, and this he has promised me to do. Schramm has had a door made in the wall between his bedroom and living-room which enables him to heat the former a bit and avoid going out into the hall in winter. This has put an end to the house-hunting. He'll hardly outlast the spring, poor devil.

Harney grows more stupid every day. Considering the nature of the feudal arrangements here,[237] he should be able to make A DEAL OF POLITICAL CAPITAL out of them, but he doesn't even begin to understand them and, moreover, ruins all the best points made by the little lawyer who supplies him with material and even complete articles. There is, by the way, much that is funny about this dead-and-alive feudal set-up, and the whole business is preposterous to a degree. A modern lawyer[c] for *Seigneur* and St. Hélier SHOPKEEPERS for vassals—the masquerade is altogether grotesque. Just now the fellows are holding feudal courts of justice; the *prévôt*[d] *du Seigneur* is a CARVER and GILDER who doesn't know a word of French and, although he's the second personage here, hasn't an inkling of what's going on. The *Seigneur* threatens to confiscate the houses of his unruly vassals, who make up some 60-70 per cent of the total number, while the vassals—DRAPERS and TALLOW-CHANDLERS—threaten to meet force with force. *Voilà*[e] the present state of affairs.

If you write to me on Monday, but IN TIME FOR THE MAIL, your letter will still find me here; whether I shall still be here on Thursday, I am not quite sure.

Warmest regards to your wife and children.

Your

F. E.

---

[a] Hermann Buck - [b] Rudolf Schramm - [c] François Godfrey - [d] the highest court and police officer in medieval France - [e] such is

The Sepoys must have defended the ENCEINTE of Delhi very badly[238]; the real joke was the house-to-house fighting when, presumably, the NATIVE TROOPS were sent in first. So the actual siege—what came afterwards could hardly be described as such—lasted from the 5th to the 14th, long enough for breaches to be made in the unprotected wall by heavy naval guns firing at a range of 300-400 yards. These were already in position by the 5th or 6th. The cannon on the walls do not appear to have been effectively manned, otherwise the English wouldn't have been able to make so swift an approach.

The AMERICAN CRASH is superb and not yet over by a long chalk. We still have to see the collapse of the better part of the import houses; so far only one here and there would appear to have crashed. The repercussion in England would seem to have begun with the Liverpool Borough Bank. *Tant mieux.*[a] That means that, for the next 3 or 4 years, commerce will again be in a bad way. *Nous avons maintenant de la chance.*[b]

I haven't got a STAMP in the house and it is now midnight.

First published abridged in *Der Briefwechsel zwischen F. Engels und K. Marx*, Bd. 2, Stuttgart, 1913 and in full in: Marx and Engels, *Works*, First Russian Edition, Vol. XXII, Moscow, 1929

Printed according to the original

Published in English in full for the first time

104

MARX TO ENGELS

IN ST. HÉLIER IN JERSEY

[London,] 31 October 1857

DEAR Frederic,

Have received two letters from Dana. Says first, that *'Army'* arrived in good time. *Secondly*, that, because of the COMMERCIAL CRISIS, notice has been given to all European correspondents except for myself and Bayard Taylor; I, however, am to confine myself STRICTLY to 1 ARTICLE PER WEEK—lately I had been trying to break

---

[a] So much the better. - [b] We're now in luck.

through this limitation—and for the time being write exclusively about the INDIAN WAR and the FINANCIAL CRISIS.

If you could let me have the HISTORY OF CANNON[235] by Friday, IT WOULD BE A GREAT BOON. As soon as the next mail arrives from India, you must write to me at some length about the Delhi affair or rather, IF POSSIBLE, do the whole article[a] since this time it has to be purely technical.

I sent the chaps ABOUT 8 sheets under the heading 'Blücher', the same being sub-titled 'THE SILESIAN ARMY IN THE CAMPAIGNS ETC.'.[239] As I had to spend so much time reading Clausewitz, Müffling,[b] etc., some degree of compensation was called for.

So far as your resolution as to Manchester is concerned, it seems to me QUITE RATIONAL, within Heckscher's LIMITATIONS. Allen, too, says that fatal consequences are likely to result only if the lung is affected but that, in the early days after such a business, it behoves anyone to take care of himself.

The doses of iron may have been somewhat too strong. At all events it should have an excellent effect on your BODY. The weather here has improved during the past few days.

I SHOULD MUCH LIKE, OLD BOY, TO SEE YOU BEFORE YOUR RETURN TO MANCHESTER. There is a certain irony of fate in my being personally embroiled in these damned crises. What SATISFACTION it would give Heinzen *s'il le savait*[c]!

The news AS TO Schramm is no less saddening for being predictable. What do you say to Cavaignac's DEATH and the idiocy of our liege-lord[d]?

With warm regards from the WHOLE FAMILY.

Your

K. M.

First published in *Der Briefwechsel zwischen F. Engels und K. Marx*, Bd. 2, Stuttgart, 1913

Printed according to the original

Published in English for the first time

[a] Engels did write it ('The Capture of Delhi'). - [b] C. von Clausewitz, *Der Feldzug von 1812 in Rußland, der Feldzug von 1813 bis zum Waffenstillstand und der Feldzug von 1814 in Frankreich* and *Der Feldzug von 1815 in Frankreich*; [F. K. F.] Müffling, *Passages from My Life....* - [c] if he knew - [d] King Frederick William IV of Prussia

105

MARX TO ENGELS

IN MANCHESTER

[London,] 13 November 1857

Dear Engels,

A week ago on Thursday[240] I waited at both the appointed places—which, however, was one too many—from 11 o'clock to 3. Then I gave the whole thing up IN DESPAIR.

I can write no more than a line or two, the article[a] having left me only a few minutes until posting time. Let me know definitely when I can have 'Cannon'.[235] It's a matter of getting the goods off to America at what is (for me) a crucial moment.

Meanwhile I haven't written a word about India. I have got to have some accurate military stuff on the subject, EVENTS having to some extent discredited myself and the *Tribune*.[241]

Though my own FINANCIAL DISTRESS may be dire indeed, never, since 1849, have I felt SO COSY as during this OUTBREAK. Furthermore you can set Lupus' mind at rest by telling him that, NOW THAT THE WHOLE STATEMENT IS BEFORE US, I have written an exhaustive ARTICLE for the *Tribune*[a] in which I show, if only on the basis of the table of DISCOUNT-RATES for 1848-54, that the crisis ought by rights to have set in 2 years earlier. Moreover the DELAYS are now explicable in such rational terms that even Hegel might, to his great SATISFACTION, have rediscovered the 'concept' in the 'empirical diversity of the world of finite interests'.

Salut.

Your
K. M.

Go on sending me, as you started to do, as many Manchester papers as possible. Not only for the *Tribune*. I am thinking of writing about the crisis for the benefit of the fatherland.

First published abridged in *Der Briefwechsel zwischen F. Engels und K. Marx*, Bd. 2, Stuttgart, 1913 and in full in: Marx and Engels, *Works*, First Russian Edition, Vol. XXII, Moscow, 1929

Printed according to the original
Published in English for the first time

[a] K. Marx, 'The British Revulsion'.

106

ENGELS TO MARX

IN LONDON

Manchester, 15 November 1857

Dear Marx,

I'm sorry about your waiting for me last Monday—I didn't arrive at Euston Square until after 6, THANKS TO BAD ARRANGEMENTS OF THE RAILWAY COMPANY IN BRIGHTON, and travelled on to Manchester the same evening.

I'm in good health and everyone, even Heckscher, is surprised that I should have recovered so well. My memory is still poor, the DULLNESS persists to some extent, and alcohol no longer agrees with me. My last sore is healing up beautifully, a process which riding and a reduction of work at the office cannot fail to help; as to the latter I have agreed with our factory to put myself on SHORT TIME.

You should have 'Cannon'[235] for certain by next Friday's post. It can't be done before that and will amount to about 10 full sheets. The rest of C ought to follow shortly; most of it is trifling stuff which can be done quickly with the books I have here.

As soon as I can see daylight in my financial affairs (now in great confusion) I shall send you some money.

This time the crisis is developing in rather a curious way. For almost a year now, speculative share dealings in France and Germany have been in a state of what might be described as pre-crisis; only now, with the collapse of the main speculative share dealings in New York, has everything come to a head. As always, of course, the Yankees have been doing their swindling with foreign capital, but the really remarkable thing is that this time the capital has come predominantly from the Continent. The bureaucrats and rentiers in Germany, who have been eagerly buying up everything provided it was American, will be well and truly bled. Because of the above-mentioned pre-crisis and the few direct points of contact between continental and American stock-exchange swindles, the destructive repercussions of the latter are not immediately making themselves felt. But they soon will.

Speculation has affected not only shares but all raw materials and colonial produce, hence also all manufactured goods where the cost of the raw material is still strongly reflected in the price; hence the closer they are to the raw material and the dearer the raw material, the more they are affected. Yarns more than grey goods, the latter more than printed or coloured goods, silk goods more than cotton goods. Here, we have had a pre-crisis in silk since August; approximately 20 manufactures have failed for an amount I would hesitate to put at less than £200,000 and of which only 35% to 40% at the most will be recovered. We are in for £6,000, which makes my share £300!!! or, taking the most optimistic view, £180 after payment of dividends. In these circumstances I shall probably have to come to a new agreement with my old man. That is by the way. The crisis in silk continues. The failure of Bennoch, Twentyman & Rigg (competitors of Blank's) has caught 5 silk ribbon manufacturers in Coventry to the tune of £100,000, the biggest sum being £40,000 and the smallest £6,000. In addition T. S. Reed & Co. of Derby, important silk spinners, doublers and manufacturers, became insolvent immediately after, and in consequence of, Bennoch's failure. In Glasgow a whole crowd of small and medium firms, besides those mentioned in the papers, have come a cropper without eliciting the least comment or inquiry. Whether the Maison Ernst Dronke is among them I don't know. Maybe he didn't have the sense to take advantage of the moment to make an honourable exit.

The enclosed chart,[a] which I have prepared from official printed reports supplied by our broker, will show you how the cotton market has fared this year. *Whenever the horizontal* black line passes between two of the eighths this means that the price was midway between, or $^1/_{16}$th, thus e.g. between 7 $^3/_8$d and 7 $^1/_2$d means 7 $^7/_{16}$d.

As far as industrial production itself is concerned, America's excess stocks would seem to be mainly in the west; from all I hear, stocks of manufactured goods in the eastern ports are very low. But that these are already A DRUG ON THE MARKET is borne out by the return of entire shipments from New York to Liverpool. $^3/_4$ of the local spinners are making for stock and only $^1/_4$ *at the most* have orders on their books. SHORT TIME pretty well general. A very active yarn commission house here, which 3 weeks ago had contracts worth £45,000, now has only £3,000 worth, so quickly have the spinners been able to deliver, despite SHORT TIME.

The peculiarly favourable advices from Madras and Bombay (sales with profit, which has not been the case since 1847) have revived the Indian trade. Everyone who possibly can is rushing into it. To the annoyance of the other commission houses, S. Mendel, INDIAN agent, has the whole of his big WAREHOUSE lit up

---

[a] See this volume, p. 205.

until 10 o'clock every night and sends out stuff for all he's worth. NO DOUBT hundreds of spinners and weavers are shipping goods there on consignment. So we have a reserve crisis up our sleeve there in case this first impact proves incapable of overturning the old muck.[242]

The general appearance of the Exchange here was truly delightful last week. The fellows are utterly infuriated by my sudden and inexplicable onset of high spirits. INDEED, the Exchange is the one place where my current DULLNESS is transformed into resilience and BOUNCING. On top of that my predictions are, of course, always gloomy, which makes the asses doubly furious. On Thursday the situation was at its most dismal, on Friday the gentlemen were mulling over the possible effects of the suspension of the Bank Act[132] and, with COTTON rising another ld., word went round that the worst was over. By yesterday, however, the most delectable DESPONDENCY again prevailed; all the hosannas had been so much hot air and, since hardly anyone wanted to buy, the market here remained as bad as ever.

What promises this crisis a brilliant future is the immediate necessity of suspending the Bank Act at the *first impact*. The direct effect of this will be to land the Bank itself in Queer Street. In 1847 it was still possible to let things drag on as they had done since 1845, and not to resort to this measure until the very last and grimmest moment.

The extension and prolongation of the crisis are also assured. The combination of SHORT TIME and the silk crisis, which latter has already deprived the vast mass of the silk (HAND-LOOM) weavers of their livelihood, will of itself suffice to ruin the HOME TRADE completely this winter—up till the end of October it was still doing well. The American crisis is playing havoc with the Barmen and Elberfeld SMALLWARE MANUFACTURERS, the Elberfeld, Krefeld and Lyons silk manufacturers and the German, French and Belgian cloth manufacturers. The SMALLWARE MANUFACTURERS of Barmen are suffering particularly also due to Bennoch and Twentyman, while Draper, Pietroni & Co. are causing difficulties in Italy, especially Milan, the Duchies,[a] Bologna, etc.

Unless cotton comes down to 6d per pound even a momentary revival of the cotton industry here is out of the question. And at present it is still as high as 7 to 7 ¹/₄d. From this you will see how remote here is the prospect of any change in the state of affairs. Nevertheless a momentary change in the spring is possible and,

---

[a] Tuscany, Parma and Modena

indeed, probable. Not that this will mean 'good business', but rather that business can again be done so that the machinery of trade keeps turning and doesn't rust up. Never before has any crisis exhausted itself so rapidly and abruptly, and this one, coming after 10 years of prosperity and speculation, is least apt to do so. Nor is there another Australia or California to come to the rescue, while China will be in the doldrums for the next 20 years.[243] However the violence of this initial blow shows what colossal dimensions the thing is assuming. And in view of the recent enormous output of gold and the correspondingly vast expansion of industry, it could not be otherwise.

We can only hope that this 'improvement' in the crisis from the acute to the chronic stage sets in before a second and really decisive blow falls. A period of chronic pressure is needed to get the people's blood up. The proletariat will then fight better, with better *connaissance de cause*[a] and in greater unison, just as a cavalry attack succeeds much better if the horses have to cover the first 500 paces at the trot before arriving within charging distance of the enemy. I shouldn't care for anything to happen prematurely before Europe as a whole has been affected; the subsequent struggle would be harder, more tedious and fluctuating. Even May or June would be somewhat too early. The long period of prosperity is bound to have made the masses damned lethargic. However, sight drafts for a revolution will now be presented to us by our friends Kinkel & Co. for payment; that is to be expected, but NEVER MIND, we shall honour them soon enough, as these gentlemen will see.

It's capital that you should be collecting material on this crisis. I am sending you another 2 *Guardians* today. You shall have it regularly, and the *Examiner and Times* too now and again. I shall also advise you as frequently as possible of everything I learn so that we have a good STOCK OF FACTS.

I must say I feel just as you do. When the bubble burst in New York I grew very restless in Jersey and in the midst of this GENERAL DOWNBREAK I fell tremendously cheerful. The bourgeois filth of the last seven years has undoubtedly clung to me to some extent; now it will be washed away and I shall become a changed man. Physically, the crisis will do me as much good as a bathe in the sea; I can sense it already. In 1848 we were saying: Now our time is coming, and so IN A CERTAIN SENSE it was, but this time it is coming properly; now it's a case of do or die. This will at once give a more

---

[a] knowledge of what they are doing

practical slant to my military studies. I shall apply myself without delay to the existing organisation and elementary tactics of the Prussian, Austrian, Bavarian and French armies, and apart from that confine my activities to riding, i.e. fox-hunting, which is the best school of all.

My kindest regards to your wife and children. They, too, will be in high spirits despite your bad luck. Day and night I worry over my inability to get you out of it.

Your
F. E.

In Failsworth, 4 miles from here, a manufacturer by the name of Liddle was yesterday hanged in effigy *optima forma*[a] while a weaver dressed as a parson read the BURIAL SERVICE. In place of the words 'MAY THE LORD HAVE MERCY UPON YOUR SOUL' he read: 'MAY THE LORD BLAST YOUR SOUL'.—NOW IS THE TIME FOR JONES, if only he knows how to make use of it.

First published abridged in *Der Briefwechsel zwischen F. Engels und K. Marx*, Bd. 2, Stuttgart, 1913 and in full in: Marx and Engels, *Works*, First Russian Edition, Vol. XXII, Moscow, 1929

Printed according to the original

Published in English for the first time

107

ENGELS TO MARX

IN LONDON

Manchester, 16 November 1857
7 Southgate

Dear Marx,

Enclosed the table[b] I forgot yesterday. I have just seen that today's *Guardian* has everything on Delhi. I'm going home now (6 o'clock) and shall do my best to go through it and get the article,[c] if only a short one, done for you; it can go off by the 2nd post as I think I shall have finished it by 12 o'clock. At such short NOTICE there can be no question of tidying it up or correcting the style.

---

a with due formality - b See p. 205. - c F. Engels, 'The Capture of Delhi'.

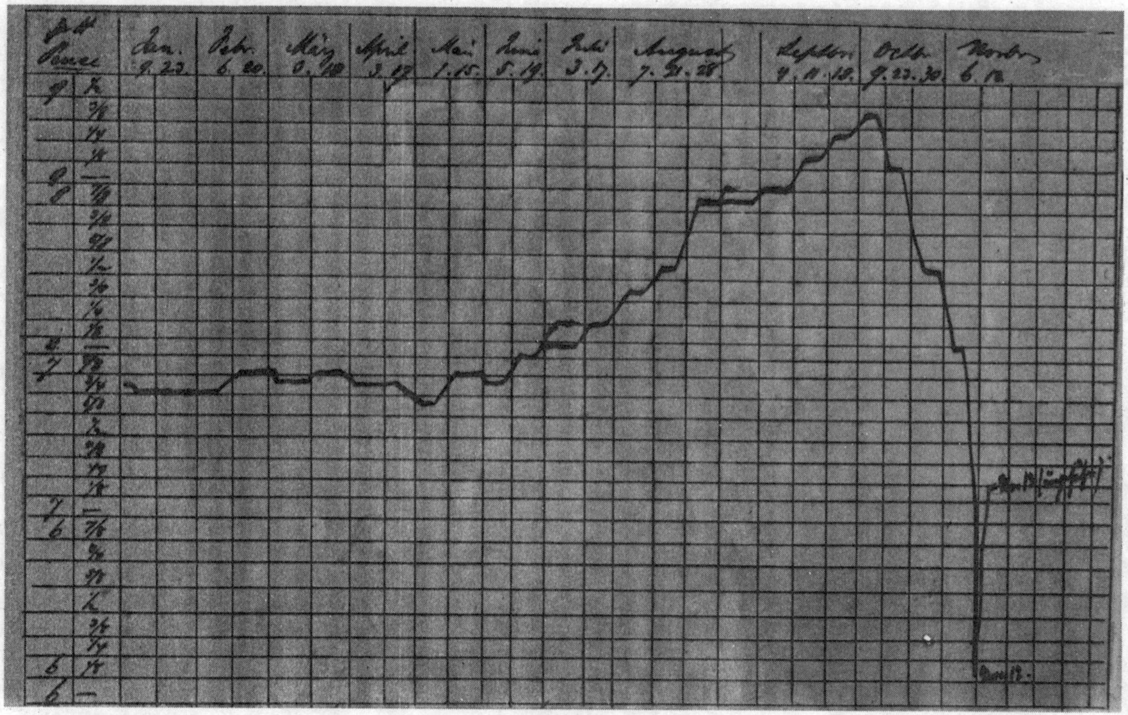

Movements in the Price of Middling Orleans Cotton since 1 January 1857

Two dates per month shown up to the end of July, 3 dates thereafter. Lowest level on 12 November when the Western Bank of Scotland disposed of its stocks *à tout prix.* On 13 November approximate level 7d; brokers were not quoting

[*Engels' explanation to the chart*]

In these circumstances it's most doubtful whether I shall be able to send you 'Cannon'[235] by Thursday. I have only two evenings left and I can't write every evening without my head starting to spin. So it will have to wait until a week today.

Your

F. E.

First published in *Der Briefwechsel zwischen F. Engels and K. Marx,* Bd. 2, Stuttgart, 1913

Printed according to the original

Published in English for the first time

108

ENGELS TO MARX

IN LONDON

Manchester, 17 November 1857
7 Southgate

Dear Marx,

I doubt whether yesterday's article[a] reached you soon enough. When I went to the post it had just turned midnight and the BOX was closed, so I dropped it in the EXTRA BOX, which means it must have left here at 9.15 this morning and arrived in London at 3:45, hence been delivered to you at about 6 o'clock.

About a month ago there was a share CRASH in Vienna, on which occasion 105 houses are said to have failed there to the tune of Fl. 14,000,000, or £1,400,000.

Nothing has been done here today. Tomorrow you will receive a whole bundle of *Guardians* and also some money from me, I hope.

Your

F. E.

First published in: Marx and Engels, *Works,* First Russian Edition, Vol. XXII, Moscow, 1929

Printed according to the original

Published in English for the first time

[a] F. Engels, 'The Capture of Delhi'.

109

MARX TO ENGELS[1]

IN MANCHESTER

[London,] 24 November 1857

Dear Frederick,

You must excuse me for not having acknowledged receipt either of the money, or of the article[a] or of various letters. The comings and goings connected with DOMESTIC AFFAIRS have made such demands on my time that little was left for work.

The MONETARY PANIC in London has SUBSIDED to some extent during the past few days but will soon begin afresh with the assistance of, among others, Fould, who has come over here with a French bank director in order to regulate the export of gold from England to France. The actual SUSPENSION of the Bank Act[132] could, of course, only be effective in so far as it did away with the PANIC SURPLUS artificially created by the Bank Act. The BANKING DEPARTMENT should have had to declare itself insolvent the following day since the reserve fund amounted to no more than four or five hundred thousand pounds, whereas DEPOSITS—PUBLIC and PRIVATE—exceeded 17 millions. On the other hand this danger was created solely by the Act itself in that the metal reserve in the ISSUING DEPARTMENT was not much below one-third of the ISSUED NOTES. The Act precipitated the outbreak of the MONEY PANIC, thereby perhaps reducing its intensity. However, lendings by the Bank up to a maximum of 10% (on FIRST-RATE PAPERS) will keep a mass of transactions going which must ultimately lead to another CRASH. If, for instance, the price of corn, sugar, etc., is currently being maintained it is because their OWNERS are discounting the bills drawn on them for the same instead of selling the commodities. A fall in the price of these commodities seems to me inevitable and hence I believe that these chaps are simply heading straight for serious bankruptcies. That was EXACTLY THE CASE [IN] MAY 1847. As distinct from earlier crises, what is still to some extent supporting the so-called MONEY-MARKET in London is the existence of JOINT-STOCK BANKS which didn't really begin to expand until the last ten years. The interest they pay the philistines, small rentiers, etc., is 1% less than the Bank of England's official rate. The lure of 9% is too great to meet with any serious resistance. So the City mob has the philistines' small capital at its disposal to a greater degree than

[a] F. Engels, 'The Capture of Delhi'.

ever before. If just one of these BANKS were now to collapse, there would be a general uproar. Hence it is greatly to be regretted that the ROYAL BRITISH BANK should have crashed prematurely.

As for America, it seems almost certain that the PROTECTIONISTS will prevail as a result of the crisis. This will have lasting and disagreeable repercussions so far as the worthy English are concerned.

I don't know whether Steffen has already told you that he is leaving England. This is because the crisis has caused his sister (how, I don't know) to lose what little money she had. He is going to Germany to join forces with her, so that they can scrape along together. I think he's doing quite the wrong thing. I have it from a reliable source that Mrs Ruge (all she speaks is a kind of Saxon *patois*) is the only teacher of German in Brighton and, so greatly does demand exceed supply, that she is now launching her daughter[a] in the same TRADE. So Steffen's sister would find good EMPLOYMENT in Brighton were Steffen himself able to get on better with people. Apropos Ruge. Some months ago the old jackass sent out a prospectus for the resuscitation of the *ci-devant*[b] *Deutsche Jahrbücher*,[244] the main object of which is to combat materialism in the natural sciences and in industry; *idem* the proliferation of comparative linguistics, etc.—everything, in short, that calls for exact knowledge. To carry out his scheme he requires 1,000 subscribers *à* 10 talers. Over a period of 2 months *summa summarum* 40, I repeat 40, enthusiasts for 'intellectual freedom' have come forward. The muster-roll of his adherents in Germany is, CONSEQUENTLY, far from creditable.

I know nothing about Mr Dronke save that some months ago he urged Freiligrath to play the middleman (viz. the discounter) in a kite-flying operation upon which he thought to embark with old Naut. Freiligrath, of course, sent him away with a flea in his ear. Shortly afterwards he wrote saying that, though his circumstances were 'quite good', he was prepared to work anywhere as a clerk at a salary of £200-250, and asked Freiligrath to look out for a post of this kind. All this would seem to indicate that he is about to make his exit from the world of commerce.

Becker[c] has been released from prison; Bürgers, on the other hand, has been subjected to additional restrictions.

In one of your letters you say that the manufacturers will be able to make headway only when cotton is at 6d.[d] But won't the substantial curtailment of production soon bring COTTON prices down to that point anyway?

---

[a] Hedwig Ruge - [b] former - [c] Hermann Heinrich Becker - [d] See this volume, p. 202.

Jones is playing a very inane role. As you know, long before the crisis and with no particular end in view unless to provide a pretext for agitation during the lull, he proposed to hold a Chartist conference to which bourgeois radicals (not just Bright, but even men like Cunningham) were also to be invited.[245] The general idea was to come to a compromise with the bourgeois whereby *they* were to be given the BALLOT and, in return, accord MANHOOD SUFFRAGE to the workers. This proposal gave rise to splits in the Chartist Party and these in turn involved Jones even more deeply in his project. Now, instead of making use of the crisis and substituting genuine agitation for an ill-chosen pretext for agitation, he clings to his NONSENSE; he shocks the working-men by preaching co-operation with the bourgeois while in no way inspiring in the latter the slightest degree of confidence. To complete his ruin he is being cajoled by some of the radical papers. In his own sheet[a] that old ass Frost, whom he himself proclaimed a hero and appointed chairman of his conference, has attacked him in a brutally outspoken letter in which *inter alia* he tells him that if he considers that the co-operation of the MIDDLE CLASS is necessary—and *nothing* can be done *without* it—he should speak out *bona fide*. Who, Frost goes on to ask, gave him the right to draw up the programme for the conference *without* consulting his allies, and who empowered him to appoint Frost chairman and himself to play the dictator, etc.?[b] So now he's in hot water and, for the first time, is playing a role that is not merely *inane* but also *ambiguous*. I haven't seen him for some while but now intend to call on him. I believe him to be an honest man and, since in England it is impossible for *A PUBLIC CHARACTER* to render himself 'impossible' by his stupidities, all he has to do is extricate himself as soon as he can from his self-laid snare. The ass should begin by *forming* a party, for which purpose he must go to the manufacturing districts. Then the radical bourgeois will come to him in search of compromise.

Salut.

Your

K. M.

First published abridged in *Der Briefwechsel zwischen F. Engels und K. Marx*, Bd. 2, Stuttgart, 1913 and in full in: Marx and Engels, *Works*, First Russian Edition, Vol. XXII, Moscow, 1929

Printed according to the original

Published in English in full for the first time

---

a *The People's Paper* - b 'Mr. John Frost to the Secretary of the Chartists of Nottingham', *The People's Paper*, No. 289, 14 November 1857.

110

ENGELS TO MARX

IN LONDON

Manchester, 7 December 1857

Dear Marx,

Last week, what with prices eternally fluctuating and stocks building up, I was forced by the crisis to do a great deal of quill-pushing and so couldn't write to you but only send you *Guardians*.

In your last there's a SLIGHT MISTAKE. You say that if 'the price of corn, sugar, etc., is currently being maintained it is because their OWNERS are discounting the bills drawn on them for the same instead of selling the commodities'.[a] They, as the *drawees*, cannot discount the bills; all they have to do with bills is accept them and pay them when they fall due. The HOLDERS of commodities can only protect themselves against forced selling by obtaining advances on the commodities. UNDER THE CIRCUMSTANCES this will be difficult, and in any case the amount of these advances will be reduced by the tremendous fall in the price of commodities (35% in the case of sugar!) and the certain knowledge that, as soon as *some degree* of forced selling becomes unavoidable, the value of the commodities will fall still further. So whereas the HOLDERS formerly received advances amounting to $^2/_3$ or $^3/_4$ of the *higher* value of the commodities, they will now receive at most $^1/_2$ of the *reduced* value, i.e. about half the previously obtainable advance. This will inevitably precipitate the crash. But there is also a possibility that the MINCING LANE AND MARK LANE TRADE[b] will continue a little longer in a slow decline before a few major bankruptcies occur. And come they will, as surely as in Liverpool and other ports. The amounts being lost on sugar, coffee, cotton, hides, dye-stuffs, silk, etc., etc., are colossal. The whole LOT of the 1857 cotton crop, estimated at 3 mill. bales (will be $3\,^1/_4$), is now worth £15,000,000 less than in September. One of the houses here has in transit 35,000 sacks of coffee on each of which there will be a loss of £1. The loss on Indian cotton is just as great—33%. As the bills

[a] See this volume, p. 208. - [b] Mincing Lane—a street in London, centre of wholesale trade in colonial goods; Mark Lane—a street in London where the Corn Exchange is situated.

drawn in respect of these goods fall due, bankruptcies cannot fail to occur.

The big American house which, after 2 days of negotiation with the Bank of England, recently obtained a million-pound advance, thereby saving its skin, belonged to Mr Peabody, the 4TH JULY ANNIVERSARY DINNER man. [246] Latterly even Suse & Sibeth, the soundest of houses and the only people besides Frühling & Göschen whose bills continued to be negotiable in India after 1847 without a bill of lading as guarantee, have *allegedly* been compelled to appeal to the Bank for help. This firm, S. & S., are the greatest skinflints and so easily scared that they'd rather do no business at all than run any kind of risk.

Here things still look much as they did before. Some 8 to 10 days ago Indian and Levantine buyers suddenly appeared in the market, procured what they wanted at the lowest prices and thus helped some manufacturers heavily overstocked with cotton, yarn and cloth out of the worst of their predicament. Since Tuesday (Nov. 4th?[a]) everything has been quiet again. As for the manufacturers their expenses go on, SHORT time AND FULL TIME, coal and lubricants, etc., etc., remain just as before, and only WAGES have been reduced by $^1/_3$ to $^1/_2$. Moreover, nothing is being sold, most of our SPINNERS AND MANUFACTURERS are getting very short of FLOATING CAPITAL and many of them are rotten to the core. 8 to 9 of the smaller ones have already come a cropper in the past few days, but that is only the first sign that the crisis has caught up with this class. Today I heard that the Cookes, who own the huge factory in Oxford Road (Oxford Road Twist Company), have sold their HUNTERS, FOXHOUNDS, GREYHOUNDS, etc., etc., and that one of them has dismissed his servants and left his palace, which is now *TO BE LET*. They haven't gone bust yet, but will undoubtedly be in for it soon. Another fortnight, and the dance will really be in full swing here.

Sewell's and Neck's failure will have serious repercussions in Norway, which has not been affected hitherto.

Things in Hamburg look splendid. Ulberg and Cramer (Sweden), whose debts when they failed amounted to 12,000,000 banco marks (of which 7 mill. were bills on themselves!), *had a capital of not more than 300,000 marks!!* A whole lot of chaps have got into hot water simply for want of sufficient cash when a single bill fell due, although they might have had in their desks a hundred times that amount in currently worthless bills. Never has panic assumed so perfect and classic a form as in Hamburg just now. *Everything is*

---

[a] (Nov. 4th?) added by Marx

worthless, utterly worthless, save for silver and gold. Last week also saw the failure of Christ. Matth. Schröder, a very old and wealthy house. J. H. Schröder & Co., London (his brother), telegraphed saying that if 2 million banco marks would be enough, he would send the equivalent in silver. Came the reply: 3 millions or nothing. He couldn't spare the 3 millions and Christian Matthias crashed.[247] We have debtors in Hamburg and have no idea whether they still exist or whether they've gone bust. In Hamburg the whole imbroglio is the result of the most colossal kite-flying operations that have ever been seen. They were at their most outrageous in the dealings between Hamburg, London, Copenhagen and Stockholm. Then, with the American CRASH and the fall in the price of goods, the whole business came to light and, for the moment, Hamburg is done for commercially. The German industrialists, especially those in Berlin, Saxony and Silesia, will be very hard hit.

Cotton is now 6 $^{9}/_{16}$d for MIDDLING and will no doubt soon come down to 6d. But the mills here will only be able to go on full time again provided increased production does not promptly force the price *above* 6d. Yet that is what would immediately happen just now.

Among our local philistines the crisis has induced a strong desire for the bottle. No one can bear to stay at home alone with his cares and his family. The clubs are livening up and the consumption of LIQUOR is rising sharply. The worse of a jam a chap is in, the more frenzied his efforts to cheer himself up. And then, the morning after, what more striking example of remorse, both alcoholic and moral!

This week I shall again apply myself to the *Cyclopaedia* and do as many of the C articles as possible. Just now I can't work much or for very long at a stretch, but I'll do what I can.

Warmest regards to your wife and children.

Your

F. E.

Lupus is also involved in the crisis—but it will be his luck: his Samson has gone bankrupt, so his mornings are free.

First published abridged in *Der Briefwechsel zwischen F. Engels und K. Marx*, Bd. 2, Stuttgart, 1913 and in full in: Marx and Engels, *Works*, First Russian Edition, Vol. XXII, Moscow, 1929

Printed according to the original

Published in English for the first time

111

MARX TO ENGELS

IN MANCHESTER

[London,] 8 December 1857

Dear Frederick,

While I was upstairs busy writing my last letter to you,[a] my wife down below was besieged by hungry wolves all of whom used the PRETEXT of the 'HEAVY TIMES' to dun her for money which she had not got. (Luckily £15 arrived from Germany a few days afterwards, thus enabling us TO SHIFT OFF THE EVIL DAY FOR A WEEK OR A FORTNIGHT.) WELL, in the above-mentioned circumstances I may have been a RATHER confused correspondent, but not too confused to recall my confusion that self-same evening, after posting the letter, and remark to my wife what a wry face you would pull at my bit about debtors receiving money on bills payable by themselves, etc. Ever since I have been keeping up her spirits, which have been much depressed by this *'petite guerre'*[b] with sundry scoundrels, by reflecting on how you would break it to me in the most gracious possible way. But I could hardly go so far as to expect that you would tone down the RIDICULOUS BLUNDER to a 'SLIGHT MISTAKE'.[c] MY BEST THANKS FOR THIS GRACE, SIR.

But to return to the matter in hand. According to *The Economist* it is true that the chaps in Mincing Lane and Mark Lane[d] had again been receiving LOANS on their PRODUCE, but this MOVE ceased last *Wednesday* or thereabouts. Corn, in particular, even showed an UPWARD TENDENCY for a day or two, but (flour actually) then dropped 3/- per 280 lbs as a result of the FRENCH DECREES permitting the free export of corn and flour, and significantly so yesterday as a result of the DOWNBREAK of corn prices in the Baltic. (*Nota bene*: In France, Bonaparte's measure had no more than a transient effect; though prices rose a little there, the rise immediately resulted in INCREASED SUPPLIES, which have still to find their way on to the French market.) A few corn merchants have failed here, but as yet only insignificant houses and then only OPERATORS UPON GRAIN FOR DISTANT DELIVERY. The big American SHIPMENTS arrive in the SPRING; the French will bombard England with corn AT ANY PRICE as soon as PRESSURE over

---

[a] See this volume, pp. 208-10. - [b] guerrilla warfare - [c] See this volume, p. 211. - [d] Mincing Lane—a street in London, centre of wholesale trade in colonial goods; Mark Lane—a London street where the Corn Exchange is situated.

there grows MORE SERIOUS. In my opinion—and always supposing that, in accordance with the old adage, there are several good autumns in succession—*only now* will the effects of the REPEAL of the CORN LAWS[150] begin to tell on LANDLORDS and FARMERS in England and the ANTIQUATED AGRICULTURAL DISTRESS recur in no mean fashion. The satisfactory state of the HOME TRADE resulting from industrial PROSPERITY, and the succession of bad autumns have combined to make the experiment of 1847-57 inoperative and turn REPEAL TO A DEAD LETTER.[248]

I've had a gratifying experience with the *Tribune*. On 6 November I wrote an exposé for them of the 1844 Bank Act,[132] in which I said that the next few days would see the FARCE of SUSPENSION, but that not too much should be made of this MONETARY PANIC, the real *affaire* being the impending INDUSTRIAL CRASH.[a] The *Tribune* published this as a LEADER. 3 DAYS LATER *The New-York Times* (which has entered into a feudal relationship with the London *Times*) replied to the *Tribune* to the effect that, firstly, the Bank Act would *not* be suspended, extolled the Act after the manner of the MONEY-ARTICLE WRITERS of Printing House Square,[b] and declared the TALK of an 'INDUSTRIAL CRASH' in England to be 'SIMPLY ABSURD'. This was on the 24th. The following day the *N.Y.T.* received a telegram from the *Atlantic* with the news that the Bank Act had been *suspended*, and likewise news of 'INDUSTRIAL DISTRESS'. It's nice, by the by, to see Loyd-Overstone coming out with the true reason for his fanatical advocacy of the 1844 legislation—because it permitted the 'HARD CALCULATORS' to squeeze 20-30% out of the COMMERCIAL WORLD.[c]

Nice, too, that the capitalists, who so vociferously opposed the '*droit au travail*',[d] are now everywhere demanding 'public support' from their governments and hence advocating the '*droit au profit*[e] at public expense in Hamburg, Berlin, Stockholm, Copenhagen and even England (in the form of SUSPENSION of the Acts). Also, that the philistines of Hamburg should have refused to hand out any more alms to the capitalists.

The astonishing thing about the whole business is the *affaire* in France and the attitude adopted towards it by most of the English press. Just as, after the American COLLAPSE, John Bull was represented as the calm, SELF-POSSESSED MERCHANT vis-à-vis his brother

---

[a] K. Marx, 'The English Bank Act of 1844 and the Monetary Crisis in England'.
[b] Square in London where the offices of *The Times* are situated. - [c] S. J. Loyd's speech in the House of Lords on 3 December 1857 (*The Times*, No. 22855, 4 December 1857). - [d] right to work - [e] right to profit

Jonathan, so now Jacques Bonhomme vis-à-vis John Bull. The Paris correspondent of the London *Economist* comments most ingenuously:

*'There has been not the slightest *disposition to have a panic,* though circumstances certainly appeared to justify one, and though the French have heretofore been extremely ready to rush into panics on the smallest pretexts.'*[a]

The PANIC now felt by the French bourgeoisie, despite their sanguine temperament, at the very notion of panic, is surely the best indication of what panic means in France on this occasion. The virtuous disposition of the Parisian bourgeois will, however, prove no more effective than the Hamburg ASSOCIATION FOR DISCOUNTING THE PANIC.[249] Last Sunday's *Observer* relates how the dissemination of horrible rumours about the Crédit mobilier[45] sent everyone rushing to the Bourse to rid themselves *à tout prix*[b] of their SHARES. French capital, despite the *cosmopolitan* nature therein descried by Mr Péreire, is still timid, niggardly and cautious in actual COMMERCE as it has always been. Crooked dealing (which, to be sure, has IN ITS TURN become the *sine qua non* of *respectable* trade and industry) actually exists only in branches in which the State is the *real* EMPLOYER, whether directly or indirectly. But there is no doubt that even an inherently—or, as Hegel would say, 'in himself'—bankrupt capitalist of the magnitude of the French GOVERNMENT can make SHIFT for rather longer than a PRIVATE CAPITALIST. The police measures against BULLION EXPORTS, now pretty well IN FULL VIGOR in France, and to an even greater extent the export, AT WHICH PRICES WHATEVER, of the products of the corn, silk and wine harvests, etc., have put off for a week or two the drain of BULLION from the Bank of France. Nevertheless, THE DRAIN WILL SET IN and even if, as in 1856 (October), it gets no further than the gutter, the catastrophe will be complete. Meanwhile French manufacturers are treating their workers as ruthlessly as though there had never been a revolution. THIS WILL DO GOOD. On the other hand Mr Bonaparte is using the bank as an entrepreneur for the construction of railways, now at a standstill. Doubtless the next step will be the issue of *assignats*[c] as soon as the DRAIN begins. If the fellow has the courage, and always providing he *can* pay the army properly, we may yet witness a pretty prologue.

Your information about conditions in Manchester is of the greatest interest to me, the newspapers having chosen to draw a veil over them.

---

[a] Quoted from a report in *The Economist*, No. 744, 28 November 1857. - [b] at any price - [c] Paper money issued by the French revolutionary government in 1789; withdrawn in 1797.

I am working like mad all night and every night collating my economic studies so that I at least get the outlines clear before the *déluge.*[250]

Salut.

Your

K. M.

How is your *health*? It's a long time since you supplied a bulletin.

Since Lupus keeps a regular record of our *crisis* forecasts, tell him that last Saturday's *Economist* maintains that, during the final months of 1853, throughout 1854, the autumn of 1855 and 'THE SUDDEN CHANGES OF 1856', Europe has never had more than a HAIR-BREADTH ESCAPE from the IMPENDING CRASH.[a]

First published abridged in *Der Briefwechsel zwischen F. Engels und K. Marx*, Bd. 2, Stuttgart, 1913 and in full in: Marx and Engels, *Works*, First Russian Edition, Vol. XXII, Moscow, 1929

Printed according to the original
Published in English for the first time

112

MARX TO CONRAD SCHRAMM[251]

IN ST. HÉLIER IN JERSEY

London, 8 December [1857]
9 Grafton Terrace, Maitland Park, Hampstead

Dear Schramm,

Write soon and tell us how Jersey suits you. I did not see Engels when he passed through London on his return journey because he gave me the wrong time for our meeting at the RAILWAY STATION.[b] Did that ass Reventlow reply? Not that I suppose there's anything at all to the whole affair, since in any case these AMERICANS are incapable of paying just now; I only ask because of the BEHAVIOUR of this mighty hero. And how about Mr Faucher? Has he paid up yet? That CRAZY *Berlinois*[c] GROWS FROM DAY TO DAY STUPIDER. WITNESS THE FOREIGN

---

[a] 'The Deeper Causes of the Recent Pressure', *The Economist*, No. 745, 5 December 1857. - [b] See this volume, p. 199. - [c] Berliner

NEWS OF *THE MORNING STAR*, a name that bears a certain analogy with *lucus a non lucendo*.[a] In fact the entire English press gets worse every day, even without German assistance. Quite apart from the seismic effects of the GENERAL CRISIS which must delight every connoisseur, it is truly a relief when one is no longer forced to listen every day to the ENGLISH SELF-LAUDATIONS AS TO THE 'BRAVERY' OF 'THEIR ENGLISH IN INDIA'. It was really getting on one's nerves, *this overtrading in other people's courage on the part of the English paterfamilias and penny-a-liner who lives quietly at home and is uncommonly averse to anything threatening him with the remotest chance of obtaining military glory*.

Apart from the family circle, I am now pretty well cut off here. I seldom see my few acquaintances nor, on the whole, is this any great loss. The life you lead in Jersey can hardly be much quieter. I fear that as time goes on you will weary of your stay, or have you struck up acquaintanceships OF ANY KIND? True, Harney is SO FAR quite a companionable fellow, but *toujours perdrix*[b] is, of course, apt to pall. I hope to see you again in the spring, provided you don't move further south. In any case DROP ONE OR TWO LINES.

Salut.

Your

K. M.

First published in: Marx and Engels, *Works*, First Russian Edition, Vol. XXV, Moscow, 1934

Printed according to the original

Published in English for the first time

113

ENGELS TO MARX

IN LONDON

Manchester, 9 December 1857

Dear Moor,

In haste, a few more particulars about the crisis. In Hamburg, where the crisis has been grossly exacerbated by the pedantry of

---

[a] Literally: 'a grove from not being light'. The expression, first used by Quintilian in *De institutione oratoria* (I, 6, 34), illustrates the practice ascribed to ancient Roman etymologists of deriving words from their semantic opposites, as *lucus* ('grove') from *lucere* ('to shine, be light') because a grove is not light. Marx means that despite its name *The Morning Star* is rather unilluminating. - [b] Literally: always partridge. Here: always the same thing. The phrase is attributed to the confessor of King Henry IV of France.

the old and much-famed clearing bank, this is what has happened: Schunck, Souchay & Co. here had drawn bills on Hamburg. So as to be *really* on the safe side, and although the bills were on goods, etc., etc., they sent the drawees BANK OF ENGLAND SEVEN DAY BILLS. These were indignantly returned AS SO MUCH WASTE PAPER, and the bills drawn on Hamburg duly protested with the comment that only silver now had any value! Bills bearing the endorsements of Schunck, Souchay & Co. and 2 other equally good houses, maturing in 2 months, could not be discounted last week at less than $12^1/_2$ per cent.

NB. If I give you the names of the houses concerned, it is on the understanding that this remains strictly between ourselves. I could get into the devil of a row if such an abuse of confidential information were to come to light.

The Liverpool and London PRODUCE houses will come a cropper before long. Things look grim in Liverpool; the chaps are stone broke and can't even summon up the energy to go bankrupt, while at the Exchange, or so I am told by someone who was there on Monday, faces are three times as long as they are here, though here too the storm clouds are growing steadily darker. Spinners and manufacturers are paying wages and buying coal with the money they get in for their goods and when that's gone they're sure to collapse. Yesterday the market was more listless and depressed than it had ever been before.

Someone told me he knew of 5 or 6 Indian houses whose stocks are such that they *cannot fail* to go to the wall in the very near future.

Only now are the fellows beginning to realise that the monetary speculation was the least important factor in the crisis, and the more they see this, the gloomier they look.

Health good. More tomorrow or the day after. Herewith a bundle of *Guardians*. Take a look at the little bits of local news, in which you'll find some very interesting facts.

Your

F. E.

First published abridged in *Der Briefwechsel zwischen F. Engels und K. Marx*, Bd. 2, Stuttgart, 1913 and in full in: Marx and Engels, *Works*, First Russian Edition, Vol. XXII, Moscow, 1929

Printed according to the original

Published in English for the first time

114

ENGELS TO MARX

IN LONDON

Manchester, 11 December 1857

Dear Moor,

Still VERY BUSY with bad debts and price reductions.

Never before has overproduction been so general as during the present crisis, and there's no denying that this applies to colonial produce and also to corn. That's what's so splendid, and is bound to have tremendous consequences. After all, so long as overproduction was confined to industry the thing was only half-way there, but as soon as agriculture is also affected, and in the tropics as well as in the temperate zone, it will become spectacular.

The outward and visible sign of overproduction is more or less always expansion of credit, but this time it's especially *kite-flying*: This system of making money by means of drafts on bankers or 'bill-brokers', which are either met or not before maturity according to how the thing has been arranged, is the *rule* on the Continent and among the continental houses in England. The commission houses here all do it. The system was taken to the most enormous lengths in Hamburg, where bills amounting to more than 100 million banco marks were in circulation. But there was some fearful kite-flying elsewhere and it was because of this that Sieveking, Sillam, Karr, Josling & Co., Draper, Pietroni & Co. and other London houses went under. For the most part they were the *drawees* in this LINE. Among the manufacturing businesses over here and in the HOME TRADE the thing was so arranged that instead of paying CASH IN A MONTH the fellows negotiated bills on themselves at 3 months and paid the interest. In silk manufacturing the practice increased proportionately to the rise in the price of silk. In short everyone operated in excess of his resources, *OVERTRADED*. Admittedly OVERTRADING is not synonymous with overproduction, but it amounts to exactly the same thing. A MERCANTILE COMMUNITY which has a capital of £20,000,000 thereby possesses an ability to produce, trade and consume measured by this sum. If, on this capital and as a result of kite-flying, it does business presupposing a capital of £30,000,000, production will rise by 50% and consumption will also rise as a result of prosperity, but by no means to the same degree, *disons*[a] 25%. At the end of a certain period there will inevitably be an accumulation of goods of an order 25% in excess of *bona fide,* i.e. of average requirements, *even at a time of prosperity.* This alone would be bound to precipitate the crisis, even if the money market, the weathercock of trade, were not already pointing in that direction. All that's needed is a CRASH and then, in addition to this 25%, a further 25% at least of STOCKS of all NECESSARIES will become A DRUG ON THE MARKET. The present crisis provides an opportunity for a detailed study of how overproduction is generated by the expansion of credit and by OVERTRADING. There's nothing new about the thing as such, save for the remarkably clear-cut lines along which it is now developing. In 1837-42 and 1847 they were by no means so clear-cut.

That is the pretty situation in which Manchester and the cotton industry now find themselves. Prices are low enough to permit of what the philistines call A SOUND BUSINESS. But as soon as there is the slightest increase in production, cotton will start going up, since there's none to be had in Liverpool. So they'll have to carry on working SHORT TIME, orders or no orders. Now admittedly there are orders, but they're *from places that have not yet felt the intensity of the crisis*; the commission houses know this and so they aren't buying, for to do so would involve endless wrangles, and bad debts into the bargain.

Today the market was again very depressed. Yarn worth 14 to $14^1/_2$d is offered at $11^1/_4$d and anyone offering $10^3/_4$d can have it. The Indians are out of the market. The Greeks are stuck with their corn—almost all of them deal in this, it being their chief return freight (from Galatz and Odessa). The Germans can't buy for the reasons just mentioned. The HOME TRADE houses have *forbidden* their BUYERS to order anything at all. AMERICA OUT OF THE QUESTION. Italy is suffering from the general fall in price of her raw materials. Another month, and there'll be a very nasty situation here. Small spinners and manufacturers are going under every day.

Mercks in Hamburg only survived because of the 15 mill. advance from the government and on *one* day at least their house here sent away the spinners whose accounts were due. Mercks' head man in Hamburg is the ex-imperial minister Dr Ernst Merck, a lawyer but also partner.

---

[a] let's say

Kindest regards to your wife and children. There's been no time today to go into your letter about France, etc., etc; *il faudrait trop réfléchir*.[a]

Your
F. E.

First published abridged in *Der Briefwechsel zwischen F. Engels und K. Marx*, Bd. 2, Stuttgart, 1913 and in full in: Marx and Engels, *Works*, First Russian Edition, Vol. XXII, Moscow, 1929

Printed according to the original

Published in English for the first time

115

ENGELS TO MARX

IN LONDON

Manchester, 17 December 1857

Dear Marx,

This crisis is keeping me hellishly *en haleine*.[b] Prices falling every day. Moreover we ourselves are already beginning to feel it. My old man was in a fix not long ago and we had to advance him money. However I don't imagine that it will prove serious, but that's neither here nor there just now.

Manchester is becoming ever more deeply involved. The effect of the constant pressure on the market is really tremendous. Nobody can sell anything. Every day we hear of lower offers, and anyone with a sense of the proprieties stops offering his goods for sale. Things look grim among the spinners and manufacturers. Yarn agents are no longer selling to factories except for CASH or against security. A few of the smaller people have already come a cropper but that's nothing compared with what's in store.[252]

Despite two substantial subventions, Mercks are in a complete fix, both here and in Hamburg. They are expected to go under any day, and only an extraordinary fluke could save them. The capital of the Hamburg house is said to total 4 to 5 million banco marks against LIABILITIES of 22 million (13 marks=£1). According to other reports the crisis has already whittled down the capital to 600,000 marks.

---

[a] it would require too much thought - [b] on the alert

We shall have 4 more distinct crises: 1. colonial produce, 2. corn, 3. spinners and manufacturers, 4. HOME TRADE—this not before next spring. In the woollen districts things are already beginning, and very nicely too.

Don't forget to make a note of the BALANCE-SHEETS of the firms that have failed—Bennoch, Twentyman, Reed of Derby, Mendes da Costa, Hoare, Buxton, etc. All of them most edifying.

Your views on France have since been borne out by the newspapers almost to the letter. There is sure to be a CRASH over there and the first to be involved will be the speculators of central and northern Germany.

You will presumably have made a note of the proceedings relating to Macdonald, Monteith, Stevens (London and Exchange Bank).[a] The story of the London and Exchange Bank and the BORROWED NOTES counting as SECURITY is the most splendid I have ever read.

Apart from Hamburg, northern Germany has hitherto hardly been drawn into the crisis at all. But it's beginning there now too. Heimendahl (silk doubler and merchant) has gone under in Elberfeld, and Linde & Trappenberg (SMALL WARE MANUFACTURERS) in Barmen. Both respectable firms. So far the north Germans have suffered virtually nothing but losses; in their case, as over here, the temporary disruption of the money market has a less severe effect than the protracted period over which goods have been unsaleable.

Vienna's turn will also come.

Lupus is eating humble pie; we were right.

Distress has also begun to set in among the proletariat. There are as yet few signs of revolution, for the long period of prosperity has been fearfully demoralising. The unemployed on the streets continue to beg and to idle away their time. ROBBERIES by garrotters are on the increase, but not to any serious extent.

I now have to do so much running round seeing people in order to keep track of the crisis that there's damned little time left to do any work for Dana. That, too, must be attended to in the intervals. What has he to say? And how are his payments going?

Warm regards to your wife and children.

Your

F. E.

---

[a] Reported in *The Times*, Nos. 22860, 22861, 22865 and 22866, 10, 11, 16 and 17 December 1857.

The *Guardian* always publishes the Manchester market reports on Wednesdays and Saturdays. A whole bundle goes off to you today. This morning it also published some more labour statistics.

Congratulations on your prediction about the Bank Act.[a]

First published abridged in *Der Briefwechsel zwischen F. Engels und K. Marx*, Bd. 2, Stuttgart, 1913 and in full in: Marx and Engels, *Works*, First Russian Edition, Vol. XXII, Moscow, 1929

Printed according to the original

Published in English for the first time

116

MARX TO ENGELS[20]

IN MANCHESTER

[London,] 18 December 1857

Dear Frederick,

Just a few lines written in great haste. I've just received a *3rd and final warning* from the rotten rate collector to the effect that, if I haven't paid by Monday, they'll put a BROKER in the house on Monday afternoon. If possible, THEREFORE, send me a few pounds before Monday. Financial PRESSURE is now even greater than is USUALLY the case with me because, for ABOUT 3 weeks, I have had to pay for everything *in cash* and ANYTHING LIKE CREDIT has ceased, while at the same time $^2/_3$ of all the money I receive immediately goes to meet floating DEBTS. Moreover, there is only a very little coming in, since I have hitherto been unable to send the *Tribune* more than one article.[b] So FAR AS TO PRIVATE MATTERS.

I am working enormously, as a rule until 4 o'clock in the morning. I am engaged on a twofold task: 1. Elaborating the outlines of political economy.[250] (For the benefit of the public it is absolutely essential to go into the matter *au fond*,[c] as it is for my own, INDIVIDUALLY, TO GET RID OF THIS NIGHTMARE.)

2. The *present crisis.* Apart from the articles for the *Tribune*, all I do is keep records of it, which, however, takes up a considerable amount of time. I think that, somewhere ABOUT the spring, we ought to do a pamphlet *together* about the affair[253] as a *reminder* to the German public that we are still there as always, and ALWAYS THE SAME. I have started 3 large record books—ENGLAND, GERMANY, FRANCE. All the material on the American affair is available in the

[a] See this volume, p. 215. - [b] See this volume, p. 111. - [c] thoroughly

Tribune, and can be collated subsequently. By the by, I should be glad if you would send me the *Guardian*, if possible, *every day*. It not only doubles the work but also disrupts it if I have to deal with a week or so's arrears all at once.

In France, and specially at *Havre*,[a] the fun (commercial) will probably be started by the 'Germans', whom one cannot altogether help taking into account now. Moreover—apart from the GENERAL ROTTENNESS of the bankrupt State—trade itself would seem to be exceptionally rotten in Marseilles and Bordeaux, everywhere, that is, where infiltration and intervention by foreign elements has stung the beastly *crapauds*[81] out of their lousy, mean penny-pinching and TIMIDITY. *Au fond*,[b] only in such an immobile country was a Crédit mobilier[45] both possible and inevitable. THE MORE YOU BECOME ACQUAINTED WITH THE MESSIAS OF NATIONS', THE LESS YOU LIKE HIM.

Write to me whenever you have the time, for later on you're sure to forget all the *'chronique scandaleuse'* of the crisis which is so invaluable to us. I make excerpts from your letters and enter them in the principal record books.

Salut. Kind regards to Lupus. Pieper has the satisfaction of knowing that his ex-principal Saalfeld, with whose wife he had such a tremendous row, HAS GONE TO THE WALL.

Your

K. M.

First published in *Der Briefwechsel zwischen F. Engels und K. Marx*, Bd. 2, Stuttgart, 1913

Printed according to the original

Published in English in full for the first time

117

MARX TO FERDINAND LASSALLE[82]

IN DÜSSELDORF

London, 21 December 1857
9 Grafton Terrace, Maitland Park,
Haverstock Hill

Dear Lassalle,

Of the various letters you mention I have received only one, that sent *via* Freiligrath. I didn't answer, or rather was awaiting a

[a] Le Havre - [b] at bottom

private occasion for answering which, for reasons that cannot very well be committed to paper, did not present itself. I would point out, by the by, that it was you who *first* broke off the correspondence by failing for such a long time to answer a letter dated Manchester.[a]

My thanks for *Heraclitus*.[b] I have always felt a great tenderness for this philosopher, whom I prefer above all the Ancients save Aristotle. [Later][c] philosophy—Epicurus (him in particular), Stoa and Scepticism—[I] had made the object of *special* study,[d] but for [political] rather than philosophical [...] reasons. While [tendering] my thanks, [I] must at the same time [say] that the work has *not* yet reached me.

Doubtless [Nutt's] will send it as soon as it comes into their [...] [...] to write [... Mi]nistry. My views on Palmerston you know, and these have not changed. Besides, I know nothing whatever about the paper[e] since Austrian journals are nowhere on display here, and am thus quite ignorant of its general line. Whatever the case, I should be interested to see one or two numbers.[254]

I live in great isolation here, all my friends except Freiligrath having left London. Anyway, I have no desire for intercourse. *Relativement parlant*,[f] Freiligrath is doing quite well as manager of the Swiss Bank and is still the same good-natured, sterling fellow he has always been. Lupus and Engels are in Manchester as before. We still lament the loss of Weerth.

The present commercial crisis has impelled me to set to work seriously on my outlines of political economy,[250] and also to prepare something on the present crisis. I am forced to fritter away [...] my days earning a living. [Only] the nights remain free for *real* work and that is disrupted by ill-health. I [have] not yet looked round for a publisher as I know from experience the [...] come of it [...] when I [...]. I cannot send you any news, living as I do like a hermit. Throughout last winter and summer my wife was very unwell, but has now recovered in some measure.

If you know Dr Elsner's address please send him my regards.

---

[a] Marx means his letter to Lassalle of 8 November 1855 (see present edition, Vol. 39). - [b] F. Lassalle, *Die Philosophie Herakleitos des Dunklen von Ephesos*. - [c] The manuscript of this letter is seriously damaged. The words in square brackets are editorial reconstructions. The marks of omission stand for passages that cannot be restored. - [d] Marx is referring to his *Nobebooks on Epicurean Philosophy* compiled in 1839 and his doctoral dissertation, *Difference Between the Democritean and Epicurean Philosophy of Nature* written in 1840-41. - [e] *Die Presse* - [f] relatively speaking

That old ass Ruge has, I am told, made an attempt to resuscitate his *Deutsche Jahrbücher*.[244] History will not put the clock back far enough to make this feasible.

Your
K. M.

First published in: *F. Lassalle. Nachgelassene Briefe und Schriften*, Bd. III, Stuttgart-Berlin, 1922

Printed according to the original

118

MARX TO ENGELS[20]

IN MANCHESTER

[London,] 22 December 1857

Dear Frederick,

Thou hast triumphantly snatched me out of the clutches of the Exchequer, praised be thy name—halleluiah!

Herewith a letter (with enclosure) from the great Lassalle[254] who now positively assures me that he is SERIOUSLY beginning to be known in Berlin by reason of his fame. These EFFUSIONS of a beautiful soul will amuse you and Lupus. The worthy Lassalle took up philosophy and Heraclitus[a] as he took up the Hatzfeldt case[35] and, if he is to be believed, eventually won his 'case'. It would, indeed, seem that the old school—both philologists and Hegelians—were surprised to see such a *posthumous* blossoming of a by-gone epoch. But we shall be seeing the thing for ourselves and, gift-horse or no, shall look it long and searchingly in the mouth—ON THE EXPRESS CONDITION, OF COURSE, that Heraclitus doesn't reek of garlic. *Fancy only this fellow going up and down the streets of Berlin and 'asking for himself' strutting like a peacock, a stride and a stand: biting his lips, with 'a political regard' as who should say: 'This is the man who has written Heraclit.'* The laddie might be of some service to us in finding a publisher, unless, perhaps, he's afraid that competition might endanger the reputation to which he also aspires in the field of economics, thereby losing him his 'case'. I have replied to Friedländer

[a] F. Lassalle, *Die Philosophie Herakleitos des Dunklen von Ephesos.*

through Mr Lassalle saying that, while I, too, am 'anti-French', I am no less 'anti-English', and that the last thing I could do would be to write in favour of 'Lord Pam'. So I have turned the thing down. Should Friedländer send me the *Presse* so that I can see beforehand whose spiritual offspring it is, and if the fellows want no more than one MONEY ARTICLE a week—for which they would, of course, have to shell out—I might perhaps agree. There can be no question of POLITICS in this CASE.

I have written to Lassalle, brief and cool, to say that, while I had received the letter sent through Freiligrath, I hadn't answered it for reasons that could hardly be committed to paper. For the rest a few words, no more.[a]

Schramm has written to my wife from Jersey; an extremely witty letter. For his sins, Kosmos Leiden has lost 3 of his children; 2 daughters (including Mrs Mevissen) died of consumption and one of his sons went down with the *Pacific.*

In last Sunday's issue of *Reynold's* there is a significant attack upon those APOSTATES who advocate UNION with the MIDDLE CLASS. Meaning Jones. I haven't seen the laddie for a long time. He seems to be avoiding me, for which he must have his 'raysons'. However, I shall probably surprise him—ONE FINE MORNING.

Regards to Lupus.

Your

K. M.

First published abridged in *Der Briefwechsel zwischen F. Engels und K. Marx,* Bd. 2, Stuttgart, 1913 and in full in: Marx and Engels, *Works,* First Russian Edition, Vol. XXII, Moscow, 1929

Printed according to the original
Published in English in full for the first time

119

MARX TO ENGELS

IN MANCHESTER

[London,] 25 December 1857

DEAR Frederick,

Since our first task now is to get a clear idea of conditions in France, I have been re-examining all my extracts on FRENCH

[a] See this volume, pp. 225-27.

COMMERCE, INDUSTRY AND CRISES and reached certain conclusions which I shall briefly outline for you:

1. English, North European and American crises have *never* **directly** given rise in France to a 'French crisis'; rather the effects have been entirely *passive*—chronic DISTRESS, LIMITATION OF PRODUCTION, STAGNATION OF TRADE, and GENERAL UNEASINESS. The reason: France has a favourable balance of trade with the United States, the HANSEATIC TOWNS, England, Denmark. With Sweden and Norway the balance is unfavourable, but this is more than offset by Hamburg. CONSEQUENTLY these crises can never generate a *DRAIN OF BULLION* from France and hence will *not* create A PROPERLY SO-CALLED MONETARY PANIC there. If the Bank, notwithstanding, increases the bank rate, as has happened this time, it does so merely to prevent the capitalists from placing their money more advantageously in those countries. But so long as the EXPORT OF BULLION is the inevitable consequence, not of the balance of trade but simply of the avarice of the PROFITMONGERS, it can, as Bonaparte has now once more demonstrated, be stopped by the gendarmerie. If the country with the favourable balance of trade has not granted long-term credits or ACCUMULATED PRODUCE FOR THE EXPORT TO THE CENTRES OF THE CRISES—and both are repugnant to the PEDLAR-like[a] nature of your French manufacturer and merchant—it will have to endure losses, etc., but not an *acute* crisis. Louis Philippe, too, was misled by the apparent good fortune with which France emerges from the *first* phase of a GENERAL CRISIS. In his inaugural address before the Chambers on the eve of the February revolution, he congratulated *'la belle France'* UPON THIS PRIVILEGE.

2. Admitting all this, the first phase of the crisis has already affected FRENCH INDUSTRY and COMMERCE more seriously than on any similar occasion in the past.

3. In France the first effect of the crisis—AGREEABLE TO THE NATURE OF THE *crapaud*[81]—is the timorous curtailment of EXPENDITURE and BUSINESS. Hence an accumulation of money in the Bank of France coinciding with a huge drop in the circulation of BANK DISCOUNTS. Hence—owing to the circumstance that crises always happen in the *autumn* and that every French government fears political disturbances at the year's end should the bank rate be high at the SETTLEMENT of ACCOUNTS—reduction of the bank rate in December. In December 1847 Louis Philippe ordered the Bank to reduce the bank rate to 4%.

---

[a] Marx used the word 'pedlarmassig' here, formed of the English word 'pedlar' and the German 'massig' meaning 'after the fashion of'.

4. The greater availability of capital in COMMERCE and industry simultaneously gives rise to greater BUOYANCY on the Bourse. This has been the case under Boustrapa[40] to an even greater extent than under Louis Philippe because he compelled the Bank by the Decree of 1852 to make ADVANCES ON RAILWAY SECURITIES and *fonds*[a] and Crédit foncier *papiers*, to rediscount the speculative BILLS discounted by the *Comptoir National d'escompte*,[255] and likewise to make him a further advance on the SECURITIES on which that institution had made advances already. Hence, e.g. the high price of French RAILWAY SHARES and BONDS although the RECEIPTS of the French railways since the outbreak of the crises in England have fallen disproportionately more than those over here. E.g. Orleans Railway RECEIPTS dropped by 24% between 29 October and 26 November and subsequently even further. Nevertheless on 22 December Orleans Railway was quoted at 1,355 whereas on 29 October it was at 2,985.[b] It also emerges from the MONTHLY REPORT of the BANK OF FRANCE for December that, while DISCOUNTS in December have dropped by 94,236,520 frs compared with October and 49,955,500 compared with November, ADVANCES ON RAILWAY SECURITIES have risen.[c]

5. The French crisis proper does not break out until the GENERAL CRISIS has attained a certain level in Holland, Belgium, the Zollverein,[256] Italy (including Trieste), the Levant and Russia (Odessa), because in these countries the balance of trade is distinctly *unfavourable* to France; hence the direct effect of PRESSURE is MONETARY PANIC in France. Once it has hit France, it recoils on those countries *d'une manière vraiment admirable*.[d] With *Switzerland*, France is on the same footing as the United States with England. The short-term balance of trade is consistently in France's favour. But since France is substantially *in debt* to Switzerland, the latter is always apt HEAVILY TO DRAW UPON IT in times of crisis.

6. When the French crisis proper breaks out, it will play the very devil both with the SECURITY MARKET and the SECURITY of that market, the State. (This will also TELL UPON England, which AT THE

---

a stocks - b See 'Bourse du Jeudi 26 novembre 1857', *Le Moniteur universel*, No. 331, 27 November 1857; 'Bourse du Mardi 22 décembre 1857', *Le Moniteur universel*, No. 357, 23 December 1857; 'Bourse du Jeudi 29 octobre 1857', *Le Moniteur universel*, No. 303, 30 October 1857. In these sources the figure 2,985 refers to the shares of the Bank of France. The corresponding figure for Orleans Railways is 1,300, which bears out Marx's argument on the buoyancy of railway stock. - c 'Situation de la banque de France et de ses succursales', *Le Moniteur universel*, Nos. 282, 317, 345, 9 October, 13 November, 11 December 1857. - d in truly grand style

PRESENT MOMENT is again gambling in FOREIGN SECURITIES in a manner splendid to behold.) The swindling, which in Hamburg, England, the United States has been the province of PRIVATE CAPITALISTS, is practised in France by the State itself, and the French PEDLARS IN TRADE were all of them GAMBLERS on the Bourse. The RECOIL from the Anglo-American crisis sufficed to bring the railways TO A DEAD-LOCK. What does Mr Bonaparte do? Compels the Bank TO BECOME IN FACT [A] RAILWAY CONTRACTOR and to make advances to the fellows on the BONDS they were authorised to ISSUE by the SETTLEMENT of 30 November 1856. In 1858 these BONDS will run to ABOUT £9 million. Thus the Crédit mobilier,[45] which on 3 December was up to its ears in trouble, is preparing to amalgamate with the Crédit foncier and the Comptoir National d'escompte. Why? Because both the latter are legally entitled to receive ADVANCES from the Bank on their SECURITIES and to have their DISCOUNTS REDISCOUNTED. So Boustrapa's plan is clear, namely to make the BANK OF FRANCE the entrepreneur for all his fraudulent schemes with the help, not of its own capital, but of the capital which it has merely on deposit and which will drain away ON THE FIRST SIGNAL GIVEN IN THE NEIGHBOURING COUNTRIES. IN FACT, this is also an admirable way of ruining the Bank. However it would hardly occur even to Mr Bona to have the *CALLS of the SHAREHOLDERS* paid by the BANK OF FRANCE. In 1858 these CALLS will amount to over £10 million for *French* railways alone under the SETTLEMENT of 30 November 1856. They will run to at least £30 million for the host of speculative concerns SUCH AS the MERCANTILE AND INDUSTRIAL CO OF MADRID (Rothschilds), the French-American Shipping Company, the Victor Emmanuel Railway, Herserange Ironworks Co., Austrian Railways, Saragossa Co., French-Swiss Railway, LAUSANNE-FRIBOURG RAILWAY, NASSAU COMPANY, Société Générale des Tanneries, Compagnie de la Carbonisation des Houilles, CHIMAY TO MARIENBOURG RAILWAY, Lombard-Venetian RAILWAY, South American STEAM NAVIGATION CO., etc. The French haven't an earthly hope of paying these CALLS. Moreover the GERMANS, HOLLANDERS, SWISS, the LARGE HOLDERS OF FR[ENCH] SECURITIES, will sell them AT ANY PRICE on the Paris Bourse at the first sign of SERIOUS ALARM, be it in France or due to PRESSURE AT HOME. So it seems that Boustrapa will hardly be able to extricate himself in 1858 unless he holds out for a bit longer with the help of martial law and *assignats*.[a] The whole rotten old structure is falling to pieces and the ludicrously rash surge hitherto manifested

---

[a] Paper money issued by the French revolutionary government in 1789; withdrawn in 1797.

by the SECURITY MARKET in England, etc., will likewise end in disaster.[257]

Salut.

Your

K. M.

Pieper arrived today on a visit.

As regards the *Comptoir National d'escompte de Paris,* be it also noted that this institution, which was set up by the provisional government for the purpose of making bills discountable on the basis of only two signatures and similar less stringent requirements, was empowered by Boustrapa in 1851, only a day or two after the coup d'état, TO MAKE ADVANCES ON *Rentes Françaises, les actions et obligations industrielles ou de crédit constituées en sociétés anonymes.*[a] Advances on these SECURITIES amounted to £940,000 in 1854/55 and nearly £1,500,000 in 1855/56. Moreover, in 1851 it was given the right TO ESTABLISH *un 'Sous Comptoir des Chemins de Fer',*[b] whose sole BUSINESS was to make advances on RAILWAY SHARES and BONDS. At the end of JUNE 1852 its ADVANCES were £520,000, at the end of 1852 £1,240,000, 1852/53—£3,600,000; at the end of 1854: £4,560,000, i.e. ABOUT 9×the ADVANCES in 1851. It's the same delectable business that broke the neck of the *Scotch Exchange Banks* in 1846/47.

Has Dr Borchardt not yet suspended his payments?

I trust you won't go out tippling too much during the holiday and these exciting times in Manchester and that you'll pay due attention to your health. Warmest regards to Lupus.

WHAT IS FRIEND CHARLEY[c] about? and OLD Hill?

First published slightly abridged in *Der Briefwechsel zwischen F. Engels und K. Marx,* Bd. 2, Stuttgart, 1913 and in full in: Marx and Engels, *Works,* First Russian Edition, Vol. XXII, Moscow. 1929

Printed according to the original

Published in English for the first time

[a] French government stocks, the shares and bonds of industrial and banking concerns incorporated with limited liability. - [b] a railway suboffice - [c] presumably Charles Roesgen

120

MARX TO ENGELS

IN MANCHESTER

[London,] 30 December [1857]

Dear Frederick,

Come what may I shall have to deal with the Lucknow-Oudh affair on FRIDAY (1ST OF JANUARY). Could you let me have ANY ARTICLE, HOWEVER SHORT, on this subject by the day after tomorrow.[a] IT WOULD BE EXTREMELY SEASONABLE.

A happy New Year to you.

Your

K. M.

The enclosed greetings are not to be handed to *Lupus* until New Year's Day.

First published in: Marx and Engels, *Works*, First Russian Edition, Vol. XXII, Moscow, 1929

Printed according to the original

Published in English for the first time

121

ENGELS TO MARX[184]

IN LONDON

[Manchester,] 31 December 1857

Dear Moor,

I have searched the whole town for newspapers containing INDIAN NEWS, having sent you my *Guardians* on the subject the day before yesterday. I can't get hold of the relevant numbers, either from the *Guardian* itself or from the *Examiner & Times,* nor has Belfield any left. I thought you had already dealt with this affair on Tuesday. In the circumstances I cannot do the article,[b] which is

[a] In reply to this request Engels wrote the article 'The Siege and Storm of Lucknow'. - [b] The article in question, 'The Siege and Storm of Lucknow', was written later and published in the *New-York Daily Tribune* on 30 January 1858. In it Engels used some of the ideas expressed in this letter.

all the more vexing in that this is the first afternoon in 4 weeks on which I'd have been able to do it without having to neglect urgent business. In future, let me know as early as possible what your intentions are as to military articles; just now 24 hours makes quite a difference to me.

In any case, detailed information is so frightfully scarce, what there is being based almost wholly on telegraphic despatches from Cawnpore to Calcutta, that it's virtually impossible to write a critical analysis.[258] The only points I can think of are these: It is 40 MILES from Cawnpore to Lucknow (Alam Bagh)—Havelock's forced marches show that in India 15 miles a day over a protracted period is a very long march. Accordingly, with only 2-3 marches ahead of him, Colin[a] ought to have arrived at Alam Bagh no later than the 3rd day after his departure from Cawnpore, WITH PLENTY OF DAYLIGHT STILL LEFT TO ATTACK AT ONCE. It is by these standards that Colin's march must be judged; I can no longer recall the dates. 2. He had, after all, some 7,000 men (far more had been counted on, so between Calcutta and Cawnpore the march must have gone atrociously badly and a great many men been lost) and if he beat the Oudhi with approximately 7,000 men (including the garrisons of Alam Bagh and Lucknow), it was no great feat. *An army of 5-7,000 Englishmen has always been thought fully sufficient to go anywhere and do anything in the open field in India. That stamps the opponents at once.* A further consideration is that the Oudhi, although the most warlike race of the Ganges valley, were greatly inferior to the Sepoys as regards discipline, cohesion, weapons, etc., etc., precisely because they had never come under direct European organisation. Hence the main battle took the form of *a running fight, that is to say a skirmishing engagement in which the Oudhians were pushed back from post to post. Now it is true the British are, with the Russians, the worst light infantry in Europe, but they have learnt something in the Crimea, and at all events they had this great advantage over the Oudhians that their line of skirmishers was properly and regularly supported by pickets and lines the whole under one individual commander and cooperating towards a single end; while their opponents in the normal Asiatic manner, dispersed in irregular clusters, everyone pressing to the front, thus offering a sixfold aim to the British, having no regular supports or reserves and each cluster commanded by its own clannish chief, acting independently of every other clan. For it must be repeated, up to now we have not heard

---

[a] Colin Campbell

in a single instance that any insurrectionary army in India had been properly constituted under a recognized chief.* No other indication as to the nature of the fighting is given in the despatches nor, for that matter, any description of the terrain or particulars about the employment of troops, so that it's absolutely impossible for me to say anything further (let alone from memory).

As to France, you are right IN EVERY PARTICULAR, so far as I can judge. There, too, things have taken a normal course up till now. Over here the affair is in its infancy so far as HOME TRADE is concerned; it is to this category that the two London houses in the Manchester TRADE belong. But that's only a beginning. This kind of firm can only become seriously embroiled when the pressure has lasted for 8-12 months. The course of the present crisis would seem to me to have more affinity with that of 1837-42 than with any other—if one disregards the splendid universality and all-embracing nature of the present one. Just now people here are deluding themselves into thinking that THE CRISIS IS OVER because the first phase, the monetary crisis with its immediate consequences, is over. *Au fond*[a] each individual bourgeois still believes that *his particular* branch of business, and notably his own business, has been THOROUGHLY SOUND and, being able to measure themselves against the STANDARD of such splendid swindlers as Monteith, Macdonald, etc., etc., they naturally imagine themselves to be uncommonly virtuous. Nevertheless, this will not compensate Mr. Troost for losing $^2/_3$ to $^3/_4$ of his fortune on his 35,000 sacks of coffee, nor Mr SENATOR Merck for the fact that his shipments and other such operations to the tune of 22 million banco marks will eat up the whole of his capital. John Pondu, a Scot who has shot up here like a gigantic mushroom over the past 5 years, has, together with 5 others, 7,000 bales of silk in transit on which the loss will be £300,000. All this will not come to a head until March or April, and the tremendous efforts to push up prices on the commodity market will be frustrated at regular intervals as vessels arrive. It would seem that icy weather and east winds are at present preventing ships from arriving here. Should this continue for a week or a fortnight, the price of all produce will undoubtedly rise, only to fall all the more precipitously as soon as a west wind brings in an entire fleet. *Voilà ce qui s'appelle l'offre et la demande en temps de crise.*[b] STOCKS of cotton, too, are beginning to pile up in Liverpool—400,000 bales by today's count, A RATHER MORE

---

[a] at heart - [b] That's what supply and demand is like in time of crisis.

THAN AVERAGE STOCK. There's still better to come and COTTON is sure to fall again in the spring; it has just risen $^{1}/_{2}$d because de Jersey & Co.—a local firm which supplies almost the whole of the Russian market—having heard last week that their cancellation of all the orders they had placed in America had duly arrived—went and bought about 6,000 bales in Liverpool. That livened up the market, and any spinners who could afford to do so went in and bought something so as to supply their needs at the low prices. This alarmed, or rather put heart into, some other houses here and they, too, bought yarn and cloth so as to come in at the 'bottom'. It won't last long; to start with we shall, I think, have moderate UPS AND DOWNS here, the tendency being generally downward, perhaps also rising a little—one can't say exactly—until somewhere or other the lightning strikes again. At all events, there's a bad year ahead for spinners and manufacturers, if only because of insufficient demand and excessive supply. Stagnating pressure—that is the greatest danger so far as our local bourgeois are concerned. Monetary crises are of small account here, since all credits are extremely short-term (2-6 weeks).

On Saturday I went fox-hunting—7 hours in the saddle. That sort of thing always keeps me in a state of devilish exhilaration for several days; it's the greatest physical pleasure I know. I saw only 2 out of the whole FIELD who were better horsemen than myself, but then they were also better mounted. This will really put my health to rights. At least 20 of the chaps fell off or came down, 2 horses were done for, 1 fox killed (I was in AT THE DEATH); otherwise no mishaps. Admittedly there were no real fox-hunters at the meet; they ride far better than I do, of course. I shall pass your thing on to Lupus.

And now, a happy New Year to all your family and to the year of strife 1858.

Your

F. E.

First published abridged in *Der Briefwechsel zwischen F. Engels und K. Marx*, Bd. 2, Stuttgart, 1913 and in full in: Marx and Engels, *Works*, First Russian Edition, Vol. XXII, Moscow, 1929

Printed according to the original

Published in English in full for the first time

1858

122

MARX TO ENGELS

IN MANCHESTER

[London,] 1 January 1858

Dear Engels,

No article having arrived from you today, I have sent *none* to New York and shall therefore send 2 next week. I hope you will have one READY by Tuesday,[a] it being absolutely essential to write about India since a great STRUGGLE over military no less than commercial matters is taking place between the *Tribune* and *The New-York Times*. The *Times*, you see, RETAINS the London *Times*.

Enclosed:

1 *Star*,

1 *Daily News*,

1 *Overland Mail* (the most recent not yet out).

No doubt this will be sufficient.

Your

K. M.

First published in: Marx and Engels, *Works*, First Russian Edition, Vol. XXII, Moscow, 1929

Printed according to the original

Published in English for the first time

123

MARX TO ENGELS

IN MANCHESTER

[London,] 5 January [1858]

Dear Engels,

Have had your note. You don't say whether you have received my letter *enclosing those of Lassalle and Friedländer*.[b] I'd like to be sure that both will be preserved.

---

[a] F. Engels, 'The Siege and Storm of Lucknow'. - [b] See this volume, pp. 227-28

As to C, I am IN FACT in a considerable quandary. Nothing more has been sent to Dana since 27 November,[259] as I finished my own share of it (i.e. the non-military stuff) long ago. If circumstances in Manchester don't admit of your seriously applying yourself to the business this month, I shall have to give it up altogether and tell Dana on some PRETEXT or other that I can't go on with the *Cyclopaedia*. The fact that I send him long, new lists before polishing off the old ones cannot fail in the end to arouse his suspicions and compromise me. CONSEQUENTLY he's not even answering, let alone sending anything fresh. Nor can work of this kind be remunerative when there are constant hiatuses of a month or more.

STILL, I try to avoid mentioning the matter to you because the last thing I want is to subject you to any strain that might damage your health. YET sometimes it seems to me that, if you could manage to do a *little* every two days or so, it might act as a CHECK on your junketings which, from what I know of Manchester and AT THE PRESENT EXCITED TIMES, seem to me 'unavoidable' and far from good for you.

Nor can there be any question at present of my taking over the military stuff, which would entail spending a great deal of time at the Museum[a] to no real effect, for it's absolutely essential that I should finish off my other work[250]—and it takes up *all* my time—even if the house should come tumbling about my ears!

So, *my boy, try to come to a definitive resolution—one way or the other*.

Warm regards.

Your

K. M.

First published abridged in *Der Briefwechsel zwischen F. Engels und K. Marx*, Bd. 2, Stuttgart, 1913 and in full in: Marx and Engels, *Works*, First Russian Edition, Vol. XXII, Moscow, 1929

Printed according to the original

Published in English for the first time

---

[a] the British Museum Library

124

ENGELS TO MARX

IN LONDON

Manchester, 6 January 1858

Dear Moor,

You will have had the article[a] in good time, at any rate, as I posted it *before midnight* on Monday, which means that it must have been delivered between 12 and 1 o'clock.

I received Lassalle's letter and also wrote to tell you how amused Lupus and I were at the man who wrote Heraclitus.[b] Can my letter have gone astray?[260]

During the worst of the crisis it was absolutely impossible for me to think of anything but the GENERAL CRASH. I could neither read nor write and was, moreover, still irritable as a result of my illness. Then came the HOLIDAYS with fox-hunting and other such frivolities, but now that's all over and I am beginning to feel in need of a quieter occupation and way of life. Such being the case—with the added inducement of a good bout of catarrh—the letter C has come as a boon to me, and I shall embark on it this very evening. I don't imagine it will take me very long; at any rate I shall put my best foot forward and you will be able to send something off each week. Come to that, if '*Army*' arrived in October and in time for Volume I[261] then surely C, arriving in January, will be in time for Volume III. In view of the crisis the chaps won't be hurrying into print, otherwise Dana would have written long ago. If you hear from him, by the way, let me know.

Incidentally the crisis, presently at a standstill, is about to take a new turn, at least so far as Manchester and the COTTON industry are concerned. On Monday a great many spinners went to Liverpool and bought 12,000 bales in order to restock to some extent, since many of them had nothing left. This pushed up the price of cotton, and at the same time the Greeks entered the market here and bought a fair amount, which brought about a corresponding rise locally. In Manchester and in Liverpool, the price has already risen by $^3/_4$d (per lb) above the lowest point. Now the buyers are shying away again but, if the easterlies persist, cotton and yarn will

---

[a] F. Engels, 'The Siege and Storm of Lucknow'. - [b] F. Lassalle, *Die Philosophie Herakleitos des Dunklen von Ephesos.*

get even lower before the arrival of full shiploads round about February or March. What a thing to do, pushing up the price of yarn and cotton WITH FACTORIES ON SHORT TIME! It can only result in restricting demand more than ever and, if this has no immediate effect on prices, it is merely because production rises and falls *with* demand. The price of MIDDLING is again somewhere between $6^1/_4$ and $6^3/_8$—today probably $6^1/_2$d, although I haven't yet seen the closing prices.

As regards produce, too, the difficulty of investing money seems to have enabled the chaps to effect once again a small, temporary rise which will last until the wind goes round to the west.

The vast amount of surplus capital in the market is, by the way, truly astounding and proves yet again what colossal dimensions everything has assumed since 1847. It would not surprise me in the least if, even before the crisis has passed through its remaining phases, this superfluity of FLOATING CAPITAL were to bring about renewed speculation in shares. This superfluity of disposable capital has undoubtedly helped to keep speculation going in France, and to such good effect that now, having survived the panic, the Crédit mobilier[45] can claim to be one of the soundest institutions in the world.

The letter about Lassalle must have reached you; have another look for it. I wrote it 2 or 3 days after receiving Lassalle's letter.

Enclosed with my day-before-yesterday's article were a few lines from Lupus to your wife and the girls. Cordial regards to them from me.

Your

F. E.

Today a line or two from Schramm saying that he had been rather worse but has now improved again. His worthy brothers now seem to be making the crisis a pretext for leaving him very much in the lurch. He talks of going either to Krefeld or to Virginia so as not to have to worry about where his next meal is coming from! I shall send him five pounds.

First published abridged in *Der Briefwechsel zwischen F. Engels und K. Marx*, Bd. 2, Stuttgart, 1913 and in full in: Marx and Engels, *Works*, First Russian Edition, Vol. XXII, Moscow, 1929

Printed according to the original

Published in English for the first time

125
ENGELS TO MARX
IN LONDON

Manchester, 7 January 1858

Dear Moor,

Herewith the beginning of C.[262] I shall try and do a few more articles tomorrow evening. It seems to me that there are only 2 articles for which material will be difficult to obtain—perhaps impossible in sufficient quantity—namely, CAPS (PERCUSSION)[263] and 'CAMP' (ROMAN, HEBREW, GREEK). The excerpts I made from Rüstow about Caesar's camp[a] amount to *very little* for, though I had ordered my own copy of Rüstow, the bookseller supplied an altogether different book. In the case of PERCUSSION CAPS, what I chiefly need is the story of the discovery of potassium tetrachlorate and its explosive qualities, likewise the dates when percussion fire-arms were introduced into the various armies. These two things would be useful to have. If you could manage to go to the British Museum and rout out something on this for me I could soon have these articles ready also, otherwise they'll hang fire since the libraries I use up here have no information on the subject.

If, by the way, Monsieur Dana can't be bothered to reply when we send him our lists, he has only himself to blame. He could have sent a list for D long ago. Now I shall make one out myself. At all events the chap seems to be taking the whole business very lightly; I only hope he's sent you some money for it, otherwise it's high time to start kicking up a fuss.

Charley[b] is in Holland and will be going to Switzerland. Luckily the shortage of orders makes it possible for me to leave most of the tasks connected with the year's end to the office boys, so that I'm not unduly burdened with work. THAT'S ONE GOOD JOB.

I enclose today's *Guardian* from which you will see that there is still a lot of SHORT TIME here. Next week it may ease again somewhat. At present I am sending you only those *Guardians* in which there's something of commercial interest.

I am reading, *inter alia*, Clausewitz's *Vom Kriege*. An odd way of philosophising, but *per se* very good. On the question as to whether one should speak of the art or the science of war, he says that, more than anything else, war resembles commerce. Combat is

---

[a] W. Rüstow, *Heerwesen und Kriegführung C. Julius Cäsars*. - [b] Charles Roesgen

to war what cash payment is to commerce; however seldom it need happen in reality, everything is directed towards it and ultimately it is bound to occur and proves decisive.[a]

Many regards to your wife and little ones.

Your

F. E.

First published abridged in *Der Briefwechsel zwischen F. Engels und K. Marx*, Bd. 2, Stuttgart, 1913 and in full in: Marx and Engels, *Works*, First Russian Edition, Vol. XXII, Moscow, 1929

Printed according to the original

Published in English for the first time

126

MARX TO ENGELS

IN MANCHESTER

[London,] 7 January 1858

Dear Frederic,

I received your article[b] at 5 o'clock on Tuesday afternoon. It is HIGHLY AMUSING and will delight the Yankees. The news from India, by the by, is no longer quite so favourable to the worthy English. POOR Havelock!

I have definitely not had your letter about Lassalle.[c] So it has either got held up somewhere in Manchester or has been intercepted down here.[260]

Lupus' letter to the family, who send you their regards, HAS PRODUCED A GREAT SENSATION.

Pieper was here during the Christmas holidays. He arrived in a state of alcoholic remorse and was more vapid and boring THAN EVER. The older the fellow grows the worse he becomes. He seems to have acquired the pleasant habit of drinking first thing in the morning, not tea or coffee, but a PINT [OF] STOUT, which gives him A SHEEP'S EYE for the rest of the day. Indeed, the combination of dilettantism and sententiousness, *fadaise*[d] and pedantry makes him ever harder to stomach. And, as often in the case of such laddies,

---

[a] C. von Clausewitz, *Vom Kriege*. Vol. I, Book 2, Chapter 3. - [b] F. Engels, 'The Siege and Storm of Lucknow'. - [c] See this volume, p. 240. - [d] vapidity

there lurks, beneath an apparently sunny temperament, much irritability, moodiness and crapulous despondency. He has presented the children with two daguerreotypes of his charming person which are truly sublime and might be entitled 'Pieper with countenance exposed'. Both confected on the very morning of his arrival by rail in London. The first, still drunk with sleep, A MOST ABJECT PICTURE OF MENTAL AND MORAL DEJECTION: great, big mouth, flaccid jowl, blurred, sprawling features, in his eyes A STUPENDOUS EXPRESSION OF NOTHINGNESS. In the 2nd our friend had already pulled himself together and remembered that he was the handsome and *aimable* Pieper. It is the awakening of complacency and its victory over UTTER DEGRADATION. The first portrait—PIEPER AS HE *IS*, the 2nd AS HE *APPEARS* TO HIMSELF and the world in general. As little Jenny aptly remarked, all that was wanting to put the fellow in a nutshell was his drama, *WHAT IS THE MATTER?*

I enclose an interesting document which the Urquhartites, with that IMPERTURBABLE importunity of theirs, have extracted from the BOARD OF TRADE.[264] In addition to the BAD STATE of England's balance of trade during the past 3 years, it will show you *inter alia* how much money was being made by *Prussia* at the time of the Russian war; further, that our *HANSA TOWNS* are AT THE HEAD of those regions whose balance of trade *favours* England.

The momentary LULL in the crisis is, or so it seems to me, most advantageous to our interests—PARTY INTERESTS, I mean. Even in 1848, after the first LULL, England suffered some very severe blows at 2 or 3 INTERVALS, and at that time the crater had already shifted from where it had been in April 1847, etc.

The 'Neapolitan Question',[103] which has caused earnest politicians such a lot of head-scratching, has now been resolved by the EARTHQUAKE IN A MOST DELIGHTFUL MANNER. At least that's what the POT-HOUSE POLITICIANS OF *THE MORNING ADVERTISER* say.

You won't forget to send the *Guardian*, will you?

Above all I beg you to take care of your health. Times will get better and will make considerable CLAIMS on your BODY. So temper it and see that it comes to no harm.

Salut.

Your

K. M.

Apropos. In his last number of the *Pionier* Heinzen remarks that, while it was quite comprehensible that the stultified workers in Germany should have been deluded by two sophists into believing they formed a *distinct class because* they plied a *plane*, it was altogether too much of a good thing when, as now, the cry of class was raised among the workers at every MEETING in America! He shouts about the obfuscation of the masses, who are not susceptible of wisdom. Proclaims 'spiritual revolution' and, in opposition to the class prophets, a new triumvirate—*Goethe, G. St.-Hilaire and Karl Heinzen!!!*

In recent weeks the *Crédit mobilier*[45] has pushed up the price of its shares to an exceptional height by the ANNOUNCEMENT OF A DIVIDEND OF 25 P.C., THIS TIME undoubtedly paid OUT OF CAPITAL.

First published abridged in *Der Briefwechsel zwischen F. Engels und K. Marx*, Bd. 2, Stuttgart, 1913 and in full in: Marx and Engels, *Works*, First Russian Edition, Vol. XXII, Moscow, 1929

Printed according to the original

Published in English for the first time

127

MARX TO ENGELS

IN MANCHESTER

[London,] 11 January [1858]

Dear Frederick,

'Campaign', etc.[262] received. In the next day or so I shall go to the Museum[a] to look up the matters in question.[b]

Affairs in India—with Windham for HERO—are again taking an interesting TURN. If we have fuller particulars this week, by Wednesday or thereabouts, I shall have to send off something on the subject to the *Tribune*.[265]

In elaborating the PRINCIPLES of economics[250] I have been so damnably held up by errors in calculation that in DESPAIR I have applied myself to a rapid revision of algebra. I have never felt at home with arithmetic. But by making a detour via algebra, I shall quickly get back into the way of things.

Your health bulletins are too cursory. I'd like you to go into more detail, FOR INSTANCE, have all your sores healed up?

More in my next.

Your

K. M.

---

[a] the British Museum Library - [b] See this volume, p. 241.

The reading-room of the British Museum, London, where Marx worked

I hunted through Clausewitz,[a] more or less, when doing Blücher. The fellow possesses a COMMON SENSE bordering on the ingenious.

First published in *Der Briefwechsel zwischen F. Engels und K. Marx,* Bd. 2, Stuttgart, 1913

Printed according to the original

Published in English for the first time

128

ENGELS TO MARX

IN LONDON

Manchester, 14 January 1858
7 Southgate

Dear Marx,

Herewith the article,[b] though it has just occurred to me that by a ludicrous slip I have written Wilson throughout instead of *Inglis*; perhaps you would alter this as there's no time to do so now.

I shall do a few more C's for Tuesday, and finish 'Cavalry', which should make a good article and also be somewhat longer.

Apropos, have you done 'Coehoorn' (Baron)? If not I have some excellent material.

NB. I've *no material whatever* on *'Catapults'*—there should be something in Ersch and Gruber.[c]

The Lucknow garrison's greatest act of heroism consisted in the fact THAT THEY HAD TO FACE EVERY DAY THE 'COARSE BEEF' COOKED BY THE LADIES, *'ENTIRELY UNAIDED'*. Must have been damned badly cooked. *The Daily News* has something on Windham, but not enough.

Kindest regards to your wife and children.

Your

F. E.

My health is good. The sores have all been healed for the last 6 weeks. Heckscher is very satisfied with the way the thing is

---

[a] C. von Clausewitz, *Der Feldzug von 1812 in Rußland, der Feldzug von 1813 bis zum Waffenstillstand und der Feldzug von 1814 in Frankreich* and *Der Feldzug von 1815 in Frankreich.* - [b] F. Engels. 'The Relief of Lucknow'. - [c] *Allgemeine Encyclopädie der Wissenschaften und Künste* ... bearbeitet und herausgegeben von J. S. Ersch und J. G. Gruber.

progressing, but he's still limiting what I eat and drink—not so much in quantity as in kind.

First published in *Der Briefwechsel zwischen F. Engels und K. Marx*, Bd. 2, Stuttgart, 1913

Printed according to the original

Published in English for the first time

129

ENGELS TO MARX

IN LONDON

[Manchester,] 15 January 1858

Dear Marx,

Judging by the enclosed letter from Harney, it seems most doubtful whether Schramm is still alive. I wrote to Harney straight away. As soon as I hear anything further I shall let you know.

Your

F. E.

First published in *Der Briefwechsel zwischen F. Engels und K. Marx*, Bd. 2, Stuttgart, 1913

Printed according to the original

Published in English for the first time

130

MARX TO ENGELS[266]

IN MANCHESTER

[London,] 16 January 1858

Dear Frederick,

You, too, will have had a letter from Harney about friend Schramm. There was no prospect of recovery. A pity, though, that money worries—for which the fat London philistine[a] is to blame—should have clouded his last days.

a Rudolf Schramm, brother of Conrad Schramm

Your article[a] is SPLENDID and IN STYLE and MANNER altogether reminiscent of the *Neue Rheinische Zeitung* in its heyday. As for Windham, he may be a very bad general, but on this occasion the man was undone by what was the making of him at the Redan[267]—unseasoned troops. I am generally of the opinion that in terms of bravery, self-reliance and STEADINESS this, the second army England has committed to India (and of which not a man will return), will not be able to hold a candle to the first, which seems to have dwindled away almost entirely. As regards the effect of the climate on the troops, while temporarily in charge of the military DEPARTMENT I showed in various articles by exact calculations that mortality was DISPROPORTIONATELY higher than stated in the official English despatches.[268] In view of the DRAIN OF MEN and BULLION which she will cost the English, India is now our best ally.

On Monday I shall again visit the Museum,[b] after which I shall send you 'Catapult'—along with the other stuff you ask for—drawn from the best sources. I have *not* done *'Coehoorn'*, as it would have taken me too much time to unearth the correct sources.

I am EXCEEDINGLY glad to learn that your health is progressing WELL. For the past 3 weeks I, too, have again been dosing myself and only stopped doing so today. I had been overdoing very much my nocturnal labours, accompanied, it is true, by mere lemonade on the one hand, but AN IMMENSE DEAL OF TOBACCO on the other. I am, by the way, discovering some nice arguments.[250] E.g. I have completely demolished the theory of profit as hitherto propounded. What was of great use to me as regards *method* of treatment was Hegel's *Logic* at which I had taken another look BY MERE ACCIDENT, Freiligrath having found and made me a present of several volumes of Hegel, originally the property of Bakunin. If ever the time comes when such work is again possible, I should very much like to write 2 or 3 sheets making accessible to the common reader the *rational* aspect of the method which Hegel not only discovered but also mystified.

Of all recent economists, Monsieur Bastiat with his *Harmonies économiques* represents the very dregs of fatuity at their most concentrated. Only a *crapaud*[81] could have concocted an harmonious *pot-au-feu*[c] of this kind.

What do you think of our friend Jones[245]? I still refuse to believe that the chap has sold himself. Perhaps his experience of

---

[a] F. Engels, 'The Relief of Lucknow'. - [b] the British Museum Library - [c] stew

1848 lies heavy on his stomach. So great is his faith in himself that he may think himself capable of exploiting the MIDDLE CLASS or imagine that if only, ONE WAY OR THE OTHER, Ernest Jones could be got into Parliament, world history could not fail to take A NEW TURN. The best of it all is that—out of SPITE against Jones, OF COURSE—Reynolds is now posing in his paper[a] as the most rabid opponent of the MIDDLE CLASS and of all compromise. Mr B. O'Brien has likewise become an IRREPRESSIBLE CHARTIST AT ANY PRICE. Jones' only excuse is the enervation now rampant among the working class in England. However that may be, if he goes on as at present he will become either DUPE of the MIDDLE CLASS or RENEGADE. The FACT that he should now seek to avoid me as anxiously as he once used to consult me over the merest trifle is evidence of anything but a good conscience.

Herewith a letter for Lupus from Laura and Jenny. The two GIRLS naturally imagine that you might take umbrage at Lupus appearing to be preferred as a correspondent. Hence they have earnestly admonished me not to forget to tell you THAT YOURS SHALL BE THE NEXT TURN.

I shall wait another 3 weeks until the situation has pretty well come to a head and then write to Mr Dana saying that I cannot go on working for the *Tribune* if I'm restricted to *4 articles a month,* and that *6* is the minimum. In fact I am now invariably obliged to compress into 1 article sufficient material for 2, and hence am doing double the work for HALF THE PRICE. THIS WILL NEVER DO.

Did you enclose Lassalle's and Friedländer's letters[b] in the one about Lassalle[260] which went astray? For political reasons, it would be desirable to preserve them.

Salut.

Your

K. M.

First published abridged in *Der Briefwechsel zwischen F. Engels und K. Marx*, Bd. 2, Stuttgart, 1913 and in full in: Marx and Engels, *Works*, First Russian Edition, Vol. XXII, Moscow, 1929

Printed according to the original

Published in English in full for the first time

---

a *Reynolds's Newspaper* - b See this volume, pp. 227-28.

131

MARX TO ENGELS

IN MANCHESTER

[London,] 23 January 1858

Dear Engels,

I have received: 1. Copies of the *Guardian*; 2. C ('Carabine', etc.[269]). You have not told me whether you got my letter, together with an enclosure for Lupus, sent off a week ago today.[a]

Herewith a letter from Dana which you must return as it has not yet been answered. One disagreeable consequence so far as I am concerned is that I am already considerably in the fellows' debt, having miscalculated what was due to me and drawn a further amount after sending off 'Cannon'.[235] The PAY, by the by, isn't even A PENNY THE LINE.

As regards the new B articles Dana is asking for—and for me the main thing is to pay off as quickly as possible what I have overdrawn on Appleton, otherwise I shall be unable to draw anything on the *Tribune* and hence be stone broke—they are, with *one* exception, taken from the list you drew up. As regards that *one exception*—'THE HISTORY OF THE BENGAL REBELLION'—I suggest the most appropriate course would be tell Dana straight out it can't be done. How get hold of the sources at such short notice? Since it 'SHALL BE SENT AT ONCE' and must be 'AS BRIEF AS POSSIBLE', the work involved would be out of all proportion to the PAY and it would simply prevent us from getting on with the other articles. What is your opinion? The military side is the more important, but it seems to me that the whole, whether military or political, has not yet reached the stage where it could be 'sent AT ONCE'.

I cannot recall the MISTAKE IN [THE] BATTLE OF 'ALBUERA' to which Dana refers.[270]

Freiligrath writes to say that the great Ernst Dronke has arrived in London from *Paris,* having left the latter place for the first time on account of the attempted assassination.[271]

Salut.

Your

K. M.

---

[a] See this volume, p. 250.

There were some nice things from the Paris correspondent in *The Manchester Guardian* you sent me. How is business in Manchester? Everything seems to be going better than expected.

First published abridged in *Der Briefwechsel zwischen F. Engels und K. Marx*, Bd. 2, Stuttgart, 1913 and in full in: Marx and Engels, *Works*, First Russian Edition, Vol. XXII, Moscow, 1929

Printed according to the original

Published in English for the first time

132

ENGELS TO MARX

IN LONDON

Manchester, 25 January 1858

Dear Marx,

The letters have all arrived safely. It will be utterly impossible to do the BENGAL REBELLION in the time stipulated and I would advise you, while you are about it, to point out to Mr Dana that, had he been more prompt in agreeing to our proposals and the list we sent him, he would have had all these articles long ago. He can perfectly well fit in BENGAL REBELLION as HINDUSTAN REBELLION or something of the sort.[272] As to the alleged howler,[270] I can't look into it this moment, there being no time, but shall do so tomorrow. The item was taken from *Brockhaus*,[a] so it will probably be correct.

Lassalle's letter is still up here.

I have the material ready for 'Blenheim', 'Borodino' and many more and you will be receiving a LOT on Friday, provided the Indian MAIL doesn't necessitate my doing an article, which seems unlikely judging by the telegraphic despatch. I shall have to look up 'Bidassoa', etc. But what is all this about Dana saying he had already asked for *these articles*? It's the first I've heard of it.

Harney will have written to tell you that poor Schramm died a week ago on Friday. I have no details yet. I wrote and asked

---

[a] *Brockhaus' Konversations-Lexikon*

Harney,[273] should he find anything in your handwriting or mine, to take it away and hold it at our disposal—it would be too bad if anything of that kind were allowed to fall into the hands of Mr Rudolf,[a] who has become an out-and-out Prussian. I had not thought Schramm would have any serious attacks before the spring. The poor fellow was putting up a splendid fight against the disease while I was there and, from what I hear, continued to do so until the end. Our old guard is rapidly dwindling away during this long spell of peace!

Business here is very shaky. Every fortnight an attempt is made to push up cotton prices, the moment chosen being when a few spinners have to buy. It succeeds for three or four days and then prices fall again. Generally speaking we are now $^5/_8$d above the lowest point. It's much the same with ourselves. As soon as prices become thoroughly depressed as a result of a fortnight's stagnation, the Indian and Levantine buyers step into the market and force everything up; after that no one wants to buy and prices gradually fall again. Everything is still far from normal. The spinners are going on to full time, not because there is any real demand, but because others are doing so and because they're heartily sick of SHORT TIME. On the whole the spinners' position has deteriorated because the difference in price between raw cotton and yarn has diminished. The Germans are still buying very little. Prospects here are far from brilliant; every day trade suffers a CHECK because of attempts to force up prices and, if that doesn't happen, they say that THERE IS AN IMPROVED FEELING IN THE MARKET. IMPROVED BE DAMNED!

The enclosure for Lupus was a source of great pride and joy to the old man.[b] He sends his warmest regards to the writers. By the way I hardly saw him at all last week; we kept missing one another and later he had a slight touch of *tic douloureux*.[c]

Warm regards to the FAMILY.

Your

F. E.

First published abridged in *Der Briefwechsel zwischen F. Engels und K. Marx*, Bd. 2, Stuttgart, 1913 and in full in: Marx and Engels, *Works*, First Russian Edition, Vol. XXII, Moscow, 1929

Printed according to the original

Published in English for the first time

---

[a] Rudolf Schramm - [b] See this volume, p. 250. - [c] facial neuralgia

133

ENGELS TO MARX

IN LONDON

Manchester, 28 January 1858

Dear Moor,

Herewith 3 B articles.[274] I had meant, if possible, to do Windham[a] as well today, but in the first place the PARTICULARS are still very confused and it is absolutely essential to wait for the official report on the affair, for hitherto everything has been glossed over; and, secondly, I had no time this afternoon, was barely able to look over the 3 articles. Also, I have too bad a cold to risk going into town at midnight to post the letter. Tell Dana that the material is still incomplete.

Have you sent Dana my C list? If not, do so *now* so that he can reply in good time. Once again his C is LUDICROUSLY INCOMPLETE.

Unfortunately I couldn't make 'Borodino' any shorter since all previous accounts of the battle have been quite wrong.

Your

F. E.

First published in *Der Briefwechsel zwischen F. Engels und K. Marx,* Bd. 2, Stuttgart, 1913

Printed according to the original

Published in English for the first time

134

MARX TO ENGELS[20]

IN MANCHESTER

[London,] 28 January [1858]
9 Grafton Terrace, Maitland Park,
Haverstock Hill

DEAR Frederick,

The freezing weather which has set in here and the *real shortage of coal in this house* compels me—although there's nothing in the world I loathe more—to impose on you again. I have brought

[a] F. Engels, 'Windham's Defeat'.

myself to do so only after HEAVY PRESSURE FROM WITHOUT. My wife has pointed out to me that you had miscalculated through having sent a remittance from Jersey earlier than usual, and hence would not send anything this month unless I wrote expressly; that she had pawned her SHAWL, etc., etc., and was at a loss where to turn. In short, I *must* write, which is why I am doing so. Indeed, if these conditions persist, I'd sooner be miles under the ground than go on scraping along in this way. Always to be a burden on others while constantly tormented oneself by beastly trifles becomes unbearable in the long run. I personally can bury myself in my work and escape the *misère* by devoting my attention to universalities. My wife, OF COURSE, has no such refuge, etc., etc.

Lassalle's book arrived today[a]; it cost 2/—not the book, but the carriage. This circumstance ensured it a bad reception. 2 volumes of 30 sheets EACH. Have no more than squinted at it. In his preface the fellow deludes readers into believing that he has been gestating it since 1846. Seems altogether Old Hegelian. Very possibly the legal tradition of hermeneutics came in useful for the interpretation and comparison of passages. *Nous verrons,*[b] though the thing's too bulky to be read from cover to cover.

I have also heard from Mr Pieper. He imparts the interesting secret that, while here, he was suffering from 'abdominal difficulties' and hence 'may' have seemed a bore.

The Orsini, etc., conspiracy[271] might well put paid to the Prussian amnesty.[275] The day before yesterday the police here forced their way into Orsini's rooms *at midnight,* and INVEIGLED his maid[c] into accompanying them to Scotland Yard, where she was interrogated by Mr Richard Mayne and some French *mouchards.*[d] This escapade, besides compromising Mr Pam, failed in its purpose even more lamentably in that Martin Bernard has taken possession of all letters addressed to Orsini in London since the latter's arrest, Orsini himself having *burned* all the rest before leaving here.

Salut.

Your

K. M.

First published slightly abridged in *Der Briefwechsel zwischen F. Engels und K. Marx,* Bd. 2, Stuttgart, 1913 and in full in: Marx and Engels, *Works,* First Russian Edition, Vol. XXII, Moscow, 1929

Printed according to the original

Published in English in full for the first time

---

a F. Lassalle, *Die Philosophie Herakleitos des Dunklen von Ephesos.* - b We shall see - c Eliza Cheney - d police spies

135

MARX TO ENGELS

IN MANCHESTER

[London,] 29 January 1858

DEAR Frederick,

The 3 B articles received.[a] It's excellent that you should have made 'Borodino' longer. Since the fellows' columns are so IMMENSE and their PAY so bad, the only remedy is to lengthen the articles. I hope that when you come to do 'Cavalry' you will spin it out as much as possible so that I can get rid of my DEBTS to those curs.

In France things are splendid. The COOLNESS with which the *épiciers*[b] responded to the news of the attempted assassination[271] has exasperated the fellow.[c] The secret of this indifference of the *épiciers* is doubtless the unspoken desire of many of them that some sudden political event should get them out of their mess. The majority of the laddies had had their bills renewed by the Bank, Discount Association, etc., which were acting on the ORDERS of Boustrapa.[40] However, to put off is not to write off. A large number of French bourgeois, with commercial ruin staring them in the face, are anxiously awaiting the day of reckoning. They now find themselves in much the same STATE as Boustrapa *before* the coup d'état.[276] ANY POLITICAL PRETEXT FOR MAKING AN HONOURABLE EXIT WILL, CONSEQUENTLY, BE EAGERLY SEIZED UPON BY THE DAMNED FELLOWS—just as it was 10 years ago. Boustrapa knows this and now wishes to act the real 'despot'. *Nous verrons*.[d] If he pins his faith on Magnan, Castellane, etc., he will be left high and dry.[277]

In my economic work[250] I have now reached a point at which I could do with some information on practical matters from you, since nothing of the kind is to be found in theoretical writings. I mean, the *circulation* of capital—how it varies in various kinds of business; the effect of the same on profit and prices. If you can provide me with any information on the subject, it would be VERY welcome.

Mr Lassalle, in his preface to *Die Philosophie Herakleitos des Dunklen von Ephesos*, says *inter alia*:

'All but a small part of the same' (the book) 'was completed early in 1846, and I was on the point of putting the concluding touches to it when suddenly an interest of a different kind—how true in *every* respect is Sophocles' dictum:

---

[a] F. Engels, 'Berme', 'Blenheim', 'Borodino'. - [b] grocers - [c] Napoleon III - [d] We shall see.

"πολλὰ τὰ δεινὰ, κοὐδὲν
ἀνθρώπου δεινότερον πέλει"[a]

—precipitated me into a welter of practical strife and prevented me over a period of nearly 10 years from devoting myself to the completion of this work.'

Do you suppose that Sophocles' verse, put into German by Lassalle, means: 'There's no more frightful specimen of *humankind* than the Countess Hatzfeldt!'[35]

Salut.

Your
K. M.

First published abridged in *Der Briefwechsel zwischen F. Engels und K. Marx*, Bd. 2, Stuttgart, 1913 and in full in: Marx and Engels, *Works*, First Russian Edition, Vol. XXII, Moscow, 1929

Printed according to the original

Published in English for the first time

136

ENGELS TO MARX

IN LONDON

Manchester, 30 January 1858

Dear Marx,

Your two letters arrived together this morning. I enclose a fiver; unfortunately I'm very tight for money myself and Schramm touched me for five pounds at the beginning of January—in the circumstances there was absolutely no question of refusing, but in consequence I was even more broke. 'Windham'[b] will be ready for Tuesday.

Apropos, would you send me another copy of the B articles Dana asked for (both the original ones and those subsequently ordered) as I have mislaid mine.

How goes it with 'Camp', 'Catapults' and 'Caps' (Percussion)?[263]

Well, the would-be assassins[271] may not have bagged Bonaparte, but they caught K. Heinzen all right. You will recall his bloodthirsty threats of destruction in 1848 and his big talk about

---

[a] There are many wonderful things, and nothing is more wonderful than man' (Sophocles, *Antigone*, Lines 339-40). - [b] F. Engels, 'Windham's Defeat'.

the deadly weapons of modern science concerning which he, of course, knew nothing. Kossuth is a great man, but Kossuth forgot fulminating silver, etc. *Eh bien,*[a] after this business we shall hear no more of fulminating silver. I said at once, judging by the appalling number of injured and relatively few dead, that the bombs had been overfilled and had therefore burst into a mass of small splinters, none of which had much force. The asses went about it with more stupidity than cunning. With a filling of ordinary powder the bombs would inevitably have had a much greater effect. Instead they cram in as much fulminating mercury as the things will hold, thereby producing a hail of small, relatively innocuous splinters. Dr Larrey confirms my view. SO MUCH FOR Heinzen.

On the 21st *courant*[b] there was another attempt on Bonaparte's life in the Bois de Boulogne, with a pistol; the fellow was arrested before he could pull the trigger. The affair has been hushed up. As soon as I can dispense with the relevant *Guardian* you shall have it.

I shall send for Charras' *Cent jours.*[c] Mightn't we go in for literary criticism in America? An article on the subject would certainly be interesting and not difficult to do.

Warm regards to your wife and children.

Your

F. E.

First published in *Der Briefwechsel zwischen F. Engels und K. Marx,* Bd. 2, Stuttgart, 1913

Printed according to the original

Published in English for the first time

137

MARX TO ENGELS[1]

IN MANCHESTER

[London,] 1 February 1858
9 Grafton Terrace, Maitland Park,
Haverstock Hill

Dear Frederick,

£5 arrived. The simultaneous arrival of two letters, of which I sent off one on Thursday, the other on Friday, would seem to

---

a Well - b instant - c J. B. A. Charras, *Histoire de la campagne de 1815.*

indicate that refugees' letters are being held back, examined, etc., by the Post Office.

New B's are: *'Bidassoa'* (BATTLE OF), *'Blenheim'* (ditto), *'Burmah'* (WAR IN), *'Bomarsund'* (SIEGE), *'Borodino'* (BATTLE), *'Brescia'* (ASSAULT), *'Bridge-head', 'Bülow', 'Buda'* (SIEGE OF), *'Beresford', 'Berme'.*[a] When Dana says, 'MOST OF THEM I ASKED YOU BEFORE', he is mistaken, and is confusing *your* list of B's with *his own.* All he himself ordered was:

'Barbette', 'Bastion', 'Bayonet', 'Barclay de Tolly', 'Battery', 'Battle', 'Bem', 'Bennigsen', 'Berthier', 'Bernadotte', 'Bessières', 'Bivouac', 'Blindage', 'Blücher', 'Blum', 'Bolivar', 'Bomb', 'Bombardier', 'Bombardment', 'Bomb (Ketch, Proof, Vessel)', 'Bonnet', 'Bosquet', 'Bourrienne', *'Bridge'* (pontoon), Brown (Sir George), 'Brune', 'Bugeaud'.[a] (The ass has received the lot.)

I have done *'Catapult'* for you (not very much). Likewise the better part of *'Castrum'*[b] (but I still have to look up Greek camps in Wachsmuth, *Hellenische Alterthumskunde,* and Jewish in de Wette[c]). It's a lengthy business where *PERCUSSION CAPS*[263] are concerned because there are so many different types of gun-locks, etc., to be listed. I'd have already finished the job if it hadn't been for the new order from Dana. I'll send you all the rubbish at the same time. Besides, whenever I'm at the Museum,[d] there's such a LOT of stuff to look up that it's closing-time (now 4 o'clock) before I've so much as looked round. Then there's the journey there. So much time lost.

Heraclitus, the Dark Philosopher by Lassalle the Luminous One is, *au fond,*[e] a very silly concoction. Every time Heraclitus uses an image to demonstrate the unity of AFFIRMATION and NEGATION—and this is often—IN STEPS Lassalle and makes the most of the occasion by treating us to some passage from Hegel's *Logic* which is HARDLY improved in the process; always at great length too, like a schoolboy who must show in his essay that he has thoroughly understood his 'essence' and 'appearance' as well as the 'dialectical process'. Once he has got this into his speculative noddle, one may be sure that the schoolboy will nevertheless be able to carry out the process of ratiocination only in strict accord with the prescribed formula and the *formes sacramentales.*[f] Just so our Lassalle. The fellow seems to have tried to puzzle out Hegelian logic via Heraclitus, nor ever to have tired of beginning the process all over again. As for learning, there is a tremendous

---

[a] All names and parentheses written in English by Marx. - [b] 'Camp' - [c] Probably a reference to W. M. L. de Wette's *Lehrbuch der hebräisch-jüdischen Archäologie...* - [d] the British Museum Library - [e] basically - [f] hallowed forms

display of it. But, as any well-informed person will know, provided one has the time and the money and, like Mr Lassalle, can have Bonn University Library delivered *ad libitum* to one's home, it is easy enough to assemble such an array of quotations. One can see what an amazing swell the fellow himself thinks he is in this philological finery, and how he moves with all the grace of a man wearing FASHIONABLE DRESS for the first time in his life. Since most philologists are *not* possessed of the speculative thinking dominant in Heraclitus, every Hegelian has the incontestable advantage of understanding what the philologist does not. (It would, by the by, be strange indeed if, by learning Greek, a fellow were to become a philosopher *in Greek* without being one *in German.*) Instead of simply taking this for granted, Mr Lassalle proceeds to lecture us in a quasi-Lessingian manner. In long-winded, lawyer's style he vindicates the Hegelian interpretation as opposed to the erroneous exegeses of the philologists—erroneous for want of specialised knowledge. Thus we are accorded the twofold gratification, first, of having dialectical matters which we had all but forgotten expounded to us at considerable length and, secondly, of seeing this 'speculative heritage' vindicated (qua special province of Mr Lassalle's philological-jurisprudential astuteness and erudition) vis-à-vis the unspeculative philologists. Despite the fellow's claim, by the way, that hitherto Heraclitus has been a book with 7 seals, he has to all intents and purposes added *nothing whatever that is new* to what Hegel says in the *History of Philosophy.*[a] All he does is to enlarge on points of detail which could, of course, have been accomplished quite adequately in two sheets of print. Still less does it occur to the laddie to come out with any critical reflections on dialectics as such. If all the fragments by Heraclitus were put together in print, they would HARDLY fill half a sheet. Only a chap who brings out his books at the expense of the frightful 'specimen of humankind'[b] can presume to launch upon the world 2 volumes of 60 sheets on such a pretext.

Heraclitus, the Dark Philosopher, is quoted as saying in an attempt to elucidate the transformation of all things into their opposite: 'Thus gold changeth into all things, and all things change into gold.' Here, Lassalle says, gold means money (*c'est juste*[c]) and money is value.[d] Thus the Ideal, Universality, the One (value), and things, the Real, Particularity, the Many. He makes use of this surprising insight to give, in a lengthy note, AN EARNEST OF HIS

[a] G. W. F. Hegel, *Vorlesungen über die Geschichte der Philosophie.* - [b] Sophie von Hatzfeldt (see this volume, p. 257) - [c] that is correct - [d] F. Lassalle, *Die Philosophie Herakleitos des Dunklen von Ephesos,* Bd. I, S. 222-23.

DISCOVERIES IN THE SCIENCE OF POLITICAL ECONOMY. Every other word a howler, but set forth with remarkable pretentiousness. It is plain to me from this one note that, in his second grand opus, the fellow intends to expound political economy in the manner of Hegel.[278] He will discover to his cost that it is one thing for a critique to take a science to the point at which it admits of a dialectical presentation, and quite another to apply an abstract, ready-made system of logic to vague presentiments of just such a system.

But, as I remarked immediately after receipt of his first self-complacent letter, the Old Hegelians and philologists must indeed have been PLEASED to discover such old-fashioned virtues in a young man who passes for a great revolutionary.[a] On top of that, he bows and scrapes to all and sundry in the hope of assuring himself a favourable reception. As soon as I've skimmed through the stuff, I'll send it too.

Salut.

Your

K. M.

First published abridged in *Der Briefwechsel zwischen F. Engels und K. Marx*, Bd. 2, Stuttgart, 1913 and in full in: Marx and Engels, *Works*, First Russian Edition, Vol. XXII, Moscow, 1929

Printed according to the original

Published in English in full for the first time

138

ENGELS TO MARX

IN LONDON

Manchester, 8 February 1858

Dear Moor,

At times last week I wasn't well. There would seem to be some slight vestige of my former complaint which, though too mild to take a serious hold, plagues me with all kinds of little miseries—a peculiarly sensitive skin, cuts slow to heal, abscesses on the fingers, and similar boring and idiotic things. Fortunately there is no longer any sign at all of septic glands, so I have nothing to fear on

---

a See this volume, p. 227.

that score. These little miseries crop up whenever I have a cold, and will doubtless continue to bother me off and on until I go to bathe in the sea again. Pending that I shall, at any rate, have to be careful. My piles, by the way, which have become something of a problem since I got back, act as a diversion; this may help at the time, but makes sitting impossible for the next day or two, except on horseback. Hence my silence last week and the dearth of contributions since Monday. Most evenings I could only *lie down.* However my cold is now SUBSIDING—so much so that yesterday I was again able to ride 28 miles, which means we shall be able to pitch in again tomorrow.

Au fond[a] Mr Lassalle doesn't seem to have taken much trouble over the dark Heraclitus. Lupus was much amused by your description of his method; it gave him some satisfaction to learn that Greek scholarship is not this gentleman's forte. When the book[b] arrives I shall let him study it.

Today friend Belfield again presented himself for election to the city council and suffered a resounding defeat. 196 votes against 143 in his favour.

I still have a few *Guardians* at home with some nice reports from Paris and shall send them to you in the next few days.

Warm regards to the FAMILY. There'll be some more *Cyclopaedia* stuff for Friday.

Your

F. E.

First published in: Marx and Engels, *Works,* First Russian Edition, Vol. XXII, Moscow, 1929

Printed according to the original

Published in English for the first time

139

MARX TO ENGELS

IN MANCHESTER

[London,] 10 February [1858]

Dear Engels,

That ass Dana (in a letter which I shall send you later and in which he leaves it UNDECIDED WHETHER OR NOT to honour the bill I drew

[a] in the main - [b] F. Lassalle, *Die Philosophie Herakleitos des Dunklen von Ephesos.*

at the end of December) writes *inter alia*: *'In the article *"Artillery"* in speaking of the equipment of the Prussian army, you use the words *seam*-horses; what are they? I do not find them in any dictionary.'* Answer by return, so that I can write to the ass about it on Friday.

I suspected that all was not quite well with you. You really must take care of yourself. You've been overdoing things during the Manchester 'period of *Sturm und Drang*'.[279] More soon.

Your

K. M.

Did Harney DEAR send you also his *Independent*[a] NONSENSE? Who do you suppose concocted Schramm's life story? Harney makes out that THE CELEBRATED POET Freiligrath—alongside whom Engels ESQ. looks odd—was the publisher of the *Revue der Neuen Rheinischen Zeitung*.[b]

First published abridged in *Der Briefwechsel zwischen F. Engels und K. Marx*, Bd. 2, Stuttgart, 1913 and in full in: Marx and Engels, *Works*, First Russian Edition, Vol. XXII, Moscow, 1929

Printed according to the original

Published in English for the first time

140

ENGELS TO MARX

IN LONDON

Manchester, 11 February 1858

Dear Moor,

Dana can't read—the word is *TEAM*-HORSES, i.e. THE HORSES HARNESSED TO ANY GUN OR CARRIAGE IN ORDER TO DRAW IT. The expression 'TEAM' crops up frequently elsewhere in the article[c] and if he wants an authority let him look up the article on 'Artillery' in the *Encyclopaedia Britannica*.

Unfortunately I can't send you anything today. Yesterday I let myself be talked into attending a COURSING MEETING at which hares are hunted with greyhounds, and spent 7 hours in the saddle. All

---

[a] *The Jersey Independent* - [b] *Neue Rheinische Zeitung. Politisch-ökonomische Revue* - [c] F. Engels, 'Artillery'.

in all, it did me a power of good though it kept me from my work, and I haven't got far enough with the stuff I've begun—'Burmah', etc., etc.—to have a hope of getting it ready in time for tonight. It's sickening to read long works on 'Burmah', yet be unable to make a decent job of the thing, AS IT MUST BE PRETTY SHORT. But I shall have my revenge with 'Cavalry'. Dana will be getting Griesheim[a] *in toto* in so far as it applies.

Lupus has apparently retired from the world of pubs. During 4 visits to the Chatsworth, his regular haunt, I only ran into him once. Since I only go there on his account, it has been a great waste of time and something will have to be done about it.

I too have been sent Harney DEAR'S rubbish.[b] For this Harro Harring, who lives in Jersey (though I never saw him), must take the chief blame. The description of Krefeld is killing. Real vintage Harney. He has turned Schramm's death into yet another great melodramatic spectacle, the principal role being played by G. J. H.[c] of course. The whole affair, funeral and all, his letters headed HASTE! IMMEDIATE!, etc., and then the presumption of asking me to come to Jersey to figure among the *crapauds*[81] and Waschlapskis[d]—I find the whole affair repugnant. He's a rotten little blighter and Jersey is just the right place for him; moreover he is absolutely delighted at having involved his paper in a libel action brought by François Godfrey, Jersey's feudal lord.[237]

The 'Engels ESQ' certainly does look very odd. I ought never to forgive Harney, if only because the best he has to say of me boils down to *Esq. Grosse bête!*[e]

Jones, too, is evidently up to some pretty tricks. The obese Livesay, whom he appointed CHAIRMAN of his conference,[245] is a wretched little bourgeois who swears by Miall and who, in company with Sturge & Co., engineered the COMPLETE SUFFRAGE SECESSION as long ago as 1842 when all the petty bourgeois withdrew.[280]

But NEVER MIND. Mr Bonaparte *travaille pour nous.*[f] The way he is running things, we couldn't possibly ask for anything better. Espinasse, Minister of the Interior! THAT BEATS COCK FIGHTING. And on top of that, the idiocy of publishing those addresses.[281]

---

[a] G. von Griesheim, *Vorlesungen über die Taktik*. - [b] See previous letter. - [c] George Julian Harney - [d] *Waschlapski,* of which the English equivalent would be Dishragski, is the name of a down-at-heel nobleman in Heine's satirical poem *Zwei Ritter*. By the *crapauds* and *Waschlapskis* Engels means French and Polish petty-bourgeois refugees in Jersey. - [e] Silly ass! (Engels wrote this paragraph in the margin.) - [f] is working for us

By the way, so that you don't start getting wrong ideas about my physical condition, let me tell you that yesterday I took my horse over a hedge and bank measuring 5 feet and some inches, the highest jump I've ever done. Clearly, EFFORTS of this kind presuppose moderately sound limbs if they are to be made without discomfort. After all, we want to show the Prussian cavalry a thing or two when we get back to Germany. The gentlemen will find it difficult to keep up with me for I've already had a great deal of practice and am improving every day. I'm getting quite a reputation, as time goes on. But only now am I getting to grips with the real problems of riding over difficult country; it's a highly complicated business.

Kind regards to your wife and children. A few articles at any rate will arrive by Monday. As regards India I think we might wait for one more mail, unless anything of real interest crops up.

Your

F. E.

First published abridged in *Der Briefwechsel zwischen F. Engels und K. Marx*, Bd. 2, Stuttgart, 1913 and in full in: Marx and Engels, *Works*, First Russian Edition, Vol. XXII, Moscow, 1929

Printed according to the original

Published in English for the first time

141

MARX TO ENGELS[20]

IN MANCHESTER

[London,] 14 February 1858

Dear Engels,

You had promised to send me the *Guardian*. I was therefore expecting to get it today since France is now the only possible topic for reports and the fellows prefer a few gossipy anecdotes to ANY AMOUNT OF IDEAS. I assume the numbers you promised me will arrive tomorrow but would most urgently beg that in future you always let me have the things for Thursday or for Friday at the latest. *After* the appointed day they are, OF COURSE, no longer of any use to me for my reports.

For 3 days I shall now be on tenterhooks until I know whether or not my bill, which does not appear to have been despatched from here until several weeks AFTER ITS DRAWING, has been honoured. At very best I shan't be able to draw anything more on the *Tribune* against the articles I have sent in until the matter with Appleton is SETTLED.[a] My estimate of the value of the last goods despatched to him was badly out. Moreover, a longish article on '*Bolivar*'[b] elicited objections from Dana because, he said, it is written IN A PARTISAN STYLE and he asked me to cite my AUTHORITIES. This I can, of course, do, although it's a singular demand. As regards the PARTISAN STYLE, it is true that I departed somewhat from the tone of a cyclopaedia. To see the most dastardly, most miserable and meanest of blackguards described as Napoleon I was altogether too much. Bolivar is a veritable Soulouque.[282]

I CONGRATULATE YOU UPON YOUR EQUESTRIAN PERFORMANCES. Only don't take too many breakneck jumps, as there will soon be more important occasion for risking your neck. You seem TO RIDE SOMEWHAT HARD THIS HOBBY-HORSE. In any case I don't believe that the CAVALRY is the speciality in which you will be of the greatest service to Germany. I would venture another little objection, viz. whether OVER-EXERTION IN ANY LINE is compatible with your health. *Aurea mediocritas*[c] in all types of exertion, or so at least a doctor assures me, should remain the norm for you for some time yet.

The Bonaparte affair[271] had indeed put a sorry end to the proposed Prussian amnesty.[275] Louis, by the way, is merely aping his putative uncle.[283] He is, in fact, not only *Napoléon le Petit* (in Victor Hugo's sense[d] as opposed to *Napoléon le Grand*) but he PERSONATES IN A MOST ADMIRABLE WAY THE LITTLENESS of the great Napoleon. I have looked up Cobbett for 1802-03 where I discover that the 'DEN OF ASSASSINS' AND ALL THAT LITERALLY appeared in the *Moniteur* of that time.[284] *Inter alia*, the *Moniteur* of 9 August 1802 declares word for word:

*'Either the English government authorises and tolerates these public and private crimes, in which case it cannot be said that such conduct is consistent with British generosity, civilisation, and honour; or it cannot prevent them, in which case it does not deserve the name of government; above all, if it does not possess the means of repressing *assassination* and calumny and protecting *social order*.'*[e]

Salut.

Your

K. M.

---

[a] See this volume, p. 251. - [b] K. Marx, 'Bolivar y Ponte'. - [c] The golden mean - [d] V. Hugo, *Napoléon le petit* (Hugo first used the phrase in a speech in the Legislative Assembly in 1851). - [e] This passage from an article in *Le Moniteur universel*, No. 320, 9 August 1802 (datelined 'Paris, le 19 thermidor') is quoted by Marx in English according to *Cobbett's Annual Register*. From July to December, 1802, Vol. II.

If you haven't yet sent off the *back* numbers of the *Guardian*, try and let me have them by Monday, and the next ones by Friday.

First published slightly abridged in *Der Briefwechsel zwischen F. Engels und K. Marx*, Bd. 2, Stuttgart, 1913 and in full in: Marx and Engels, *Works*, First Russian Edition, Vol. XXII, Moscow, 1929

Printed according to the original

Published in English in full for the first time

142

ENGELS TO MARX

IN LONDON

[Manchester,] 18 February 1858

Dear Moor,

Every day this week I have meant to write to you, and every day the steady rise in prices has stopped me from doing so. You will remember my telling you[a] that 6d for Middling Orleans was the highest price compatible with FULL TIME. Now, with Middling Orleans at $5^3/_4$d, $^7/_8$ of all spinners have gone on to FULL TIME, and the result of this asininity is that, out of sheer impatience, they've pushed Middling Orleans up to $7^3/_4$d in 6 weeks! Yarn and cloth haven't followed in the same proportion, of course; the manufacturer's MARGIN between the price of his raw material and the finished product has been reduced to below cost price and now the asses want to revert to SHORT TIME, which they ought never to have abandoned!

The *Guardians* will go off today at the same time.

I trust that your bill has been honoured. Since you had in any case advised them so long in advance, they should certainly have told you long ago had there been any intention of returning it.

Enclosed another little thing for Dana.[285] If the fellow wants to lay down the law on the strength of his paltry 2 dollars, then he deserves some rough words. At all events he can't expect more than we are already providing—largely original work instead of the measly compilations he is getting from elsewhere. Urge him to pay better and *que puis nous verrions.*[b] As regards Badajos,[270] the wretched *Brockhaus*[c] really led me astray.

---

[a] See this volume, p. 231. - [b] then we shall see - [c] *Brockhaus' Konversations-Lexikon*

'Burmah' is A VERY LABORIOUS ARTICLE. Could you not take over 'Bülow' and 'Beresford'? Up here even the bare bones of the biographies are lacking, but I could let you have the chief points on the military side.

I shall discuss equitation another time. *Au fond*[a] the thing is the material basis for all my military studies, as you know. The *crapauds*[81] regard the sordid Bonaparte as a hero because he sits elegantly on a horse though only a passable rider; there are plenty of witnesses over here who know that he is A VERY INDIFFERENT FENCER[b] and that he shirks many an obstacle which YOUR HUMBLE SERVANT would tackle without a second thought. Moreover riding is the only physical accomplishment in which I have acquired a modicum of competence and anyway the element of danger in hunting and jumping is so small (probability 1:10,000) that it has an irresistible attraction. Anyway, *sois tranquille*,[c] if I break my neck it won't be by falling off a horse. Warm regards to all the FAMILY.

Your
F. E.

First published abridged in *Der Briefwechsel zwischen F. Engels und K. Marx*, Bd. 2, Stuttgart, 1913 and in full in: Marx and Engels, *Works*, First Russian Edition, Vol. XXII, Moscow, 1929

Printed according to the original

Published in English for the first time

143

MARX TO FERDINAND LASSALLE[286]

IN DÜSSELDORF

London, 22 February 1858
9 Grafton Terrace, Maitland Park, Haverstock Hill

Dear Lassalle,

Nutt has now sent me *Heraclitus*.[d] As soon as I have read it all I shall let you have my opinion. But you will have to wait a while

---

[a] at bottom - [b] i.e. jumper - [c] don't worry - [d] F. Lassalle, *Die Philosophie Herakleitos des Dunklen von Ephesos.*

since I have exceptionally little spare time just now. As regards the Stoics, I did not myself study their relationship to Heraclitus in the matter of natural philosophy, because of the novice-like earnestness of their approach to this discipline. Of Epicurus, on the other hand, it can be shown *en détail* that, although he bases himself on the natural philosophy of Democritus, he is for ever turning the argument inside out. Cicero and Plutarch can hardly be blamed for not having grasped this since it has eluded even men of intellect such as Bayle, not to speak of Hegel *ipsissimus.*[a] Nor, for that matter, could one expect Hegel, the first to comprehend the entire history of philosophy, not to commit errors of detail.

From the papers you will have seen that Palmerston has fallen. Those best acquainted with the old rascal are generally inclined to suspect that his last BLUNDERS were *deliberate*, so that he could make his exit *pro tempore.* They affirm that *le dernier but de toute sa vie*[b] was to engineer a war between England and France, that he now believes he has managed to do so, that at first other hands are to be concerned with the execution of *his* plan and that, when the imbroglio has become sufficiently involved and is far enough advanced, THE NATION WILL BE FORCED TO CALL AGAIN UPON HIM. This latter opinion may be too recherché, but that Pam did not resign in any way *against his will* seems to me unquestionable.

Now, as to your cousin,[c] there's one thing I am willing to do, but the *Presse,* I assume, would not.[254] All I could commit myself to would be *one* article a week on trade, finance, etc., in any one of the three countries, England, France and the United States of America, depending on which is INTERESTING. This is also the *most practicable* form in which to attack Bonaparte. It is also a form which would permit me to have absolutely nothing to do with the *Presse* politically. It seems to me that just now there is widespread ignorance, especially about *French* financial affairs and French economic conditions in general. The question is whether the subject will be of sufficient interest to the *Presse,* or RATHER, to its readers. They, of course, must be the best judges of that. For a weekly article of this kind I would ask £1 STERLING. Moreover, it would be necessary for me to have a few copies of the *Presse* beforehand so that I could see whether MY PRINCIPLES would at all permit me to work for the paper. HOWEVER THAT MAY BE, will you thank your cousin on my behalf for having remembered me in this connection.

---

[a] his very self - [b] the ultimate aim of his whole life - [c] Max Friedländer

Now let me tell you how my political economy[250] is getting on. I have IN FACT been at work on the final stages for some months. But the thing is proceeding very slowly because no sooner does one set about finally disposing of subjects to which one has devoted years of study than they start revealing new aspects and demand to be thought out further. On top of which I am not master of my time but RATHER its slave. Only the nights are left for my own work, which in turn is often disrupted by bilious attacks or recurrences of liver trouble. All things considered it would be most convenient for me to bring out the whole work in instalments without any rigid datelines. This might also have the advantage of making it easier to find a publisher, since less working capital would be tied up in the venture. You would, OF COURSE, oblige me by trying to find someone in Berlin prepared to undertake this. By 'instalments', I mean fascicles similar to those in which Vischer's *Aesthetik* came out.

The work I am presently concerned with is a *Critique of Economic Categories* or, IF YOU LIKE, a critical exposé of the system of the bourgeois economy. It is at once an exposé and, by the same token, a critique of the system. I have very little idea how many sheets the whole thing will amount to. Had I the means, the time and the leisure to finish the whole thing off completely prior to placing it before the public, I would condense it a great deal, a method for which I have always had a predilection. But printed thus, in successive instalments—easier for readers to understand perhaps but certainly detrimental to the form—it is bound to be rather more diffuse. *Nota bene:* As soon as you know definitely whether *or not* the thing can be done in Berlin, kindly write to me, since if it's no go there I'll try Hamburg. A further point is that I must be *paid* by the publisher who takes the thing on—a stipulation over which it might come to grief in Berlin.

The presentation—the manner of it, I mean—is entirely scientific, hence unobjectionable to the police in the ordinary sense. The whole is divided into 6 books: 1. On Capital (contains a few introductory CHAPTERS). 2. On Landed Property. 3. On Wage Labour. 4. On the State. 5. International Trade. 6. World Market. I cannot, of course, avoid all critical consideration of other economists, in particular a polemic against Ricardo in as much as even he, *qua* bourgeois, cannot but commit blunders *even from a strictly economic viewpoint.* But generally speaking the critique and history of political economy and socialism would form the subject of another work, and, finally, the short *historical outline* of the development of economic categories and relations yet a third. Now that I am at last ready to set to work after 15 years of study, I have an uncomfortable feeling that turbulent movements from without will probably INTERFERE AFTER ALL. NEVER MIND. If I finish too late and thus find the world no longer attentive to such subjects, the fault is clearly MY OWN.

I was greatly amused by your remarks about Rudolf Schramm.[a] Sad to say, a worthier Schramm, Conrad, brother of the above and one of my best friends, died of consumption in Jersey some 4 weeks ago. The death within the past few years of Weerth, Schramm and Dr Daniels has been a blow to their friends, amongst whom I was happy enough to count myself.

There are turbulent times in the offing. If I were merely to consult my own private inclinations, I would wish for another few years of superficial calm. There could, at any rate, be no better time for scholarly undertakings and, after all, what has happened over the last ten years must have increased any RATIONAL BEING'S contempt for the masses as for individuals to such a degree that *'odi profanum vulgus et arceo'*[b] has almost become an inescapable maxim. However all these are themselves philistine ruminations which will be swept away by the first storm.

Your

K. M.

The connection between the latest events in France[271] and the commercial crisis is, perhaps, apparent only to a few. It becomes EVIDENT, however, if one considers 1. THE REAL ECONOMICAL STATE PRODUCED IN FRANCE BY THE LAST CRISIS; 2. asks oneself and *consciencieusement*[c] answers, why the attempted assassination brought forth the effects it did, effects which APPARENTLY STOOD IN NO PROPORTION WHATEVER, AND EVEN IN NO NECESSARY RELATION TO THE ALLEGED CAUSE.

First published in: *F. Lassalle. Nachgelassene Briefe und Schriften*, Bd. III, Stuttgart-Berlin, 1922

Printed according to the original

---

[a] in Lassalle's letter to Marx of 10 February 1858 (see this volume, p. 272) - [b] I detest and repudiate the common people (Horace, *Odes*, III, I, 1). - [c] conscientiously

144

MARX TO ENGELS

IN MANCHESTER

[London,] 22 February 1858

Dear Engels,

Herewith a letter from Lassalle, INTERESTING on account of the bit about Rudolf Schramm. What the chap says about my 'logic' amounts to nothing more than a *refusal* to understand me. All I did was *simplement* inform him that I *hadn't* written to him because MATTERS HAD COME TO A POINT at which a verbal explanation was necessary if written INTERCOURSE were to continue. IN FACT I had DONE this ticklish PASSAGE IN A VERY DIPLOMATICAL STYLE.[a]

In my reply I asked him, of course, to look round for a publisher in Berlin. It is my intention to bring the thing out by *instalments*,[b] having neither the time nor the means to complete the whole of it at leisure. This initial form may be detrimental to the form. Better for distribution, at any rate. Also makes it easier to find a publisher.

As for the lousy Yankees nothing, of course, could have given me greater pleasure than to write and tell Messrs Dana and Appleton to—. But the STATE OF AFFAIRS IS SIMPLY THIS:

I had overdrawn £20 on Appleton. According to my reckoning, the amount overdrawn was at most £5. However I had no alternative, since some accounts which were due at the end of December had to be paid. WELL. For the time being Mr Dana has now credited the *à compte*[c] of the *Tribune* with £20—a sum which I was to draw on the *Tribune* EXACTLY TOMORROW—in this way virtually cutting off all my resources until the manuscript sent to Appleton has paid off the damned thing. So until then I am IN A DEADLOCK. As soon as this chap Appleton has been paid in kind, thus enabling me to dip into the *Tribune*'s treasure-chest again, I am all for dropping him altogether—more especially if the Vienna *Presse* accedes to my suggestion of a weekly article on finance.[254] At all events I am of the opinion THAT EVEN THE MENACE TO STOP SUPPLY WOULD BRING ROUND DANA AND APPLETON, AND INDUCE THEM TO OFFER A BETTER PAYMENT. But this move can only be made when the present DEADLOCK has been resolved. By my reckoning some 30 or 32 columns will

---

[a] See this volume, p. 228. - [b] See previous letter, p. 270. - [c] account

still remain to be sent if the swine have taken 'Bolivar'. Until then I shall be quite literally in the air. Moreover, the rascals know that they now have me in their power. Hence, none of the stuff that now remains to be done should be condensed more than is absolutely necessary to avoid making it insipid.

As far as 'Bülow' and 'Beresford' are concerned, I can write the biographies, but the *military part should be written entirely by you, in English,* in order that these articles should not stand out from the rest. Besides, mere indications are of no use to me in this case since following them up would, after all, involve research—an impossibility just now. As soon as you have finished with B, you must get to work on 'Cavalry', since this will pay off the debt.

SUCH, MY BOY, IS THE SITUATION. Fortunately events in the outside world offer a good deal of solace just now. Otherwise, in private I THINK I lead THE MOST TROUBLED LIFE THAT CAN BE IMAGINED. NEVER MIND! What could be more asinine for people of wide aspirations than to get married at all, thus letting themselves in for the *petites misères de la vie domestique et privée.*[a]

What will the good *Guardian* say now? The REVENGE of Milner Gibson and Bright is INDEED classic.[287] Between ourselves, I think that Pam HAD his *'raysons'*[b] for dissolving his own ministry and that all the apparent BLUNDERS which led to this RESULT were calculated ones so far as he was concerned.

From a PAPER which recently appeared in the *Moniteur* it transpires that, IF COMPARED WITH 1855 and '56, the STORED UP COMMODITIES IN THE FRENCH CUSTOMS *entrepôts*[c] are enormous,[d] while the *Economist*'s correspondent declares outright that Bonaparte caused the Bank TO MAKE ADVANCES on the same and thus ENABLED THEIR HOLDERS TO RETURN THEM. But with the approach of spring they will inevitably BE THROWN ON THE MARKET, AND THEN, THERE IS NO DOUBT, THERE WILL BE A *CRASH* IN FRANCE, ANSWERED BY CRASHES IN BELGIUM, HOLLAND, RHENISH PRUSSIA ETC.[e]

In Italy the economic situation is truly frightful. Side by side with INDUSTRIAL CRISIS, AGRICULTURAL DISTRESS. (This last, according to the CONCLUSIONS of an AGRICULTURAL CONGRESS IN FRANCE, very bad there too. The congress declared that THEY COULD NOT GO ON WITH 17 FRS. THE HECTOLITRE OF WHEAT.[288])

---

[a] petty miseries of domestic and private life - [b] The original has *Grind,* a distorted form of the German *Gründe* (reasons). - [c] depots - [d] 'Situation des entrepôts à la fin du mois de décembre', *Le Moniteur universel,* No. 24, 24 January 1858. - [e] 'From Our Own Correspondent. Paris, Thursday', *The Economist,* No. 756, 20 February 1858.

TAKEN ALL IN ALL, the crisis has been burrowing away like the good old mole it is.[a]

Salut,

Your

K. M.

First published in *Der Briefwechsel zwischen F. Engels und K. Marx,* Bd. 2, Stuttgart, 1913

Printed according to the original

Published in English for the first time

145

ENGELS TO MARX

IN LONDON

[Manchester,] 24 February 1858

Dear Moor,

Enclosed a fiver[b]—unfortunately I couldn't shell out yesterday, otherwise you would have had it 24 hours earlier—and the article 'Brescia'. Now there are only 'Burmah' (half-finished—it's long job searching out the reports on the latest war[289]) and 'Bomarsund' to be done for B, and after that the two biographies. As to these I can soon get together what is needed on 'Beresford', but I'm in a quandary with 'Bülow' because I find it absolutely impossible to get hold of a good book on the wars of liberation.[c] His resolution at Grossbeeren (he beat the French against Bernadotte's wishes) is to be commended and the victory at Dennewitz was a most remarkable one: 40,000 Prussians beat 70,000 Frenchmen.[197] However I shall have another look round. Once the stuff for B is finished I shall go on to 'Cavalry'.

I don't agree with the idea of dropping Appleton—unless that is, we have to go to the Continent. I find the encyclopaedic course most useful and, after all, the thing is going so slowly that it could be done entirely at one's leisure were financial circumstances not

---

[a] Cf. references to the 'mole' in Marx's *The Eighteenth Brumaire of Louis Bonaparte* and 'Speech at the Anniversary of *The People's Paper*' (present edition, Vol. 11, p. 185 and Vol. 14, p. 656). - [b] Crossed out in the original: 'R/J 56641, Manchester, 16 Jan. 1857' (see next letter). - [c] the 1813-14 military campaigns against Napoleonic France

so pressing. Anyway you should threaten to resign as soon as the situation permits. I too believe that it would prove instantly beneficial.

In these circumstances the great Lassalle might be very useful. I trust he does what is necessary as regards the political economy, and likewise the Vienna *Presse.* He must have been very dilatory in the latter case, seeing that you had already written to him before about the financial article. I am keeping his letter here to show Lupus, since you've answered it anyway.

The historical irony whereby Mr Pam received his notice at the hands of Gibson and Bright is very pretty.[287] What the *Guardian* has to say about it you will be able to see from the 3 copies I am sending off at the same time as this letter. Pam, by the way, evidently intends to eliminate any possibility of his return—the prosecution of the wretched little publisher[a] in London, the witch hunt that ended in the cellar in Birmingham (see day before yesterday's *Sun,* A CAPITAL HOAX) and other gestures of subservience to Bonaparte that crop up every day cannot fail in the long run to infuriate John Bull.

In Italy the outlook can't be so very bad after all. Admittedly there are complaints about the delay in recovering outstanding debts but on the whole it's no worse than here in the HOME TRADE. We don't have very many more overdue accounts than is usually the case in Italy. Indeed the fellows are starting to order more freely again. Admittedly our own article can't be regarded as an absolute criterion, but it nevertheless provides a few pointers. Business is still *bad* over there, of course, but not exceedingly so. But all that can still come.

The Bonapartists must have become tremendously nervous. At Fould's *bal masqué* 75 *sergents de ville*[b] were ON THE PREMISES dressed as dominos. See the *Guardian.*

Warmest regards to the whole FAMILY.

Your
F. E.

First published abridged in *Der Briefwechsel zwischen F. Engels und K. Marx,* Bd. 2, Stuttgart, 1913 and in full in: Marx and Engels, *Works,* First Russian Edition, Vol. XXII, Moscow, 1929

Printed according to the original

Published in English for the first time

[a] Edward Truelove - [b] policemen

146

ENGELS TO MARX

IN LONDON

Manchester, 1 March 1858

Dear Marx,

On Wednesday, 24 February, I sent you a registered letter containing R/J 56641, Manchester, 16 Jan. 1857; a five-pound note. I trust that it reached you. If not, STOP PAYMENT at the Bank IMMEDIATELY. This evening I shall also send DIVERSE *Guardians*; another batch went off last Wednesday at the same time as the letter. In today's you'll find some interesting stuff about Orsini.

The shabby way in which Pam, as he made his exit, unleashed all manner of political persecution—first Bernard and Allsop and now that poor devil of a PUBLISHER[a]—was quite a lark. But even this hasn't put John Bull off his TRULY BRITISH MINISTER,[141] just a little grumbling here and there about the 2 *cives Romani* in Naples.[290] VERILY, the fellow has left an offensive stench behind him.

In today's *Guardian* you will see that in Preston, etc., etc., SHORT TIME is still the order of the day. Will soon be general again. At present prices MANUFACTURERS are losing on most things, while spinners are just able to subsist, and to subsist well in the case of a few articles. As soon as rising prices CHECK demand (hitherto the fear of *still* higher prices has momentarily increased it), that too will cease and the fun begin all over again.

Your

F. E.

First published in: Marx and Engels, *Works*, First Russian Edition, Vol. XXII, Moscow, 1929

Printed according to the original

Published in English for the first time

[a] Edward Truelove

147

MARX TO ENGELS

IN MANCHESTER

[London,] 2 March 1858

Dear Frederick,

I sent you *by return* a note acknowledging receipt of the £5. The scrawl contained nothing else save a few political comments, ALTOGETHER NOT 20 LINES.[291] But all the same, I find it exceedingly irritating that the post office here should be taking an immediate interest in my correspondence. Not long ago I wrote to Collet, that most respectable of men, and the letter vanished. Complaints availed me nothing. I SHALL NOW WATCH THE PROGRESS OF POST OFFICE INTERFERENCE. If there is a 3rd CASE of this kind I shall proclaim the fact above my signature in the London press. The canaille are welcome to read what I write about POLITICS. But my PRIVATE AFFAIRS are not such that I would care to have any old German POST OFFICE SPY go poking his nose into them; 50 swine of various nationalities are, it seems, regularly employed as interpreters by the London *cabinet noir*,[292] AT LEAST, THE URQUHARTITES SAY SO.

The information I sent you recently about the STATE of TRADE IN ITALY, and Milan in particular, was taken from the Turin papers, which are well supplied with correspondents in that region. While it is, of course, in the interests of Turin to paint the situation in Austrian Italy in the blackest possible colours, the reports from Milan went into details which had the real ring of truth.—As regards the STATE of FRENCH TRADE, you should read the contribution from the Paris CORRESPONDENT in today's *Times*.[a] True, the chap now seems to be blaming the thing on Orsini and the FRENCH COLONELS, *mais c'est ridicule*.[b]

I enclose a wretched scrawl by Pyat, Talandier and Co.,[c] which laddies couldn't rest for the fame accorded to Ledru-Rollin and Mazzini and Bernard, whereas they themselves had apparently been quite passed over by the French government. They believe that a revolution is in the offing and after all their 'activity' in London—Talandier had shouted himself as hoarse as *quondam*

---

[a] The contribution datelined 'Paris, Saturday, Feb. 27, 6 p.m.', *The Times*, No. 22930, 2 March 1858. - [b] but it's ridiculous - [c] F. Pyat, A. Besson, A. Talandier, *Letter to the Parliament and the Press* (Marx seems to have used the French version of the letter).

Bornstedt—it was INDEED galling for the great men to have the attention of revolutionary Europe diverted from them by other INCIDENTS. Therefore, JUST IN THE NICK OF TIME, THEY ISSUED the clap-trap enclosed herewith.[293] No style, no sense, not even French, altogether in the style of the Porte St. Martin streetwalker so typical of the former *Charivari* contributor and COMPOSITOR of little TOASTS.[294] In order that this publication should not fail in its *purpose,* they sent the beastly little thing to all the PAPERS. Persigny-Palmerston Jenkins OF *THE MORNING POST* was instantly CAUGHT in the TRAP. In a LEADER written by himself he denounced the chaps and their opusculum TO THE HONOURABLE MR WALPOLE and, as an additional precaution, HE DID THE WHOLE PAMPHLET INTO BAD ENGLISH. More than that. In his INAUGURAL SPEECH Derby informed the HOUSE OF LORDS that the CROWN advocates had been instructed to look into the thing and see if legal proceedings could be taken against it.[a] In this way CITIZENS Talandier, Pyat and Besson have, with their insane concoction, succeeded in puffing themselves TO A DEGREE they could hardly have dared hope for.

As for Bernard, he will presumably have to spend a little longer in jug.

The insolence and IMPUDENCE with which Pam has placed himself at the head of the liberal opposition and nominated himself an HONOURABLE GENTLEMAN OPPOSITE,[295] IS TRULY WONDERFUL, but he can, of course, do exactly what he pleases with a House of Commons of his own creation.

Apropos. Can you tell me how often machinery has to be replaced in, say, your factory? Babbage maintains that in Manchester THE BULK OF MACHINERY IS RENOVATED on average EVERY 5 YEARS.[b] This seems to me somewhat STARTLING and not QUITE TRUSTWORTHY. The average period for the replacement of machinery is *one* important factor in explaining the multi-year cycle which has been a feature of industrial development ever since the consolidation of big industry.

What is Lupus up to? Give him my regards.

Your

K. M.

[a] Derby's speech in the House of Lords of 1 March 1858 published in *The Times,* No. 22930, 2 March 1858. - [b] Ch. Babbage, *On the Economy of Machinery and Manufactures,* p. 285.

Another BATCH OF *Guardians* arrived today. 'Bidassoa' also received last week.

First published abridged in *Der Briefwechsel zwischen F. Engels und K. Marx*, Bd. 2, Stuttgart, 1913 and in full in: Marx and Engels, *Works*, First Russian Edition, Vol. XXII, Moscow, 1929

Printed according to the original

Published in English for the first time

148

ENGELS TO MARX

IN LONDON

Manchester, 4 March 1858

Dear Moor,

So once again the *cabinet noir*[292] has well and truly honoured you with its attentions. I had expected something of the sort but it's a bit steep to go and intercept letters. I think you would do better to have the address done in another hand, in which case they will only open the letters sent *to* you. I was expecting an acknowledgment from you and therefore took PARTICULAR care to ask our messenger daily and in so many words whether there were any letters for me—each time the answer was in the negative. And yet we have the asinine Félix Pyat announcing to the world *qu'il n'y a pas de police politique proprement dite, en Angleterre.*[a] Rarely have I come across a more bungled concoction, style and all.[293] Still the same old faith in the Constitution of 1848; one might almost be face to face with our own jackasses of the Imperial Constitution.[296] And what a ghastly style! *Après tout*[b] the idiots have achieved their aim and will, perhaps, earn themselves a cheap form of martyrdom. *Cette bête de*[c] Derby, falling straight into the trap like that, and allowing the riff-raff to have their way.

As to the question of machinery, it's difficult to say anything positive; at all events Babbage[d] is quite WRONG. The most reliable criterion is the PERCENTAGE by which a manufacturer writes down his

[a] that properly speaking there are no political police in England - [b] However - [c] That ass - [d] Ch. Babbage, *On the Economy of Machinery and Manufactures.*

machinery each year for wear and tear and repairs, thus recovering the entire cost of his machines within a given period. This PERCENTAGE is normally $7^1/_2$, in which case the machinery will be paid for over $13^1/_3$ years by an annual deduction from profits, i.e. will be replaceable without loss. E.g. I have £10,000 worth of machinery. At the end of the first year, when I draw up my balance-sheet, I enter

	£10,000
from which I deduct $7^1/_2$% for wear and tear	» 750
	£9,250
Expenditure on repairs	£100
Cost of machinery	£9,350
At the end of the 2nd year I deduct $7^1/_2$% [of] £10,000, and $7^1/_2$% [of] £100	» 757 10
	£8,593 10
Expenditure on repairs	» 306 10
Present cost of entire machinery	£8,900

etc. Now, $13^1/_3$ years is admittedly a long time in the course of which numerous bankruptcies and changes occur; you may enter other branches, sell your old machinery, introduce new improvements, but if this calculation wasn't more or less right, practice would have changed it long ago. Nor does the old machinery that has been sold promptly become old iron; it finds takers among the small spinners, etc., etc., who continue to use it. We ourselves have machines in operation that are certainly 20 years old and, when one occasionally takes a glance inside some of the more ancient and ramshackle CONCERNS up here, one can see antiquated stuff that must be 30 years old at least. Moreover, in the case of most machines, only a few of the components wear out to the extent that they have to be replaced after 5 or 6 years. And even after 15 years, provided the basic principle of a machine has not been superseded by new inventions, there is relatively little difficulty in replacing worn out parts (I refer here to spinning and flyer frames), so that it is hard to set a definite term on the effective life of such machinery. Again, over the last 20 years improvements in spinning machinery have not been such as to preclude the incorporation of almost all of them in the existing *structure* of the machines, since nearly all are minor innovations. (Admittedly, in the case of carding, the enlargement of the carding cylinder was a major improvement which supplanted the old machines where *good* qualities were concerned, but for ordinary qualities the old machinery will be perfectly adequate for a long time yet.)

Babbage's assertion is so absurd that were it true, England's industrial capital must continually diminish and money simply be thrown away. A manufacturer who turns over his capital 5 times in 4 years, hence $6^{1}/_{4}$ times in 5 years, would, in addition to his average profit of 10%, have to earn annually a further 20% on approximately $^{3}/_{4}$ of his capital (the machinery) if he was to recoup without loss his outlay on the old machinery—i.e. would have to make 25%. This would, of course, vastly increase the cost price of all articles—more, almost, than it would be increased by wages—in which case where is the advantage of machinery? Annual WAGES amount to perhaps $^{1}/_{3}$ the cost of the machinery—undoubtedly less in the case of the smaller spinners and weavers, and wear and tear is supposed to amount to $^{1}/_{5}$—the thing is ludicrous. There is certainly not a single establishment in England in the regular LINE of big industry which replaces its machinery in 5 years. Anyone foolish enough to do so would go to the wall at the first CHANGE; the old machines, even though much inferior, would certainly have the advantage over the modern ones and would be able to produce much more cheaply, for the market follows not the people who charge 15% for wear and tear on every pound of twist, but those who charge only 6% (approx. $^{4}/_{5}$ of an annual depreciation of $7^{1}/_{2}$%) and hence sell at cheaper prices.

Ten to twelve years are enough to bring about changes in the character of the BULK of machinery, thereby necessitating its replacement to a greater or lesser extent. The period of $13^{1}/_{3}$ years will vary, of course, depending on bankruptcies, breakage of essential parts where a repair would prove too expensive, and similar contingencies, so one could make it a bit shorter. But certainly not less than 10 years.

I had finished 'Burmah' when I was compelled to make DIVERSE necessary ADDITIONS from another source. So I haven't done with it yet and the thing will have to wait until Tuesday. It will run to nearly 3 pages. There are still a few details to be looked up for 'Bomarsund'. On top of that I have to snatch whatever opportunity I can, since library hours are so similar to office hours that I can't always get there. As soon as I've dealt with these wretched things—likewise 'Bülow' and 'Beresford', which suffer from the same snag—I shall again have A FAIR GALLOPING COUNTRY ahead of me and be able to clap on spurs with 'Cavalry', etc.

Many regards to your wife and children.

Your

F. E.

First published in *Der Briefwechsel zwischen F. Engels und K. Marx*, Bd. 2, Stuttgart, 1913

Printed according to the original

Published in English for the first time

149

MARX TO ENGELS

IN MANCHESTER

[London,] 5 March 1858

DEAR Frederic,

As regards the enclosed, which has clearly been delayed,[297] you might be so good as to discuss with Lupus the kind of answer you think would be suitable. *Don't* return the thing (but keep it) because such things are safer with you than with me just now. At present London is a gathering-point for *mouchards*[a] of all nations. Hardly a day goes by when the curs aren't *plus ou moins*[b] lynched.

MY BEST THANKS FOR YOUR *éclaircissements*[c] about machinery. The figure of 13 years corresponds closely enough to the theory, since it establishes a *unit* for ONE EPOCH OF INDUSTRIAL REPRODUCTION which *plus ou moins* coincides with the period in which major crises recur; needless to say their course is also determined by factors of a quite different kind, depending on their period of reproduction. For me the important thing is to discover, in the immediate material postulates of big industry, *one* factor that determines cycles. In considering the reproduction of machinery, as distinct from *capital circulant*, one is irresistibly reminded of the Moleschotts who also pay insufficient attention to the period of reproduction of the bony skeleton, contenting themselves RATHER, like the economists, with the average time taken by the human body to replace itself completely. Another question in respect of which I require only one example (approximate), is how, e.g. in your own mill OR RATHER

---

[a] police spies - [b] more or less - [c] explanations

manufacturing business, FLOATING CAPITAL is apportioned over raw material and WAGES, and what portion on average you leave with your BANKER. Further, how you *calculate* turnover in your books. Here the theoretical rules are extremely simple and SELF-EVIDENT. But it is nevertheless just as well to have some inkling of how the thing looks in practice. The method of calculation used by businessmen is, of course, PARTLY based on illusions even greater than those of the economists; on the other hand it rectifies the latter's theoretical illusions by means of practical ones. You speak of 10% profit. I SUPPOSE THAT YOU DO NOT TAKE INTO ACCOUNT THE INTEREST and that this is doubtless shown along with the profit. IN THE 'FIRST REPORT OF THE FACTORY COMMISSIONERS' I have found the following STATEMENT, which serves as an average example:

*Capital sunk in building and machinery	£10,000
Floating capital	£ 7,000

£500 interest on 10,000 fixed capital
£350 interest on floating capital
£150 Rents, taxes, rates
£650 Sinking fund of $6^1/_2$ p.c. for wear and tear of the fixed capital

£1,650
1,100 contingencies (?), carriage, coal, oil

£2,750
£2,600 wages and salaries

£5,350
£10,000 for about 400,000 lbs raw cotton at 6d

£15,350*

16,000 for 363,000 LBS TWIST SPUN. VALUE 16,000. *Profit* 650, OR ABOUT 4.2 P.C. Hence WAGES of OPERATIVES here ABOUT $^1/_6$.

It is true that in this case the total profit only amounts to ABOUT 10%, including interest. Mr Senior, however, who after all represents the manufacturers' interests, states that in Manchester the average profit including interest amounts to 15%.[a] It is a great pity that the above STATEMENT does not show the *number* of operatives, or the proportion of actual *WAGES* to what appears as *SALARIES.*

By the by, the manner in which even the best economists, SUCH AS Ricardo *ipsissimus*,[b] descend into sheer juvenile poppycock

[a] N. W. Senior, *Letters on the Factory Act...*, pp. 12, 13. - [b] himself

whenever they find themselves on the treadmill of bourgeois thought, struck me very forcibly in the following passage of Ricardo's, which I happened to come across yesterday. You will recall that A. Smith, who is still very old-fashioned, declares that by comparison with trade at home, overseas trade only gives ONE HALF OF THE ENCOURAGEMENT TO THE PRODUCTIVE LABOUR OF A COUNTRY ETC. To this Ricardo replies with the following example:

'Smith's argument appears to me to be fallacious; for though two CAPITALS, one Portuguese and one English, be employed, as Smith supposes, still a capital will be EMPLOYED in the foreign trade, double of what would be employed in the home trade. Suppose that Scotland employs a capital of a thousand pounds in making linen, which she exchanges for the produce of a similar capital employed in making silks in England, two thousand pounds, and a proportional quantity of labour will be employed by the two countries. Suppose now, that England discovers that she can import more linen from Germany, for the silks which she before exported to Scotland, and that Scotland discovers that she can obtain more silks from France in return for her linen, than she before obtained from England,—will not England and Scotland immediately cease trading with each other, and will not the home trade of consumption be changed for a foreign trade of consumption? But although two additional capitals will enter into this trade, the capital of Germany and that of France, will not the same amount of Scotch and of English capital continue to be employed, and will it not give motion to the same quantity of industry as when it was engaged in the home trade?'[a]

The assumption that in such circumstances Germany would buy her silks in England instead of France, and France her linen in Scotland instead of Germany is hardly what one would expect OF A FELLOW LIKE RICARDO.

Friend Thomas Tooke has died, and with him the last English economist OF ANY VALUE.

Did you overlook, in one of the *Guardians* you sent me, the item in which David Urquhart figures as an infanticide? The FOOL treated his 13-month-old baby to a Turkish bath which, as chance would have it, contributed to congestion of the brain and hence its subsequent DEATH. The CORONER'S INQUEST on this CASE lasted for 3 days and it was only by the skin of his teeth that Urquhart escaped a verdict OF MANSLAUGHTER. *Quel triomphe pour*[b] Pam.

Salut.

Your

K. M.

First published abridged in *Der Briefwechsel zwischen F. Engels und K. Marx*, Bd. 2, Stuttgart, 1913 and in full in: Marx and Engels, *Works*, First Russian Edition, Vol. XXII, Moscow, 1929

Printed according to the original

Published in English for the first time

---

[a] D. Ricardo, *On the Principles of Political Economy, and Taxation*, p. 420. (Marx quotes the passage in his own German translation.) - [b] What a triumph for

150

ENGELS TO MARX

IN LONDON

[Manchester,] 11 March 1858

Dear Moor,

Herewith something on 'Beresford' which I've been able to abstract from Napier.[a] I couldn't find anything about his expedition to Buenos Aires at the beginning of the century, but it was a glorious one and would be worth investigating. He capitulated, RUMP AND STUMP, with the whole English force.[298]

'Bülow' is IN HAND. Ditto 'Cavalry'. Still some particulars to be looked up on 'Bomarsund'. In India there's another article brewing for which I shall be on the *qui vive*.

Charras' *Campagne de 1815* is no longer obtainable in Brussels; said to be out of print and with no definite prospect of a reprint. In other words, Bonaparte has bought the publisher.[b] If you can run to ground a cheap (i. e. not exorbitant) copy in London, I'd like you to let me know; just now I'm studying this campaign.

I suspect that friend Dana is abridging our articles considerably, otherwise you couldn't possibly have miscalculated so badly. Go to Trübner's some time and have a look at the *Cyclopaedia*.

No news here, except that it's a ghastly winter; the weather changes I don't know how many times a day. Health very good. Am also taking iron.

Warm regards to your wife and children.

Your

F. E.

A bundle of *Guardians* goes off today. As often as not there's nothing from their foreign correspondents just now. In today's more statistics on the UNEMPLOYED.[c]

First published abridged in *Der Briefwechsel zwischen F. Engels und K. Marx*, Bd. 2, Stuttgart, 1913 and in full in: Marx and Engels, *Works*, First Russian Edition, Vol. XXII, Moscow, 1929

Printed according to the original

Published in English for the first time

---

[a] W. F. P. Napier, *History of the War in the Peninsula...* - [b] Alphonse Dürr - [c] This paragraph was added in pencil in the original.

151

MARX TO FERDINAND LASSALLE[299]

IN BERLIN

London, 11 March 1858
9 Grafton Terrace, Maitland Park,
Haverstock Hill

Dear Lassalle,

I was confined to bed when your letter arrived, [hence][a] the delay in replying. Now I am ALL RIGHT again. *D'abord*,[b] whatever the outcome of the NEGOTIATION ini[tiated] by you, whether successful or otherwise, I would like to express my warmest thanks for your exertions whose value is doubled by the fact that you yourself were in poor health. I hope that you are now perfectly well again. Friend Quételet[c] has calculated that, after Petersburg and Madrid, Berlin is the most insalubrious capital in Europe—as, indeed, having lived there 5 years, I personally can confirm by comparison with London, Brussels and Paris.

But to come to business. You will, perhaps, permit me to reply to question 4 first and then proceed in reverse.

1. The publisher shall have the right to cease publication *on receipt of the second instalment*, always provided I am given due notice. A proper contract, assuming he intends to publish *more than one* instalment, shall not be concluded before delivery of the third.[d]

2. As regards the fee, I shall, if necessary, agree to a minimum of 0 for the first instalment, for while I certainly cannot write the whole work gratis, I am even less prepared to see its publication come to grief over the question of money. I have no idea what authors are paid in Germany. But if you do not think 30 talers per sheet is too much, that is what you should ask,—less, if you think it excessive. Once the thing has been launched we shall see on what conditions the publisher can and will go on with it.

---

[a] Ms. damaged. - [b] First of all - [c] A. Quételet, *Sur l'homme et le développement de ses facultés....* Marx used an English translation of the book, *A Treatise on Man and the Development of the Faculties*. - [d] This refers to the large economic work planned by Marx. Only one instalment was published. It appeared under the title *A Contribution to the Critique of Political Economy* in 1859.

3. Minimum length of the instalments SAY 4 sheets; maximum 6. It is to be desired, of course, that each instalment should form a relative whole. But the separate sections vary greatly in length.

Whatever the circumstances, the first instalment would have to constitute a relative whole and, since it lays the foundations for all that follows, it could hardly be done in under 5 or 6 sheets. But that is something I shall find out when I come to finish it off. It contains 1. Value, 2. Money, 3. Capital in General (the process of production of capital; process of its circulation; the unity of the two, or capital and profit; interest). This constitutes a pamphlet in its own right. As you yourself will have discovered from your economic studies, Ricardo's exposition of profit conflicts with his (correct) definition of value, thus giving rise among his followers either to a complete departure from his basis, or to the most objectionable eclecticism. I believe that I have cleared the matter up. (On closer examination the economists will, to be sure, find that ALTOGETHER IT IS A DIRTY BUSINESS.)

4. As to the total number of sheets I am myself very much in the dark since, in my notebooks, the material for the work is entirely in the form of monographs,[250] many of which go into a wealth of detail that would disappear in the course of compilation. Nor is it my intention to elaborate to an equal degree all the 6 books into which I am dividing the whole, but rather to give no more than the broad outline in the last 3, whereas in the first 3, which contain the actual nub of the economic argument, some degree of amplification will be unavoidable. I hardly think that the whole can be done in under 30 or 40 sheets.

With kind regards.

Your

K. M.

PS. If the publisher is agreeable, I could arrange for him to have the first instalment ABOUT the end of May.

First published in: *F. Lassalle. Nachgelassene Briefe und Schriften*, Bd. III, Stuttgart-Berlin, 1922

Printed according to the original

152

MARX TO ENGELS

IN MANCHESTER

[London,] 15 March [1858]

Dear Frederick,

'Burmah', 'Beresford', *Manchester Guardian* received. You haven't mentioned receiving a letter from me enclosing one from New York,[297] etc. Considering how things are with the post just now, it's important that I should know. DROP, THEREFORE, TWO LINES.

A longer letter soon.

Your

K. M.

First published in *Der Briefwechsel zwischen F. Engels und K. Marx*, Bd. 2, Stuttgart, 1913

Printed according to the original

Published in English for the first time

153

ENGELS TO MARX

IN LONDON

[Manchester, 16 March 1858]

Dear Moor,

The letter with enclosure from New York[a] arrived here safely—when I sent off 'Beresford' last week I was in such a hurry that I completely forgot to acknowledge its receipt.

For the same reason I haven't yet been able to see Lupus and at this moment my head is again so full of damned COMMERCE that I can hardly summon what few wits I have, let alone work on Appleton's things. I shall finish 'Bomarsund' and if possible 'Bülow' in time for Friday, i. e. send off 'Bülow' tomorrow if possible, so that you'll have time to add the biographical part; the

[a] See previous letter.

only sources I have, by the way, are Siborne and Jomini.[a] For 'Bomarsund' I have to refer to the press again; there's nothing further about it in my papers.

Then I'll set to work with a will on 'Cavalry'. Unfortunately I can't lay my hand on anything about the Seven Years War,[300] the heyday of the cavalry. However, *nous verrons.*[b]

I'm annoyed at being unable to get through the things faster; but the second lot of B's was really a very tiring job and I quite definitely cannot work far into the night without suffering from insomnia for several days afterwards. Two evenings in succession is the maximum I can manage but, all the same, it's easier now than it was in the beginning.

Since Saturday, *nothing* whatever from Paris in the *Guardian.*

Your

F. E.

First published abridged in *Der Briefwechsel zwischen F. Engels und K. Marx,* Bd. 2, Stuttgart, 1913 and in full in: Marx and Engels, *Works,* First Russian Edition, Vol. XXII, Moscow, 1929

Printed according to the original

Published in English for the first time

154

ENGELS TO MARX

IN LONDON

[Manchester,] 17 March 1858

Dear Moor,

When you get this letter and today's *Guardian,* sent off at the same time, give your wife the Paris report to read. It gives one quite a turn to hear a Bonapartist and official relate how 100,000 *ouvriers*[c] in the Faubourg St. Antoine responded to Orsini's execution[271] with the cry *'Vive la République'.*[d] So deportations and arrests *à tort et à travers*[e] have borne as little fruit as the *cités ouvrières*[f] and the national *ateliers en gros,*[g] and it is gratifying, on the eve of the grand ball, to see such a roll-call take place and hear

[a] W. Siborne, *History of the War in France and Belgium, in 1815;* A. H. Jomini, *Vie politique et militaire de Napoléon...* - [b] we shall see - [c] workers - [d] Long live the Republic. - [e] wholly at random - [f] workers' settlements - [g] workshops on a large scale

100,000 men reply, *'Present!'* I'm only sorry Orsini couldn't hear that cry.

A local philistine who was lately in Paris has returned with the news that since Orsini's attempt on Monsieur Boustrapa's[40] life two more had been made. The first was also mentioned in the English press; the fellow was arrested in the Bois de Boulogne at the moment he took aim with his pistol; the second was news to me; it appears that the fellow shot at or tried to stab him in the Tuileries gardens and was summarily shot by soldiers of the Guard in the gallery of June 1848 fame beneath the *terrasse du bord de l'eau.*[a] [301]

It seems that all threadbare patriotic notables want to make fools of themselves: mad old Landor must needs go and write to *The Times* today.[302] All that remains now is for Venedey to protest against Orsini.

But Boustrapa has indeed come to a pretty pass, and it is a pity that the *Constitutionnel* should no longer be in a position to declare that *l'horizon politique s'obscurcit.*[b] [95] What could be funnier than to find in the *Moniteur,* no less, a story about the officers at Châlon who, before risking rank and skin for the *empereur,* hurried to the *sous-préfet* to ask whether or not a republic had really been proclaimed in Paris?[c] But one can also see how, even in the army, the only genuine Bonapartists are the men at the top because these are compromised and lured on by the prospect of truly splendid bounties. For, after all, what has Boustrapa to offer the bulk of subalterns? The blackguard doubtless knows as well as we do that, aside from his Guard, there are few troops he can rely on. Unfortunately the Guard is strong and knows that, under *any* other government, it would either be relegated to the line or disbanded. It consists, as far as infantry is concerned, of 4 regiments of grenadiers, 2 of riflemen, 1 of gendarmes, 1 of Zouaves, 1 battalion of light infantry (17 infantry battalions all told); further, 2 regiments of cuirassiers, 2 of dragoons, 1 of mounted grenadiers, 1 of hussars, 1 of chasseurs—21 squadrons and a strong force of artillery. In all 18,000-20,000 men with 40-50 cannon, a nucleus solid enough to stiffen a somewhat wavering line. In addition everything has been so organised as to provide for a speedy concentration of troops from the Provinces (you only have to look at a railway map of France) so that a movement, if *anticipated,* would undoubtedly find itself confronted by 60,000-80,000 men. Victory over such vast numbers is to be

---

[a] waterside terrace - [b] the political horizon is lowering - [c] 'A Châlon-sur-Saône, dans la soirée...', *Le Moniteur universel,* No. 68, 9 March 1858.

achieved in 2 ways only: either by secret societies within the army itself—and these are said to be numerous—or by a determined anti-Bonapartist stand on the part of the bourgeoisie, as in February.[a] I don't believe that victory is possible in the absence of one, let alone both, of these conditions. There is no doubt that the lower echelons of the army are undermined by reds and the higher by Orleanists[124] and Legitimists,[303] nor that the *loi des suspects*[304] in conjunction with other repressive measures is making life impossible for the bourgeoisie. Boustrapa's mounting difficulties are daily forcing him into ever more desperate straits; he dare not risk war with Prussia, he has shut himself out of Italy; no one any longer believes in Boustrapian socialism; Algeria has no more campaigns to offer. All diversions being excluded, *reste la répression croissante*,[b] i. e. the virtual driving of the bourgeoisie into revolution. For the Orleanists and Legitimists the restoration of the constitutional republic under their joint rule must already be LOOMING IN THE DISTANCE as the most probable *pis aller*[c] should circumstances not hold out an immediate prospect of victory for either party. *Le cas de soulèvement donné*[d]—and it's bound to come in the course of this year—there is every chance that they will follow the pattern of February 1848, *sauf à lancer plus tard les troupes sur les faubourgs*.[e] And we know what will happen then. As soon as their fear of Bonaparte has made the troops unsteady enough to render the success of the insurrection *inevitable*, their fear of the *prolétaires* will make them induce the troops to put down the insurrection—*trop tard*[f]*!*—the flood will surge over them regardless, the troops will stand gaping—and then we shall see how much ground the water has gained since the last springtide of 1848.

Fortunately commerce in France is in such a state that it *cannot* improve until the chronic crisis has culminated in political revolution. I don't believe that the state of trade in France can possibly improve so long as Boustrapa remains at the helm. While the crisis lasts all the talk about 'confidence' being undermined by Orsini, Espinasse, etc., is mere idle euphemism; but under a régime of this nature it will become sober truth should the conditions responsible for the crisis cease to obtain. By the way, I have quite come round to your opinion that in France the Crédit mobilier[45] was no haphazard swindle but an altogether necessary institution, and that Morny's pilferings which it spawned were no

[a] i.e. during the February Revolution of 1848 - [b] there remains growing repression - [c] expedient - [d] Given an insurrection - [e] save that later they may send troops against the suburbs - [f] too late

less inevitable, for it was only the prospect of getting rich quick which made the Crédit mobilier viable in France. Under these circumstances it's a TOSS-UP which falls first—Boustrapa or the Crédit mobilier.—The prolongation of bills must inevitably give rise to enormous losses. The use of such means to overcome a crisis can be of avail only if the *reprise des affaires*[a] is a *real* one in industry too, but the mere fact of an EASY MONEY-MARKET cannot help anyone who has no credit—and I believe that in France credit is no longer accorded save by prolonging what has already been given.

Things in Prussia look pretty rotten to me. The tinpot little Chamber has greatly inflamed the parochial Prussian patriotism of the philistines there and even the arch-philistine, I fear, looks forward with assurance to the advent, along with the English marriage,[305] of an English constitution, albeit democratised. If only the corporal[b] were to make a fool of himself, and that right soon! In Prussia, I fear, it won't be too easy to get rid of the ROYAL FAMILY—unless, that is, the proletariat has made really enormous strides. The bourgeois and philistines have, at any rate, got even worse since 1848. In German Austria, too, nothing much seems to be happening. Plainly your good, honest German has not yet emerged from the hibernation that followed the strenuous exertions of 1848. Slav insurrections and the loss of Hungary and Italy will, by the way, serve their turn in Austria, and on top of that, in the big towns and industrial districts, the crisis will have repercussions which, just now and at this distance, are impossible to gauge. *Après tout*,[c] it's going to be a hard struggle.

But what if Boustrapa were to subdue the first big attempt at an uprising? I regard this as practically impossible, precisely because the measures he has adopted are such that things would not become serious save on a really major occasion. But supposing Boustrapa were to succeed, he'd be doubly in the soup. Pélissier would be *empereur*. The troops of the line, who would in any case show signs of weakness and irresolution, would be declared *non grata* and the Guard alone remain in favour—indeed more so than ever before. A sure means of fostering conspiracy in the army. Next, Boustrapa would have to go directly for the Orleanists and Legitimists, nor would Thiers get away with a couple of days in the Mazas burnishing his Brown Bess.[306] A sure means of utterly ruining commerce. If Boustrapa were ever to triumph, his downfall would be all the more assured.

---

a resumption of business - b the Prince of Prussia - c After all

I only hope the fellow won't be assassinated. In which case I believe things would turn out in the way Morny once described to him: 'Nous commencerions par jeter tous les Jérôme par la fenêtre et puis nous tacherions de nous arranger tant bien que mal avec les Orléans.'[a] Before the *faubourgs* had had time to collect their wits, Morny would have effected his palace revolution and, although the revolution from below would only be postponed for a short while, its basis would no longer be the same.

To return to our own private affairs, I've been able to find virtually nothing about Bülow in Jomini and Cathcart[b] and must see if I can unearth some other source. I shall try and get 'Bomarsund' done tonight. These two articles are preying on my mind.

As soon as the Indian mail brings details about Campbell's Lucknow expedition (in maybe a week or a fortnight's time), send me all the material you can lay hands on, so that I can make an *immediate* start. I shall be able to buy *The Times* up here, but *not* the other London papers, i. e. in single numbers.

Warm regards to your wife and children. I'd like to send you some more money but shall have to wait and see what further payments I shall have to make this month; as soon as I get some idea of this I shall do what I can, you may be sure of that.

Your

F. E.

Lupus has the solemn document from New York.[297] Isn't Kamm that Kinkelian 'proletarian' who used to run a brothel? F. Jacobi is a ridiculous little barrister from Münster who was the butt of everyone's jokes in Switzerland.

First published abridged in *Der Briefwechsel zwischen F. Engels und K. Marx*, Bd. 2, Stuttgart, 1913 and in full in: Marx and Engels, *Works,* First Russian Edition, Vol. XXII, Moscow, 1929

Printed according to the original

Published in English for the first time

---

[a] 'We would begin by throwing all the Jérômes out of the window and then get along as best we could with the Orleans.' - [b] A. H. Jomini, *Vie politique et militaire de Napoléon...*; G. Cathcart, *Commentaries on the War in Russia and Germany in 1812 and 1813.*

155

MARX TO ENGELS

IN MANCHESTER

[London,] 19 March [1858]

Dear Engels,

My article[a] leaves no time for a letter today. Only this much. Rather than let yourself be held up any longer by a search for material, DROP 'Bülow', about whom *I* have sufficient *for* A COMMON BIOGRAPHY (brief), and get ON WITH 'CAVALRY'. *Periculum in mora.*[b] Secondly, I enclose a few delectable DOCUMENTS on the ITALIAN CONGRESS HOAX from the *Star.*[307]

Your letter of today[c] largely used in my article.

Salut.

Your

K. M.

First published in: Marx and Engels, *Works*, First Russian Edition, Vol. XXII, Moscow, 1929

Printed according to the original

Published in English for the first time

156

ENGELS TO MARX

IN LONDON

[Manchester, 26 March 1858]

Dear Moor,

Herewith a five-pound note, number as below.[d] 'Cavalry' progressing well. I have again found some good stuff in Mommsen's *Römische Geschichte* (Hannibal's cavalry). Unfortunately it's difficult to get hold of anything about the Seven Years War.[300]

---

[a] K. Marx, 'Bonaparte's Present Position'. - [b] Danger in delay (Livy, *History of Rome*, Vol. XXXVIII, Chap. 25). - [c] See this volume, pp. 289-93. - [d] The number of the note is no longer to be found in the original.

You'll have received the *Guardians* I sent off yesterday. They were the only ones containing reports from Paris or anything at all of special interest.

In haste—it's half past seven—and the office-boys are waiting to lock up.

Your

F. E.

First published abridged in *Der Briefwechsel zwischen F. Engels und K. Marx*, Bd. 2, Stuttgart, 1913 and in full in: Marx and Engels, *Works*, First Russian Edition, Vol. XXII, Moscow, 1929

Printed according to the original

Published in English for the first time

157

MARX TO ENGELS

IN MANCHESTER

British Museum
[London,] 29 March 1858

Dear Frederic,

The £5 most gratefully received.

Today a letter from Lassalle.[a] Duncker is prepared to publish my political economy on the following conditions. Every few months I am to supply instalments of 3 to 6 sheets (this was my suggestion). He is to have the right to cancel the arrangement at the third instalment. Indeed, no contract is to be definitely concluded until then. In the meantime he is to pay 3 friedrichsdors per sheet. (According to Lassalle, professors in Berlin get only 2.) The first instalment[b] is to be READY at the end of May, i. e. the manuscript.

In my next I must let you have an outline of the first instalment so that you can tell me what you think of it. For the past two weeks I have again been VERY SICKLY and have been taking medicine for my liver. I have been much subject to relapses of late owing to prolonged work by night and, by day, a multitude of petty annoyances RESULTING FROM THE ECONOMICAL CONDITIONS OF MY DOMESTICITY.

[a] of 26 March 1858 - [b] K. Marx, *A Contribution to the Critique of Political Economy.*

I hope that you are quite well again. Write to me about this POINT.

Have had a letter from Harney today, returning my wife's letter to Schramm,[a] which is nice. The little man seems annoyed at my failure to write. He no longer addresses me as DEAR M. but as Dr M. WELL. Maybe I shall send him 4 lines or so, TO CONSOLE THE LOUSY LITTLE FELLOW.

In France, the dance is proceeding most satisfactorily. Conditions are very unlikely to remain peaceful throughout the summer. What do you think of the 5 pashaliks?[308] Originally it was intended to make Pélissier their supreme CHIEF. But on closer consideration Bonaparte decided THAT THIS WOULD BE IN FACT AN ABDICATION OF POWER ON HIS PART. So it's only a half-measure, and one whereby the Spanish institution of CAPTAIN-GENERALSHIP[309] has been introduced into France lock, stock and barrel. Now doesn't this imply a collapse of centralisation and, IN FACT, a diminution of the power of the army? WE MUST HOPE that the French business won't take a SPANISH TURN, but rather that this decentralisation will merely reduce the resistance to be encountered by the revolution.

Salut.

Your

K. M.

Have you ATTENDED [noticed] that of late most of the French companies set up on the pattern of the Crédit mobilier[45] have appeared before the *tribunal criminel*?

First published abridged in *Der Briefwechsel zwischen F. Engels und K. Marx*, Bd. 2, Stuttgart, 1913 and in full in: Marx and Engels, *Works*, First Russian Edition, Vol. XXII, Moscow, 1929

Printed according to the original

Published in English for the first time

158

MARX TO ENGELS[1]

IN MANCHESTER

[London,] 2 April 1858

DEAR Frederick,

The *Guardian* stories highly AMUSING.[b] A correspondent of the *Daily Telegraph* (DIRECTLY UNDER PAM'S AUSPICES) writes of the great

---

[a] See this volume, pp. 566-68. - [b] Ibid., p. 289.

danger of being 'DEAF' in Paris, and says that all 'DEAF ENGLISHMEN' were being hounded by the police as Allsops. Also that ENGLISHMEN were leaving Paris *en masse,* partly because of police chicanery, partly for fear of an outbreak. For if the latter were to happen and the Bonapartists be victorious, the John Bulls feared they might be massacred by the MADDENED SOLDIERS, whereat the correspondent himself naively comments that IN SUCH A CASE [HE] SHOULD LIKE TO BE ANYWHERE ELSE BUT IN PARIS. This DESERTION by the Bulls AT THIS MOMENT OF COMMERCIAL DEPRESSION is queering the pitch of the Parisian *épicier*[a] and householder, whores, etc. Have you seen that 300 million francs have *AVOWEDLY* 'DISAPPEARED' FROM THE BUDGET, AND NOBODY KNOWS WHAT HAS BECOME OF THEM? There will, BY AND BY, be further REVELATIONS about Bonapartist FINANCE, and then the asses on the *Tribune* will realise the wisdom of *not* having published the very ELABORATED ARTICLES I sent them on the subject six months ago.[219] The fellows are asses and anything which is not, in the crudest sense, a 'question of the day' they tend to cast aside as UNINTERESTING, only to go and compile the most egregious rubbish about the selfsame subject as soon as it does become *à l'ordre du jour.*[b]

Nota bene: in the military clubs here it is being rumoured that EVIDENCE has been discovered among the papers left by Raglan that, 1. at the battle of the Alma[209] *he* rightly suggested to attack the Russians, not from the direction of the coast, but from the opposite flank, and drive them into the sea; 2. that he proposed to advance on Simferopol after the battle of the Alma; 3. that at Inkerman[34] it was only by dint of the most urgent pleas and MENACES that he extorted from Canrobert the order for Bosquet to hasten to his [Raglan's] assistance. It is further said that, if the boasting on the other side of the Channel were to continue, these PAPERS would be published, providing proof that the French were ever ready TO BETRAY THEIR DEAR ALLIES. Indeed, a few HINTS which de Lacy Evans dropped in the HOUSE OF COMMONS seem to indicate something of the kind.

I've been so ill with my bilious complaint this week that I am incapable of thinking, reading, writing or, indeed, of anything SAVE the ARTICLES for the *Tribune.* These, of course, cannot be allowed to lapse since I must draw on the curs *as soon as possible.* But my indisposition is disastrous, for I can't begin working on the thing for Duncker[c] until I'm better and my fingers regain their VIGOUR and GRASP.

---

[a] grocer - [b] the order of the day - [c] K. Marx, *A Contribution to the Crtique of Political Economy.*

The following is a SHORT OUTLINE OF THE FIRST PART. The whole thing is to be divided into 6 books: 1. On Capital. 2. Landed Property. 3. Wage Labour. 4. State. 5. International Trade. 6. World Market.

1. *Capital* falls into 4 sections. a) Capital *en général.* (*This is the substance of the first instalment.*) b) *Competition,* or the interaction of many capitals. c) *Credit,* where capital, as against individual capitals, is shown to be a universal element. d) *Share capital* as the most perfected form (turning into communism) together with all its contradictions. The transition from capital to landed property is also historical, since landed property in its modern form is a product of the action of capital on feudal, etc., landed property. In the same way, the transition of landed property to wage labour is not only dialectical but historical, since the last product of modern landed property is the general introduction of wage labour, which then appears as the basis of the whole business.

WELL (IT IS DIFFICULT FOR ME TO-DAY TO WRITE), let us now come to the *corpus delicti.*[a]

I. *Capital. First section: Capital in general.* (Throughout this section wages are invariably assumed to be at their minimum. Movements in wages themselves and the rise and fall of that minimum will be considered under wage labour. Further, landed property is assumed to be zero, i. e. landed property as a special economic relation is of no relevance as yet. Only by this procedure is it possible to discuss one relation without discussing all the rest.)

1. *Value.* Simply reduced to the quantity of labour; time as a measure of labour. Use-value—whether regarded subjectively as the USEFULNESS of labour, or objectively as the UTILITY of the product—is shown here simply as the material prerequisite of value, and one which for the present is entirely irrelevant to the formal economic definition. Value as such has no 'substance' other than actual labour. This definition of value, first outlined by Petty and neatly elaborated by Ricardo,[b] is simply bourgeois wealth in its most abstract form. As such, it already presupposes 1. the transcending of indigenous communism (India, etc.), 2. of all undeveloped, pre-bourgeois modes of production which are not in every respect governed by exchange. Although an abstraction, it is an historical abstraction and hence feasible only when grounded on a specific economic development of society. All objections to

---

[a] the incriminating evidence. Here, the main topic. - [b] W. Petty, *A Treatise of Taxes and Contributions...*; D. Ricardo, *On the Principles of Political Economy, and Taxation.*

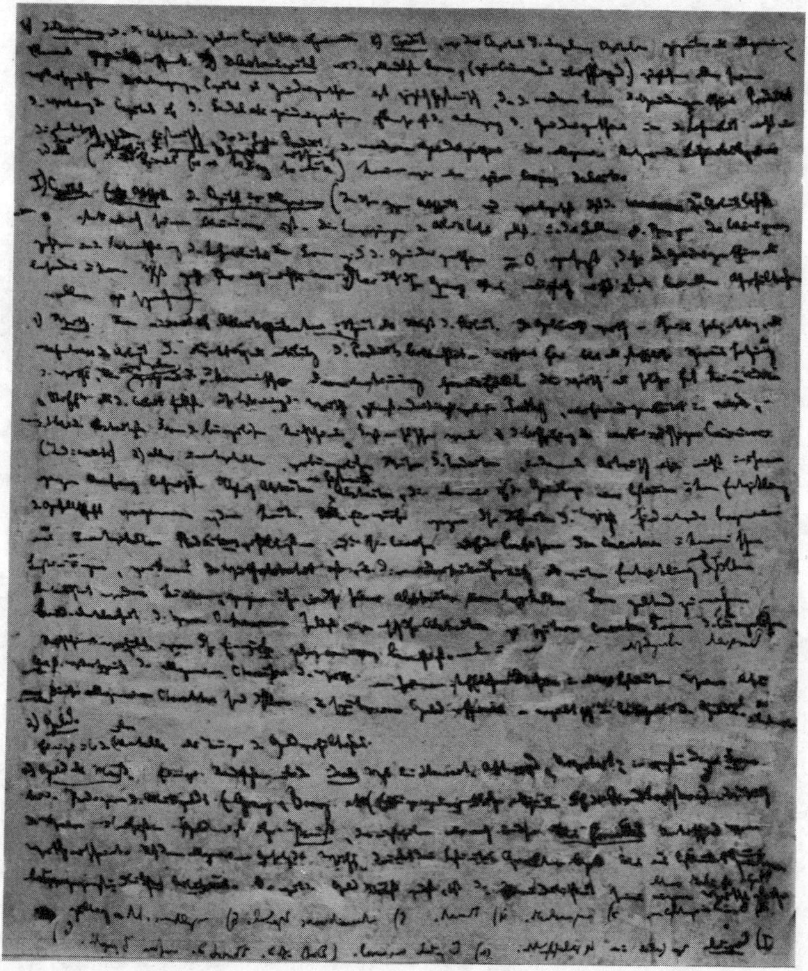

The second page of Marx's letter to Engels of 2 April 1858

this definition of value derive either from less developed relations of production or else are based on confused thinking, whereby the more concrete economic definitions from which value has been abstracted (and which may therefore also be seen, on the other hand, as a further development of the same) are upheld as against value in this its abstract, undeveloped form. In view of the uncertainty of *messieurs les économistes* themselves about the precise relation of this abstraction to later, more concrete forms of bourgeois wealth, these objections were *plus ou moins*[a] justified.

The contradiction between the general characteristics of value and its material existence in a particular commodity, etc.—these general characteristics being the same as those later appearing in money—gives rise to the category of money.

2. *Money*.

Some discussion of precious metals as vehicles of the money relation.

a) *Money as a measure*. A few comments on the *ideal* measure in Steuart, Attwood,[310] Urquhart; in more comprehensible form among the advocates of labour money (Gray, Bray,[b] etc. An occasional swipe at the Proudhonists). The value of a commodity translated into money is its *price*. For the moment price appears only in this *purely formal* distinction between it and value. Thus, in accordance with the general law of value, a specific amount of money merely expresses a specific amount of objectified labour. In so far as money is a measure, the variability of its own value is of no importance.

b) *Money as a means of exchange, or simple circulation*.

Here we need only consider the simple form of circulation as such. All the other conditions by which it is determined are external to it, and hence will not be considered till later (presuppose more highly developed relations). If the commodity be C and money M then, although simple circulation evinces the two circuits or final points: C—M—M—C and M—C—C—M (this latter constituting the transition to c), the point of departure and the point of return in no way coincide, save by chance. Most of the so-called laws put forward by economists do not consider money circulation within its own confines, but as subsumed under, and determined by, higher movements. All this must be set

---

[a] more or less - [b] Marx means the following works: J. Steuart, *An Inquiry into the Principles of Political Oeconomy...*; D. Urquhart, *Familiar Words...*; J. Gray, *Lectures on the Nature and Use of Money, The Social System...*; J. F. Bray, *Labour's Wrongs and Labour's Remedy....*

aside. (Belongs in part to the theory of credit; but also calls for consideration where money appears again, but further defined.) Here, then, money as means of circulation (*coin*). But likewise as *realisation* (not simply evanescent) of price. From the simple statement that a commodity, in terms of *price*, has already been exchanged for money in theory before it is so exchanged in fact, there naturally follows the important economic law *that the volume of the circulating medium is determined by prices, not vice versa.* (Here, some historical stuff on the polemic concerning this point.) Again it follows that velocity may be a substitute for volume, but that a *certain volume* is essential to simultaneous acts of exchange in so far as the relation of these themselves is not that of + and −, an equalisation and consideration which will only be touched on at this juncture by way of anticipation. At this point I shall not go further into the development of this section and would only add that the lack of congruence of C—M and M—C is the most abstract and superficial form in which the possibility of crises is expressed. If the law concerning the determination of circulating volume by prices be developed, it will be found that the assumptions made here are by no means applicable to all states of society; hence the fatuity of comparing e.g. the influx of money from Asia into Rome and its effect on prices there *tout bonnement*[a] with modern commercial relations. On closer examination, the most abstract definitions invariably point to a broader, definite, concrete, historical basis. (OF COURSE, since to the extent that they are definite they have been abstracted therefrom.)

c) *Money qua money.* This is a development of the formula M—C—C—M. Money, the independent existence of value as opposed to circulation; material existence of abstract wealth. Already manifested in circulation in so far as it appears, not only as a means of circulation, but as realising price. In this capacity c), in which a) and b) appear to be no more than functions, money is the universal commodity of contracts (here the variability of its value acquires importance: value being determined by labour time); it becomes an object of HOARDING. (This would still seem to be an important function in Asia, as formerly in the ancient world and in the Middle Ages GENERALLY. Now persists only in a subordinate capacity within the banking system. In times of crisis money in this form again acquires importance. In this form money considered along with the world-historical DELUSIONS which it engenders, etc. Destructive properties, etc.) As the realisation of all

---

[a] just like that

higher forms in which value will appear; definitive forms in which all relations of value are externally concluded. Money, however, once fixed in this form, ceases to be an economic relation which is lost in its material medium, gold and silver. On the other hand, in so far as money comes into circulation and is again exchanged for C, the final process, the consumption of the commodity, again falls outside the economic relation. The principle of self-reproduction is not intrinsic to simple money circulation, which therefore implies something extrinsic to itself. Implicit in money—as the elaboration of its definitions shows—is the postulate *capital*, i.e. value entering into and maintaining itself in circulation, of which it is at the same time the prerequisite. This transition also historical. The antediluvian form of capital is commercial capital, which always generates money. At the same time the emergence of real capital, either from money or merchant capital, which gains control of production.

d) This simple circulation, considered as such—and it constitutes the surface of bourgeois society in which the underlying operations which gave rise to it are obliterated—evinces no distinction between the objects of exchange, save formal and evanescent ones. Here we have *the realm of liberty, equality and of property based on 'labour'*. Accumulation, as it appears here in the form of HOARDING, is merely greater thrift, etc. On the one hand then, the fatuity of the economic harmonists, modern free traders (Bastiat, Carey,[a] etc.), in upholding this most superficial and most abstract relation of production as *their* truth, as against the more advanced relations and their antagonisms. Fatuity of the Proudhonists and suchlike socialists, in contrasting the ideas of equality, etc., corresponding to this exchange of equivalents (or presumed AS SUCH), to the inequalities, etc., to which this exchange reverts and from which it emanates. In this sphere, appropriation by labour, the exchange of equivalents, appears as the law of appropriation so that exchange simply returns the same value in another material form. In short, while everything may be 'lovely' here, it will soon come to a sticky end and this as a result of the law of equivalence. For now we come to

3. *Capital.*

This is really the most important part of the first instalment and one on which I particularly need your opinion. But today I can't go on writing. My bilious trouble makes it difficult for me to ply

---

[a] Fr. Bastiat, *Harmonies économiques*; H. Ch. Carey, *Essay on the Rate of Wages....*

my pen, and keeping my head bent over the paper makes me dizzy. So FOR NEXT TIME.

Salut.

Your

K. M.

First published in *Der Briefwechsel zwischen F. Engels und K. Marx*, Bd. 2, Stuttgart, 1913

Printed according to the original

Published in English in full for the first time

159

ENGELS TO MARX

IN LONDON

Manchester, 9 April 1858

Dear Moor,

The study of your ABSTRACT of the first half-instalment[a] has greatly exercised me; IT IS A VERY ABSTRACT ABSTRACT INDEED—inevitably so, in view of its brevity,—and I often had to search hard for the dialectical transitions, particularly since ALL ABSTRACT REASONING is now completely foreign to me. The arrangement of the whole into 6 books could hardly be better and seems to me an excellent idea, although the dialectical transition from landed property to wage labour is not yet quite clear to me. The development of the monetary business, too, is really excellent, though again there are individual bits I can't quite make out, at least until I have looked up the historical background. However, I think that I shall get a better idea of the DRIFT when I've had the last part of capital in general, and shall then write to you at greater length about it. The abstract, dialectical tone of your synopsis will, of course, disappear in the development.

Yesterday I sent you two more *Guardians.* Now that the price has been reduced to 1d, the chaps are evidently cutting down on all expenses such as foreign correspondents, etc. Their attempt to produce a FIRST-CLASS PROVINCIAL PAPER failed completely. Hence the dearth of foreign news and the rarity of contributions from Paris.

---

[a] K. Marx, *A Contribution to the Critique of Political Economy.*

The thing about Fould in yesterday's *Guardian* isn't bad. But what's even better is the COTTON SUPPLY ASSOCIATION'S[311] report. How splendid that, 10 years after its introduction, FREE TRADE[150] should be repudiated outright by the free traders themselves. For all that this COTTON SUPPLY ASSOCIATION amounts to is an institution set up by these selfsame free traders with the object of boosting the cultivation of cotton everywhere in the world where soil and climate are not entirely unsuitable—and this, in direct opposition to FREE TRADE principles, by means of rewards, advances, gifts of seed, loans of machinery, etc., etc. If the State does something of this sort, it's all wrong, but if the MANCHESTER COTTON SPINNERS, who are much further removed from the NIGGERS, Bedouins, etc., in Africa than their own monarch, do the selfsame thing, then IT'S ALL RIGHT. This report is as pretty a satire on *laissez-faire*[312] clap-trap generally as one could hope to find. Very pretty, too, the admission that the import of English goods manufactured from American cotton has disrupted cotton cultivation in almost all other countries and that this last will now have to be restored by artificial means! These wretched English regard their monopoly in cotton spinning and weaving as something fine and natural to which no one could object; whereas the cotton-growing monopoly of the United States, engendered by the selfsame world market, must be smashed, even if this means ANTI-FREE TRADE measures. The thing ought to be called *Association for enabling the single spinners to buy cotton in the dearest market, the collective spinners paying the producer the difference between the market value and his cost of production*. Of course, this is to go on only until subsidised cotton growing can stand on its own legs; but after all that is exactly what Monsieur List is also seeking to do with his protective tariffs! The thing might supply you with material for an article, since the Yankees have a direct interest in it and the *Tribune*, too, is ANTI-FREE TRADE.

My prognostications that fluctuations in produce would be entirely dependent on the east and west winds and that, with MIDDLING ORLEANS COTTON above 6d, there could be no question of trade being either normal or brisk, have proved remarkably accurate.[a] As regards cotton, the fulfilment of my first prognostication will be apparent from the enclosed table which is a continuation of the one I sent you earlier on the price of Middling Orleans, and brings it up to date.[b] Sugar, coffee and tea have gone

---

[a] See this volume, pp. 202, 213, 235-36, 239-40. - [b] Ibid., p. 205. The continuation of the table is not extant.

the same way, save that the existence of considerable stocks inhibited the temporary steep rise which the shortage of stocks made possible in the case of cotton. As for the second prognostication, there's still quite a lot of SHORT TIME, STRIKES, and stoppages due to unprofitable production and, since the crop will provide 3,000 M[a] bales whereas full production would now demand a minimum of 3,500 M (same ratio for other cotton producing countries), any attempt at revival by the cotton industry up to the end of this year will be hampered—quite aside from political convulsions—by the rising price of raw material, as indeed already happened at the end of February and the beginning of March (see table). Prices in general—even though there may be an initial fall—will rise, but at the same time there will be a CHECK to production proportionate to the rise. This, always SUPPOSING THAT [THERE IS] NO ROW ON THE CONTINENT, though the latter is a virtual certainty.

In one week, 19-26 February, *only 62 bales* of cotton of all qualities arrived in Liverpool! Normally they are counted in thousands.

What's this about the 300 million francs which are admitted to have vanished? All I remember having read is that, instead of a surplus of 40 million, Magne has a deficit—but I don't know the details. It really is priceless. Now the *'prince impérial'*[b] is also to be given his own household and a dotation—CASH MUST BE DEVILISH SCARCE!

I hope your bilious trouble is better. Obviously all this excitation caused by the crisis is to blame. In the evenings I am sometimes plagued by toothache as a result of the weather; but nothing worse.

Kind regards to your wife and children.

Your

F. E.

First published in *Der Briefwechsel zwischen F. Engels und K. Marx*, Bd. 2, Stuttgart, 1913

Printed according to the original

Published in English for the first time

---

[a] M stands for *mille* (Latin: thousand). - [b] Eugène, son of Napoleon III

160

ENGELS TO JENNY MARX[313]

IN LONDON

Manchester, 14 April 1858

Dear Mrs Marx,

I trust that Moor is at last on the road to recovery and will soon be able to return unhampered to his labours on political economy.[250] I was also plagued with toothache last week. By Sunday it had gone, only to return with added virulence this evening just as I was settling down to sort out some preliminary stuff on the conquest of Lucknow[a] for the *Tribune*. Whether I shall succeed in these circumstances seems very doubtful. At any rate I shall try and read up the subject this evening and if possible concoct something, even if not much, tomorrow midday while I'm at the office. But it would at any rate be a good idea if Moor were to have a *sujet in petto*[b] so that, if the worst comes to the worst, there's something to send the fellows.

I still find working in the evenings very tiring and, if I go on for too long or for two evenings running, I get over-excited and suffer from insomnia, particularly when I've had a lot of writing to do during the day. And I also feel very stupid and lethargic in the evenings until I wake myself up by forcing myself to concentrate on some subject. My memory is better on the whole, although every day I still find that things I have done or heard the day before vanish so completely from my mind that they might never have happened, and it's only when I've been reminded of *individual details* that it all comes back to me. Otherwise I am physically strong and healthy again, able to stand up to strains and stresses and—*sauf le*[c] TOOTHACHE—to any kind of weather.

Lupus is still very lame and is having to spend more on CABS in one week than he usually does in a year. But he is improving visibly and in a week's time he'll probably again be able to stand a certain amount of walking. He sends everyone his best wishes.

How do you like the Bernard trial[314]? The French *mouchards*[d] and their worthy *confrère* MR Rogers are cutting a pretty figure.

---

[a] F. Engels, 'The Fall of Lucknow'. - [b] subject up his sleeve - [c] save for the - [d] police spies

Yesterday's *Morning Post* drew a very nice picture of the trial's physiognomy. That Chevalier Estien was excellently portrayed.[a]

I have today received from DEAR Harney 3 more *Independents*[b] from which it transpires that his arch-enemy, Seigneur Godfrey, has begun a fresh libel suit against him.[237] The man will soon be thinking himself as 'greet' as the 'greet'[c] Lassalle.

'OUR FAITHFUL ALLY'[d] is now weighing on English commerce like a nightmare. Nobody wants to speculate or buy more than his immediate requirements because the whole of Philistia is expecting war, revolution or even more outlandish things in France.

Very best wishes to the girls and Moor,

Yours ever,

F. Engels

First published in: Marx and Engels, *Works*, First Russian Edition, Vol. XXII, Moscow, 1929

Printed according to the original

Published in English for the first time

161

ENGELS TO MARX

IN LONDON

Manchester, 22 April 1858

Dear Moor,

I wrote to your wife last week and the following day sent an article on Lucknow[e] and also *Guardians* (or cuttings, I don't remember exactly). I hope everything arrived safely. 2 more *Guardians* go off today. Russell's report in Tuesday's *Times*[f] did not have the makings of an article, but I'm saving it up until the arrival of the next mail; this is sure to bring the last part of the Lucknow story, when the whole thing can be polished off all at one go—with, I hope, the help of Campbell's despatches as well. Meanwhile I have thrown myself into 'Cavalry' again—shall leave

[a] 'Trial of Simon Bernard', *The Morning Post*, No. 26298, 13 April 1858. - [b] *The Jersey Independent* - [c] Engels has *grauss*—South-German for *gross* (great). - [d] Napoleon III - [e] F. Engels, 'The Fall of Lucknow'. - [f] [W. H. Russell,] 'The Capture of Lucknow', *The Times*, No. 22972, 20 April 1858.

open bits of the historical section for the present until I can unearth the relevant sources, and shall get on with the tactical side. The article will probably take up 10 or 12 of my long double pages, and maybe more.

The *affaire* Bernard[314] will greatly mortify Monsieur Bonaparte and make quite an impression on the refugee *crapauds*[81] in London. James' speech, by the way, was feeble and *décousu*[a] and as usual old Campbell's summing up went against the PRISONER. The old donkey is vexed at losing the chance of an interesting legal case when he could have presided over 15 other judges.

The revelations made by Cavour and La Marmora[b] about their relations with Cavaignac and the latter's fear of Austria[315] will be of interest to the *républicains purs*. The more that comes to light about the *National's* period of supremacy, the more pitiful it seems.

Your
F. E.

First published in: Marx and Engels, *Works*, First Russian Edition, Vol. XXII, Moscow, 1929

Printed according to the original
Published in English for the first time

162

MARX TO ENGELS

IN MANCHESTER

London, 29 April 1858

DEAR Frederick,

My long silence can be explained in one word—inability to write. This existed (AND TO SOME DEGREE EXISTS STILL) not only IN THE LITERARY, but IN THE LITERAL SENSE OF THE WORD. The few obligatory articles for the *Tribune*[c] were dictated to my wife, but even that was only possible by APPLYING STRONG STIMULI. Never before have I had such a violent *attaque* of liver trouble and FOR SOME TIME there was a

[a] disjointed - [b] C. B. Cavour's speech of 16 April 1858 in the Chamber of Representatives of the Kingdom of Piedmont, *The Times*, No. 22973, 21 April 1858; A. F. La Marmora's speech of 17 April 1858 in the Chamber of Representatives of the Kingdom of Piedmont, *The Times*, No. 22974, 22 April 1858. - [c] K. Marx, 'The French Trials in London', 'The Financial Position of France', 'Mr Disraeli's Budget', 'The English Alliance'.

fear that it might be sclerosis of the liver. The doctor wanted me to travel but *d'abord*[a] that was incompatible with the STATE OF FINANCE, and secondly I hoped from day to day to be able to start work again. The persistent urge to get down to WORK coupled with inability to do so helped aggravate my condition. However there's been an improvement during the past week. But I'm not yet capable of working. Whenever I sit down and write for a couple of hours I have to lie quite fallow for a couple of days. I hope to heaven that this state of affairs comes to an end next week. It couldn't have happened at a more inconvenient time. Obviously I overdid my nocturnal labours last winter. *Hinc illae lacrimae.*[b]

Your letters and *Guardians* arrived safely.

A book has appeared by Louis Blanc on the revolution of 1848.[c] Evinces the most candid admiration for the *'petit'*[d] which, or so he says, is what the workers call him. If read carefully, however, it makes the fellow look an ass for it shows that on every crucial occasion the workers acted without his knowledge or consent and generally returned him sentiment for 'sentiment', taking the view that they had thereby paid the oracle of Luxembourg his FULL PRICE.[316]

The movement for the emancipation of the serfs in Russia strikes me as important in so far as it indicates the beginning of an internal development that might run counter to the country's traditional foreign policy. Herzen, of course, has discovered afresh that 'liberty' has emigrated from Paris to Moscow.

Friend Bangya, AS IT SEEMS, has been caught out by Sefer Pasha's son[e] engaging in unauthorised correspondence with Philipson, the Russian general. It is said that he HAS BEEN SHOT together with a number of his Hungarian and Polish accomplices.[317]

Regards to Lupus.

Your

K. M.

First published abridged in *Der Briefwechsel zwischen F. Engels und K. Marx*, Bd. 2, Stuttgart, 1913 and in full in: Marx and Engels, *Works*, First Russian Edition, Vol. XXII, Moscow, 1929

Printed according to the original

Published in English for the first time

---

[a] first of all - [b] Hence these tears (Terence, *Andria*, I, i, 99). - [c] L. Blanc, *1848. Historical Revelations...* - [d] the little one - [e] Prince Ibrahim Karabatir

163

ENGELS TO MARX

IN LONDON

Manchester, 30 April 1858
7 Southgate

Dear Moor,

If travel you must, why not travel to Manchester, THAT'S EASY ENOUGH. Should the note I sent you yesterday have already disappeared, *ce qui serait bien possible*,[a] let me know; for 21/- you can now get an 8-day RETURN TICKET FIRST CLASS, and then, of course, you just disregard the RETURN. I shall try and arrange for a spare bed at my house, which should be possible for a few days, *anyhow*. For the rest we shall see. If you still have the money for the journey, come up straight away. We shall immediately send off to your wife anything you borrow from her; I've had no time to get a POST OFFICE ORDER today. I shall give the necessary instructions when I get home this evening. Come straight to *No 6 Thorncliffe Grove*, Oxford Road. If you don't actually leave tomorrow evening (there's a train at about 5 o'clock), let me know on Monday morning when you are arriving and I'll pick you up at the station—but say whether by NORTH WESTERN OR GREAT NORTHERN RAILWAY.

If you are arriving on Sunday, telegraph me tomorrow—it costs 2/6d for 20 words excluding the address. Send the telegram to my house.

Your
F. E.

First published abridged in *Der Briefwechsel zwischen F. Engels und K. Marx*, Bd. 2, Stuttgart, 1913 and in full in: Marx and Engels, *Works*, First Russian Edition, Vol. XXII, Moscow, 1929

Printed according to the original

Published in English for the first time

[a] which is quite possible

164

MARX TO ENGELS

IN MANCHESTER

[London,] 1 May [1858]

Dear Frederick,

*I shall part on Thursday[a] by the Great Northern, leaves London at half past 2, arrives at Manchester at 7 p.m.[318]

Yours*

K. M.

Since yesterday I have been feeling much better and *au fond*[b] it was my intention to start work *sérieusement* on Monday. However AFTER CONSULTATION WITH THE DOCTOR, who thinks that I still need a week of gadding about, I have let my duty go hang.

First published in: Marx and Engels, *Works*, First Russian Edition, Vol. XXII, Moscow, 1929

Printed according to the original

Published in English for the first time

165

ENGELS TO RUDOLF SCHRAMM

IN LONDON

[Draft]

Manchester, 6 May 1858

To Mr R. Schramm in London

I have just received your note dated the 3rd.

After the death of my friend, Conrad Schramm,[188] I instructed Mr Harney to return to *us*, not you, the letters from Marx and myself found among his papers,[c] since those letters were not intended for you. And this indeed was done.

I can see no reason whatever why I should discuss with you matters which concerned no one but myself and my late friend

---

a 6 May 1858 - b by and large - c See this volume, pp. 252-53.

and party comrade. While Conrad was still alive your own friends were surprised at the indifference you showed towards his financial circumstances.

In so far as I had anything to say about the disposal of Conrad's effects, I have said it to his only possible executor, Mr Harney.

As to my 'sense of justice', which has nothing whatever to do with the case, you may perhaps have occasion to become better acquainted with it some day in Germany.

I am, Sir, your obedient servant,

F. E.

First published in: Marx and Engels, *Works*, First Russian Edition, Vol. XXV, Moscow, 1934

Printed according to the original

Published in English for the first time

166

ENGELS TO JENNY MARX

IN LONDON

Manchester, 11 May 1858

Dear Mrs Marx,

Moor has been out riding for two hours today and feels so well after it that he's waxing quite enthusiastic about the thing. He has left town and gone home, and has asked me to drop you a line about that fool Cluss.[a] He thinks it might be a good thing for you to go and see Pfänder, who would probably elicit something from him. The main thing is that Monsieur Cluss should *come up here*, for we have got to know how we stand with him, and either he must declare himself IN A SATISFACTORY MANNER or else we must break with him. What good is the ass to us if he's so unreliable as first to come to you, his heart brimful and overflowing, stay for 3 hours with no other apparent object than to get back on to the old footing again, and then suddenly write you a letter as confused as it is ill-bred in which he retracts? We're only sorry that, in the midst of what is a far from rosy spell, such dolts should come and add to *your* troubles.

---

[a] See this volume, pp. 374-75, 571.

If at all possible, see that the man comes up here so that we at least have the satisfaction of telling him exactly what we think of him.

I hope that Moor will persevere with his riding, for if he does he'll be able to write again in a week. Lupus' leg is much better too.

Your devoted
F. Engels

First published in *Der Briefwechsel zwischen F. Engels und K. Marx*, Bd. 2, Stuttgart, 1913

Printed according to the original

Published in English for the first time

167

ENGELS TO JENNY AND LAURA MARX

IN LONDON

Manchester, 11 May 1858

Dear Jenny and Laura,

I cannot allow this note to go off to your mama without thanking you for the two lovely portraits which you asked Moor to bring me. They have found a temporary home on the CHIMNEY-PIECE in front of the looking-glass, but in a day or two will be given a splendid place of their own on the wall.

I hope Mr Schleiden suits you all right[a]; the man's far more solemn than you are, and I only hope you won't see fit to imitate him.

Dai ritratti vedo con piacere che avete molto grandito tutte le due e che, benchè siate grande signorine adesso, vi sono sempre le vecchie faccie piene di franchezza ed ingenuità; e credete pure chè anch' io per voi sarò sempre il vecchio[b]

Engels

First published in: Marx and Engels, *Works*, First Russian Edition, Vol. XXII, Moscow, 1929

Printed according to the original

Published in English for the first time

---

[a] Probably a reference to the book: M. J. Schleiden, *Die Pflanze und ihr Leben*. - [b] I see with pleasure from your portraits that you have both grown a lot and that, although you are now grown-up young girls, your faces are still as frank and artless as of old; and you must believe me still to be your old

168

MARX TO FERDINAND LASSALLE[82]

IN BERLIN

London, 31 May 1858
9 Grafton Terrace, Maitland Park,
Haverstock Hill

Dear Lassalle,

Post tot discrimina rerum[a] at long last a sign of life. As for me, what's been happening since my wife wrote to you[b] is simply this:

Having been totally incapable of writing—not only IN A LITERARY, BUT IN THE LITERAL SENSE OF THE WORD—for several weeks, and striven in vain to rebel against my illness; having, moreover, been pumped full of medicine and all TO NO USE, I was positively assured by my doctor that I must have a change of air, secondly that I must DROP all INTELLECTUAL LABOUR FOR SOME TIME and, finally, engage in riding as the main form of treatment. In itself the illness wasn't dangerous—enlargement of the liver—but on this occasion the accompanying symptoms were particularly revolting; moreover, in my family it has nasty implications in that it was the starting-point of the illness which led to my father's death. WELL. With the utmost reluctance I eventually gave way to the insistence of doctor and family, joined Engels in Manchester,[318] went in for riding and other physical EXERCISES and, after spending a month up there, finally returned to London fully restored. The illness—altogether a very expensive LUXURY in my circumstances—was all the more inopportune in that I had already begun to prepare the first instalment[c] for publication. I shall now settle down to this with a will. I trust you will be so kind as to tell the publisher[d] all about these ADVENTURES. You will readily be able to imagine the state of mind I was in during my illness when I tell you that liver complaints as such tend to make one hypochondriacal and that, in addition, my life was bedevilled by all manner of domestic circumstances, not to speak of the hitch over publication. Now I have recovered my accustomed good humour.

---

[a] After so many setbacks (Virgil, *Aeneid*, I, 204). - [b] See this volume, p. 570. - [c] K. Marx. *A Contribution to the Critique of Political Economy*. - [d] Franz Gustav Duncker

During this time of tribulation I carefully perused your *Heraclitus*.[a] Your reconstruction of the system from the scattered fragments I regard as brilliant, nor was I any less impressed by the perspicacity of your polemic. In so far as I have any fault to find, it is largely formal. I believe your exposé could have been rather more condensed without in any way jeopardising the import. I should, moreover, have liked to find in the text proper some *critical* indications as to your attitude to Hegelian dialectic. This dialectic is, to be sure, the ultimate word in philosophy and hence there is all the more need to divest it of the mystical aura given it by Hegel. Finally, there are some details upon which I do not agree with you; e.g. your interpretation of Democritus' natural philosophy. These, however, are all minor points. I am all the more aware of the difficulties you had to surmount in this work in that ABOUT 18 years ago I myself attempted a similar work on a far easier philosopher, Epicurus[b]—namely the portrayal of a complete system from fragments, a system which I am convinced, by the by, was—as with Heraclitus—only *implicitly* present in his work, not consciously as a system. Even in the case of philosophers who give systematic form to their work, Spinoza for instance, the true inner structure of the system is quite unlike the form in which it was consciously presented by him. It is incomprehensible to me, by the by, how you found the time in the midst of all your other work to acquire so much Greek philology.

On the whole the present moment of time is a pleasing one. History is clearly about TO TAKE AGAIN A NEW START, and the signs of dissolution EVERYWHERE ARE DELIGHTFUL FOR EVERY MIND NOT BENT UPON THE CONSERVATION OF THINGS AS THEY ARE.

Salut.

Your

K. M.

First published in: *F. Lassalle. Nachgelassene Briefe und Schriften*, Bd. III, Stuttgart-Berlin, 1922

Printed according to the original

---

[a] F. Lassalle, *Die Philosophie Herakleitos des Dunklen von Ephesos*. - [b] Marx means his doctoral dissertation *Difference Between the Democritean and Epicurean Philosophy of Nature*.

Jenny Marx, daughter of Karl Marx. Late 1850s-early 1860s

169

MARX TO ENGELS

IN MANCHESTER

London, 31 May 1858
9 Grafton Terrace, Maitland Park,
Haverstock Hill

Dear Frederick,

It took me a week to acclimatise myself again; moreover, the abrupt discontinuation of riding did me no good to begin with. Not until this very day have I at last begun to feel as fit as I did on the day I left Manchester. I am now IN WORKING ORDER and shall at once start getting the stuff ready for publication.[a] All I wrote last week was 2 articles for the *Tribune*.[b] The rest of the time I kept constantly on the move, since the feeling of heaviness in my head and trouble with my bowels made me fear a relapse.

Ad vocem[c] *Cluss*. Before leaving, this young man visited Schapper again. When he got back from my house the worthy fellow discovered to his dismay that he had brought something back with him from Paris, viz. a chancre with all sorts of nasty secondary symptoms. He took to his bed and this, he told Schapper, was the reason for his withdrawal from the civilised world.

Ad vocem Pélissier. What we jokingly suggested in Manchester, namely that Pélissier would promptly enter into relations with the Orléans, has now happened IN REAL GOOD EARNEST, and become the talk of the town here.

What do you think of Bonaparte's thirst for confiscation?[319]

During my absence a book by Maclaren covering the entire history of CURRENCY came out in London[d]; to judge by the excerpts in *The Economist* it is FIRST-RATE.[e] The book isn't in the library[f] yet—nothing ever turns up there until months after publication. I, of course, am bound to read it before writing my treatise. So I sent my wife to the PUBLISHER[g] in the City. To our dismay, however, we discovered that it costs 9/6d—more than the whole of our

[a] K. Marx, *A Contribution to the Critique of Political Economy*. - [b] 'Lord Canning's Proclamation and Land Tenure in India' and 'The Financial Manoeuvres of Bonaparte.—Military Despotism' - [c] As regards - [d] J. Maclaren, *A Sketch of the History of the Currency*... - [e] *The Economist*, No. 768, 15 May 1858, pp. 536-37. - [f] of the British Museum - [g] Groombridge

fighting funds. Hence I should be most grateful if you could send me a POST OFFICE ORDER for that amount. There probably won't be anything that's new to me in the book, but after all the fuss *The Economist* has made about it and the excerpts I myself have read, my theoretical scruples won't permit me to proceed without having looked at it.

Don't you think you might have sufficient material to do something general on the STATE OF THE BRITISH FORCES IN INDIA and also something conjectural for Friday? IT WOULD BE A GREAT BOON FOR ME since reading over my own manuscript[a] will take me the better part of a week. The damnable part of it is that my manuscript (which in print would amount to a hefty volume) is a real hotchpotch, much of it intended for much later sections. So I shall have to make an index briefly indicating in which notebook and on which page to find the stuff I want to work on first.

I have at long last written to Lassalle.[b] You must grant me absolution for the plaudits I was obliged to accord *Heraclitus, the Dark Philosopher.* In a few unobtrusive asides—for praise is taken seriously only when offset by censure—I have to some extent, if very *piano-piano,* hinted at the real shortcomings of the *entreprise.*

Tomorrow or the day after I shall be getting some more Bangya numbers,[c] 2 of which I shall send to Manchester, 1 for you and 1 for Lupus. Apropos, in an issue of the *Tribune* I see that Pulszky is endeavouring to forestall the nauseous REVELATIONS by representing Bangya as *Metternich*'s spy and as one who betrayed General Stein.[d] So statesman Blind, WHILE GIVING A *TESTIMONIUM PAUPERTATIS* TO KOSSUTH, 'THE ILLUSTRIOUS GOVERNOR OF HUNGARY', in the *Advertiser,* nevertheless found himself obliged to invite him in so many words to make a 'counter-statement'. Kossuth, OF COURSE, held his tongue.

How is Gumpert progressing in the noble art of equitation? As for me, the pity of it is that I always have to break off just when I'm again making enough progress to take an interest in the thing.

Salut.

Your

K. M.

First published in *Der Briefwechsel zwischen F. Engels und K. Marx,* Bd. 2, Stuttgart, 1913

Printed according to the original

Published in English for the first time

---

[a] *Economic Manuscripts of 1857-58* - [b] See this volume, pp. 315-16. - [c] 'Recent Treachery in Circassia', *The Free Press,* No. 16, 12 May 1858. - [d] [F. Pulszky,] 'From Our Own Correspondent. London, April 23, 1858', *New-York Daily Tribune,* No. 5319, 8 May 1858.

170

MARX TO ENGELS[20]

IN MANCHESTER

[London,] 7 June 1858

Dear Frederick,

Enclosed 2 Bangya numbers,[a] ONE FOR YOU, THE OTHER FOR Lupus.

Have received from you 1. letter with the POST OFFICE NOTE; 2. SECOND LETTER; 3. ARTICLE FOR THE *TRIBUNE* (VERY AMUSING ONE, TOO[b]). Did not acknowledge receipt before because each day I was expecting the 2 Bangya numbers; also a lot of PRIVATE TROUBLES which took up my time.

Enclosed a letter from Lassalle.[c] It's an extremely odd business. I cannot reply until I have your own and Lupus' opinion. So I should like you to consult together at once and send me your *avis*[d] without delay. My own view is that Lassalle should not engage in a duel with that ass Fabrice and that, even from the standpoint of the duel, the assault by the two gentlemen from the 'High Court' has put any duelling OUT OF THE QUESTION. GENERALLY, it is my view—though having to decide whether or not the duel *as such* accords with *principle* seems to me ludicrous, OF COURSE—that in the PRESENT CIRCUMSTANCES, AT THIS PARTICULAR JUNCTURE, etc., etc., in contemporary history, members of the revolutionary party may respond to their PRIVATE ENEMIES with clubs, kicks and punches, but not engage in duels. But it would seem to me totally wrong if, after he has come out so categorically against all duelling, Lassalle WOULD ALLOW HIMSELF TO BE BULLIED by feudal GOSSIP.

Schapper came to see me yesterday. Told me, *inter alia*, that friend Caussidière, arriving drunk in a disreputable alley in New York one evening, apparently attacked a wench with his stick; her yells attracted half a dozen LOAFERS who promptly set upon Caussidière and beat him almost to death. The fat lout was PICKED UP unconscious by the police early next morning and it was 6 weeks before he was fit enough to be up and about again.

Seiler had a CASE [attack] of paralysis; at death's door for

---

[a] 'Recent Treachery in Circassia', *The Free Press*, No. 16, 12 May 1858. - [b] F. Engels, 'The British Army in India'. - [c] Lassalle's letter to Marx of 4 June 1858 - [d] opinion

10 weeks; but weeds are indestructible. Heise is said to be dangerously ill again.

Salut.

Your

K. M.

First published abridged in *Der Briefwechsel zwischen F. Engels und K. Marx*, Bd. 2, Stuttgart, 1913 and in full in: Marx and Engels, *Works*, First Russian Edition, Vol. XXII, Moscow, 1929

Printed according to the original

Published in English in full for the first time

171

ENGELS TO MARX

IN LONDON

[Manchester,] 9 June 1858

Dear Moor,

I return Lassalle's letter herewith.[a] Borchardt had already told me on Saturday with a look of triumph that our little Jew Braun had been in a brawl. It's extremely useful to know these details. As for our opinion, it's as clear as day that, by making so despicable an attempt on a person's life, both the gentlemen, the *Intendanturrat* no less than the *Assessor*, have adopted *in toto* the standpoint of the bludgeon, and that the only duel one *might* engage in with such laddies has already *taken place* during the brawl itself. If 2 chaps waylay a third and *both* of them set on him, I don't believe that any duelling code in the world would *permit* a subsequent duel with such riff-raff. If Mr Fabrice intended forcibly to provoke a duel by means of the horse-whip affair, either Mr Bormann ought to have looked on purely passively as a *witness*, or his presence was altogether superfluous. But when two men simultaneously set upon *one*, then we are dealing with *canaille*[b] for whom honour and FAIR PLAY do not exist and who have given proof that A FAIR DUEL cannot be fought with them. Indeed one would run the risk of being treacherously murdered.

So much for my own and Lupus' opinion, if we are to take the duelling code as the basis in law.

---

a See this volume, p. 319. - b rabble

This apart we share your view that 1. duels are, on the whole, untimely for revolutionaries just now and 2. that Lassalle, having declared himself unequivocally against duelling 'on principle', would be greatly discredited were he now to engage in a duel.

So far as we are concerned, therefore, you can safely go ahead and tell our Ephraim Artful[a] not to fight but rather tranquilly restore his 'unshakable determination' with the help of the bottle, take the moon by the horns again as soon as may be and risk annihilation for the hundred and first time. As to the discovery that he appears to possess an adequate store of vanity, silence is, I think, the best form of congratulation.

Did you read the story about Fould's son[b]? He decamped to London with Mademoiselle Valérie[c] of the Gymnase and 1,600,000 francs. His old man[d] wrote to Pélissier and told him that he should *au cas de besoin, user d'autorité.*[e] Pélissier invited the loving couple to *déjeuner*[f] and told them: *Je vous donne ma bénédiction*[g] and wrote to the old man: *Que voulez-vous? Les jeunes gens seront toujours de jeunes gens!*[h] Whereat old Fould became the laughing-stock of Paris.

Your

F. E.

First published in *Der Briefwechsel zwischen F. Engels und K. Marx*, Bd. 2, Stuttgart, 1913

Printed according to the original

Published in English for the first time

172

MARX TO FERDINAND LASSALLE[82]

IN BERLIN

London, 10 June 1858
9 Grafton Terrace, Maitland Park, Haverstock Hill

Dear Lassalle,

You would have had an immediate answer to your letter, but it seemed to me advisable—not in order to formulate my own views

---

[a] Lassalle - [b] Gustave Eugène Fould - [c] Wilhelmine Joséphine Simonin - [d] Achille Fould - [e] if need be, exercise his authority - [f] lunch - [g] I give you my blessing. - [h] What do you expect? Young people are all alike.

but because *tres faciunt collegium*[a]—to put the CASE to Engels and Lupus in Manchester and obtain their opinion. Since their views and my own coincide at every point, you may regard the following as our unanimous OPINION.

1. *From the standpoint of the duel.* It is as clear as day that by their despicable attack in the street the two gentlemen, the *Intendanturrat* and the *Assessor*, have adopted *in toto* the standpoint of the bludgeon and that the only duel which one *might* engage in with such laddies has already *taken place* during the brawl itself. If 2 chaps waylay a third and *both* of them set on him, we don't believe that any duelling code in the world would *permit* a subsequent duel with such riff-raff. If, by flourishing a horse-whip, Mr Fabrice intended forcibly to provoke a duel, either Mr Bormann ought to have looked on purely passively as a *witness*, or his presence was altogether superfluous. But when two men simultaneously set upon *one*, and one of them actually operates IN THE REAR of the person attacked, then we are dealing with *canaille*[b] who have given proof that A FAIR DUEL cannot be fought with them.

2. *Principle of the duel.* We don't believe that, generally speaking, an affair as relative as a duel can be subsumed under the category *good* or *bad*. That duelling as such is not rational there can be no doubt. Nor that it is a relic of a bygone stage of civilisation. However, a concomitant of the one-sidedness of *bourgeois* society is that, in opposition to the latter, certain feudal forms maintain the rights of the individual. The most striking proof of this is to be found in the United States where duelling is a civil right. Individuals may become locked in a mutual conflict so insupportable that a duel seems to them the only solution. However such deadly tension is not IN FACT possible vis-à-vis an indifferent person such as an *Intendanturrat*, an *Assessor*, or a lieutenant. This would demand a significant personal relationship. Otherwise a duel is an utter farce. It is invariably a farce when performed in deference to so-called 'public opinion'.

3. We therefore regard duelling as being purely dependent on circumstances; hence recourse may be had to it as an exceptional *pis aller*[c] in exceptional circumstances. In the CASE under discussion, however, all the circumstances argue quite emphatically against it, even if the attack in the street had not put it ALTOGETHER OUT OF THE QUESTION.

4. The really decisive factor is that you are not only opposed to all duelling on principle but have proclaimed this principle, and in

---

[a] three constitute a panel - [b] rabble - [c] expedient

Fabrice's presence at that. So you would discredit yourself were you nevertheless to engage in a duel through fear of 'public opinion'.

5. In the case under discussion, a duel would have absolutely no meaning save as the observance of a *conventional* formality recognised by certain privileged classes. Our party must resolutely set its face against these class ceremonies and reject with the most cynical contempt the presumptuous demand that we submit to them. The present state of affairs is far too serious to permit of your consenting to such puerilities and it would be sheer puerility to engage in a duel with Mr Fabrice because he is an *'Intendanturrat'* and belongs to the clique qualified to fight duels, whereas if e.g. a tailor or cobbler were to set about you in the street, you would simply hand him over to the courts without any infringement of 'honour'. In the case under consideration you would not be fighting a duel with Fabrice, an individual who is indifferent to you, but with the *'Intendanturrat'*—which would be an absurd manoeuvre. In general, the fellows' insistence that differences with them must be settled by a duel as a *privilege* due to them—and all FASHIONABLE duels fall under this head—should be laughed to scorn. To acknowledge this claim would be altogether counter-revolutionary.

I have given you our view *in nuce*.[a] We shall be interested to hear how the affair progresses.

Salut.

Your

K. M.

First published in: *F. Lassalle. Nachgelassene Briefe und Schriften*, Bd. III, Stuttgart-Berlin, 1922

Printed according to the original

173

MARX TO ENGELS

IN MANCHESTER

London, 2 July 1858
9 Grafton Terrace, Maitland Park, Haverstock Hill

Dear Engels,

The delay in acknowledging your 'Cavalry'[320] due to great domestic TROUBLE. For weeks our youngest child[b] has been

a in a nutshell - b Eleanor Marx

suffering from HOOPING-COUGH, a most alarming illness, besides which my wife is very seedy. So my work has been damnably disrupted by this and all kinds of other domestic upsets.

You will remember that, while our friend Schramm was in Jersey, I secured him the position of correspondent to an American paper. Now that he's dead and after he had dunned them on several occasions, his fee of SOME 6 POUNDS has arrived and has, of course, fallen to Mr Rudolf[a] as pocket-money.

Otherwise nothing new here. That little London German rag once run by Gumpert has, I believe, now fallen to 'united democracy', *sub auspiciis*[b] of the great Blind under the title *Neue Welt*.[c]

I assume you have read the statements made in the *Star* by Mr Türr and by the Hungarian émigrés in Constantinople. If not, I shall send you *The Free Press*.[d] Meanwhile Kossuth still remains obdurately silent. Our excerpt from Bangya's story has appeared in the *Tribune*.[e] The row in New York will force Kossuth to speak. Thus I may have to come right out into the open in this matter. Pulszky had *de longue main*[f] provided a loophole in the *Tribune* when he described Bangya as a former spy of *Metternich's* (!).[g] Klapka, whom I met for a moment or two at Freiligrath's, remarked drily of Bangya: '*Finis coronat opus.*'[h] He seems to be very blasé about Kossuth. Is presently dabbling in Turkish shares.

Herewith two letters from New York.[321]

I have had no word from Ephraim Artful[i] for a fortnight. Being convinced, OF COURSE, that there was small likelihood of my letter being put to discreet use by him, I worded it with the utmost caution SO THAT IT WILL BE EXTREMELY DIFFICULT FOR HIM TO ABUSE IT. Apart from the special CIRCUMSTANCES of the CASE, concerning which I gave him your opinion pretty well verbatim, I censured duelling only in so far as it is claimed as privilege of caste by fellows who believe that their insults *must* be punished otherwise than those of a tailor, cobbler, etc. The revolutionary thing to do, I told him, when confronted with such inane presumption and laddies of this ilk, was to adopt the 'standpoint of the lout' and the 'code of the bludgeon'. On the other hand, in reply to Ephraim's pedantry, I said that duelling was among the things Aristotle described as being 'indifferent' and which one could either take or leave as one

---

[a] Rudolf Schramm - [b] under the auspices - [c] presumably *Die Neue Zeit* - [d] I. Türr, 'To the Editor of the *Presse d'Orient*', *The Free Press*, No. 18, 30 June 1858. - [e] K. Marx, 'A Curious Piece of History'. - [f] long ago - [g] [F. Pulszky,] 'From Our Own Correspondent. London, April 23, 1858', *New-York Daily Tribune*, No. 5319, 8 May 1858. - [h] 'The end crowns the work.' - [i] Ferdinand Lassalle

pleased; I told him he was right in saying that it was a relic of a bygone stage of development but that, 'given the one-sidedness and narrow-mindedness of *bourgeois* relations, individuality could sometimes assert itself only in feudal form'.[a]

I trust that, come what may, you will send me an article on India[b] next week. There is ample material for an article for the *Tribune,* which will otherwise reprint stuff from *The Times,* etc. Anyway, all that matters is that articles should be sent.

Salut.

Your

K. M.

Regards to Lupus.

Humboldt has published a very 'flattering' letter in the *Tribune* addressed to Fröbel,[c] who has published a book of his American travels.[d]

First published abridged in *Der Briefwechsel zwischen F. Engels und K. Marx,* Bd. 2, Stuttgart, 1913 and in full in: Marx and Engels, *Works,* First Russian Edition, Vol. XXII, Moscow, 1929

Printed according to the original

Published in English for the first time

174

ENGELS TO MARX[1]

IN LONDON

Manchester, 14 July 1858

Dear Moor,

Up here we are now in the middle of the balance-sheet and hence I haven't had the leisure to write to you at greater length. I hope that your little Tussy[e] is better. Gumpert tells me that in the English climate whooping-cough is seldom dangerous and, though usually chronic, is benign. All the cases they've had in the hospital so far have ended well. He gave me both the reports (Marei's) this hospital has so far produced. They are highly scientific and I wish

[a] See also this volume, p. 322. - [b] F. Engels, 'The Indian Army'. - [c] A. Humboldt, 'A Private Letter to Mr. Julius Froebel', *New-York Daily Tribune,* No. 5335, 27 May 1858. - [d] J. Fröbel, *Aus America.* - [e] Eleanor Marx

I had had material of this kind when I was writing my book.[a] I also have copies of it for you which I shall be sending; individual bits may come in useful for your chapter on wage labour. No doubt you will derive some amusement from Marei's grandiose conception and sanguine expectations.

Have neither seen nor heard of the statements by Mr Türr, etc. The *Star* is not much read up here. So I'd be glad if you would just send *The Free Press*[b] and also, if possible, a copy for Lupus, who is still in Buxton, whither he was sent by Borchardt, and where, out of boredom, he may well do more walking than is good for his leg.

The two letters from New York which you mention in your last were *not* enclosed.[321]

Apropos. Kindly let me have Hegel's *Philosophy of Nature*[c] as promised. I am presently doing a little physiology which I shall combine with comparative anatomy. Here one comes upon highly speculative things, all of which, however, have only recently been discovered; I am exceedingly curious to see whether the old man may not already have had some inkling of them. This much is certain: were he *today* to write a *Philosophy of Nature,* subjects would come flocking in on him from all directions. One has no idea, by the way, of the progress made in the natural sciences during the past 30 years. Two things have been crucial where physiology is concerned: 1. the tremendous development of organic chemistry, 2. the microscope, which has been properly used only during the past 20 years. This last has produced even more important results than chemistry; what has been chiefly responsible for revolutionising the whole of physiology and has alone made comparative physiology possible is the discovery of the cell—in plants by Schleiden and in animals by Schwann (about 1836). Everything consists of cells. The cell is Hegelian 'being in itself' and its development follows the Hegelian process step by step right up to the final emergence of the 'idea'—i.e. each completed organism.

Another result that would have delighted old Hegel is the correlation of forces in physics, or the law whereby mechanical motion, i.e. mechanical force (e.g. through friction), is, in given conditions, converted into heat, heat into light, light into chemical affinity, chemical affinity (e.g. in the voltaic pile) into electricity, the latter into magnetism. These transitions may also take place

---

[a] *The Condition of the Working-Class in England* - [b] I. Türr, 'To the Editor of the *Presse d'Orient', The Free Press,* No. 18, 30 June 1858. - [c] G. W. F. Hegel, *Vorlesungen über die Naturphilosophie...*

differently, backwards or forwards. An Englishman[a] whose name I can't recall has now shown that these forces pass from one to the other in quite specific quantitative proportions so that e.g. a certain quantity of one, e.g. electricity, corresponds to a certain quantity of each of the others, e.g. magnetism, light, heat, chemical affinity (positive or negative—combining or separating) and motion. The idiotic theory of latent heat is thus disposed of. But isn't this splendid material proof of how the reflex categories dissolve one into the other?

This much is certain—comparative physiology gives one a healthy contempt for man's idealistic arrogance in regard to other animals. At every step it is forcibly brought home to one how completely his structure corresponds to that of other mammals; he has basic features in common with all vertebrates and even—if less distinctly—with insects, crustaceans, tapeworms, etc. Here too Hegel's stuff about the qualitative leap in the quantitative sequence fits in very nicely. Finally, with the most primitive infusoria, one reaches the original form, the single cell existing independently, which again is not perceptibly distinguishable from the lowest vegetable life (single-celled fungi such as those causing disease in potatoes, the vine, etc., etc.) or, at a higher stage of development, from the germ right up to and including the human ovum and spermatozoon, and is identical in appearance to the separate cells in the living body (blood corpuscles, the cells of the epidermis and mucous membrane, secreting cells in the glands, kidneys, etc., etc.).

Some time you might also let me know what sort of a disease *dyspepsia crapulosa*[b] is. This isn't, as it happens, a bad joke but a scientifically recognised term.

If *The Times* has any particulars about India tomorrow, we shall see what can be done for the *Tribune*, otherwise it will be no go. So you'll see from tomorrow's *Times* more or less what can be expected.

Warm regards to the FAMILY.

Your

F. E.

The acceptance business successfully concluded.

First published abridged in *Der Briefwechsel zwischen F. Engels und K. Marx*, Bd. 2, Stuttgart, 1913 and in full in: Marx and Engels, *Works*, First Russian Edition, Vol. XXII, Moscow, 1929

Printed according to the original

Published in English in full for the first time

[a] James Joule - [b] digestive upset caused by over-eating

175

MARX TO ENGELS[82]

IN MANCHESTER

[London,] 15 July 1858
9 Grafton Terrace, Maitland Park

Dear Engels,

D'abord[a] I would beg you not to take fright at the contents of this letter since it is not in any way intended as an APPEAL to your already unduly overloaded exchequer. On the other hand it behoves us to put our heads together to see if some way cannot be found out of the present situation, for it has become absolutely untenable. It has already resulted in my being COMPLETELY DISABLED from doing any work, partly because I have to waste most of my time running round in fruitless attempts to raise money, and partly because my abstract thinking—due rather, perhaps, to my being physically run down—is no longer a match for domestic miseries. The general unpleasantness has made a nervous wreck of my wife, and Dr Allen who, of course, suspects where the shoe PINCHES but doesn't know the real state of affairs, has now told me repeatedly and positively that he cannot rule out brain fever or something of the sort unless she is sent to a seaside resort for a longish stay. I for my part know that circumstances being what they are, this course, even if feasible, would do her no good so long as she continues to be the victim of daily pressures and haunted by the spectre of final and unavoidable catastrophe. This last, however, cannot be long postponed and, even if it be staved off for a few weeks, there still remains the unbearable day-to-day struggle for MERE NECESSARIES and a general situation such as will inevitably bring everything to wrack and ruin.

There are in London so-called LOAN-SOCIETIES[182] which advertise LOANS of £5-200, *without* SECURITIES and on the strength of REFERENCES alone. I therefore attempted an operation of this kind, Freiligrath and an *épicier*[b] having offered to act as REFEREES. The result was that some £2 went on FEES. The final, negative, answer arrived the day before yesterday. I don't know whether I should make a further attempt of this kind.

To give you an idea of the real state of affairs, I have asked my wife to draw up a statement in respect of the £20 advanced by you

a First - b grocer

and the £24 I drew on the *Tribune* (of which £2 were overdrawn) on 16 June. From it you will see that, as soon as a fairly substantial sum such as this arrives, not a penny is left over even for the most urgent day-to-day expenses, let alone enjoyment of any kind; that exactly the same sickening STRUGGLE recommences the following day, and within a very short time the creditors, having received only the most meagre payments on account, once more begin to exert exactly the same pressure in respect of other bills which have accumulated in the meantime. At the same time you will see that my wife hasn't spent a FARTHING on clothes, etc., for herself, while the situation as regards the children's summer DRESSES is subproletarian. I think it is essential that you should go through these particulars since it would not otherwise be possible to arrive at a correct opinion of the CASE.

Statement in respect of £20 received 19 May. Paid out:

Rates (water, gas)	£7	—
Pawnshop, interest	3	—
Redeemed from pawnshop, for	1	10
Wages	2	—
TALLYMAN (who had to be paid weekly for a coat and trousers)	—	18
Shoes and hats for the children	1	10
Baker	1	—
Butcher	1	10
Epicier	1	—
CHEESEMONGER	—	10
Coal	—	10

Statement in respect of £24 received 16 June from the 'Tribune'

School for QUARTER February, March, April	£8	—
Loaned by *Schapper* for daily expenses over 4 weeks, repaid	3	—
Linen redeemed from pawnshop	2	—
Wages	1	—
TALLYMAN	1	4
Butcher	2	—
Epicier	2	—
GREENGROCER	1	—
Chemises, dresses, etc., for the children	2	—
Baker	2	—

Thus, after 17 June there was again not a single penny in the house and, to cover for four weeks day-to-day expenses which had to be paid in cash, we borrowed £4 from Schapper, about £2 of which, however, went on the abortive LOAN OPERATION IN FEES.

The full state of indebtedness, as it now stands in London, is as follows. (It will show you that a large part of the same consists in debts to small *épiciers* who have stretched their credit as far as it will go.)

Rates, due 25 June	£9	—
School, due 2 August	6	—
Newspaper man (for a year)	6	—
TALLYMAN	3	9
Butcher	7	14
Baker	6	—
Epicier	4	—
GREENGROCER and coal	2	—
Milkman	6	17
Owing to previous milkman and baker in Soho	9	—
Dr Allen (£7 paid out of last but one *Tribune* money)	10	—
Lina Schöler	9	—
Schapper	4	—
Pawnshop	30	—

Of these debts, the only ones I don't consider urgent are those owing to Dr Allen, Lina Schöler, the old creditors in Soho and part of what is due to the pawnshop.

Thus the whole business turns on the fact that what little comes in is never earmarked for the coming month, nor is it ever more than just sufficient—after deducting regular outgoings on house, school, rates and pawnshop—to reduce debts to a level that will preclude one's actually being thrown out into the street. In some 4-5 weeks' time I shall have ABOUT £24 to draw on the *Tribune*. Of this £15 will immediately go on rates and rent alone. If only a minimum is paid out in respect of other debts—and it is very questionable whether the BUTCHER, etc., will be prepared to wait so long—the predicament will, on the other hand, again be compounded by the 4 weeks which have to be got through *d'une manière ou d'une autre*.[a] The LANDLORD is himself being harried by creditors and is dunning me for all he's worth. I fail to see what I am to do, unless it is possible to obtain a LOAN from a LOAN-SOCIETY or

[a] somehow or other

LIFE-INSURANCE SOCIETY. Even were I to seek to reduce expenditure to the utmost—e.g. take the children away from school, move into a wholly working-class lodging, get rid of the maids, live on potatoes—not even the auction of my household goods would suffice to satisfy the creditors in the vicinity and ensure an unhampered removal to some hidey-hole. The SHOW of RESPECTABILITY which has so far been kept up has been the only means of avoiding a collapse. I for my part wouldn't care a damn about living in Whitechapel,[322] provided I could again at last secure an hour's peace in which to attend to my work. But in view of my wife's condition just now such a metamorphosis might entail dangerous consequences, and it could hardly be suitable for growing girls.

I HAVE NOW MADE A CLEAN BREAST OF IT and I assure you that it has cost me no small effort to do so. But *enfin*,[a] I must speak my mind to somebody. I know that you yourself can do nothing to help. All I ask is your opinion on WHAT TO DO. I would not wish my worst enemy to have to wade through the QUAGMIRE in which I've been trapped for the past two months, fuming the while over the innumerable vexations that are ruining my intellect and destroying my capacity for work.

Salut.

Your

K. M.

I shall send you the things you ask for.[b]

First published slightly abridged in *Der Briefwechsel zwischen F. Engels und K. Marx*, Bd. 2, Stuttgart, 1913 and in full in: Marx and Engels, *Works*, First Russian Edition, Vol. XXII, Moscow, 1929

Printed according to the original

176

ENGELS TO MARX

IN LONDON

Manchester, 16 July 1858

Dear Moor,

It is very decent of you to have laid your difficulties plainly before me. Obviously there is need for immediate action. By my

---

[a] after all - [b] See this volume, p. 326.

reckoning then, about £50 *à* £60 is urgent, and the rest can wait a while. I could at once raise £30 towards this amount by means of a fresh acceptance, provided the fellow agrees to make out the acceptance at *4 months minimum*, otherwise I wouldn't be in a position to find the money. If he is willing it might also be possible to draw £20 at 4 months and another £20 at 6 months (plus interest) so that I should have to pay in November and January and you would at once get £40 clear. So go and see Freiligrath straight away and find out what can be done. It is, of course, absolutely essential that *the discounter retains the acceptances in his own portfolio, otherwise I shall be ruined.* The rascal ought not to ask more than the 20% I am calculating on, which already represents a loss of nearly £5.

In this way, or so it seems to me, you would be covered to the extent that you could, at a pinch, wait until it's time to draw your next bill. But in view of your wife's state of health even more will be needed, of course, and unfortunately I can't manage it. I can't even step across to Watts here in connection with his Provident Institution as I've fallen out with the fellow. However he only has a BRANCH-OFFICE up here; the head-OFFICE is in London and you can look it up in any DIRECTORY. The business is called the PEOPLE'S PROVIDENT ASSURANCE SOCIETY AND LIFE AND EQUITABLE INSTITUTION[323] Freiligrath will easily get hold of a prospectus, TERMS, etc., for you and if there is anything to be done, which I doubt, he could also set the matter in train.

Though I've racked my brains I can think of no other method of raising money in England. It seems to me that the moment has come for you to have a go at your mater[a] or one or other of the Dutchmen.[b] Ultimately it is a question of wiping the slate clean and making A FRESH START; all this business of LOANS merely puts matters off and ultimately leads to an even worse crisis, quite apart from all the money—what with FEES, etc.—and time that is expended in attempts to raise the cash. Moreover, an acceptance on my part anticipates the money which I would otherwise have been able to send you over a period in small amounts and, although a lump sum is worth more to you than the ODD five-pound note now and again, this will certainly mean a corresponding loss of regular income.

You must really cast aside any reservations—*s'il y en aurait*[c]—in this case and attempt a *coup*. It's a question of finding a further

---

[a] Henriette Marx - [b] the Philips family, Marx's Dutch relations - [c] if there are any

£50 or so and I can see absolutely no way of getting it other than through your relations.

Meanwhile I shall mull the thing over for a couple of days and see if anything occurs to me. At all events it would be as well to burn *this* correspondence so that the matter remains between ourselves.

Your
F. E.

If *absolutely necessary* I would accept £20 at 3 months and £20 at 6; anything shorter wouldn't do. Interest on top of this, so you would have £40 net.

First published abridged in *Der Briefwechsel zwischen F. Engels und K. Marx*, Bd. 2, Stuttgart, 1913 and in full in: Marx and Engels, *Works*, First Russian Edition, Vol. XXII, Moscow, 1929

Printed according to the original

Published in English for the first time

177

MARX TO ENGELS [20]

IN MANCHESTER

London, 20 July 1858
9 Grafton Terrace, Maitland Park,
Haverstock Hill

Dear Engels,

When your letter arrived on Saturday I did not reply immediately because I first wanted to see what response I got to another 'ATTEMPT' before taking advantage of the authorisation you gave me. On Monday, however, I received an answer in the negative. Hence any further delay seemed impracticable. Accordingly to Freiligrath. Today he informed me in writing that the thing could be proceeded with on the TERMS you proposed, but not until 3 August since his USURER was unable to go ahead any earlier. I shall therefore write and tell him to put the business in hand by 3 August.

On Saturday I had a long letter from my mother. For I had asked Mrs Liebknecht, who was going to Germany, to take the old girl a portrait of our youngest child [a] with a brief note in which I

[a] Eleanor Marx

mentioned my being frequently ill but said nothing about our other circumstances.[324] The old girl's letter is such as to suggest the possibility of a meeting between us a few weeks hence. IF SO, I SHOULD ARRANGE THINGS. But I mustn't be too pressing IN THIS RESPECT. Otherwise she will promptly draw BACK.

Thank you for the *Tribune* article.[325] More tomorrow.

Your

K. M.

First published in *Der Briefwechsel zwischen F. Engels und K. Marx*, Bd. 2, Stuttgart, 1913

Printed according to the original

Published in English in full for the first time

178

MARX TO ENGELS

IN MANCHESTER

[London,] 25 July [1858]

Dear Engels,

From the enclosed letter of Freiligrath you will see that further DIFFICULTIES have arisen. But the 'new' terms seem to me *au fond*[a] better than the old, for though payment is nominally required in 3 months it need, IN FACT, only be made in 6 and the cost is 10% less.

Kindly reply at once ONE WAY OR THE OTHER. The matter is PRESSING. If it can be arranged in this way I shall, AT ANY RISK, immediately send my wife to a nearby seaside resort for a couple of weeks and, in the meantime, see what I can fix up with my mater—after the more unruly creditors have been placated, OF COURSE.

Salut.

Your

K. M.

First published in: Marx and Engels, *Works*, First Russian Edition, Vol. XXII, Moscow, 1929

Printed according to the original

Published in English for the first time

---

[a] in the main

179

MARX TO ENGELS[326]

IN MANCHESTER

London, 8 August 1858
9 Grafton Terrace, Maitland Park,
Haverstock Hill

Dear Engels,

If I haven't written before, this was because it wasn't till yesterday that the matter was decided *for certain* and, indeed, in the affirmative. Every time I sat down to write to you, another letter arrived from the City to say there was nothing doing and that I should try and carry out the transaction with SOMEBODY ELSE. However, I wanted to tell you something definite ONE WAY OR THE OTHER. After he had negotiated with 6 different USURERS, and every time the fellows went back on their promise when it came to the point, Freiligrath eventually discounted the bill with his own tailor, after he had agreed to act as collateral. He had, *ab initio,*[a] made it *payable at his own bank.* The old chap went to a great deal of trouble over the matter, even to the extent of taking certain steps not altogether in keeping with his 'professional' status. So if you should happen to write to him, give him a little PAT on the back, an action to which he is not wholly impervious. The bill has been deposited with Freiligrath himself. The tailor declares that he is prepared to renew it, *whatever the circumstances.* But he would prefer to receive £20 in November so that he would only have to make out a new bill for the remaining £20 payable in January. (After receiving your letter,[327] I immediately informed Freiligrath that the thing could not be proceeded with *unless* there was a *certainty of renewal.*)

To my alarm I saw from your letter that you were ill again, and in the circumstances it was all the more embarrassing to me to have ANNOYED you. Please write *by return* saying how you are, or else get Dr Gumpert to write.

After receiving the money, I promptly paid off as much as possible and yesterday sent my wife to Ramsgate, since there was not another day to be lost. She really is extraordinarily unwell. If Ramsgate isn't too expensive, and she is thus able to have several weeks of sea bathing, I believe all will soon be RIGHT again.

[a] from the start

MEANWHILE I shall see if there's anything to be done with my mother. How I should answer the old girl in regard to my relations with Prussia is a very ticklish point. It's just *possible* that she might fork out if she thought my inheritance was under threat from the authorities. But again it's just *possible*—since she seems to me to be making her will—that she might in that case put everything in the care of the Dutchman,[a] which wouldn't suit me at all. *Que faire dans cette situation?*[b] She writes saying her days are numbered, but I believe that's just a manner of speaking. She probably wanted me to invite her to London, as indeed I would certainly have done had my time not been precious to me just now. For the past 2 months I have hardly been able to work, and the Duncker business is becoming urgent.[c]

I have written a lot for the *Tribune* of late so as to replenish my account a bit, but I'm getting damnably short of material. India isn't my department. Cherbourg[328] would have provided me with ample opportunity for political epigrams, except that I'm too ignorant of military matters to give the thing the proper depth. To me—though it's an altogether subjective opinion, not to say a prejudice—Cherbourg would seem to be no more than a DODGE, like all Boustrapa's[40] grand doings, a mere SLEIGHT OF HAND. At any rate, the *Moniteur*, no less, contained certain ominous hints to the effect that the military authorities are by no means happy about the choice of the spot and have raised a host of circumstantial objections to the lay-out of the works. It is, furthermore, FAR FROM BEING FINISHED and, in its present state, represents rather what's *to be* than what *is*. The only thing that is completely finished is the big equestrian statue of Napoleon. In Central India, or so it seems to me, the fall of Gwalior settles the matter. The Indian papers are all very hostile to Campbell and critical of his 'tactics'.

Enclosed a letter from Lassalle.[d] Ephraim Artful is a curious fellow. He demands of me AN IMMENSE DEAL OF DISCRETION and puts on a great show of secrecy, yet the whole scrawl[e] appears substantially in the *Kölner Zeitung*! There's a vein of absurd grandiloquence running through the man's letters. 'Then I addressed, etc., a trenchantly cutting memoir, etc.' 'I set Böckh and Humboldt in motion.' Humboldt wrote 'a fulminating letter'. 'I myself made a complaint direct to the Prince[f] couched in the *bluntest German*.' 'Truly *foudroyant*[g] arraignment of the minister[h].' 'Urgent plea.' 'In

[a] Lion Philips - [b] What's to be done in this situation? - [c] Marx means the preparation for the press of *A Contribution to the Critique of Political Economy*. - [d] Lassalle's letter to Marx of 23 July 1858 - [e] See this volume, pp. 321-23. - [f] William, Prince of Prussia - [g] crushing - [h] Ferdinand von Westphalen

absolute confidence.' 'My biggest pistol.' 'Hopeless.' 'Utmost secrecy *and* discretion.' 'If that's not sauce for the gander, etc.'

Our friend Bürgers will soon be out of prison again now. His main idea, it seems, is to play father to Daniels' children and to that end, first take over the post of bedfellow to Mrs Daniels. The latter has, however, written to Lina[a] saying that Bürgers isn't to be compared with her husband.

Apropos, Lupus will be interested to hear that little Jenny has received THE FIRST GENERAL PRIZE IN THE FIRST CLASS (which also includes the *English* prize), and little Laura the second. They are the youngest in the class. Jenny also got the prize for French.

Salut. I hope to hear some *good* news about your STATE OF HEALTH.

Your

K. M.

The *Telegraph* (enclosed) is also to be kept.

First published abridged in *Der Briefwechsel zwischen F. Engels und K. Marx*, Bd. 2, Stuttgart, 1913 and in full in: Marx and Engels, *Works,* First Russian Edition, Vol. XXII, Moscow, 1929

Printed according to the original

Published in English in full for the first time

180

ENGELS TO MARX

IN LONDON

Manchester, 10 August 1858
7 Southgate

Dear Moor,

Back at the office again since yesterday. I wasn't ill, by the way, merely wounded SURGICALLY and, though the wound is not yet quite healed, the purpose has been achieved. In no circumstances shall I be in a condition to do a *Tribune* article before next week.

How's the Appleton affair going? You once wrote saying you were enclosing two letters from America,[321] but you forgot to do so. Did they have any bearing on it? In a fortnight's time I shall probably be going to the seaside, where I might be able to get down to some hard work on the thing.

---

[a] Caroline Schöler

Ephraim's[a] letter is strange indeed. How can anyone be so stupid as to part with something like that, actually put down in black and white? That's what I really call dubbing oneself a fool *à perpétuité*.

Lupus and I send our hearty congratulations to the two girls[b] on their achievements. The old chap was delighted about it. His leg is still not up to much. Borchardt undoubtedly treated the thing the wrong way and Lupus has mucked up matters by undue zeal and unnecessary foot-slogging. The thing might have other disagreeable, if not serious, consequences later on. He was in Buxton and then in Devonshire where he again had to endure the horror of bad hotels, got nothing to drink and was colossally fleeced.

I hope your wife, too, is now better. The tailor will be able to have half the amount in October.

Your

F. E.

First published in: Marx and Engels, *Works*, First Russian Edition, Vol. XXII, Moscow, 1929

Printed according to the original

Published in English for the first time

181

MARX TO ENGELS

IN MANCHESTER

[London,] 13 August 1858

Dear Engels,

I am delighted to hear that my fears about your health were unfounded.

Of the two letters I meant to send you, one was from Weydemeyer (Milwaukee, Wisconsin) and the other from one A. Komp (New York), both of which arrived under the same cover. I had put them down on the table (my writing-table) to enclose them in my letter to you, forgot, and then couldn't find them. They are probably tucked away in one of the many

[a] Ferdinand Lassalle's - [b] Jenny and Laura Marx

notebooks that are strewn around, and will reappear when I leaf through them.[321]

I know nothing about the *Cyclopaedia* save that I've seen an advertisement for the second volume in the *Tribune*.[a] So it's still coming out and, if you have the leisure, you might occasionally do something for C.—subject, however, to two reservations: 1. I cannot go to the Museum[b] just now; 2. it would be of more immediate advantage to me to increase my balance at the *Tribune*. This has already decreased slightly since my wife went away and I cannot in any case write twice for them myself, as it's impossible for me to deal with subjects such as India, Montenegro, China, Bonaparte's military railway system and his installations at Cherbourg.[328] Hence, as soon as time permits (and, OF COURSE, without physical HARM to yourself), I would greatly prefer it if, in the immediate future, you were to write more often for the *Tribune*, ON ANY SUBJECT WHATEVER.

The sea is doing my wife a lot of good; at the beginning of this week she sent for all the children and Lenchen.[c] SO FAR SO GOOD; the only snag is that, UNDER THE CIRCUMSTANCES, I shall hardly be able to let her stay there beyond next week. Mentally she is very much refreshed, but physically (save that her nerves are stronger) she is not yet all that she might be. In Ramsgate she has made the acquaintance of refined and, *horribile dictu*,[d] clever Englishwomen. After years during which she has enjoyed only inferior company, if any at all, intercourse with people of her own kind seems to agree with her.

Have you read the review in *The Times* of Gladstone's book on Homer?[e] There is much that is amusing in it (the review). A work such as this is, by the by, typical of your Englishman's incompetence in matters of 'philology'.

I presume that TRADE IN MANCHESTER is again LOOKING UP? Indeed, over the past few weeks the world has grown damned optimistic again.

Mr Pyat, still oppressed by the fact that his name was not given due prominence during the recent political prosecutions, has published a fresh *'lettre'*[f] about his *'lettre'* to the Parliament, containing a vindication of 'regicide'.[329] In order to compel the government to prosecute, he has flouted police regulations by

---

[a] *New-York Daily Tribune*, No. 5319, 8 May 1858 - [b] the British Museum Library - [c] Helene Demuth - [d] horrible to mention - [e] W. E. Gladstone, *Studies on Homer and the Homeric Age* (the review appeared in *The Times*, Nos. 23070 and 23071, 12 and 13 August 1858 under the title 'Mr. Gladstone's Homeric Studies'). - [f] F. Pyat, *Lettre au jury. Défense de la lettre au Parlement et à la Presse.*

letting the scrawl come out without the printer's name. But the government is inexorable. Pyat is not to be made a martyr, even to the tune of a 2/6d fine with COSTS in a magistrate's court. *Le pauvre Sire!*[a]

Warm regards to Lupus.

Your

K. M.

First published abridged in *Der Briefwechsel zwischen F. Engels und K. Marx*, Bd. 2, Stuttgart, 1913 and in full in: Marx and Engels, *Works*, First Russian Edition, Vol. XXII, Moscow, 1929

Printed according to the original

Published in English for the first time

182

MARX TO ENGELS

IN MANCHESTER

[London,] 18 August 1858

Dear Engels,

If at all possible, let me have 1 ARTICLE on India *or* Cherbourg by Friday.[328] *It's absolutely impossible for me to carry on any longer* without an *entremets* of this kind. You will understand how bereft of material I am when I tell you that yesterday I wrote (*via* Ramsgate, where the fair copy was made[b]) about the SLAVE-TRADE in Cuba.[330] On the other hand, it is now more than ever essential that I should jack up my credit a little.

Salut.

Your

K. M.

Apropos. I inserted—not directly, but through a channel *viz.* that of Liebknecht, who himself made use of yet another channel—Kinkel's advertisement of a trip to the LAKES in the

---

[a] Poor devil - [b] Jenny Marx, who usually made the fair copies of Marx's articles for the *New-York Daily Tribune*, was in Ramsgate at the time.

Neue Zeit (a German rag in London).[a] The thing caused a scandal. Kinkel now denies it. Important you should write to me about it.

First published in: Marx and Engels, *Works*, First Russian Edition, Vol. XXII, Moscow, 1929

Printed according to the original

Published in English for the first time

183

MARX TO ENGELS

IN MANCHESTER

[London,] 21 September 1858
9 Grafton Terrace, Maitland Park,
Haverstock Hill

DEAR Frederick,

You must exercise your customary forbearance and excuse my long silence. The indisposition from which I was suffering even before leaving Manchester again became chronic—persisting throughout the entire summer—so that any kind of writing costs me a tremendous effort. For the same reason my manuscript[b] is only now about to go off (IN 2 WEEKS), but there will be 2 instalments AT ONCE. Even though I had nothing to do but correct the style of what had already been written, I might sometimes sit for hours before getting this or that phrase right. For ABOUT 8 DAYS, by the by, I have been much better and on the whole I find the cooler time of year more beneficial. Moreover, there is every prospect that, with my mother's help, I shall be able to put my domestic affairs entirely in order and also start to take HORSE EXERCISE again. The latter will be my prime concern, as soon as the BUSINESS has been attended to.

Meanwhile I have been writing very regularly for the *Tribune*, as I have no desire to make these chaps a gift of any money.

Find out from Lupus or (directly or indirectly) from Borchardt whether they know a Mrs von Paula (might sign herself Paulaw) who once lived in Breslau.[c] If so, I have something curious to tell you.

---

[a] K. Marx, 'To the Editor of the *Neue Zeit*'. - [b] *A Contribution to the Critique of Political Economy* - [c] Wrocław

Re Bangya, I had in my possession (but, alas, only for a few hours) some material relating to him—letters from Constantinople as well as cuttings from the Constantinople papers. The excerpts in *The Free Press* don't give such a clear idea of the thing.[a] It's the *affaire* of the 'CHIEF of the dynasty'[b] all over again. Kossuth would appear to be directly compromised. I have now SUMMONED him in the *Tribune*[c] TO DECLARE HIMSELF!

Apropos. I've had an amusing experience with the *Tribune*. By way of evaluating the 'REPORT of the COMMITTEE'[d] on the late crisis I sent the paper several articles specifically relating to banking, CURRENCY, etc., which they published as LEADERS.[331] Along comes a BANKER, a self-styled 'BULLIONIST', and writes a letter to the *Tribune*[e] in which he says 1. that never has so COMPREHENSIVE A SUMMARY of the whole subject been PENNED, etc., but 2. raises all kinds of objections and challenges the editors to reply. So reply the POOR DEVILS must needs do[f] and INDEED VERY SAD WORK they made of it. But such incidents can only do me good.

Our friend Jones HAS DECIDEDLY SOLD HIMSELF (BUT AT THE LOWEST POSSIBLE PRICE) TO THE BRIGHT COTERIE. The idiot has ruined himself politically without rescuing himself commercially. I'll cut out the articles relating to him in *Reynolds's* and send them to you. But how little his apostasy—the laddie is preaching UNION OF THE MIDDLE AND WORKING CLASSES—has availed him (he has sold *The People's Paper* to the *Morning Star* fellows, has retained a mere couple of columns in the sheet for himself and is, moreover, already at loggerheads with his new allies over the financial terms) will be evident to you from the fact that the day before yesterday he went to Freiligrath and handed him a letter in German in which he asked for £4, failing which he would be 'locked up'. Freiligrath told him to address himself 'TO OUR FRIEND GILPIN'. That Gilpin is MANAGING DIRECTOR of the SWITZERLAND BANK and of the paper with which Jones has incorporated himself.

If you possibly have time, write ANYTHING for Friday. I wrote about the Chinese Treaty yesterday.[332]

Lina[g] is now STAYING with us, having lost her position again. *Salut.* Regards to Lupus.

Your

K. M.

---

[a] 'The Russian Agent in Circassia', *The Free Press,* No. 20, 25 August 1858. - [b] See this volume, p. 109. - [c] K. Marx, 'Another Strange Chapter of Modern History'. - [d] *Report from the Select Committee on Bank Acts...* - [e] 'To the Editor of *N. Y. Tribune', New-York Daily Tribune,* No. 5420, 4 September 1858. - [f] The editors' reply was published in the same issue as the Banker's letter. - [g] Caroline Schöler

Come what may, you must arrange to spend a few days here over Christmas or the New Year.

According to the latest report in *The Economist*, French trade has got worse rather than better over recent months.[a] (*Give the enclosed to Lupus.*)

First published abridged in *Der Briefwechsel zwischen F. Engels und K. Marx*, Bd. 2, Stuttgart, 1913 and in full in: Marx and Engels, *Works*, First Russian Edition, Vol. XXII, Moscow, 1929

Printed according to the original

Published in English for the first time

184

ENGELS TO MARX[1]

IN LONDON

Manchester, 7 October 1858

Dear Moor,

No doubt you will be writing about the Canning despatch tomorrow[333]; THE THING IS OUT OF MY LATITUDE ALTOGETHER. I have not read the newspapers at all regularly of late and have had a great deal to do, since Ermen has been over there for the past fortnight and I am having to cope with the whole shop on my own. Business here is tremendously good; for the past 6 weeks the spinners have been making 1d *à* 1¼d more per pound on coarse and medium counts than for the past 3 years and—quite unprecedented this—the local market in yarn rose 1d before the Liverpool chaps were able to get another ¼d for cotton. During the past 10-12 days the rise has slowed down somewhat, but all the spinners are booked up well ahead and demand is still quite strong enough to sustain prices. If it goes on like this much longer there'll be MOVEMENTS for increased wages. In France, too, the cotton spinners have for sometime been earning more than in recent years (this is positive; I have it from a cotton agent who was over there himself); how things look in other branches of commerce there I can't say exactly, but the state of the Bourse suggests a considerable improvement. All this looks damned rosy and the

---

[a] 'Accounts Relating to Trade and Navigation for the Seven Months Ended July 31, 1858', *The Economist*, No. 783 (supplement), 28 August 1858.

devil only knows how long it will last unless there is substantial overproduction with India and China in view. Trade must be absolutely splendid in India just now; the last Bombay MAIL but one advised sales—over a 14-day period—of 320,000 pieces of cotton cloth, and the last one a further 100,000. The chaps have already sold the whole lot forward, knowing only that it had been purchased in Manchester and not yet even shipped. Judging by the way the local philistines are talking and also by the state of the market, it seems to me that India and China will provide an immediate excuse for overproduction and, if we have a good winter, it may confidently be expected that kite-flying and the unbridled granting of credit will again go ahead merrily in the spring.

The Jones business is most distasteful. He held a meeting here and the speech he made was entirely in the spirit of the new alliance.[334] After that affair one might almost believe that the English proletarian movement in its old traditional Chartist form must perish utterly before it can evolve in a new and viable form. And yet it is not possible to foresee what the new form will look like. It seems to me, by the way, that there is in fact a connection between Jones' NEW MOVE, seen in conjunction with previous more or less successful attempts at such an alliance, and the fact that the English proletariat is actually becoming more and more bourgeois, so that the ultimate aim of this most bourgeois of all nations would appear to be the possession, *alongside* the bourgeoisie, of a bourgeois aristocracy and a bourgeois proletariat. In the case of a nation which exploits the entire world this is, of course, justified to some extent. Only a couple of thoroughly bad years might help here, but after the discoveries of gold these are no longer so easy to engineer. For the rest it is a complete mystery to me how the massive overproduction which caused the crisis has been absorbed; never before has such heavy flooding drained away so rapidly.

Reynolds will become a prominent personage thanks to Jones' manoeuvre; he is the only 'educated' man (*vulgo* 'scholar') who still poses as the representative of the proletariat—*au fond*[a] he is as bourgeois as Monsieur Jones has now become, though in a different way. For him this is a GODSEND. Be sure to send me the cuttings from his paper[b] you promised me.

There is still something wrong with Lupus' leg; he still can't walk fast without suffering for it, though he is walking passably well again.

---

[a] in the main - [b] *Reynolds's Newspaper*

The little German poetaster whose account of his adventures with Kinkel and Freiligrath appeared last summer in the *Augsburger* is called Isaak Levi, alias Julius Rodenberg, a schoolfellow of Gumpert's.

If at all possible I shall come up for Christmas. It's splendid to hear that you will be arranging money matters with your mater. I hope this has meanwhile been done or is at least cut and dried. I am writing to Freiligrath today about the bill.

Warm regards to your wife and the girls.

Your

F. E.

Has the manuscript gone off[a]?

First published abridged in *Der Briefwechsel zwischen F. Engels und K. Marx*, Bd. 2, Stuttgart, 1913 and in full in: Marx and Engels, *Works*, First Russian Edition, Vol. XXII, Moscow, 1929

Printed according to the original

Published in English in full for the first time

185

MARX TO ENGELS[1]

IN MANCHESTER

London, Friday, [8 October[b]] 1858

DEAR Frederick,

You will today be receiving two packages AT ONCE since not all the stuff could go into one letter. It consists of:

1. Cuttings from *Reynolds's* relating to Jones. You will see for yourself where Reynolds is conveying FACTS, and opinions based on FACTS, and where he is venting his spleen. Reynolds is a far greater rogue than Jones, but he is rich and a good speculator. The mere FACT THAT HE HAS TURNED AN OUT AND OUT CHARTIST shows that this position must STILL be a 'profitable' one. I have read the speech Jones made in Manchester.[334] Since you did not see his earlier SPEECHES in Greenwich, etc., you couldn't have detected that he is making another TURN and seeking again to bring the 'alliance' more into accord with his former attitude.

2. Pyat's new *lettre*,[c] which contains one or 2 FACTS that are INTERESTING, otherwise in his former manner.[329] The marks in the

[a] K. Marx, *A Contribution to the Critique of Political Economy*. - [b] Date inserted by Engels. - [c] F. Pyat, *Lettre au jury. Défense de la lettre au Parlement et à la Presse.*

margin have been scribbled by my BABY[a] and do not, therefore, have any bearing on the contents.

3. Mazzini's new manifesto.[b] Still the same old jackass. Save that now he is gracious enough not to consider *le salariat*[c] any longer as the absolute and final form. There's nothing funnier than the way he contradicts himself, on the one hand saying that in Italy the revolutionary party is organised according to his views and, on the other, proving after 'his own' fashion not only that it has the nation behind it, but also that there is every outward prospect of success—and finally *fails to explain* why, despite *Dio e Popolo* AND MAZZINI INTO THE BARGAIN, all is calm in Italy.

4. A little cutting from the Cincinnati *Hochwächter* containing a letter from 'General' Willich.

Considering the optimistic turn taken by world trade AT THIS MOMENT (although the vast accumulations of money in the BANKS of London, Paris and New York show that things cannot by any means be ALL RIGHT yet), it is some consolation at least that the *revolution has begun* in Russia, for I regard the convocation of 'NOTABLES' to Petersburg[335] as such a beginning. Similarly in Prussia things are worse than they were in 1847, and the ridiculous DELUSIONS AS TO THE MIDDLE CLASS PROPENSITIES OF THE PRINCE OF PRUSSIA will be exploded in an outburst of rage.[336] It will do the French no harm to see that, even without them, the world 'mov't' (Pennsylvania-fashion).[d] At the same time exceptional movements are on foot amongst the Slavs, notably in Bohemia, which, though counter-revolutionary, yet provide ferment for the movement. The Russian war of 1854-55,[e] wretched though it was and little though its consequences damaged the Russians (but rather the Turks), nevertheless clearly precipitated the present turn of events in Russia. The only circumstance which turned the Germans into mere satellites of France so far as their revolutionary movement was concerned, was the ATTITUDE of Russia. This absurdity will cease with an internal movement in MOSCOVY. As soon as the thing assumes clearer shape there, we shall have proof of the full extent to which the worthy Regierungsrat Haxthausen has allowed himself to be hoodwinked by the 'authorities' and by the peasants those authorities have trained.[337]

There is no denying that bourgeois society has for the second time experienced its 16th century, a 16th century which, I hope,

---

a Eleanor Marx - b Published in *Pensiero ed Azione,* 14 September 1858 (for details see Marx's article 'Mazzini's New Manifesto'). - c wage labour - d Marx has (*pennsylvanisch*) which presumably is a comment on 'mov't' and means: the way Germans in Pennsylvania speak English. - e the Crimean war will sound its death knell just as the first ushered it into the world. The proper task of bourgeois society is the creation of the world market, at least in outline, and of the production based on that market. Since the world is round, the colonisation of California and Australia and the opening up of China and Japan would seem to have completed this process. For us, the difficult QUESTION is this: on the Continent revolution is imminent and will, moreover, instantly assume a socialist character. Will it not necessarily be CRUSHED in this little corner of the earth, since the MOVEMENT of bourgeois society is still in the ASCENDANT over a far greater area?

So far as China in particular is concerned, I have, by carefully analysing the movement of trade since 1836, established *first* that by 1847 the surge in English and American exports between 1844 and 1846 had proved a complete fraud and that, in the 10 years that followed, the average remained pretty stationary whereas imports from China into England and America rose enormously; *secondly*, that the only result of the opening up of the 5 ports[338] and the annexation of Hong Kong was a shift of trade from Canton to Shanghai. The other 'EMPORIUMS' do not count. The main reason for the FAILURE of this market would seem to be the opium trade—to which, indeed, every increase in the export trade to China has invariably been confined; however, another factor is the country's internal economic organisation, its MINUTE AGRICULTURE, etc., to demolish which will take an enormously long time. England's present TREATY with China[332] which, in my view, was worked out by Palmerston jointly with the cabinet in Petersburg and was given to Lord Elgin to take with him on his journey, is A MOCKERY FROM BEGINNING TO END.

Can you give me your sources for the PROGRESS of the Russians in Central Asia? I shall use the article[a] for *The Free Press*, at any rate.

My mother has suddenly and unexpectedly withdrawn into what, to me, is an inexplicable silence. I am inclined to think that third persons have put a spoke in the wheel. But the matter will resolve itself.

Regards to Lupus.

Your

K. M.

First published in *Der Briefwechsel zwischen F. Engels und K. Marx*, Bd. 2, Stuttgart, 1913

Printed according to the original

Published in English in full for the first time

[a] F. Engels, 'Russian Progress in Central Asia'.

186

ENGELS TO MARX

IN LONDON

Manchester, 21 October 1858

Dear Moor,

For the past fortnight I've been VERY MUCH PUT OUT OF THE WAY by sundry slings and arrows—a rumpus at my LODGINGS necessitating a move and all that entails and, for good measure, a mass of other tiresome happenings. I haven't even found new LODGINGS yet and am hardly likely to be out of the TROUBLE before the end of next week.

Much obliged for the stuff relating to Jones, Mazzini and Pyat, likewise the 'enthusiastic general'.[a] The latter seems to have surrendered entirely to the vulgar German-American day-dream; *habeat sibi,*[b] let him go hang. *Quoad*[c] Jones, I should say that *Reynolds's* is a bit short on FACTS and presupposes some degree of familiarity with preceding events. This turn things have finally taken is hardly surprising in view of the contemptible way Monsieur Jones has already long been behaving. But simply to throw oneself away like that! Duncombe did at least get his debts paid and a good position into the bargain.

Pyat and Mazzini, even by comparison with formerly, are distinguishing themselves by a surprising poverty of intelligence.

Prospects for Mr Rudolf Schramm seem exceedingly poor. Now as always, the corporal[d] is confiscating newspapers and, if the telegraphic despatches are to be believed, did not even swear an oath on the Constitution yesterday. At any rate, the joyous day-dream which the Prussian bourgeois have deluded each other into believing will very soon evaporate, but I agree with you when you say that this won't be the end of the affair.[336] However, I'm not yet clear as to what course it will take. I should say that the bourgeoisie has not yet got over 1848 and 1849 to such an extent as to summon up sufficient courage simultaneously to confront on the one hand the aristocracy and bureaucracy, and, on the other, proletarian unrest. However, it's possible that, so long as nothing is going on in France, the proletarian movement will for a time seem too slight a threat to be very intimidating; but in that case its

---

[a] August Willich - [b] for all I care - [c] As for - [d] William, Prince of Prussia

progress will have to be damned slow. If nothing happens in France—which, in view of the present state of the Crédit mobilier's[45] shares, is hardly to be expected—Prussia might, of course, see the formation of a movement similar to the one in Italy during the years 1846-48, with a proletarian background. But otherwise I'm afraid the bourgeoisie may come round again before it's too late.

The Russian affair is turning out very well.[335] There is unrest in the South now, too. Apropos. Could you obtain for me from Tchorzewsky, or whoever Herzen's agent is now, a few of his more recent publications? After all, these ought to contain something, e.g. his *Голоса изъ Россіи (Voices from Russia)* and the *Колоколъ* (*Bell*). Some material might be found in them, though hardly very much—but certainly now and again in the correspondents' reports, etc., etc.

My sources for the Central Asiatic stuff were Brockhaus' new volume *Unsere Zeit*[a] (partly copied from the *Preußisches Wochenblatt*) and Petermann's geographical *Mittheilungen*.[b] The material is all derived from Russian state papers. If you like I could write an article about the Russian treaty with China[339] (what a slap in the face for England and France!) for Tuesday, or thereabouts,[c] i.e. if not prevented by my exodus. Let me know, and also send your further comments on the connection you suspect exists between the Elgin treaty and Pam.[d] Or perhaps you have already dealt with this yourself?

India is now quite outside my LATITUDE. From the military point of view nothing at all remains to be said. So desultory has everything become that it's not even possible to do a survey of one month's events. Altogether, I'm in a quandary about subjects for articles to send you.

What's the position about the manuscript for Duncker[e]? Now's YOUR TIME. Come what may, there'll be a new ministry which will probably be rather more hesitant about *making its début* with the confiscation of a *scientific* work. I hope it has gone off. But let me know for sure, so that I can reassure Lupus too. Last Sunday he arrived at my place very much the worse for drink, but was safely escorted home. Since then his leg has been rather worse again; no doubt it took a knock.

---

[a] *Unsere Zeit. Jahrbuch zum Conversations-Lexikon*, Bd. 2. - [b] *Mittheilungen aus Justus Perthes' Geographischer Anstalt....* - [c] F. Engels, 'Russia's Successes in the Far East'. - [d] See this volume, p. 347. - [e] K. Marx, *A Contribution to the Critique of Political Economy*.

For the past four weeks, trade here has been going through a sticky period during which the spinners have had their profits cut by $^1/_2$d per lb as a result of a fall in yarn and a rise in cotton. However, they are still doing good business and, if cotton again comes down a bit, as is quite possible, it will take only a minimal increase in demand to restore the situation. Moreover, there are signs here and there of moves by the workers to obtain higher wages and, if business continues good, these will gather force.

How are things going with your mater? Best regards to your wife and children.

Your

F. E.

First published abridged in *Der Briefwechsel zwischen F. Engels und K. Marx,* Bd. 2, Stuttgart, 1913 and in full in: Marx and Engels, *Works,* First Russian Edition, Vol. XXII, Moscow, 1929

Printed according to the original

Published in English for the first time

187

MARX TO ENGELS

IN MANCHESTER

[London,] Friday [22 October 1858][340]

Dear Engels,

I haven't a moment to lose today, for it's already 2 o'clock and I've still not begun the article.[341] I am just writing you these few lines to inform you that you must send something next week. Two articles a week means my spending an enormous amount of time hunting for material. Write about China. Another subject might be the ludicrous RIFLED CANNONS article in today's *Times.*[a].

Yesterday, after ages of silence, a letter arrived from Pieper—from *the hospital in Dalston* (London).

My mother has written me a fatuous letter. She has *postponed* our discussion until such time as *I* 'shall' visit her. Obviously there has been interference by a third party.

---

a 'The theory of war ...', *The Times,* No. 23131, 22 October 1858.

The manuscript[a] has not gone off yet and, Lupus or no Lupus, it will be weeks before I am able to send it.

Your

K. M.

First published in: Marx and Engels, *Works*, First Russian Edition, Vol. XXII, Moscow, 1929

Printed according to the original

Published in English for the first time

188

MARX TO ENGELS

IN MANCHESTER

[London,] 2 November 1858

Dear Frederick,

'Montalembert'[b] WILL DO. Yesterday I wrote about Quasimodo's goings-on with the Portuguese.[342]

Enclosed you will find works by the great Blind, who now functions as a 'united' friend of the people. The £100 has also been remitted to him by Kinkel. Keep the stuff. You will observe that Pyat and Mazzini still stand head and shoulders above these German democrats in the matter of style, etc. Blind has also set his hand over here to the trade he learnt on the *Mannheimer Abendzeitung*. He gets a couple of acquaintances in Hamburg to send to *English papers* letters (composed by himself) in which mention is made of the stir created by his anonymous pamphlets.[343] His friends then write more letters, this time to the German press, saying what a fuss has been made by the English papers, etc. That, you see, is what it is to be a man of action.

Paid a visit to 'unhappy' Pieper in hospital. Has a syphilitic boil on his forehead. Otherwise the same old Pieper. Probably won't be cured before the end of December, when he proposes to take a trip to Hanover.

---

[a] K. Marx, *A Contribution to the Critique of Political Economy*. - [b] F. Engels, 'The Prosecution of Montalembert'.

I have the most damnable toothache and so can't write any more today.

Regards to Lupus.

Your
K. M.

First published in: Marx and Engels, *Works*, First Russian Edition, Vol. XXII, Moscow, 1929

Printed according to the original

Published in English for the first time

189

MARX TO ENGELS

IN MANCHESTER

[London,] 10 November 1858

Dear Frederick,

For the past 10 days I have had the most appalling toothache and ulcers all over my mouth, i.e. inflammation of the gums, etc. Hence in very bad humour, these having come on top of all my other troubles.

Your article[a] went off yesterday *as of Friday*, since I had sent nothing on that day. I myself wrote about the new Prussian ministry. Have now sent about six articles on Prussia dated Berlin to the *Tribune*.[b] So I don't imagine that you will be able to have any new matter concerning Prussia for next Tuesday. One subject that might be worth writing about, though in this case I fear our common material goes not very far, would be the growth of industry in Prussia over the last 10 years. But whence obtain the 'material'? As regards Japan I imagine the Yankees know more about it than we do, though in fact their knowledge is always exceedingly superficial. Those engaged in high politics (e.g. Mr Pulszky in the *Tribune*) are blathering away about a possible war in Italy between Austria on the one hand and Bonaparte and Piedmont on the other. I regard all that as nonsense. Might it not, on the whole, be a good idea to say something sensible for once about Bonaparte's

[a] F. Engels, 'The Prosecution of Montalembert'. - [b] K. Marx, 'The King of Prussia's Insanity' (2 articles), 'The Prussian Regency', 'Affairs in Prussia' (2 articles), 'The New Ministry' (2 articles).

military position vis-à-vis Germany generally? If you don't like that topic, do something on France, say, or Russia, or ANYTHING ELSE.

I had forgotten to enclose Blind's 'pamphlets'.[343] Unfortunately I can't lay my hands on the most idiotic one, *Aufruf an Schleswig-Holstein*—yes, here it is at last. In addition I am sending you a speech by that clown Edgar Bauer from the London *Neue Zeit*.[a] Keep the things.

Next week I have to pay more than one pound interest at the pawnshop. As it's impossible for me to draw on the *Tribune* just now, I'd be grateful if you would send me the pound.

Mind you write and tell me your opinion of Mr E. Bauer's 'Philosophy of History'.

Salut. Regards to Lupus.

Your

K. M.

First published in *Der Briefwechsel zwischen F. Engels und K. Marx*, Bd. 2, Stuttgart, 1913

Printed according to the original

Published in English for the first time

190

MARX TO FERDINAND LASSALLE

IN BERLIN

London, 12 November 1858
9 Grafton Terrace, Maitland Park,
Haverstock Hill

Dear Lassalle,

Post tot pericula![b] My answer to your last letter[c] was held up by an infamous toothache. I didn't answer your letter from Frankfurt[d] because you gave no address.

Well, *d'abord: beatus ille*[e] who is not seen through Köster's eyes but who sees with the eyes of Köster. I and Freiligrath had explained at length to Köster himself that throughout the summer

---

[a] E. Bauer, 'Vorträge über die Geschichte der Politik...', *Die Neue Zeit*, No. 20, 6 November 1858. - [b] After so many dangers! - [c] of 22 October 1858 - [d] This letter is not extant. - [e] first: Blessed is he (Horace, *Epodes*, II, 1).

the most severe liver trouble had virtually incapacitated me for work. And as for my 'splendid circumstances', Freiligrath and I had deemed fit to conjure up the brightest of pictures for the benefit of this average German bourgeois, while altogether concealing the darker side, since we both opined that even the best bourgeois of this type could not fail to derive a certain malicious satisfaction from the knowledge of what the *fuorusciti*'s[a] circumstances were really like. So FAR Köster.

As regards the delay in sending off the manuscript,[b] I was first prevented from doing so by illness, and subsequently had to catch up on the other 'bread and butter' work. But the real reason is this: the material was to hand and all that I was concerned with was the form. But to me the style of everything I wrote seemed tainted with liver trouble. And I have a twofold motive for not allowing this work to be spoiled on medical grounds:

1. It is the product of 15 years of research, i.e. the best years of my life.

2. In it an important view of social relations is scientifically expounded for the first time. Hence I owe it to the Party that the thing shouldn't be disfigured by the kind of heavy, wooden style proper to a disordered liver.

My aim is not to produce an elegant exposé, but only to write as I usually do, which, during these months of sickness, was impossible—at least on this subject, although over the same period I was compelled to write, and hence did write, the equivalent of at least 2 printed volumes of English leading articles *de omnibus rebus et quibusdam aliis*.[c]

I believe that even if someone less intelligent than you were to acquaint Mr Duncker with this state of affairs, he could not but sanction a mode of conduct which, so far as he as a publisher was concerned, merely signified the endeavour to give him the best value for his money.

I shall have finished about 4 weeks from now, having only just begun the actual writing.

There is a further circumstance which, however, you should not put to him until the arrival of the manuscript. The first section, *'Capital in General'*, is likely to run to *2 instalments* since I have discovered while elaborating it that here, at the very juncture where the most abstract aspect of political economy is to be discussed, undue brevity would render the thing indigestible to the public. But on the other hand this second instalment must come

[a] refugees' - [b] K. Marx, *A Contribution to the Critique of Political Economy*. - [c] about everything under the sun and more

out *at the same time* as the first. This is demanded by their intrinsic coherence, and the whole effect depends upon it.

Apropos. In your letter from Frankfurt you said nothing about your economic work.[278] As far as our rivalry is concerned, I don't believe that the German public suffers from an *embarras de richesses* in this field. In fact economics as a science in the German sense of the word has yet to be tackled and to that end not just the two of us but a dozen will be needed. I hope, at any rate, that my work will result in drawing a number of better brains into the same field of research.

I should be infinitely obliged to you if you could write to me from time to time about conditions in Prussia and send me the relevant newspaper clippings.

My wife sends her regards and says she is afraid Köster is as mistaken about 'her beauty' as he is about her husband's health.

Freiligrath likewise sends his regards. He is completely immersed in his profession of banker. Hence you should not hold his silence against him.

Salut.

Your

K. M.

First published in: *F. Lassalle. Nachgelassene Briefe und Schriften,* Bd. III, Stuttgart-Berlin, 1922

Printed according to the original

Published in English for the first time

191

MARX TO ENGELS

IN MANCHESTER

[London,] 24 November 1858

Dear Frederick,

Yesterday I wrote about Prussia.[a] So for Friday you have all the rest of the world at your disposal.

Have received the £1. The 'particular' pickle in which I find myself at the moment arises from the fact that I was compelled to pay out all at once more than £8 to the newspaper man, who had

---

[a] 'Affairs in Prussia'

been giving me credit for over a year. I'm stone broke, which in this weather is not COMFORTABLE. In Trier, my sister[a] would now seem to have frustrated my mother's perfectly rational INTENTIONS, or at least to have postponed THEIR REALISATION *sine die.*

Blind was here the day before yesterday with wife.[b] It was over a year since I had seen this FAMILY. From them I learnt sundry pieces of gossip.

1. Mrs Kinkel threw herself out of the window a week ago last Monday and has since been buried. Gottfried,[c] with a sublimity all his own, attended the post-mortem and delivered an 'oration' at the graveside. Freiligrath is so moved that he'll shun me, as a 'frivolous' man, for a fortnight at least.

2. Fröbel is over here. Has married a rich wife. Is returning to America. According to him Russia and America must share the world between them, a point of view that makes him feel very superior. He enthuses over American 'luxury' and GENTLEMAN-LIKENESS, despises the Germans and gives practical proof of this by engaging in the German slave trade to Central America. It's really too comical that, because deeply impressed by bourgeois society in its American reality, this son of Rudolstadt should believe himself more 'advanced' than the 'REST OF EUROPE'. Once they HAVE FOUND THEIR BREAD AND CHEESE, all these scoundrels require is some blasé pretext to bid farewell to the struggle.

3. Asinine Ruge, in a piece for Prutz, has proved that 'Shakespeare was not a dramatic poet' because he 'had no philosophical system', whereas Schiller, being a Kantian, is a TRULY 'dramatic poet'.[d] Prutz then wrote a 'vindication of Shakespeare'.[e] In addition, Ruge described Moleschott in the American papers as 'a silly ass', whereupon Heinzen sacked him from the *Pionier.* However, the old bounder is now finding a place for his inanities in Börnstein's *Anzeiger des Westens.*

4. The foolish Ewerbeck returned to Paris two years ago, corresponds regularly with Blind. Had let himself be inveigled by Ribbentrop into marrying Ribbentrop's maid, only to discover that the former was tumbling the latter, after which came divorce, lawsuit, etc. He was assistant in a Paris library, and was sacked by the priests. Writes to say he only has 1,200 frs left, threatens to come to England having read in the *Univers,* etc., that 'socialism and atheism' are flourishing in the latter country.

---

[a] Emilie Marx - [b] Friederike Blind - [c] Gottfried Kinkel - [d] A. Ruge, 'Idealismus und Realismus im Reich des Ideals', *Deutsches Museum,* Nos. 14, 15, 19, 1 and 8 April, 6 May 1858. - [e] R. E. Prutz, 'Literaturgeschichte', *Deutsches Museum,* No. 24, 10 June 1858.

5. Dr Freund is said to be so down on his luck that he has allegedly approached people in the street for a shilling.

6. Loutish Landolphe has reappeared in England as a beggar and through Blind's intervention, has been engaged by Dr Bronner at a German school in Bradford.

Salut.

Your

K. M.

First published abridged in *Der Briefwechsel zwischen F. Engels und K. Marx*, Bd. 2, Stuttgart, 1913 and in full in: Marx and Engels, *Works*, First Russian Edition, Vol. XXII, Moscow, 1929

Printed according to the original

Published in English for the first time

192

MARX TO ENGELS

IN MANCHESTER

[London,] 29 November 1858

Dear Frederick,

Article received.[a] Very good. *Quoad*[b] Bonaparte, I have lately dealt with two separate points—the sham provocation of England in the Portuguese affair[342] and how the fellow is generally avenging Waterloo[217] only in so far as he can do so by sham demonstrations within the 'limits of the English alliance' and hence, in fact, with the permission of the English government, although he is, in reality, England's underling. Secondly, his edict *re* the corn-granaries,[c] by which this 'socialist' proposes to remedy the ruinously low prices of corn—dangerously low, in view of the grumbles of the peasantry—by creating an artificial demand at the bakers' expense.[d] Generally, a very dangerous experiment this, to raise the price of corn through government ukases. Increasing the cost of bread will do more harm to his popularity in the towns than it can do good in the country.

[a] F. Engels, 'Europe in 1858'. - [b] As regards - [c] Napoleon III's decree on grain reserves of 16 November 1858, *Le Moniteur universel*, No. 322, 18 November 1858. - [d] K. Marx, 'Project for the Regulation of the Price of Bread in France'.

I have not written about the GENERAL RISING of the bourgeoisie in Europe but did, of course, allude to it in what I wrote about Prussia. I have dealt with the Russian peasant movement ABOUT twice in 6 months,[a] the second time simply to show that on the first occasion my diagnosis was correct.

As regards the reform movement in England, all I have discussed latterly is Bright's meeting in Birmingham,[b] the gist of the article being THAT HIS PROGRAMME IS A REDUCTION OF THE PEOPLE'S CHARTER TO THE MIDDLE CLASS STANDARD.[344] Earlier on, ABOUT 8-12 WEEKS ago (I think Parliament was actually still sitting), a piece to the effect that WHIGGISM MUST DISSOLVE AND COALESCE WITH TORYISM INTO THE PARTY OF *THE* ARISTOCRACY.[c] That is all.

My wife is copying the manuscript[d] and it's hardly likely to go off before the end of this month. The reasons for the delay: long intervals of physical indisposition which, with the cold weather, has now come to an end. Too much domestic and financial TROUBLE. Finally, the first section is now longer because the two initial chapters, of which the *first, The Commodity,* did not appear at all in the rough draft while the *second, Money, or Simple Circulation,* was only sketched in the briefest outline, have been written at greater length than I originally planned.

Salut.

Your

K. M.

Mr Edgar Bauer is now the real, and Mr Lout and Weitlingian Scherzer the nominal, editor of the London *Neue Zeit.* Mr Edgar, of course, has a great deal to say on the subject of Mr Edgar and his lectures to the working men,[e] for he himself writes about everything concerning Mr Edgar. This CLOWN deems it necessary to take a revolutionary TURN. He presided at the Robert Blum ceremony. In an essay in the last issue the CLOWN makes the discovery that 'imperialism' has now been introduced into Prussia

[a] K. Marx, 'Political Parties in England.—The Situation in Europe', 'The Question of the Abolition of Serfdom in Russia'. - [b] A reference to J. Bright's speech at a meeting of Birmingham constituents on 27 October 1858 (the meeting was reported in *The Times,* No. 23136, 28 October 1858). - [c] Marx expressed this idea in his article 'Political Parties in England.—The Situation in Europe'. - [d] K. Marx, *A Contribution to the Critique of Political Economy.* - [e] E. Bauer, 'Vorträge über die Geschichte der Politik...', *Die Neue Zeit,* No. 20, 6 November 1858.

in constitutional form.[a] This same issue is not uninteresting by reason of an article from Struve's *Sociale Republik*[b] which was, however, written over here by a certain Feibel and in which Freiligrath; on the occasion of the publication of his poems in America, had himself extolled AS THE TRUE HERO OF THE PROLETARIAN PARTY.

First published abridged in *Der Briefwechsel zwischen F. Engels und K. Marx*, Bd. 2, Stuttgart, 1913 and in full in: Marx and Engels, *Works*, First Russian Edition, Vol. XXII, Moscow, 1929

Printed according to the original

Published in English for the first time

193

MARX TO ENGELS[20]

IN MANCHESTER

[London,] 11 December 1858

Dear Engels,

Can you let me have an account of Bright's MEETING by Tuesday, so worded as to make it clear THAT THE WRITER WAS AT MANCHESTER?

Herewith Kinkeliana.[345] Freiligrath seems to think that, because the Kinkel woman has broken her neck, her husband has become a great man, or at very least a noble one. So melodramatically did Kinkel organise the funeral—with 'trembling hand' and 'laurel wreath', etc.—that Freiligrath, who could not wring from his lyre a single note of sorrow for the 'tragic' events, either in his own party (as at Daniels' death) or in the world GENERALLY (Cayenne,[346] Orsini AND SO FORTH), suddenly goes and hymns the wretched humbug. From *The Daily Telegraph* cutting you will see how the coterie is exploiting the death of the NASTY, 'acrimonious shrew' (for such was the affected, speciously clever, essentially coarse personage whose meanness was GLARINGLY displayed in, e.g., her ingratitude to Strodtmann and to Mrs von Brüningk once she had squeezed the latter dry, etc.) in just the same way as the creature herself exploited 'KINKEL'S HAT, SHOT THROUGH AND THROUGH', and wrote to Germany from London: *'Have you an idea what it is to be looked upon as a sort of mother to all emigrants?'* That was what

---

[a] E. Bauer, 'Preußens constitutioneller Imperialismus', *Die Neue Zeit*, No. 22, 27 November 1858. - [b] [G. Struve,] 'Bildung macht frei!', *Die Neue Zeit*, No. 22, 27 November 1858.

the creature wrote at a time when she and Gottfried, AS A SORT OF BEGGAR, were knocking at the doors of all the Jews in the City.

And there's something else I don't like in the palliative letter Freiligrath wrote me. I am expected to regard his opposition to the general craze for amnesty, i.e., IN FACT, to Rudolf Schramm's idiosyncrasy, as something revolutionary. But a few weeks ago our Freiligrath got himself *naturalised* English and would be a fool indeed were he to yearn nostalgically for the post of a badly paid clerk in Germany so long as those nice Crédits mobiliers[45] LAST. Very vividly do I remember Mrs Freiligrath—at a time when people were already drivelling about amnesty but the GENERAL BANK OF SWITZERLAND had as yet no place in the ROYAL EXCHANGE BUILDINGS—most earnestly seeking to persuade me not to raise any objection to the acceptance of amnesty.

All these people sense THAT THERE IS SOMETHING MOVING AGAIN. And, of course, are pushing their way onto the stage bearing banners of liberty.

Keep the enclosed poem and letter.

In this house things look MORE DREARY AND DESOLATE THAN EVER. Since my wife cannot even arrange Christmas festivities for the children—instead, she is beset on all sides by dunning letters, on top of which she is having to copy my manuscript[a] and, in between whiles, to run errands to the pawnshop in town—the atmosphere is gloomy in the extreme. Moreover, my wife is quite right when she says that, after all the *misère* she has had to go through, the revolution will only make things worse and afford her the gratification of seeing all the humbugs from here once again celebrating their victories over there. Women are like that. And the womanish behaviour of Freiligrath, etc., and other acquaintances justly embitters her. *À la guerre comme à la guerre,*[b] she says. But THERE IS NO *guerre.* It's day-to-day routine.

Salut.

Your

K. M.

First published abridged in *Der Briefwechsel zwischen F. Engels und K. Marx,* Bd. 2, Stuttgart, 1913 and in full in: Marx and Engels, *Works,* First Russian Edition, Vol. XXII, Moscow, 1929

Printed according to the original

Published in English in full for the first time

[a] *A Contribution to the Critique of Political Economy* - [b] One must take the rough with the smooth (literally: that's how it is in wartime).

194

MARX TO ENGELS

IN MANCHESTER

London, 16 December 1858

Dear Engels,

My best thanks. How welcome the money was you will see from the enclosed letter, which arrived at the same time. It is my belief that Schapper and I and 100 others know better what it is to 'fight' in London than do the 'scattered remnants' beside the old harridan's[a] grave. The Heckscher story calls for further investigation. Nice of Freiligrath to give the signal for a Kinkel revival in Germany. For Lupus' amusement I enclose some of my Berlin gossip articles[b] which I have cut out of the *Tribune*; also your article on Montalembert, which Dana included under 'Paris', so that in *that* particular issue of the *Tribune* we represent the whole of Europe at once.[c]

Salut.

Your

K. M.

News will soon reach Lupus that the manuscript[d] has gone off, but I'll be blowed if anyone else in similar circumstances and with as rotten a liver could have got it done as soon.

First published abridged in *Der Briefwechsel zwischen F. Engels und K. Marx*, Bd. 2, Stuttgart, 1913 and in full in: Marx and Engels, *Works*, First Russian Edition, Vol. XXII, Moscow, 1929

Printed according to the original

Published in English for the first time

---

[a] Johanna Kinkel - [b] See this volume, p. 352. - [c] A reference to Engels' article 'The Prosecution of Montalembert' and Marx's 'The New Ministry'. - [d] K. Marx, *A Contribution to the Critique of Political Economy.*

195

MARX TO ENGELS

IN MANCHESTER

[London,] 17 December [1858]

Dear Frederick,

£2 received with THANKS.

I knew about Blind's confection (just the kind of thing, as he told me himself, that Hecker used to do), although I wasn't, of course, aware of some of the nicer details. *D'abord*,[a] this *Telegraph Morning Express* is edited by several English Seilers, and all its telegraphic despatches, or at any rate the better part of them, are *reprinted* from London morning papers. I can vouch for the FACT that Blind smuggled a bogus '*TELEGR. DESPATCH*' (dated Brussels) into *The Morning Advertiser*. This was, OF COURSE, instantly appropriated by the *Telegraph Morning Express*. Secondly, Dr Bronner is not merely *an* but *the* agent of Blind, [he] having 'no other' to send. I also believe it was he himself who 'decreed' that [the missive] be sent to Lupus, since Bronner never does anything [without] official sanction. In today's *Daily Telegraph* also, you will find in the letter from Berlin: *'Similar petitions have been presented to the (Holstein) Diet by the German merchants resident at Bradford and Liverpool.'* The industry of these little Baden fleas hatched in the democratic midden is touching. Even the Ancients indulged in sundry edifying reflections on the subject of flea jumps.

I've had a satisfying experience with the *Tribune*. For months that rotten sheet had published as LEADERS all my articles on China (a complete history of Anglo-Chinese trade,[b] etc.) and had even been complimented on them. But when the *official* text of the Anglo-Chinese treaty[332] was finally released, I wrote an article in which I said *inter alia* that the Chinese 'would now legalise the import of opium, likewise put an IMPORT DUTY on opium and, LASTLY, might even permit the cultivation of opium actually in China', and thus the 'SECOND OPIUM WAR' would SOONER OR LATER deal a DEADLY BLOW to the English OPIUM TRADE, and notably to the INDIAN EXCHEQUER.[c] WELL! Mr Dana printed this article as being from an 'OCCASIONAL CORRESPONDENT' in London, and himself wrote a bombastic LEADER

---

[a] First - [b] K. Marx. 'History of the Opium Trade' (two articles). - [c] K. Marx, 'The British and Chinese Treaty'.

refuting his OCCASIONAL CORRESPONDENT.[a] Now, [the day before yesterday][b] (on *Monday,* RATHER), my predictions were confirmed *word for word* in the HOUSE OF COMMONS by Fitzgerald and Stanley in the name of the Ministry.[347] So on Tuesday, qua OCCASIONAL CORRESPONDENT I wrote a SOMEWHAT mocking though, of course, restrained piece about my 'castigator'.[348]

Apropos. My brother-in-law,[c] a tall and tedious if worthy Dutchman, is coming up to Manchester on business. And notably to ascertain the solvency of certain individuals. Send me *your private address,* as he wishes to contact you. But avoid any allusion to my PRIVATE AFFAIRS.

Salut.

Your

K. M.

Little by little philistine Freiligrath is coughing up sundry things about Gottfried.[d] 1. that Gottfried is sending Gerstenberg to see various MERCHANTS in the City, suggesting they subscribe to the *Hermann.* After all, says he, the poor man has got to 'live' and make up for the *'loss'* incurred through the death of his wife. 2. He tells me that Gottfried, immediately after the Mockel woman's death, approached him and asked whether (and how big) *a deal* might be done with Cotta over her literary estate. 'After all', says Gottfried, 'I enjoy *the favour* of the public.'

It could be that Blind himself is again hoodwinking *The Morning Advertiser* and getting friend *Schütz* to send bogus telegraphic despatches from Brussels.

Cluss has married someone he met at Dr Wiss's in Baltimore.

Apropos, on the strength of Blind's recommendation, Bronner has found Landolphe the *grec*[e] a schoolmaster's post in Bradford.

Mr *Liebknecht* has introduced Edgar Bauer into the Workers' Society.[50] I WATCH HIM.

First published abridged in *Der Briefwechsel zwischen F. Engels und K. Marx,* Bd. 2, Stuttgart, 1913 and in full in: Marx and Engels, *Works,* First Russian Edition, Vol. XXII, Moscow, 1929

Printed according to the original

Published in English for the first time

[a] 'Our London correspondent suggests...', *New-York Daily Tribune,* No. 5455, 15 October 1858 - [b] 'the day before yesterday' is deleted. - [c] Johann Carl Juta - [d] Kinkel - [e] swindler

196

MARX TO ENGELS

IN MANCHESTER

[London,] 22 December 1858

Dear Engels,

Yesterday I wrote about Buchanan's MESSAGE[349]—REVIEWED the English PAPERS' criticism thereof.[a] I should be very glad if you could let me have an article by Friday on, say, Campbell's latest campaign, or ANYTHING ELSE. Since the manuscript[b] must go off to Duncker before the end of this year there is, quite literally, no time to lose.

Salut.

Your
K. M.

First published in: Marx and Engels, *Works*, First Russian Edition, Vol. XXII, Moscow, 1929

Printed according to the original

Published in English for the first time

197

MARX TO ENGELS

IN MANCHESTER

London, 28 December 1858

A Happy New Year!
Ditto to Lupus.
HOW WITH SERVIA?[350]
Salut.

K. Marx

First published in: Marx and Engels, *Works*, First Russian Edition, Vol. XXII, Moscow, 1929

Printed according to the original

Published in English for the first time

---

[a] J. Buchanan, 'The President's Message to the XXXVth Congress', *The Times*, No. 23181, 20 December 1858. The paper reviewed the 'Message' in the same issue, in a leader beginning with the words, 'There is nothing in the Message of President Buchanan...'. - [b] K. Marx, *A Contribution to the Critique of Political Economy*.

198

MARX TO ENGELS

IN MANCHESTER

[London,] 30 December 1858

Dear Frederick,

Of Colonel Hodges it has been observed—and this puts the seal on Pam's participation in the Serbian affair—that he was a sort of Palmerstonian Bangya.

I shall for a time again be writing articles on economics for the *Tribune* and also on Prussia,[a] so all the rest of the world is at your disposal. In addition, yesterday I wrote about Ireland and the conspiracies there and the government's dodge.[b] Whenever I deal with a theme other than the two mentioned above I shall always advise you.

Will you be so good as to send me Lupus' private address.

Salut, and for the 2nd time, this time seasonably, a Happy New Year.

Your

K. M.

First published abridged in *Der Briefwechsel zwischen F. Engels und K. Marx*, Bd. 2, Stuttgart, 1913 and in full in: Marx and Engels, *Works*, First Russian Edition, Vol. XXII, Moscow, 1929

Printed according to the manuscript

Published in English for the first time

[a] This probably refers to Marx's articles 'Project for the Regulation of the Price of Bread in France' and 'Affairs in Prussia' (three instalments). - [b] 'The Excitement in Ireland'

1859

199

MARX TO ENGELS

IN MANCHESTER

[London,] 6 January 1859[a]

Dear Engels,

Will you be so good as to send me Lupus' address.

If you have done with Serbia,[350] there is fresh material READY to hand in the (proposed) changes in the *Landwehr* in Prussia, on which I shall have to report.[351] Today's *Times* contains a detailed account dated Vienna of the latest *brouhaha* in Serbia.[b]

While Mr Edgar Bauer is editor[c] under THE AUSPICES of Scherzer and is even adopting 'class contradictions' and giving them a Berlin twist, Mr Gottfried Kinkel, who can't afford to let slip the opportunity presented by the Kinkel REVIVAL, is bringing out a weekly in London, to wit, the *Hermann* (not the Cheruscan, I presume, but Goethe's SIMPLETON).[352] Freiligrath, or so it *seems* from a brief note he sent me, is already REPENTANT of the BLUNDER[d] he committed. If you write, tell him (but *most politely*, OF COURSE, for he complains about the *crude, brash tone of your letters*) that in Manchester there is much talk among the Germans about *his* alliance with Kinkel; you might also slip in Heckscher's anecdote, quoting your source. At *this* particular time it is *of moment to us* that Freiligrath should break with these swine for good.

Apropos, Willich is now editing the gymnasts' paper in Cincinnati.[e] Was 'selected' as editor there. He accepted the appointment (doubtless obtained for him by Cluss so as to rid himself of the man) in a superb circular letter in which he says

---

[a] 1858 in the original - [b] 'The Revolution in Servia', *The Times*, No. 23196, 6 January 1859. - [c] of *Die Neue Zeit* - [d] See this volume, pp. 359-60. - [e] *Die Turn-Zeitung*

that the time has come for him to take charge of propaganda since the people are not in need of military leaders just now.

Salut.

Your
K. M.

First published abridged in *Der Briefwechsel zwischen F. Engels und K. Marx*, Bd. 2, Stuttgart, 1913 and in full in: Marx and Engels, *Works*, First Russian Edition, Vol. XXII, Moscow, 1929

Printed according to the original

Published in English for the first time

200

MARX TO ENGELS

IN MANCHESTER

[London,] 8 January 1859

Dear Frederick,

Herewith letter from Freiligrath. (I had written him something about the Kinkel affair.) Prospectus for the *Hermann*.[353] Mr Willich's letter.

Salut.

Your
K. M.

First published in *Der Briefwechsel zwischen F. Engels und K. Marx*, Bd. 2, Stuttgart, 1913

Printed according to the original

Published in English for the first time

201

MARX TO ENGELS

IN MANCHESTER

[London, between 13 and 15 January 1859][354]

Dear Engels,

If possible, let me have an article by Tuesday (I would then do *next Friday's*[a]); this is *crucial,* as I'd like to be able to send Duncker

[a] On Tuesdays and Fridays Marx sent articles to New York.

my manuscript[a] by Wednesday, which would be impossible unless I have Tuesday free.

The manuscript amounts to ABOUT 12 sheets of print (3 instalments) and—don't be bowled over by this—although entitled *Capital in General*, these instalments contain ***nothing*** as yet on the subject of capital, but only the two chapters: **1.** *The Commodity*, **2.** *Money or Simple Circulation*. As you can see, the part that was worked out in detail (in May, when I was staying with you[318]) is not to appear at all yet.[355] This is good on two counts. If the thing is a success, the third chapter on capital can follow very soon. Secondly, since the matter in the published part will, by its very nature, prevent the curs from confining their criticism solely to tendentious vituperation, and since the whole thing has an EXCEEDINGLY serious and scientific air, the canaille will later on be compelled to take my views on capital RATHER SERIOUSLY. Besides, I believe that, all practical considerations apart, the chapter on money will be of interest to experts.

I have had to alter your article on Bonaparte-Italy[b] somewhat, having myself written about the *same* subject on Tuesday.[c] Among the AGENCIES which are egging Bonaparte on you forget *Russia*. Pam did not visit Paris for nothing, nor were the Russian MOVES IN ITALY without significance, nor yet Russia's coquetry with Bonaparte since the Peace of Paris.[356] If Russia does no more than compel the Austrians, through Bonaparte, to sack their minister Buol and replace him with a Pan-Slav Russian agent, she will have achieved a great deal.

As Berlin correspondent I have promised an article on the *Prussian army* which you might do ONE OF THESE DAYS.[351]

In the American press Ruge is emerging as the fanatical champion of the Prince of Prussia. Schramm[d] has been given permission to return to Prussia (the warrant against him having been withdrawn) and to appear before a new jury without undergoing preventive detention.

Your

K. M.

First published abridged in *Der Briefwechsel zwischen F. Engels und K. Marx*, Bd. 2, Stuttgart, 1913 and in full in: Marx and Engels, *Works*, First Russian Edition, Vol. XXII, Moscow, 1929

Printed according to the original

Published in English for the first time

[a] *A Contribution to the Critique of Political Economy* - [b] K. Marx and F. Engels, 'The Money Panic in Europe'. - [c] K. Marx, 'The War Prospect in Europe'. - [d] Rudolf Schramm

202

MARX TO ENGELS[82]

IN MANCHESTER

[London,] 21 January [1859]

Dear Engels,

The ill-fated manuscript[a] is ready but can't be sent off as I haven't a FARTHING for postage or insurance. This last is essential since I have no copy of it. Hence I must ask you to let me have a little money by Monday (POST OFFICE IN TOTTENHAM COURT ROAD CORNER). If you could send £2 it would be most welcome as I have put off paying various small tradesmen until Monday, after which any further postponements will be absolutely out of the question. As you can imagine, it is far from pleasant for me to burden you again just now when you have paid, or have got to pay, Freiligrath's bill. BUT IRON NECESSITY. Next week—as I am giving myself a week's holiday *quoad*[b] the *next part* of the manuscript—I shall see if I can't manage to pull off some financial coup or other. I don't suppose anyone has ever written about 'money' when so short of the stuff. Most *autores* on this SUBJECT have been on terms of the utmost amity with THE SUBJECT OF THEIR RESEARCHES.

Should the thing prove a success in Berlin, there's a chance that I might get out of all this mess. It's HIGH TIME I did.

Salut.

Your

K. M.

If the thing proves a success in Berlin, it might be possible to strike a bargain with a London publisher in respect of an *English* translation, and there's no comparison between what one is paid over here and in Berlin. Besides, such an EVENT would dreadfully annoy our worthy enemies. The canaille believed that we were both of us done for—the more so just now when Mr Clown 'Edgar Bauer' has 'supplanted' us 'in the eyes of working-men', as Gottfried Kinkel is telling all and sundry in the City. With every word they publish, the canaille are making out their own death warrants and well may they wonder what 'SORT OF LIFE' we have preserved.

---

[a] K. Marx, *A Contribution to the Critique of Political Economy*. - [b] as regards

I'm uncertain whether I should mark the thing 'THE AUTHOR RESERVES TO HIMSELF THE RIGHT OF TRANSLATION'. (As you know, there's a copyright agreement between Prussia and England.) My aversion to all humbug and semblance of vanity or pretentiousness says 'No'. On the other hand my own interests say 'Yes'. The more so since some scrawl about monetary matters is published almost weekly in England. WHAT DO YOU THINK, SIR? This point requires an immediate answer since I myself must decide by Monday.

First published in *Der Briefwechsel zwischen F. Engels und K. Marx*, Bd. 2, Stuttgart, 1913

Printed according to the original

203

ENGELS TO FERDINAND FREILIGRATH[357]

IN LONDON

[Draft]

Manchester, 25 January 1859

Dear Freiligrath,

The bloody boy who was to have got the POST OFFICE ORDER yesterday idled away the time instead, which is why the 22/- will only arrive today. Many thanks for your trouble and for the outlay.

As to the *Neueste Rheinische Zeitung*,[358] due provision has been made, never fear. We have in the meanwhile learnt a great deal and forgotten nothing,[359] and that's more than the others can say. Of this you could find no better illustration than the *Hermann* (clearly a misprint for *Gottfried*, otherwise the title's meaningless[a]), which you recently described as the *Rheinische Zeitung*'s John the Baptist. It's a long time since I've read rubbish as insipid, namby-pamby, tail-wagging, lavish of compliments, conciliatory, propitiatory and atrociously written as is found in this, the latest product of the pseudo-noble sometime *Maikäfer*[360] which, to judge by its style and content, is aimed solely at and tailored to the tastes of the Camberwell philistines and the German ditto in the City. The man has even forgotten what little he managed to pick up in 1848 and has become a real bourgeois windbag. Now, since it was you who brought up the topic of this cheery customer,

[a] An allusion to Gottfried Kinkel's weekly *Hermann*.

presently touting round his 'grief', I will not conceal from you the fact that I have recently been asked by various philistines how it is that you have formed such a bond of friendship with Monsieur Kinkel. Though an exaggeration, this placed me, as you can imagine, in something of a quandary. Needless to say, I attributed it largely to the malicious exaggeration with which Kinkel and clique had seized on what was a mere encounter with you and blazoned it in all the papers as an offensive and defensive alliance—directed against us—and this I roundly denied. As for your social intercourse with the worthy citizen, all I could do was crack bad jokes, such as that, since poets live in a world apart, Kinkel could only pass himself off as a poet by citing his intercourse with you, etc. Suffice it to say that, although a poor diplomat, I succeeded well enough in defending the party's position. Moreover, it eventually transpired that one of the Jewish females who patronised the gentle Gottfried when he was last up here, had said: 'Ah, just let Kinkel, the naughty man, visit Manchester again—he seduced a girl of good family in London and keeps her as his mistress, and that's the reason why his wife....'[a]

First published in: Marx and Engels, *Works*, First Russian Edition, Vol. XXV, Moscow, 1934

Printed according to the original

Published in English for the first time

204

MARX TO ENGELS[361]

IN MANCHESTER

[London, 26 January 1859]

Dear Frederick,

The £2 safely received; the manuscript[b] gone off; wrote ECONOMICAL REVIEW for the *Tribune* yesterday.

More tomorrow, and SOMETHING VERY AMUSING TOO.

Your

K. M.

First published in *Der Briefwechsel zwischen F. Engels und K. Marx*, Bd. 2, Stuttgart, 1913

Printed according to the original

Published in English for the first time

---

[a] The manuscript breaks off here. - [b] K. Marx, *A Contribution to the Critique of Political Economy.*

205

ENGELS TO MARX

IN LONDON

[Manchester,] 27 January 1859

Dear Moor,

I look forward keenly to your communication. Meanwhile herewith some bits of Paris gossip.

Yesterday I wrote to Freiligrath about Kinkel, the pretext being provided by the good fellow himself. I had written to him about the matter of the bill, adding a few comments on the political and economic aspects of the international situation, and this inspired him to declare: 'The *Hermann* will undoubtedly be followed one day by a *Neueste Rheinische Zeitung*.'[358] What led him to mention Kinkel's rag I cannot imagine, unless he hoped to induce me to speak my mind on the subject of Johann Gottfried,[a] in which case he was not disappointed. I must say that his attempt to establish some sort of connection between ourselves and that rotten little paper annoyed me very much. The day before yesterday I tried twice to write him a letter,[b] but it was too crude, I was too angry, so I left the thing over until yesterday. I treated *him* very decently, but Monsieur Gottfried with considerable asperity. I told him that Kinkel was exploiting him in order to establish his credentials as a poet, since his own literary fame, spuriously acquired as a result of his wife's importunate advertising, would not otherwise endure; that the *Hermann* had only served to increase the contempt I had always felt for this vacuous, affected, dandyish jackanapes, and that I'd not forgiven the 'cur' the dirty tricks which he had played on you and me in America and was too cowardly to admit.[362] It was a three page letter; as I said, Freiligrath can have no complaint about the way I treated *him* but, indirectly and by reading between the lines, he will learn a great deal. I'm curious to see what he will do.

I have had another visitor in the person of a Wuppertal poet and distant relation[c] of mine; in London he made straight for Freiligrath, of course, who wrote saying that he seemed to be a nice chap. I replied that he was at any rate robust, healthy and neither vain nor affected—qualities which, modern German poets

---

[a] Gottfried Kinkel. Engels ironically calls him Johann after his wife, Johanna Kinkel. - [b] See this volume, pp. 370-71. - [c] Carl Siebel

being what they are, made up for a comparative lack of talent. Freiligrath told this chap that his salary was a thousand pounds.

I was terribly annoyed at Freiligrath's surreptitious introduction of the *Hermann* into his letter, but he'll never play another trick of that kind on me, you may be sure of that.

Many regards to your wife and children.

Your

F. E.

Just for a joke I enclose one of the rejected drafts of my letter to Freiligrath.

First published in *Der Briefwechsel zwischen F. Engels und K. Marx*, Bd. 2, Stuttgart, 1913

Printed according to the original

Published in English for the first time

206

MARX TO ENGELS

IN MANCHESTER

[London,] 28 January 1859

Dear Engels,

All manner of TROUBLES prevented me from writing to you yesterday. Today is article day.[a] Till tomorrow, then. But I enclose the 'joke'.

I am writing today about Clotilde mild, angelic child.[363] I expect an article from you on Tuesday. Couldn't you write about the cotton trade, industrial prospects, etc., in Manchester? I deliberately left this field open in my economic article on Tuesday.[361]

Salut.

Your

K. M.

Freiligrath showed me your letter. It's *splendidly* written.

First published in *Der Briefwechsel zwischen F. Engels und K. Marx*, Bd. 2, Stuttgart, 1913

Printed according to the original

Published in English for the first time

[a] 28 January was a Friday. On Tuesdays and Fridays Marx sent articles to New York.

207

MARX TO JOSEPH WEYDEMEYER[1]

IN MILWAUKEE

London, 1 February 1859
9 Grafton Terrace, Maitland Park,
Haverstock Hill

Dear Weiwi,

Your letter is dated 28 February 1858, arrived here (or at any rate reached me) at the end of May and is being answered in February 1859.[321] This is easily explained: During the whole of the spring and summer I suffered from liver trouble and it was only with difficulty that I found time for essential work. Hence such writing as was not absolutely necessary was OUT OF THE QUESTION. Later in the year, however, I was overwhelmed with work.

Well, to start with, I must convey cordial regards to you and yours from all members of the family, likewise from Engels, Lupus and Freiligrath. In particular I would wish to be most kindly remembered to your dear wife.

Engels is still in Manchester, also Lupus, who is giving lessons and doing moderately well; Freiligrath is MANAGER of a branch of the Swiss Crédit mobilier[364] in London; Dronke is a commission agent in Glasgow; Imandt (I'm not sure if you know him) is a teacher in Dundee; our dear friend Weerth died in Haiti,[365] alas,—an *irreplaceable* loss.

Things have gone badly rather than well for me during the past 2 years; for on the one side the good old *Tribune* made the crisis a pretext for halving my income although in times of prosperity they never gave me an extra penny; on the other, the time demanded by my work on political economy (of which more anon) compelled me (if with a heavy heart) to turn down very remunerative offers made me in London and Vienna. But I have got to pursue my object through thick and thin and not allow bourgeois society to turn me into a MONEY-MAKING MACHINE.

Mr Cluss was over here last May. I happened to be staying with Engels in Manchester at the time. Cluss called on my wife and accepted an invitation for the following day; and who failed to put in an appearance? Why, Cluss! He [dis]appeared from London and never showed his face again. Instead he sent my wife a scrawl to which 'embarrassment' had given an uncouth *tournure.*[a] He didn't turn up in Manchester either. Subsequently we learned that he had allied himself with Mr Willich. This, then, also explains the mysterious discontinuation of his correspondence. If we were conceited we would feel duly chastened by the news that a fool like Willich had been able to oust us from the good graces of a shrewd chap like Cluss. But as it was, the whole story was so funny that it eliminated any bitter feelings.

I have broken with Ernest Jones.[245] Despite my repeated warnings, and although I had predicted exactly what would happen—namely that he would ruin himself and disorganise the Chartist Party—he took the course of trying to come to terms with the BOURGEOIS RADICALS. HE IS NOW A RUINED MAN, but the harm he has done to the English proletariat is incalculable. The fault will, of course, be rectified, but a most favourable moment for action has been missed. Imagine an army whose general goes over to the enemy camp on the eve of battle.

You'll have heard that Mr Kinkel has become a famous man again because Mrs Kinkel fell out of a window and broke her neck. The 'cheery' customer—never has he felt so jolly as since the death of the old Mockel woman—promptly decided to tout round his 'grief'. Freiligrath allowed himself to be misled by Gottfried's melodramatic scenes into writing a poem about Johanna[b] which he already regrets. For he has come to realise, firstly, that Gottfried is merry as a grig, and secondly that he immediately used the poem to disseminate to all and sundry the lie that Freiligrath had entered into an alliance with him and broken with us. A week later, in an attempt to exploit the Kinkel REVIVAL sparked off by his wife's death, Gottfried published in London a weekly dubbed the *Hermann*; unless this is the *Hermann* sung by Schönaich[c] and crowned by Gottsched,[366] the title ought to be *Gottfried.* In the first place the rag preaches peace with God and the world,[d] and secondly it is nothing more than a puff for Mr Gottfried vis-à-vis German Philistia in the City of London. Nothing more pitiful has ever seen the light of day, and we can thank our stars that the 10 years of exile have so completely laid bare the hollowness of our democratic friends. The *Kölnische Zeitung* is witty and daring by comparison.

---

[a] twist - [b] F. Freiligrath, 'Nach Johanna Kinkels Begräbnis', 20 November 1858. - [c] Ch. O. von Schönaich, *Hermann, oder das befreyte Deutschland...* - [d] A pun: Gottfried (Kinkel's surname)=Gott (God)+Friede (peace)

What is really choice about Kinkel's exploitation of his wife's death is that the latter creature, who was suffering from heart disease, was outraged because our suave parson had seduced a Jewess by the name of Herz, and generally treated her 'coldly'. In Manchester the Jewish women swear that this is the reason why Johanna Mockel of blessed memory fell out of the window. Anyhow, this would show that, inane though Gottfried may be in other respects, he is cunning enough to exploit public CREDULITY. But that's enough about this humbug.

The wind of revolution which is blowing across the Continent of Europe has, of course, awakened all the great men[367] from their winter sleep.

At the same time as this letter, I am sending one—indeed, my first—to Komp. I have given up associations—*organised* ones. They were, I thought, compromising for our friends in Germany. *Over here*, on the other hand, after the dirty tricks I have suffered at the hands of the louts who have allowed themselves to be used as mere tools against myself by a Kinkel, a Willich or some other such humbug, and since the Cologne trial,[71] I have withdrawn completely into my study. My time was too precious to be wasted in fruitless endeavour and petty squabbles.

And now for essentials. My *Critique of Political Economy* is to be published in instalments (the first ones in a week or ten days' time[a]) by Franz Duncker of Berlin (Bessersche Verlagsbuchhandlung). It was only thanks to Lassalle's extraordinary zeal and powers of persuasion that Duncker was induced to take this step. He has, however, left himself a loophole. *A firm contract depends on the sale of the first instalments.*

I divide the whole of political economy into 6 books.

Capital; landed property; wage labour; the State; foreign trade; world market.

Book I, on capital, comprises 4 sections.

Section I: *Capital in general* comprises 3 chapters, 1. *The Commodity*; 2. *Money, or simple circulation*; 3. *Capital*. 1 and 2, ABOUT 10 sheets, make up the contents of the first instalments to be published. You will understand the *political* motives that led me to hold back the third chapter on 'Capital' until I have again become established.

The contents of the instalments now being published are as follows:

---

[a] *A Contribution to the Critique of Political Economy*

Chapter One: *The Commodity*

A. *Historical notes on the analysis of commodities.* {William Petty (Englishman, Charles II's reign); Boisguillebert (Louis XIV); *B. Franklin* (first of his early works 1729)[a]; the Physiocrats; Sir James Steuart; Adam Smith; Ricardo and Sismondi.}

Chapter Two: *Money or simple circulation*

1. *Measure of value*

B. *Theories of the standard of money.* (Late 17th century, Locke and Lowndes, Bishop Berkeley (1750)[b]; Sir James Steuart; Lord Castlereagh; Thomas Attwood; John Gray; Proudhonists.)

2. *Medium of circulation*
   a) *The metamorphosis of commodities*
   b) *The circulation of money*
   c) *Coin. Token of value*
3. *Money*
   a) *Hoarding*
   b) *Means of payment*
   c) *Money of the world*
4. *The Precious metals*

C. *Theories of the medium of circulation and of money.* {Monetary system; *Spectator,*[368] Montesquieu, David Hume; Sir James Steuart; A. Smith, J.-B. Say; Bullion Committee,[c] Ricardo, James Mill; Lord Overstone and school; Thomas Tooke (James Wilson, John Fullarton).}

In these two chapters the Proudhonist socialism now FASHIONABLE in France—which wants to retain private production *while organising* the exchange of private products, to have *commodities* but not *money*—is demolished to its very foundations. Communism must above all rid itself of this 'false brother'.[d] But apart from all polemical aims, the analysis of simple money forms is, you know, the most difficult because the most abstract part of political economy.

I hope to win a scientific victory for our party. But the latter must itself now show whether its numbers are great enough to buy enough copies to banish the publisher's 'moral scruples'. The continuation of the venture depends on the sale of the first

---

[a] B. Franklin, *A Modest Inquiry into the Nature and Necessity of a Paper Currency.* - [b] G. Berkeley, *The Querist...* - [c] This refers to *Report from the Select Committee on the High Price of Gold Bullion...* - [d] Cf. 2 Corinthians 11:26

instalments. Once I've got a firm contract, everything will be ALL RIGHT.

Salut.

Your
K. M.

First published abridged in *Die Neue Zeit*, Bd. 2, No. 32, 1906-07 and in full in: Marx and Engels, *Works*, First Russian Edition, Vol. XXV, Moscow, 1934

Printed according to the original

Published in English in full for the first time

208

MARX TO FERDINAND LASSALLE[82]

IN BERLIN

London, 2 February 1859
9 Grafton Terrace, Maitland Park,
Haverstock Hill

Dear Lassalle,

The manuscript[a] went off from here on 26 January; by 31 January notification had already got back *here* from Berlin that the manuscript had arrived. The parcels company received this notification from their correspondent. On the other hand there is your letter dated 31 January in which you say the manuscript hasn't arrived. So *whatever the circumstances* the Prussian government—friend Stieber perhaps—has spent 3 days rummaging through[b] the manuscript. Legally, so far as I am aware, all they were empowered to do was ascertain whether the parcel contained Brussels lace, other parcels being no concern of theirs. Who is going to assure me that some junior official hasn't amused himself by using a page or 2 for spills?

I presume that, in its own interest, the Prussian government hasn't taken any FALSE STEPS with my manuscript. Otherwise I should see to it that all hell was let loose in the London press (*Times*, etc.).

---

[a] K. Marx, *A Contribution to the Critique of Political Economy*. - [b] Marx makes a pun on the name *Stieber* and the verb *durchstöbern* (rummage through).

I shall write you a *proper letter* tomorrow or the day after. This is simply a business notification, and it's nearly time for the post.

Your piece, BY THE BY, pleased me enormously.

My wife sends her kindest regards; now that her *cher frère* has been dismissed,[a] she believes that manuscripts, at any rate, may safely be sent to Berlin.

Salut.

Your
K. Marx

I may bring out an *English version* of the first instalments straight away. Duncker must put on the title-page: *'*The author reserves to himself the right of translation*'.*

First published in: *F. Lassalle. Nachgelassene Briefe und Schriften,* Bd. III, Stuttgart-Berlin, 1922

Printed according to the original

209

MARX TO ENGELS

IN MANCHESTER

[London,] 2 February 1859

DEAR Frederick,

The *Constitutionnel* wins since, according to *The Times,* the author was none other than Mr Boustrapa.[369]

Today came a letter (which I'll send you later) from Lassalle saying that the manuscript[b] has *not yet* arrived. Now take note: It went off on Tuesday (25); I was notified as early as *30th* January by the PACKET COMPANY here that the manuscript had arrived in Berlin. Lassalle's letter is dated 31 January. *Hence* the government has been *holding back* my manuscript for 3 or 4 days at least (if Duncker got the manuscript *after* Lassalle's letter went off). Maybe Mr Stieber has been rummaging through[c] it, or Mr von Patow has been endeavouring to make a hasty acquaintance with economics.

[a] This refers to Ferdinand von Westphalen, Jenny Marx's stepbrother, who until October 1859 was Prussian Minister of the Interior. - [b] K. Marx, *A Contribution to the Critique of Political Economy.* - [c] Marx makes a pun on the name *Stieber* and the verb *durchstöbern* (rummage through).

Wrote to Lassalle straight off. *Your philistines* have *intercepted* the stuff you were sending me (for Tuesday). It didn't arrive. I waited until 3 in the afternoon. Then I dashed off another article.

Salut.

Your
K. M.

First published in: Marx and Engels, *Works,* First Russian Edition, Vol. XXII, Moscow, 1929

Printed according to the original

Published in English for the first time

210

MARX TO FERDINAND LASSALLE[100]

IN BERLIN

London, 4 February 1859
9 Grafton Terrace, Maitland Park,
Haverstock Hill

Dear Lassalle,

I've not yet had an acknowledgment of receipt from Mr Duncker and am therefore still in doubt whether the manuscript[a] is yet out of the clutches of the *authorities.* You will see from the enclosed note that it left London on 26 January.

Ad vocem bellum[b]: The *general* view here is that war in Italy is inevitable.[370] This much is certain: Mr Emmanuel[c] is in earnest and Mr Bonaparte was in earnest. What has swayed the latter is 1. *Fear of Italian daggers.*[371] Since Orsini's death, he has been constantly engaged in secret intrigues with the Carbonari, the go-between being *Plon-Plon,* the husband of 'Clotilde'.[d] 2. *An exceedingly bleak financial situation*: it is, in fact, impossible to go on feeding the French army 'in peacetime'; Lombardy is fat and fertile. Moreover a war would again make 'war loans' possible. Any other loan is 'impossible'. 3. Over the last two years Bonaparte's repute has dwindled daily amongst all parties in France, and his diplomatic TRANSACTIONS have also been a succession of FAILURES. So

[a] K. Marx, *A Contribution to the Critique of Political Economy.* - [b] As regards the war - [c] Victor Emmanuel II - [d] Clotilde, the Princess of Savoy

something has *got* to happen if his prestige is to be restored. Even in the rural areas there is a great deal of grumbling about the ruinously low price of grain and Mr Bonaparte has tried in vain to push up the price of wheat artificially by means of his decrees on granaries.[a] 4. The parvenu in the Tuileries is being egged on by Russia. Given the Pan-Slav movement in Bohemia, Moravia, Galicia, southern, northern and eastern Hungary, Illyria, etc., and a war in Italy, Russia would almost certainly break the resistance that Austria continues to offer her. (Russia regards the prospect of an internal agrarian revolution with horror, and war abroad might come as a welcome diversion to the government, quite apart from any diplomatic objectives.) 5. Mr Plon-Plon, son of the ex-King of Westphalia,[b] and his clique (headed by Girardin and a very mixed bag of Hungarian, Polish and Italian pseudo-revolutionaries) are doing all in their power to force the issue. 6. A war against Austria in Italy is the only one in which England, who cannot take a direct stand *for* the Pope, etc., and *against* so-called liberty, would remain neutral, at least at the start. Russia, however, would keep Prussia in check should the latter feel inclined, which I doubt, to intervene at the very outset of the campaign.

On the other hand one may be perfectly sure that Mr Louis Bonaparte is devilishly afraid of a really serious war. 1. The man is always full of misgivings and, like all gamblers, is far from resolute. He has always inched his way to the Rubicon,[372] but those standing behind him have invariably had to chuck him in. In every case—Boulogne, Strasbourg, December 1851[373]—he was, in the end, *forced* to proceed in earnest with his plans. 2. The exceptionally cool reception accorded his scheme in France is not encouraging, of course. The masses appear to be INDIFFERENT. On the other hand there have been outright and earnest remonstrations against it on the part of high finance, trade and industry, the clerical party and, finally, the senior generals (Pélissier, for example, and Canrobert). Indeed, prospects on the military side are far from rosy, even if the braggadocio in the *Constitutionnel*[c] is taken at its face value. Assuming France can muster all in all 700,000 men, 580,000 of these, at the very highest estimate, will be fit for military service. Deduct 50,000 for Algiers; 49,000 gendarmes, etc.; 100,000 (minimum) for guarding the cities (Paris,

---

[a] Napoleon III, Decree on grain reserves of 16 November 1858, *Le Moniteur universel*, No. 322, 18 November 1858. - [b] Jérôme Bonaparte - [c] This refers to the article marked 'L. Boniface. Paris, le 29 janvier' in *Le Constitutionnel*, No. 30, 30 January 1859.

etc.) and fortresses of France; 181,000 at least for the army keeping watch on the Swiss, German and Belgian frontiers. This leaves 200,000 which, even if you add the minuscule Piedmontese army, is by no means AN OVERWHELMING FORCE to employ against the Austrians in their fortified positions on the Mincio and the Adige.

However that may be, if Mr Bonaparte draws back now, he will be done for so far as the bulk of the French army is concerned; and this might ultimately induce him to go ahead after all.

You apparently believe that in the event of such a war Hungary would rise. I very much doubt it. Austria will, of course, place a corps on the Galician-Hungarian frontier to observe the Russians, and this will simultaneously keep the Hungarians in check. The Hungarian regiments (in so far as they have not—and many of them already have—been dispersed among their enemies, e.g. the Czechs, Serbs, Slovenes, etc.) will be stationed in German provinces.

The war would, of course, have serious, and without doubt ultimately revolutionary consequences. But initially it will maintain Bonapartism in France, set back the internal movement within England and Russia, revive the pettiest nationalist passions in Germany, etc., and hence, in my view, its initial effect will everywhere be counter-revolutionary.

Be that as it may, you should expect *nothing* of the émigrés here. Apart from Mazzini who, at least, is a fanatic, they're a bunch of confidence tricksters whose one ambition is to extract money from the English. Mr Kossuth has positively sunk to the level of an itinerant LECTURER who hawks the same old nonsense round the various PROVINCES of England and Scotland and sells it over and over again to ever new audiences.[a]

The scoundrels here have all become so conservative that they would indeed deserve to be amnestied. Mr Gottfried Kinkel, for example, is publishing a weekly here, *Hermann* by name, compared with which even the *Kölnische Zeitung* is a daring and witty paper. (By indulging in sundry flirtations with aesthetic Jewesses, the suave, melodramatic parson is said, amongst other things, to have driven his wife to fall out of the window and break her neck. Freiligrath, being a kind-hearted fellow, was so taken in by the scenes of grief that he wrote a poem about the late Johanna Mockel,[b] only to discover a day or two later that the grief was

---

[a] Kossuth's lectures were published in Brussels in 1859 under the title *L'Europe, l'Autriche et la Hongrie*. - [b] F. Freiligrath, 'Nach Johanna Kinkels Begräbnis'.

merely *feigned* and that never had Mr Gottfried felt so FREE and EASY as since the death of his spouse.) The fellow preaches '*optimism*' in a namby-pamby, hat-doffing, somewhat breathless manner. The paper should be called *Gottfried.* For my part I would rather write under Manteuffel's yoke than under that of the German philistines in the City of London. To Mr Kinkel, however, the yoke is all the sweeter and lighter for the fact of his being not one jot superior to the said philistines where character and insight are concerned. The to-do made by the 'Lewald' woman, *alias* 'Stahr', about the late Mockel has compromised the latter person still further.[374]

Salut.

Your
K. M.

It would be a great help to me if you could obtain in *Breslau*,[a] and let me have *as soon as possible*, particulars about a person of the female sex by the name (allegedly) of von Paula-Kröcher, who used to live there and is *now over here.*

First published in: *F. Lassalle. Nachgelassene Briefe und Schriften*, Bd. III, Stuttgart-Berlin, 1922

Printed according to the original

Published in English in full for the first time

211

MARX TO ENGELS

IN MANCHESTER

[London,] 8 February 1859

Dear Engels,

It's a *fortnight ago* today since I sent the manuscript[b] to Berlin; since then 2 letters have gone off to Lassalle; up to this moment I've had no acknowledgment of receipt. Moreover, I had made this 'acknowledgment of receipt' a condition for the despatch of

---

[a] Wrocław - [b] K. Marx, *A Contribution to the Critique of Political Economy.*

the *preface*. As you can imagine, one begins to lose all patience when everything goes so wrong. I am quite ill with vexation.

Herewith Lassalle's letter. *Let me have it back.*

Today I have written about Bonaparte's rotten speech and his pamphlet.[a] [375]

Salut.

Your
K. M.

First published in *Der Briefwechsel zwischen F. Engels und K. Marx*, Bd. 2, Stuttgart, 1913

Printed according to the original

Published in English for the first time

212

MARX TO ENGELS

IN MANCHESTER

[London,] 9 February 1859

Dear Engels,

At last a letter from Duncker *today*. *He* didn't receive the manuscript[b] until 1 February. Not printed *this* week, because just completing some work or other—I don't know which—of Lassalle's.[c]

Enclosed a letter from Eccarius and Pfänder from which you will see that poor Eccarius is down with consumption. This is the most tragic thing I have yet experienced here in London.

Pieper, who had been discharged as cured, is back from Bognor again and in the German hospital. This time starvation treatment. SERVES HIM RIGHT.

I meant to send you the enclosed letters from Weydemeyer and Komp long ago.[321] I have at last replied to them.[d]

Dronke has been to Bonn, where one of his brothers was dying. Having obtained Flottwell's permission, he attended a ball given by

---

[a] This refers to 'Discours de S. M. L'Empereur. Session législative de 1859' (*Le Moniteur universel*, No. 39, special edition, 7 February 1859) and the pamphlet inspired by Napoleon III: [A. La Guéronnière,] *L'Empereur Napoléon III et l'Italie*. - [b] K. Marx, *A Contribution to the Critique of Political Economy*. - [c] F. Lassalle, *Franz von Sickingen*. - [d] See this volume, pp. 324, 338 and 374-78.

his [students'] 'corps' in Bonn. The little man[a] has written to Dingelstedt (*of Fulda*), through whom he hopes to arrange a performance of a *play* he himself has written. In addition, the little man writes 'Glasgower Briefe' for Prutz's *Museum*.[b] I had all this news from philistine Freiligrath.

From the latter, who came to see me yesterday (I myself being confined to the house with a bad throat), I also learned that Gottfried's—or Hermann's[c]—behaviour towards ladies is invariably so ludicrous (the buffoon now supposes he need only throw down his handkerchief) that he has become an object of general *dégoût*.[d] Moreover, Freiligrath has now also tumbled to the fact that Gottfried feels exceptionally 'FREE AND EASY' now that the Mockel woman[e] is dead and—strangest of all—*it now transpires* that, even *before the day of the funeral*, philistine Freiligrath and wife had discovered brother Hermann's 'lack of concern'.

According to Gottfried, the *Hermann*, to which the Prussian government has, as the Berlin *National-Zeitung* announces, granted a licence for postal distribution, is to cover the '*loss*' to his funds occasioned by his wife's death.

In due course, no doubt, Mrs Daniels will become Mrs Bürgers. She has written to Lina[f] saying that 'Bürgers has grown *still more* energetic and self-confident'. In proof of that 'self-confidence' she writes, '*we are* delighted by Freiligrath's poem about Mrs Kinkel,[g] which was mutilated by the "perfidious" *Kölnische Zeitung*'.

Steffen has written to Freiligrath asking for your address and mine as he has lost them. Steffen's address is: *W. Steffen, Harrison Square near Boston, Mass. U. St.*

Salut.

Your
K. M.

First published abridged in *Der Briefwechsel zwischen F. Engels und K. Marx*, Bd. 2, Stuttgart, 1913 and in full in: Marx and Engels, *Works*, First Russian Edition, Vol. XXII, Moscow, 1929

Printed according to the original

Published in English for the first time

---

[a] Ernst Dronke - [b] *Deutsches Museum* - [c] An allusion to the weekly *Hermann* published by Gottfried Kinkel. - [d] disgust - [e] Johanna Kinkel - [f] Caroline Schöler - [g] F. Freiligrath, 'Nach Johanna Kinkels Begräbnis'.

213

ENGELS TO MARX

IN LONDON

Manchester, 10 February 1859

Dear Moor,

The news about Eccarius is truly staggering. What a heroic letter he wrote you![376] That such a fine chap should come to such a pitiful end! We are losing our best men during this wretched period of peace, and the new blood is very *pauvre*.[a]

Herewith Lassalle's letter. I'm glad the manuscript[b] has arrived.

What did Freiligrath have to say concerning my letter about Kinkel[c]? To me he wrote, 'ALL RIGHT, ALL RIGHT' and said he had given his answer to *you*. So you still owe it to me.

I am going home now and shall get an article on the Austrian and German federal army[d] done in time for the 2nd post.

Your

F. E.

First published in *Der Briefwechsel zwischen F. Engels und K. Marx*, Bd. 2, Stuttgart, 1913

Printed according to the original

Published in English for the first time

214

ENGELS TO MARX

IN LONDON

Manchester, 14 February 1859

Dear Marx,

Something I forgot to mention. Certainly you must reserve the translation rights on your book.[e] Even if only to stop some jackass or industrialist from massacring the thing. Moreover it is now a

---

[a] poor - [b] K. Marx, *A Contribution to the Critique of Political Economy*. - [c] See this volume, pp. 370-71. - [d] F. Engels, 'German Resources for War'. - [e] K. Marx, *A Contribution to the Critique of Political Economy.*

mere legal formality which anyone can accomplish without any hesitation.

Statesman Blind has a friend in the telegraph office who occasionally sends the provincial papers some pretty tall stories by telegraph. More about this anon.

Your

F. E.

First published in *Der Briefwechsel zwischen F. Engels und K. Marx*, Bd. 2, Stuttgart, 1913

Printed according to the original

Published in English for the first time

215

MARX TO ENGELS

IN MANCHESTER

[London,] 15 February 1859

Dear Engels,

Herewith:

1. Letter from my brother-in-law (the CAPE MAN)[a] from which you will see that the fellow will be landing in London tomorrow. Since I am *sans sou*[b] (only last Saturday I had to pawn my wife's last 'spare' skirt in order to send Eccarius SOME COMFORTS) and have got to entertain the man decently—he is going to Trier and carries some weight in the TRANSACTIONS with my mother[c]—I must once again press you to mail me AT LEAST £1. Luckily I have what is known as mumps, which means that I only have to entertain the man here at home and, as an invalid, can refuse to do any gadding about.

2. Letter from Eccarius. I had told the latter (who seemed, I thought, to be improving a little) that if he needed wine he was to let me know. So you should send him ABOUT 2 BOTTLES OF port wine.

3. 2 enclosures from *The Free Press* (the more important for having been reprinted from *The New York Herald*) will give you some idea of the Chinese war[332] and Mr Palmerston's policy.[d]

---

[a] Johann Carl Juta - [b] penniless - [c] Henriette Marx - [d] 'Revelation by a Russian of the Object of the Chinese War and Treaty', *The Free Press*, No. 24, 22 December 1858.

Ad vocem[a] *Freiligrath*. I came, most opportunely for him, on the very day he got your letter.[b] He gave it to me to read and excused himself for the non-political nature of the poem[c] on the grounds that he was a 'poet'. Also said he had written to you about the *Hermann* simply as a 'joke'.[d] WELL, AFTER THESE VERY MEAGRE EXPLANATIONS, he said he would write and tell you that he had made everything ALL RIGHT with me. By the by, your letter 'tickled' him tremendously. I told him that it was 'very well written' and he, of course, couldn't help laughing at me for looking to 'style' first of all ON SUCH AN OCCASION. The FACT is, Freiligrath realises that Kinkel has *used* him and, having used him, is actually becoming somewhat uppish towards him. (Thus, to Freiligrath's intense annoyance, the '*Schriften von Gottfried und Johanna Kinkel*' figure in large type among the *Hermann*'s advertisements and, under the *same* heading, '*F. Freiligraths Gedichte*' in small type, so that Freiligrath's poems are annexed to the works of Gottfried and Johanna. This greatly riles our philistine.) On the other hand, Freiligrath is very much beholden to Kinkel for having, apparently against all expectations, again put him in the way of a *political purgative* which, BY THE BY, and if I am not mistaken, has earned him high praise and even, it is said, presents from philistines in Germany. *Nota bene:* Mrs Daniels wrote to Lina[e] (in reply to some quips about the Kinkel CASE the latter had sent her): '*We*' (she and Heinrich, the quiet one[f]) '*are delighted* and *entranced* by Freiligrath's poem' and the day-dreaming Heinrich, who had grown 'still more self-confident and still more energetic', had actually discovered that 'the perfidious' *Kölnische Zeitung* had suppressed the 'most important verse', a verse which existed only in Heinrich's Olympian imagination.

What's this about Blind?

Apropos. Did you and Lupus see in the papers (maybe a month or six weeks ago) that *Madame* Bangya in Paris had been sentenced to six months hard labour for soliciting?

Salut.

Your

K. M.

I've lost Lupus' address again. It's 59 Boundary Street, Greenheys, isn't it? At any rate I sent him a letter to that address.[377]

---

[a] As regards - [b] See this volume, pp. 370-71. - [c] F. Freiligrath, 'Nach Johanna Kinkels Begräbnis'. See also this volume, p. 359. - [d] See this volume, p. 372. - [e] Caroline Schöler - [f] Heinrich Bürgers

Schapper's wife has produced a son, and the old fool, who now goes in for phrenology, has discovered that the seven days'-old IMP has a sanguine-choleric temperament.

First published in: Marx and Engels, *Works*, First Russian Edition, Vol. XXII, Moscow, 1929

Printed according to the original

Published in English for the first time

216

MARX TO ENGELS

IN MANCHESTER

[London, about 22 February 1859][378]

Dear Frederick,

My brother-in-law[a] will be travelling to Manchester on Thursday and will probably come and see you on Friday. But you must let me have your exact address. On closer acquaintance, by the by, Juta proves to be a far from [healthy][b] chap. He suffers damnably from his liver, and hence must go to Carlsbad.[c] I should be glad if Gumpert would examine him and, since his liver is presently giving him a great deal of pain, do something to alleviate this. But *if the thing is really serious, Gumpert must not give any indication of the fact.*

Tomorrow I am writing about the Factory Report,[d] and expect an article from you, the more so as I am now working out *Capital.*[355]

Your

K. M.

Nota bene.

I have written asking Dana whether he can find me a Yankee for the English edition of the *Political Economy.*[e] In which case, if the

---

[a] Johann Carl Juta - [b] Ms. damaged. - [c] Karlovy Vary - [d] Marx means his article 'The State of British Manufactures', for which he used data from *Reports of the Inspectors of Factories to Her Majesty's Principal Secretary of State for the Home Department, for the Half Year Ending 31st October 1858.* - [e] K. Marx, *A Contribution to the Critique of Political Economy.*

thing looks like being *lucrative*, I should have to spend a few weeks in Manchester, putting it into English with you.

First published in: Marx and Engels, *Works*, First Russian Edition, Vol. XXII, Moscow, 1929

Printed according to the original

Published in English for the first time

217

MARX TO ENGELS

IN MANCHESTER

[London,] 22 February 1859

Dear Engels,

The bearer of these lines is my brother-in-law Juta, whom I most warmly recommend to you.

Your

K. Marx

Eccarius received the wine on Saturday and *believes* he can already feel the benefit of it. It seems probable that the wine will help him pull through.

First published in: Marx and Engels, *Works*, First Russian Edition, Vol. XXII, Moscow, 1929

Printed according to the original

Published in English for the first time

218

MARX TO FRANZ DUNCKER

IN BERLIN

London, 23 February 1859

Dear Sir,

The 'Preface'[a] enclosed herewith.

Yours very faithfully,

Karl Marx

First published in *International Review of Social History*, Vol. X, Part 1, 1965

Printed according to the original

Published in English for the first time

[a] to *A Contribution to the Critique of Political Economy*

219

MARX TO FERDINAND LASSALLE

IN BERLIN

London, 23 February 1859

Dear Lassalle,

I have today sent off the preface[a] to Duncker. Perhaps you would be good enough to ensure that I am sent the fee *as soon as the manuscript has been printed.* I would certainly not write to you about this point had it not become a *question brûlante*[b] due to unforeseen circumstances.

I hope to have a letter from you soon and, notwithstanding your coyness, something about 'conditions in the homeland', or at least the gossip there, this being essential for forming an opinion.

Salut.

Your
K. M.

First published in: *F. Lassalle. Nachgelassene Briefe und Schriften,* Bd. III, Stuttgart-Berlin, 1922

Printed according to the original

Published in English for the first time

220

MARX TO FERDINAND LASSALLE[1]

IN BERLIN

London, 25 February 1859
9 Grafton Terrace, Maitland Park, Haverstock Hill

Dear Lassalle,

Iterum Crispinus.[c]

It is Engels' intention to publish—*anonymously* to begin with—a short pamphlet entitled *Po and Rhine.*[379]

---

[a] to *A Contribution to the Critique of Political Economy* - [b] burning question - [c] *Iterum Crispinus*—Crispinus again (Juvenal, *Satires,* I, 4). Here: It's me again.

Main content: Military proof, i.e. based on military science, that all the reasons advanced to the effect that Austria must have the Mincio line in order to protect *Germany*, correspond precisely to the argument that France must have the Rhine frontier in order to protect herself; further that, whereas *Austria*'s interest in the Mincio line is considerable, that of Germany, as a single power, is nil, and that Italy will always be dominated militarily by Germany so long as the whole of Switzerland isn't French. The thing is mainly directed against the strategists of the Augsburg *Allgemeine Zeitung*, but otherwise against Mr Bonaparte—from a national viewpoint, of course.

I am willing to stake all my 'powers of discernment'[a] on the fact that the publication of this pamphlet, which will entail hardly any outlay because consisting of only a few sheets, would, at the present time, actually be a ***speculation*** (IN THE EMINENT SENSE OF THE WORD) for a bookseller.

Since taking part in the Baden campaign,[380] Engels has made military matters his special study. Added to which his writing, as you know, is exceedingly plausible.

However, the publisher must preserve the secret of the writer's identity until the AUTHOR himself chooses to disclose it. You may be sure that the most eminent military writers of Prussia will be suspected of being at the bottom of the thing.

Now here we have something the publication of which is intimately related to the times—a question of the day. Hence it must be pushed through quickly. Do you think that Duncker will agree to do it? It would undoubtedly be in his own interests. One can never know in the case of purely scientific stuff whether and to what extent the philistines will buy it. Where questions of the day such as these are concerned, this can be calculated with almost mathematical exactitude.

Should Duncker agree, Engels authorises you to conclude the transaction in his name and on whatever terms you think fit. Should he refuse, might there not be some other possibility? I know a publisher in Hamburg who would take it.[b] But this fellow was always personally hostile to the *Neue Rheinische Zeitung*, as he plainly told our friend Heine, and hence it would vex me sorely were he to obtain so much as a single line from any of us. Besides, he treated our never-to-be-forgotten and irreplaceable friend Weerth in the most outrageous fashion.

---

[a] Marx has 'kritische Urteilskraft', an allusion to the title of Kant's book *Kritik der Urteilskraft*. - [b] Marx probably refers to J. Campe.

Let me have an answer as soon as possible, and please don't begrudge the considerable time and effort I cost you. I can only plead the GENERAL PARTY INTEREST.

Your
K. M.

First published in: *F. Lassalle. Nachgelassene Briefe und Schriften*, Bd. III, Stuttgart-Berlin, 1922

Printed according to the original
Published in English in full for the first time

221

MARX TO ENGELS[1]

IN MANCHESTER

[London,] 25 February[a] 1859

Dear Engels,

Po and Rhine is a first-class idea and must be put in hand straight away.[379] You must *set to* **at once**, time being *everything* in this case. I have written to Lassalle this very day and am sure that little Jew Braun will put the thing through.

The pamphlet (HOW MANY SHEETS? Let me have the answer to this *by return*) must first appear *anonymously* so that the public believes the author to be an eminent general. In the *second* edition, which you may account a certainty provided the thing comes out on time, you will reveal your identity in a 6-LINE foreword, and then it will be a triumph for our party. In my 'Preface'[b] I have done you a few *honneurs*; and thus it is all to the good if you yourself take the stage immediately afterwards.

Those dogs of democrats and liberal riff-raff will see that we're the only chaps who haven't been stultified by the ghastly period of peace.

In any case, you'll get the *copies* of the *Tribune*. *Not one* of the military articles[c] has so far been published. Mr Dana *didn't* print the first, which you wrote A LONG TIME AGO, but will probably do so now. I too constantly experience the like. It's often three months before the asses discover that we've foretold EVENTS for them, whereupon they print the relevant articles.

---

[a] A slip of the pen in the original: 29 February. - [b] to *A Contribution to the Critique of Political Economy* - [c] Marx presumably means Engels' articles 'German Resources for War' and 'The Austrian Hold on Italy'.

My brother-in-law's[a] address is correct save that he forgot to add 'CITY (NEAR THE GENERAL POST OFFICE)'. But I imagine he'll be in Manchester by now and able to tell you about himself.

Salut.

Your

K. M.

First published abridged in *Der Briefwechsel zwischen F. Engels und K. Marx*, Bd. 2, Stuttgart, 1913 and in full in: Marx and Engels, *Works*, First Russian Edition, Vol. XXII, Moscow, 1929

Printed according to the original

Published in English in full for the first time

222

MARX TO ENGELS

IN MANCHESTER

[London,] 25 February 1859

Dear Engels,

I am writing to you again this evening because TIME PRESSES. I am morally convinced that, *in view of what I've written to Lassalle*, Duncker will accept the pamphlet.[b] Admittedly, little Jew Braun hasn't written to me since my manuscript[c] arrived, and that was over four weeks ago. For one thing, he was busy with the publication of his own immortal, 'inflammatory' work[d] (STILL, the little Jew, even his *Heraclitus*,[e] although atrociously written, is BETTER THAN ANYTHING THE DEMOCRATS COULD BOAST OF), and then he will probably have to do the final proof-reading of my scrawl. For another thing, he may be a trifle stunned by the terrible knock on the head dealt him indirectly by my analysis of money. For his *Heraclitus* contains the following note which I shall now quote verbatim despite its interminable length (you've got to read it, though):

'If we remarked above that in the said fragment Heraclitus has specified the true nature and function of money in political economy' (Heraclitus in fact says:

---

[a] Johann Carl Juta - [b] F. Engels, *Po and Rhine*. - [c] *A Contribution to the Critique of Political Economy* - [d] F. Lassalle, *Franz von Sickingen*. - [e] F. Lassalle, *Die Philosophie Herakleitos des Dunklen von Ephesos*. Further on Marx quotes Note 3 to p. 224 of Vol. I of this work.

'πυρὸς τ'ἀνταμείβεσδαι πάντα καὶ πῦρ ἁπάντωγ ὥσπερ χρυσοῦ χρήματα, καὶ χρημάτων χρυσός'[a]), 'this, we need hardly point out, is not to make a political economist of him, and hence it is far from our intention to suggest that he had grasped any of the wider implications of that fragment. But although this science neither existed nor could have existed at that time and therefore was not the object of Heraclitus' thought, it is correct to say that, precisely because he never goes by reflex categories but only by the speculative concept, Heraclitus has, in that fragment, discerned the nature of money in all its profundity and this more truly than many a modern economist. And it may not be altogether without interest or, indeed, so irrelevant as might at first appear, to observe how what is simply a consequence of that thought *automatically gives rise to the modern discoveries in this field.*'[b] (*Nota bene.* Lassalle doesn't know the first thing about these discoveries.)

'When Heraclitus suggests that money as a medium of exchange is the *antithesis* of all real products entering exchange and owes its *real existence* solely to the same' (I underline where Lassalle has underlined), 'this is not to say that money as such is itself a product invested with a material value of its own, one *commodity* among other commodities, as Say's school' (a nice Continental DELUSION that there is such a thing as Say's school) 'persists in regarding coin up to this very day; rather it is but the ideal *representative* of circulating real products, a *symbol of value* for the latter, which merely *stands for them.* And that is only in part a conclusion drawn from the fragment, in part only the concept implicit in it for Heraclitus himself.

'But if *all* money is merely the ideal unit or expression of value of all real circulating products and owes *its real existence* solely *to these,* which are at one and the same time its antithesis, it follows from the very consequence' (nice style! It follows from 'the very consequence') 'of this concept that a country's sum of values or its wealth may be increased only by an increase in real products, but never by an increase in money since money, of course, far from being even merely a factor of wealth and value' (now we have wealth *and* value; before it was sum of values *or* wealth), 'never expresses, as an abstract unit, more than the value which is situated in the products' (and a nice district, too[c]), 'and is *real* only *therein.* Hence the error of the balance of trade system.' (This is worthy of Ruge.) 'It further follows that *All* money is always equal in value to all circulating products, since it merely reduces the latter to an ideal unit of value, hence merely gives expression to *their* value; hence that, by an increase or decrease in the amount of money available, the value of this total sum of money will never be affected and will always remain equal only to that of all circulating products; that strictly speaking it is never possible to talk of the *value* of all money as compared with the *value* of all circulating products, because such a comparison supposes that the value of money and the value of products are *two* values in their own right, whereas only *one* value exists, which is realised in concrete form in the material product, and expressed as an abstract unit of value in money; or rather, *value* itself is nothing but a unit abstracted from real things, in which it does not exist *as such,* and finding its special expression in money; not only, then, does the value of all money *remain equal to* the value of all products but, properly speaking, all money **is** only the *value* of all circulating products.' (This ultra-bold type is the author's.) 'Hence it follows that, with an increase in the

---

[a] 'All things are exchanged for fire and fire for all things, as wares are exchanged for gold and gold for wares.' Here and below the insertions in parentheses are Marx's. - [b] Marx's italics - [c] An allusion to a joke current at the time: one woman tells another of her son's death in action near Leipzig (1813), whereupon the other remarks: 'And a nice district, too!' ('Auch eine schöne Gegend!')

quantity of coin, since the value of the total remains the same, that of each individual coin can only fall, just as it will rise again with a decrease in the quantity of coin. It further follows that, since money is merely the unreal theoretical abstraction of value and represents the *antithesis* of *real products* and materials, money as such does not need to have any intrinsic *reality*, i.e. need not consist of any truly valuable material, but may equally be paper money, and it is precisely then that it corresponds most closely to its concept. All these and many other conclusions, which have only been reached, and along entirely different lines, since *Ricardo*'s studies and have by no means found universal acceptance, follow from the mere consequence of that speculative concept discerned by Heraclitus.'

I, of course, paid not the slightest heed to this Talmudic wisdom but roundly slated Ricardo for his theory of money which, by the way, did not originate with him but with Hume and Montesquieu. So Lassalle may feel this to be a personal insult. There was actually no harm in it, for in my anti-Proudhon piece[a] I myself adopted Ricardo's theory. But I'd had a perfectly ridiculous letter from little Jew Braun in which he said that he had 'the early publication of my manuscript at heart, *although* he himself was engaged in writing a major work on political economy'[278] for which he had 'allocated two years'. But if I were to 'deprive him of too much that was new, he might abandon the whole thing'. WELL, to this I replied that there was no fear of rivalry since this 'new' science could accommodate himself and me and a dozen more besides.[b] My disquisition on money will now show him, either that I know nothing of the subject—although if I'm wrong, so is the whole history of the monetary theory—or else that he is an ass, since, with a few empty abstract expressions such as 'abstract unit', he presumes to lay down the law about empirical matters which, if one wishes to hold forth about them, call for study, and prolonged study INTO THE BARGAIN. For this reason he may, in the innermost recesses of his heart, be nourishing something of a grudge against me just now. But—and this is what I have been leading up to—firstly, Lassalle has really too great a stake 'in the cause' and, secondly, he is too much of an 'Ephraim Artful' not to keep in with us *coûte que coûte*,[c] which is all the more necessary to him because of his quarrel with the Düsseldorf people.[d] Moreover, living in Berlin has made him see that, for an energetic fellow like himself, the bourgeois party holds out no prospects whatever.[381]

So with clever MANAGEMENT the man will be ours, body and soul, no matter how much he indulges in 'inflammatory' antics or makes

---

[a] *The Poverty of Philosophy. Answer to the Philosophy of Poverty by M. Proudhon* - [b] See this volume, p. 355. - [c] cost what it may - [d] See this volume, pp. 23-24 and 27.

Heraclitus pay for being the most succinct of philosophers by providing him with the most prolix of commentaries. For the same reason I am *sure* that *en cas de besoin*[a] he will *force* Duncker to take your pamphlet. I have, by the by, so framed my letter that he can show the whole of it to Duncker. It was, in fact, written for Duncker rather than Lassalle, though for all his artfulness Ephraim is unlikely to notice the fact.

Hence I consider it *certain* that Duncker will take the pamphlet, so the main thing now is for you to set to work on it *at once*, for this is like a newspaper article. There's no time to be lost. For the same reason—immediacy of impact—I believe you shouldn't exceed 4 or 5 sheets (if as much is needed). So you may regard yourself as totally absolved from the *Tribune* work (unless some martial occurrence steals a march on your pamphlet, which is improbable), until you've finished the thing. The most *sensible* thing to do would be to plead sudden illness and stay away from the office, so as to write the thing all at one go.

Amicus Engels Senior, amicus Ermen (Gotofredus!), sed magis amicum τὸ φρονεῖν'.[b]

> 'φεῦ, φεῦ, φρονεῖν ὡς δεινὸν, ἔνθα μὴ τέλη
> λύει φρονοῦντι,'[c]

as your old man might say to you, like Tiresias did to King Oedipus, to which, however, you would reply that he

> '«ἐν τοῖς κέρδεσι
> μόνον δέδορκε, τὴν τέχνην δ'ἔφυ τυφλός»'.[d]

Salut.

Your
K. M.

First published abridged in *Der Briefwechsel zwischen F. Engels und K. Marx*, Bd. 2, Stuttgart, 1913 and in full in: Marx and Engels, *Works*, First Russian Edition, Vol. XXII, Moscow, 1929

Printed according to the original

Published in English for the first time

---

[a] in case of need - [b] Engels Senior is dear to me, Ermen (Gottfried!) is dear to me, but knowledge is dearer still. An adaptation of 'Amicus Plato, amicus Socrates, sed magis amica veritas'—'Plato is dear to me, Socrates is dear to me, but truth is dearer still' (Ammonius Saccas, *Vita Aristoteles*). - [c] 'Alas, 'tis terrible to be wise when it brings the wise man no reward' (Sophocles, *Oedipus Tyrannus*, 324, 325). - [d] 'In usury but sharp-eyed, yet in his sooth-saying blind' (Sophocles, *Oedipus Tyrannus*, 396, 397).

223

MARX TO ENGELS

IN MANCHESTER

[London,] 3 March 1859

Dear Engels,

From the enclosed letter of Lassalle's[382] you will see that I know my men and what MANAGEMENT means.

As regards the letter, I would make the following observations:

1. You must now really follow my advice and *shun the office altogether for a few days.* I did, of course, put the thing in such a way as to suggest that I'd already read your manuscript.[a] A few days here or there are of no importance, but if you only work in the evenings you won't finish *in time.*

2. In your position you cannot agree to the small fee but must, if only *honoris causa,* settle for the alternative of half the net profits.

3. Lassalle's direction that you send the *title* (i.e. *not* write it on the manuscript), the foreword (which I'd suggest you don't write) and the table of contents to him personally (F. Lassalle, 131 Potsdamer Strasse, Berlin), is a sensible one. For parcels are being opened by the Post Office, and the government mustn't know the title, which would give them the key to the whole secret.

The manuscript, on the other hand, I shall send from here, as I sent my own manuscript[b] (i.e. insured), to Duncker *via* Fräulein Ludmilla Assing. Only I'll get *Pfänder* to put himself down as the sender.

4. You should indeed include something national, anti-Bonapartist, but the tone should be careful and gentlemanly. You can the more readily employ this colour in that the intention of your pamphlet is, IN FACT, a great victory for Mazzini vis-à-vis the National Assembly of 1848 (Radowitz[c]-Mincio),[383] and you enable Germans for the first time to interest themselves with a good conscience in Italy's emancipation.

NOW, GOOD-BYE, OLD BOY.

Your

K. M.

---

[a] *Po and Rhine* (see this volume, pp. 391-92) - [b] *A Contribution to the Critique of Political Economy* - [c] Marx refers to J. M. von Radowitz's speech of 12 August 1848 in the Frankfurt National Assembly.

In his latest *Gottfried* Mr Gottfried[a] kow-tows to Suse-Sibeth, whom he describes as a model merchanting house, likewise to that wretched publisher, Trübner, who has compiled a worthless American bibliography.[b] *Macte puer virtute.*[c]

First published abridged in *Der Briefwechsel zwischen F. Engels und K. Marx*, Bd. 2, Stuttgart, 1913 and in full in: Marx and Engels, *Works*, First Russian Edition, Vol. XXII, Moscow, 1929

Printed according to the original

Published in English for the first time

224

ENGELS TO MARX

IN LONDON

[Manchester,] 4 March 1859

Dear Moor,

Little Jew Braun[d] has managed things well; I agree to half the net profits. The work is going ahead fairly quickly,[e] 9 long double pages of the kind I send you for the *Tribune* are ready, 2 or 3 more will see the finish of the Po and then comes the Rhine, which won't be as long—barely 3 sheets in all. This evening, Saturday and Sunday will certainly dispose of the better part of the thing, and I shall let you have it by Wednesday, provided all goes smoothly. However I must be on my guard since I'll have all the official military writers against me, and if they can pick any holes in the thing they'll certainly do so. So better too short than too long, and the historical examples can be done quite briefly. Besides, if the manuscript arrives in Berlin at the end of next week, it will be soon enough; after all, there's going to be war.[370] So there's no need to worry about time. It's *impossible* just now to absent myself from the WAREHOUSE for several days. There's no real need and it wouldn't be much help. What holds one up is poring

---

[a] A reference to the weekly *Hermann* edited by Gottfried Kinkel. - [b] 'Commerzielle Briefe' and 'Amerikanische Literatur. Trübner's Bibliographical Guide to American Literature', *Hermann*, No. 7, 19 February 1859. - [c] Persevere in thy valour, o youth! (Virgil, *Aeneid*, IX, 641.) - [d] Ferdinand Lassalle - [e] Engels' work on *Po and Rhine*

over the map, which *must* be done *staccato*,[a] otherwise one gets bemused.

I'm not doing a foreword. That would be asking for too much.

Your

F. E.

First published in *Der Briefwechsel zwischen F. Engels und K. Marx*, Bd. 2, Stuttgart, 1913

Printed according to the original

Published in English for the first time

225

MARX TO ENGELS

IN MANCHESTER

[London,] 10 March 1859

Dear Engels,

Pamphlet[b] received. Will run to about 4 printed sheets if not more, considering the way pamphlets are printed. Have read it all; EXCEEDINGLY CLEVER; the political side is also splendidly done and that was damned difficult. THE PAMPHLET WILL HAVE A GREAT SUCCESS.

I've deleted nothing but one short sentence about Reuss-Schleiz; not where you discuss the 'natural frontiers' of that state[c] but in the first passage where it makes for *double emploi*[d] and detracts from the effect.

I suggest that the subtitle 'Military Studies' detracts from the effect and should be deleted.

Should you be writing to Lassalle tomorrow I'd like you to do something in your own name which I can't do in mine. The FACTS are as follows: Last Monday (7 March) something arrived from Berlin! What do you think it was? *The first proof-sheet*[e] and since then I have not had another. *Contrary to what Mr Duncker expressly said in his letter*, they did nothing at all about my manuscript for 6 weeks and would now seem to be printing 1 sheet a week. When your manuscript arrives they'll perhaps break off again and thus the thing may drag on for months. I find this quite deplorable,

a with breaks in between - b F. Engels, *Po and Rhine*. - c See present edition, Vol. 16, p. 250. - d duplication - e of K. Marx's *A Contribution to the Critique of Political Economy*

and you might DROP SOME WORDS in your own name to Lassalle about the matter.[a] Do the fellows want to put the piece off until the very eve of war,[370] thereby ensuring that it comes to nothing and giving Mr Duncker an excuse to refuse the sequel?

Besides, I was counting on the money, and this delay has rendered intolerable my already distressing mode of existence. On this occasion Freiligrath (who is seeking IN EVERY WAY to reestablish himself)[b] was decent enough to try and negotiate bills for me here in London. However the thing came to nothing.

Apropos the *Tribune*. For the past 6 weeks they have not published one article either of yours or mine. The intrigues associated with a presidential election are already BEGINNING. In the light of experience I should say that the omission of our articles was a preliminary manoeuvre enabling them to notify me that they will only be requiring one article per week for the time being.

Salut.

Your

K. M.

I believe there will be war. However, a diplomatic intermezzo is necessary, partly on account of the clamour in Germany, partly on account of the vociferousness of the French bourgeoisie, lastly on account of the English Parliament; perhaps also in order that Russia may in the meantime extort sundry concessions from Austria. The Russians have achieved one main object. In 1846, when, for the first time, Austria's finances showed no deficit, Russia used the Cracow affair[384] to plunge her back into the most appalling financial predicament. In 1858 the Austrians appeared to have got their finances in some sort of order and announced an immediate payment by the Bank, which is why Bonaparte was promptly sent into the field and Austria's finances are back where they were in 1848. The dissolution of Parliament, the absence of government here in the interim, and subsequently Palmerston as FOREIGN MINISTER[385] are similarly moves required by Russia for the purpose of war.

First published in *Der Briefwechsel zwischen F. Engels und K. Marx*, Bd. 2, Stuttgart, 1913

Printed according to the original

Published in English for the first time

[a] See this volume, pp. 402-03. - [b] See this volume, pp. 360 and 366.

226

ENGELS TO FERDINAND LASSALLE

IN BERLIN

Manchester, 14 March 1859
6 Thorncliffe Grove, Oxford Street

Dear Lassalle,

First of all my thanks for your *bons offices*[a] with Duncker, which have met with such outstanding success and will, for the first time in nearly ten years, give me the opportunity of appearing before the German public. I sent the manuscript to Marx last Wednesday[b] and he will have forwarded it on Thursday. The title page should read simply *Po and Rhine*, Berlin, Published by ... etc., etc. Marx and I both consider it better that the thing should first appear anonymously because specialised and, at the start, the name of a civilian could only be detrimental to a military paper. If the thing is successful, as I hope, it will be time enough to put my name to it. There's no need for a table of contents, the sections being merely numbered. Nor have I written a foreword.

Marx thinks it will amount to 4 sheets, which I doubt, but it all depends on the printing, of course.

As regards terms, I have decided in favour of half the net profits; it goes without saying, of course, that there should be the usual number of free copies, one of which you must naturally bespeak in advance. They can be sent through publisher's channels, though I'd like one (or else proofs) to be sent direct to me by post. I might bring it out in English. The matter lends itself less readily to a French translation which would, furthermore, be difficult to place; however, I shall see.

How is the printing of Marx's manuscript[c] getting on? So far I've only heard of *one* sheet having been printed, and yet the manuscript has been in Berlin for over a month. This seems to me very slow. One or two instalments at least should be out in time for the Leipzig Fair[386] and there's not long to go.

Reiterated promises notwithstanding, Marx hasn't yet sent me your *Heraclitus*,[d] which I greatly look forward to seeing, although both my Greek and the speculative concept have grown exceedingly rusty. I am equally anxious to read your play,[e] which I have

---

[a] good offices - [b] 9 March - [c] *A Contribution to the Critique of Political Economy* - [d] F. Lassalle, *Die Philosophie Herakleitos des Dunklen von Ephesos*. - [e] F. Lassalle, *Franz von Sickingen*.

seen advertised. Despite your versatility, I would never have expected you to take up this speciality as well.

Since I've been here I have been devoting myself largely to militaria, also dallying at intervals with an old love, comparative philology. But when one has engaged in noble commerce all day long, it's impossible to go beyond sheer dilettantism in so vast and extensive a discipline. And even though I once cherished the brash idea of writing a comparative grammar of the Slavonic languages, I gave it up long ago, the more so since Miklosich[a] has undertaken the same thing with such brilliant success.

So once again very many thanks and kind regards from your

F. E.

First published in: *F. Lassalle. Nachgelassene Briefe und Schriften*, Bd. III, Stuttgart-Berlin, 1922

Printed according to the original

Published in English for the first time

227

MARX TO ENGELS

IN MANCHESTER

[London,] 16 March 1859

Dear Frederick,

£5 received. Thanks.

Yesterday proof sheet II[b] arrived. If it goes on like this it'll take them three months. There can't possibly be more than one type-setter employed on this affair.

I don't know what to write about on Friday. Can you do something—on Armstrong's gun, perhaps?

Mr Bruno Bauer has, I am told, written a pamphlet on the 'question of the day', pro-Russia and France and anti-Austria and England. He is now the ally of Manteuffel, in support of whom he has already written recently in the *Zeit*.[c]

I am sending you that clown Edgar Bauer's paper. The man has become a great communist and working men's representative. He and his little rag are almost finished. The first article, 'Zank',[d] is a

---

[a] F. Miklosich, *Vergleichende Grammatik der slawischen Sprachen*. - [b] of Marx's *A Contribution to the Critique of Political Economy* - [c] *Die Neue Zeit* - [d] *Die Neue Zeit*, No. 37, 12, March 1859.

direct attack on me. I am, it seems, quietly to join up with Mr Edgar and emerge from my 'surly' and 'distrustful' isolation. The CLOWN has turned into a real preacher. He doesn't dare attack the *Hermann* for fear the fellows may disclose his 'PAST'.

Kinkel's paper is doing excellent business. Prudently, he has quite given up writing himself. The money comes partly from a Dr Juch and partly from the Portuguese Jew, Castello (an old Portuguese financial house), who was talked into it by the great Gerstenberg.[a]

First published abridged in *Der Briefwechsel zwischen F. Engels und K. Marx*, Bd. 2, Stuttgart, 1913 and in full in: Marx and Engels, *Works,* First Russian Edition, Vol. XXII, Moscow, 1929

Printed according to the original

Published in English for the first time

228

MARX TO FERDINAND LASSALLE

IN BERLIN

London, 16 March 1859
9 Grafton Terrace, Maitland Park, Haverstock Hill

Dear Lassalle,

Your latest work[b] and accompanying letter have not yet arrived, nor are they to be here so soon. Despatch through publisher's channels is about as expeditious as if you were to send me the things via Petersburg, Kamchatka and North America.

If it's not too late, get them to print 'THE RIGHT OF TRANSLATION IS RESERVED' on the last manuscript[c] I sent you. Otherwise some of the German clowns over here might massacre the thing.

Owing to circumstances which I can't go into today (for I am dictating an article in English[d] while writing this note to you), I am very hard pressed for money. Might it be possible for you to carry out some sort of bill transaction for me in Berlin having a currency of a few weeks, in return for which you could subsequently take the fee Duncker owes me?

---

[a] The letter is unsigned. - [b] *Franz von Sickingen* - [c] F. Engels, *Po and Rhine.* - [d] K. Marx, 'The War Prospect in Prussia'.

Yesterday I had a visitor from Paris, a man by whose judgment I set tremendous store. Speaking of war,[370] he said: *'Il n'y a pas deux opinions à Paris. Nous avons la guerre.'*[a] He was quite convinced that, were Bonaparte to draw back, he would crack up and, LIKE the *Empereur* Soulouque, would be betrayed by the army itself. Even the Parisian bourgeois, though rabid for peace, are already beginning to mutter that the fellow has no more courage than Louis Philippe.

There's one factor, by the by, which you must not overlook; Russia is stirring up the whole thing, and her ally, Palmerston (you only have to look at *The Times*) is doing all he can to drive Bonaparte to war. On top of that there'll soon be a change of ministry here, and then Palmerston will run the thing direct.[385] The pro-Poerio, etc., demonstrations here are wholly inspired by him. He has placed his son-in-law, Lord Shaftesbury, at the head of these, AS RESPONSIBLE EDITOR.[387]

I am now, AFTER ALL, beginning to believe that the war might hold out some prospects for us as well.

Salut.

Your

K. M.

Don't forget, by the by, that if you write to me about certain conditions,[b] it will benefit a vast public, amongst whom a great many Germans. The *Tribune* numbers some 200,000 regular subscribers.

First published in: *F. Lassalle. Nachgelassene Briefe und Schriften,* Bd. III, Stuttgart-Berlin, 1922

Printed according to the original

Published in English for the first time

229

MARX TO FRANZ DUNCKER

IN BERLIN

[London,] 17TH MARCH 1859

Dear Sir,

I am returning the proofs[c] in an envelope because advised by the Post Office over here that, while proofs may be sent from

---

[a] 'There's no two opinions about it in Paris. We shall have war.' - [b] i.e., about the position in Germany (see this volume, p. 391) - [c] of the book *A Contribution to the Critique of Political Economy*

Berlin to London, they must go from London to Berlin as letters.

Page 32, in the final lines I forgot to amend 'more profound *economic* differences between English and French, etc., political economy' to 'more profound *fundamental*, etc.'

My memory may be deceiving me, but it seems to me that the beginnings of the sentences on p. 33, both in the text and in the first note, were missing on p. 32.

Yours very faithfully,
K. M.

First published in *International Review of Social History*, Vol. X, Part 1, 1965

Printed according to the original
Published in English for the first time

230

MARX TO ENGELS[388]

IN MANCHESTER

[London, 22 March 1859]

Dear Engels,

Herewith Eccarius' letter. Unfortunately he had to return to his tailor's sweat-shop for which, or so it seems to me, he is by no means sufficiently recovered.

I wrote about the Reform Bill today[389]; you should write (if your eyes [are alright], as I hope—otherwise, OF COURSE, DON'T THINK OF IT) about the likelihood of war.[a] This I regard as necessary, if the rascals on the *Tribune* are not to reprint anything.[390] Nothing from Berlin. Only 3 proof-sheets received[b] in *8* weeks.

Salut.

Your
K. M.

First published in *Der Briefwechsel zwischen F. Engels und K. Marx*, Bd. 2, Stuttgart, 1913

Printed according to the original
Published in English for the first time

[a] In response to this request Engels wrote the article 'War Inevitable'. - [b] of Marx's *A Contribution to the Critique of Political Economy*

231

MARX TO ENGELS

IN MANCHESTER

[London,] 25 March [1859]

Dear Engels,

I think you have misunderstood Lassalle's letter.[a]

All he says is:

'I'm most anxious to see what the pamphlet[b] *contains.* Marx's work[c] will *also* be appearing soon, etc.' By this he means he has *not read* your pamphlet. *Voilà tout.*[d] The same affectation as in the case of my manuscript which he purports *not to have read.* I had a letter from him this morning which I shall send on to you later. Had your manuscript not arrived he would at least have told me.

Your manuscript left London *the same* day as it arrived. Pfänder was given a receipt for it. Anyway it *is* sure to have arrived. Duncker is A SLOW COACH. To date (8 WEEKS) I have had only 3 proof-sheets.

Your

K. M.

First published in *Der Briefwechsel zwischen F. Engels und K. Marx,* Bd. 2, Stuttgart, 1913

Printed according to the original

Published in English for the first time

232

MARX TO FERDINAND LASSALLE[20]

IN BERLIN

London, 28 March 1859
9 Grafton Terrace, Maitland Park,
Haverstock Hill

Dear Lassalle,

Ad vocem[e] *financial predicament*: *D'abord*[f] many thanks for your offers of help. In the meantime, however, I have tried other

[a] Marx refers to Lassalle's letter to Engels of 21 March 1859. - [b] F. Engels, *Po and Rhine.* - [c] *A Contribution to the Critique of Political Economy* - [d] That's all. - [e] As regards - [f] First

means, namely writing to my mother asking her if she will lend me the money for a few weeks. *Je verrai.*[a] Here in London a bill could have been negotiated only through Gerstenberg. But the latter, a petty pompous gentleman and Kinkel's patron, shall not have the gratification of being asked to do me a service, even a purely formal one.

Ad vocem Duncker: This Wednesday (day after tomorrow), the man will have had the manuscript[b] for almost 9 weeks. So far I've been sent only *3 proof-sheets.* Between ourselves I should say quite frankly that Duncker is regretting having undertaken the business and that's why he is handling it in this dilatory, Wetzlar chancellery fashion.[391] If he goes on like this the thing won't even be out by Easter. And this puts me in another quandary. I am negotiating with an Englishman over the English rendering of these first instalments. This last depends, of course, on the publication of the work in German, and since everything is done at high pressure in London, the Englishman is growing mistrustful. You absolutely cannot make an Englishman understand the German way of doing business.

You will see that the first section does not comprise the principal chapter, i.e. the 3rd, on *capital.* I thought this advisable on *political* grounds, for it's in III that the battle really begins and it seemed to me better not to frighten people *de prime abord.*[c]

Ad vocem telegraphy. I ACCEPT THE OFFER.[392] The matter isn't as simple as you think. Obtaining the information is nothing, but takes up *a great deal of time.* I shall set up office near the Exchange (where the telegraphic companies who despatch the things also have their offices). However, your cousin[d] must now let me know: 1. By what route does he want the despatches sent? There are 3 companies, one sends via France, the second via Ostend and the third via Antwerp. The only things which should be sent via France, I think, are those for which no French censorship can present a danger. This is, incidentally, the shortest route. 2. *What* does he want telegraphed? Different papers base their views of what is important on very different principles. 3. How frequently does he want me to telegraph? 4. Besides NEWS from England, do these people want news from America, in short, from outside Europe? He must give me exact instructions about all this since telegraphy demands first and foremost that all non-essentials should be omitted. 5. Finally, I must know at what hour of the day

---

[a] I shall see. - [b] K. Marx, *A Contribution to the Critique of Political Economy.* - [c] at the very outset - [d] Max Friedländer

the *Presse* prefers to receive its news (in the English provinces, at any rate, this varies with individual newspapers, according to the time they come out). In the case of extraordinary events no time could, of course, be laid down, as it could, presumably, for ordinary despatches. For stock-market news I would, of course, have an exceptional source of information in Freiligrath.

Ad vocem 'Presse': I accept this offer, too: *Firstly,* because, unlike last time, no conditions are imposed on me as regards the treatment of specific political personalities. I make it an absolute principle never to assent to a *condition.* On the other hand, every newspaper has a right to expect tact of its correspondents. *Secondly,* because times have changed and I now consider it essential that our party should secure positions wherever possible, even if only for a time, so that others should not gain possession of the terrain. For the time being, of course, it must be used cautiously, but the most important thing is to acquire influence at various points against more crucial contingencies. I never received the copies of the *Presse* which you say Friedländer sent me, probably because they were wrongly addressed. I ought, by the by, to be sent a few numbers immediately; one has to find out from the actual paper *how,* not *what,* one should write for the Viennese public.

Ad vocem your writing for the 'Presse'. I am quite convinced you should write for them. True, it would be 'improper' for you, as a *Prussian,* to write for an *Austrian* paper just now. But on principle we should, as Luther says of God, 'use a thief to catch a thief',[a] and whenever we get the chance, contribute to the general state of disintegration and confusion. *Before* the start of the present troubles I would neither have written for the *Presse* myself, nor have advised you to do so. But the fermentation process has begun and now it's up to everyone to do what he can. It is now advisable to infiltrate poison, no matter where. Should we confine ourselves to writing for papers which *on the whole* share our viewpoint, we'd have to postpone all journalistic activity indefinitely. And should one really allow so-called 'PUBLIC OPINION' to have nothing but counter-revolutionary stuff pumped into it?

Ad vocem 'Tribune': You certainly misunderstood me if you thought I was asking you to take the *Tribune*'s subscribers into account. The fact of the matter is this: My real business with the *Tribune* consists in writing leaders about anything I choose. Here, England heads the bill and France comes second. Much is of an

[a] M. Luther, *Von Kauffshandlung und Wucher.*

economic nature. But since the change of course in Prussia,[336] I have amused myself on the sly by writing an occasional report from 'Berlin' and owing to my 'internal' ties with the Hohenzollern homeland I have been able to assess conditions there with great assurance. Among the said subscribers to the *Tribune* there are a great many Germans. Moreover, the German-American newspapers, whose name is legion, reprint stuff from it. This being so, it was important for me to give local colour to the occasional article I wrote from 'Berlin' in order that my polemic with the Prussian State might also be pursued in the New World. A little gossip is indispensable to local colour of this kind. Besides, present Prussian history consists largely of *chronique scandaleuse. Hinc illae lacrimae.*[a] In this respect your last letter served me to good purpose.

Salut.

Your

K. M.

P.S. Have just received a letter from Nutt, the City booksellers, advising me that your parcel has arrived. I shall collect it without fail today.

What is happening about Engels' pamphlet[b]? I sent it off on the 10TH OF MARCH. I'd have thought this kind of thing could have been done in 5 days.

First published in: *F. Lassalle. Nachgelassene Briefe und Schriften*, Bd. III, Stuttgart-Berlin, 1922

Printed according to the original

Published in English in full for the first time

233

MARX TO ENGELS

IN MANCHESTER

[London,] 1 April 1859

Dear Engels,

Herewith letter from Lassalle. Herewith letter from Dana, which you must return. I shall wait to hear from you before answering it.[393]

---

[a] Hence these tears (Terence, *Andria*, I, i, 99). - [b] *Po and Rhine*

Have written articles on the Reform Bill, MINISTRY.[389] My article for next week: *Indian Finances.*[a] All the rest of the world is therefore at your disposal.

So Palmerston, as was decided at Compiègne[356] (but in effect at Petersburg), is to return to the MINISTRY whatever its denomination. Without him Russia could not allow a war. Now, as in 1852 and 1855, Bright and Russell have pulled the chestnuts out of the fire for him.[394]

By the by, the debate in parliament was very funny. The Whigs and Radicals attacked the Tories largely on the grounds of their being REVOLUTIONISTS. Here, Bright's and Gibson's role most abject. (The latter even went so far as to declaim romantically *against* ELECTORAL DISTRICTS.[395]) On the other hand, the farce of Tories, in the name of the MIDDLE CLASS, advocating their own rubbish in opposition to Whigs and MIDDLE CLASS, who advocate theirs in the name of the WORKING CLASS. A sign of great progress in England.

Salut.

Your

K. M.

First published abridged in *Der Briefwechsel zwischen F. Engels und K. Marx*, Bd. 2, Stuttgart, 1913 and in full in: Marx and Engels, *Works*, First Russian Edition, Vol. XXII, Moscow, 1929

Printed according to the original

Published in English for the first time

234

MARX TO FERDINAND LASSALLE

IN BERLIN

London, 4 April 1859

Dear Lassalle,

All my attempts to raise money have failed. I have also had an answer in the negative from home—you know how much attached

[a] K. Marx, 'Great Trouble in Indian Finances'.

old people are to 'things finite'. Unpleasant though it is for me to approach you—since your own funds are on the ebb just now—I have no other choice. If 20 friedrichsdors is too much, send less. But draw the money from Duncker later on.

Has Engels' pamphlet[a] come out?

I shall write to you from here at length next week (this week there's absolutely no time). In the meantime my thanks for the play[b] and the accompanying letter.

Salut.

Your

K. M.

First published in: *F. Lassalle. Nachgelassene Briefe und Schriften*, Bd. III, Stuttgart-Berlin, 1922

Printed according to the original

Published in English for the first time

235

MARX TO ENGELS[396]

IN MANCHESTER

[London,] 9 April 1859

Dear Frederick,

Have written to Dana telling him he can have the articles if he pays better.[397]

Pieper, finally cured and out of hospital (after a serious relapse), is off to Bremen. He has an ugly inflammation on his forehead.

Have you been following the exposure of Palmerston over the Italian question (1848)?[c]

Anstey is back from Hong Kong and is threatening to have his revenge on Palmerston. As an opponent, the latter will find Anstey not a little dangerous—more so, at any rate, than Urquhart.[398]

The financial muddle in India must be seen as the real result of

---

[a] *Po and Rhine* - [b] F. Lassalle, *Franz con Sickingen* - [c] See this volume, pp. 431-32.

the Indian Mutiny.[178] A GENERAL financial BREAKDOWN seems inevitable unless those classes are taxed which to date have been England's most solid supporters. However, even that will be of no substantial help. The joke is that John Bull will now have to pay out annually between 4 and 5 million cash in India in order to keep the wheels turning, and will in this nice roundabout way restore his national debt to the proper progressive RATIO. It must certainly be admitted that the Indian market is being paid a damned high price for Manchester COTTONS. According to the report of the Military Commission 80,000 EUROPEANS as well as some 200,000 to 260,000 NATIVES will have to be maintained in India for years to come. This costs ABOUT £20 million and the total NET REVENUE amounts to no more than £25 million. Moreover, the mutiny has added a PERMANENT DEBT of £50 million or, according to Wilson's calculations, a permanent annual deficit of 3 million. In addition, there is the GUARANTEE of £2 million per annum to the RAILWAYS until they are running and, indefinitely, a smaller sum if their NET REVENUE falls short of 5%. So far (apart from the short stretch of railway that has been completed) India has got nothing out of the thing save the privilege of paying English capitalists 5% for their capital. But John Bull has cheated himself, or rather has been cheated by his capitalists. India's payments are merely nominal, whereas those of John Bull are real. E.g. a substantial part of Stanley's LOAN[399] was simply to be used for paying 5% to English capitalists, even in respect of railways the building of which has not yet begun. Finally, the revenue from opium, amounting hitherto to £4 million per annum, is under serious threat as a result of the Chinese treaty.[400] Whatever happens the monopoly is bound to collapse and in China itself the cultivation of opium will soon be in full swing. Revenue was derived from opium precisely because it was an article of contraband. To my mind the present financial catastrophe in India is a more serious affair than was the war in India.

What do you make of Duncker? Was there ever such a rascally slow coach?

Salut.

Your

K. M.

First published abridged in *Der Briefwechsel zwischen F. Engels und K. Marx*, Bd. 2, Stuttgart, 1913 and in full in: Marx and Engels, *Works*, First Russian Edition, Vol. XXII, Moscow, 1929

Printed according to the original

Published in English in full for the first time

236

ENGELS TO MARX

IN LONDON

[Manchester,] Monday, 11 April 1859

D.M.,

Article for *Friday* on war.[a] The Austrians evidently intend to seize the initiative after all. Very sensible. If I'm not mistaken I have already sent the plan of the war to the *Tribune*[b]: An Austrian offensive to defeat, first, the Piedmontese and then the invading French severally as they debouch from Mont Cenis, Mont Genèvre, the Col di Tenda and Bocchetta—was that it? I can no longer remember exactly. It'll be a very jolly affair.

What clever-clever SLOW COACHES they are in Berlin. They can't even print a pamphlet[c]! I've heard absolutely nothing more—it's enough to drive one insane.

En attendant, vive la guerre![d] In 10 days' time they will, I hope, be at each other's throats in Alessandria or Casale, and then who knows what kind of foxes I shall be hunting next SEASON!

Your

F. E.

First published in: Marx and Engels, *Works,* First Russian Edition, Vol. XXII, Moscow, 1929

Printed according to the original

Published in English for the first time

237

MARX TO ENGELS

IN MANCHESTER

[London,] 12 April 1859

Dear Engels,

Yesterday Lassalle wrote to me about your pamphlet[e] as follows:

---

[a] F. Engels, 'War Inevitable'. - [b] F. Engels, 'Chances of the Impending War'. - [c] This refers to Engels' *Po and Rhine.* - [d] In the meantime, three cheers for war! - [e] *Po and Rhine*

'Engels' pamphlet came out 3 days ago. Today I am sending him two copies by book post, as I shall do each day for 6 days in succession. For this is the only way we could devise' (!) 'of *avoiding* heavy postal charges on the one hand and, on the other, *preventing certain persons from guessing who was the pamphlet's author.* Write and tell him this.'[a]

Have you ever known such tomfoolery? To *distract* attention from you, they send you copies by book post '6 days in succession'!

Of the thing itself Lassalle writes:

'The pamphlet is truly impressive by reason of the pungency and sterling quality of the strategic knowledge evinced therein.'

(The 'pungency' of 'knowledge' may be regarded as a *lapsus pennae.*[b])

As to my own affair,[c] Lassalle writes:

'Duncker tells me that the instalments will be ready by mid-May.'

(So that's another month's delay.)

'He maintains he is getting on with the printing as quickly as he can. At any rate you are *utterly* wrong in supposing that he is deliberately dragging his feet. He's always rather slow.'

What I *do* know, however, is that another 10 days have gone by without my getting a proof-sheet.

Apropos. The *Neue Zeit* is on its last legs. Mr Edgar, who actually ended up by gracing its columns with a short story of his own contriving,[d] resigned a week ago—realising that the world was thoroughly unamenable to his genius. Last Saturday[e] it came out as a half number, and this week will probably see the end of it. The *Hermann,* too, according to current rumour, will soon depart this life. A good thing the curs snatched so eagerly at the opportunity of thus shamelessly laying bare their nonentity before all the world. Kinkel has KILLED the Kinkel humbug with his own hand. The CLOWN,[f] for his part, has found out just how 'easy' it is to take our place in communist literature.

Salut.

Your

K. M.

---

[a] Here and below Marx quotes Lassalle's letter to him of 8 April 1859 (the italics are Marx's). - [b] slip of the pen - [c] i.e. the publication of the book *A Contribution to the Critique of Political Economy* - [d] E. Bauer, 'Das Kloster', *Die Neue Zeit,* Nos. 38-42, 19 and 26 March and 2, 10 and 16 April 1859. - [e] 9 April - [f] Edgar Bauer

You explained the Austrian plan of attack in the *Tribune*[a] just as you describe it.

Pas trop de zèle![b]

First published abridged in *Der Briefwechsel zwischen F. Engels und K. Marx*, Bd. 2, Stuttgart, 1913 and in full in: Marx and Engels, *Works*, First Russian Edition, Vol. XXII, Moscow, 1929

Printed according to the original

Published in English for the first time

238

MARX TO ENGELS

IN MANCHESTER

London, 16 April [1859]

Dear Engels,

I trust that by the time you get this note your toothache will have gone. It's a fiendish thing.

MEANWHILE I have made arrangements which, within a short time, will double my income and thus put an end to the habitual misery. Friedländer, Lassalle's cousin (sometime editor along with Elsner and Co. of the *Neue Oder-Zeitung*), present editor of the *Presse* in Vienna (which, *en passant*, has 24,000 subscribers), offered, in January 1858, to appoint me correspondent to his paper.[254] I turned this down at the time because he stipulated that only Bonaparte, not Palmerston, be attacked. Now he has renewed the offer, ALL CONDITIONS LAID ASIDE. Since, however, this will *as a rule* involve only 1 article (20 frs) per week, it is comparatively unimportant. But I am at the same time to be their despatcher of telegrams (in French), 10 frs per telegram, and this, though time-consuming, is lucrative.

The only point that remains to be settled is that of instructions to a banking house in London, since telegraphing necessitates considerable expenditure. Negotiations—before the terms were SETTLED—extended over 3 weeks. It was only yesterday that I sent a definite answer to a letter received the same day from Vienna. So it will be 8-10 days before the thing gets under way.

---

[a] F. Engels, 'Chances of the Impending War' - [b] Not too much zeal! (The dictum is attributed to Talleyrand.)

MEANWHILE the interest on our most valuable silver, watches, etc., is due for payment next Tuesday. By private TRANSACTIONS with the PAWNBROKER my wife has already put off the date of foreclosure for 3 weeks, but Tuesday is the *ultimus terminus*. So my request that you send me a few pounds goes hand in hand with the hope that this will definitely be the last time and the tax upon you will cease for good.

Be so kind as to send 1 copy[a] for me. As soon as you are in possession of several, Freiligrath and Pfänder ought each to have one.

Salut.

Your

K. M.

First published abridged in *Der Briefwechsel zwischen F. Engels und K. Marx*, Bd. 2, Stuttgart, 1913 and in full in: Marx and Engels, *Works*, First Russian Edition, Vol. XXII, Moscow, 1929

Printed according to the original

Published in English for the first time

239

MARX TO ENGELS

IN MANCHESTER

[London,] 19 April [1859]

Dear Engels,

1. £5 ARRIVED. BEST THANKS.
2. I shall look out the *Tribunes* for you and send them IN THE COURSE OF THIS WEEK.
3. The *Tribune* which arrived today (dated *5 April*) contains an attack (enclosed),[b] probably by some idiot of a Hungarian, which you should answer by *Friday at the latest*. The ANSWER of the '14TH INST'[c] to which the idiot alludes is not to hand. However his own REPETITION will tell you everything he said in 'HIS SHORT ANSWER'.[401]
4. What did the Augsburg *Allgemeine Zeitung* say about your *Tribune* articles[402]?

---

[a] F. Engels, *Po and Rhine*. - [b] [A.] Asbóth, '"Chances of the Impending War". To the Editor of *The N. Y. Tribune*'. *New-York Daily Tribune*, No. 5602, 5 April 1859. - [c] [A.] A[sbóth,] '"The Austrian Hold on Italy". To the Editor of *The N. Y. Tribune*', *New-York Daily Tribune*, No. 5581, 11 March 1859.

5. Yesterday I saw Duncker's advertisement for *Po and Rhine* in the *Hamburger Correspondent*.

6. I myself have so far received 8 proof-sheets.[a] So the thing's approaching its end, but no doubt it will be another fortnight before Duncker sends any more.

7. *Ad vocem*[b] Lassalle, I shall deal with this *inter alia* in a longer letter tomorrow.

Salut.

Your
K. M.

First published in *Der Briefwechsel zwischen F. Engels und K. Marx*, Bd. 2, Stuttgart, 1913

Printed according to the original

Published in English for the first time

240

MARX TO FERDINAND LASSALLE[403]

IN BERLIN

London, 19 April 1859

Dear Lassalle,

I sent no separate acknowledgment of the £14 10/- because the letter was registered. But I should have written earlier had I not been plagued by a damned 'cousin from Holland',[c] who laid claim to my surplus working time in THE MOST CRUEL MANNER.

HE IS NOW GONE, and so I can breathe again.

Friedländer has written to me.[d] The terms are not as favourable as those originally communicated to you, but are nonetheless 'RESPECTABLE'.[254] Once a few subsidiary points have been settled between us—which will, I think, be done in the course of this week—I shall write to him.

Here in England the class struggle is progressing in a most gratifying way. Unfortunately there is no longer any Chartist paper in existence and hence I had to give up literary collaboration with that movement ABOUT two years ago.

Now I come to *Franz von Sickingen*. *D'abord*,[e] I must applaud

---

[a] K. Marx, *A Contribution to the Critique of Political Economy*. - [b] As to - [c] Johann Carl Juta - [d] See this volume, p. 416. - [e] First

both composition and action, and that's more than one can say of any other modern German play. IN THE SECOND INSTANCE, and aside from any reactions of a purely critical nature, the work excited me very much at the first reading and hence will induce this reaction to an even greater degree in more emotionally inclined readers. And that is another and very important aspect.

Now for THE OTHER SIDE OF THE MEDAL: *Firstly*—and this is purely a question of form—since you have chosen to write in verse, you could have put a touch more artistry into the iambics. However, though your neglecting to do so might well shock a *professional poet*, I regard it by and large as a merit, our breed of poetical epigones having retained nothing but formal polish. *Secondly*, the implicit conflict is not just tragic; it is the tragic conflict upon which the revolutionary party of 1848-49 justly foundered. Hence making it the fulcrum of a modern tragedy can only meet with my wholehearted approval. But then, I ask myself, is the theme in question suitable for the portrayal of that conflict? Balthasar may indeed imagine that had Sickingen not pretended that his rebellion was a knightly feud, but had instead raised the standard of opposition to the emperor and open war against the princes, he would have won. But are we able to share that illusion? Sickingen (and with him Hutten, more or less) went under, not because of his cunning, but because, as a *knight* and as *representative of a declining class*, he rebelled against existing reality, or rather against the new form of existing reality. Strip Sickingen of the appurtenances of the individual and his particular education, natural disposition, etc., and you have—Götz von Berlichingen. In this latter, *miserable* fellow the tragic opposition between knights on the one hand and emperor and princes on the other is adequately personified and that is why Goethe rightly made him his hero.[a] In so far as Sickingen—and even Hutten up to a point, although in his case, as in that of all ideologists of a class, such assertions call for substantial modification—is fighting the princes (he turns against the emperor[b] only because the emperor of knights has become the emperor of princes), he is, in fact, nothing more than a Don Quixote, if with some historical justification. The fact that he begins his rebellion in the guise of a knightly feud merely means that he begins it in *knightly fashion*. Were he to begin it in any other way, he would have to appeal directly and at the very outset to the towns and the peasants, i.e. the very classes whose development=the negation of knighthood.

---

[a] J. W. Goethe, *Götz von Berlichingen*. - [b] Charles V

Unless, therefore, you wished to reduce the conflict to no more than what is portrayed in Götz von Berlichingen—and such was not your plan—Sickingen and Hutten were bound to go under because they imagined themselves to be revolutionaries (which cannot be said of Götz) and, just like the *cultivated* Polish aristocracy of 1830, turned themselves on the one hand into the organs of modern ideas while on the other actually representing a reactionary class interest.[404] The *aristocratic* representatives of revolution—behind whose catch-words of unity and liberty there still lingers the dream of the imperial past and of club-law—ought not in that case to monopolise the interest as you make them do; rather the representatives of the peasants (of these in particular) and of the revolutionary elements in the towns should provide an altogether significant and dynamic background. This would have enabled you to give expression in far greater measure precisely to the most modern ideas in their most unsophisticated form; whereas, in fact now, the dominant idea, apart from *religious* freedom, is civic *unity*. Then you would automatically have had to *'Shakespearise'* more, whereas your principal failing is, to my mind, *'Schillering'*, i.e. using individuals as mere mouthpieces for the spirit of the times. Have not you yourself—like your Franz von Sickingen—succumbed, to some extent, to the diplomatic error of regarding the Lutheran-knightly opposition as superior to the plebeian-Münzerian?

Again, I miss what is characteristic in the characters. I except Charles V, Balthasar and Richard of Trier. And was there ever a time of more robust character traits than the 16th century? To my mind Hutten is, to far too great a degree, merely a representative of 'enthusiasm', which is boring. Wasn't he also witty, an infernal wit, and hence hasn't he been done a grave injustice?

The extent to which even your Sickingen—who, by the way, is portrayed much too abstractly—suffers as a result of a conflict that is quite independent of all his personal calculations is evident from the necessity he is in of urging friendship with the towns, etc., upon his knights and, on the other hand, from the satisfaction with which he himself imposes club-law upon those same towns.

To come down to details, I would censure the sometimes excessive preoccupation of individuals with themselves—the result of your predilection for Schiller. E.g. on p. 121, when Hutten is telling Marie the history of his life, it would have been quite natural to make Marie say:

'The whole gamut of sensations',

etc., up to the words,

'And weighs more heavily on me than did the years'.

The preceding verses, from 'They say' to 'grown older', might follow *at this point*, but the comment, 'The virgin in a single night matures into a woman' (although showing that the love Marie knows is more than a mere abstraction), is completely pointless; still less should Marie have begun by reflecting upon her own 'ageing'. After recounting all that she had said during the 'one' hour, she might have given general expression to her feelings in the phrase about her "ageing'. Again, what offends me in the lines that follow is: 'I thought it was my *right*' (i.e. happiness). Why give the lie to the ingenuous view of the world which Marie has hitherto professed to hold, by turning it into a doctrine of rights? Maybe some other time I shall give you my opinion in greater detail.

I consider the scene between Sickingen and Charles V to be particularly felicitous, although the dialogue on both sides is rather too much in the nature of pleading; also the scenes in Trier. Hutten's lines about the sword I thought very fine.

Well, that's enough for this time.

You have made my wife into a special admirer of your play. Only Marie doesn't satisfy her.

Salut.

Your

K. M.

Apropos. There are some bad misprints in Engels' *Po and Rhine.* I append a list of them on the last page of this letter.[a]

First published in: *F. Lassale. Nachgelassene Briefe und Schriften*, Bd. III, Stuttgart-Berlin, 1922

Printed according to the original

[a] The list is in Marx's handwriting.

241

ENGELS TO ELISABETH ENGELS

IN ENGELSKIRCHEN

Manchester, 20 April 1859

Dear Mother,

At last a modicum of peace and quiet in which to write to you again. I got both your dear letters and am glad to hear that you are all well and that the Blank children have recovered from the measles. I am very well; my back teeth are gradually breaking up, but not too painfully on the whole, otherwise there's absolutely nothing wrong with me; my appetite and digestion are first-rate and there hasn't been a trace of the old troubles.

So little Delius has finally been unable after all to help coming the Bradfordian over you. I should have thought he would mind his p's and q's a bit more, but since he has evidently begun to stir up these little troubles, I can only tell you that in Bradford talking big is in the very air, and that, in the long run, it's a sheer impossibility for a Bradfordian to tell the truth. Now that the little chap shares lodgings with Wilhelm Kutter, who is the greatest tall story teller under the sun, he seems increasingly to be acquiring the same virtue. If a Bradfordian were to tell me that twice two makes four, I would immediately begin to doubt the accuracy of the multiplication table. I'm warning you of this in advance, so that you're not too hard on the little chap; Bradfordians are all alike, they're fluent liars. The story about the horse originated simply from my having told the owner that, if he would sell the animal for less than £120, he was to *let me know*—nothing more. It's a long way from there to buying. Were it now to be offered me at £120, I would think twice before giving £100 for it, since it is in fact rather too light for me and for the same money I could get a very fine, strong hunter. Come to that, it's not such a tall story about his bolting into a shop. Any horse that's really mettlesome and has done little or nothing for a whole week will, with an indifferent rider, engage in all manner of strange antics, and whether the pair of them break their necks is entirely a matter of luck. But no horse is going to find it easy to take me into a shop against my will, you may be sure of that.

The other story, the one about Carl Siebel, is still more of a fabrication. Far from leading a dissipated life, he spends nearly every evening at home, hardly ever goes out and has hardly any acquaintances. I don't believe there are twenty young men of his age in the whole of Manchester who live as soberly as he does. True, in the early days he did once or twice drink a glass too many, and indulged in all kinds of childish pranks but, being in the company of myself and a few acquaintances and seeing that we found nothing to admire in these puerilities, he gave it up. Altogether he's still half a child, terribly immature and incapable of coping with the most everyday problems. But time will take care of that. We Barmen lads all seem to have this in common—that it takes us a long time to emerge from uncouth adolescence; I must have been just as queer a fish when I was 23. His parents, by the way, must have gone about it very oddly if they could do nothing with the lad, for he has an excellent side to him, namely awareness of his own weaknesses, and, far from being self-willed, is on the contrary very amenable to persuasion. What prepossesses me in his favour is that, despite all the fulsome praise that has been lavished on his verses, he knows at the bottom of his heart that these are nothing but immature, unfinished, superficial affairs, and the nice young chap was awfully grateful to me when I explained this to him good-humouredly but no less clearly for that; for after he had presented me with the whole of his immortal works, I told him outright that, while they showed talent, it was wasted talent, and that none of his stuff was of any value as a work of art. The lad must really have been very much of a dilettante in Berlin, and in danger of going to the dogs among the belletristic riff-raff of the literary world there. Whenever I see him, I regularly take him to task on the subject and tell him he should turn his back on versifying for a time and make a thorough study of the classical poets of all nations in order to educate his very confused taste a little, and to learn German, of which he still knows nothing. If he does this, he may yet become a very steady sort of chap. His parents, by the way, ought to have sufficient gumption to place themselves on a rational footing with him—one that he can tolerate—or so arrange matters that he can gradually find the means and the opportunity of setting himself up, here or elsewhere, as an independent business man. The boy knows that he can at any time earn sufficient to live on by his writing, and if his dear papa has neither the intelligence nor the tact to treat him like a grown-up person, he has only himself to blame if the chap finally gets sick of the whole thing and decides to do nothing but write, when he would quite certainly *go completely to the dogs*. Old Siebel may perhaps imagine that I'm putting all kinds of nonsense into his son's head, but he can rest assured that I am bringing my whole influence to bear on him to deter him from over-much writing (because the boy isn't yet ripe for it) and to make him realise that there's no more wretched existence than dependence on earnings from literary work, and that the sooner he comes to terms with his prosaic, bourgeois trade, the better (for without it, since he is *au fond*[a] reluctant to learn, there would be nothing to restrain him and he'd go to the dogs altogether). If he does this and gains a little more experience of life and sheds his awkwardness, I have no doubt he will become a very steady sort of chap and achieve something worthwhile in the literary field too. I like the boy very much since he is exceedingly good-natured, not at all conceited and very frank and straightforward. I normally see him twice a week or so.

I didn't know that E. Blank was in London and hope that he'll come up here one of these days; anyhow, a few months ago he promised he would. War or no war, by the way, let nothing prevent you from coming over here this summer—I'm counting firmly on it. As you know, we're bound for Scotland this summer, and in the meantime you can take another look at your Walter Scott so that you'll know what's what.

But now I must stop as it's 7 o'clock and I still have sundry business letters to write. I had really meant to enclose a note for Father, but it is absolutely impossible and I must have the statements done for him as well. So I'll write to him as soon as I can, in two or three days' time.

Meanwhile give him my love, and also to my brothers and sisters and their families.

With much love from your son,

Friedrich

You needn't, of course, tell Mrs Siebel every word I've said about Carl.

From the bottom of my heart I wish you many happy returns of the day, and hope that I shall be able to do so many, many times again.

First published in *Deutsche Revue*, Jg. 46, Bd. 2, 1921

Printed according to the original

Published in English for the first time

[a] at bottom

242

MARX TO ENGELS

IN MANCHESTER

[London,] 22 April 1859

Dear Frederick,

I have MODIFIED your ARTICLE[a] to accord with the latest NEWS.

You didn't, I suppose, waste your time (as I was obliged to do) wading through last Monday's parliamentary debates.[b] Their GIST was as follows:

1. England has been duped throughout the negotiations.
2. England is decidedly pro-Austrian.

ad 1. The English ministers had announced once before that everything was SETTLED. This was when the news of the evacuation of Rome[405] was appearing in all the papers. From statements made in the House of Lords it follows: that the Pope[c] really had requested that his territory be evacuated. France had repeatedly complained to the English about the falsity of her position in Rome. She had wished to withdraw but was prevented, on the one hand, by the Pope's apprehensions and, on the other, by the Austrians' refusal similarly to withdraw. This was actually the *official* PRETEXT Boustrapa[40] gave England to justify the scene with the Austrian ambassador on 1 January.[406] WELL, the Pope scotched that PRETEXT. Austria *ACTUALLY* withdrew 2 battalions from Bologna and had given ORDERS for the remaining troops to leave. Then Bonaparte discovered a pretext for *not* evacuating, and thus the whole business fell through. This put Mr Derby into a very BAD TEMPER and, TO SOOTH HIM, Bonaparte unbosomed himself about the 'ITALIAN QUESTION' to Lord Cowley, who telegraphed London saying he found his demands 'SATISFACTORY'. Thereupon Cowley was sent to Vienna bearing Bonaparte's demands which *England* had accepted. (This man Cowley is the selfsame swine who, in Vienna in 1848/49, intrigued against the German revolution.) This was at the end of February. Austria, being exceedingly reluctant to engage in a war and having at the time not progressed nearly so far in the matter of armaments as by the middle of March, *accepted*

---

[a] 'The State of the Question.—Germany Arming' - [b] An account of the debates in the British Parliament on 18 April 1859 was published in *The Times*, No. 23284, 19 April 1859. - [c] Pius IX

everything. When Cowley arrived in London on his way back to Paris, both 'he' and the 'Ministry', as Derby himself says, were fully convinced that everything was SETTLED, and *again discredited themselves* by making a fresh statement to that effect before Parliament. So Cowley departs in sanguine mood for Paris. Here he learns that they've been playing blind man's buff with him and that, *at Russia's suggestion,* Boustrapa has agreed to A GENERAL CONGRESS at which, again *at Russia's suggestion,* only the 5 great powers were to be represented, i.e. Sardinia was to be excluded. Derby declared outright that *Russia's intervention* (although agreed with France; but *Bonaparte,* of course, could not reject CONDITIONS put to Austria by England in *his* name) was alone to blame for the fact that peace had not been achieved. On the same day Palmerston said in the House OF COMMONS that he didn't (OF COURSE) blame Russia; had England's mediation been successful Russia would not have played the role she would certainly play at a congress and which was her due where European questions were concerned. Although with very bad grace, Derby accepted the Russian proposal under certain conditions, of which THE PRINCIPAL was that the TERRITORIAL SETTLEMENTS of the Treaty of Vienna of 1815[407] should not be infringed. Austria, who had already assumed that everything was settled, now clearly perceived that war had been *decided upon* and that an attempt was being made to lead her by the nose. Hence her reply to the new English proposal was the outrageous demand that, by way of a preliminary to the congress, Sardinia must disarm. Whereupon Derby proposed to Bonaparte that Sardinia should be induced to consent to this outrage on condition that both France and England simultaneously undertook to guarantee her against a breach of the peace by Austria during the congress. That ass Bonaparte rejected this. Had he accepted he could have got his agents to stage some sort of fracas on the Austro-Piedmontese border, when England would have been BOUND DOWN TO AN OFFENSIVE TREATY WITH FRANCE AND SARDINIA AGAINST AUSTRIA, and Palmerston would have certainly compelled the Tories TO BE AS GOOD AS THEIR WORD. The Austrians, for their part, were alarmed by the ease with which, under certain circumstances, England was prepared to enter into an offensive alliance against them. They therefore promptly declared themselves in favour of the English proposal, and made Sardinia's disarmament a general disarmament. Then came the row as to whether disarmament should take place before the MEETING of the CONGRESS, as maintained by Austria, or after it, as maintained by Bonaparte, and then as to whether or not Sardinia should be admitted, etc. In short, all the new difficulties stemmed from Bonaparte, 1) the QUIBBLES about disarmament; 2) after all, *he* and *Russia* had *proposed* the exclusion of Sardinia from the congress. So enraged was Derby last Monday that he is said to have literally shouted when he declared that England would now make one more, *ULTIMATE* proposal; but he was weary of TRIFLING and if that one failed he would no longer act as mediator, etc.

ad 2. Bonaparte could accept these latter proposals since they were *detrimental* solely to Austria in so far as she was in the lead with her armaments. He *had* to accept them if Derby was not to be given a pretext for taking an outright stand against him. Austria had to reject them if she was not to deprive herself of every advantage, etc. Bonaparte, who had counted on Derby's fall and Palmerston's accession, was IN A PLIGHT THE WORSE since in their speeches Derby and Disraeli had plainly indicated that they were tired of being duped by Bonaparte and Russia and had, moreover, definitely sided with Austria. Malmesbury said he failed to understand *upon what pretext* Bonaparte had intervened in the Italian imbroglio. Derby said that England would at first observe ARMED NEUTRALITY, but turn against any power which 'for no good reason' instigated a war. Derby said that England's interests in the Adriatic did not permit him to look on with folded arms; and that he would regard an attack on Trieste almost as a *casus belli.* Disraeli said that Austria had behaved with 'DIGNIFIED MODERATION' and that Sardinia was 'AMBIGUOUS, VEXING AND EVEN AMBITIOUS'. Finally they all said that the treaties of 1815 must be MAINTAINED, and repeatedly emphasised, with immediate reference to the TERRITORIAL SETTLEMENT IN ITALY, that those treaties 'INTENDED PUTTING A CHECK UPON THE ENCROACHING AMBITION OF FRANCE'.

This much is certain: The ruse whereby Derby, instead of resigning, consigned Parliament to the devil, thus temporarily banishing Palmerston into private life, has placed the Russo-French game in a serious dilemma.

There are only two alternatives.

Either Austria allows herself to be intimidated by minatory TELEGRAMS from London and Berlin, and WITHDRAWS Gyulay's ultimatum to Piedmont,[408] in *which* case not even God will be able to help Bonaparte. For then he will, IN FACT, be compelled to *disarm* and be treated by the army as a Soulouque. As it is, the workers in Paris have been infuriated by the turpitude of Blanqui's deportation to Cayenne.[409] Or else Austria wearies of diplomatic trifling and marches on Turin. In which case Mr Bonaparte has won a diplomatic victory in as much as Austria will have been the first to declare war; but that diplomatic victory will have been bought at the expense of AN UGLY MILITARY DEFEAT. In which case I don't give 4 MONTHS PURCHASE FOR HIS CROWN AND DYNASTY.

I'll send you the *Tribunes* tomorrow.

Apropos.

The great imperial Vogt[410] has written Freiligrath an epistle in which he informs him that this imperial gang is bringing out a new newspaper in Zurich (or Berne, I forget which).[411] He invited Freiligrath to write for the feuilleton and to enlist the profound Bucher as political correspondent.

The platform upon which imperial Vogt proposes to build a new 'party' and which has, as he himself puts it, been most warmly welcomed by A. Herzen, is this: Germany surrenders her extraterritorial possessions. Does not support Austria. French despotism is transitory, Austrian permanent. Both despots to be allowed to bleed to death. (Even some predilection for Bonaparte in evidence.) Armed neutrality for Germany. A revolutionary movement in Germany, as Vogt 'knows on the best authority', is not to be thought of DURING OUR LIFETIME. CONSEQUENTLY, as soon as Austria has been ruined by Bonaparte, the fatherland will experience the spontaneous beginnings of a moderate, liberal-national development *à la* imperial Regency, and Vogt may yet become Prussian court jester. From Vogt's letter it is evident that he believes Freiligrath to be no longer connected with us in any way. The ignorance of this imperial Vogt about the people he is dealing with! Bucher, as an Urquhartite, is an *Austrian*. The great Blind, ON THE OTHER HAND, finding himself in the dilemma of being anti-Bonaparte as a German and anti-Austria as √Rotteck, is AT THE PRESENT MOMENT convening a 'German Parliament',[a] as the telegraph will soon announce in Manchester.[412]

Salut.

Your

K. M.

First published in *Der Briefwechsel zwischen F. Engels und K. Marx*, Bd. 2, Stuttgart, 1913

Printed according to the original

Published in English for the first time

[a] K. Blind, 'Der Befreier Napoleon', *Hermann*, No. 15, 16 April 1859.

243

MARX TO FERDINAND LASSALLE[82]

IN BERLIN

London, 5 May 1859
9 Grafton Terrace, Maitland Park,
Haverstock Hill

Dear Lassalle,

From the enclosed letter dated April 12,[a] which I should like to have back, you will see that there is a very considerable difference between the terms offered me by your cousin Friedländer and the terms you originally communicated to me.[b] Nevertheless I replied *by return* accepting them.[413] I merely noted:

1. that I could not make disbursements for telegrams, a point, by the by, that hardly needed mentioning and had been anticipated in your letter;

2. that, if we came to an arrangement, I should like (though I did not make it a *conditio sine qua*[c]) to be able to draw on them with a BANKER here for articles, etc., sent, as is done in the case of the *Tribune*.

So far there has been no answer, which I find strange. If the editors have changed their minds, they might have had the decency to inform me. As you are aware, I did not in any way thrust myself forward in this matter. But, having accepted, I made one or two preliminary approaches to English newspapers, etc., and I am specially anxious not to be compromised in the eyes of these people and other acquaintances whom I have informed of the matter for business reasons. That I, for my part, have not yet sent off any article is only natural, since there is still no firm engagement.

The elections here have not, alas, turned out to be sufficiently Tory.[385] Had this been the case there would, BY and BY, have been the beginnings of a revolutionary movement here. Palmerston's return to the FOREIGN MINISTRY can now, AFTER SOME SHUFFLING, be

---

[a] A letter from M. Friedländer inviting Marx to contribute to the Vienna newspaper *Die Presse*. - [b] See this volume, pp. 408-09. - [c] necessary condition

regarded as certain and hence Russia will again be in direct control of English policy.

Salut.

Your

K. M.

First published in: *F. Lassalle. Nachgelassene Briefe und Schriften*, Bd. III, Stuttgart-Berlin, 1922

Printed according to the original

244

MARX TO ENGELS[20]

IN MANCHESTER

[London,] 6 May 1859

DEAR Frederick,

Your article received.[414] You will have seen from a telegraphic despatch that Hess has come out against Gyulay's plan (perhaps one should describe it as *absence of plan*). Looked at from our—i.e. a revolutionary—POINT OF VIEW, it would be by no means undesirable if Austria were to begin either by suffering a reverse or, which is morally the same thing, by withdrawing into Lombardy again. This will greatly complicate matters and thus allow sufficient time for things to come to a head in Paris. All in all the state of affairs is such that, no matter on what side BLUNDERS occur, they will necessarily redound to our advantage. If, at the outset, Austria were to beat the Piedmontese army, take Turin and thrash the French as they debouched from the Alps, Russia might immediately turn against Bonaparte[415]—having in any case not yet *actually* entered into any obligations against Germany, and our rotten Prussian government would be extricated from the only dilemma that might cost it its neck. Again: Such a devastating defeat at the very beginning could bring about a mutiny in the French army and an anti-Bonaparte revolution in Paris. What then? At *this* juncture the upshot would be victorious armed intervention by the Holy Alliance[416] against a potential revolutionary government in Paris, something which certainly doesn't come into our *calcul.*[a]

[a] calculations

Even Radetzky had the revolutionary ardour of 1848 in his veins. On the other hand I believe that on both sides, Austrian and French, the war will now be conducted with reactionary mediocrity.

It was wrong of you not to have sent us at least two more pamphlets[a]—for Pfänder, who sent off your manuscript under his own name, and for Freiligrath. It would also be fitting to send a copy to P. Imandt (DUNDEE SEMINARY, *Dundee*). You must pay some heed to party relations and keep the chaps in good humour.

Apropos, I deleted the whole of the preamble to your last Friday's article,[b] firstly because I had my MISGIVINGS about the Austrians; secondly because it is absolutely essential that we do not identify our cause with that of the present German governments.

In my view, the worthy Palmerston will very shortly be back at the helm as FOREIGN MINISTER or War Minister. Those dolts of Tories are indeed making things too easy for him. First they go and spoil the Austrians' game by their miserable SHOW OF MEDIATION. Then, as soon as the Franco-Russian treaty has been made known, they bend every FORCE to deny its existence, so as to prove THAT THEY HAVE NOT BEEN TAKEN BY SURPRISE. This in turn gives *The Times* the opportunity to deride them and adopt a patriotic attitude towards Russia.[c] But the LONG AND SHORT of it is that *The Times*, like all the rest of Palmerston's papers (though these, depending on their allotted role, either oppose or support the various powers involved), is hinting at the necessity of reappointing THE TRULY BRITISH MINISTER[141] (*The Morning Advertiser* and *The Daily Telegraph*, which write for the MOB, are saying it openly). The wretched Tories ought instead to have 'lent credence to' the Russo-French treaty and seized on the chance of going for Pam. They had the best of OPPORTUNITIES. Firstly, Pam was in Compiègne[356] when the whole plan was hatched. Secondly, Mr Whiteside, speaking on behalf of the ministry, had in fact already told silly old John Bull[d] what had long been apparent from the Blue Books,[38] namely that in 1848 Austria approached Palmerston and offered to *relinquish the whole of Lombardy* but to install an Italian government in Venice under an Austrian ARCHDUKE, if he would mediate.[e] Piedmont had approached him at the same time, France ditto. What did Pam do?

---

[a] F. Engels, *Po and Phine*. - [b] 'Prospects of the War' - [c] 'In our long list of telegrams...', *The Times*, No. 23295, 2 May 1859. - [d] A reference to J. Whiteside's speech in the House of Commons delivered on 25 March 1859, *The Times*, No. 23264, 26 March 1859. - [e] Marx refers to the Blue Book *Correspondence Respecting the Affairs of Italy* published in 1849.

He rejected the proposal, on the PRETEXT that Venice, too, must be given up altogether. He gave this answer after a three weeks' silence. As soon as Radetzky was victorious he called upon the Austrians to carry out the plan they had divulged to him. In the Hungarian affair (with reference this time to the CONDITIONS upon which the already desperate Hungarians were willing to submit) he performed the same manoeuvre. The fellow's return to the ministry constitutes A REAL DANGER. In Germany, by the by, the fellows are beginning to see through him. In a book by Prof. Wurm of Hamburg (a history of the war in the East),[a] and a book on Nicholas by another German, whose name I can't recall, Pam is attacked outright as a Russian agent.

Ad vocem BUSINESS.[b] That ass Friedländer wrote to me on 12 April but had forgotten the crucial point, i.e. instructions to a banking-house. Instead, he spoke of an 'advance'. This last is NONSENSE. £8-10, and often £15, will be needed each week for telegrams. I wrote and told the ass so. Up till now no answer, although he regularly sends me the Vienna *Presse* (from which I gather that it now has 26,000 subscribers). Yesterday I wrote Lassalle a fulminating letter.[c] I see from the *Presse* that Lassalle has embarked on his articles and telegraphic despatches for that paper with great zeal albeit small talent. However he did not accept this post until I had 'given him permission' in writing,[d] not wanting—or so he says—to take the political risk without my CONSENT. It would be a rum business, would it not, if all the transaction led to was Lassalle's installing himself in that quarter? It's possible, however, that the delay is due to Friedländer's difficulty in arranging the financial side in Vienna during the present TROUBLES. MEANWHILE, out of impatience, I am devoting myself to algebra.

Salut.

Is Lupus in Manchester?

Your

K. M.

First published abridged in *Der Briefwechsel zwischen F. Engels und K. Marx*, Bd. 2, Stuttgart, 1913 and in full in: Marx and Engels, *Works*, First Russian Edition, Vol. XXII, Moscow, 1929

Printed according to the original

Published in English in full for the first time

---

[a] F. Wurm, *Diplomatische Geschichte der Orientalischen Frage*. - [b] See this volume, p. 416. - [c] Ibid., p. 409. - [d] Ibid., pp. 429-30.

245

MARX TO MAX FRIEDLÄNDER

IN VIENNA

London, 16 May 1859
9 Grafton Terrace, Maitland Park,
Haverstock Hill

Dear Sir,

I have been receiving the Vienna *Presse* regularly and my debt to you for sending it is the greater in that it throws light on conditions in Austria at this important juncture.

I have not yet had a reply to the letter I wrote you some weeks ago.[413] If, by chance, the proposed arrangement[a] has come to nothing as a result of the DERANGEMENTS of the Vienna money market,[417] *I would beg you to advise me of this by return*, for I have made certain agreements regarding telegrams with newspapers over here which commit me to financial outlays and which I shall accordingly terminate forthwith.

Yours very truly,
Dr K. Marx

First published in: Marx and Engels, *Works*, Second Russian Edition, Vol. 29, Moscow, 1962

Printed according to the original

Published in English for the first time

246

MARX TO ENGELS

IN MANCHESTER

[London,] 16 May 1859

Dear Engels,

From the enclosed letter of Lassalle's,[418] which I must have back *by return*, you will see how far things have progressed with the

[a] Marx's work for the Vienna newspaper *Die Presse* (see this volume, p. 432).

Vienna BUSINESS. I wrote to Friedländer at once. The fact is that Lassalle doesn't know that I get the *Presse* every day—I enclose a few excerpts from it—and thus have seen that, up to the time of my letter,[a] he regularly contributed to the paper, but that the latter stopped his telegrams from Berlin on account of their inordinate length; moreover his articles were inept and would be something of an embarrassment to *any* paper. It is possible that the whole business is off, but it is also possible that the COMMERCIAL PANIC in Vienna, comparable only to the one in Hamburg,[419] has so far prevented the chaps from making any ARRANGEMENT. *Nous verrons.*[b]

More in my next—highly comical, too. This much today: our[c] *ex-gérant*[d] Korff has been sentenced in New Orleans to 12 years penal servitude for FORGERY OF A BILL.

Ex-imperial regent Vogt[410] has sold himself to Bonaparte.[420]

Salut.

Your

K. M.

First published abridged in *Der Briefwechsel zwischen F. Engels und K. Marx*, Bd. 2, Stuttgart, 1913 and in full in: Marx and Engels, *Works*, First Russian Edition, Vol. XXII, Moscow, 1929

Printed according to the original

Published in English for the first time

247

MARX TO ENGELS[1]

IN MANCHESTER

[London,] 18 May 1859

Dear Engels,

Lassalle's letter[418] contains several POINTS upon which I shall haul him over the coals. *D'abord,*[e] the laddie talks about what he 'is to do for me'. But all I asked of him was that he, who set the whole thing in train and whose articles I was constantly seeing in the *Presse,* should enlighten me as to the mysterious silence from Vienna.[f] This was *his* BUSINESS. Secondly, he makes it look as

---

[a] See this volume, pp. 407-09. - [b] We shall see. - [c] A reference to the *Neue Rheinische Zeitung*. - [d] ex-manager - [e] First - [f] See this volume, p. 429.

though he had contributed to the *Presse* only after a tremendous struggle, on 'my' insistence. But at one point in the same letter he admits that he had already begun sending articles to Vienna *before* I had stated my case. Then, however, he proceeds to reverse the 'nexus'. When he sent me Friedländer's offer he drivelled away for two pages about whether or not he should write to Vienna, and made the thing dependent on my decision. *D'abord*, it went without saying that, if I thought writing for the *Presse* good enough for me, I wouldn't think it beneath Lassalle. Moreover, I could see from his letter how anxious he was to obtain my CONSENT. Why then do we now have this self-aggrandizing misrepresentation of the causal nexus? What he says about 'bias' and having written to Friedländer 'telling him off' about it, is NONSENSE. As Austrian papers go and considering the circumstances, the Vienna *Presse* is edited cleverly and fairly, with far greater tact than Lassalle would be able to command. Finally, I did not invite the laddie's instructions as to what is or is not 'worthy' of me. I consider it RATHER ARROGANT of him to drop hints to me on the subject. If Friedländer manages to SETTLE the financial side, I shall *positivement* stand by my decision, which is in no way altered by the fact that Lassalle's articles don't seem to suit Friedländer. From recent issues of the *Presse* I see that the number of its subscribers has risen to 27,000.

Lassalle's pamphlet[a] is an ENORMOUS BLUNDER.[421] The publication of your 'anonymous' pamphlet[b] made him envious. Admittedly the position of the revolutionary party in Germany is difficult at present, yet a little critical analysis of the CIRCUMSTANCES suffices to make it plain. As regards the 'governments', it is clear from all points of view, if only in the interests of Germany's *existence*, that they must be urged *not* to remain *neutral* but to be, as you rightly say, *patriotic*. But the affair can be given *revolutionary* pertinence simply by stressing opposition *to Russia* more strongly than opposition to Boustrapa.[40] That's what Lassalle should have done vis-à-vis the *Neue Preussische Zeitung*'s anti-French clamour. Indeed, it is *this* point which, as the war goes on, will in practice involve the German governments in high treason and at which it will be possible to seize them by the throat. Incidentally, if Lassalle takes it upon himself to speak in the name of the party, he must in future either resign himself to being publicly disavowed by us, since circumstances are too grave to take account of feelings, or else he must first ascertain the views held by others besides himself before following

[a] *Der italienische Krieg und die Aufgabe Preußens* - [b] *Po and Rhine*

the joint inspiration of fire and logic.[422] We must now absolutely insist on party discipline, otherwise everything will be in the soup.

The confusion presently reigning in men's minds has reached a curious peak. *D'abord*, THERE IS that traitor to the Empire, the 'imperial regent',[410] who has received cash payments from Paris.[420] In the Hamburg *Freischütz*, Mr Meyen praises Vogt's piece.[a] There is a type of vulgar democrat (some sincere ones among them believe that an Austrian defeat, complemented by revolution in Hungary+Galicia, etc., would bring about revolution in Germany. The dolts forget that revolution in Germany *now*=disorganisation of her armies and would benefit, not the revolutionaries, but Russia and Boustrapa), a type, I say, of vulgar democrat who delights in being able to pipe the same tune as the decembristising[138] Hungarians (Bangyas all) and Poles (in the Prussian chamber a few days ago Mr Cieszkowski called Nicholas the Poles' 'great Slav ally') and Italians. Another lot—e.g. Blind who seeks to combine patriotism and democratism—are making asses of themselves (and old Uhland too among their number) by demanding war *with* Austria against Bonaparte and, at the same time, an imperial parliament. *D'abord*, the asses fail to see that the conditions for the fulfilment of this repellent wish are entirely wanting. Secondly, however, they pay so little heed to what is really happening as to be wholly unaware that, in the only part of Germany which counts, namely *Prussia*, the bourgeois are proud of their Chambers, whose power is bound to grow with the growing embarrassment of the GOVERNMENT; that these bourgeois are justifiably (as recent transactions in the Chambers go to show) disinclined to be dictated to by Badeners and Württembergers under the style of 'parliament', just as the Prussian government is reluctant to be ruled by Austria under the style of 'Federal Diet'[423]; that these bourgeois know from the experience of 1848 that a parliament alongside their Chambers destroys the power of the latter while itself remaining nothing more than a phantasm. In fact there is much more revolutionary purchase in the Prussian Chambers, which have to vote budgets and which, in certain EVENTUALITIES, have part of the ARMY and the Berlin mob behind them, than in a DEBATING CLUB under the style of 'Imperial Parliament'. That Badeners, Württembergers and OTHER SMALL DEER take a different

---

[a] E. Meyen's review of K. Vogt's book *Studien zur gegenwärtigen Lage Europas* was published anonymously under the title 'Oesterreich und Deutschland' in *Der Freischütz*, Nos. 55 and 56, 7 and 10 May 1859.

view because of their own importance goes without saying. There is a very real fear among our own party friends and other sincere revolutionaries that war against Boustrapa would mean a reversion to 1813-15. Finally, those who speak for the Crédit mobilier[45] in Germany (*Kölnische Zeitung*, Fould-Oppenheim, etc.) naturally share the democrats' apprehensions and pin their hopes on the Prussian dynasty's traditional short-sighted perfidy (Peace of Basle,[424] etc.). On the other hand, a section of the democratic and revolutionary party feels bound for patriotic reasons to adopt a Jahn-Arndtian tone. In view of all these CONFUSIONS, and since I believe that Germany's fate is hanging in the balance, I think it behoves the two of us to issue a party manifesto.[425] If the Vienna business[a] is settled, you must come up for the purpose at Whitsun. If not, I shall come to Manchester.

From these GENERAL THINGS I NOW come to the STATE OF PARTIES (German) in London, and here I must recapitulate certain matters which I considered too boring to recount to you so long as they were still in progress.

First, you will recall that Mr Liebknecht introduced the CLOWN E. Bauer into the so-called Communist Society[426] just when I had publicly broken with Bauer and that the CLOWN took over the *Neue Zeit* in which the ignorant blockhead, by his EXAGGERATION of the few communist catch-phrases he had picked up from Scherzer, turned our party into a laughing-stock. For me it was a most disagreeable affair—not because of the few louts in London, but because of the malicious glee of the democratic crew, because of the FALSE APPEARANCES evoked by smartly sending COPIES of the filthy rag to Germany and the UNITED STATES, because of the knowledge the CLOWN gained of the rotten state of the party; finally, because of the contacts he made with the International Committee here.[427] Throughout the time the CLOWN was editing the *Neue Zeit* and lecturing to the Society, Mr Liebknecht remained in the latter and, moreover, talked a great deal of nonsense about having to defend me against the great odium felt for me by the workers (i.e. louts), etc. Well, after only half a number (I sent it to you) of the *Neue Zeit* had appeared because of lack of money, Liebknecht acted as CHAIRMAN at a meeting to which the various associations had been invited for the purpose of saving the paper.[428] The result, of course, was nil. After this performance, I convened our people (a small gang, Pfänder, Lochner, etc., and a few newcomers, whom

---

[a] The question of Marx's contributing to the Vienna newspaper *Die Presse*.

Liebknecht had for a long time—ever since my removal out of town[429]—treated as his private club) and took the occasion to pitch into Liebknecht in a manner far from pleasing to him until he declared himself a contrite sinner. He said that an attempt had been made to bring out the *Neue Zeit* again, but had been frustrated by *his* vigorous intervention. I was therefore surprised to receive, a day or two later, what appeared to be a successor to the *Neue Zeit*, entitled *Das Volk.*[430] However, the matter was elucidated in a curious way, as follows (see also enclosed letter):

Mr CLOWN had finally written to Biskamp (you have a letter to him from Biskamp) saying that Kinkel had ruined the *Neue Zeit* by his intrigues, appeared to be seething with vindictive feelings, etc. WELL. Biskamp comes up to London and is *d'abord* STARTLED BY THE FACT that one of *his own* articles intended for the *Neue Zeit* has appeared in the *Hermann* somewhat watered down. He hurries to the CLOWN, who seems far from PLEASED to see him, says he is ill, simulates disillusionment and ends up by telling him that the whole thing is a mess, that he (Biskamp) should not get involved in it, that Kinkel is too strong, etc. But Biskamp, struck by the fact that Kinkel had transferred his *Hermann* to the *Neue Zeit*'s press, having given up his former press, and that he was printing *his* manuscripts, hastily sought out Hirschfeld at the press where he discovered—*Edgar Bauer*'s manuscript and proof corrections. IN ONE WORD, Mr Edgar had used the *Neue Zeit* to *sell himself to Kinkel* and—evidence of the man's fecundity—made the most of the occasion by printing Biskamp's manuscripts as contributions of *his own.* That oaf Kinkel! He seeks to ruin the *Neue Zeit*, not by giving the CLOWN money and allowing him to continue as editor, but by buying the said CLOWN who, throughout his editorship, had eschewed all polemic! But in this way Gottfried thought to rid himself once and for all of competition, however small. One more word about the activities of this same Gottfried. A third German paper made its appearance here, first under the title *Londoner Deutsche Zeitung*, then under the title *Germania.* This paper, edited by a certain Ermani, had Austrian leanings. Gottfried revealed that the editor had committed some felony, got Dr Juch to threaten him, bought up his paper and press for a mere song (whether out of the Revolutionary Fund or with money supplied by the Prussian Embassy isn't known) and, they say, intends to continue publishing the sheet under Juch's management and a different title. Kinkel's paper has 1,700 subscribers, is coming to be a source of income, and the fellow wishes to secure it against any competition or polemics.

After the CLOWN's betrayal, Biskamp, etc., founded *Das Volk*, and he and the louts first approached me indirectly through Liebknecht. Then Biskamp came to see me.

I told him that *we* could not contribute directly to a *small* paper nor, for that matter, to *any* party paper *which we did not ourselves edit*. However, the latter was a move for which every prerequisite was lacking at the moment. On the other hand *Mr Liebknecht* might give Biskamp the benefit of his collaboration. I appreciated, of course, that Gottfried has not been left in command of the field and that his dirty schemes should be BAFFLED, but all I would undertake to do was to let them have from time to time 'published' *Tribune* ARTICLES which they could use; to urge my acquaintances to take the paper; and, finally, to give them *verbally* any information that reached me and 'pointers' about this and that. On the other hand I stipulated that Biskamp should forthwith publish (he will do so in the very next number) a documented account of Bauer's and Kinkel's dirty work.[a] (I shall thus have killed 2 birds with one stone, even if the little paper ceases publication.) Further, that the CLOWN's objective heights must be abandoned and that the tone adopted must IN EVERY RESPECT be aggressive and polemical and, indeed, as amusing as possible.

CONSEQUENTLY, I would ask you, Lupus, Gumpert and anyone else you can get hold of (point out that our only interest in the thing is that it's anti-Kinkel) to subscribe to *Das Volk*, OFFICE: 3 Litchfield Street, Soho. (Quarterly subscription 3/6d post free.) Gumpert and Biskamp both come from Hesse-Cassel and since the former may have an occasional *bon mot* up his sleeve, he might send it to his compatriot. Finally, let me have the name of some fellow (a STATIONER) in Manchester to whom *Das Volk* could be sent for distribution. (Write to the Bradfordian[b] as well.)

I consider *Das Volk* to be a dilettante rag like our Brussels and Paris papers.[c] But covertly and without intervening directly, we can use it to worry the life out of Gottfried, etc., etc. Again, *the moment may come,* and that very soon, *when it will be of crucial importance that, not just our enemies, but we ourselves* should be able to publish our views in a London paper. Biskamp works for nothing and hence is all the more deserving of support.

What is really choice is that in No. 18 of the *Hermann*, the CLOWN wrote a highly inane, piddling sort of article in which he 'proves' that, because of 'England's neutrality', the present war is con-

[a] An item on the subject appeared in *Das Volk*, No. 4, 28 May 1859 ('Vereins-Nachrichten'). - [b] Wilhelm Strohn - [c] the *Deutsche-Brüsseler-Zeitung* and *Vorwärts!*

demned to be a 'hole and corner war'.[a] 'Conclusive' deeds are no longer possible on the unhappy Continent, which is the *reason why* noble England remains 'neutral'. In No. 19 the CLOWN is given a dressing-down by Blind from the indignant democratic-patriotic standpoint and by Bucher from the Urquhartite and thus, having been stamped upon by all parties, he will doubtless soon get the sack, even from the *Hermann*.[b]

This has been a very good lesson for the louts. Scherzer, that old-Weitlingian jackass, imagined that *he* could nominate party representatives. At *my* meeting with a deputation of the louts (I have refused to visit any association, but Liebknecht is CHAIRMAN of one and Laplander[c] of another[431]) I told them straight out that we owed our position as representatives of the proletarian party to nobody *but ourselves*; this, however, had been endorsed by the exclusive and universal hatred accorded us by every faction and party of the old world. You can imagine how taken aback the oafs were.

If you haven't any *Po and Rhine* left, you must order some. COPIES are also needed for Steffen, Weydemeyer and several reviews here.

Might it be possible to send poor Eccarius, who is again going to pieces in his sweat-shop, a fresh consignment of port?

Salut.

Your

K. M.

Have received a letter from Weydemeyer and Komp.[432] Shall send it you very soon. Thanks to them Duncker has already had orders for about 100 copies of my *Economy*[d] from the UNITED STATES.

Tell Lupus that, FROM THE BEGINNING, Beta (Bettziech), editor of *How do you do?*, was also Gottfried's real editorial factotum.

First published abridged in *Der Briefwechsel zwischen F. Engels und K. Marx*, Bd. 2, Stuttgart, 1913 and in full in *MEGA*, Abt. III, Bd. 2, Berlin, 1930

Printed according to the original

Published in English in full for the first time

[a] [E. Bauer,] 'Englische Neutralität', *Hermann*, No. 18, 7 May 1859. - [b] K. Blind, 'Der lokalisierte Krieg und die deutsche Volkspartei' and L. B[ucher], Louis Napoleon's Laufbahn', *Hermann*, No. 19, 14 May 1859. - [c] Albert August Anders - [d] K. Marx, *A Contribution to the Critique of Political Economy.*

248

ENGELS TO FERDINAND LASSALLE[433]

IN BERLIN

Manchester, 18 May 1859
6 Thorncliffe Grove

Dear Lassalle,

You will have found it somewhat strange that I haven't written to you for so long, the more so since I owe you an opinion on your *Sickingen*.[a] But that is precisely what has kept me from writing to you for so long. With the current and universal barrenness of fiction I seldom have a chance to read such a work, and for years I have never had a chance to read one of this kind *in such a way* that the reading of it resulted in a detailed judgment, a precisely stated opinion. The rubbish isn't worth the trouble. Even the few better English novels I read from time to time, e. g. those of Thackeray, have never been able to elicit this interest in me, despite their undeniable literary and cultural significance. But, having lain fallow for so long, my judgment has lost most of its edge and I need a good deal of time before I can permit myself to express an opinion. Your *Sickingen*, however, deserves better treatment than that sort of stuff and so I've taken my time. The first and second readings of what is in every sense, both as regards material and treatment, a German national drama, stirred my emotions to the extent that I was compelled to put it aside for a while, the more so as my taste has become so vitiated in these lean times that it has reduced me, I'm ashamed to say, to a state in which sometimes even stuff of inferior quality inevitably has some effect on me at the *first* reading. So in order to be wholly unbiassed, wholly 'critical', I put *Sickingen* away, i. e. allowed a few of my acquaintances to borrow it (there are still a few Germans here who are more or less knowledgeable about literature). *Habent sua fata libelli*[b]—if they're borrowed one rarely sets eyes on them again, and so I actually had to recover my *Sickingen* by force. I can tell you that, after the third and fourth readings, my impression has remained unaltered and, in the knowledge that your *Sickingen* can stand up to criticism, I shall now speak my mind.

---

[a] F. Lassalle, *Franz von Sickingen*. - [b] Books have their destinies—from Terentianus Maurus, *De litteris, syllabis et metris* ('Carmen heroicum', 258).

I know that I am not paying you any particular compliment when I state the fact that not one of Germany's present official poets would be remotely capable of writing such a play. However, fact it is and one all too characteristic of our literature not to be voiced. Taking the formal aspect first, your skilful manipulation of the plot and the thoroughly dramatic nature of the piece came as a very pleasant surprise. Admittedly you have taken a good many liberties with the versification but this is more bothersome in the reading than it would be on the stage. I should very much like to have read the stage version[434]; as the play stands here it could certainly not be performed; I have had with me here a young German poet (Carl Siebel), a distant relative who hails from my neighbourhood, and has had a good deal to do with the stage. He may be coming to Berlin as a reservist in the Prussian Guard, in which case I may take the liberty of giving him a note for you. He thought highly of your play but considered a performance quite impracticable by reason of the long speeches in which only one actor is occupied while the others may run through their entire miming routine 2 or 3 times so as not to stand there like dummies. The last two acts give adequate proof that you experience no difficulty in making your dialogue brisk and lively and since, with the exception of a few scenes (as happens in any play), the same thing would seem to be feasible in the first 3, I don't doubt you have taken this circumstance into account in your stage version. The *intellectual content* must, of course, suffer as a result—but that's inevitable, and the complete fusion of greater intellectual profundity, of a consciously historical content (both of which you ascribe, not without reason, to the German drama[435]), with Shakespearean vivacity and wealth of action will probably not be achieved—and perhaps not even by the Germans—until some time in the future. Indeed, that, to my mind, is where the future of the drama lies. Your *Sickingen* is entirely on the right lines; the chief protagonists in the action *are* representative of certain classes and tendencies, hence of certain ideas of their time, and derive their motives not from the petty appetites of the individual but from the very historical current by which they are borne along. But there is one advance that might yet be made in that these motives should emerge more of themselves, in a live, active, as it were spontaneous manner, more through the development of the action, while on the other hand reasoned debate (in which, by the way, I rediscovered with pleasure your old eloquence before the Assizes and the popular meeting[436]) becomes increasingly superfluous. You yourself seem to recognise this ideal as a goal, since you draw a distinction between stage drama and literary drama; I admit that *Sickingen* could be turned into a stage drama along the lines indicated, difficult though this would be (for it is truly no mean accomplishment). The characterisation of the protagonists is linked with this. You quite rightly oppose the *cheap* individualisation now prevalent, which amounts to nothing more than petty intellectual fireworks and is an essential characteristic of ineffectual imitative literature. At the same time it seems to me that a person is not characterised merely by *what* he does, but also by *how* he does it; and in this respect it would, I think, have done the intellectual content of the play no harm had clearer distinctions and stronger contrasts been drawn between individual characters. The characterisation of the *ancients* no longer suffices today, and it is here, I think, that you might to your own advantage have paid rather more attention to the importance of Shakespeare in the historical development of the drama. But these are minor points which I bring up only to show you that I have also concerned myself with the formal aspect of your play.

Now, as regards the historical content, you have presented what to you were the two most important aspects of the movement of that period very vividly and with justifiable reference to subsequent developments: the national aristocratic movement represented by Sickingen, and the humanist-theoretical movement, with its more extensive ramifications in the theological and ecclesiastical field, the Reformation. The scenes I like best are those between Sickingen and the Emperor[a] and between the Legate and the Archbishop of Trier[b] (here, in the contrast between the narrow-minded German prince of the church and the worldly Legate with his aesthetic and classical culture and political and theoretical foresight, you have, too, pulled off a nice piece of individual characterisation which nevertheless stems directly from the *representative* character of the two protagonists); in the scene between Sickingen and Charles the characterisation is also very striking. However, in making Hutten tell his life-story,[c] the *content* of which you rightly describe as essential, you have chosen a desperate means of introducing that content into the play. Also of great importance is the conversation in Act V between Balthasar and Franz during which the former remonstrates with his master about the *genuinely revolutionary* policy he should have followed. It is here that the real tragedy becomes apparent; and, precisely

---

[a] Charles V - [b] Richard von Greifenklau - [c] a scene between Hutten and Maria in Act III

because of this significance, it seems to me that it should have been rather more strongly indicated as early as Act III, in which there are several opportunities for this. But again I digress.

The attitude of the towns and the princes at that time is likewise portrayed more than once with great clarity, thereby pretty well exhausting what might be called the *official* elements of the movement as it then was. But something upon which I should say you had failed to lay due emphasis are the non-official, plebeian and peasant elements, with their concomitant theoretical representation. In its own way the peasant movement was just as national, just as hostile to the princes, as that of the aristocracy, and the colossal dimensions of the struggle in which it succumbed contrast most significantly with the levity with which the aristocracy, leaving Sickingen in the lurch, gave itself up to its historical calling of sycophancy. Even allowing for your concept of the drama which, as you will have seen, is rather too abstract, not realistic enough, in my opinion, I should say that the peasant movement deserved closer attention; certainly, the peasant scene with Joss Fritz is true to type and the individuality of this 'agitator'[437] is very accurately portrayed but, relative to the aristocratic movement, it does not represent with sufficient force what was then already a surging torrent of peasant agitation. In accordance with *my* view of the drama, which consists in not allowing the ideal to oust the real, or Schiller to oust Shakespeare, the introduction of society's plebeian section, so wonderfully colourful at the time, would have provided material of a quite different kind with which to animate the play, an incomparable backdrop for the national aristocratic movement going on down-stage, which would itself thus appear in its true light for the first time. What bizarre portraits does this period of dissolving feudal ties not bring forth! Vagabond beggar kings, hungry mercenaries and adventurers of all kinds—a Falstaffian[a] backdrop which, in a historical play in *this* sense, must needs be even more effective than in Shakespeare! But apart from that, I should say more particularly that neglect of the peasant movement is what has led you to give an incorrect idea, or so it seems to me, of one aspect of the national aristocratic movement also, while at the same time allowing the *truly* tragic element in Sickingen's fate to escape you. In my view, it never occurred to the bulk of the nobility then subject directly to the emperor to form an alliance with the peasants; their dependence on the income deriving from oppression of the peasants did not admit of this. An

[a] Falstaff is a character in Shakespeare's *Henry IV* and *The Merry Wives of Windsor*.

alliance with the towns would have been rather more feasible, but this did not come about either, or only in isolated instances. The national aristocratic revolution could, however, only have been effected by means of an alliance with the towns and the peasants, particularly the latter; and to my mind the tragic element lies precisely in the fact that this essential condition, alliance with the peasants, was impossible; that the policy of the aristocracy was therefore necessarily petty; that at the very moment when the aristocracy sought to take its place at the head of the national movement, the *bulk* of the nation, the peasants, protested against its leadership and hence ensured its downfall. To what extent there is any historical foundation for your assumption that Sickingen really did have some contact with the peasants, I am not able to judge, nor is it in any way relevant. So far as I can recall, by the way, whenever Hutten's writings are addressed to the peasants, they skate over the ticklish question of the aristocracy and seek to focus the peasants' wrath primarily on the clergy. But in no way do I dispute your right to portray Sickingen and Hutten as though it had been their intention to emancipate the peasants. However, this immediately presented you with the tragic contradiction whereby these two found themselves placed between the aristocracy on the one hand, who definitely did *not* want this, and the peasants on the other. Here, in my view, lay the tragic clash between the historically necessary postulate and the impossibility of its execution in practice. By discarding this element you reduce the tragic conflict to the fact that Sickingen does not join battle straight away with Emperor and Empire, but with one prince only[a] (although here too your tact rightly leads you to introduce the peasants), while his downfall is made to ensue from nothing more than the indifference and pusillanimity of the aristocracy. This would, however, have been quite differently motivated had you laid more stress at an earlier stage on the mounting peasant movement and the mood of the aristocracy, inevitably grown more conservative as a result of the earlier *Bundschuh* and Poor Konrad movements.[438] All this, incidentally, represents only one way in which the peasant and plebeian movement might be brought into the play; one could think of at least ten others which would be just as good, if not better.

As you can see, I am judging your work by a very high standard, indeed the *highest there is*, from both the aesthetic and the historical point of view, and the fact that I have to do so in

---

[a] Richard von Greifenklau

order to raise an objection here and there will provide you with the best proof of my appreciation. *Between ourselves* criticism has, of course, for years been necessarily as outspoken as possible in the interests of the party itself; but this aside, it is always a great pleasure to me and all of us when we are given fresh proof that our party, irrespective of the field in which it makes an appearance, invariably does so with distinction. And that is what you, too, have done on this occasion.

In other respects it would seem that world events are about to take a truly delectable course. It would be difficult to imagine a better basis for a thorough-going German revolution than that provided by a Franco-Russian-alliance. The water has to be right up to our necks before we Germans are gripped *en masse* by the *furor teutonicus*[a]; and this time we would seem to be in sufficient danger of drowning. *Tant mieux.*[b] In such a crisis all existing powers must necessarily be ruined and all the parties crumble one after another, from the *Kreuz-Zeitung* to Gottfried Kinkel, and from Count Rechberg to 'Hecker, Struve, Blenker, Zitz and Blum'[439]; in such a struggle the moment must necessarily come when only the most ruthless and resolute party is in a position to save the nation and, at the same time, the conditions be given which alone make it possible to jettison completely all the old trumpery—internal dissension on the one hand and, on the other, the Polish and Italian appendages which are the legacy of Austria. We must not cede an inch of Prussian Poland and what...[c]

First published in *Die Neue Zeit*, Bd. 1, Nr. 18, 1922

Printed according to the original

Published in English in full for the first time

249

MARX TO FRANZ DUNCKER

IN BERLIN

London, 21 May [1859]

Dear Sir,

From a communication I have received from North America[432] I see that about 100 copies of the first instalment[d] have been ordered

---

[a] From Lucan's *Pharsalia*, I, 255. - [b] So much the better. - [c] End of letter missing. - [d] K. Marx, *A Contribution to the Critique of Political Economy.*

by party friends of mine. Whether you have already received the order, I do not know. However, I was advised at the same time that we can count on 100 more copies being ordered in the same circles as soon as the *price* is known. I would therefore request you to advise me of the latter *by return*. This does not, of course, mean that the work could not be advertised for the benefit of the general public in North America at some later date.

The slowness with which the matter is being handled would not appear to be in your own interest. It is certainly not in mine.

In the *list of printer's errors* for the sheets I have had I would request you to include the following: ...[a]

First published in *International Review of Social History*, Vol. X, Part 1, 1965

Printed according to the original

Published in English for the first time

250

ENGELS TO MARX

IN LONDON

Manchester, 23 May 1859

Dear Moor,

I entirely agree about the manifesto.[b] What ought we to do about printing it? It will probably have to be printed in London; make some inquiries about costs and other PARTICULARS so that we can launch it immediately it's been written.[425]

The *Völkchen*[c] business is very amusing, very satisfactory, and may turn out to be extremely useful.[430] As regards its distribution here, the following should be noted: While I could easily find an English 'STATIONER', he would never stand a chance of catching even a STRAY subscriber. To get hold of them we must have recourse to the FOREIGN BOOKSELLERS here, Dunnill and Palmer, Princess Street, and Franz Thimm, Princess Street. Lupus is taking out a subscription with Dunnill and Palmer, Gumpert and I with Thimm, who is our bookseller. The *Hermann* is very much on the wane here and there is a whole load of back-numbers; Thimm's manager, who doesn't seem overfond of Kinkel, tells me that the

---

[a] The end of the letter is missing. - [b] See this volume, p. 437. - [c] diminutive of *Volk*

subscribers get fewer every week. So send Thimm a dozen copies of the early numbers, particularly the one dealing with the Kinkel affair,[a] and another half-dozen or so to Dunnill and Palmer; as soon as it appears I shall set that chatterbox Heckscher in motion and he will start the thing circulating here as sure as 2×2=4. But the stuff for Thimm must be sent *direct* to the Thimm up here; the London chap would be perfectly capable of intercepting the things. Then, as soon as Thimm gets subscriptions here, the local salesmen will perhaps take a greater interest in the matter.

I shall deal with the battle of Casteggio next Friday; the affair is too insignificant to warrant 2 articles and the telegrams are too vague to permit of anything worthwhile being said about it.[b] Your old map of Lombardy has stood me in very good stead, the scale being approx. 1/160,000, hence quite large. Unfortunately the delineation of the ground is very poor.

Many regards,

Your

F. E.

First published in: Marx and Engels, *Works*, First Russian Edition, Vol. XXII, Moscow, 1929

Printed according to the original

Published in English for the first time

251

MARX TO ENGELS[20]

IN MANCHESTER

[London,] 24 May 1859

Dear Engels,

If you could possibly let me have some 'TIN', you would *greatly* oblige me. That wretched Duncker, whom I had been counting on, appears to be putting the thing[c] off *ad infinitum*. Once again 11 days have gone by without my receiving anything from the dolt. Who do you think it is STOPS MY WAY? None other than Lassalle. First,

---

[a] See this volume, p. 439. - [b] The *New-York Daily Tribune* published two articles by Engels on the battle of Casteggio (or Montebello) fought by the French and Austrians on 20 May 1859: 'Fighting at Last' and 'The Battle of Montebello'. They may have been two instalments of what was originally one article. - [c] Marx's *A Contribution to the Critique of Political Economy*

my thing was held up for 4 weeks on account of his *Sickingen*. Now that it is nearing its conclusion, the fool must needs cut in yet again with his 'anonymous' pamphlet,[a] which he only wrote because your own 'anonymous' pamphlet[b] gave him no respite. Can't the scoundrel see that decency, if nothing else, demands that my thing be brought out first? I shall wait a day or two, but after that write a really filthy letter to Berlin.

I have seen to your orders for Manchester. If you can possibly find the time tomorrow, write 20-30-40 lines for me in German on the subject of the war; I shall pass them on to Dishrag Liebknecht, not in your writing but by dictating them. There is no time to be lost since the *Volk* boasts only *one* type-setter and everything has to be ready by the morning of each Friday.

A point not to be overlooked. With something more original from the theatre of war we ought TO CATCH at least 50 more customers in London.[c] I shall MANAGE the thing in such a way that initially you and I are not directly responsible.

You will be able to judge Gottfried's[d] manoeuvres from the fact that last week in the East End the parson was selling his *Hermann* to the Whitechapel[322] public for a HALFPENNY, solely in order to stop the sale of the *Volk*. But where did the *fonds*[e] come from? Schapper tells me that *Willich* has been over here. In which case the fellows must have shared out the money and flung the small change to watchdog Heinzen, for the dog has ceased to bark. We shall get to the bottom of it.

As regards the business of publishing our manifesto[f] I SHALL LOOK OUT.[425]

Salut.

Your

K. M.

Imandt is marrying his landlady's daughter, a Scotswoman. A nice district, too.[g]

First published abridged in *Der Briefwechsel zwischen F. Engels und K. Marx*, Bd. 2, Stuttgart, 1913 and in full in: Marx and Engels, *Works*, First Russian Edition, Vol. XXII, Moscow, 1929

Printed according to the original

Published in English in full for the first time

---

[a] *Der italienische Krieg und die Aufgabe Preußens* - [b] *Po and Rhine* - [c] Engels wrote an article entitled 'The Campaign in Italy' for the *Volk*. - [d] Gottfried Kinkel's - [e] funds - [f] See this volume, p. 437. - [g] An allusion to a joke current at the time: one woman tells another of her son's death in action near Leipzig (1813), whereupon the other remarks: 'And a nice district, too!' ('Auch eine schöne Gegend!')

252

MARX TO ENGELS

IN MANCHESTER

[London,] 25 May 1859

Dear Fred,

As things stand here just now, it's doubtful whether I shall be able to leave London, certainly not at the beginning of next week.

It is now a whole fortnight, or so I see from a note in my DIARY, since I sent that scoundrel Duncker *the last 3 proof-sheets* (i. e. sheets 9-11). The thing[a] was *ready*, therefore, and all the chap had to do was send me the clean proofs of *the last 3 sheets* for the *list of misprints*. Instead of that, what do I get? Lassalle's pamphlet[b] and, as we hadn't any money in the house and pretty well everything has been pawned that can be pawned, I had to send my last wearable coat to the pawnshop since there was 2/- to pay on this rubbish, which might perhaps cost 8d in Berlin. But to come to the point:

It is now EVIDENT, then, that a further fortnight's embargo has been placed on my thing in order to make way for Mr Lassalle. The work still to be done on it would take 3 hours at the most. But that infernal and conceited fool has decreed the embargo in order to secure the undivided attention *publici*.[c] Duncker, the swine, is happy as a sandboy, however, since it gives him a further excuse to postpone payment of my fee. I shan't forget the trick the little Jew has played. The speed with which his tripe was printed shows that he was *magna pars*[d] responsible for our stuff being delayed. Besides the oaf is so enamoured of his laborious emanations that he takes it for granted that I'm burning with impatience to see *his* 'anonymous' pamphlet and am 'objective' enough to take the killing of my stuff as a matter of course.

The confounded Jew in Vienna[e] hasn't written either.

Lupus is greatly mistaken about Liebknecht if he imagines that this worthy citizen could himself have composed a piece such as 'Der Reichsregent'.[410] Biskamp wrote it[f] (I gave him the FACTS) and it must be Biskamp that writes *everything*. Nothing is attributable to Liebknecht save the 'Politische Rundschau', dated London with the

---

[a] K. Marx, *A Contribution to the Critique of Political Economy*. - [b] *Der italienische Krieg und die Aufgabe Preußens* - [c] of the public - [d] in large measure - [e] Max Friedländer - [f] [E. Biskamp,] 'Der Reichsregent', *Das Volk*, No. 2, 14 May 1859.

symbol π, and not even all of that.[a] Liebknecht's uselessness as a writer is only equalled by his unreliability and weakness of character, about which I shall have more to say later. The fellow would have been kicked out for good this week had there not been special circumstances that necessitated his being kept on for a while as a scarecrow.

Even if my private circumstances—apart from waiting for Duncker—were not likely to preclude my coming up to Manchester next week, there would be the further consideration that, were I to abandon my post, everything might easily go to rack and ruin in view of the vast intrigues being conjured up here, there, and everywhere by the émigré democrats, the merchants of Camberwell, the Weitlingians, etc., etc., and in view of the extraordinary feebleness of the people who are supposed to represent us here. Yesterday, by the by, I got Pfänder to give categoric instructions to that inert hunk of flesh, Schapper, to the effect that if he did not rejoin the Workers' Society (the so-called communist one)[50] forthwith and take over the MANAGEMENT thereof, I would sever all 'connections' with him. This is the one sphere in which we could make use of the hippopotamus, yet the fool thinks it beneath him. *Mais nous verrons.*[b] Never have we had a poorer STAFF. Pieper would have been very useful just now, instead of which he is in Bremen and doesn't even write.

Salut.

Your

K. M.

First published in: Marx and Engels, *Works*, First Russian Edition, Vol. XXII, Moscow, 1929

Printed according to the original

Published in English for the first time

253

MARX TO ENGELS

IN MANCHESTER

[London,] 27 May [1859]

Dear Engels,

£5 received.

You must COLOUR YOUR WAR-ARTICLES A LITTLE MORE seeing that you are writing for A GENERAL NEWSPAPER, not for a scientific military journal.

---

[a] *Das Volk*, No. 3, 21 May 1859. - [b] But we shall see.

Something more descriptive and individual could easily be gleaned from the *Times* CORRESPONDENT, etc. I can't interpolate it myself as this would lead to unevenness of style. Failing this Dana will go and insert some utter nonsense off his own bat.

Today I am sending you 2 numbers (the last ones) of the *Presse* as samples, so that you can see whether you can use the PAPER.

At 7 o'clock yesterday evening Mr Liebknecht turned up with 6 lines for *Das Volk* having, by his failure to appear (and the idiot is always taking on all manner of things), thrown the entire setting INTO DISORDER, or so Biskamp tells me. I had told the blockhead exactly which bits of your pamphlet[a] were to be reproduced. Instead he tries to make a LEADER of it, in which, of course, he doesn't succeed. Bürgers *redivivus*[b] but far WORSE, since Bürgers could at least be used for purposes of attack in societies, etc.

Garibaldi has, in my opinion, deliberately been consigned to a position that will spell his ruin.

Unlike Kossuth who, with Klapka, has already 'recognised' 'Constantine' as the Russian king of Hungary, Mazzini (undoubtedly a greater authority on Italian patriotism than Mr Lassalle) is behaving very well.[440] I shall try and lay hands on the last, concluding number of his *Pensiero ed Azione*.[c] Send me your last copy of *Po and Rhine* for *Mazzini*. I shall write a short accompanying note, or *better still, write it yourself*.

Salut.

Your
K. M.

Still nothing from Berlin today. I. e. 16 days to correct the misprints in the last 3 sheets[d]!

First published abridged in *Der Briefwechsel zwischen F. Engels und K. Marx*, Bd. 2, Stuttgart, 1913 and in full in: Marx and Engels, *Works*. First Russian Edition, Vol. XXII, Moscow, 1929

Printed according to the original

Published in English for the first time

---

[a] *Po and Rhine* - [b] reborn - [c] In his article 'Mazzini's Manifesto' Marx reproduced in English Mazzini's manifesto 'La Guerra' which appeared in *Pensiero ed Azione*, No. 17, 2-16 May 1859. - [d] Marx means his *A Contribution to the Critique of Political Economy*.

254

MARX TO ENGELS

IN MANCHESTER

[London,] 28 May [1859]

Dear Engels,

Herewith a letter I have received from Dana. What should I answer?

Apropos. I have just learned from Biskamp, on the authority of the CLOWN[a] himself, that Bruno Bauer was definitely in the pay of Russia. He received 300 friedrichsdors from von Budberg, the Russian ambassador. The CLOWN was brought in as accomplice. Bruno dropped the thing because Budberg didn't treat him 'respectfully' and left him to *chambrer*[b] in the *antichambre*. He came to England for the purpose of attempting, with his brother—*par nobile fratrum*[c]—a similar transaction with the English government. Fell through, OF COURSE. WHAT DO YOU SAY TO THIS?

Salut.

Your
K. M.

First published in *Der Briefwechsel zwischen F. Engels und K. Marx*, Bd. 2, Stuttgart, 1913

Printed according to the original

Published in English for the first time

255

MARX TO FRANZ DUNCKER

IN BERLIN

London, 28 May 1859

Dear Sir,

You have not thought fit to reply to the letter in which I requested you to advise me of the price of the book.[d] Since the American mail leaves only twice a week, I have thus been

---

[a] Edgar Bauer - [b] cool down - [c] a noble pair of brothers (Horace, *Satires*, II, III, 243) - [d] K. Marx, *A Contribution to the Critique of Political Economy* (see this volume, p. 447).

prevented from replying to my friends.[432]

After your receipt of my manuscript a fortnight elapsed before I got any acknowledgment. In it you said that printing was to commence a week later. That week turned into more than three weeks. About eight weeks ago Lassalle wrote to say that the thing would be finished by the middle of May. More than three weeks ago I received the last three proof-sheets. The amendments that were called for could easily have been made in a *single* day. Instead, work would again seem to have been completely suspended during that time, although printing was *complete.* I hereby declare that I am tired of this *systematic and deliberate procrastination* and that I hereby demand, and indeed categorically, that you desist from these machinations, the purpose of which seems to me exceedingly suspect. All my acquaintances in England are of the same opinion and have earnestly enjoined me to take the above step.

Yours faithfully,

Dr K. Marx

First published in *International Review of Social History,* Vol. X, Part 1, 1965

Printed according to the original

Published in English for the first time

256

MARX TO FRANZ DUNCKER

IN BERLIN

[London,] 30 May 1859

Dear Sir,

I can find no misprint in the sheets sent to me.[a]

I am sending you the enclosed envelope so that you may, if you deem it worth while, have the postage refunded by the Prussian post. I paid 4/-and some d for this parcel and 2/-, etc., for the last but one. The envelope of the latter is in the hands of the English postal authorities, who declare that all such items, even if stamped, must be paid extra unless sent *via Calais.*

Yours faithfully,

Dr K. Marx

First published in: Marx and Engels, *Works,* Second Russian Edition, Vol. 50, Moscow, 1981

Printed according to the original

Published in English for the first time

---

[a] The proofs of Marx's *A Contribution to the Critique of Political Economy.*

257

MARX TO ENGELS

IN MANCHESTER

[London,] 1 June 1859

Dear Engels,

Enclosed 1 copy of the *Presse* containing some particulars that may be of interest to you. No answer from that fellow, Friedländer,[254] needless to say. However, my present explanation for this is as follows: When he lectured Friedländer about bias,[a] Lassalle did so, OF COURSE, not only in his but also in my name. Friedländer believes that I am hand in glove with Heraclitus the Dark Philosopher.[b] So he naturally can't imagine that under PRESENT CIRCUMSTANCES I can write for a Viennese paper. Every day the Vienna *Presse* contains veiled attacks upon the Berlin wiseacre. Thus, for instance, in a leading article on 29 May:

> 'But how can one demand a sense of national self-respect of those speculative minds which see in Napoleon III the avenging arm of history and, in his alleged genius for liberating the peoples, complacently admire the reflection of the ineptitude, pedantry and aridity of their own categorising intellects.'

The very insistence with which Lassalle required of me not to write any more to his cousin[c] is evidence that the fellow carried on his intrigues *in my name also*. Thus the blockhead has frustrated the best prospect I had for the summer. Besides, in certain eventualities it would be a good thing if I had some say in the Vienna *Presse*.

When you next write about Garibaldi, WHATEVER MAY BE HIS FATE, crack a joke about the curious position in which only 'his uncle's nephew'[d] could have found himself, namely that beside him the leader of the volunteer corps figures as a HERO. Can you imagine anything of the kind happening under the old Napoleon? By the by, in today's *Times* the Paris correspondent writes that the Bonapartists are already GRUMBLING loudly about Garibaldi's 'fame', and that 'A FEW SELECT POLICE' have been smuggled into his corps and send in detailed reports about him.[e] Adhering strictly to Mazzini's instructions, Garibaldi *omitted* all mention of Bonaparte in his proclamation.[441] Mazzini's latest thing[f] is not, by the by, as good as

---

[a] See this volume, p. 434-35. - [b] Ferdinand Lassalle, author of *Die Philosophie Herakleitos des Dunklen von Ephesos*. - [c] Max Friedländer - [d] Napoleon III - [e] *The Times*, No. 23321, 1 June 1859. - [f] Mazzini's manifesto 'La Guerra' published in *Pensiero ed Azione*, No. 17, 2-16 May 1859.

I thought. I had only run my eye over some excerpts. His old complaints about socialism. *We* can do nothing with him direct. But he could with advantage be used as an authority against Kossuth, etc. By the by, in his last number,[a] which I shall send you at the end of this week, you will reacquaint yourself with Mr Karl Blind's importance.

Salut.

Your
K. M.

Incidentally, Blind is no longer with the *Hermann,* but is greatly mistaken if he's hoping to get onto the *Volk.* Feeble though the little sheet may be, it has made the entire emigration down here froth at the mouth with rage. Among others Tausenau and Co., who are paid by Kossuth-Bonaparte to form German 'OPINION' in London.

First published abridged in *Der Briefwechsel zwischen F. Engels und K. Marx,* Bd. 2, Stuttgart, 1913 and in full in: Marx and Engels, *Works,* First Russian Edition, Vol. XXII, Moscow, 1929

Printed according to the original

Published in English for the first time

258

MARX TO FRANZ DUNCKER

IN BERLIN

London, 2 June 1859

Dear Sir,

I am indeed very sorry if I wrote you an offensive letter.[b] Please allow me, therefore, to say a few words in extenuation. To begin with I have in fact been away from Germany for too long and have grown too accustomed to conditions in London to form a correct estimate of the way business is conducted in Germany. Secondly, as I informed Lassalle some two months ago,[c] I am engaged in negotiations with a London publisher with regard to an English rendering of the first instalment.[d] The constantly misleading information which I, constantly labouring as I was

---

[a] *Pensiero ed Azione* - [b] See this volume, pp. 453-54. - [c] See this volume, pp. 407-10. - [d] K. Marx, *A Contribution to the Critique of Political Economy.*

under a false assumption, have been forced to give this man regarding the appearance of the book, has more than sufficed to show me up as a REGULAR HUMBUG in the eyes of the aforesaid John Bull. The repeated and impatient inquiries of my friends and in the end, the rumour that the thing will not be coming out at all—a rumour carefully disseminated, out of what motives I cannot say, by a Berlin clique *here*—finally proved too much for my patience.

Lastly, I trust that, in consideration of these reasons, you will regard my letter merely as the hasty expression of an irritability aroused by all manner of circumstances and absolve me of any intention of wishing to give offence.

Yours very faithfully,

Dr K. Marx

First published in *International Review of Social History,* Vol. X, Part 1, 1965

Printed according to the original

Published in English for the first time

259

MARX TO ENGELS

IN MANCHESTER

[London,] 7 June [1859]

DEAR Frederick,

You must excuse me for not writing to you before, and only these few lines. My time has been completely taken up with work and with running private and party errands.

D'abord[a] I was delighted to hear that you liked the first instalment,[b] for your opinion is the only one I value in this matter. To my wife's considerable AMUSEMENT, I awaited WITH SOME ANXIETY YOUR JUDGMENT.

Ad vocem[c] *'Volk'*: Admittedly its administration leaves a great deal to be desired, since there is only one type-setter, no errand-boy, etc., on top of which not a single 'trustworthy' despatch clerk has yet presented himself, and above all, no money. Nevertheless, recent issues have been virtually sold out and if ways and means

[a] First - [b] K. Marx, *A Contribution to the Critique of Political Economy.* - [c] As regards

can be found of appointing a reasonably reliable despatch clerk, the thing will survive. Moreover, the 'little sheet', although only indirectly given a TURN by us, has set the whole of democracy by the ears. Not just here, but also in Switzerland, where Vogt-Kinkel have pitched into me in the *Handels-Courier* with one of those blackguardly little articles with which you are familiar.[a] I'll get them to reproduce it in the next number.[b]

I shall speak to Biskamp on the Manchester question. For his part, *he* asked me yesterday to write and tell *you* that *not a single* copy had been ordered in Manchester. It looks to me as though *Hollinger* (the printer) has already been bribed by Kinkel. *Nous verrons.*[c]

Kinkel, following an audience with Kossuth and money payments from Vogt, has gone over to the camp of high treason. Bucher and Blind have resigned in 'indignation'. Kinkel's colleagues are now as follows: Bamberger, Ed. Bauer, Beta (*How do you do?*) and Born[d] (our ex-Born's[e] brother). A fine lot. Add to which one or two old whores.

Ad vocem Freiligrath. Between ourselves, a rotter. Having now seen that things are taking a revolutionary TURN (you must have heard about the labour RIOT in Berlin[442]) and that Kinkel is becoming DISRESPECTABLE, he reviles him. But the sixth and last volume of his collected works (3/4 of it translated rubbish) published in America, which he has just received and sent me, concludes with the poem about Johanna Mockel,[f] whereas he has suppressed the *anti*-Kinkel poem.[g] This is a filthy thing to do and it was with very sceptical mien that I listened to his excuses on the subject. The devil take the bardic profession.

Ad vocem Vogt. Has placed himself at Prussia's 'disposal' in the *Volks-Zeitung* (Berlin).

Ad vocem Duncker. That dolt Duncker, to whom I had written in exceedingly rude terms about his dilly-dallying, has sent me a letter admitting outright that the last delay of 3 weeks (when *everything* had been completed save for the list of misprints) was *due to the publication* of the 'anonymous pamphlet',[h] the one concocted of 'sweat, fire and logic'.[422] I *deliberately* divulged to the press the fact that you were the author of *Po and Rhine,*[443] because

[a] [K. Vogt,] 'Zur Warnung', *Schweizer Handels-Courier,* No. 150 (supplement), 2 June 1859. - [b] The article was reprinted with editorial comments in *Das Volk,* No. 6, 11 June 1859. - [c] We shall see. - [d] David Born - [e] Stephan Born - [f] F. Freiligrath, 'Nach Johanna Kinkels Begräbnis' (see this volume, p. 359). - [g] F. Freiligrath, 'An Joseph Weydemeyer'. - [h] [F. Lassalle,] *Der italienische Krieg und die Aufgabe Preußens.*

I had good reason to suppose that the author of the 'anonymous pamphlet' was quietly 'switching places' with you. I must say, it's a bit thick, Mr Lassalle placing an embargo on me at will! The thing is coming out in Berlin this week—my first instalment, I mean.

Finally, whatever happens and as soon as the MEANS READY, I shall come to Manchester for a few days as we have all sorts of things to settle.[444]

Salut.

Your

K. M.

Regards to lupullum.[a]

Tomorrow I shall send you copies of the *Presse* (in which quarter the 'anonymous one' has put a spoke in my wheel good and proper).

The rotten STAFF here is no joke, I assure you. Biskamp at least writes quickly and has a ready wit. Liebknecht is AN AWFUL NUISANCE. Due to his over-ingenious manoeuvrings, the little sheet was only able to publish the gossip about Kinkel and Bauer in a much attenuated form.[b]

Your article[c] appeared in the *Volk* on the same day it arrived. The last number contains the preface to my affair,[d] i. e. with such omissions as Mr Biskamp thought fit.

First published abridged in *Der Briefwechsel zwischen F. Engels und K. Marx,* Bd. 2, Stuttgart, 1913 and in full in: Marx and Engels, *Works,* First Russian Edition, Vol. XXII, Moscow, 1929

Printed according to the original

Published in English for the first time

260

MARX TO FERDINAND LASSALLE[20]

IN BERLIN

[London,] 10 June 1859

Dear Lassalle,

Since I wrote to you last I have had to prepare and send off 15 printed sheets for the English-American cyclopaedia, which is

[a] the little wolf, i.e. Lupus (Wilhelm Wolff) - [b] *Das Volk,* No. 4, 28 May 1859 ('Vereins-Nachrichten'). See also this volume, p. 439. - [c] F. Engels, 'The Campaign in Italy'. - [d] *A Contribution to the Critique of Political Economy*

appearing in New York.[a] This is no joke, what with my other work. Today is the day for the *Tribune* articles.[b] So there's not a minute to spare. Hence I'm merely writing to let you know that I got your letters as well as the pamphlet.[c]

This much for the present:

Ad vocem[d] *Sickingen*: Shall read it as soon as I have time and let you have a reply.[445]

Ad vocem pamphlet: In no way corresponds with my own view or that of my party friends in England. It is probable, by the by, that we shall express our view in print.

Ad vocem Duncker: Have written to tell him I'm sorry if my letter offended him. However it's a scandalous piece of procrastination. I received the last proof-sheet[e] as much as 5 weeks ago. You can't expect me—*once I have a contract*—to behave towards a publisher or permit myself to be treated by him as though he were printing the thing only as a 'favour' to yourself. One good turn he has already done me, and that is to lose me my *English* publisher until further notice.

Ad vocem Vogt (Imperial bailiff)[410]: *We possess evidence*, not only that the man has received money for himself from Bonaparte, but also money to suborn Germans in the interests of Franco-Russian propaganda.[420] Up till now he has succeeded only in the case of that politically negative quantity, Gottfried Kinkel.

Ad vocem Proudhon: Is said to have gone out of his mind and been put in a lunatic asylum in Brussels.

Salut.

Your

K. M.

First published in: *F. Lassalle. Nachgelassene Briefe und Schriften*, Bd. III, Stuttgart-Berlin, 1922

Printed according to the original

Published in English in full for the first time

---

[a] *The New American Cyclopaedia* - [b] 10 June 1859 was a Friday. On Tuesdays and Fridays Marx sent off his articles to New York. - [c] [F. Lassalle,] *Der italienische Krieg und die Aufgabe Preußens.* - [d] As regards - [e] K. Marx, *A Contribution to the Critique of Political Economy.*

261

MARX TO ENGELS[20]

IN MANCHESTER

London, 10 June 1859

Dear Frederick,

Two manuscripts received today. *One of them splendid*—yours on 'fortification', though I must say I feel some twinges of conscience about having made such demands on the little spare time you have. *One grotesque*, viz. Lassalle's reply to myself and you respecting his *Sickingen*.[445] A whole sheaf of closely written pages. Incredible that at this season and in the present historical circumstances, a man should not only find time to produce stuff of this kind himself, but actually presume that we have time to read it.

Ad vocem[a] *Volk*. Should your booksellers actually deliver the little paper to you, which I doubt, you and Lupus will be surprised to see in tomorrow's issue an announcement that there is some 'prospect' of our, etc., collaboration.[b] The diplomatic reasons which decided me to take this step will be communicated by word of mouth.

Duncker: Nothing yet received, neither money nor copies.[c] Tell Lupus about this; he'd already have had one otherwise.

Ad vocem Schramm[d]: This great man was a failure in Berlin. His wife's family council therefore decided that he should take a minor commercial post in Krefeld. Thereupon the 'failure' addressed a long scrawl to the Ministers in Berlin saying he had considered it his political duty to join combat with Minister Manteuffel, whom he abhorred, but now, having fulfilled that duty, and finding that Prussia was not *à sa hauteur à lui*,[e] requested to be released from the commonwealth of subjects. Granted, and Schramm arrived in London along with the other PARCELS. Now intends, as he warned the Hohenzollern cabinet, to get himself 'naturalised' an Englishman. The worst blow that has befallen Prussia since the battle of Jena.[46]

Ad vocem Lassalle. In reply to his gigantic manuscript, wherein, by the by, he also mentions the 'anonymous' pamphlet[f] he wrote

---

[a] As regards - [b] 'Statement by the Editorial Board of the Newspaper *Das Volk*' - [c] K. Marx, *A Contribution to the Critique of Political Economy*. - [d] Rudolf Schramm - [e] good enough for him - [f] [F. Lassalle,] *Der italienische Krieg und die Aufgabe Preußens*.

'in the name of the party', I sent him (today) a letter about $^1/_3$ as long as the present one.[a] As regards the pamphlet, all I said was: 'Not our view at all. No point in writing about it, as we should be expressing our opinion publicly in print.'[446]

Salut.

Your

K. M.

First published abridged in *Der Briefwechsel zwischen F. Engels und K. Marx*, Bd. 2, Stuttgart, 1913 and in full in: Marx and Engels, *Works*, First Russian Edition, Vol. XXII, Moscow, 1929

Printed according to the original

Published in English in full for the first time

262

MARX TO FRANZ DUNCKER

IN BERLIN

Manchester,[444] 22 June [1859]

Dear Sir,

I would request you to send the balance of the fee for my book[b] *without delay* to my wife in London.

In the letter you wrote me at the end of May you said that the book would come out and the fee be paid '*next week*'. Neither the one nor the other was done until today, 22 June. Your principle would seem to be that a 'strictly scientific work' can never come out too late and, more particularly, that one should wait until such time as the general spread of the war[370] has stimulated a 'strictly scientific' interest.

The same circumstances as have induced you to sanction this further postponement might, perhaps, justify a postponement until 1860, particularly in view of what you say in your letter, namely that, in the case of scientific works *in respect of which there is no undertaking as to the time of publication*, it is customary for German publishers to place an embargo on their appearance in favour of topical works whenever this would seem to be opportune.

---

[a] See this volume, pp. 459-60. - [b] *A Contribution to the Critique of Political Economy*

Since it is impossible for me to reply privately to the many inquiries I receive—in connection with these delays—I shall, after waiting a few days longer, issue a *public statement*.[447]

Yours very faithfully,

Dr K. Marx

First published in *International Review of Social History*, Vol. X, Part 1, 1965

Printed according to the original

Published in English for the first time

263

MARX TO ENGELS

IN MANCHESTER

[London,] 14 July 1859

Dear Frederick,

You must have been wondering about my long silence, but there was a perfectly natural explanation for it. During the first week[448] I had to scurry round like mad in an attempt to get *Das Volk* into some kind of order, and this week PRIVATE MATTERS obtruded.

WELL. The state of the *Volk* when I got back was as follows: Kinkel had been felled by our latest quips. (Since then I have gone on with the 'GATHERINGS'.[449] In the current issue I'll do this section by myself. Unless, of course, some piece of news gives Biskamp occasion to introduce a few more drolleries.) But at the same time *Das Volk* showed every sign of disintegrating, and it was doubtful whether it would continue to appear. During my absence debts had been contracted amounting to over £6, since the 'agents', printer,[a] old Uncle Tom Cobley and all suspected that my return would put an end to the fun. Biskamp was IN THE MOST DEJECTED STATE. He had been given notice by the *Kölnische*[b] (having been denounced by a competitor); to receive charity from Speck went against the grain, and he had therefore spent several nights camping out in the 'park'. Finally, the printer had been approached by 'genuine democrats, *likewise* socialists, but moderate, and inimical to any kind of personal politics (Blind?)', who were prepared to take over *Das Volk* and provide the necessary subsidies. SUCH WAS THE GENERAL STATE OF THINGS WHEN I ARRIVED AT LONDON.

---

[a] Fidelio Hollinger - [b] *Kölnische Zeitung*

First I gave Biskamp £3, at the same time persuading him to accept a schoolmaster's post in Edmonton which, since he won't be required to live in, do any supervision or give more than 4 lessons, *will permit him to write just as much for the paper as hitherto.* OTHERWISE he would soon have been DISARMED by misfortune and idleness. He is moving there on the first of August. Actually he won't be any further away from London than I am.[429] On the other hand, it will be better for me if he is *not* present *in person* when I myself have more to do with the paper, as I intend to do BY and BY. I only paid out £1 5/- for the paper (debts) and compelled Garthe, Speck and a few louts to get together the sum of £3 15/- as part payment for Hollinger. In addition I had to repay Mr Liebknecht the 16/- he had advanced to Hollinger during my absence. Hence £5 1/- had to be expended before 'current' operations began. These included 15/- paid to Carstens,[a] 5/- for rent of the despatch room, 4/- for STAMPS, 2/6d advanced to Mr Hollinger in respect of No. 9. So as you can see, I've pretty well scraped the bottom of the barrel before I've begun. However, if we maintain the pressure for a few more weeks there is every prospect that the *Hermann* will go under and leave us in complete possession of the field. Moreover, with the new despatch arrangements the thing will become SELF-PAYING. I am of the firm opinion that, even if we have to set the little paper's sights rather lower for a time, we must, AT A CERTAIN MOMENT, give it a meaningful line. Should the *Hermann* go under we shall change over to Hirschfeld's press. (Cheaper, gives more credit, more expeditious.) FOR THE MOMENT, however, it's absolutely essential that a few more subsidies be sent from Manchester.

Napoleon's peace[450] exceeds all my expectations. Yesterday the French revolutionary gang in London were all of them exultant and Louis Blanc was running around like a madman; the Italians, however, are gnashing their teeth. Even Mazzini, although he *foretold* the result 6 weeks before the end of the war, succumbed AFTERWARDS all the same to the illusion that Bonaparte would at least throw THE AUSTRIANS out of Italy. I have read a letter (*PRIVATE* LETTER) from an Irishman who sleeps with the Duchesse de Padua in Paris. According to this man, the secret articles of the treaty stipulate two Turkish provinces for Austria; the amalgamation of the Prussian Rhine Province and Belgium into a 'Catholic state', or rather the use of this 'new empire' as a pretext for snapping up the delicious titbits.

---

[a] Friedrich Lessner

The over-ingenuity of Prussia, with the support of Lassalle,[a] etc., has got Germany (and Prussia) into such hot water that the *only hope* of salvation lies in a ferocious revolution.

I would draw your attention to the first article in *The Free Press*,[b] which I am sending you.

Salut.

Your

K. M.

First published in *Der Briefwechsel zwischen F. Engels und K. Marx*, Bd. 2, Stuttgart, 1913

Printed according to the original

Published in English for the first time

264

ENGELS TO MARX

IN LONDON

[Manchester,] Friday, 15 July[c] 1859

Dear Moor,

I'd have written something about the peace[450] for the *Volk*, but since I neither see nor hear anything of what's going on, I conclude that you are dealing with the subject yourself and hence that my article would be *double emploi*.[d]

Excepting the continuation of the war, nothing could be more welcome to us than *this* peace. Prussia discredited, Austria discredited, Bonaparte discredited, Sardinia and vulgar Italian liberalism discredited, England discredited, Kossuth ruined, Vogt & Co. discredited, no gains for anybody except the Russians and the revolutionaries, i. e. what little Jew Braun[e] would call a 'tidy revolutionary situation'.[451] But His Excellency Ephraim Artful[e] is the most discredited of all.

Your

F. E.

First published in *Der Briefwechsel zwischen F. Engels und K. Marx*, Bd. 2, Stuttgart, 1913

Printed according to the original

Published in English for the first time

---

[a] A reference to Lassalle's pamphlet *Der italienische Krieg und die Aufgabe Preußens*. - [b] 'Memoir on Russia, for the Instruction of the Present Emperor', *The Free Press*, No. 7, 13 July 1859. - [c] A slip of the pen in the original: 14 July. - [d] needless duplication - [e] By 'little Jew Braun' and, below, 'Ephraim Artful' Engels means Ferdinand Lassalle.

265

MARX TO ENGELS

IN MANCHESTER

[London,] 18 July 1859

DEAR Frederick,

Since the last number of the *Volk* proved so very exiguous, I intend this week to put something in about Russia. It would please me greatly if an article by you could appear at the same time. Wouldn't it be possible to do something military summing up the campaign, or else ridiculing the whole affair?[a] But it would have to be here by Thursday. If the little sheet fails to appear on Friday, it always means a serious loss of revenue; last time this fell off appreciably, another reason being that we suddenly had to change *all our agents* and get rid of Scherzer among others. The CLOWN Edgar Bauer (an admirer of Bonaparte) has uttered a mighty threat, viz. that *we* are to be attacked in the next *Hermann. Nous verrons*[b]....

Have you seen my book[c] advertised anywhere yet?

Salut.

Your

K. M.

Little Jenny has been awarded THE GENERAL PRIZE, Laura two special prizes.

First published in: Marx and Engels, *Works,* First Russian Edition, Vol. XXII, Moscow, 1929

Printed according to the original

Published in English for the first time

[a] In compliance with Marx's request Engels wrote an article entitled 'The Italian War. Retrospect'. - [b] We shall see. - [c] *A Contribution to the Critique of Political Economy*

266

ENGELS TO MARX

IN LONDON

Manchester, 18 July 1859

Dear Moor,

I shall send you tomorrow or the day after the £5 still required to pay off the *Volk*'s arrears. It was too late for me to do it today, and besides I have the company of the 'little man', *scilicet* [a] Dronke, who sidled up to me at the Exchange; the little chap's business seems to be doing passably well. Apart from current day-to-day gossip, on which he holds forth like a pothouse politician, he seems reluctant to talk about *politicis*, particularly of the past, and this I encourage, for after all I treat him as an *extraneus*.[b] His knowledge, however, has not increased, and the profundity of his politics may be summed up in his remark that the Italians 'have *got* to hit out *now*, or they're not worth a thing'.

But to revert from the little man to the *Volk*; we must at once discuss what is to be done. If the £7 you took with you has vanished so quickly, and the louts' £3 15/- as well, the £3 I have in reserve will doubtless soon be gone too. *Que faire?* [c] I've heard nothing about Strohn's return. There's not much more to be done with Borchardt. As soon as Lupus returns—but heaven knows where he is—I shall at all events get him to carry out a reconnaissance. Before that I wouldn't care to approach him personally. Nor do I run across him any more, though I've several times kept half an eye open for him in Oxford Road.

At any rate you must let me know sometime exactly how matters stand financially under the new administration, so that I can have an answer ready to eventual queries. How many copies are now being sold? Have you cut down the newsboys, etc., to $^1/_2$d per copy? What do the total weekly expenses amount to and what is the income—hence what is the deficit?

Mr Thimm has been talked round very nicely. *Das Volk* is now displayed in his window IN A CONSPICUOUS POSITION, a much better one than the *Hermann* and the *Колоколъ*, which flank it. A few more 'Gatherings' and the last-named [d] will doubtless be done for

---

[a] to wit - [b] outsider - [c] What is to be done? - [d] Engels has 'den letzteren', probably a slip of the pen; 'den ersteren' ('the first-named') would fit the context better, as the 'Gatherings' were directed against the *Hermann*, not against the *Колоколъ*.

altogether.[449] The way in which Kinkel has suddenly taken to his heels is very funny.[a]

Next week's LEADER on the peace ought to be done by you. It's important, I think, since we've been lucky enough to get hold of the secret articles,[b] that this point be fully exploited. As you are making a *Tribune* article[c] out of it anyway, that should be easy for you. This point may well give the *Volk* a significance of quite a different order, and *exact* for it a position in the press. Think this over.

Let me know also *by return* what you people would like me to write about this week; then I shall do it on Wednesday evening.

I have sent for the *Portfolio* and am studying these and other Russian documents and Palmerstoniana; shall also get hold of as many BACK NUMBERS of *The Free Press* as possible. It's really high time I went through the stuff, seeing what importance the thing is now assuming. Can you tell me where the Russian memorandum on Russian policy[d] originated and which Prussian ministerial crisis brought it to the light of day[452]? So far as I am concerned the internal EVIDENCE and the classic phraseology are, of course, more than sufficient, but I need these FACTS for the debate with Philistia; anyway it is stupid of Urquhart to be so unnecessarily secretive.

Is there anything to be wormed out of Blind *quoad*[e] Vogt[420]? The 'little man' doesn't believe the thing, of course, and asks 'why, then, didn't *we* see to it that the documents were printed'?

Generally speaking the documents in Vol. 1 of the *Portfolio* are not the most important, though there are some nice things among them, particularly those by Pozzo di Borgo and the memorandum to the German governments.[f] What idiots they are and how the Russians must laugh at them!

The memorandum in *The Free Press* is a true classic from start to finish, including the almost comical way in which the worthy diplomats make out that regicide is at once self-sacrifice and a republican virtue. Still, it seems to be going a bit far when Nicholas[g] gives his son[h] this kind of lesson with regard to the

---

[a] G. Kinkel, 'An unsere Leser', *Hermann*, No. 26, 2 July 1859. - [b] See this volume, p. 464. - [c] K. Marx, 'The Treaty of Villafranca'. - [d] 'Memoir on Russia, for the Instruction of the Present Emperor', *The Free Press*, No. 7, 13 July 1859. - [e] concerning - [f] 'Copy of a Despatch from Count Pozzo di Borgo, Addressed to Count Nesselrode. Dated Paris, 10th (22nd) December, 1826'; 'Copy of a Very Secret Despatch from Count Pozzo di Borgo, dated Paris, the 28th November, 1828'; 'Memoir on the State and Prospects of Germany, Drawn up under the Direction of a Minister at St. Petersburgh, and Confidentially Communicated to Several of the German Governments'. - [g] Nicholas I - [h] future Emperor Alexander II

Chetham's Library in Manchester where Marx worked in the 1840s and Engels in the 1840-60s. General view and part of the reading-room

murder of his own father; I should say this passage has been altered.[453]

Is it not possible to get hold of the complete document? Dronke tells me that in Glasgow there is a STATIONER by the name of Love in St. Enoch Square who sells the *Hermann* and would be a very suitable man to sell *Das Volk*. It might be a good idea to send him a few copies and a letter.

Have you sent it to America? It's about time you did. To Weydemeyer, Steffen and the chap in New York[a] who once wrote to you about communist matters.[297]

Warmest regards to your wife and the girls.

Your

F. E.

First published abridged in *Der Briefwechsel zwischen F. Engels und K. Marx*, Bd. 2, Stuttgart, 1913 and in full in: Marx and Engels, *Works*, First Russian Edition, Vol. XXII, Moscow, 1929

Printed according to the original

Published in English for the first time

267

MARX TO ENGELS

IN MANCHESTER

[London,] 19 July 1859

DEAR Frederick,

I would gladly have written the article on the peace, for it would simply have meant combining last Friday's *and today's* articles for the *Tribune*.[b] They were, moreover, good articles, for *ira facit poetam*.[c] However, as Biskamp has *begun* the thing, has already *announced* No. II,[d] and is effectively, or at least nominally, in command, *decency* precludes one interfering in this way. Once he is in Edmonton, his very remoteness will ensure that at crucial moments such as this the

[a] Friedrich Kamm - [b] Marx refers to his articles 'The Peace' and 'The Treaty of Villafranca'. - [c] Anger gives wings to one's words. An allusion to 'Facit indignatio versum'—'Indignation makes verse' (Juvenal, *Satires*, I, 79). - [d] [E. Biskamp,] 'Der Friede von Villa Franca', *Das Volk*, No. 11, 16 July 1859. The second instalment was published in the next issue of *Das Volk* on 23 July.

LEADER can be taken out of his hands without hurt to his *amour propre*—which is all he gets out of it.

But what the two of us *can* do to put some stiffening into the next issue, is support him on his left and right flanks. On the pretext of discussing Urquhart's document,[a] I shall briefly sum up Russia's PART in this tragi-comedy and at the same time disparage Bonaparte.[454] You, on the pretext of writing a final article on military affairs,[b] must also set about Bonaparte, etc. (and on the same occasion take a swipe at Prussia). In my view it is of the utmost importance *morally* that a belief in Bonaparte's greatness should not be allowed to *arise* among the Germans. As for Austria, the agreed LINE we have adopted of blaming everything on the sovereign[c] is SUFFICIENT.

Ad vocem[d] the *document*. Fell into the hands of the 'Prince of Prussia'[e] during the regency crisis on the occasion of Manteuffel's sudden removal.[336] More than that is not to be coaxed out of Urquhart's idiots. Certain passages have been *forged* because they didn't get hold of the *complete document*.[452] The *authenticity* of the whole is vouched for by the style peculiar to all, even 'secret', Russian documents, in which certain stereotyped, conventional untruths take turn and turn about. It is a LINE even Pozzo di Borgo adopts in his writing. The plain truth about Russia's machinations comes to light only with the chance publication of the documents of Russian agents not in the direct employ of the Russian state. E.g. Theyls' (a Dutchman) and Patkul's (came out in Berlin in 1796) memoirs and correspondence.[f]

Portfolio. I shall obtain for you (and myself) from Paris the complete edition published there of the PAPERS of which the *Portfolio* was allowed to contain only those authorised by Palmerston.

Volk. Agents' remuneration reduced to $^1/_2$d. Expenditure has been heavy because Biskamp required personal sustenance; because the rows the fellows were having with each other during my absence[444] meant that the administration was at sixes and sevens; because the entire staff has been changed since my return. By the end of the week I shall have a *full statement of accounts*. This involves a great deal of work in view of the way the thing has been run hitherto. £4-£5 worth of advertising will have to be obtained

---

[a] 'Memoir on Russia, for the Instruction of the Present Emperor', *The Free Press*, No. 7, 13 July 1859. - [b] F. Engels, 'The Italian War. Retrospect'. - [c] Francis Joseph I - [d] As regards - [e] William - [f] W. Theyls, *Mémoires pour servir à l'histoire de Charles XII, roi de Suède*; J. R. von Patkul, *Berichte an das Zaarische Cabinet in Moscau, von seinem Gesandschafts-Posten bei August II, Könige von Polen*, Th. I-III.

this week in order to liquidate the debt to Hollinger for Nos 9 and 10.

Biskamp wanted to write a short review of my *Critique of Political Economy*, etc. I dissuaded him, for he knows nothing about the subject. But since he has undertaken (in the *Volk*) to say something about it, I should like you to do it for him[a] (say next week, but not this). Briefly on the method and what is new in the content. In this way you would set the tone for the correspondents down here. And likewise help frustrate Lassalle's plan to KILL me.

Salut.

Your

K. M.

First published abridged in *Der Briefwechsel zwischen F. Engels und K. Marx*, Bd. 2, Stuttgart, 1913 and in full in: Marx and Engels, *Works*, First Russian Edition, Vol. XXII, Moscow, 1929

Printed according to the original

Published in English for the first time

268

ENGELS TO MARX[455]

IN LONDON

[Manchester, 20 or 21 July 1859]

Dear Moor,

Herewith the article.[b] If it's too long cut it short somewhere and return me the manuscript of the *unprinted* portion so that I know where to start again.

Also a POST OFFICE order made out to you, this being the three pounds for the *Volk.*

The little man[c] pushes off tomorrow. He has bought the entire *Free Press* for 1859 as I have, ditto 1858. However much the Piccolo may chew away at it he won't digest a great deal. I asked him whether any money could be raised for the *Völkchen* in Glasgow; he thought *not.* I did this deliberately *en passant.* However, if you think it would serve some purpose I shall write to him; since he has just been partially restored to grace, it may

---

[a] Engels did write a review: 'Karl Marx. *A Contribution to the Critique of Political Economy*'. - [b] F. Engels, 'The Italian War. Retrospect'. - [c] Ernst Dronke

perhaps bear fruit and he can fork out at least a few pounds himself. But I wouldn't care to do this without consulting you, for there's no knowing what boasts the little fellow might not subsequently make with a letter like that in his pocket. This apart, *père* Freiligrath, too, ought to fork out a £5 note. If the louts can pay, so can he, and after all if our party has to support the paper out of its own money for the present, the fat philistine must also do his bit.

Many regards to the FAMILY.

Your
F. E.

First published in *MEGA*, Abt. III, Bd. 2, Berlin, 1930

Printed according to the original

Published in English for the first time

269

MARX TO ENGELS

IN MANCHESTER

[London,] 22 July 1859

Dear Engels,

£3 received. Immediately paid out £2 to Hollinger and 15/- to Lessner. Out-of-town subscriptions are increasing (there are already 60) but are not payable until the end of the quarter and call for a weekly outlay on STAMPS. I am now convinced, 1. that there was a debt of ABOUT £7 of which I was not told before I left for Manchester[444]; 2. that the advertisements (instead of £5, receipts were ABOUT 20/-) and Mr Scherzer's London subscriptions—I have sacked him—were just a piece of private skulduggery. With proper MANAGEMENT, which is now under way but whose results won't make themselves felt for weeks to come, the advertisements alone will pay for the little sheet. Since more money is needed immediately, write to Dronke. If you tell the little man that for the time being the paper can only exist by party sacrifices and hence we are asking *all* party members to make such sacrifices, he can, if he wishes, get the letter printed. I am convinced that, within 6 weeks, the thing will be on a solid footing. But there can be no question of giving it up now that Gagern and

Co., in short the entire 1848 gang, are again taking the stage. Thimm has asked us to put his name in the paper as our distributor in Manchester. I could not carry out my intention this week, for I was overcome by a kind of cholera as a result of the heat and was vomiting from morning till night. Being able to write again today, I have written for the *Tribune,* A GLORIOUS VINDICATION of your military article,[a] basing it on Francis Joseph's and Bonaparte's manifestos.[b] The paper had been so much intimidated that it suppressed all your articles for a time. During my absence *Blind* was scheming to gain control of the *Volk.* I wrote him an exceedingly rude letter, which was followed by an INTERVIEW. After that, however, there'll be no dunning the man for money for a while. Philistine Freiligrath *hasn't even paid* his subscription, although pressed *twice.* Instead, when speaking to Mr Juch, he deprecated the 'undignified' tone of the *Volk,* although he tells *us* that he is *'delighted'* with it. *By and by we shall take our revenge upon these diplomatical fellows.*

You forgot to let me know whether you wish to do a review of my piece.[c] There is great rejoicing among the fellows here. They imagine the thing's a failure *because* they are ignorant of the fact that Duncker hasn't even advertised it yet. Should you write something, don't forget, 1. that it extirpates Proudhonism root and branch, 2. that the *specifically* social, by no means *absolute,* character of bourgeois production is analysed straight away in its simplest form, that of the *commodity.* Mr Liebknecht informed Biskamp that 'never has a book *disappointed* him so much', and Biskamp himself told me that he didn't see *'à quoi bon'.*[d] Is Lupus back?

In your second article on the war[e] you will not, I am sure, forget to stress the inadequate strength of the pursuit after victory had been won, and the pitiful whining of Bonaparte, who had at last got to the point where Europe did not, as hitherto, out of fear of revolution, permit him to *play* the old Napoleon within given limits. In this connection it would be pertinent to recall the 1796-97 campaign, when France was not able to take her time

---

[a] Marx probably means Engels' article 'Historical Justice'. - [b] K. Marx, 'Truth Testified'. In this article Marx cites Francis Joseph's manifesto of 15 July 1859 (reported in *The Times,* No. 23364, 21 July 1859) and Napoleon III's speech at a reception for members of the State Council, the Senate and the Corps législatif in the Palace of Saint-Cloud on 19 July 1859 (*Le Moniteur universel,* No. 201, 20 July 1859). - [c] K. Marx, *A Contribution to the Critique of Political Economy.* - [d] 'what use it was' - [e] 'The Italian War. Retrospect' (was published in three instalments in *Das Volk*)

preparing all her resources for 'A LOCALISED WAR' but, with her finances completely disrupted, had to fight not only beyond the Rhine, but also beyond the Mincio and the Adige. Bonaparte is actually complaining that his '*succès d'estime*' are now begrudged him.

Salut.

Your
K. M.

Can't anything be got out of Heckscher?

Have you written *to Duncker*?

Ask Dronke to write for us as well.

First published in *Der Briefwechsel zwischen F. Engels und K. Marx,* Bd. 2, Stuttgart, 1913

Printed according to the original

Published in English for the first time

270

ENGELS TO MARX

IN LONDON

Manchester, 25 July 1859

Dear Moor,

Have written to Duncker.[456] Also about the total absence up till now of any advertisements of your book[a] in the Augsburg *Allgemeine Zeitung* and *Kölnische Zeitung*. I can't possibly do an article on it *this week*; it is quite an *undertaking* and I should have had NOTICE of it somewhat earlier. Besides, I've begun the military article[b] and want to get it finished quickly. However, I promise to do the article for next week.[c]

Some nonsense was edited into my last article. I said that, during the march from Pavia, the 5th corps so exerted itself on the 3rd and 4th[d] that, had the $4^1/_2$ hours lost through the halt been put to use, the result would not have been materially different, nor would the corps have arrived on the battle-field

[a] *A Contribution to the Critique of Political Economy* - [b] 'The Italian War. Retrospect' - [c] 'Karl Marx. *A Contribution to the Critique of Political Economy*' - [d] 3 and 4 June 1859. Engels speaks of the first instalment of his article 'The Italian War. Retrospect'.

appreciably earlier. In print it says that it was the halt alone which made that exertion possible, which 1. is just the opposite and 2. is nonsense. In the first place the troops were not in the least tired at 6 o'clock in the morning of the 3rd, having only *just moved off*, so that the halt could be of no benefit to them, and secondly the halt deprived them of the cool hours of the morning and forced them to march when the midday heat was at its greatest. To any military man, the sentence as it now stands would seem quite preposterous. Much good all these stylistic improvements do me anyway, if printing errors are responsible for the most egregious nonsense, e.g. *rest* for *thrust* (!) and so forth. My articles are particularly distinguished by this kind of nonsense, the remainder being tolerably well corrected.

How, by the way, could you permit Herwegh's lousy poem[a] to be included?

Quanto al danaro,[b] Dronke will be back here again in a fortnight's time (about 10 days from *now*, that is), so I shall have to put everything off till then. Nor have I any news of Lupus. Where to get money from in the meantime is difficult to say. I'll try Heckscher, but just now I have *my hands full* and a great deal of my time is taken up with the article on your book. If only Strohn were here! Gumpert is at home, confined to bed with laryngitis and unable to speak. However, I shall see; if at all possible Heckscher will have to keep the paper going this week. But the miserly Freiligrath should certainly be made to cough up.

How funny that you should have obtained so flattering an opinion from Mr Liebknecht too.[c] It's just like these folk. The gentlemen are so used to our doing their thinking for them that invariably and without exception they want to have everything presented to them not only on a platter, but already pre-digested, not only the quintessence in the smallest possible space, but also a detailed exposition, READY COOKED AND DRIED. One is expected to perform miracles, *ni plus ni moins*.[d] What does an ass of that species really want? As though he couldn't discover for himself from the first 3 lines of the preface that this first instalment was to be followed by at least 15 others before he got to the final conclusions. Naturally, the solutions to ticklish monetary problems, etc., mean nothing whatever to Liebknecht, seeing that such problems simply don't exist for him. But the least one could ask of

---

[a] Engels refers to Georg Herwegh's poem written on the occasion of the Federal Marksmen's Festival in Zurich and published in *Das Volk*, No. 12, 23 July 1859. - [b] As for money - [c] See this volume, p. 473. - [d] neither more nor less

such a blockhead is that he should take in at least those few points that happen to suit his book. However, what recks a cow of Sunday?

The Russian document[452] ought not to be reprinted in such short BITS, otherwise one completely loses the thread.[a] Mr Petersen's lucubrations also become tedious in the long run.[b 457] It's true you were in difficulty last week.

Mr Bonaparte's speeches get ever more comical. The one he made before the diplomatic corps is really too funny.[c] And the fellow kept clapping his hand to his sword all the while! The fool seems quite seriously determined to impose himself on the world as the 'old one',[d] at least so far as *le dehors*[e] is concerned.

Kossuth has been spreading it about that he's been away in Lussinpiccolo![f]

Many regards.

Your

F. E.

First published abridged in *Der Briefwechsel zwischen F. Engels und K. Marx*, Bd. 2, Stuttgart, 1913 and in full in: Marx and Engels, *Works*, First Russian Edition, Vol. XXII, Moscow, 1929

Printed according to the original

Published in English for the first time

271

MARX TO ENGELS

IN MANCHESTER

[London,] 1 August 1859

DEAR Frederick,

D'abord[g] I must acknowledge the £2 10/-. This time I myself corrected the proofs of your article.[h] If it still contains misprints,

---

[a] A reference to 'Russisches Memoir zur Belehrung des gegenwärtigen Kaisers' (*Das Volk*, Nos. 12-16, 23 and 30 July and 6, 13 and 20 August 1859), a German translation of 'Memoir on Russia' published in *The Free Press*, No. 7, 13 July 1859. - [b] [N.] P[etersen,] 'Feierstunden-Arbeit eines Arbeiters', *Das Volk*, Nos. 8-10, 12 and 16, 25 June; 2, 9 and 23 July; 20 August 1859. - [c] Napoleon III made this speech on 21 July 1859 and it was published in *Le Moniteur universel*, No. 203, 22 July 1859. - [d] Napoleon I - [e] outward appearance - [f] Town in Lussin island in the Adriatic, then under Austrian rule. - [g] First - [h] 'The Italian War. Retrospect'

the printer is the only one to blame. Herwegh's rotten poem[a] got in without my knowing about it. I therefore compelled Biskamp to give an explanation in the last issue[b] and, INTO THE BARGAIN, I got him to publish the Landwehr soldier's song (as a fitting sequel to Herwegh).[458]

What is catastrophic so far as I'm concerned is that Biskamp isn't going to Edmonton but (it would seem) has accepted the post of tutor *chez* Bibra (the innkeeper) in the middle of the West End. If this is so I shall press for a written agreement with the gentleman. For, like all professional humorists he's a capricious, hysterical old woman, and we're not going to right the apple-cart so that someone else can drive it away. We must make sure we get *possession* of the thing.

Lina[c] is back here from Cologne. Bürgers has grown quite 'high-minded' since his release. He reprobates the *Volk*'s 'reversion' to the old manner of using 'bad jokes' to split the 'party'. For him, it would seem, the 'party' comprises anyone who is 'not' official, and that includes Vogt and Kinkel. Needless to say these 'hints' were given merely out of tender regard for 'me'. 'One' copy of my work[d] had arrived at Bermbach's for the dozen or so party friends in Cologne. Bürgers hadn't read it, of course, nor will he, 'but in my interests' expressed his indignation that the thing should be coming out 'by dribs and drabs' and not all 60 sheets AT ONCE. For the rest, he's tutor at some 'merchant's', which only takes up a few hours each morning, and apart from that he gives one other lesson. All in all, he earns 700 talers. His 'work' is confined to mornings. After the midday meal he starts 'recovering' from his half day's work and lounges about chatting by the hour at Mrs Daniels' house where, however, he has a serious rival in Dr Klein. But in the evenings he hurries to Löllchen's to preside with great dignity over the Cologne debating club until far into the night. He 'esteems' Lassalle's activities but hasn't 'read' anything of his, not even *Franz von Sickingen*. The spurious pretext of having contracted a serious chest complaint during his time in prison has provided him with a splendid means of masking his habitual idleness. In addition, the 'high-minded man' frequents 'music clubs'. As regards the Cologne trial[71] he actually repeated to Lina several most infamous and far from unwitting lies, e.g. that it was *us* not *him* and the other asses in Cologne who sent that ass

[a] ['On the Occasion of the Federal Marksmen's Festival in Zurich',] *Das Volk*, No. 12, 23 July 1859. - [b] This explanation by the Editorial Board was published in *Das Volk*, No. 13, 30 July 1859. - [c] Caroline Schöler - [d] *A Contribution to the Critique of Political Economy*

Nothjung to Germany as emissary.[459] He has, it seems, grown 'even more handsome' than he used to be. *En passant*, Georg Jung has become a gambler and has apparently pretty well dissipated his fortune. A few weeks ago Countess Hatzfeldt again took up residence in Berlin.

As soon as you have some hours to spare, it would be a good thing to go ahead with 'Infantry'.[a] My finances are closely linked with this. I should like to send my wife to the seaside for a few weeks. But that would be feasible only if I could draw an additional sum on *America*.

Salut.

Your

K. M.

First published abridged in *Der Briefwechsel zwischen F. Engels und K. Marx*, Bd. 2, Stuttgart, 1913 and in full in: Marx and Engels, *Works*, First Russian Edition, Vol. XXII, Moscow, 1929

Printed according to the original

Published in English for the first time

272

ENGELS TO MARX

IN LONDON

Manchester, 3 August 1859
7 Southgate

Dear Moor,

Herewith the beginning of the article about your book.[b] Take a good look at it and, if you don't like it *in toto*, tear it up and let me have your opinion. Through lack of practice I have grown so unused to this sort of writing that your wife will be greatly tickled by my awkwardness. If you can knock it into shape, do so. A few convincing examples of the materialistic viewpoint would not come amiss, in place of my indifferent reference to the February revolution.[c]

As soon as I've done with this thing, I shall set to work on 'Infantry', which will, however, demand a good deal of time and

[a] an article for *The New American Cyclopaedia* - [b] F. Engels, 'K. Marx. *A Contribution to the Critique of Political Economy*'. - [c] Engels means the 1848 revolution in France and subsequent revolutionary events in other European countries.

trouble, despite Rüstow, who must, of course, be treated with some reserve.[a]

Can you shed any further light on the particulars contained in Crawshay's letter in *The Free Press* of 27 July regarding the Russian document?[b] Surely the 'German' isn't Mr Bucher? And in which German paper is the thing supposed to have appeared?[460]

When you saw Blind, did you speak to him about the Vogt affair?[461] *N'y avait-il rien à faire?*[c]

The gentle Heinrich[d] is acquitting himself well in his new role. Gloomy as ever, but all the lazier for that, redeeming the world by his courageous and intelligent GRUMBLING.

Lupus has had another adventure, this time with a parson who swapped travelling bags with him. The deadly earnestness of the affair was, however, alleviated by the fact that the bag that had been left behind contained the said parson's MAIDEN SERMON which he was due to rattle off the following day. This lent the thing certain humorous *extérieurs*,[e] otherwise Lupus was again on the point of exclaiming: *'There are so many rogues in this country, and not of the working class, but of the middle class.'*

Your
F. E.

First published abridged in *Der Briefwechsel zwischen F. Engels und K. Marx*, Bd. 2, Stuttgart, 1913 and in full in: Marx and Engels, *Works*, First Russian Edition, Vol. XXII, Moscow, 1929

Printed according to the original

Published in English for the first time

273

MARX TO ENGELS

IN MANCHESTER

[London,] 8 August 1859

Dear Engels,

As a result of an attack of vomiting that has now lasted for two whole days, I am as weak as a fly and hence cannot write more than a few lines.

---

[a] W. Rüstow, *Geschichte der Infanterie*. - [b] G. Crawshay, 'The Russian Memoir of 1837', *The Free Press*, No. 8, 27 July 1859. - [c] Could nothing be done about it? - [d] Heinrich Bürgers - [e] aspects

Would it be possible to scrape together some money for the *Volk* by *Wednesday morning*?

Last Monday (Monday is always settlement day; i.e. a week ago today) the *total deficit* had been reduced to no more than about £2. (This did not, of course, include the charge for No. 13, which only has to be met today, and still less for No. 14, where payment doesn't fall due until today week. The issues are, of course, only charged at the end of the week following publication.) So things are in good shape. But today there is further expenditure to be met, in addition to the usual £1 extra (15/- for Lessner, 5 for the OFFICE). I myself am under so much PRESSURE that I cannot at this moment advance a *single* FARTHING and am, moreover, wasting an inordinate amount of time over the business. As for philistine Freiligrath, he imagines that he is giving adequate proof of his 'convictions' by maintaining a 'neutral' attitude towards ourselves and the *Hermann*.

Ledru and L. Blanc have united to publish a paper, the *Union Républicaine*. It is to appear at the beginning of next month from the same press as the *Volk*, and would benefit the latter in as much as Hollinger would then print by machine instead of by hand as heretofore.[462] It makes the continued existence of the *Volk* all the more essential, by the by.

Later on (as soon as I'm fit again), I shall write to Germany about the business. And to Borchardt too?

To make the thing a PAYING proposition more quickly, fresh outlays would be necessary in a town like London: errand-boys besides Lessner, etc.

Strohn not back yet?

No answer yet from Duncker, the swine?

Regards to Lupus and Gumpert.

Salut.

Your

K. M.

First published abridged in *Der Briefwechsel zwischen F. Engels und K. Marx*, Bd. 2, Stuttgart, 1913 and in full in: Marx and Engels, *Works*, First Russian Edition, Vol. XXII, Moscow, 1929

Printed according to the original

Published in English for the first time

274

ENGELS TO MARX

IN LONDON

Manchester, 10 August 1859

Dear Moor,

Just now I'm in such a jam, paying off private debts which have accumulated in respect of the new financial year, that only in the case of direst need shall I be able to advance any money to the *Volk* during the next few weeks. I neither see nor hear anything of Strohn, but should know at once if he returned to Bradford. If the worst comes to the worst you could always write to Borchardt—I don't see why not. Then you could let me know and, if necessary, Lupus might also drop in on him. I neither see nor hear anything of Borchardt.

Yesterday evening, when about to write the 2nd article on your book,[a] I was interrupted in such a way as to preclude further work. I shan't be able to make up for lost time today and so the article will have to be put off till next week, greatly to my annoyance.

I was out of town from Saturday to Monday, and on Monday evening found the enclosed scrawl from Duncker.[463] The note I enclose will enable you to obtain the 6 copies of *Po and Rhine*; send me those you don't need. *Freiligrath has had one.* It's really high time the fool was forced to adopt a less equivocal position, or at very least to *shell out.*

Duncker is frankly trying to do me down. Lassalle mentioned 2,000 copies; now he claims to have printed only 1,000. Siebel, who is back here again, tells me that, to judge by his own experience of the pamphlet's success with booksellers, this must be a lie. *Que faire?*[b]

What do you think of the pretty excuse for failing to advertise your book?

So Mazzini has finally made his diplomatic revelations in a frightful tirade in *The Times.*[c] All the same, the facts are

---

[a] F. Engels, 'Karl Marx. *A Contribution to the Critique of Political Economy*'. - [b] What's to be done? - [c] G. Mazzini, 'To the Editor of *The Times*', *The Times,* No. 23381, 10 August 1859.

important and confirm our information and conclusions. Perhaps this will shake Urquhart's view that Mazzini's a RUSSIAN.[464]

Salut.

Your
F. E.

First published abridged in *Der Briefwechsel zwischen F. Engels und K. Marx*, Bd. 2, Stuttgart, 1913 and in full in: Marx and Engels, *Works*, First Russian Edition, Vol. XXII, Moscow, 1929

Printed according to the original

Published in English for the first time

275

MARX TO ENGELS

IN MANCHESTER

[London,] 13 August 1859

Dear Engels,

I received the enclosed note[a] on Thursday afternoon. I therefore hastened into town. Matters could only be arranged by my borrowing £4 from Garthe, which *will have to be returned.* On Monday I shall write to Borchardt. To abandon the paper now would seem to me foolish on several counts: 1. because this would save the now foundering *Gottfried*[b]; 2. because after the King of Prussia's[c] death there will be radical changes in Germany, when *we* must have a paper of our own; 3. because of the growing number of subscribers (although *for the time being* this is simply a disadvantage financially, since the cost in STAMPS increases weekly while payments aren't due until the *end of the quarter*). The *Volk* already wields considerable influence in the United States. For instance the preface to my book[d] has been reprinted from the *Volk* and variously commented on by German papers from New England to California.

You couldn't, I suppose, arrange to let me have your article[e] by Wednesday, there being nothing 'topical' about it this time?

---

[a] The note is not extant. - [b] the weekly *Hermann*, of which Gottfried Kinkel had been publisher until July 1859 - [c] Frederick William IV - [d] *A Contribution to the Critique of Political Economy* - [e] F. Engels, 'K. Marx. *A Contribution to the Critique of Political Economy*'.

Might it be possible to raise some money from German business employees in Manchester through your cousin Siebel?

I shall certainly succeed in getting some money out of Berlin and New York. But there's the next 6 to 8 weeks to be taken care of.

As TO Freiligrath, just come and TRY extracting one shilling from him if you can!

Incidentally, and between ourselves, we'd have done better over money if new deficits hadn't continually arisen as a result of renewed thefts. But these were perpetrated by the old agents. Beginning with Scherzer, I've thrown out *all* those who *had* compromised themselves. But what remained of the old leaven[a] wasn't any good and, even if these uncouth louts have been well-behaved hitherto, they blot their copybook when they make their *exit.* I finally threw out *the last* of them—Mr Lange—last week. It would have been relatively much easier to start up a completely new paper from scratch rather than, as Biskamp and Liebknecht did, *continue,* if only nominally, the existence of an organ that was rotten through and through.[b]

Herewith a letter from Dana.

Though I don't think much of his POETRY, could your RELATIVE Siebel do some little piece of verse for the *Volk*? But nothing sublime, please! So as to nettle Freiligrath, we simply must unearth some poet or other, even if we have to write the verse for him ourselves.

Salut.

Your

K. M.

Copies of *Po and Rhine* next week.

First published abridged in *Der Briefwechsel zwischen F. Engels und K. Marx,* Bd. 2, Stuttgart, 1913 and in full in: Marx and Engels, *Works,* First Russian Edition, Vol. XXII, Moscow, 1929

Printed according to the original

Published in English for the first time

---

[a] I Corinthians 5:7 - [b] See this volume, pp. 437-39.

276

MARX TO ENGELS

IN MANCHESTER

London, 26 August [1859]

Dear Fred,

'*Das Volk' is no more.* I had already advanced to Hollinger the £2 you sent at the end of last week, for otherwise last Friday's issue (a week ago today) would not have come out. I have therefore paid it back to myself. In addition I owe Garthe £4 (for the paper) and ABOUT £2 more to Lessner, *£6 in all.* Moreover in Hollinger's case the deficit has accumulated—which doesn't, of course, concern us so immediately. However, it ought not to be allowed to grow any more. This can only be charged when the money for the subscriptions has come in. The *French* paper is not going to appear because of the amnesty.[465]

Borchardt, the braggart, wrote to say there was nothing doing in Manchester. First, because of the peace, then because of the amnesty. But more especially—and this was something he had not *himself* felt able to refute—because *Das Volk* was a scurrilous paper (oh, you idiot of a philistine!). I.e. not nice enough for the Steinthals and other such Ikeys. On the other hand a letter arrived at the same time from Lupus in which he spoke very highly of *Das Volk.* But the FACT is that as the paper improved, losses increased and readers fell off. Besides, that idiot Biskamp, with all sorts of people on at him, appeared to be jealous on account of his dwindling importance on the paper.

Lastly, in view of Liebknecht's ineptitude and Biskamp's instability and weakness, it would have become increasingly necessary for me to intervene directly in the editorial work (for if sales were low among the louts, they were correspondingly high among the German *diplomatic haute volée*[a] in London). Distances being what they are here, the thing was in any case taking up too much of my time, and my own circumstances ARE IN SUCH A DESPERATE STATE THAT I MUST LOOK TO THEM.

---

[a] upper crust

That wretch Dronke hasn't even subscribed for one copy. Your cousin Siebel, however, as you will see from the enclosed, is the *Hermann*'s bard under Beta's management.[a]

Salut.

Your

K. M.

First published abridged in *Der Briefwechsel zwischen F. Engels und K. Marx*, Bd. 2, Stuttgart, 1913 and in full in: Marx and Engels, *Works*, First Russian Edition, Vol. XXII, Moscow, 1929

Printed according to the original

Published in English for the first time

277

MARX TO ENGELS[466]

IN MANCHESTER

[London, 5 September 1859]

Dear Engels,

Could you possibly send me a military piece on China by Friday? I have written today (but not last Friday since I had a tiresome visitor) about Italy and Hungary.[b] The purely political stuff is AT AN END until the opening of Parliament.

Salut.

Your

K. M.

First published in: Marx and Engels, *Works*, First Russian Edition, Vol. XXII, Moscow, 1929

Printed according to the original

Published in English for the first time

[a] Probably a reference to the item 'Sprüche von Carl Siebel' in *Hermann*, No. 33, 20 August 1859. - [b] 'Kossuth and Louis Napoleon'

278

ENGELS TO MARX[467]

IN LONDON

Manchester, [8 September 1859]
7 Southgate

Dear Moor,

Unfortunately the article can't be sent today. It's now 7 o'clock and I still have at least half an hour's work at the office; it takes me $^1/_2$ hour to get home and, what is more, I haven't yet set eyes on *The Times*, nor should I be able to borrow it for this evening. I'd have to finish the whole thing by 11.30 at the latest if I were to get it off—it's *clairement impossible*, particularly in the case of names which have been wrongly telegraphed and can only be deciphered after one has spent ages poring over the map. However, I'll go over the material for Tuesday and, should the Calcutta MAIL be in by Monday, rectify it accordingly.

First published in: Marx and Engels, *Works*, First Russian Edition, Vol. XXII, Moscow, 1929

Printed according to the original

Published in English for the first time

279

MARX TO WILHELM LIEBKNECHT

IN LONDON

London, 17 September 1859

Dear Liebknecht,

I should ere now have returned Blind's letter of 8th September,[468] which you passed on to me, had not various passages therein made it *necessary* for me to take further steps to ascertain the facts of the case.

In this letter Blind maintains that he had had '*nothing whatever to do with the problem in question*' (i.e. with the *public* denunciation of Vogt). He further maintains that 'the remarks' he made '*in the course of a private conversation...*'[461] (implying that he's only spoken about Vogt '*in private*') '*were completely misinterpreted*'. The words 'completely misinterpreted' are used with reference to *myself*. It was *I* who '*completely misinterpreted*' Blind's 'remarks made in the course of a *private conversation*' and hence '*completely misrepresented*' them to you and Biskamp. The misrepresentation in question is not *witting, deliberate* misrepresentation, but misrepresentation due either to the inherent difficulty of Blind's account, or to the feebleness and natural perversity of my powers of comprehension.

As to which I would observe:

1. Vogt was a tool used by Bonaparte to corrupt liberals in Germany and German revolutionaries abroad. Vogt further offered 30,000 gulden to a certain liberal writer in Germany in order to win him over in the interests of Bonapartist propaganda.—These two *on-dit*[a] were imparted to *me* IN THE MOST SERIOUS MANNER by Blind on 9 May, the day of Urquhart's first meeting. He imparted them to Freiligrath. He imparted them to *others*. He repeated, or rather *reaffirmed*, them in your presence, in Hollinger's presence, in my presence, on the day we all three of us had AN INTERVIEW with him. In regard to these two points, therefore, there can be no question of any interpretation, false or otherwise. They have been admitted. They can be proved by evidence. They are FACTS in so far as we consider Blind's *statements* as *FACTS*.

2. Now as to Blind's '*interpretation*'—minus the *name* Vogt *qua* agent of Bonapartist corruption, and minus the affair of the 30,000 gulden—it is to be found in an article in the London *Free Press* dated 27 May with the heading: 'The Grand Duke Constantine to be King of Hungary'. Blind ***is*** the author of this article in which he says that **he* 'knows the name of a Swiss Senator to whom he (Prince Jerome Napoleon) broached the subject'*, and even knows what Plon-Plon DID BROACH TO THE SWISS SENATOR; in which he further *knows of 'the attempts made ... to win over to the Russo-Napoleonic scheme some of the exiled German Democrats, as well as some influential Liberals in Germany'*; in which he further *KNOWS* that *'***large pecuniary advantages*** were held out to them as a ***bribe***'*; and in which, finally, he is *'glad that these offers were rejected with indignation'*. This 'interpretation' is *printed* and did not therefore occur 'in the course of a *private conversation*'. Again, it would seem from this that Blind, far from having had nothing to do with 'the problem', played the part of initiator.

3. Add together 1. the *facts* related, and admitted to have been related, by Blind and 2. the 'interpretation' which Blind had

[a] rumours

printed and which is *legally verifiable* as such, and what do you get?

The anonymous pamphlet *Zur Warnung* minus a few irrelevant phrases. Whether or not Blind composed this pamphlet is therefore *completely immaterial*. He is *responsible for publishing* the elements which go to make it up.

He mentioned the *name* Vogt and the affair of the 30,000 gulden 'in the course of a private conversation'. Not only with me but with Freiligrath and others. And not as a private and '*confidential*' matter but as political denunciation. He *himself* had the 'interpretation' relating to these two POINTS printed.

It is quite immaterial, therefore, whether or not the pamphlet which subsequently came out was composed by him! All it contains is the sum total of verbal Blind and printed Blind. It *is* Blind added together. Hence it was not only *I* who regarded him as its author. Freiligrath did too. He even questioned him about it.

Author or otherwise, it in *no way* alters the case. He is still the *instigator* responsible.

You will recall that at the above-mentioned meeting he stated on his *word of honour* that he had not *composed* the pamphlet. *Composing* and *writing* are in effect two separate things. I now have *documentary, legally valid* evidence (*which is at your disposal*) to the effect that the pamphlet was printed by F. Hollinger, was handed to him by Blind, was written in Blind's *hand*, and was regarded by F. Hollinger as Blind's product.[469]

What remains, then, is *my* interpretation, described not merely as a 'misinterpretation' but a 'complete misinterpretation'.

As regards the Augsburg *Allgemeine Zeitung*, the relationship between myself and that paper has always been one of outright *hostility*. What is at issue in the law-suit that is to be heard in open court at Augsburg on the 28th of October[470] is not a QUARREL between the A. *A. Z.* and Vogt but a *legal ruling* on the relationship between the German ex-imperial regent[410] Vogt and the French EMPEROR Louis Bonaparte. In my view, then, what is at issue for *every* German revolutionary, even if not a member of a 'Fatherland Association',[471] is *not*, in this instance, 'the affairs of a newspaper with which he had *nothing whatever* to do'; rather it is *his own* affair. That, however, is a matter of taste. *De gustibus*, etc.[a]

Salut.

Your

K. M.

First published in: Marx and Engels, *Works*, First Russian Edition, Vol. XXIX, Moscow, 1946

Printed according to the original

Published in English for the first time

---

[a] *De gustibus non est disputandum*—Tastes are not matters for discussion.

Wilhelm Liebknecht

Conrad Schramm

Ferdinand Lassalle

280

MARX TO ENGELS

IN MANCHESTER

[London,] 21 September 1859

Dear Engels,

I have received your letter[472] together with the enclosure. My domestic AFFAIRS, by the by, have again reached the inevitable point of crisis, worse this time than ever before, because I can't see any way out. A go at my brother-in-law[a] ended IN NOTHING. Freiligrath's business is WINDING UP. Whether the Swiss will set up a new London agency, and for him, in 1860 is still in doubt. So he now has a better excuse than ever to refuse to handle any bill transactions. Dana has warned me about OVERDRAWING. Consequently I'm in a complete FIX. Apart from minor hazards (e.g. this week they are threatening to cut off the gas and water) the more considerable debts have all been mounting up and a substantial portion of these can no longer be put off. E.g. house, school, etc.

As I shall have to write to Duncker shortly about the second instalment, let me know whether he has advertised the first instalment in the press. It seems to me that he would gladly let THE WHOLE MATTER DROP.[473]

The damnable thing about it is that I no longer have a Bamberger in London. Otherwise I could certainly arrange a few ACCOMMODATION BILLS which I would subsequently pay with the money from America. In these CIRCUMSTANCES it can never be a question of anything but [MAKE]SHIFTS.

You must forgive me for telling you this tale of woe. But down here there is absolutely no-one to whom I can freely unburden myself.

As I've already told Lupus in my letter,[474] you will both be hearing from me shortly about some odd political scandals.

Salut.

Your

K. M.

First published in *Der Briefwechsel zwischen F. Engels und K. Marx,* Bd. 2, Stuttgart, 1913

Printed according to the original

Published in English for the first time

---

[a] Johann Carl Juta

281

ENGELS TO MARX

IN LONDON

Manchester, 22 September 1859

Dear Moor,

Lupus has just brought me your letter. I only got back the evening before last from a tour of Scotland with my parents[a] and have now packed them off home again.

A day or two before my old man arrived I had the most damnable bit of bad luck. At a drunken gathering I was insulted by an Englishman[b] I didn't know; I hit out at him with the umbrella I was carrying and the ferrule got him in the eye. The chap immediately put the matter in the hands of his LAWYER. I made the necessary counter-moves, and since his eye wasn't permanently damaged and he has now recovered, it at first seemed probable that the affair would be settled—though I would still be responsible for the costs. Now, however, the swine has suddenly done a *volte-face* and is threatening me with an ACTION; and if it came to that the thing would cost me over two hundred pounds, on top of which there would be a public scandal and a ROW with my old man, who would have to put up the money. However I still hope to get round the JOBBING LAWYERS; if all goes *really well* the DRUNKEN BRAWL will cost me forty or fifty pounds. The worst of it is that I'm completely in the hands of this swine and his SOLICITOR, can do nothing to force the issue and must put up with everything to avoid a scandal, otherwise the costs will be even heavier. Needless to say these blasted English don't want to deprive themselves of the pleasure of getting their hands on a BLOODY FOREIGNER.

So this time my troubles have certainly not come singly. I simply don't know what to do until I can see how the business is going to turn out. My English acquaintances are behaving very honourably and instantly took the thing up, but I'm going to be bled, that's certain, and how much, heaven only knows.

At all events I shall send you a five-pound note about Saturday or Monday to prevent the worst happening; meanwhile I can get it carried over to the October account. You may rest assured that I

---

[a] Friedrich and Elisabeth Engels - [b] Daniells

shall do whatever I can, but as you can see for yourself I don't really know where I am myself at the moment.

Warm regards to your wife and children.

Your

F. E.

First published in *Der Briefwechsel zwischen F. Engels und K. Marx*, Bd. 2, Stuttgart, 1913

Printed according to the original

Published in English for the first time

282

MARX TO ENGELS

IN MANCHESTER

London, 23 September [1859]

Dear Frederic,

Bad news. This time I'm in some doubt whether the business down here can be got over. There are *very nasty* difficulties in the way.

I'm also in some doubt about your own *affaire. Apart from the scandal*—if the fellow's eye is better, if it can be proved that he offended you first and, further, that he had already agreed to your compromise, etc.—I don't see that, under English law, there is very much he can do. In London you would at worst be fined £2-£5. It seems to me that the purpose of the whole thing is *to obtain money on false pretences.*

If the situation here is not to get *any worse,* I believe it essential that I should be able to send off 'Infantry' to Dana in about a week or 10 days from now. Although he said 15 September it certainly won't be too late and in any case he must admit that we have shown good will. The main thing is that it should be not so much profound as prolix.

If, immediately after your arrival in Manchester [475] and after having made inquiries about the 'Englishman',[a] you had departed again, *for London, say,* and made it known to the swine through a third party that you were on your way *to the Continent,* you would have been able to come to *any* arrangement you wanted. *This might still be possible* for, judging by Allen, etc., all Englishmen now believe that there will be a general amnesty [476] on the Continent and

[a] Daniells

hence are afraid that their debtors will QUIT THE COUNTRY. (After all, the Prussian amnesty is to be on the 15th of October.) Every stratagem should be used against a chap like that.

Salut.

Your

K. M.

First published abridged in *Der Briefwechsel zwischen F. Engels und K. Marx*, Bd. 2, Stuttgart, 1913 and in full in: Marx and Engels, *Works*, First Russian Edition, Vol. XXII, Moscow, 1929

Printed according to the original
Published in English for the first time

283

ENGELS TO MARX[477]

IN LONDON

Manchester, 7 Southgate
[between 24 and 26 September 1859]

Dear Moor,

Enclosed fiver B/B 95281 Manchester, 1 January 1859.

Shall deal with the other matters very shortly.

For the present just one more point to which an answer is required by return if possible.

1. How much money is needed to return to those subscribers to the *Volk* who have paid direct, the few pence due to them in respect of undelivered copies?

2. What arrangement was made about this with Thimm and others? Have the booksellers deducted what was not delivered, OR HOW? Or not paid at all yet?

I must have clarification of these matters, if possible *at once*, and I shall, if possible, raise the money—it can't amount to much—to settle the sorry business of the direct subscribers. Up here the bourgeois are complaining like mad that they've been cheated, and Lupus and I have to swallow it all. So let me have an answer at once. The day before yesterday Lupus was involved in a row on this account and I shall have to see the 'third party' as soon as possible.

'Infantry' is in hand and if at all possible I shall finish it before the week is out.

As to my own affair up here, surely you don't imagine that I, for my part, didn't also have SENSE enough to hand the thing over to a LAWYER and listen to his opinion. It's not a case of some miserable fine imposed by a magistrate but of an ACTION AT NISI PRIUS FOR DAMAGES, in which the *costs* alone could be as high as £200. You surely don't imagine that I shall let myself be swindled like this without lifting a finger; as to running away, I need hardly say that, my circumstances being what they are, there can be no question of it, even for a fortnight; and being as well known in Manchester as I am, no one here would imagine that I would run away from the firm, etc., in order to escape a lawsuit of this sort.

The real joke is that the use of pretty well any instrument gives a LAWYER a HANDLE with which to sway a BRITISH JURY, namely moral indignation at BLOODY FOREIGNERS who don't use their fists, etc. In which case the verdict goes against the FOREIGNER as sure as 2×2=4, and on top of that he has to fork out the costs. Anyway you can count on it that I shall fork out no more than is absolutely necessary. As yet the affair hasn't progressed an inch but I hope it will soon be settled so that I may at least get a clear idea of what can be done to help you through the crisis.

Many regards to your wife and the girls.

Your

F. E.

First published abridged in *Der Briefwechsel zwischen F. Engels und K. Marx*, Bd. 2, Stuttgart, 1913 and in full in: Marx and Engels, *Works*, First Russian Edition, Vol. XXII, Moscow, 1929

Printed according to the original

Published in English for the first time

284

MARX TO BERTALAN SZEMERE[478]

IN PARIS

London, 26 September 1859

My dear Franck,

In reply to your letter d.d. Sept. 23 I beg to state: 1) On the arrival at London of the *N. Y. T.* containing P's declaration, which to sign with his name he had not dared,[a] I sent the

---

[a] [F. Pulszky,] 'From Our Own Correspondent. Monday, August 7, 1859', *New-York Daily Tribune*, No. 5720, 23 August 1859.

N. Y. T. two letters with a full statement of the case. Simultaneously, I addressed a *private note* to the Editor in which I insisted upon the necessity of exposing the manoeuvres and intrigues of the wide-mouthed charlatan.[479] *We shall, by and by, ascertain, whether or not my letters were published by the* N. Y. T.[a]

As to the great London Daily Papers, it is quite out of the question to induce them to give publicity to a full exposure of Kossuth. The statement, in the first instance, would imply a *libel case,* which to stand the editors are, or at least affect to be, afraid of, considering the difficulty to prove such charges of bribery, and to summon the witnesses before a British tribunal. In the second instance, Kossuth is too unmitigated a humbug to not share the secret sympathies of the venal London press-gang. I have, however, put down a summary for the *'Free Press'* (the Urquhartite paper which appears on the last Wednesday of every month)[b] I have authorised them, if they think it necessary, 'to dress the salad' in their own style, and I think myself warranted in supposing that the 'thing' is to come out *this very week.* In that case I shall forward you a copy. Although circulated among a very exclusive public, the *Free Press* finds its way to all the cabinets and capitals of Europe. It is well known at Constantinople. Besides, the statement having once appeared in the *Free Press,* some London correspondents, connected with the German press, and more or less influenced by me, will find it easier to transplant the thing to the Teutonic soil.

I enclose Asboth's declaration from the *N. Y. T.*[c] The turn now given to K's proceedings is, that that 'illustrious' patriot attempted only to prevent 'a premature *rising* in Hungary', and that the clever 'statesman' altogether succeeded in this 'difficult' task.

Some time ago, Urquhart had his correspondence with Kossuth (which I alluded to, as you will recollect) translated into Italian, and copiously distributed throughout Italy.[d]

2) *In regard to the wine-affair,* I became informed, soon after your departure from London, that my brother-in-law[e] was not to return to Amsterdam before October. I have, therefore, *not yet* written to him on the business.

For England I have till now vacillated between two men, both of whom, though in different ways, appear fit for undertaking the

[a] K. Marx, 'Kossuth and Louis Napoleon'. - [b] [K. Marx,] 'Particulars of Kossuth's Transaction with Louis Napoleon'. - [c] A. Asbóth, 'The Peace of Villafranca and the Hungarian Cause', *New-York Daily Tribune,* No. 5727, 31 August 1859. - [d] Letters of L. Kossuth and D. Urquhart published in *The Free Press,* No. 16, 12 May 1858. - [e] Johann Carl Juta

task. The one is a German, without capital, but very energetical, speculative, and industrious. The other is an Englishman, who deals in French and German wines, a *'respectable'* merchant, although no large one. At all events, he has contrived to get on with his wine-business and to rise, in the short period of 6-7 years, from very small beginnings to comparative affluency. The former candidate would have been exclusively given to the business in question; the latter has the advantage of greater means, a settled concern, and established connexions. If, as will be decided in a few days, the German is, for the present, not yet ready to enter on the affair (and I have reason to think so), I shall make a conditional offer to the Englishman. You will then be informed of his conditions and may decide yourself.

Yours truly

A. Williams [a]

P.S. At this moment I receive your second letter. I think it is already answered by the preceding lines.

27. Sep. The proof-sheet of the 'thing' in the *Free Press* has been forwarded to me.

First published in *Revue d'histoire comparée*, t. IV, Nos. 1-2, 1946

Reproduced from the original

285

MARX TO ENGELS [480]

IN MANCHESTER

[London, 27 September 1859]

Dear Engels,

Your letter with enclosure received.

I knew as soon as the letter had gone off that some of my critical remarks were idiotic.[b]

I myself am involved in a COUNTY-COURT PROCESS on account of the *Volk*. As regards the 'direct' subscribers in Manchester, these were only Lupus and a 'cobbler' who had already cancelled his order *before* the paper ceased to be.

---

[a] conspiratorial pseudonym of Karl Marx - [b] See this volume, p. 491.

Thimm has *not yet* paid and was, moreover, requested to pay only for the NUMBERS RECEIVED. How can we have done anything to the prejudice of the philistines in Manchester when they have not yet paid *a single* FARTHING?

Send the names of the fellows with claims. Tell Thimm (on Biskamp's behalf) that he must not send another FARTHING here until he hears from us again. You may instruct him to pay 'bona fide' claimants in Manchester.

Biskamp has now taken lodgings at my expense here in Hampstead. The POOR DEVIL has had an operation for PLEURISY at the German hospital, where he spent $1^1/_2$ weeks—*sans sou.*[a] All in all a nice state of affairs.

Today is article day, so I shall close.

Salut.

Your

K. M.

First published abridged in *Der Briefwechsel zwischen F. Engels und K. Marx*, Bd. 2, Stuttgart, 1913 and in full in: Marx and Engels, *Works*, First Russian Edition, Vol. XXII, Moscow, 1929

Printed according to the original

Published in English for the first time

286

MARX TO ENGELS

IN MANCHESTER

London, 28 September [1859]

Dear Engels,

Yesterday evening I had a visit from Lessner, whom I had sent for in connection with the Manchester subscribers to the *Volk*.

Like Biskamp, he assures me that (apart from Lupus) there wasn't a single direct subscriber to the *Volk*. And up till now no one has sent a FARTHING to London.

After the *Volk* ceased publication Thimm wrote to Lessner asking for an account. Lessner replied that he could send him an account only in respect of the period in which he, Lessner, had been despatch clerk. He then sent him an invoice for the *individual numbers*. Up till yesterday there had been no reply from Thimm.

---

a without a penny

So I'd like to know what fellows are kicking up the fuss in Manchester and on what PRETEXT.

Down here we (and I especially) have unpleasantnesses enough in respect of the *Volk* without that.

The 'Particulars' about Kossuth in *The Free Press* are mine. (I have made 2 articles out of them for the *Tribune*[479] and shall see whether they are accepted.) I got them from Szemere, partly in writing, partly by word of mouth. Szemere was here a few weeks ago.

Salut. Regards to Lupus.

Your

K. M.

It's doubtful whether Biskamp will pull through. The poor devil is as low as can be. We seem to attract every damned spot of bother that's going.

First published abridged in *Der Briefwechsel zwischen F. Engels und K. Marx*, Bd. 2, Stuttgart, 1913 and in full in: Marx and Engels, *Works*, First Russian Edition, Vol. XXII, Moscow, 1929

Printed according to the original

Published in English for the first time

287

MARX TO FERDINAND LASSALLE [481]

IN BERLIN

London, [not before 2 October 1859]
9 Grafton Terrace, Maitland Park,
Haverstock Hill

Dear Lassalle,

It is very good of you to be the first to take up the pen again, and this in a matter touching my interests, despite the fact that appearances speak against me.

As for my silence, let me say briefly:

First, I didn't get either of your letters until weeks after their despatch, namely on my return to London from a journey to Scotland *via* Manchester, made for business reasons.[444] Meanwhile events had moved so fast that they had, as it were, removed the point of our debate.[a] For the POINT IN QUESTION did not relate—nor, between you and me, could it have related—to the nationalities issue, but rather to the most suitable policy to be pursued by the German revolutionaries towards their own governments and other countries. Now I would nevertheless have sent a reply, if a belated one, had there not been fresh grounds for delay. In one of your letters you asked for evidence relating to Vogt. That evidence was in the hands of Karl Blind. The 'worthy democrat', however, though privately inclined to play at moral indignation as well as stir up scandal, resisted all expostulations TO COME OUT. Consequently I broke with him. (He even denied authorship of *Zur Warnung*, the anonymous pamphlet published in London[461] and reproduced in the *Augsburger*.[b] However, I have succeeded in obtaining documentary evidence against him (Blind) in this matter,[469] to which I shall revert 'at the right time and the right place'.) This provided a fresh occasion for prolonging my silence. And, since 'the evil deed is accursed in that it must constantly engender evil'[c] my silence itself became an obstacle to my breaking it. On top of that—and I beg you not to regard this simply as a figure of speech—there was a whole series of domestic complications, as yet by no means eliminated, which in fact robbed me of all desire to write. So much for my silence, which, however, and despite all APPEARANCES TO THE CONTRARY, was in no way motivated by ill-will.

Now as to Duncker,

on my return to London I found a letter from him which apparently rendered it impossible for me to make any further direct approach to the man regarding the sequel.[473] On the other hand, not having written to you for so long, I couldn't possibly start off by suddenly writing to you about my own concerns. So I let the matter DROP, on the tacit assumption that, if I hadn't heard from Duncker by a certain date, I should have to approach another publisher.

However, one of your earlier letters led me to suppose that Duncker had undertaken to publish 2 instalments, or rather the first section ('Capital in General') in its entirety.[d] But on the other hand the first instalment[e] was much more compendious than had

---

[a] See this volume, p. 460. - [b] [K. Blind.] *Zur Warnung, Allgemeine Zeitung*, No. 173 (supplement), 22 June 1859. - [c] An allusion to the following lines from Schiller's drama *Wallenstein. Die Piccolomini*, V, 1: 'Das eben ist der Fluch der bösen That,/Daß sie, fortzeugend, immer Böses muß gebären' ('This is the curse of every evil deed,/That, propagating still, it brings forth evil'). - [d] See this volume, pp. 270 and 368. - [e] K. Marx, *A Contribution to the Critique of Political Economy*.

been originally planned, nor, for that matter, did I want him to be a 'publisher *malgré lui*[a]'. However, since the first 2 instalments form a whole, it would be desirable for them at least to appear under the same imprint.

I shall now be obliged to remodel the thing completely, as the manuscript for this second instalment is already a year old[250]; and, since my circumstances do not permit me to devote much time to the matter just now, I hardly think I shall be able to finish it before the end of December. That, however, would be at the *very outside*.

I am busy with an *English* rendering of the first instalment and this, too, has been disrupted by a bad domestic spell. At any rate I am assured of a better reception in England than in Germany where, so far as I am aware, nobody inquires after the thing or gives a straw for it. All I want is to place the whole of this *first section*, at least, before the German public. Should the latter continue to pay no heed to the work, I intend to put all subsequent sections straight into English and no longer concern myself with the German philistines.

Vale faveque.[b]

K. M.

First published in: *F. Lassalle. Nachgelassene Briefe und Schriften*, Bd. II, Stuttgart-Berlin, 1922

Printed according to the original

Published in English in full for the first time

288

ENGELS TO MARX

IN LONDON

Manchester, 3 October 1859

Dear Moor,

What you wrote and told me about *Das Volk* was most welcome news. It now transpires that the philistine who raised an outcry had taken out a subscription with Thimm *après tout*.[c]

What's this about proceedings in the COUNTY COURT[d]?

---

[a] against his will. Cf. Molière's *Le Médecin malgré lui*. - [b] Good-bye and farewell. - [c] after all - [d] See this volume, p. 495.

Because of sundry interruptions and an (otherwise insignificant) inflammation of the left eye which prevents me doing much writing by gas-light, 'Infantry' is not quite finished. You'll get it by Friday for sure.

My quarrel not settled yet and might still be damnably long-drawn-out. But I've got the scoundrel[a] pretty well pinned down and believe I can now stand back and watch; whatever happens, though, it's going to cost money—that's the most annoying thing about it; moreover, the LAW being what it is here, one can never be quite sure of one's case. At all events, things look a good deal better now.

The Free Press hadn't arrived the day before yesterday; I shall go and have another look presently. What sort of a branch is it that Urquhart has opened in Berlin?

So it now transpires that the Russian memorandum appeared in the *Preussisches Wochenblatt*! (I've only just seen the August number of *The Free Press.*)[482] Apart from what's in *The Free Press,*[b] have you any other scandalous stuff about great men[367]?

Your

F. E.

Have a complete account made out for Thimm as soon as possible, i.e. covering the pre-Lessner period as well; the fellow apparently intends to pocket the money. But send me a full list of the people who subscribed through Thimm, so that I can keep a check on reimbursements and send round a circular telling people that they can reclaim their money from Thimm.

Siebel's indifferent verse[c] was sent to the *Hermann* behind Siebel's back by a chap in Germany to whom he had written enclosing it. He promptly wrote to the editors, and only then did he learn how this had come about.

First published in *Der Briefwechsel zwischen F. Engels und K. Marx,* Bd. 2, Stuttgart, 1913

Printed according to the original

Published in English for the first time

---

a Daniells - b Engels means Marx's article 'Particulars of Kossuth's Transaction with Louis Napoleon'. - c 'Sprüche von Carl Siebel', *Hermann,* No. 33, 20 August 1859. See this volume, p. 485.

289

MARX TO ENGELS

IN MANCHESTER

[London,] 5 October [1859]

Dear Engels,

In view of the way things are managed here (Speck has gone bankrupt and disappeared; Garthe, the cashier, is in Brighton) and always have been managed so far as the *Volk* is concerned, it is impossible to obtain an accurate account AS TO FOREIGN [out-of-town] SUBSCRIBERS during the pre-Lessner period. Biskamp maintains that, with the exception of the very first issues, Thimm was always sent a dozen copies.

Hollinger is suing me for £12 and a couple of shillings arrears in respect of *Das Volk*, together with the type for the last issue, which did not appear. The dirty dog is trying to make out all of a sudden that I'm the 'proprietor', although the whole business, I won't say foundered (for your philistine here is a hopeless proposition), but closed down with a deficit because I *wasn't* the proprietor and was unable to knock the slipshod management into shape despite all the time I spent on it. Still less did I ever give the chap a legal guarantee. I think his account is wrong, for apart from the other moneys received, the fellow had had £7 from me *for the 3 penultimate issues alone* (his account covers the last 2 issues).—The 15/- for Lessner did not go through his hands but was paid direct by me.—However, I'm not going to engage in any controversy on the subject since I would thereby immediately acknowledge his right to sue *me*. The dirty dog will swear on oath and get one of his type-setters to swear on oath that I gave a guarantee. (Even were this the case he should have sued Biskamp first.) I shall call in Biskamp, etc., to give counter-evidence. Had I the means, I should have avoided all *public* proceedings, not by paying Hollinger, but by buying the debt he incurred with one Lisle, Hollinger's LANDLORD and *owner* of the press. Hollinger owes this man some £60 and has never paid him a FARTHING.

But circumstances being what they are, there can be no question of anything of the kind.

Unless I bring off some sort of coup—and I simply cannot see *how* I can do so—my position will become *completely* untenable. Freiligrath made another attempt at negotiating a bill. But yesterday evening, at the same time as threatening letters from the LANDLORD, etc., etc., a letter arrived from him saying it was definitely no go. The enclosed letter from Lassalle, which I answered by return,[a] looks like good news to me. The thing[b] appears to be selling despite the *conspiration de silence.* Otherwise I wouldn't have received this *indirect* request from Duncker. I shall, by the by, be totally incapable of going on with the thing[473] until I've CLEARED up the worst of the domestic mess *d'une manière ou d'une autre.*[c] *Your articles* on my affair[d] have been reprinted in German papers from New York to California (with the tiny little *Volk* we hooked the whole of the German-American press). To show you the kind of rubbish that's appearing in Germany, I enclose a cutting of the advertisements in the Vienna *Presse. Il suffit*[e] TO READ the index. (BY THE BY, I am giving lectures about the first instalment to a *select* circle of artisans.[f] It seems to interest the chaps a great deal.[483])

Lastly, a report on two 'great men'.[367]

Ad vocem[g] *R. Schramm.* Some while ago this pitiful blockhead was in Ostend, whence he sent a contribution to the *Hermann.*[h] Not that I'm in the habit of reading that trashy sheet; I heard about this through Freiligrath. In his contribution R. Schramm declares that one could gauge the depths to which the Germans had sunk simply by listening to their conversations on the beach. Thus he had, for instance, overheard two ladies chattering away in broad Wuppertal accents and one of them had addressed the other as 'Mrs Engels'. So that's the kind of revenge this wretch takes! But by way of retribution the blockhead recently lost £2,000 (*teste*[i] Freiligrath), having, like a fool, entered the 'precious stones business'. This had, moreover, frustrated his scheme of starting a German paper of his own in London (was to have come out this month). To the chap's intense annoyance and as a riposte to his childish MALICE, I got Biskamp to see that the FACTS—non-appearance of the paper, gem trade and loss of money—were published in the *Weser-Zeitung.*

Ad vocem K. Blind. With regard to this *homme d'état,* I must go into greater detail.

About a fortnight after my return to London from Manchester, Biskamp told me that Blind had proposed, through Hollinger, that he (i.e. *Das Volk*) amalgamate with Blind and company but

---

[a] See this volume, pp. 497-99. - [b] K. Marx, *A Contribution to the Critique of Political Economy.* - [c] one way or another - [d] F. Engels, 'Karl Marx. *A Contribution to the Critique of Political Economy*'. - [e] It suffices - [f] Marx has: *Knoten.* - [g] As to - [h] [C. Schramm,] 'Ostende 31. August', *Hermann,* No. 36, 10 September 1859 ('Vermischte Nachrichten'). - [i] witness

that I, and the communist element generally, must go. In our stead—sensible socialism. At that time I had, as you know, written nothing for the *Volk* save for a pleasantry or two.[a] However, I forthwith wrote Blind, not a letter, but a communication of ABOUT 10 LINES[484] in which I called him amongst other things an *'homme d'état'* and an 'important man', and alluded to his henchman 'Fidelio'[b] (i.e. Hollinger). Next day along comes Liebknecht, and tells me that Blind and Hollinger are sitting in the pub on the corner. The former, he said, was expecting me. I therefore went there with Liebknecht. Blind gave his word of honour that there was *nothing* in the thing. That swine Hollinger ditto. Hence I could only believe them. However, the meeting gave me a chance of finding out about other machinations of Blind's. *Inter alia*, the conversation came round to Vogt. Blind assured me on his *word of honour* (as he had already assured Freiligrath, though omitting his word of honour) that he had neither written the anonymous *Zur Warnung* nor launched it upon the world. I said this surprised me, since it contained no more than what he had told me *by word of mouth* on the occasion of Urquhart's meeting on 9 May.[461] I reminded him that he had assured me at the time that he possessed *tangible evidence*, knew the name of the man to whom Vogt had offered 30,000 or 40,000 gulden, but 'unfortunately' could not divulge it, etc. Well, Blind hadn't the face to deny this but expressly admitted it more than once in Liebknecht's and Hollinger's presence.

WELL! A few weeks ago the Augsburg *Allgemeine Zeitung* wrote to Liebknecht, who had sent them *Zur Warnung*. Liebknecht came to me.[470] I told him to go and find Blind, and that I should await the *homme d'état* 'in the pub at Blind's corner'. Blind was at some resort—St. Leonard's, I think. Liebknecht wrote to him; wrote once, twice. At last a letter from the *homme d'état*. In the coolest and most 'diplomatic' manner the latter regretted that 'I' should have called to see him in vain. Liebknecht, he went on, must understand that he (Blind) had no desire to intervene in the affairs of a 'paper with which he had absolutely nothing to do' and in a matter with which he had absolutely nothing to do. As for Liebknecht's allusions to 'remarks' let fall 'in the course of a private conversation', these could only be attributed to a 'complete' misunderstanding. And that, or so the *'homme d'état'* imagined, was that.

---

[a] Marx means his reviews published in the section 'Gatherings from the Press'. - [b] Fidelio—the assumed name of Leonore, heroine of Beethoven's opera *Fidelio*.

I now took Liebknecht with me to Collet. I recalled that *The Free Press* of *27 May* ('The Grand Duke Constantine',[440] etc., p. 53) had contained a paragraph which I immediately suspected to be Blind's handiwork and which, taken in conjunction with Blind's *verbal* admissions before Liebknecht, Hollinger and myself, constituted the entire contents of the anonymous pamphlet, besides providing *proof* that it was not just *en passant*, in the course of a 'private conversation', that Blind had touched on this 'matter with which he had absolutely nothing to do'. Hence to Collet, who *instantly* declared Blind to be the AUTHOR. He still had Blind's letter in which the latter had enclosed his card but had asked that his *name* should not be disclosed. This was convincing evidence.

By a series of manoeuvres which it would take too long to describe here, I further extracted the enclosed (*which you must let me have back by return*. I have also shown it to Freiligrath). So much for the respectable citizen's 'word of honour'!

Well, last Saturday Liebknecht sent the *homme d'état* a letter (modelled on a letter from myself to Liebknecht in which I had summed the matter up in somewhat forceful terms[a]). We are awaiting the answer and will let you know the details.

Salut.

Your

K. M.

First published abridged in *Der Briefwechsel zwischen F. Engels und K. Marx*, Bd. 2, Stuttgart, 1913 and in full in: Marx and Engels, *Works*, First Russian Edition, Vol. XXII, Moscow, 1929

Printed according to the original

Published in English for the first time

290

MARX TO BERTALAN SZEMERE[478]

IN PARIS

London, 8 October 1859

My dear Franck,

I have received your last letter, in which you appear to suppose that, as yet, nothing has been done in the affair K. Now, this is altogether a mistake.

---

[a] See this volume, pp. 486-88.

1) On Thursday (Sept. 29), I sent you a copy of the *London Free Press* d.d. 28 Sept., containing a statement headed: *Particulars of K's Transaction with L. N.* On the very day of its issue that number of the *F. P.* was forwarded to *all* the newspaper offices of London. *The Times* published its article in K's favour[a] only *after* having made sure from the *F. P.*, that K. is as venal a fellow as the *Times* writers.

For the case of the number of the *F. P.*, sent to you, having been intercepted by the French Post-Office, I enclose the article above said in this letter.

2) The statement of the *F. P.* has been reprinted in English, Scotch and Irish provincial papers. A literal translation of it has, by friends of mine, been inserted in the Augsburg *Allgemeine Zeitung*[b] and the Bremer *Weserzeitung*. Another German translation is said to have appeared in the Berlin 'Nationalzeitung'.

3) Simultaneously with your letter, I received to-day the *New York Tribune d.d. September 24* which, under the title 'K. and L. N.', brings an elaborate article of mine, filling two and a half columns, and put forward in a prominent place of the paper. The *Tribune* having always had a *faible*[c] for K., and P. being its London correspondent, this publication is a real success, the more so, since P. is nominally denounced in the article, and the apologetical passages of his own letter to the *New Y. T.*[d] are ridiculed. There exist at least some hundred smaller American papers, published in the English language, which receive their *mot d'ordre*[e] from the *Tribune*, and, consequently, will reprint that article. The German American press, from New York to San Francisco, will, by this time, have translated the article into the Teutonic vernacular.

Moreover, it should not be forgotten that New York is the centre of the Hungarian emigration in America.

If you [should] be unable to get the *Tribune* d.d. Sept. 24., I shall send you the article *on the condition of your remitting it*, since I possess no other copy, and stand in need of it should it be replied to by P.

4) K's letter to Mac Adam,[f] on which the *Times* leader remarks, has been generally ridiculed by the London papers, so much so

---

[a] 'One of the most remarkable results...', *The Times*, No. 23428, 4 October 1859. - [b] [K. Marx,] 'Ludwig Kossuth und Louis Napoleon', *Allgemeine Zeitung*, No. 276, 3 October 1859 (supplement). - [c] weak point - [d] [F. Pulszky,] 'From Our Own Correspondent. Monday, August 7, 1859', *New-York Daily Tribune*, No. 5720, 23 August 1859. - [e] cue - [f] Kossuth's letter to J. M'. Adam was published in *The Times*, No. 23428, 4 October 1859.

that K. induced that same Mac Adam to declare in the same papers, that the letter was a *private* letter and not meant for publication.[a] As a specimen, of the manner in which K's letter was handled, I enclose a leader from the London *Daily Telegraph.*

5) If you can forward me any further particulars on K's proclamations and intrigues in Hungary, they will be very welcome, and are sure to find their way into the Press.

6) My stationer was unable to get the *Times'* copies you ask for. Generally, some days after their issue, London Daily papers are difficult of procuring.

7) The remark on *Perczel* in the *F. P.* article is based on a public declaration of his. I thought fit to allude to it, in order to throw confusion into the ranks of K's partisans as to the source from which the information proceeds.

8) From the note enclosed, you will see that the English merchant, on further consideration, declines entering upon the wine-affair. The German, I spoke of, has returned to the Continent. Thus I see no prospect of pushing on this affair in England.

As to my brother-in-law,[b] I have written to him, but not yet received his answer.

Yours truly
Williams[c]

First published in *Revue d'histoire comparée,* t. IV, Nos. 1-2, 1946

Reproduced from the original

291

MARX TO ENGELS

IN MANCHESTER

London, 10 October 1859

DEAR Frederick,

The money arrived on Saturday and really 'saved our lives', for on that day the gang of creditors, or part of it, launched a concerted attack. MY BEST THANKS. Likewise for the manuscript.[d]

---

[a] J. M' Adam, 'To the Editor of *The Times', The Times,* No. 23431, 7 October 1859. - [b] Johann Carl Juta - [c] conspiratorial pseudonym of Karl Marx - [d] F. Engels, 'Infantry'.

I enclose herewith my *Tribune* article on Kossuth.[a] Let Lupus have a look at it as well. *Then send it back to me.* There'll be a major rumpus, since Pulszky is the *Tribune*'s London correspondent. The words[b] I *cite* re 'AUSTRIAN SYMPATHIES', 'ANTI-NAPOLEONIC RAGE', etc., are taken from Pulszky's LETTER *in* the *Tribune* in which he sought to defend Kossuth and Co.[c] IN FACT I'm surprised that, in THESE CIRCUMSTANCES and in view of its general *faible* for Kossuth, the *Tribune* printed the article. True, I enclosed a brief note in German which put heart into Dana.[479]

Collet has sent Kossuth 5 COPIES of the last *Free Press.* The Augsburg *Allgemeine Zeitung* has reproduced the thing.[d] Likewise the *Weser-Zeitung.*

Collet came to see me yesterday. Statesman Blind had called on him and complained forcefully about his (Collet's) having failed to preserve editorial secrecy vis-à-vis myself. He (Collet) must call on me to prevent my doing any more MISCHIEF. The Augsburg *Allgemeine Zeitung* was 'A RUSSIAN (!) ORGAN', which was why he (Blind) would not hold out a helping hand to it.[470] To me, Collet said: *'At the outset, he made upon me the impression of a very sneakish fellow.'* Statesman Blind, like the gentleman he is, has not deigned to answer Liebknecht, and imagines he's been able to spike my guns through Collet. THE FOOL! At the same time he tried to get Collet to tell him who had written about Kossuth in the [*Free*] *Press.*

Salut.

Your

K. M.

First published abridged in *Der Briefwechsel zwischen F. Engels und K. Marx*, Bd. 2, Stuttgart, 1913 and in full in: Marx and Engels, *Works*, First Russian Edition, Vol. XXII, Moscow, 1929

Printed according to the original

Published in English for the first time

---

[a] 'Kossuth and Louis Napoleon' - [b] Marx has 'Werke' (works). - [c] [F. Pulszky,] 'From Our Own Correspondent. Monday, August 7, 1859', *New-York Daily Tribune*, No. 5720, 23 August 1859. - [d] [K. Marx,] 'Ludwig Kossuth und Louis Napoleon', *Allgemeine Zeitung*, No. 276 (supplement), 3 October 1859. (It was a German translation of Marx's article 'Particulars of Kossuth's Transaction with Louis Napoleon' published in *The Free Press*, No. 10, 28 September 1859.)

292

MARX TO ENGELS

IN MANCHESTER

[London,] 26 October 1859

Dear Engels,

I trust that you aren't ill or that some other misfortune hasn't befallen you, but would beg you, whatever the case, TO DROP SOME LINES since your protracted silence worries me.

Do please return me the cutting from the *Tribune*[a] which I enclosed in my last.

Duncker has now definitely declared himself willing to bring out the second instalment.[473] Lassalle speaks of his 'Italian' tactics *quasi re bene gesta*[b] and, in the course of pressing me to make a statement, lets fall the modest hope that perhaps I have revised 'my' opinion.[485]

The Kinkel or Schiller festival here, a festival, by the by, that will turn out to be an altogether wretched affair, is something Freiligrath, 'as a German poet', could not but associate himself with, though I warned him that he was required simply as an accessory to Gottfried.[486]

As regards the *Volk* I have avoided the COUNTY COURT PROCESS[c] by sacrificing ABOUT £5 while, on the other hand, getting Hollinger to recognise Biskamp as *PROPRIETOR* on the receipt; he (Biskamp) is therefore responsible for the balance, but since he possesses no property whatsoever, he is absolved of any further liability. This step—a highly unpleasant one under the ACTUAL CIRCUMSTANCES—had to be taken because Kinkel's gang was only waiting for the case in order to raise a public scandal, and not one of the paper's hangers-on was presentable enough to be exhibited in court.

At the request (ENCOMPASSED in two very plaintive, abject letters) of the *Augsburger Zeitung* I sent them the document relating to Blind.[487] It served the laddie right, the more so because he went to Collet and 1. tried to make use of him for sundry subterfuges, 2. denounced Liebknecht to Collet as 'BELONGING TO THE COMMUNIST PARTY'

---

a the clipping with Marx's article 'Kossuth and Louis Napoleon' - b as a well-conducted action - c See this volume, p. 495.

and, finally, in order to blacken him completely, 3. described the Augsburg *Allgemeine Zeitung* as a 'Russian' organ.

Remind *Thimm* to settle his account with us.

Salut.

Your

K. M.

First published abridged in *Der Briefwechsel zwischen F. Engels und K. Marx*, Bd. 2, Stuttgart, 1913 and in full in: Marx and Engels, *Works*, First Russian Edition, Vol. XXII, Moscow, 1929

Printed according to the original

Published in English for the first time

293

ENGELS TO MARX [a]

IN LONDON

Manchester, 28 October 1859

[...] The Blind affair is very funny indeed; it's always a particularly agreeable spectacle when a would-be diplomatic wiseacre comes a cropper. The fellow could be terribly discredited as a result. Needless to say he gave his 'word of honour' simply IN THE DIPLOMATIC SENSE OF THE WORD, just as it is no insult to call someone a swine IN A PARLIAMENTARY SENSE.[b] This enrichment of the language by Blind is worthy of recognition. What would be nicest of all, by the way, would be to discover that Mr Blind's 'evidence' had no basis other than hot air which, this sinister saviour of his country being what he is, I think highly probable.

Lupus is in despair over the deterioration of BITTER BEER, which is forcing him to drink PORTER and HALF AND HALF; this apart, he is keeping pretty well and is still living in Chatsworth.

Not long ago Siebel had a letter from a ludicrous German *literatus*[c] who, for lack of money, was seeking to sell himself to the revolution and wanted him to negotiate the deal, I being supposedly the purchaser. At the same time he threatened, should the revolution refuse to buy him, to throw himself into the arms

---

[a] The beginning of the letter missing; the date is at the end of the letter. - [b] See this volume, pp. 502-04. - [c] Hugo Oelbermann

of the Jesuits. They, however, wouldn't accept him *gratis*, for I need hardly tell you that the fellow is a colossal blockhead.

Warm regards to your wife and children.

Your

F. E.

First published abridged in *Der Briefwechsel zwischen F. Engels und K. Marx*, Bd. 2, Stuttgart, 1913 and in full in: Marx and Engels, *Works*, First Russian Edition, Vol. XXII, Moscow, 1929

Printed according to the original

Published in English for the first time

294

ENGELS TO E. J. FAULKNER

IN MANCHESTER

[Draft]

Manchester, 2 November 1859

Dear Faulkner,

Will something like the enclosed do? I shall call here again before 7 o'clock.

Yours

F. E.[a]

Mr Daniells

Sir,

After what happened between you and me on a certain evening,[b] I should have been the first to make to you that apology which one Gentleman owed to another under the circumstances, if you had not at once taken such steps as precluded me entirely from doing so. Indeed I at once requested a friend of mine to call upon you for the purpose but when he arrived it was too late. If Mrs Daniells as I hear feels aggrieved at anything I may have said, I should be very sorry not to withdraw most emphatically any expression which may have given umbrage to a lady whom I have not the honour of knowing and upon whose character it could

[a] In the rough copy this note to Faulkner was written after the draft of Engels' letter to Daniells. - [b] See this volume, p. 490.

therefore never enter into my intention to cast the slightest imputation.

As to the other matter between you and me, I am only sorry that it ever should have occurred and am prepared to pay to you £30.—in the shape of compensation.

I am Sir

Your obedient servant

First published in: Marx and Engels, *Works*, First Russian Edition, Vol. XXV, Moscow, 1934

Reproduced from the original

Published in English for the first time

295

MARX TO ENGELS

IN MANCHESTER

[London,] 3 November 1859

Dear Frederick,

Lessner hasn't got the names of the people to whom *Das Volk* was sent. All he knows is the number of copies (12) which he regularly despatched to Thimm.

Biskamp maintains that the books he ordered from Thimm were not for his own account but for that of the parson who employed him as a schoolmaster. Nor, come to that, had Thimm ever said a word about the matter. He will be writing to him about it, likewise about Panzer's acquisitive propensities. A few days ago he was taken on by the *Weser-Zeitung* at 50 talers a month.

My work is making poor progress.[473] I'm plagued by too many domestic disruptions and too many worries. You'll have heard about the 'grand' Schiller festival here.[486] Freiligrath and Kinkel, or rather Kinkel and Freiligrath, are to be its heroes. Seeing that the whole thing emanated from the Kinkel clique here and that even the invitations to form a committee were sent out by that wretch Beta, Gottfried's factotum, I wrote to Freiligrath weeks ago saying I hoped HE WOULD KEEP ALOOF FROM THE KINKEL DEMONSTRATION.[488] In reply I received a not exactly unequivocal letter from the fat philistine in which, *inter alia*, he said:

'Even should Kinkel secure Briseis in the shape of the festive address, this would be no reason for Achilles to withdraw sulking into his tent.'

So Kinkel is Agamemnon and Freiligrath Achilles[a]! Moreover, he says that the festival 'is relevant *in more ways than one*' (in what ways we shall presently see), and finally that he has written a poem on Schiller[b] commissioned by the city of Boston (United States).

Later I discovered from the *Hermann* that Freiligrath was acting as a member of the committee and that there was some talk of his having written a cantata on Schiller (set to music by Pauer)[c]; in other words, that the philistine had kept something back from me. Later still I got another letter from him in which he said I would seem to have been right after all, though his participation had partially frustrated Gottfried's plans.

Well, when I saw the man he told me with bated breath about all that had happened. Beta and Juch, Kinkel's agents, had heard from America that Freiligrath had written the poem on Schiller for Boston. Gottfried had, besides the address, reserved the festive cantata for himself. Believing, however, that *non bis in idem*,[d] and that it wouldn't be feasible to co-opt Freiligrath without conceding, or rather offering, him the poetic part (though they counted on his turning down the offer), Juch and Beta invited Freiligrath, on behalf of Kinkel's committee, to join that committee and write the cantata. Freiligrath said he had already composed a poem for Boston, gave an inconclusive reply but promised to serve on the committee. This last treated the matter as a mere formality and did not renew its request. Freiligrath, however, hastily sets to work (no such difficulties here as in the case of the *Volk* for which he never *could* manage as much as 3 lines), writes a cantata (in the same metre as Schiller's dithyrambs[e]; he read me the stuff—pomp and circumstance), hurries to Pauer, has it set to music and, through his friends in the Schiller festival choir, compels Kinkel and Co. to renew their invitation to him. Then he sends them the rubbish which, 'by an anachronism', happened to be already finished and complete, not only written but actually set to music, and likens himself at the end of his epistle to a 'menial' who has served his 'master' without waiting for orders (Messrs Kinkel, Beta, Juch and Co.)! (And it's the philistine himself who tells me this.)

---

[a] In Homer's *Iliad* Agamemnon and Achilles quarrelled for the possession of Briseis, the captive queen of Lyrnessus. - [b] Here and below Marx refers to Freiligrath's poems 'Zur Schillerfeier. 10. November 1859' which are subtitled 'Festlied der Deutschen in Amerika' and 'Festlied der Deutschen in London'. - [c] 'Die Sitzungen des Schiller-Comité's', *Hermann*, No. 43, 29 October 1859. - [d] the same thing must not be done twice (from Roman law) - [e] F. Schiller, 'Dithyrambe'.

However the 'tension' between him and Gottfried was not yet at an end. Freiligrath attended the committee, where Gottfried behaved very coolly towards him. Now Freiligrath—'quite fortuitously' or so he says—had introduced into his cantata a passage during which it was 'essential' for Schiller's bust to be *unveiled*. Gottfried, no less fortuitously, had arranged for the climax of his sermon to coincide with the *'moment of unveiling'*. After a prolonged tussle, throughout which philistine Freiligrath sat in silence and let his friends (riff-raff of all kinds) do the talking, it was at length decided that the 'unveiling' should fall to Freiligrath, whereupon Gottfried, sighing heavily, declared that in that case he would now be obliged to address his entire oration to 'the veiled portrait'. Whereupon one of Freiligrath's pals rose to his feet and said that this difficulty could be overcome if Kinkel were to make his speech *after* the cantata. Gottfried, however, voiced his unqualified opposition to this, declaring with the utmost indignation that 'he had already made so many concessions over the affair that this could not possibly be demanded of him'. And that was the end of that. So the sermon will come first.

And Freiligrath told me all this rubbish with great seriousness and gravity; on the other hand he finds it perfectly natural that he should never have breathed a word to the committee about the Kinkel gang's having taken it for granted that his (Freiligrath's) supposed 'party friends' should not be invited to join the committee, thus making a Kinkel demonstration of it. Though he knew perfectly well that I wouldn't attend, he should never have permitted such 'ostracism' on the part of a committee on which he himself sits. Blind is on it, of course.

Ever since his poem about the Mockel woman,[a] Freiligrath has treated us 'strictly in private' as his friends while openly walking arm-in-arm with our enemies. *Qui vivra verra.*[b]

Ad vocem[c] *Blind*: The scoundrel has now been to see Hollinger. For the Augsburg *Allgemeine Zeitung* had written to him saying that, if he persisted in his reticence, he would be brought out into the open in the most unpleasant manner, and that they possessed a document incriminating him.[487] He accused Hollinger of having let the cat out of the bag. Hollinger, with justice, said *quod non*[d] and asked why Blind refused to admit responsibility for it. The latter told him that, while he had indeed written the manuscript, a friend of his had composed it. The fact of the matter is that while Blind wrote and composed it, Goegg supplied the most inculpating

[a] F. Freiligrath, 'Nach Johanna Kinkels Begräbnis'. - [b] He who survives will see. - [c] As to - [d] that such was not the case

bits. Now the respectable Goegg is 'apparently' Vogt's friend, as he needs must be since Fazy, through the Swiss bank, owns shares worth 25,000 frs in his looking-glass factory and generally serves him as BANKER. Hence Goegg's indignation at the act of 'high treason' can only be ventilated *sotto voce.* Such are the 'serious republicans'.

Couldn't you do me an ARTICLE on the recent changes in the Prussian army[a]?

Regards to Lupus.

Salut.

Your

K. M.

First published abridged in *Der Briefwechsel zwischen F. Engels und K. Marx,* Bd. 2, Stuttgart, 1913 and in full in: Marx and Engels, *Works,* First Russian Edition, Vol. XXII, Moscow, 1929

Printed according to the original

Published in English for the first time

296

ENGELS TO MARX

IN LONDON

Manchester, 4 November 1859

Dear Moor,

Freiligrath really deserves to be severely chastised for once and I hope that an opportunity will present itself before the Schiller nonsense is over (or its after-pains).[486] Such poet's vanity and literary presumption combined with toadyism is altogether too much, and on top of that the *Augsburger*[b] credits him with political virtue!

I suppose you read about Vogt's law-suit[470] in the Augsburg *Allgemeine Zeitung,* No. 297 *et seq.*[c]? The thing went quite well, but Biskamp's letter is shockingly discreditable. The fellow could

---

a In compliance with this request, Engels wrote, at the end of January and beginning of February 1860, the article 'Military Reform in Germany'. - b *Allgemeine Zeitung* - c The *Allgemeine Zeitung* carried reports on the case on 25 October 1859 and on the following days.

perfectly well have dealt with his private affairs in a separate note but, as things are, it is exceedingly distasteful that the editor of the *Volk* should send the Augsburg *Allgemeine Zeitung* a testimonial, begging to be taken on as correspondent, and that this should appear in print.[a] Vogt will make a great noise about it. Why do we always have such tactless idiots hanging round us?

But most satisfactory is the discrediting of Blind. The statement in your letter[b] and the document[487] have now obliged the worthy diplomat to come creeping out into the open, if only to save himself being discredited still further. He has boasted about the evidence he possesses and, if he holds his tongue, will seem an unmitigated liar.

Vogt is in no less nice a mess. Case dismissed for lack of jurisdiction, ordered to pay all the costs, and referred to a jury—what can he do?

He will have to sue either the Augsburg *Allgemeine Zeitung* before a Bavarian jury—in which case he will be doomed in advance—or the *Volk*—and then Blind will be SUBPOENAED—or else Blind himself. In any case, it will turn out badly for him, and I don't see how he can do anything but discredit himself still more.

All this is most consoling.

Garibaldi would seem to be playing a somewhat ambiguous role. A general of that ilk is in a difficult position. Once he had been forced to compound with the devil, there was no turning back. For Victor Emmanuel the obvious thing is, of course, first to exploit Garibaldi and then ruin him. *Altro esempio*[c] of how far you get with a 'practical attitude' in a revolution. It's a pity about the chap, though. Excellent, on the other hand, that Piedmont should lose its spurious character as representative of Italian unity.[489]

I shall do you an article about army reform in Germany when this affair has progressed a little further. Far-reaching things are happening in the sphere of military organisation, not only in Prussia but elsewhere, in Austria, etc. Everywhere the French style of uniform, etc., is being adopted, and in many respects this even means quite definitely putting the clock back. But so far everything's still rather confused; as soon as I can clarify my ideas a little I'll do the article for you.[d]

I also hope that soon there'll be something further for me to report on in China and the Far East GENERALLY. Likewise Morocco.[490]

---

[a] Biskamp's letter, dated 20 October 1859, was published in the *Allgemeine Zeitung*, No. 300, on 27 October 1859. - [b] to the Editor of the *Allgemeine Zeitung* - [c] Another example - [d] Somewhat later Engels wrote an article on the subject, entitled 'Military Reform in Germany'.

But none of this has come to a head yet. About Morocco next week perhaps.[a] Have you already written about it, or could you, perhaps, let me have some political information *ad vocem*[b] Pam on the subject so that I am *au fait*.

At the moment I'm deep in Ulfilas.[491] It was really high time for me to polish off that damned Gothic, which I'd always been so desultory about. To my surprise I find I know far more than I thought; if only I can get hold of another reference book, I think I shall polish this off completely in a fortnight. Then I shall go on to Old Norse and Anglo-Saxon, with which I've never been on more than nodding terms. So far, I've been working without a dictionary or other reference book save the Gothic text and Grimm.[c] However, that old fellow is really splendid.

What I need badly here is Grimm's *Geschichte der deutschen Sprache*. Could you let me have it back?

I think I shall see Lupus this evening.

We are having a Schiller festival up here too (programme enclosed). Needless to say, I have nothing whatever to do with the thing. Mr Alfr. Meissner is sending a prologue, and Siebel will do the epilogue, straightforward recitation, of course, but done in proper form. In addition, this *flâneur* is producing a performance of 'Wallensteins Lager' [d]; I've been to two of the rehearsals and, if the chaps keep their nerve, it might be quite passable. The committee members are, without exception, a bunch of fools; among the public Borchardt plays at being in opposition. He's no less negatively pompous than the others are positively so, except that his negation is based on the same point of view as the position of the others, i.e. he admits that he is essentially one of their number.

Salut.

Your

F. E.

Nil novi ab Ephraim Artful? [e]

First published abridged in *Der Briefwechsel zwischen F. Engels und K. Marx*, Bd. 2, Stuttgart, 1913 and in full in: Marx and Engels, *Works*, First Russian Edition, Vol. XXII, Moscow, 1929

Printed according to the original

Published in English for the first time

---

a Early in December 1859 Engels wrote the article 'Progress of the Moorish War' and later several more articles on the subject. - b as regards - c J. Grimm, *Deutsche Grammatik*, Th. I-IV. - d first part of Schiller's trilogy *Wallenstein* - e No news from Ephraim Artful (Ferdinand Lassalle)?

297

ENGELS TO JENNY MARX[a]

IN LONDON

Manchester, 5 November 1859

Dear Mrs Marx,

I must really beg you to forgive me for having been so shockingly remiss that Moor finally had to get you to extract the article in question[b] from me. However, I had no idea that it was needed for anything except staving off possible ructions on Mr Pulszky's part and hence was in no hurry at all about returning it.[c] But this time it really is enclosed.

Freiligrath, the fat philistine, is really behaving in a most disgraceful way and deserves to be well and truly chastised, for which an opportunity will, I trust, soon present itself. Most amusing is the Trojan War over the momentous question as to who should have the cantata and who the festive speech, and which is to come first, the speech or the cantata.[d] The philistines up here are greatly vexed by Lupus' and my refusal to get mixed up in the Schiller do. Only yesterday evening I had another sparring match with three enthusiastic Schillerians. These folk are quite unable to comprehend how anyone could fail to jump at such a beautiful opportunity for self-advertisement. They want to found a 'Schiller Institute'[492] here, i.e. a German club in which to read, eat, drink, hold lectures, do gymnastics, act plays, make music and goodness knows what else. Borchardt was silly enough to attend the preliminary meeting and to speak against it (he urged me to go too but for that very reason I stayed away) and when it was put to the vote, Hoyoll the crippled painter and one other man voted with him, and Borchardt, of course, suffered a spectacular defeat. Subsequently he subscribed £4 10/- to the thing, which makes him a member for 3 years. You have no idea what German erudition has suddenly come to light here on this occasion. There's a Dr Götze, a Dr Marcus, a Dr Dolch, a Dr Samelson, all fellows of whom one had never heard before. These and a few aesthetic Jews have taken charge of the whole thing, and once again erudition plays mentor to the Jews—save in the

[a] written in reply to Jenny Marx's letter of 4 November 1859 (see this volume, p. 573) — [b] K. Marx, 'Kossuth and Louis Napoleon'. - [c] See this volume, p. 507. - [d] Ibid., pp. 511-12.

case of Samelson, he's a doctor who, for the past four years, has 'quite recently settled in Manchester'. Nothing but self-advertisement and tittle-tattle, and they actually expect one to take part in it.

For that matter, I myself am indulging in tittle-tattle, as you see, and hence it would be best for me to break off altogether. Please give my warmest regards to the girls, and do not forget Moor.

Your

F. Engels

First published in: Marx and Engels, *Works*, First Russian Edition, Vol. XXII, Moscow, 1929

Printed according to the original

Published in English for the first time

298

MARX TO FERDINAND LASSALLE[20]

IN BERLIN

London, 6 November 1859

Dear Lassalle,

You'd have had a reply from me sooner if my spare time hadn't been entirely taken up with a mass of repulsive domestic business.

1. Thank you for your good offices with Duncker.[493] You're mistaken, by the by, if you think that I expected glowing tributes from the German press, or gave a rap for them. I expected to be attacked or criticised but not to be utterly ignored, which, moreover, is bound to have a serious effect on sales. Considering how vehemently these people have, at various times, railed against my communism, it was to be expected that they would now unleash their wisdom against the theoretical argument in support of the same. For after all, Germany is not without its specialised journals on economics.

In America the first instalment[a] was discussed at length in the entire German press from New York to New Orleans. I only fear that it is too theoretical in tone for the working-class public there.

2. *ad vocem*[b] *Vogt*.

---

[a] K. Marx, *A Contribution to the Critique of Political Economy*. - [b] as to

You'll have been surprised by the information in the Augsburg *Allgemeine Zeitung* concerning Vogt's law-suit[470] and by the strange company in which I find myself in that journal.[a]

Here, in brief, is the story:

Besides the *Hermann*, there used to be a so-called working-men's paper here, *Die Neue Zeit*, whose last editor was Edgar Bauer. One of his colleagues on that paper was Biskamp, who was a schoolmaster out in the country. The paper was opposed on what is called principle to the *Hermann*. For Edgar Bauer thought it was time he *played* at being a communist. I, needless to say, had *nothing* to do with this. Bauer wrote and told Biskamp that, in order to rid himself of a rival, Kinkel had transferred his sheet to the printer of the *Neue Zeit*[b] which last, depending as it did on that printer's credit, was completely in his power. On receipt of this letter, Biskamp rushed up to London to discover, not only that Kinkel had destroyed the *Neue Zeit* by swapping printers, but also that Edgar Bauer, the editor of the so-called 'working-men's paper', had joined the editorial staff of the *Hermann* and gone over to Kinkel.

A brief note re Biskamp: He was at one time a co-publisher of the *Hornisse*. He edited the *Bremer Tages-Chronik* in company with Dulon and Ruge. In Switzerland he joined the Communist League.[494] His relationship with Ruge meant that we never saw each other while he was in London. I took no notice of him, but he occasionally took notice in a polemical way of me. This man is a strange mixture of noble instincts, innate (and also physical) weakness, asceticism and idleness, Kantian moral consciousness and tactless whimsicality. His nervous irritability makes him liable to surrender any position 'on principle', to precipitate himself suddenly into the most hopeless situation, to endure it passively and stoically for a while, and then suddenly perpetrate stupidities bordering on the iniquitous. The man as I paint him here is not, of course, the man I used to know. I am painting a portrait which experience has gradually pieced together for me.

But to return to my story. Biskamp at once gave up his schoolmaster's post to take up 'the struggle of labour against capital' (i.e. Kinkel), started *Das Volk* without any means whatsoever except subsidies from a workers' society, etc. So long as the thing lasted he was, of course, on the verge of starvation. He had secured work as correspondent to a couple of papers in Germany, but lost this as soon as his new function became known. A few

[a] *Allgemeine Zeitung*, No. 298, 25 October 1859. - [b] Fidelio Hollinger

private lessons barely enabled him to eke out the life of a *Bohémien*.

Before continuing I should point out that I have had *no* connection whatever with any of the public workers' associations (including the so-called communist one[50]) since 1851. The only workers with whom I foregather are 20-30 picked men to whom I give *private* lectures on political economy.[483] Liebknecht, however, is chairman of the workers' society which helped Biskamp to start *Das Volk*.

A few days after the birth of this paper Biskamp and Liebknecht came to see me and invited me to collaborate. At the time I declined outright, partly for want of time and partly because I was about to leave London for a longish spell.[444] All I promised was to obtain a few financial contributions from friends in England, which in fact I did. On that same day I related to both of them what Blind had told me with great moral indignation the day before about Vogt, and also named my source. Biskamp used this for an article,[a] as I later saw. During my absence he reprinted in *Das Volk* Blind's anonymous pamphlet,[b] which was printed by the same press as *Das Volk*. At the same time Liebknecht sent a copy of the pamphlet to the Augsburg *Allgemeine Zeitung*[470] for which he supplies the English article. (As to this last circumstance, I should point out that the refugees here contribute to all papers indiscriminately. I believe myself to be the only exception to this, as I do not contribute to *any* German paper. Be it noted, by the by, that Palmerston, through the channel of the *Prussian* embassy, which in turn used *Williams*—the English bookseller—for its organ, has tried to get Liebknecht removed from the *A. A. Z.* on account of his ANTI-GOVERNMENTAL tendencies.)

After my return to London, *Das Volk* received from myself and Engels various contributions wholly unrelated to the *affaire* Vogt. Apart from a few attacks on Schleinitz's diplomatic circulars,[c] all I supplied was a humorous comment or two on Kinkel's aesthetic dissertations in the *Hermann*, viewed from a *grammatical* standpoint.[d] Life here in London is too tough for one not to indulge in distractions of this kind every 8 years or so.

---

[a] [E. Biskamp,] 'Der Reichsregent', *Das Volk*, No. 2, 14 May 1859. - [b] [K. Blind,] 'Warnung zur gefälligen Verbreitung', *Das Volk*, No. 7, 18 June 1859. - [c] Schleinitz's despatches to the Prussian embassies in Britain, Russia and Germany (Berlin, June-July 1859) were reported in the *Neue Preußische Zeitung*, No. 170, 24 July ('Zu der "Vermittlung"'), No. 171, 26 July ('Preußische Depeschen'), No. 174, 29 July 1859 ('Deutschland'). - [d] Marx refers to his series of articles *Quid pro quo* and his reviews published in the section 'Gatherings from the Press'.

The paper came to a sudden end, mainly for lack of money. Biskamp, besides being wholly without means of subsistence, contracted a painful disease and had to go into the German hospital. When he was discharged he must literally have starved to death if I hadn't taken care of him. During this period he wrote to several German papers in the hope of becoming their correspondent, but to no effect. Then he got a letter from the editorial board of the *A. A. Z.*, whereupon he wrote them that shockingly discreditable epistle—behind the backs of his friends, of course.[a] Naturally he believed he was writing a private letter. The idiot is now overcome with contrition and for a couple of days has neither eaten nor slept. I don't know what will become of him. If I have told you all this at some length, it is not in order to justify the man's behaviour, but to explain it. If he were so venal a fellow as most of the 'democrats' here, he wouldn't have precipitated himself into a situation which he hadn't the strength to endure.

As to my statement in the *A. A. Z.*,[b] the circumstances are as follows:

As you know, Blind published his denunciation of Vogt. At the same time an anonymous article by him[c] appeared in the London *Free Press* (Urquhart's PAPER), containing much the same information—I enclose the article with this letter—but omitting Vogt's name and sundry other particulars.[440] Now when Vogt brought his action against the *A. A. Z.*, and the latter appealed to Liebknecht, he, being responsible to the *A. A. Z.*, naturally appealed to me and I to Blind. The latter refused to answer for his statements. It was all due to a misunderstanding, he said. The whole thing had nothing to do with him. He even went so far as to give his *word of honour* that he had had nothing to do with the anonymous pamphlet. Repeated requests were of no avail. This conduct was all the more infamous in that the worthy fellow knew that Vogt was citing *me*—privately in London and publicly in Switzerland—as the source of the denunciation so as to represent the whole thing as deriving from the malicious ill-will borne by the communist towards the 'eminent democrat' and 'ex-imperial regent'.[410] I therefore began by turning to Collet, who made no bones about stating that *Blind* had written the article in *The Free Press.* Next, I obtained a statement from the type-setter[d] who had set the type for the pamphlet.[487] Blind's duplicity called for

[a] E. Biskamp, [Letter to the Editor of the *Allgemeine Zeitung*, dated 20 October 1859,] *Allgemeine Zeitung*, No. 300, 27 October 1859. - [b] K. Marx, [Letter to the Editor of the *Allgemeine Zeitung*]. - [c] [K. Blind,] 'The Grand Duke Constantine to Be King of Hungary', *The Free Press*, No. 5, 27 May 1859. - [d] A. Vögele

castigation. I had absolutely no intention of pulling this 'republican's' chestnuts out of the fire for him. Indeed, it is only by forcing him and Vogt to attack one another that the truth will come out. Finally, like any paper which accepts a denunciation of this kind, the *A. A. Z.* deserves to be supplied with any information that can possibly help to throw light on the facts.

I shall now have the whole of Germany's vulgar democracy about my ears, and Biskamp's folly will make this all the easier for them. Needless to say, it would never occur to me to skirmish in insignificant journals with all these insignificant scoundrels. However, I believe it necessary to make an example of *one* of them, namely Mr Eduard Meyen of the *Freischütz*,[a] *pour encourager les autres*.[b] I'm sending one copy to the *A. A. Z.*, one to the *Reform*[c] in Hamburg and I'd like the copy I sent you to appear in a Berlin paper.

I must save up my exposé of the Italian war,[485] an affair upon which I have in no way changed my views, for my next letter[d] (shortly).

Salut.

Your
K. M.

P.S. Much as I detest alluding to this point, my financial affairs are in a dangerously critical state—so much so that I can hardly find time for my articles for the *Tribune*, let alone the political economy.[473] Admittedly I shall be receiving over £40 in 8 to 10 weeks' time. But for me the essential and crucial point is to *anticipate* its receipt. Can you help me with a bill transaction towards that end? In 8, or at most 10, weeks' time I shall be good for £50.

First published in: *F. Lassalle. Nachgelassene Briefe und Schriften*, Bd. III, Stuttgart-Berlin, 1922

Printed according to the original

Published in English in full for the first time

---

[a] E. Meyen, 'Der Proceß Carl Vogt's gegen die Augsburger *Allg. Ztg.*', *Der Freischütz*, No. 132, 3 November 1859. - [b] to encourage the others - [c] K. Marx, 'Statement to the Editors of *Die Reform*, the *Volks-Zeitung* and the *Allgemeine Zeitung*. - [d] See this volume, pp. 536-39.

299

MARX TO ENGELS

IN MANCHESTER

London, 7 November 1859

Dear Engels,

I shall send you the Grimm.[a]

I have not written anything yet about Morocco,[490] or about the Caucasus,[495] or any military stuff on Asia. I have no diplomatic particulars about Morocco, so you will have to pick up your pen again. My circumstances are such as to preclude my doing sufficient work on the 2nd instalment, which I regard as of crucial importance.[473] It does, in fact, contain the pith of all the bourgeois stuff.

Biskamp's letter[b] is infinitely discreditable; in view of his situation one can explain but not excuse it. The whole of vulgar democracy is seeking to hush up the Blind affair in the German press while assailing me. E.g. Mr Meyen, present editor of the *Freischütz*.[c] I have now sent a sharply-worded statement to the Augsburg *Allgemeine Zeitung* and the *Reform* in Hamburg.[d] I shall bring Vogt and Blind face to face even if it has to be done at gun point.

In a couple of lines in the *Tribune* the wretched Pulszky dismisses my letter[e] as emanating from the camp of the 'CRACKED' Urquhart.[f] The fellows dare not open their traps. For they don't know what kind of evidence we have at our disposal. For Kossuth, or so Szemere wrote and told me, secretly decamped after the treaty of Villafranca without a word to Klapka and the other officers. For he was afraid of being handed over to the

---

[a] J. Grimm, *Geschichte der deutschen Sprache*, Bd. 1-2. - [b] E. Biskamp, [Letter to the Editor of the *Allgemeine Zeitung*, 20 October 1859,] *Allgemeine Zeitung*, No. 300, 27 October 1859. - [c] [E. Meyen,] 'Der Proceß Carl Vogt's gegen die Augsburger *Allg. Ztg.*', *Der Freischütz*, No. 132, 3 November 1859. - [d] K. Marx, 'Statement to the Editors of *Die Reform*, the *Volks-Zeitung* and the *Allgemeine Zeitung*'. - [e] K. Marx, 'Kossuth and Louis Napoleon'. - [f] Marx refers to Pulszky's report of 11 October 1859 published in the *New-York Daily Tribune*, No. 5775, 26 October 1859.

Austrians.[496] *Hence the greatest animosities against him in the Hungarian camp.* I shall give Pulszky a thorough lambasting.

Your

K. M.

First published abridged in *Der Briefwechsel zwischen F. Engels und K. Marx*, Bd. 2, Stuttgart, 1913 and in full in: Marx and Engels, *Works*, First Russian Edition, Vol. XXII, Moscow, 1929

Printed according to the original

Published in English for the first time

300

MARX TO FERDINAND LASSALLE[20]

IN BERLIN

London, 14 November 1859
9 Grafton Terrace, Maitland Park, Haverstock Hill

Dear Lassalle,

I am answering your by return.

It isn't a question of *your* finding the money, but of a bill transaction. Would you allow me to draw on you at 3 months? *If so* you would be provided with *security* (guaranteed not only by myself, *but also by Engels*) *before* the bill fell due. It's a question, therefore, of an accommodation bill or, to put it more crudely, kite-flying. It still remains very doubtful, of course, *whether* I could manage to negotiate a bill of this kind over here. However there might be some CHANCE of it. Engels would have procured what was necessary had not all his liquid assets been tied up as a result of an action for causing bodily harm to an Englishman.[a] The affair is costing more than £100 and accommodation bills drawn in London on Manchester are only possible between businessmen.

I think it is now too late to insert the anti-Meyen statement.[b] Assuming the *Reform* and the Augsburg *Allgemeine Zeitung* accept it, it would arrive too late in Berlin.[c] Assuming they don't accept it, it will in any case be too late for any consideration of the great Meyen's article,[d] which will by then be outdated.

---

[a] Daniells. See this volume, p. 490. - [b] K. Marx, 'Statement to the Editors of *Die Reform*, the *Volks-Zeitung* and the *Allgemeine Zeitung*'. - [c] i.e. the editorial office of the *Volks-Zeitung* - [d] [E. Meyen,] 'Der Proceß Carl Vogt's gegen die Augsburger *Allg. Ztg.*', *Der Freischütz*, No. 132, 3 November 1859.

As regards Vogt, it behoves our party—as opposed to vulgar democracy—to force him to pick up the gauntlet thrown down by Blind. Both gentlemen seem to be equally anxious to keep their distance. It was very clever of Vogt to make me out to be the source of the denunciation, but also to select as his target the *A. Z.* in Augsburg rather than the *Volk* in London. As regards myself, he can attribute the thing to rancour, if only because of the erstwhile opposition to him on the part of the *Neue Rheinische Zeitung*. (You are doubtless aware that, when Lupus came to the National Assembly in Frankfurt, he opposed Uhland's vote of thanks to John, the imperial regent. Vogt seized this opportunity to vent his spleen and made an abusive speech attacking the *N. Rh. Z. en général* and Lupus in particular.[497] Lupus thereupon called him out. But Vogt thought his skin too valuable to the Fatherland to risk it in this way. Lupus thereupon threatened to box his ears publicly in the street. Thereafter Vogt never made an appearance unless flanked by his sister on one side and a woman acquaintance of his sister's on the other. And Lupus was too courteous, etc.) But again, Mr Vogt knew that Germany's vulgar democrats regard me as their *bête noire*. Furthermore, had he sued *Das Volk* instead of the *A. Z.*, Blind, etc., would have been legally compelled to give evidence on oath and the matter would have *been bound* to come to light. Finally, it was one thing to break a lance with a revolutionary paper direct, and quite another to do so with the reactionary *A. Z.* The way in which the 'noble' Vogt (Vogt the 'well-rounded', as his barrister described him,[498] is rather more TO THE POINT) attacked me in the Biel *Handels-Courier*[a] rejoiced my heart. I am, it seems, in communication with 'the police', live off the workers, and such-like inanities.

As to Kossuth, all the particulars about his transaction with Bonaparte were provided by Szemere (formerly Hungarian Prime Minister, presently in Paris).[479] I sent him my anti-Kossuth article[b] in the *Tribune* and shall let you have it as soon as he returns me the cutting from Paris. The nicest part of it is that Kossuth's agent, Pulszky, is the *Tribune*'s London correspondent.

The Schiller festival here was a Kinkel festival.[486] Freiligrath himself, who took part in it despite my warning, now realises that Gottfried used him simply as a tool. He told me that Kinkel's melodramatic speech was a veritable farce which literally had to be seen to be believed. You'd laugh heartily were I to tell you what

---

[a] [K. Vogt,] 'Zur Warnung', *Schweizer Handels-Courier*, No. 150 (supplement), 2 June 1859. The article was reprinted, with editorial comments, in *Das Volk*, No. 6, 11 June 1859. - [b] K. Marx, 'Kossuth and Louis Napoleon'.

went on behind the scenes between Kinkel and Freiligrath before the public performance actually took place.[a] In the days of the *N. Rh. Z.* Gottfried invariably figured in the press with a travelling-bag for attribute. Later on, it was a musket, then a lyre, then a distaff. Now our parson never does so without a black, red and gold flag.[499] The so-called 'working men' whom he has gathered round him belong to a guild; article 1 of the rules of their society runs: 'In accordance with the rules, all politics are to be excluded from the society's debates.' Before 1848 these same fellows enjoyed Bunsen's patronage.

Well, enough of gossip, for this note was simply intended to be *de re pecuniaria.*[b]

Salut.

Your

K. M.

First published in: *F. Lassalle. Nachgelassene Briefe und Schriften,* Bd. III, Stuttgart-Berlin, 1922

Printed according to the original

Published in English in full for the first time

301

MARX TO FERDINAND LASSALLE

IN BERLIN

[London,] 15 November 1859

Dear Lassalle,

Could you possibly get the *Volks-Zeitung* to publish the following reply[c] to Blind's declaration in No. 313 of the Augsburg *Allgemeine Zeitung*? If so, please send me 2 COPIES of it. *En passant,* I would draw your attention to the hymn of self-adulation struck up by Gottfried Kinkel in the latest *Hermann*[d] to the accompaniment of general rejoicing on the part of the Germans in London.

In haste.

Your

K. M.

First published in: *F. Lassalle. Nachgelassene Briefe und Schriften,* Bd. III, Stuttgart-Berlin, 1922

Printed according to the original

Published in English for the first time

---

a See this volume, pp. 511-12. - b about financial matters - c K. Marx, 'Declaration'. - d 'Das Schillerfest in London', *Hermann,* No. 45, 12 November 1859.

302

MARX TO ENGELS

IN MANCHESTER

[London,] 16 November 1859

Dear Engels,

I hope that a Morocco will arrive from you on Friday.[a] Apart from everything else, this is the time of the presidential elections, and in any case I fear that restrictions will again be put on the quantity of articles to be delivered. This fate will befall me all the sooner if, given the present shortage of material, I don't write about THEMES like this that interest the fellows.

You must also write something for me, PRIVATELY, OF COURSE, not for the *Tribune*, about the Schiller tomfoolery in Manchester. In my next I shall tell you about the Kinkel festival down here. Just now Freiligrath is deeply resentful of Gottfried. Meanwhile you should read the latest number of the *Hermann*[b] and see with your own eyes how 'Parson Charming' drools over himself.

The Augsburg *Allgemeine Zeitung* has not, it seems, accepted my declaration because it was apparently rendered superfluous by the one sent to them by Blind.[c] I have now sent them an answer to this slyboots from Baden with a *positive* demand—for I refer at the same time to the letters they wrote me[d]—that they print my answer.[e]

Salut.

Your

K. M.

First published abridged in *Der Briefwechsel zwischen F. Engels und K. Marx*, Bd. 2, Stuttgart, 1913 and in full in: Marx and Engels, *Works*, First Russian Edition, Vol. XXII, Moscow, 1929

Printed according to the original

Published in English for the first time

---

[a] At the beginning of December Engels wrote the article 'Progress of the Moorish War'. - [b] 'Das Schillerfest in London', *Hermann*, No. 45, 12 November 1859. - [c] K. Blind, 'Erklärung', *Allgemeine Zeitung*, No. 313, 9 November 1859. - [d] See this volume, p. 508. - [e] The *Allgemeine Zeitung* did publish Marx's 'Declaration' in its issue No. 325 (supplement), 21 November 1859.

303

ENGELS TO EMIL ENGELS

IN ENGELSKIRCHEN

Manchester, 16 November 1859

Dear Emil,

Our procedure and method of adjustment are simply as follows: The rollers are removed and the yarn laid over them, after which they are replaced; the upper roller is then moved upwards by means of screws (one at either end of the machine) until there is sufficient tension on the yarn.

1. The rollers are made of iron with rectangular pegs at the ends which fit into rectangular apertures (in the axle). This, however, applies only to the lower roller, which is rotated by the machine; the upper one rests in a simple socket and runs automatically with the other.

2. As already said, the screws are at either end of the upper roller and are tightened by the machine, not by hand.

3. The brushing cylinder has fixed mountings for its axle so as to ensure that it is in the right position immediately the yarn is in place and tightened. For all but the very fine counts we now have cylinders clothed alternately with brushes and wooden slats which rub against the yarn.

4. Your final question—how the connection is effected between the roller one inserts and the part that rotates—is not clear to me; however I think it has already been answered under 1.

It's impossible for me to make you a sketch of the machine, as I can't describe the wheels from memory. But you'll have no difficulty in making one of your own, since to the best of my knowledge all the essential parts correspond exactly to yours, and we use the same machine both for coarse and fine counts, altering the PULLEYS, if anything, in order to reduce the speed. For normal use the average diameter of the PULLEYS for the brushes is 20 inches and for the rollers 14 inches, the speed of the shaft being 163.90 revolutions per minute. For *really* fine counts we increase the diameter of the PULLEY for the rollers to 18 inches. The screws are driven by an 'OPEN AND CROSS STRAP'.

Our machines are made partly by ourselves, partly by Wren & Hopkinson; you wouldn't be able to buy a complete machine or individual parts over here unless you approached G. Ermen.

Tell Father that I shall make inquiries on behalf of Linkenbach, though with little prospect of success until he comes over himself. Young fellows who come over with good recommendations (and he should bring *as many as possible* to different houses) generally fix themselves up before long, whereas no one does so by remaining over there. However there's always a risk in coming here on the off chance.

My love to Lottchen,[a] Father, Mother, Elise,[b] Adolf,[c] and the two families, also to all the cholera refugees should still lodging with you. My new horse is a splendid goer.

Your
Friedrich

First published in: Marx and Engels, *Works*, First Russian Edition, Vol. XXV, Moscow, 1934

Printed according to the original
Published in English for the first time

304

MARX TO ENGELS[500]

IN MANCHESTER

[London, 17 November 1859]

Dear Engels,

If you have nothing ready on Morocco[d] by tomorrow, there will be time enough until *Saturday* (i.e. via Cork[e]). I am writing today (not having written on Tuesday) about the Suez question.[501] The Morocco affair must follow. Otherwise they'll be compelled to copy from *The Times.*

Salut.

Your
K. M.

First published in *Der Briefwechsel zwischen F. Engels und K. Marx*, Bd. 2, Stuttgart, 1913

Printed according to the original
Published in English for the first time

---

[a] Charlotte Bredt - [b] Elise von Griesheim - [c] Adolf von Griesheim - [d] At the beginning of December Engels wrote the article 'Progress of the Moorish War'. - [e] seaport in Ireland

305

ENGELS TO MARX

IN LONDON

Manchester, 17 November 1859

Dear Moor,

As though it wasn't enough to be saddled with a Russian, I have a Genevan arriving today, and Ermen shows an increasing tendency to foist onto me the *onerous* side of representing the firm. Nevertheless I still had hopes this morning of finding time for an article, but it proved utterly impossible. Next Tuesday, however, you will get an article on Morocco,[a] *you may be sure of that.* This will be followed as soon as possible by more on the RIFLE VOLUNTEER MOVEMENT,[502] Prussian army reform[b] and diverse other matters.

The business of the ASSAULT has been settled.[c] Thirty pounds damages and twenty-five costs. It's been paid—partly by borrowing. The action was brought in London and, quite apart from the scandal up here, the publication in the German papers of *The Times* report of the affair would have been a nice juicy titbit for Kinkel & Co.

Schiller festival. Programme enclosed, likewise the original poetical creations consisting, as you will observe, of

Prologue by Meissner,
Catalogue by Samelson,
Epilogue by Siebel.

Pro- and epi- only saved by the antithesis of the catalogue.

The first part went OFF in a resounding failure. Dr Marcus (bankrupt woollen merchant with an Erlangen[d] doctorate *à* 66 talers, 20 silver groschen) read the committee's report in a lachrymose voice, Siebel declaimed the prologue passably well, but indistinctly, Theodores spoke flowery nonsense very indistinctly indeed, all that one could hear being rrrrrr—the choir sang splendidly—Morell delivered himself of platitudes in English, but audibly and fluently—'Die Kraniche des Ibykus'[e] sent the entire

---

[a] At the beginning of December Engels wrote the article 'Progress of the Moorish War'. - [b] F. Engels, 'Military Reform in Germany'. - [c] See this volume, p. 490. - [d] University town in Bavaria - [e] a poem by Schiller

audience to sleep. Fortunately this made everything so late that a full performance of the programme would have lasted until 1 o'clock in the morning. Samelson's stanzas were therefore consigned to the lumber room. The 'Armada'[a] was excellently recited by one Link, then came the play.[b] A very nice stage, but bad acoustics, excellent grouping, much—almost too much—activity constantly going on up stage. All in all, the lads acted quite well but were difficult to understand on account of the unduly voluminous beards they wore in front of their mouths and also because they didn't address the audience properly. The friar was good (Dolch, a former corps student, author of a *Geschichte des Deutschen Studententhums*, a fool and a donkey). Siebel's epilogue, delivered by Link in a most melodious voice and with much decorum, was effective. In short, part 2 saved the day; in the second part and in the piece dropped from the first the lads predominated (also indirectly attributable to a good deal of 'UNDERHAND INFLUENCE' on my part, for the introduction to *Wallensteins Lager* was composed from data supplied by me and was actually very good); the first was dominated by the wiseacres and self-assertive philistines and schoolmasters.

Now they propose to found a Schiller Institute[492] with the surplus, the surplus, however, being a deficit of £150!

On Saturday a festive guzzle which I didn't attend. Numerous toasts and readings of all the REJECTED ADDRESSES.

On Friday night the singers and actors went on carousing until four o'clock in the morning—a very merry affair.

Your

F. E.

What is all this about a brawl at the Crystal Palace[503]?

First published in: Marx and Engels, *Works*, First Russian Edition, Vol. XXII, Moscow, 1929

Printed according to the original

Published in English for the first time

---

[a] F. Schiller, 'Die unüberwindliche Flotte'. - [b] F. Schiller, *Wallensteins Lager*—first part of the trilogy *Wallenstein*.

306

MARX TO ENGELS

IN MANCHESTER

London, 19 November 1859
9 Grafton Terrace, Maitland Park,
Haverstock Hill

Dear Engels,

Today I'm sending you all sorts of curious things: 1. a letter[a] from philistine Freiligrath to me; 2. a letter from Orges (of the Augsburg *Allgemeine Zeitung*) to Biskamp; 3. an issue (No. 43) of the *Gartenlaube*,[b] published in Leipzig, and 4. a letter from Imandt to me together with a cutting from the Trier *Volksblatt*.[504] Finally, I would advise you to buy today's *Hermann* as it contains the story, devised by Mr Beta, of the Schiller festival here and casts a strange light on the conduct of our friend Freiligrath.[c]

Before going into these matters and in case I forget, I would mention that the Hungarians in New York, Chicago, New Orleans, etc., have held meetings at which they resolved to send Kossuth a letter suggesting he vindicate himself with reference to my article in the *New-York Tribune*.[d] Otherwise they would renounce their ALLEGIANCE to him. I don't know whether I have told you about the latest news I have received from Szemere.[e] *D'abord*,[f] that after the peace of Villafranca, Kossuth decamped from Italy without a word to his officers, amongst whom Klapka. Kossuth was afraid Bonaparte would hand him over to Francis Joseph.[496] *Originally*, so Szemere now writes, this same worthy had not been included in the Bonaparte business. Klapka, Kiss and Teleki had, off their own bat, agreed with Plon-Plon to instigate a revolution in Hungary. Kossuth got wind of it and, from London, *threatened* to *denounce* them in the English press should they not include him in the compact. SUCH ARE THOSE WORTHIES.

In some ways I envy you for being able to live in Manchester, cut off as you are from the war between mice and frogs.[505] Down here I have to wade through all this ordure and do so in circumstances which already consume too much of the time I

---

[a] dated 17 November 1859 - [b] containing H. Beta's article 'Ferdinand Freiligrath' - [c] [H.] B[eta,] 'Chronik unseres Schillerfestes', *Hermann*, No. 46, 19 November 1859. - [d] 'Kossuth and Louis Napoleon' - [e] See this volume, p. 523. - [f] First

should be devoting to my theoretical studies. Conversely, I'm glad that you only have to put up with all the ordure at second hand.

Last Thursday I received the enclosed letter from Freiligrath. What follows will help you understand the full extent of his depravity and pettiness. Throughout the time when that fellow (Blind) was playing his perfidious role vis-à-vis ourselves, he was on the most intimate terms with Freiligrath. He acted as his *homme d'affaires*—in the matter of the great Kinkel-Freiligrath controversy—on the organising committee for the Schiller festival. At that festival the Blind and Freiligrath families sat cheek by jowl throughout the performance. Well, on the following morning[a] *The Morning Advertiser* carried a report in which Freiligrath's poem was described as 'ABOVE MEDIOCRITY'[b]. The same critical sense (whereof, indeed, not much is needed to strip student Blind of his mask of anonymity) which told me that Blind, and Blind alone, had written the anti-Vogt paragraph in *The Free Press*,[c] also told me that he was the author of this article. The only thing which surprised me was that the obsequious sycophant had had the courage to speak about Freiligrath IN THIS COOL MANNER. I sent the latter the cutting. Whereupon I received from him the enclosed letter which, if one reads between the lines, more or less voices the suspicion that *I* was responsible for introducing a forgery into student Blind's EXERCISE—namely, the quip about Freiligrath. On Saturday I went to see Freiligrath. I didn't yet know about the statement he had made in the Augsburg *Allgemeine Zeitung* (to wit, that he was not one of Vogt's accusers, *nor had he ever written a line for the 'Volk'*).[d] He was careful, too, not to breathe a word to me about it. I told him *de prime abord*[e] that I thought it by no means a crime on Blind's part to consider Freiligrath's poem as 'ABOVE MEDIOCRITY', for this was an aesthetic judgment; but that it did seem to me altogether too much when he allowed Blind to bamboozle him into thinking I had amended Blind's task for him—through some mysterious third party—and interpolated the quip about himself (Freiligrath). Greatly embarrassed, the philistine now admitted, *d'abord*,[f] that *he* had shown Blind *my* letter, and proceeded to show me the two letters from Blind. In the first, student Blind describes a person frequently seen near me at the Urquhartite meeting of 9 May[420] and who had *skulked round* him

[a] 11 November 1859 - [b] 'Crystal Palace.—The Schiller Commemoration', *The Morning Advertiser*, No. 21344, 11 November 1859. - [c] [K. Blind,] 'The Grand Duke Constantine to Be King of Hungary', *The Free Press*, No. 5, 27 May 1859. - [d] F. Freiligrath, 'Erklärung', *Allgemeine Zeitung*, No. 319 (supplement), 15 November 1859. - [e] to begin with - [f] first

at the Crystal Palace (10 November).[503] In the second letter (Freiligrath was condescending enough to write to Blind saying he couldn't believe *I* had interpolated the insulting bit) Blind declares that that wasn't really what he'd meant to say. I next told the philistine that the only two Germans or, for that matter, persons, who had accosted me more than once on the platform on 9 May had been Blind and Faucher and NOBODY ELSE. Well now, Blind *knows* Faucher, whom he asked to be introduced to on the Schiller committee and whom he thanked on Freiligrath's behalf for backing Freiligrath's 'cantata' against the 'speech'.[a] Again, the slyboots from Baden failed to mention Faucher's name. (I immediately informed the latter of the fact.) For Faucher knows EDITOR Grant of *The Morning Advertiser*, and might help to get Blind kicked out of the LICENSED VICTUALLER PAPER were he to demand that Blind make a personal statement as to whether he (Faucher) had got him (Grant) to interpolate something in Blind's article, which is why student Blind is capable of remembering what Faucher's FEATURES were like on 9 May. He recalls that they were the same FEATURES that *skulked round* him at the Crystal Palace on 10 November. But he forgets that this individual he knows so well is that selfsame Faucher.

This whole business is so rotten—tortuous—and so typical of philistines Freiligrath and Blind that I had to go into this nonsense at some length. It's altogether typical of philistine Freiligrath that he should not deem himself accountable to *me* for his appearance in public with Kinkel and Co., for his statement in the Augsburg *Allgemeine Zeitung*, for his coquetry with the *Hermann*, for his intercourse with Blind at a time when he knew about that scoundrel's 'word of honour',[b] etc.—but believes that everything should revolve round somebody's having had the audacity to find his poem (I enclose it) 'ABOVE MEDIOCRITY' instead of crying it up AS THE VERY INCARNATION OF THE BEAUTIFUL AND SUBLIME.

I told him I didn't give a fig for *that* affair, compared with which there were far more important things at stake between myself and Blind, etc.

As for the 'machinations' against him on the part of Kinkel, etc., he had only himself to blame. Why demean himself with the fellows?

Finally I wanted to know what was contained in No. 43 of the *Gartenlaube*.[c] It then transpired that Mr Freiligrath was on very

---

[a] by Kinkel (see this volume, pp. 512-13) - [b] See this volume, pp. 502-04. - [c] It contained Beta's article 'Ferdinand Freiligrath'.

close terms with Mr Beta, had entertained him in his own house and had 'suffered' Beta to write a fulsome biography of himself and an apotheosis of his family, and was irritated only at Beta's having concluded (at Kinkel's instigation, of course) with the suggestion that Freiligrath's poetry, like his character, was being ruined—*by me.* It was I who was to blame for the fact that Mr Freiligrath, never particularly prolific in the matter of original work, had for years pursued the business of banking rather than the business of poetry. Mr Freiligrath showed no feeling of shame in my presence for having demeaned himself by consorting with that scoundrel Beta, one-time sub-editor of Louis Drucker's *How do you do?* Nor for the gross flattery ladled out by that abject creature. What shocked him was to be publicly portrayed as 'influenced' by me. He wasn't sure whether he oughtn't to make some statement on the subject, being deterred from doing so only by his fear of a counter-statement on my part. The fellow thinks it 'in the nature of things' that, if he lets out a fart, it should cause a great flurry; that on the one hand he should serve Mammon and, on the other, be 'priest to the Muse'; that his want of character in practice should be hailed as 'political virtue' in theory. The man is sensitive to the tiniest pin-prick. His petty histrionic bickerings behind the scenes with Gottfried[a] he treats as weighty intrigues. On the other hand he considers it quite in order that my family should forego, not just recognition but even *notice,* of a closely reasoned work such as the instalment on money,[b] and that, as a result of my uncompromising political attitude, they should have to endure much *misère* and, in fact, lead a joyless existence. The man thinks that my wife should, moreover, gratefully bear with the *slights* publicly inflicted on myself in the knowledge that Mrs Freiligrath is eulogised and extolled and that even his Käthchen,[c] a SILLY GOOSE who doesn't understand a word of German, is commended to your German philistines. The man has not a vestige of fellow-feeling. Otherwise he would see how my wife is suffering, and how much he and his spouse contribute thereto. How false and ambiguous his behaviour is, both from the personal and the party point of view.

Nevertheless, I cannot and dare not risk any kind of é c l a t[d] *with the fellow.* He sees to my bills on the *Tribune,* something I'm bound to regard as a favour (although the standing thus gained with Bischoffsheim is to *his* advantage, not *mine*). Otherwise I should

[a] Gottfried Kinkel - [b] K. Marx, *A Contribution to the Critique of Political Economy.* - [c] Kätche, Freiligrath's daughter - [d] row

find myself in the same old quandary about how to get my money from the *Tribune*. On the other hand, nothing would please Kinkel and Co.—the whole of vulgar democracy (*including Mrs Freiligrath*)—more than that this row should take place. If only for that reason it shouldn't be allowed to happen *just now*. However, it will be hard for me to take all these slights lying down.

About the happenings at the Crystal Palace and subsequently on the Schiller committee in my next.

Salut.

Your

K. M.

Another thing you should note in the latest rotten *Hermann* is the way Mr Blind commends himself as a prophet.[a]

The UPSHOT of all the *Hermann*'s revelations from Berlin *re* Stieber is that Duncker, the old policeman, is again trying to *take the place* of Stieber, his rival and enemy (since 1848).[b] Moreover, in the last issue but one of the *Hermann*, the reinstatement of Police Superintendent Duncker was declared by the Berlin correspondent to be the true aim of modern world history.[c]

First published abridged in *Der Briefwechsel zwischen F. Engels und K. Marx*, Bd. 2, Stuttgart, 1913 and in full in: Marx and Engels, *Works*, First Russian Edition, Vol. XXII, Moscow, 1929

Printed according to the original

Published in English for the first time

307

MARX TO FERDINAND LASSALLE[506]

IN BERLIN

[London,] 22 November 1859

Dear Lassalle,

For one thing today is mailing day for America[d]; for another I have taken medicine. So writing is difficult either way. Hence I shall be quite brief.

---

[a] [Blind,] 'Prognostikon des wahrscheinlichen Verlaufes des italienischen Krieges; geschrieben kurz vor Ausbruch desselben', *Hermann*, No. 46, 19 November 1859. - [b] [K. W. Eichhoff,] 'Stieber', *Hermann*, Nos. 36-38, 40, 42, 43; 10, 17, 24 September, 8, 22, 29 October 1859. - [c] [K. W. Eichhoff,] 'Berlin, 8. Nov. (Stieber)', *Hermann*, No. 45, 12 November 1859. - [d] It was a Tuesday. On Tuesdays and Fridays Marx sent off articles for the *New-York Daily Tribune*.

1. THANKS for your last letter but one. I shall, however, probably succeed in arranging a bill *on myself* here in London, at an exorbitant rate of interest.

2. You had best abandon your anti-Vogt statement now that the *Reform* has already printed a statement of mine.[a] My chief concern now is to compel Mr Vogt to pursue the matter in London.[b]

3. I have told Freiligrath that you have praised his poem on Schiller and criticised his conduct towards you.[507] He will now write to you. Read No. 43 of the *Gartenlaube* wherein Kinkel's sycophant, Mr Beta (sometime editor of the *How do you do?* published here by *Louis Drucker*, and presently *faiseur-en-chef*[c] of the *Hermann*, whose EDITORS are all recruited from the literary *Lumpenproletariat*), makes the discovery that Freiligrath 'seldom sang any more' after he had been 'inspired' by me.[d] During recent years Freiligrath has been whoring too much after the idols of Babylon, so great is his thirst for popularity. His wife may not be an altogether beneficent influence IN THIS RESPECT. I will dilate no further on this theme, except to say that I show more consideration for old personal and party friends than seems right to many very clever people in our party.

4. *Ad vocem*[e] *Bonaparte.* So far as I can see, the Italian war[370] has temporarily strengthened Bonaparte's position in France; betrayed the Italian revolution into the hands of the Piedmontese doctrinaires and their henchmen; made Prussia exceptionally popular with the liberal *vulgus*[f] by virtue of her Haugwitzian policy; increased *Russia's* influence in Germany; and, finally, propagated demoralisation of an unprecedented kind—a most repulsive combination of Bonapartism and drivel about nationalities. I for my part fail to see any reason why members of our party had to give dialectical support to these nauseous, counter-revolutionary illusions of philistine-liberal provenance. It is my belief that, from the moment when Disraeli publicly admitted the existence of an alliance between Bonaparte and Russia,[415] and more especially from the moment when Russia sent out her shameless circular note to the German courts,[g] the battle-cry should have been raised against the *Russo*-French

---

[a] K. Marx, 'Statement to the Editors of *Die Reform*, the *Volks-Zeitung* and the *Allgemeine Zeitung*'. - [b] See this volume, p. 525. - [c] chief impresario - [d] [H.] B[eta,] 'Ferdinand Freiligrath', *Die Gartenlaube*, No. 43, 1859. - [e] As to - [f] common people - [g] A. Gortschakoff, 'Circularschreiben an die russischen Gesandtschaften vom 15 (27) Mai 1859', *Allgemeine Zeitung*, No. 167, 16 June 1859.

alliance. Opposition to Russia would instantly have disposed of the delusion that there was anything anti-liberal about a turning against France.

Schleinitz's despatches,[a] which I have studied in detail, together with the statements made by the ministers over here, some direct to Parliament, some in the press, confirm my view that *Prussia* had no intention of intervening so long as the German frontier was not violated. Bonaparte, as the protégé of Russia and England, had at the time been given permission to conduct a 'localised' war in order to keep him in France. Prussia would not have dared lift a finger and, had she done so, there would have been war between Germany and Russia, than which nothing could be more desirable. But IN FACT there was no question of it, because Prussia would *never* have had the courage to take such a step. Rather it was a question, partly of exposing the Prussian government in all its miserable weakness, partly and above all of unmasking Bonapartist DELUSIONS. Nor would the game have been too difficult, since all the representatives of the revolutionary party from Mazzini to Louis Blanc, Ledru-Rollin and even Proudhon would have joined in. This would have meant that the polemic against Bonaparte's imposture could not have acquired the appearance of hostility to Italy or France.

I am not, of course, going into the matter thoroughly here, but merely jotting down a few points. However, I shall, with your permission, make one further observation. There is a possibility that things will come to a head again soon. In that case one of two things must prevail in our party: either no one speaks for the party without prior consultation with the others, or everyone has the right to put forward his views without any regard for the others. Now this last is certainly not to be recommended, since a public polemic would in no way benefit so small a party (which, I hope, makes up in vigour for what it lacks in numbers). I can only say that, during my travels through England and Scotland (this summer)[444]—for our old party friends are scattered about the country—I did not find anybody here who would not have wished you had modified your pamphlet[b] in many respects. I see a quite simple explanation for this, namely that foreign policy, in

[a] to the Prussian embassies in Britain, Russia and Germany (Berlin, June-July 1859); reports on the despatches appeared in the *Neue Preußische Zeitung*, No. 170, 24 July 1859 ('Zu der "Vermittlung"'), No. 171, 26 July ('Preußische Depeschen') and No. 174, 29 July 1859 ('Deutschland'). See also p. 520 - [b] F. Lassalle, *Der italienische Krieg und die Aufgabe Preußens.*

particular, presents a very different aspect according to whether you view it from English soil or from the Continent.

Salut.

Your
K. M.

First published in: *F. Lassalle. Nachgelassene Briefe und Schriften*, Bd. III, Stuttgart-Berlin, 1922

Printed according to the original

Published in English for the first time

308

MARX TO FERDINAND FREILIGRATH

IN LONDON

[London,] 23 November 1859

Dear Freiligrath,

I have just received a copy of your letter to Liebknecht[a] in which the following passage occurs:

> 'I possess only *one* letter from Vogt,[508] dated 1 April 1859. This letter, as Marx *conceded* only last Saturday, does not contain a single syllable that *might* be used to substantiate a charge against Vogt.'

Since accuracy is desirable in matters of this kind, I must register a formal protest in regard to this passage.

Firstly, I *conceded* nothing. To concede (*concédere*) presupposes a debate in which one of the assertions originally put forward is withdrawn and the opposing view accepted. Nothing of the kind happened between us. The initiative was mine. I told you something; I conceded nothing. The facts were as follows:

I recalled that you yourself had asked Mr Blind whether he was the author of the anonymous pamphlet,[b] since both the tone and the content of his verbal account tallied entirely with the pamphlet.[461] I stressed that, *before* encountering Mr Blind at Urquhart's meeting of 9 May,[420] I knew nothing of Vogt's participation in the Italian imbroglio, save only for his letter to you. I reminded you that, on the evening you showed me that letter, it never remotely occurred to me to infer therefrom that Vogt had been bribed, or anything of the kind. All I found in the letter was the same old, all too familiar, superficially liberal

[a] Freiligrath's letter to Liebknecht of 21 November 1859. - [b] *Zur Warnung*

pot-house politics of his. If I laid any emphasis on all this, it was—*à tout seigneur tout honneur*[a]—so as not to detract in any way from Mr Blind's merit in uncovering Vogt's high treason.

Secondly, however, it never occurred to me to say that 'Vogt's letter did *not contain a single syllable* that *might* be used to substantiate a charge against Vogt'. All I said was that, having read the letter, it would not occur to *me* to draw such a conclusion. But the immediate subjective impression made upon me by the letter is very far removed from an *objective judgment* on the content of the letter, or even on conjectures which *might* be made about it. I never had either the occasion or the opportunity to subject the letter to the critical examination necessary for such an objective judgment. That Mr Blind put a different construction on, for instance, the letters Vogt addressed to you, him, etc., is and was known to you. E.g. in his article in *The Free Press* (27 May)[b] *these* letters are expressly mentioned as *corpora delicti*,[c] even though no names are given. This is again the case in his statement in the Augsburg *Allgemeine Zeitung*.[d]

From Mr Vogt I now come to Mr Beta, whose No. 43 I bought after getting your letter.[e] Having perused the *opus*, I decided to do exactly what I have been doing for the past 10 years, namely ignore such stuff. But I have today heard from two very close friends (not in London) urging me to make a statement in the interests of the party. I shall first deliberate the pros and cons for twice 24 hours. If, after mature deliberation, I should decide to speak, my statement would contain essentially the following:

1. If an attempt were made *wrongly* to attribute to me any influence over you, this could at most apply to the brief life-span of the *Neue Rheinische Zeitung*, at which time you were writing what was truly splendid and indisputably your most popular poetry.

2. *A biographical sketch* in a few sentences *of Mr Betziege*,[f] *alias Hans Beta*, starting from the time when he wrote for a blackmailing theatrical rag in Berlin, going on through his editorship of the *How do you do?* under Louis Drucker, vintner and clown (including my visit to the *How do you do*'s lair[509]) and his

---

[a] honour to whom honour is due - [b] [K. Blind,] 'The Grand Duke Constantine to Be King of Hungary', *The Free Press*, No. 5, 27 May 1859. - [c] incriminating evidence - [d] K. Blind, 'Erklärung', *Allgemeine Zeitung*, No. 313, 9 November 1859. - [e] [H.] B[eta,] 'Ferdinand Freiligrath', *Die Gartenlaube*, No. 43, 1859. - [f] Literally 'praying goat', a play on the name Bettzieh.

subsequent activities in Leipzig, when he simultaneously libelled me in the *Gartenlaube*, i.e. reproduced the tripe from the *How do you do?* and appropriated my anti-Palmerston pamphlets,[a] and ending up with his present occupation of factotum to Gottfried Kinkel. It might, perhaps, do some good if the German public were to be shown what a scoundrelly bunch of lumpenproletarians it is that is croaking loudest in the foul swamp of current German literature.

3. Two letters from Heine to myself which will enable the public to decide between the authority of Heine and the authority of Beta.

4. Finally, a couple of letters written to me by Johann Kinkel[b] and Johanna Kinkel at the time of the *N. Rh. Z.* I would use these to unseat the melodramatic parson from the high horse upon which this Father Brey[c] (it is in that sense that your version of Goethe should be amended) is charging me in what is for him the typical arena of a *Gartenlaube.*

I am telling you all this so that, as is fitting between friends, you will have been informed in advance should I decide to make a statement.[510]

As for Liebknecht, Kolb is clearly seeking to justify himself in Cotta's eyes by using your letter to sacrifice Liebknecht as a scapegoat, for his own, not Liebknecht's *quid pro quo. Peccant reges, plectuntur Achivi*[d] still holds good.

To obviate all misunderstanding I have, at the same time as this letter to you, sent Liebknecht a copy of the passages in it relating to the Vogt affair.

Your
K. M.

First published in *Die Neue Zeit*, Ergänzungshefte, No. 12, 1911-1912

Printed according to the original

Published in English for the first time

---

[a] K. Marx, 'Lord Palmerston'. - [b] Gottfried Kinkel. Marx ironically calls him Johann after his wife, Johanna Kinkel. - [c] A character from Goethe's *Ein Fastnachtsspiel auch wohl zu tragieren Ostern, vom Pater Brey, dem falschen Propheten.* - [d] The chiefs sin, the Aacheans suffer. Paraphrase of *Quidquid delirant reges plectuntur Achivi* (whatever madness possesses the chiefs, it is the Aacheans who suffer), Horace, *Epistle*, I, ii, 14.

309

MARX TO ENGELS

IN MANCHESTER

London, 26 November 1859
9 Grafton Terrace, Maitland Park,
Haverstock Hill

Dear Engels,

On Monday I sent you a long letter about the wrangles down here. On Tuesday I sent you the *Gartenlaube*[a] and Beta's article.[512] Well, every day I've been waiting to hear from you since, in AFFAIRS of this kind, it is only *your letters* that revive my wife's DROOPING SPIRITS. One can simply laugh off such rubbish if the rest of one's life is tolerable. But in my CIRCUMSTANCES THEY WEIGH HEAVILY UPON THE FAMILY.

Well, today I'm sending you:

1. *A letter from Lassalle* to myself.[513] The 'statement' I sent the *Volks-Zeitung* is the same as appeared in No. 325 of the Augsburg *Allgemeine Zeitung*.[b] (Another, two columns long, about my attitude to vulgar democracy, etc., appeared in No. 139 of the Hamburg *Reform*.[c] I took the opportunity of naming you as the author of *Po and Rhine*, a fact obstinately kept dark by that same vulgar democracy.) From Lassalle's letter you will see that he, who IN POINT OF FACT was piping the same tune as Vogt, would much rather the Berlin public did not know about my opposition to Vogt and his propaganda.

From the same letter you will see that he at last intends to set to work on *his 'Political Economy'*,[278] but is clever enough to wait another 3 months until he is in possession of my second instalment.[473] The motives for the consistent failure, even on the part of one who is 'friendly', to break the *conspiration de silence* are now plain.

I have taken the opportunity of giving Lassalle a brief outline of my views on the Italian question,[d] at the same time telling him that, should anyone wish at such a critical moment to speak in the name of the party, the following alternatives must hold good. Either he consults the others beforehand, or the others (euphemis-

---

[a] 'Ferdinand Freiligrath', *Die Gartenlaube*, No. 43, 1859. - [b] K. Marx, 'Declaration'. - [c] K. Marx, 'Statement to the Editors of *Die Reform*, the *Volks-Zeitung* and the *Allgemeine Zeitung*'. - [d] See this volume, pp. 536-39.

tic for you and me) have the right to put their own view before the public, without regard for that anyone.

2. A letter from Liebknecht to Freiligrath. You will have seen from the Augsburg *Allgemeine Zeitung* that Freiligrath declared, firstly, that he had been made out to be Vogt's accuser 'without his knowledge and consent'; secondly, that 'he had never written a line for the *Volk*' (doesn't write at all).[a] Mr Kolb, who had *wrongly* construed a private letter from Liebknecht to himself and had been told off by Cotta *after* this statement of Freiligrath's, naturally sacrificed Liebknecht as a scapegoat.[511] But Freiligrath, who is a SUBALTERN of Fazy's, was outraged and wrote an exceedingly rude letter to Liebknecht.[b] I enclose Liebknecht's reply to it.[c]

Now Freiligrath's letter to Liebknecht contained the following passage:

> 'I possess only *one* letter from Vogt, dated 1 April 1859.[508] This letter, as Marx only last Saturday *conceded*' (I UNDERLINE), 'does not contain a single syllable that *might* be used to substantiate a charge against Vogt. Why on earth, then, should I be trying to prove him guilty of attempted bribery?'

Now although on the one hand Freiligrath is *indispensable* to me for drawing bills on New York, although on the other I wish for political reasons to avoid a breach with him, and, lastly, am fond of him personally WITH ALL HIS FAULTS, I could not do otherwise—it was absolutely essential—than send him a *formal protest* about the above lines. For who is to guarantee that he will not write the same thing to Vogt and that the latter will not have it published?

The matter he misrepresents was as follows:

During my meeting with him, at which the topic was Blind, not Vogt,[d] I told him (there was no question of a *debate*, and still less of *his* calling me to account, as might be inferred from the words 'Marx *conceded*') that *he himself* had considered Blind to be the author of the pamphlet,[e] the latter having told him what he had told me; also that, *before* my meeting with Blind on 9th May,[420] I had known nothing at all about Vogt's activities, save his letter to Freiligrath from which—as *he*, Freiligrath, would recall—I did not infer bribery, but rather found therein the same old, all too familiar, superficially liberal pot-house politics of his. This is, after all, not at all the same thing as '*conceding* that the letter did not

---

[a] F. Freiligrath, 'Erklärung', *Allgemeine Zeitung*, No. 319 (supplement), 15 November 1859. - [b] on 21 November 1859 - [c] Liebknecht replied on 23 November. - [d] See this volume, p. 533. - [e] *Zur Warnung*

contain a single line that *might* be used to substantiate a charge'. I pointed this out to him, at the same time expressing my astonishment at his failure to call Blind to account for having, in *The Free Press*,[a] treated similar letters (including Freiligrath's) as *corpora delicti*.[b] So far I have had no answer from him, although he usually replies at once. It is possible—and this would be disastrous—that he has taken this opportunity to sever old party ties which, or so it would seem, have long become irksome to him. HOWEVER THAT MAY BE, I was bound to protest against his account of the affair.

Enough of this rubbish.

Yesterday a Tory journalist told me it was *his* intention to provide evidence next week in a TORY WEEKLY (the *WEEKLY MAIL*, I THINK) to the effect that Garibaldi was receiving money from Bonaparte while still a merchant in South America. *Nous verrons*.[c]

Regards to Lupus.

Your
K. M.

Apropos. In my article in the *Tribune*[d] yesterday I said that I would shortly be writing about the RIFLE MOVEMENT over here. So I should be glad if you would write about it.[502]

First published abridged in *Der Briefwechsel zwischen F. Engels und K. Marx*, Bd. 2, Stuttgart, 1913 and in full in: Marx and Engels, *Works*, First Russian Edition, Vol. XXII, Moscow, 1929

Printed according to the original

Published in English for the first time

310

ENGELS TO MARX
IN LONDON

Manchester, 28 November 1859
7 Southgate

Dear Moor,

If I didn't write last week it was because I had given Lupus all the papers; nor did I recover them for several days having, in the

---

[a] [K. Blind,] 'The Grand Duke Constantine to Be King of Hungary', *The Free Press*, No. 5, 27 May 1859. - [b] incriminating evidence - [c] We shall see. - [d] K. Marx, 'The Invasion Panic in England'.

interval, repeatedly failed to get hold of him. Lupus is of the same opinion as myself, namely that Freiligrath's behaviour hardly admits of further party relations with him, but that on purely party grounds, and aside from your personal position, you are absolutely justified in avoiding any breach for the present *s'il y a moyen*[a]—it would be a triumph for Kinkel and Co. which they would trumpet abroad and exploit for all they were worth. But it's something we shan't forgive the weak-minded ass. If his relationship with Fazy really compelled him to make a statement at all, Freiligrath ought to have consulted *you*, which would at any rate have resulted in something other than the inane affair which he caused to be published in the Augsburg *Allgemeine Zeitung*.[b] He would seem to be dead keen on an amnesty, to judge by his strenuous denials of all participation in the *Volk*. But his getting on to personal terms with Mr Bettziech, receiving him in his own house, is something which Lupus, who went *with Freiligrath* to see Bettziech at the time of the *How do you do?* affair,[509] will never forgive him. And it really is a dirty trick. As things are now, however, it seems questionable whether we can go on much longer without an open breach with Freiligrath; he is increasingly subject to the literary man's itch, nor will madame[c] fail to point out morning, noon and night that Mr Beta, Kinkel and company do at least praise him publicly, whereas all he gets from us even privately is a MODICUM of recognition, and we can never be relied on to make him 'known by reason of his fame'.[d] However, Freiligrath is all too well aware that, while Kinkel and Co. may be of use to him in peacetime, he would be nothing without us at the moment of battle, and that he could never ally himself with our enemies without running all manner of unpleasant risks. He will, I think, take care not to go too far and will finally pin his hopes on our forbearance.

Your 'Declaration' in the Augsburg *Allgemeine Zeitung*[e] will put Blind into a very nasty position. How, without discrediting himself, he will lie his way out of the pass his lies have brought him to, I fail to see.

These shabby goings-on must indeed be a sore trial to your wife. However, this rubbish, too, will pass and, I hope, soon. Within a few weeks it will no doubt be possible to drop Mr Freiligrath and

---

[a] if possible - [b] F. Freiligrath, 'Erklärung', *Allgemeine Zeitung*, No. 319 (supplement), 15 November 1859. - [c] Ida Freiligrath — [d] Probably an allusion to Nicolas Chamfort's dictum: 'Celebrity: the advantage of being known by those who don't know you' (*Maximes et Pensées*). - [e] K. Marx, 'Declaration'.

leave him to stew in his own juice. But now I must say goodbye for today; I am about to go home and shall send an article on the RIFLE MOVEMENT[502] by the night mail. There will be several of them, at any rate.

Warm regards to your wife and the YOUNG LADIES.

Your

F. E.

First published abridged in *Der Briefwechsel zwischen F. Engels und K. Marx*, Bd. 2, Stuttgart, 1913 and in full in: Marx and Engels, *Works,* First Russian Edition, Vol. XXII, Moscow, 1929

Printed according to the original

Published in English for the first time

311

MARX TO FERDINAND FREILIGRATH[514]

IN LONDON

[London, about 30 November 1859]

Dear Freiligrath,

I am neither Liebknecht's letter-writer, nor his ATTORNEY. I shall, however, send him a copy of that part of your letter which relates to him.

I have decided against the statement I had briefly envisaged, bearing in mind that *'odi profanum vulgus et arceo'.*[a]

While the statement was certainly *against* Beta, it was for that very reason bound to be also *about* you, as you will have seen from the SUMMARY. If only for that reason, I gave you notice of it, quite apart from the intimacy in which your family and his appear in his *opusculum.*[b]

You find it unpleasant to have your name mixed up in the Vogt affair. I don't give a damn for Vogt and his infamous lies in the Biel *Handels-Courier,*[c] but I will not have my name used as a mask by democratic tricksters. As you know, if someone is forced to call upon witnesses, no other person can 'object' to being cited as a witness. In accordance with ancient English legal USE, RESTIVE WITNESSES may, *horribile dictu,*[d] actually be crushed to death.

---

[a] I loathe the profane rabble and shun it (Horace, *Odes,* III, I, 1). - [b] [H.] B[eta,] 'Ferdinand Freiligrath', *Die Gartenlaube,* No. 43, 1859. - [c] [K. Vogt,] 'Zur Warnung', *Schweizer Handels-Courier,* No. 150 (supplement), 2 June 1859. - [d] horrible to say

Finally, as regards party considerations, I am used to being treated on behalf of the whole party as target for mud-slinging by the press, and to seeing my private interests constantly damaged by party considerations; on the other hand, I am equally used to being unable to reckon on any kind of private consideration towards myself.

Salut.

Your

K. M.

First published in *Die Neue Zeit*, Ergänzungshefte, No. 12, 1911-1912

Printed according to the manuscript of Marx's letter to Engels of 10 December 1859

Published in English for the first time

312

MARX TO ENGELS

IN MANCHESTER

London, 10 December 1859

Dear Engels,

Article received.[a] I trust your health has improved.

As to the Freiligrath business, more in the course of this letter. I presume you saw the *Hermann* of a week ago today containing 'Vorletzte Sitzung des Schiller-Comités',[b] a self-portrait of the scoundrelly bunch of lumpenproletarians which has gathered round Gottfried Kinkel. The article was written by the worthy Beta.

What do you make of Mr Lassalle's notifying me ALL AT ONCE of his 'Political Economy'.[278] Does this not explain why my work[c] was, firstly, so much delayed and, secondly, so badly advertised? Lassalle *lives in Duncker's house,* or so I am told by Fischel of Berlin (was in England for a few days; editor of the Berlin *Portfolio*[482]—Urquhartite—of which Nos. 1 and 2 contain excerpts from my anti-Palmerston PAMPHLETS on Poland and Unkiar-Skelessi[d]). In

[a] F. Engels, 'Progress of the Moorish War'. - [b] *Hermann*, No. 48, 3 December 1859. - [c] *A Contribution to the Critique of Political Economy* - [d] K. Marx, 'Der "wahrhaft" englische Minister und Russland am Bosporus' and 'Lord Palmerston und die polnische Insurrection. 1831' (excerpts from the pamphlet *Lord Palmerston*), *Das Neue Portfolio*, Berlin, 1859, Heft I; 1860, Heft II.

Berlin, it would seem, he (Lassalle) is noted for his vanity. The stick with which he was given a drubbing[a] was *his own*—a memento bought in Paris, *Robespierre's stick* bearing the device, *liberté, égalité, fratérnité!*

I wrote and asked Lassalle whether he might not be able to get hold of some money for me (against a bill on myself which I would give him).[b] He replied saying that he himself was living on credit until July, and had appropriated Duncker's FLOATING SURPLUS. Then he suggested I draw a bill on him (Lassalle), discount it here, and send him the money before it fell due. But over here the name of Lassalle is not, of course, worth 1/100 of a FARTHING. I have latterly been cited at the COUNTY COURT by sundry fellows—quite small ones, such as the MILKMAN, etc., and can, in fact, see no way out of the crisis which has grown steadily worse for the past half year. Extra expenses, e.g. ABOUT £5 for the rotten *Volk* lawsuit, and Mr Biskamp, whom I have fed for three months (and am not yet quit of), have, indeed, contributed their mite to the predicament. But all in all that made little odds. What is really devilish is not having a Bamberger here in London any more, for there are at present considerable possibilities in regard to bill transactions. Had fat philistine Freiligrath so wished, he might even have procured me a LOAN, for after all the philistine had the security to hand. But the fellow imagined (and no doubt actually boasted) that he was doing a great deal if, a week before I drew a bill on the *Tribune*, he loaned me £2 for a week. I have, by the by, made various other attempts to find a usurer. BUT TILL NOW WITHOUT ANY RESULT.

I know that you yourself are in a fix as a result of being taken to court recently,[c] and hence am telling you about the STATE OF THINGS only because I feel a need to discuss it with SOMEBODY. I hope that our domestic misfortunes won't deter you from *coming up here for a few days.* It's absolutely essential for my girls to have a 'human being' in the house again for once. The poor children have been too early tormented by domestic misery.

Now ad vocem[d] *Freiligrath.*

Having waited a week, the philistine wrote the following letter:

'Dear Marx,

'I have received your letter of the 23 inst.' (November)[e] 'and Liebknecht's of the same date and, in order to simplify matters, am replying to both in this letter to you.

---

[a] See this volume, p. 319. - [b] Ibid., p. 524. - [c] Ibid., pp. 490, 493, 499, 530. - [d] as to - [e] See this volume, pp. 539-40.

'As far as Liebknecht's letter is concerned, neither its presumptuous and impertinent tone, nor its content—an unsuccessful attempt to turn the tables—could surprise me! Very nice, I must say! The London correspondent of the Augsburg *Allgemeine Zeitung* thinks fit to put my name at Mr Kolb's disposal *ad libitum* and without previously notifying me[a]; but I, if I protest against that abuse, must first give due notice!! The argument used by Liebknecht in support of this pretty doctrine is so jejune that it calls for no serious refutation on my part. I would simply remark that, in no circumstances and for no personal or party considerations whatsoever, shall I put up with arbitrary actions of this nature.

'That's all about and for Liebknecht!

'And now for your letter.

'I gladly allow your objection to the word "conceded" used in my letter to Liebknecht (of 21 November). I set no store by that word. Nor did it conceal any implication of any kind, and I might just as well have used "remarked" or "said". So without further contention I *concede* your *"conceded"*. If we were both of the same opinion from the start, so much the better!'

(The slyboots doesn't tumble to the fact that he is thereby *conceding my* opinion of Vogt and Blind.)

'As regards your anti-Beta statement you must, of course, do exactly as you think fit. All the same, I believe that your first impulse to ignore the thing was the better one and more worthy of you! Now that you have had more than twice 24 hours for deliberation, you will have decided one way or the other. Whether this way or that is quite immaterial to me!

'That you should have wished to inform me beforehand, "as is fitting between friends", of your anti-Beta statement is most deserving of thanks. For that matter your statement, so far as I can see, was to be directed against *Beta*, not against *myself*, and hence scarcely called for prior notification of your intention

'At all events let me not omit to mention *en revanche*[b] that I myself shall probably be publishing another statement in which I shall repeat, once and for all, that I object to the use of my name in connection with the Vogt affair.

Your

F. Freiligrath.'

UNDER THE CIRCUMSTANCES I could, of course, only reply IN A VERY MODERATE TONE to this letter, 'malicious' in intent and adorned with so many!! I therefore wrote by return:

'Dear Freiligrath,[c]

'I am neither Liebknecht's letter-writer, nor his ATTORNEY. I shall, however, send him a copy of that part of your letter which relates to him.

'I have decided against the statement I had briefly envisaged, bearing in mind that *"odi profanum vulgus et arceo"*.[d]

'While the statement was certainly *against* Beta, it was for that very reason bound to be also *about* you, as you will have seen from the SUMMARY. If only for that reason, I gave you notice of it, quite

---

[a] [W. Liebknecht,] 'Erklärung', *Allgemeine Zeitung*, No. 327 (supplement), 23 November 1859. - [b] by way of a return - [c] See this volume, p. 546. - [d] I loathe the profane rabble and shun it (Horace, *Odes*, III, I, 1).

apart from the intimacy in which your family and his appear in his *opusculum*.[a]

'You find it unpleasant to have your name mixed up in the Vogt affair. I don't give a damn for Vogt and his infamous lies in the Biel *Handels-Courier*,[b] but I will not have my name used as a mask by democratic tricksters. As you know, if someone is forced to call upon witnesses, no other person can "object" to being cited as a witness. In accordance with ancient English legal USE, RESTIVE WITNESSES may, *horribile dictu*,[c] actually be crushed to death.

'Finally, as regards party considerations, I am used to being treated on behalf of the whole party as target for mud-slinging by the press, and to seeing my private interests constantly damaged by party considerations; on the other hand, I am equally used to being unable to reckon on any kind of private consideration towards myself.

'*Salut.*

Your

K. M.'

To this Freiligrath has not replied, and I don't know EXACTLY what footing we are on now.

Regards to Lupus.

Your

K. M.

First published abridged in *Der Briefwechsel zwischen F. Engels und K. Marx*, Bd. 2, Stuttgart, 1913 and in full in: Marx and Engels, *Works*, First Russian Edition, Vol. XXII, Moscow, 1929

Printed according to the original

Published in English for the first time

313

ENGELS TO MARX[515]

IN LONDON

[Manchester, 11 or 12 December 1859]

Dear Moor,

Herewith POST OFFICE ORDER for £5 payable at Camden Town. Beta is the dirtiest dog I have ever come across. The infamous article[d]

---

[a] [H.] B[eta,] 'Ferdinand Freiligrath', *Die Gartenlaube*, No. 43, 1859. - [b] [K. Vogt,] 'Zur Warnung', *Schweizer Handels-Courier*, No. 150 (supplement), 2 June 1859. - [c] horrible to say - [d] [H.] B[eta,] 'Ferdinand Freiligrath', *Die Gartenlaube*, No. 43, 1859.

put me into a real rage. Unfortunately the chap's such a cripple already that no amount of beating could make him more misshapen than he is. However, sometime we shall have to wreak personal vengeance on the rascal. At any rate, some satisfaction can be derived from the fact that Kinkel's beautiful soul is forced to seek its mate in a filthy pig of this kind. Just think what it takes to produce one single Bettziech! Whole generations of crippled moles having, by the Darwinian process of NATURAL SELECTION, evolved to the highest degree the faculty to live on dung, with shit for their chosen element. Filthy, blatant lies and impotent malice—such are the tools with which that mendacious parson Kinkel's bad conscience seeks to keep on its legs. LET US GET THESE FELLOWS ONCE FACE TO FACE AGAIN, and you'll see what becomes of the gang of scoundrels.

Darwin, by the way, whom I'm reading just now, is absolutely splendid.[a] There was one aspect of teleology that had yet to be demolished, and that has now been done. Never before has so grandiose an attempt been made to demonstrate historical evolution in Nature, and certainly never to such good effect. One does, of course, have to put up with the crude English method.

Warm regards to your wife and children.

Your

F. E.

First published abridged in *Der Briefwechsel zwischen F. Engels und K. Marx*, Bd. 2, Stuttgart, 1913 and in full in: Marx and Engels, *Works*, First Russian Edition, Vol. XXII, Moscow, 1929

Printed according to the original

Published in English for the first time

314

MARX TO ENGELS[516]

IN MANCHESTER

[London,] 13 December 1859
9 Grafton Terrace, Maitland Park,
Haverstock Hill

Dear Engels,

MY BEST THANKS FOR THE £5. You can imagine how opportune it was, for in a day or two my wife has to pay an instalment to some fellow at

[a] Ch. Darwin, *On the Origin of Species by Means of Natural Selection....*

the COUNTY COURT. Yesterday I attempted one last FAMILY coup which may, perhaps, succeed. In which case there would be a chance of our being able to breathe again.

In Russia the movement is progressing better than anywhere else in Europe. On the one hand the constitutionalism of the aristocracy versus the Tsar, on the other of the peasants versus the aristocracy. Moreover, having at long last realised that the Poles have not the least inclination to be dissolved in Slav-Russian nationality, Alexander blustered frightfully. Thus the extraordinary successes of Russian diplomacy during the past 15 years, notably since 1849, are more than counter-balanced. Come the next revolution and Russia will oblige by joining in.

You have, I imagine, read Bonaparte's uneasy document addressed to the *préfets* in which he demands that exact returns be made of, *inter alia*, all respectable Orleanists,[124] Legitimists,[303] republicans and socialists, but more especially of 'reliable' Bonapartists?

From the enclosed note you will see that that louse, Juch—PROPRIETOR of the *Hermann*—feels entitled to approach me about the Stieber affair.[517] The rotten swine had deleted from Eichhoff's denunciation of Stieber in the *Hermann*[a] everything relating to our trial,[71] the 'small, insignificant party' being alluded to only *en passant*. I shall give the low scoundrel a proper dressing-down while, of course, doing everything in my power to damage that rascal Stieber. Eichhoff, by the by, was simply a tool where all these Stieber revelations were concerned. The business originated with ex-policeman Duncker in Berlin, whose removal in 1848 was largely brought about by Stieber's yapping from the democratic camp. From then on Duncker got his private police to watch Stieber's every step until he finally thought the moment had come for him to be kicked out. Furthermore, that ass Eichhoff was stupid enough to show his ass's ears in his last article from Berlin in the *Hermann*, in which HE WOUND UP HIS DENUNCIATIONS AGAINST STIEBER—WITH WHAT? WITH THE REQUEST OF THE *RESTITUTIO IN INTEGRUM* OF VIRTUOUS Police Superintendent Duncker.[b]

Nothing but fools and rapscallions, all these chaps, against whom Freiligrath bears *no* grudge, even if they do 'take liberties with his name'.

---

[a] [K. W. Eichhoff,] 'Stieber', *Hermann*, Nos. 36-38, 40, 42 and 43; 10, 17, 24 September and 8, 22 and 29 October 1859. - [b] [K. W. Eichhoff,] 'Berlin, 8. Nov. (Stieber)', *Hermann*, No. 45, 12 November 1859.

UNDER ALL CIRCUMSTANCES I HOPE TO SEE YOU HERE FOR SOME DAYS.
Regards to Lupus.
Salut.

Your
K. M.

Little Jenny has made a copy of a Raphael Madonna especially for you, and of 2 wounded French soldiers for Lupus.

First published abridged in *Der Briefwechsel zwischen F. Engels und K. Marx*, Bd. 2, Stuttgart, 1913 and in full in: Marx and Engels, *Works*, First Russian Edition, Vol. XXII, Moscow, 1929

Printed according to the original

315

ENGELS TO MARX [518]

IN LONDON

Manchester, [19 December 1859]
7 Southgate

Dear Moor,

I slaved away all day so as to have the afternoon free for the article and, when I came to light the gas, it burnt so low that the whole office had to stop work. At home it's been worse if anything for almost a week now; the prolonged spell of frost and fog has so increased the consumption of gas during the day that by the evening there's no pressure at all and hence no light. This makes it impossible for me to do the article today, and anyhow it may well gain by my having to wait until the day after tomorrow or Thursday, since the move from Ceuta against Tetuan should begin any day now.[519] Admittedly, this will be pretty awful for you, since it means you'll have to slave away tomorrow when you had been counting on me.

Siebel has been to Hamburg, where he was told by the literary Bohemians that 'Freiligrath has broken with Marx'. So you can see how Mr Kinkel is still carrying on the business of article-writing, self-advertising tittle-tattle even now that Mockel[a] is dead. Mr Strodtmann, presently on the Hamburg *Freischütz*, has apparently reverted to being a faithful disciple of Johann Gottfried.[b]

[a] Johanna Kinkel - [b] Gottfried Kinkel. Engels ironically calls him Johann after his wife, Johanna Kinkel.

My eyes are aching so I'll stop. Warm regards to your wife and children. I can't come at Christmas. G. Ermen has again been making changes at the office and this makes it impossible for me to go away, especially at the year's end, without incurring very great RESPONSIBILITY. I shall come for certain at Easter or Whitsun.

Your
F. E.

First published in: Marx and Engels, *Works*, First Russian Edition, Vol. XXII, Moscow, 1929

Printed according to the original
Published in English for the first time

316

MARX TO ENGELS

IN MANCHESTER

[London,] 20 December 1859

Dear Engels,

You do not appear to have read both Freiligrath's *and* Blind's statements in the Augsburg *Allgemeine Zeitung* (supplement, of presumably 8, 9, 10 or 11 December).[a] This shows that the rumour that 'Freiligrath has broken with Marx' could have got about without Kinkel's help.

I have had a meeting with Juch about the Stieber proceedings in Berlin[517] (the charge against Eichhoff concerns only his comments about the communist trial—the case comes up on the 22nd—so that the whole of that trial will be re-enacted before the public in Berlin. I've sent Eichhoff my pamphlet.[b] If Schneider, Bürgers, etc., weren't so spineless, they could now take a lovely revenge); he also asked me about the Blind-Freiligrath alliance, of which I was then not yet aware. Unfortunately I am compelled for the time being (on material and 'possibly' political grounds) to show some *égards*[c] for the chap.

---

[a] *Allgemeine Zeitung*, No. 345 (supplement), 11 December 1859. - [b] *Revelations Concerning the Communist Trial in Cologne* - [c] consideration

In the last issue of the *Hermann*, student Blind got 'Borkheim'[a] to describe him (Blind) as the Kinkel of South Germany.[520]

I must now do my article. Don't know what about.

Salut.

Your
K. M.

First published in: Marx and Engels, *Works*, First Russian Edition, Vol. XXII, Moscow, 1929

Printed according to the original

Published in English for the first time

317

ENGELS TO JENNY MARX

IN LONDON

Manchester, 22 December 1859

Dear Mrs Marx,

I take the liberty today of sending you a dozen bottles of wine for the festive season in the hope that they will be to your liking and contribute to the FAMILY'S cheer.

The champagne and Bordeaux (Château d'Arcins) can be drunk at once, while the port wine should be allowed to rest a little and won't be in proper condition until about New Year.

I have been frankly annoyed here by the Freiligrath goings-on.[b] It's forever the same old thing with that belletristic lot; they always want the newspapers to pay them homage, always want their names kept before the public, and the most inept little couplet of their own devising is of greater moment to them than the most tremendous historical event. Since none of this is attainable unless organised by a coterie, it goes without saying that the latter becomes the prime requirement, and we poor communists are, alas, completely useless in that respect; worse still, we are fully alive to the swindle, deride this *organisation du succès*, and ourselves feel almost criminally averse to becoming popular personalities. Now it shows great stupidity if, for these reasons, such a poet feels ill at ease in such a party, for here there is absolutely none of the

[a] S. L. Borkheim, 'An die Redaction des *Hermann*', *Hermann*, No 50, 17 December 1859. - [b] See this volume, pp. 532-36, 543-44 and 548-49.

competition which he is bound to encounter everywhere else—and it shows even greater stupidity if he throws in his lot with a bunch in which competition from a Kinkel is a foregone conclusion. *Mais que voulez-vous?*[a] In order to exist a poet requires incense, a great deal of incense, and Mrs Poet consumes even more. Competition or no competition, Mrs Poet will always be in raptures for the side which daily parades before the public her noble genius of a Ferdinand, herself, her interesting offspring, her cats, dogs, rabbits, canaries and other vermin, and indeed, showers them with Bengal lights, sentimentality and romantic lies. And what Mrs Poet wants, Mr Poet must needs want also, and this all the more in that madame gives expression to his own innermost thoughts. *Das Volk,* INDEED! The *Gartenlaube* is a very different kind of paper, and unctuous Bettziech a very different kind of man from the communists.[b] After all in the *Gartenlaube* they still treat us as a poet's family and accord us a weekly mention, nor does crooked Bettziech ever let slip an opportunity to pay us a little compliment or give us a puff.—True, Kinkel is praised far more highly for his poetry, which is greatly inferior to ours, and they publish many more anecdotes about him, but the man is Bettziech's patron after all, and everything will come right in the end. And then, take the Schiller festival! These communists despise and deride Schiller, so how could one run a Schiller festival with them? But the Schiller festival is more important than all the rest of history put together and, after all, why was Schiller born a 100 years ago if not for us to write a cantata about him today?[c]

And then there is the further consideration that the noble Ferdinand's poetry pretty well dried up years ago and the little he still manages to extract from his noddle is appallingly bad. This necessitates thinking up DODGES such as collected editions, etc., and that's something that can't be done every day. So, in order that one should not be forgotten, a puff becomes daily more of a necessity. Who, IN FACT, ever talked about Freiligrath between 1849 and 1858? Nobody. It was Bettziech who first rediscovered this classic writer, who had been so lost from mind that he was used only as Christmas and birthday presents and no longer figured in literature but in the history of literature. And, of course, nobody was to blame for all this save Karl Marx, with his 'inspiration'. But once F. Freiligrath has been thoroughly warmed up by the incense

[a] But what can you expect? - [b] An allusion to Beta's article 'Ferdinand Freiligrath' published in *Die Gartenlaube,* No. 43, 1859. - [c] This refers to Freiligrath's poem 'Zur Schillerfeier, 10. November 1859. Festlied der Deutschen in London'. See also this volume, p. 511.

of the *Gartenlaube*, then you'll see what poetry will come bubbling out of him!

How petty, shabby and paltry are the doings of these poets! Give me Siebel any day; he may be a rotten poet, but he does at least know that he is a thorough humbug and all he asks is to be allowed to advertise himself—nowadays a necessary *procédé* without which he would be a complete nonentity.

But you really mustn't take all this bickering too much to heart. As a 'personage'[a] Freiligrath is bound sooner or later to betray weaknesses such as will put him into our hands when the time is ripe. Meanwhile, no breach if it can be avoided.

I am very sorry that I shan't be able to come up on Friday, but there are such a lot of changes going on here that yesterday, for instance, I had to slave away till 9.45 at night, and there can be no question of getting away.

My warmest regards to Moor and the YOUNG LADIES.[b]

Your

F. Engels

First published in: Marx and Engels, *Works*, First Russian Edition, Vol. XXII, Moscow, 1929

Printed according to the original

Published in English for the first time

[a] Presumably an allusion to a line from Chapter 24 of Heine's satirical poem *Atta Troll* which describes the hero as 'no talent but a personage'. - [b] Jenny and Laura Marx

APPENDIX

1

JENNY MARX TO ENGELS[521]

IN MANCHESTER

[London, 28 March 1856]

Dear Mr Engels,

Moor wants to know whether you are coming here for Easter as we would all so very much like. In that case he would not send you the Blue Books.[38] Please drop us a line to say whether you are coming. Then we could take the thing to the Parcels Company on Monday. I have just posted your article.[522] Chaley[a] is very busy with the Kars papers[b] and is dictating to a somewhat seedy-looking Pieper. What do you make of the scandals in Berlin? Have you read the report from the Berlin correspondent[c] in today's *Times*?[d] Now we know the reason for the *Kreuz-Zeitung*'s sackcloth-and-ashes leaders.

I also have a bone to pick just now with the Minister of the Interior[e] about the little business of my inheritance. You will remember that my late uncle's[f] effects included a mass of letters and manuscripts belonging to my grandfather,[g] who was War Minister to the Duke of Brunswick. The Prussian State, with Mr von Scharnhorst for intermediary, had already entered into negotiations with my father[h] with a view to *purchasing* these manuscripts which contain material on the military history of the Seven Years War.[300] Then along comes my brother—and in the final statement relating to the estate I find the following curious entry: As regards the books which were found, the Minister of

[a] Karl Marx - [b] K. Marx, 'The Fall of Kars'. - [c] Probably G. B. Wilkinson - [d] 'From Our Own Correspondent. Berlin, March 25', *The Times*, No. 22327, 28 March 1856. - [e] Ferdinand von Westphalen, Jenny Marx's step-brother - [f] Heinrich Georg von Westphalen - [g] Christien Heinrich Philipp von Westphalen - [h] Ludwig von Westphalen

State has, 'on grounds of piety', taken over the same for the sum of 10 talers. He had the comparatively worthless portion sold by auction in Brunswick for 11 talers and now, without asking, takes over, out of piety, the more valuable, which he has valued at 10 talers, but debits me with the cost of *carriage* from Brunswick to Berlin. Funny sort of piety! But now for the real *casus belli.* In addition, he gets Florencourt, the chief clerk, to write:

> 'Besides the books, a large number of papers, amongst them a number of the late Landdrost von Westphalen's manuscripts—some on military history—have also come to light. The latter are, however, for the most part exceedingly incomplete and defective and it seems improbable that the same are of any real literary interest.'

So they imagine that, without sending me a legal inventory and without having the papers valued, they can appropriate them by a *coup de main.* I strongly suspect that my brother, fired by patriotic zeal, promptly presented the manuscripts to the State, the more so in view of my mother's[a] letter, in which she tells me she had already written to them about the value of the papers and asked what they intended to do with them. Their silence is very peculiar. He believes that I, like the rest of my submissive sisters,[b] will simply leave everything to him, the mighty 'Cheeef' of the family. But there he's mistaken.

I have begun by making 'discreet inquiries' so that bit by bit I can lay claim to my 'PROPERTY'.

I shall be curious to see what they answer. With Berlin in its present state of excitation it would be very easy for us to create a scandal. But out of consideration for my mother we shall tread somewhat cautiously before we start one.

We hope to see you here next week.

With cordial regards, yours,

Jenny Marx

First published in: Marx and Engels, *Works,* Second Russian Edition, Vol. 29, Moscow, 1962

Printed according to the original

Published in English for the first time

---

a Caroline von Westphalen - b Anna Elisabeth Franziska von Westphalen and Lisette von Krosigk

2

JENNY MARX TO ENGELS[523]

IN MANCHESTER

[London, about 12 April 1857]

Dear Mr Engels,

One invalid is writing for another by *ordre du mufti.*[a] Chaley's[b] head hurts him almost everywhere, terrible tooth-ache, pains in the ears, head, eyes, throat and God knows what else. Neither opium pills nor creosote do any good. The tooth has got to come out and he jibs at the idea. Now I am appealing to you to step into the breach with an article for Friday. No matter what subject. *There was, for instance, the sending of troops and ships for China, there was also a change in the organisation of the Russian army, or Bonaparte or Switzerland or yarn or anything else. One column will do.*[c] Assuming, of course, that you've got over your own eye-trouble. If you possibly can, drop us a note to let us know whether you are able to do the article. Did the eye lotion help at all?

Warm regards from

Jenny Marx

First published in: Marx and Engels, *Works*, First Russian Edition, Vol. XXII, Moscow, 1929

Printed according to the original

Published in English for the first time

3

JENNY MARX TO ENGELS[524]

IN WATERLOO NEAR MANCHESTER

[London, 31 July 1857]

Dear Mr Engels,

The wine has just arrived. The children's exultation knew no end. The girls examined the bottles very closely and found the

---

[a] order of the mufti—a jocular nickname for Karl Marx - [b] Karl Marx's - [c] In reply to this request Engels wrote the article 'Changes in the Russian Army'.

sherry sealed in green and the port in pale lilac. The Bordeaux cheers us with its red smile. Tussy[a] set to work at once on the hamper and now she is sitting in it as in a little hut packed in straw and hay. Let me convey to you, dear Mr Engels, our warmest thanks for your great kindness. I am so weak and wasted. The wine will do me a world of good.

We are all so very worried about your indisposition and this fresh cold you have caught. But a cold is unavoidable at the beginning of a stay by the seaside. The evenings are already quite cool. So see that you dress especially warmly in the evenings. Karl is very much affected by your indisposition. He would very much like to go and see you but it is absolutely out of the question just now and that annoys him so much. Just leave the 'drudgery' for the time being.

Karl is BUSY shaping the INDIAN NEWS into an article.[b] Dear little Jenny and Laura are now replacing me in my capacity as secretary. They have ousted me altogether with the *chi-i-ief* of the household.

On Tuesday morning[c] a cab stopped in front of our door, and who do you think stepped out? Conrad Schramm, whom we thought dead long ago. That FOOL Seiler had already written an obituary notice about him in the evening papers. The poor fellow is very very unwell. A real picture of misery. Yesterday Karl got him admitted to the German hospital, where he is being very well looked after for £1 a WEEK. In his mind, by the way, Schramm is the same as of old, just as he was in his early, good period, when we all liked him for his buoyancy and FRANKNESS. He is continually cracking very good jokes about God and the world. But of the latter, so he thinks, he must soon take his leave. Fortunately he has kept free of the 'American clarity' by which old Mirbach and my brother Edgar distinguished themselves so very much.

Karl will be writing tomorrow.[d] Warmest greetings from all of us.

Your
Jenny Marx

Published for the first time

Printed according to the original

[a] Eleanor Marx - [b] K. Marx, 'Indian News'. - [c] 28 July 1857 - [d] No letters by Marx to Engels dated earlier than 9 August 1857 have reached us.

4

JENNY MARX TO ENGELS[525]

IN WATERLOO NEAR LIVERPOOL

[London, about 14 August 1857]

Dear Mr Engels,

We are all so pleased to hear that you are getting better again and feeling stronger. But Moor still insists that the real way to cure your illness is prolonged dosage with iron. He has been conscientiously studying medicine at the Museum,[a] and all modern doctors prescribe it and rate it above cod-liver oil; they are thus wholly in agreement with English doctors who, after years of practice, have come to the same opinion. By the by, he begs you most *urgently* not to overtax your brain with the work for Dana. Loafing and dozing and doing nothing are just as necessary as IRON.

No doubt you will have had the two further letters he addressed to Manchester.[b] One contained NOTICES about ARMIES, the other about the Armada.[180]

A few evenings ago that clown Edgar Bauer came to see us; truly a dried cod—without any cod-liver oil and on top of that with pretensions to *wit*. So frightful were his EFFORTS that I almost fainted, while Karl was sick—not just figuratively but in fact.

Jones has lost his wife and is now happy as a sandboy; he hails all INDIANS as Kossuths and applauds the INDIAN PATRIOTS.[526] His opponent, the high-minded Richard Hart, a PAID Urquhartist, is now a lawyer at the Coal Hole. Karl heard him pleading there.

I hope your next letter will bring yet more good news. We are all so very anxious about you.

The wine suits me splendidly. The sherry is truly excellent. The port seems not quite so good, but I like it particularly on account of its sweetness. It will put me to rights again.

With warm regards,

Jenny Marx

First published abridged in *Der Briefwechsel zwischen F. Engels und K. Marx*, Bd. 2, Stuttgart, 1913 and in full in: Marx and Engels, *Works*, First Russian Edition, Vol. XXII, Moscow, 1929

Printed according to the original

Published in English for the first time

---

[a] the British Museum Library - [b] See this volume, pp. 147-49.

5

JENNY MARX TO CONRAD SCHRAMM[a]

IN ST. HÉLIER, JERSEY

[London,] 8 December [1857]
9 Grafton Terrace, Maitland Park, Hampstead

Dear Mr Schramm,

It is so long since we have heard from you that we are all most eager for news. We often talk about you and, more keenly than anything else, regret our inability to help beguile and enliven somewhat your long, solitary winter days and hours.

If it isn't too much trouble, do let us have a sign of life some time.—What do you feel about the general mess? Wouldn't you say there was something really quite exhilarating about the way the rotten old structure is crashing and tumbling down? It is to be hoped that your relations aren't yet using the crisis as a pretext for turning their backs on you and hence that you yourself have not as yet suffered any material ill-effects. Though the American crisis has touched our purse all too appreciably, in as much as Karl is writing for the *Tribune* only once instead of twice a week, *all* its European correspondents except Bayard Taylor and Karl having been given their notice, you can nevertheless imagine how HIGH UP[b] the Moor is. He has recovered all his wonted facility and capacity for work, as well as the liveliness and buoyancy of a spirit long since blighted by great sorrow, the loss of our beloved child,[c] whose death I shall never cease to mourn in my heart. By day Karl works for his living and by night at the completion of his political economy.[250] Now, when the times require this work, and it has come to be a necessity, it will, no doubt, find some wretched publisher. Already not only we, but also Lupus and Steffen have felt the immediate impact of the crisis. The former has lost the better part of his lessons because the house has gone bankrupt, and the latter was no longer able to remain in Brighton because the Indian business[178] put an abrupt end to his instruction of the Indian CADETS. On top of that, his sister lost what little money she had through the *faillite*[d] of a banker. Little Dronke has started up

[a] Added to Jenny's letter was one by Marx written on the same day and likewise addressed to Schramm. - [b] in high spirits - [c] Edgar Marx - [d] bankruptcy

a business of his own in Glasgow. I believe that all the ranting in the Glaswegian press against 'unscrupulous people who start up businesses without any capital whatsoever' is directed against the little fellow. For the moment Freiligrath is still securely ensconced in his diminutive Crédit mobilier.[364] But if the sinister rumours about the Parisian Crédit mobilier and its steady decline prove true, he too will soon go tumbling after and have to bid farewell to his manager's desk. So far, the crisis would not appear to have made any deep impression on our good, honest friend Liebknecht, or at least *n'a-t-elle pas encore frappé son physique*[a]; he still retains unimpaired his notorious, fearsome, famous, fabulous appetite and his pristine love for a RASHER [OF] BACON.

Yesterday we heard from Engels in Manchester.[b] He says: Among our local philistines the crisis has induced a strong desire for the bottle, no one can bear to stay at home, alone with his cares and his family, the clubs are livening up, and the consumption of liquor is rising sharply. The worse of a jam a chap is in, the more frenzied his efforts to cheer himself up. And then, the morning after, what more striking example of remorse, both alcoholic and moral! In Manchester, 8 or 9 manufacturers have already come a cropper in the past few days. But nowhere do things look so splendid as in Hamburg. Never has panic assumed so perfect and classic a form. The house of Ulberg and Cramer, whose debts when they failed amounted to 12,000,000 banco marks (of which 7 million were bills on themselves!), had a capital of not more than 300,000 marks!! Everything there is now worthless, utterly worthless, save for silver and gold. Last week also saw the failure of Christian Matthias Schröder. J. H. Schröder & Co. in London telegraphed saying that, if 2 million marks would be enough, he would send the equivalent in silver. Came the reply: 3 millions or nothing; he couldn't spare the 3 millions and Christian Matthias crashed. The big American house which, after 2 days of negotiation with the Bank of England, recently obtained a million-pound advance, thereby saving its skin, belonged to Mr Peabody.

This 4th JULY ANNIVERSARY DINNER MAN[246] calls to mind that lout Heinzen. Although the crisis has whittled down his *Pionier* to half its former size (despite the collaboration of student Karl Blind, that greatest of revolutionary statesmen), the rascal still continues to maintain that 'crises are mere Marxian inventions and figments of the brain'. Again, this gobbler-up of communists calls to mind

---

[a] it has not yet affected him physically - [b] See this volume, pp. 211-13.

red Becker,[a] who has now been released, and this means, dear Mr Schramm, that willy-nilly you will have to make giant strides across the ocean with me, from Europe to America and back again, since with red Becker we are back once more in the dear Fatherland, the violet which will not, on this occasion, escape with a black, or rather blue, eye—back, indeed, in dear old Cologne, so that I cannot resist telling you something about our old friend Mevissen and his family. Quite a short while since, old Leiden lost 2 children from consumption, then Mrs Mevissen, while one of his sons lost his life when the *Pacifique* went down.

You can imagine how sullen and sulky all the democrats are at the moment. For now that they are again faced with the much abhorred knife-and-fork problem, and can no longer lay all the blame on princes and tyrants, there must needs be an end to political fiddle-faddle and ale-house oratory.

But now my chatter has lasted so long that it's time for me to bid you adieu. Warmest regards from myself and the girls, who are growing up to be so sweet and lovable and charming.

Your
Jenny Marx

Apropos. We have photographs of Freiligrath and Engels. If it's not too much trouble, will you have one done of yourself for us? Karl would so much like to have likenesses of his best friends around him.

First published in: Marx and Engels, *Works*, Second Russian Edition, Vol. 29, Moscow, 1962

Printed according to the original

Published in English for the first time

---

a Hermann Heinrich Becker

6

JENNY MARX TO ENGELS[527]

IN MANCHESTER

[London, 9 April 1858]

Dear Mr Engels,

For the past week Karl has been so unwell as to be quite incapable of writing. He believes you will already have deduced from the laboured style of his most recent letter[a] that his bile and liver are again in a state of rebellion. I trust his medicines will finally take effect. The worsening of his condition is largely attributable to mental unrest and agitation which now, of course, after the conclusion of the contract with the publisher[b] are greater than ever and increasing daily, since he finds it utterly impossible to bring the work to a close. I now also intend to write straight away to the little Berlin Jew[c] who this time has proved a CLEVER manager. The children are well. Unfortunately they had to stay indoors all through the Easter holidays. The weather was too ghastly and the perpetual rain made our clayey soil so soft and muddy that it was like having the whole of Böckeburg clinging to one's soles. The *Guardians* with the two very interesting articles on France arrived today. From this we gather that you, too, are in Manchester and haven't risked an Easter TRIP. But fox-hunting no doubt?

Warmest regards from us all.

Your
Jenny Marx

First published in: Marx and Engels, *Works*, First Russian Edition, Vol. XXII, Moscow, 1929

Printed according to the original

Published in English for the first time

[a] See this volume, pp. 296-304. - [b] Franz Duncker; Jenny Marx refers to the contract for publishing Marx's *A Contribution to the Critique of Political Economy*. - [c] Ferdinand Lassalle

7

JENNY MARX TO FERDINAND LASSALLE[528]

IN BERLIN

London, 9 April 1858[a]

Dear Mr Lassalle,

Since Karl last wrote to you[b] the liver complaint from which he was already suffering at the time—unfortunately it recurs every spring—has got so much worse that he has had to dose himself constantly. Today he feels quite incapable of writing and has therefore asked me to convey to you his heartfelt thanks for your kind efforts on his behalf. Nor can I help but express my pleasure at the successful conclusion of the contract, from which I gather that you are not yet completely engrossed in theoretical works and that, besides immersing yourself in *Heraclitus* (which I, too, have been studying a little), you have still retained your practical aptitudes and remained, as the English say, 'A CLEVER MANAGER'. Karl would long since have written to you at length about your work, but it's so difficult for him to write at all. The mental unrest and agitation he feels through not being able to bring his work to a close all at one go contribute greatly, of course, to the aggravation of his condition, likewise the tiresome work for our 'DAILY BREAD', which is another thing that certainly can't be deferred. However we hope that he'll be able to deliver the manuscript[c] on time.

As soon as he feels a little better he will write to you and, in the meantime, perhaps you will make do with this brief note of mine.

With warm regards

Jenny Marx

First published in: Marx and Engels, *Works,* First Russian Edition, Vol. XXV, Moscow, 1934

Printed according to the original

Published in English for the first time

---

[a] 1885 in the original - [b] See this volume, pp. 286-87. - [c] of his *A Contribution to the Critique of Political Economy*

8

JENNY MARX TO MARX[529]

IN MANCHESTER

[London, about 9 May 1858]

My darling Karl,

I'm sorry I haven't anything better to send you than Sch[...][a] Koller's[b] letter; I kept it back yesterday but maybe you ought to see it after all.

I hope that you will reach some definite POINT OF FACT with Friedländer; nothing much is ever to be got out of a German newspaper and it's beyond me how you could ask the *enormous* rate of £1 10/- for more than *one* article, especially since they have a correspondent[254] for their regular BUSINESS; they certainly can't want more than an *enjolivement*.[c] The most that can be extracted from the *Presse*, as an AVERAGE MAXIMUM, will be £2—don't delude yourself on that score. Engels is sure to say 'you'll be able to make at least £10 a week out of it'; though such delusions may be very agreeable at the time, they are often doomed to disappointment in the event.

The course of the revolution in Prussia[336] tickles me tremendously; particularly the 'ships, sails, masts and [waves]' speech made by liquor Prince Smith on his Baltic estate, and the rapturous applause it received. And on top of that the *Kölnische Zeitung*'s transports over von der Heydt, and the admiration evinced even by the *Presse* for the energy and determination shown by the democratic press in Berlin??!!

The girls would have written to you long ago, but little Jenny declared that she detested the idea of what was simply a private letter being subjected to threefold censorship. Hence her silence.

---

[a] Ms damaged. - [b] Adolf Cluss (see this volume, pp. 374-75). - [c] adornment

Karl dear, it's frightful that I should have to BOTHER you amidst all your other tribulations; but, with Easter upon us, the fellows are growing rabid. Can't you manage to raise something, if only for Withers? They are the worst....

The others are better—they can still be staved off for a while. I went to see Miss Morton yesterday and explained matters to her.

Your
Jenny

First published in: Marx and Engels, *Works*, Second Russian Edition, Vol. 29, Moscow, 1962

Printed according to the original
Published in English for the first time

9

JENNY MARX TO ENGELS[530]

IN MANCHESTER

[London, after 13 August 1859]

Dear Mr Engels,

Moor has just gone to the Museum[a] and has asked me to thank you for the £5 note you sent so promptly. And now, on top of all our other misfortunes, comes the COUNTY COURT. The affair's all the more vexing because I arrived just 5 minutes too late, otherwise the judge would certainly have granted me the right to make monthly payments as on the first occasion. You cannot conceive, dear Mr Engels, how painful it is for Karl and me to be such a constant burden on you and, with every letter, to despatch a fresh jeremiad appealing to your friendship and kindness.

Karl has had 6 copies of *Po and Rhine* for some time now. He forgot to tell you. Of those 6 copies he has given away 3 to acquaintances (Imandt, Juta and Cavanagh). I shall be sending you the rest next week.

The girls—just now they are practising a duet together and

[a] the British Museum Library

singing very nicely indeed—send you their love, to which I too add my warm regards.

Your

Jenny Marx

First published in: Marx and Engels, *Works,* Second Russian Edition, Vol. 29, Moscow, 1962

Printed according to the original

Published in English for the first time

10

JENNY MARX TO ENGELS[531]

IN MANCHESTER

[London, 4 November 1859]

Dear Mr Engels,

Szemere is constantly pestering Moor for the *Tribune* article[a] he promised him. Another dunning letter arrived this morning. Karl, who is struggling with Friday's article, begs you to send him the Kossuth article as soon as possible.

Warmest regards from the girls and myself.

Your

Jenny M.

First published in: Marx and Engels, *Works,* Second Russian Edition, Vol. 29, Moscow, 1962

Printed according to the original

Published in English for the first time

11

JENNY MARX TO ENGELS[532]

IN MANCHESTER

[London, 23 or 24 December 1859]

My dear Mr Engels,

My most heartfelt thanks for the Christmas HAMPER. The champagne will be a tremendous help in tiding us over the

[a] K. Marx, 'Kossuth and Louis Napoleon'.

otherwise gloomy holiday, and will ensure a merry Christmas Eve. The sparkling bubbles of the champagne will make the dear children forget the lack of a little Christmas tree this year, and be happy and jolly for all that.

I have been terribly irritated by fleshy philistine Freiligrath and his Westphalian rectitude and respectability. On the other hand I was greatly amused today by your letter about the fat man and the lean woman,[a] and I cannot understand why I sometimes let the wretches' behaviour upset me so. Had we been 'BETTER OFF' this year, I'd have seen the funnier side of all this trouble, but humour goes by the board when one is constantly having to struggle against the pettiest *misère*; never have I found it so oppressive as now, when our dear little girls, who are blossoming so sweetly, have to endure it too. And then, on top of that, the secret hopes we had long nourished in regard to Karl's book[b] were all set at naught by the Germans' *conspiration de silence*, only broken by a couple of wretched, belletristic feuilleton articles which confined themselves to the preface and ignored the contents of the book. The second instalment[473] may startle the slugabeds out of their lethargy and then they will attack its line of thought the more ferociously for having kept silent about the scientific nature of the work. *Nous verrons*.[c] I am, too, particularly curious to see what Ephraim Artful[d] is going to hatch out. For his conduct in the matter is not altogether clear; Prussian Blue, like Ferdinand the Pure,[e] must be treated with great circumspection just now, and an official breach with the latter must still be postponed. He's only so thick with Blind because the latter was his MAN-SERVANT in the great Kinkel affair and stood up for his rights on the boozy Schiller committee. Because Blind helped by seeing to it that the bust of Schiller was unveiled (the green serge cover positively refused to come off until 4 men had tugged at and tussled with it) during his cantata[f] and not during the LOW COMEDIAN'S SEMAPHORING,[g] he now has to stand publicly side by side with the arrant liar and cover the latter's mendacity and cowardice with his own political loyalty and purity. Fazy's miserable lackey! But enough of these dratted people! I am also sending you my brother's book[h] through Chaplin. It might interest you and provide you with matter for a

---

[a] Ferdinand and Ida Freiligrath. See pp. 555-56. - [b] K. Marx, *A Contribution to the Critique of Political Economy*. - [c] We shall see. - [d] Ferdinand Lassalle - [e] Ferdinand Lassalle and Ferdinand Freiligrath - [f] F. Freiligrath, 'Zur Schillerfeier. 10. November 1859. Festlied der Deutschen in London'. - [g] Kinkel's speech, see also this volume, pp. 512-13. - [h] Chr. H. Ph. von Westphalen, *Geschichte der Feldzüge des Herzogs Ferdinand von Braunschweig-Lüneburg*... Hrsg. von F.O.W.H. von Westphalen.

review. Actually *mon cher frère*[a] has virtually done us out of the legacy and it was a downright lie when he wrote and told me some years ago that these papers were nothing but useless disjointed notes with which absolutely nothing could be done, and which didn't even have any 'exchange value'.[b] I have ample cause to pick a quarrel with him, nor would anything be easier, in view of his present precarious political position, than to compromise him thoroughly. The Schleinitzes and Dunckers would be glad to take up the matter. Well, last week, without Karl's knowledge, I approached him about money. Since every attempt Karl had made to raise money had failed, I resolved in this extreme EMERGENCY to take the unpleasant step which I had hitherto avoided, even in the darkest days. Although Ferdinand refused to make me an 'advance', 'himself restricted to his pension', my letter has put me in a FALSE POSITION in regard to him, and my hands are completely tied. For the present I shall have to confine myself to reproaching him for the peculiar way he has treated my father[c] in the preface. Even the crazy, egoistic brother,[d] who embittered my father's existence and, up to the last year of his life, extorted from my mother[e] a yearly allowance paid out of her small widow's income, is dealt with better, more decently and in greater detail than our humane, truly noble and magnanimous father. The latter, it is true, 'knew his Shakespeare better than his Bible', a crime which is not forgiven him even in the grave by his pietistic[113] son. Moreover it was exceedingly strange that, touching as he did on our family circumstances, he should have omitted all mention of my father's second marriage and failed to name the second mother, who was the light of my father's life and who tended and nurtured her step-children with loyalty and love and devotion such as a woman's own children seldom meet with. This enabled him skilfully to cheat my brother Edgar and myself of her existence which he found intrusive. But this last is a matter of complete indifference and affects me very little; only father and mother should not have been treated and passed over in this way—and for that he must do penance. I am anxious to know what you will have to say about the military part of the book. Today little Jenny is copying the article[533] in my place. I believe my daughters will soon put me out of business, and I shall then

---

[a] my dear brother - [b] See this volume, pp. 561-62. - [c] Ludwig von Westphalen - [d] Heinrich Georg von Westphalen - [e] Caroline von Westphalen

come on the register of 'those entitled to assistance'. A pity that there's no prospect of getting a pension after my long years of secretarial duties. Goodbye for today. Warmest regards from all, including your

Jenny Marx

First published in: Marx and Engels, *Works*, Second Russian Edition, Vol. 29, Moscow, 1962

Printed according to the original

Published in English for the first time

NOTES AND INDEXES

NOTES

[1] This letter was first published in an abridged English translation in Karl Marx and Friedrich Engels, *Correspondence. 1846-1895.* A Selection with Commentary and Notes, Martin Lawrence Ltd., London [1934].—3, 8, 19, 34, 37, 85, 208, 258, 296, 325, 343, 345, 374, 391, 393, 434

[2] This refers to Robert Cobden's pamphlet *What Next and Next?* published in London in early 1856. It attacked Britain's foreign policy during the Crimean War waged by Britain, France, Turkey and Piedmont against Russia (1853-56). In particular, Cobden condemned the draft peace treaty with Russia as failing to guarantee stable peace.—3

[3] This presumably refers to Marx's articles on the Danubian Principalities of Moldavia and Wallachia written for the *New-York Daily Tribune.* As can be seen from Marx's letter to Engels of 22 September 1856 (this volume, p. 68), they were not published, and have never been found. The articles touched on Swedish history, probably in connection with the conclusion on 21 November 1855 of a defence treaty aimed at Russia between the Kingdom of Sweden and Norway on the one hand, and Britain and France on the other.

Marx contributed to the *New-York Daily Tribune* from August 1851 to March 1862. At his request many of the articles for the *Tribune* were written by Engels. In fact it was not until August 1852 that Marx began sending his own articles. By agreement with the editors some of the articles dealing with individual European countries were datelined Paris, Berlin or Vienna (see this volume, pp. 352, 361, 368 and 410).

Marx's and Engels' articles in the *New-York Daily Tribune* dealt with key issues of foreign and domestic policy, the working-class movement, the economic development of European countries, colonial expansion, and the national liberation movement in colonial and dependent countries. Many of them were reprinted in the *Tribune*'s special editions—the *New-York Weekly Tribune* and the *New-York Semi-Weekly Tribune*—and were quoted by other American newspapers, in particular by *The New-York Times.* Some were reproduced in the Chartist *People's Paper,* London. The *Tribune* editors sometimes took liberties with the articles, printing them unsigned in the form of editorials, and making insertions, some of which were in direct contradiction to the content of the articles (see, e.g., this volume, pp. 81 and 100-01). A number of articles were not printed at all. Marx repeatedly protested against these practices. In the autumn of 1857 he was forced to reduce the number of his contributions in view of the *Tribune's* financial difficulties resulting from the economic crisis in the USA. After the outbreak of the American Civil War, he ceased contributing altogether, mainly because the *Tribune* had come under the sway of people who advocated a compromise with the slave-owning states and abandoned its initial progressive stand.—3, 68, 73, 81

4 Marx quotes a leading article from *The Times,* No. 22267, of 18 January 1856, which discussed the preliminary conditions for a peace treaty with Russia. The paper commented on the report, received the day before, about Russia's acceptance of the peace proposals put to her by her opponents in the Crimean war, and urged extensive military preparations to force Russia into 'unconditional acceptance' of the demands made on her.—3

5 A congress held at the Romanian town of Focşani in July and August 1772 aimed at ending the Russo-Turkish war started by Turkey in 1768. The Russian delegation proposed, in particular, that Wallachia and Moldavia should be granted independence under the joint protection of the European powers. No agreement having been reached at the congress, hostilities were resumed and continued until 1774.—3

6 This refers to an episode in the Russo-Turkish war of 1735-39, which had been provoked by incursions, in 1735, of the Crimean Tartars into the Ukraine and the invasion of the Caucasus by the Crimean Khan, a vassal of the Sultan. In May-June 1736, a Russian army under Field Marshal B. C. Münnich entered the Crimea and occupied the Western part of the peninsula, including Bakhchisarai, the Khan's capital. However, a shortage of provisions, forage and water and the outbreak of epidemics forced Münnich to withdraw to the Ukraine.—3

7 The principal works of Adam Müller, who belonged to the romantic school in political economy, are *Die Elemente der Staatskunst.* Theile I-III, Berlin, 1809 and *Versuche einer neuen Theorie des Geldes mit besonderer Rücksicht auf Grossbritannien,* Leipzig und Altenburg, 1816. Marx discussed Müller's views in Vols. I and III of *Capital* (present edition, Vols. 31 and 33).—4

8 *Synoptics*—the writers of the first three Gospels. Marx refers to Bruno Bauer's book *Kritik der evangelischen Geschichte der Synoptiker.* Bd. 1-2, Leipzig, 1841; Bd. 3, Braunschweig, 1842.—4

9 On 19 January 1856, David Urquhart's *Free Press* (No. 15) published under the heading 'The Chartist Correspondence' a number of documents on the Chartists' activities in 1839-41, including Urquhart's correspondence with the then British Prime Minister Lord Melbourne, Home Secretary Normanby and others. The letters show that Urquhart had abused the Chartist leaders' trust by giving the British government detailed information of Chartist plans and intentions.

While publishing some works attacking the foreign policy of the British ruling circles, in particular that of Lord Palmerston, leader of the Whig oligarchy, in *The Free Press* and other Urquhartite publications, Marx emphatically dissociated himself from Urquhart's conservative views and criticised them in the press.—4

10 This refers to Engels' duties as corresponding clerk and general assistant in the Ermen & Engels firm in Manchester, of which his father was co-owner. He

assumed the post in the early 1850s, largely because he wanted to be able to give material aid to the Marx family, and kept it until 1870. Engels' confidential business reports to his father mentioned in the letter have not come down to us.—5

11 Between January and May 1856 Engels wrote a series of articles on Pan-Slavism for the *New-York Daily Tribune,* which did not print them. The manuscripts have not been preserved.—5, 14, 51, 68, 73, 81, 100

12 Further in his letter Engels cites facts showing that opposition to Napoleon III's regime in France was mounting. Marx used them in his article 'The American Difficulty.—Affairs of France', published in the *New-York Daily Tribune* on 25 February 1856 (present edition, Vol. 14, pp. 602-04).—5

13 *Sire de Franc Boissy*—a French song containing satirical allusions to royalty and the government.—6

14 A reference to the repressions that were part of the Bonapartist coup d'état of 2 December 1851 in France.—6

15 Engels here refers to the discussion of the so-called Five Points or preliminary terms for peace between Russia and the coalition that fought Russia in the Crimean war (Britain, France, Turkey and Piedmont). The Five Points were presented to the Russian government through Austria in the form of an ultimatum by the Allied Powers in December 1855. They called for replacement of the Russian protectorate over the Danubian principalities by a protectorate of all the contracting parties, a revision of the Bessarabian border involving Russia's relinquishment of the territory along the Danube, neutralisation of the Black Sea, closure of the Straits to warships, a ban on the maintenance by Russia and Turkey of arsenals and navies in the Black Sea, and collective protection of the Sultan's Christian subjects by the Great Powers. The Allied Powers also reserved themselves the right to impose additional demands. The terms were accepted by the Russian government and provided the basis for the Paris peace talks.

The Turkish fortress of Kars in Transcaucasia was captured, after a long siege, by the Russians on 28 November 1855. The fall of Kars, the last major event of the Crimean war, speeded up the termination of hostilities. Under the Paris peace treaty (March 1856) Kars was returned to Turkey in exchange for the evacuation of Sevastopol and the other Russian towns held by the Allies.—7, 21

16 The *Aliens Bill* authorised the deportation of aliens from England at any time by decision of the British government. Enacted by Parliament in 1793, it was valid for one year and was renewed in 1802, 1803, 1816, 1818 and, in connection with revolutionary events on the Continent and Chartist demonstrations in England, in 1848. In later years too, conservative circles repeatedly sought its renewal. In particular, the question was discussed for several months from the autumn of 1855, following the publication on 10 October by *L'Homme,* a refugee newspaper appearing in Jersey, of an open letter by the French petty-bourgeois democrat Félix Pyat to Queen Victoria on the occasion of her visit to France in August of that year. The letter sharply attacked Britain's alliance with the Second Empire and was used as a pretext for the expulsion of the publisher of *L'Homme* and some other French refugees from the island and for press attacks on refugees in general. However, protests by progressive circles forces the authorities to refrain from further steps. On

1 February 1856 Palmerston declared in the House of Commons that the government would not seek renewal of the Aliens Bill.—7, 38

17 This may be an ironic reference to Richard Wagner, who—in his *Das Kunstwerk der Zukunft* (1856) and other writings—called his works the 'music of the future'.—8

18 Marx refers to the diplomatic correspondence between Pozzo di Borgo, the Russian Ambassador to France, and Count Nesselrode, the Russian Chancellor of State. Marx knew of it from diplomatic documents published under the title *The Portfolio, or a Collection of State Papers* by David Urquhart in London from 1835 to 1837, and from the book *Recueil des documents relatifs à la Russie pour la plupart secrets et inédits utiles à consulter dans la crise actuelle,* Paris, 1854.—9

19 This work, intended by Engels for *Putnam's Monthly,* which published his series *The Armies of Europe* in the second half of 1855, was presumably never written.—11

20 This letter was first published in an abridged English translation in *The Letters of Karl Marx,* selected and translated with explanatory notes and an introduction by Saul K. Padover, Prentice-Hall, Inc., Englewood Cliff, New Jersey, 1979.—12, 30, 45, 54, 61, 67, 70, 93, 110, 128, 132, 224, 227, 254, 265, 319, 333, 359, 407, 430, 448, 459, 461, 518, 524

21 *Queen's Bench*—here the reference is to a London jail intended mainly for insolvent debtors.—13

22 Marx means *The Lay of Igor's Host,* a monument of old Russian literature describing the ill-starred campaign undertaken by Igor, Prince of Novgorod Severski, against the nomadic Polovtsians in 1185. The work was published in German several times. One edition appeared in Berlin in 1854 under the title *Lied vom Heerzuge Igors.* As follows from Marx's later letters to Engels, he found the *Lay,* in the language of the original and in French translation, in F. G. Eichhoff's book *Histoire de la langue et de la littérature des slaves...,* and later also a bilingual German edition, which he sent to Engels in Manchester.—15, 19, 26, 31, 37

23 *Acta litteraria Bohemiae et Moraviae,* Pragae, 1774-1783, were literary and historical collections published by the Czech Enlightenment historian Mikuláš (Adauctus) Voigt.—16

24 Marx means Schlözer's recommendations, quoted on p. 261 of Dobrovský's book, for the study of the Slavonic languages and the compilation of Slavonic dictionaries. The recommendations are contained in Schlözer's book *Allgemeine Nordische Geschichte,* p. 330.—16

25 Dobrovský's words, taken from his book *Slavin* (p. 419), actually refer to *Acta litteraria Bohemiae et Moraviae* published by Mikuláš (Adauctus) Voigt, not to Johannes Voigt's *Geschichte Preußens.*—16

26 Archdeacon William Coxe, traveller, historian and writer, left his vast collection of manuscripts and books to the British Museum. Marx made excerpts from the following manuscript letters and reports of British diplomats in Russia: *Various Papers on the Genius and Character of the Russians, Rondeau to Walpole, Dispatch from Mr. Fuch (Finch) to Lord Harrington, Sir George Macartney to the Earl of Sandwich,* and *Sir James Harris to Lord Grantham.* He made ample use of them in his *Revelations of the Diplomatic History of the 18th Century* (see present edition, Vol. 15).—17

27 *Polovtsians* (Kipchaks or Cumans)—Turkic nomadic tribes who inhabited the South-Russian steppes from the eleventh to the thirteenth century. Following the Mongol invasion in the mid-thirteenth century some of them fled to Hungary and the Balkans, where they were absorbed, while those remaining were subjugated by the conquerors and merged with the peoples inhabiting the Golden Horde, the medieval Tartar-Mongol state.—19

28 This refers to the so-called *Königinhof manuscript*, a collection of patriotic poems glorifying Bohemian antiquity, which the Czech philologist and poet Vaclav Hanka claimed to have discovered in a church in the village of Králowé Dwoře (in German: Königinhof) in 1817. It was published in Czech under the title *Kralodvorský Rukopis* in 1819, and in 1829 in Czech and in German, translated by the Czech poet Vaclav Alois Swoboda. Marx probably had the latter edition in mind.

In the 1880s the manuscript was revealed to be a recent imitation.—19, 26

29 This apparently refers to 'Bogarodzica', a medieval Polish hymn to the Virgin first recorded in 1407. It is attributed to Adalbert (Wojciech), Bishop of Prague (957-997).—19

30 *Chambre introuvable* was the name given by King Louis XVIII to the French Chamber of Deputies, which in 1815-16 consisted of extreme conservatives. It attacked the government from the right and was eventually disbanded by the King because of its arch-reactionary views.

Here Marx calls the Prussian Chamber of Representatives *Chambre introuvable* because it was dominated by the Junkers, whose extreme reactionary attitudes were worrying the government which feared they might provoke revolutionary tendencies.—20

31 The expression 'the crazy year' ('das tolle Jahr') was first used by Johann Heinrich von Falkenstein in a chronicle published in 1739 to describe the popular unrest in Erfurt in 1509. Later it was widely used in literature to designate the revolutionary year 1848.—20

32 This refers to the struggle in the French National Convention (which met on 20 September 1792) between the *Girondists,* i.e. the party of the big bourgeoisie (a number of whose leaders came from the department of Gironde), and the *Montagnards,* commonly referred to as the Mountain, who occupied the upper seats in the Convention, i.e. the Jacobins, which represented the progressive bourgeoisie and the masses. As a result of the popular uprising of 31 May-2 June 1793, the Girondist government was overthrown and the Jacobin revolutionary democratic dictatorship was established.—21

33 The words 'take care of Dowb' were originally used by, and then popularly added to the name of, the British Secretary of War Panmure who, in an official dispatch of June 1855 informing General Simpson of his appointment as commander-in-chief in the Crimea, asked him to look after Panmure's nephew, the young officer Dowbiggin.—21

34 At the *battle of Inkerman* in the Crimea (5 November 1854) the Anglo-French forces defeated the Russian army, but the latter's vigorous action prevented the Allies from storming Sevastopol, to which they lay siege instead. Engels describes the battle in detail in his article 'The Battle of Inkerman' (see present edition, Vol. 13, pp. 528-35).—21, 178, 297

35 From 1846 to 1854 Ferdinand Lassalle handled Countess Sophie von Hatzfeldt's divorce suit against Count Edmund Hatzfeldt-Wildenburg. The

divorce was agreed to in July 1851. Later, the countess received 300,000 talers under the property settlement.—23, 27, 227

36 Gustav Levy's visit to Marx in London in late February 1856 was preceded by another, in the second half of December 1853, when he also came with a message from Düsseldorf workers. This shows that after the 1848-49 revolution the proletarian circles in the Rhine Province continued to regard Marx and Engels as their leaders. Already during his first visit Levy maintained that an uprising was needed in Germany and that the factory workers were ready for it. Marx, then too, argued that, with reaction rampant in Germany, an uprising would be premature, as would a resumption of the activities of the Communist League in Germany urged by Levy.—25

37 The letter is only dated 'Tuesday', but Marx's intention, mentioned in the letter, to send an article on Kars to New York on Friday is evidence that the letter was written on Tuesday, 25 March, since the article appeared in the *New-York Daily Tribune* on 8 April 1856 and had to be mailed in London not later than Friday, 28 March, to arrive in time for that issue.—28

38 *Blue Books*—periodically published collections of documents of the British Parliament and Foreign Office. Their publication began in the seventeenth century.—28, 120, 431, 561

39 'Enclosure 2' has been preserved. Written in Jenny Marx's hand, it is the record of a talk she had with Colonel Touroute, who related a number of facts compromising Lassalle. He pointed out, in particular, that the extravagant life Lassalle led in Countess Hatzfeldt's house, his use of her money for stock-exchange speculation, his arrogance towards workers, his self-assurance and dictatorial demeanour roused the indignation of the Düsseldorf workers.—31, 36

40 *Boustrapa*—nickname of Louis Bonaparte, composed of the first syllables of the names of the places where he and his supporters staged Bonapartist *putsches:* Boulogne (August 1840), Strasbourg (October 1846) and Paris (coup d'état of 2 December 1851).—31, 94, 170, 230, 256, 290, 336, 425, 435

41 Marx drew on Tassilier's letter for his article 'The France of Bonaparte the Little' (present edition, Vol. 14, pp. 615-20). Cayenne, in French Guiana, South America, a place of penal servitude for political prisoners, was dubbed the 'Dry Guillotine' on account of the high mortality among convicts caused by the harsh prison regulations and the unhealthy tropical climate. A translation of Tassilier's letter, sent by Marx to the Chartist *People's Paper,* was published on 12 April 1856.—31

42 Marx means the polemics between the Chartists and the Urquhartites, which had been exacerbated by the publication in Urquhart's *Free Press* (19 January 1856) of 'The Chartist Correspondence' (see Note 9). The Urquhartites' hostility towards the revolutionary trend in the British working-class movement found expression in attempts to represent the Chartists as demagogues and agents of the Russian Tsar. The Chartists, for their part, described the Urquhartites as reactionaries advocating a restoration of the customs and practices of the Middle Ages. A sharp controversy developed, in particular, over the future of Parliament. The Chartists held that it should be reformed on democratic principles and used as an instrument of social change, whereas the Urquhartites advocated total abolition of the representative system and a return to patriarchal forms of government.—32, 44

43 In February and March 1856 Ernest Jones, the Chartist leader, attempted to reorganise the activities of the National Charter Association. Writing in *The People's Paper*, he suggested that the Association should no longer hold conferences or elect leaders, but that he, Jones, and James Finlen should be recognised for life as the only members of its Executive. Jones believed that this form of centralisation would make for greater efficiency. His proposals were endorsed by the majority of the Chartist members, but led only to a temporary increase in membership (to about 2,000 by the beginning of March 1856) and local activation of Chartist propaganda. At the same time, Jones' attempts to act as the Association's only leader caused serious discontent among Manchester Chartists.

Marx and Engels, who maintained close ties with revolutionary Chartists, criticised Jones' efforts to galvanise the Chartist movement by such artificial measures, which, they predicted, could not ensure lasting success.—32, 34

44 This refers to the *German National Assembly* convened in Frankfurt am Main in May 1848 for the purpose of unifying Germany and drawing up an Imperial Constitution. Its mostly liberal deputies turned the Assembly into a mere debating club. In early June 1849 the Right-wing deputies and the moderate liberals left the Assembly after the Prussian King and other German monarchs had rejected the Constitution it had drafted. What remained of the Assembly moved to Stuttgart, where it was dispersed by Württemberg troops on 18 June 1849.

The petty-bourgeois democrat Löwe von Calbe was a deputy to the Assembly in 1848-49.—32, 63

45 Engels means the establishment of banks similar to the *Société générale du Crédit mobilier*, a big French joint-stock bank founded by the Péreire brothers in 1852. The Crédit mobilier was to mediate in credit transactions and help in setting up industrial concerns and building railways in France, Spain, Austria, Russia and other countries. It was closely associated with Napoleon III's government and under its protection engaged in large-scale speculation. It went bankrupt in 1867 and was liquidated in 1871.—34, 68, 119, 126, 128, 133, 142, 145, 216, 225, 231, 240, 244, 291, 296, 349, 360, 437

46 At the *battle of Jena* (14 October 1806) the French army, commanded by Napoleon, routed the Prussian army, thus forcing Prussia to surrender.

At *Austerlitz* (Czech name: Slavkov) Napoleon's army defeated the Austrians and Russians on 2 December 1805.—37, 170, 180, 461

47 *Marianne*, founded in 1850, was a secret republican society which opposed Napoleon III during the Second Empire.—37, 42

48 On 14 April 1856 Marx was invited as an official representative of the revolutionary refugees in London to a banquet commemorating the fourth anniversary of the Chartist *People's Paper*. In his address he spoke of the German and other proletarian revolutionaries' solidarity with the revolutionary wing of the Chartist movement, concentrating in particular on the historic role of the proletariat. The banquet was also addressed by the German Communist Wilhelm Pieper. The other speakers were mostly Chartists (James Finlen, Ernest Jones and others). Marx did not intend to publish his speech, but it was included in the newspaper report that appeared on 19 April 1856 under the heading 'Fourth Anniversary Banquet of *The People's Paper*' (present edition, Vol. 14, pp. 655-56).—38

49 *Straubingers*—German travelling journeymen. Marx and Engels often ironically gave the name to backward elements of the German working-class movement who were still influenced by guild prejudices and mistrusted the revolutionary intelligentsia.—38

50 A reference to the *German Workers' Educational Society* in London, which was founded in February 1840 by Karl Schapper, Joseph Moll and other leaders of the League of the Just (in the 1850s the Society had its premises in Windmill Street, Soho). After the reorganisation of the League of the Just in the summer of 1847 and the founding of the Communist League, the latter's local communities played a leading role in the Society. In 1847 and 1849-50 Marx and Engels took an active part in the Society's work, but on 17 September 1850 they and a number of their followers withdrew because the Willich-Schapper sectarian and adventurist faction had temporarily increased its influence in the Society and caused a split in the Communist League. Later Schapper realised the faultiness of his position and took steps towards a reconciliation with Marx. The resultant weakening of the sectarians' influence made it possible for Marx and Engels to resume their work in the Educational Society in the late 1850. In 1918, the Society was closed down by the British government.—41, 363, 451, 520

51 This refers to the German republican democrats who, following the capture of the fortress of Mainz by the French army in October 1792, formed the Friends of Liberty and Equality Society on the pattern of the Jacobin Club. The Mainz Clubbists joined the new administration (the Mainz Commune) and carried out a number of progressive reforms (abolition of feudal obligations, social-estate privileges and the guild system). Under the Clubbists' influence, the Rhenish German National Convention, convoked in Mainz in March 1793, proclaimed the merger of Mainz with the French Republic. The Clubbists' activity was violently terminated in July 1793, when the French army was driven out by the forces of the counter-revolutionary European coalition.—41

52 In his letter of 6 April 1856 Johannes von Miquel, a former member of the Communist League, asked Marx to state his views on the attitude the proletariat should take to bourgeois parties in the event of a revolution in Germany. Miquel's own statements on this question testified to a retreat from the consistently revolutionary standpoint. He limited the tasks of the revolution to establishing a united centralised state and ignored the need for social change. He maintained that the proletariat should ally itself not only with the petty-bourgeois democrats but also with the bourgeois liberals and refrain from such revolutionary measures as might frighten the bourgeoisie away from the revolution.

No answer by Marx to Miquel is extant.—42, 44

53 On 8 April 1856 Count Walewski, Foreign Minister of France, made a counter-revolutionary speech at a plenary session of the Congress of Paris convened to work out the peace terms following the Crimean war. He declared that British and French troops would continue to occupy Greece, while French and Austrian troops would remain in the Papal states to combat 'anarchy' (i. e. the national liberation movement). He attacked the Belgian press, describing its support for the French republicans and criticism of Napoleon III as incitement to 'insurrection and murder'.—42

54 An excerpt from this letter was first published in English in K. Marx and F. Engels, *Literature and Art*, New York, 1947.—43

55 This letter of Engels to Marx has not been found.—43

56 The reference is to a letter of 25 April 1856 in which A. Hamacher conveyed greetings from Cologne, Elberfeld and Solingen workers and expressed their desire to maintain contact with Marx.—44

57 The *Foreign Affairs Committees* were public organisations set up by the Urquhartites in a number of English cities between the 1840s and 1860s, mainly with the aim of opposing Palmerston's policy.—44

58 In 1856 Marx's series of articles *Lord Palmerston,* originally intended for and partly published in the *New-York Daily Tribune* (see present edition, Vol. 12), appeared in Sheffield under the title *The Story of the Life of Lord Palmerston* (*The Free Press Serials,* No. 5, 1856). This was a reproduction of the series as published under the same title between December 1855 and February 1856 in several issues of *The Free Press,* the Urquhartites' London paper. Apart from this, one of the articles, published in *The Sheffield Free Press* in November 1855, appeared as a pamphlet in Sheffield in 1856 (*The Free Press Serials,* No. 4a).—44, 58

59 This refers to Heine's third will, which he dictated to notaries F. L. Ducloux and Ch. L. E. Rousse on 13 November 1851.—45

60 Engels made excerpts from Bazancourt's book between June and September 1856. In the autumn of that year he summed up the results of his critical analysis in an article entitled 'Saint-Arnaud'. Marx sent the article to the American journal *Putnam's Monthly,* but the editors returned it unpublished.—45, 51, 71, 73, 80, 93, 106, 124, 126, 128

61 This refers to a work planned by Marx on the history of British and Russian diplomacy in the eighteenth century, of which he only completed five chapters of the Introduction. For these he made use of pamphlets, diplomatic documents and unpublished manuscripts, mostly of the period of the Northern War (the Russo-Swedish war of 1700-21), which he found in the British Museum Library. His negotiations with Nikolaus Trübner for publication of the work ended in failure. The chapters of the Introduction appeared by instalments in Urquhart's *Sheffield Free Press* from late June to early August 1856 as they were sent in by Marx. Eventually publication was stopped because of arbitrary editorial abridgements and printing errors. In June 1856 the London *Free Press* began reprinting the text from the Sheffield paper, and on 16 August 1856 it started reproducing the chapters from the beginning, with publication continuing until 1 April 1857. In both papers the unfinished work was printed under the title *Revelations of the Diplomatic History of the 18th Century* (see present edition, Vol. 15).

In 1899 Eleanor Aveling, Marx's daughter, published it in London in book form under the heading *Secret Diplomatic History of the Eighteenth Century.*—46, 56, 73, 81, 94, 110, 112, 120

62 This letter was first published in English in *Labour Monthly,* No. 10, 1932, London.—49

63 Engels and his wife, Mary Burns, made a trip to Ireland in mid-May 1856.—49

64 Between 1845 and 1847 potato blight caused widespread famine in Ireland. The poverty of the small tenants ruthlessly exploited by the big landowners had made the bulk of the population almost entirely dependent on a diet of potatoes grown on their own small patches. About one million people starved to

death, and the wave of emigration caused by the famine swept away another million. Large areas of Ireland were depopulated. The abandoned land was turned into pastures by the English and Irish landlords.—49

65 This refers to the mass eviction of Irish tenants, a policy pursued by the English and Irish landlords since the late 1840s to turn ploughland into pasture. It was stimulated by the falling demand for Irish corn owing to the repeal of the Corn Laws in 1846, and by England's growing need for Irish cattle and animal produce.—50

66 The *Encumbered Estates Court* was to enforce the Encumbered Estates Act for Ireland, passed by Parliament in 1849. This act was supplemented by a series of other acts in 1852 and 1853. The 1849 Act provided for the sale of mortgaged estates by auction if their owners were proved insolvent. As a result, the land of many ruined landlords passed into the hands of usurers, middlemen and rich tenants.—51

67 Engels compares Bazancourt's description of the Crimean war to *Batrachomyomachia* (The Battle of the Frogs and Mice), an Ancient Greek anonymous mock-heroic poem parodying Homer's *Iliad*.—51

68 Marx and Wilhelm Pieper travelled to Hull on 7 June 1856. From there Marx went to see Engels in Manchester, while Pieper returned to London to carry out a number of commissions for Marx, who returned to London about 20 July 1856.—54

69 Marx's wife Jenny and their three daughters stayed in Trier from 22 May to about 10 September 1856. She went there to visit her sick mother, Caroline von Westphalen, who died on 23 July. Marx's letter was sent from Manchester, where he was staying with Engels.—54

70 *Black Madonna*—a name given by some art specialists to early wood carvings of the Virgin Mary. It was used, in particular, by Karl Friedrich von Rumohr in his book *Italienische Forschungen* (Berlin, 1827), from which Marx made excerpts in Bonn in 1842 for his planned treatise on Christian art.—54

71 The *Cologne Communist Trial* (4 October-12 November 1852) was a trial of a group of Communist League members charged with 'treasonable conspiracy'. It was rigged by the Prussian police on the basis of forged documents and fabricated evidence, which were used not only against the accused but also to discredit the whole proletarian organisation. Seven of the twelve defendants were sentenced to prison terms of three to six years. Marx directed the defence from London, sending material revealing the provocative methods used by the prosecution. After the trial he and Engels exposed its organisers (see Engels' article 'The Late Trial at Cologne', published in the *New-York Daily Tribune*, and Marx's pamphlet *Revelations Concerning the Communist Trial in Cologne*, present edition, Vol. 11, pp. 388-93 and 395-457).—56, 69, 376, 477, 552

72 The *Allgemeine Zeitung* did not publish this counter-statement.—56

73 Only part of the draft of Marx's letter to Isaac Ironside, editor of *The Sheffield Free Press*, has reached us. The beginning, up to and including the words 'I shall consider myself obliged to stop the publication', is written in pencil in Engels' hand with changes in ink by Marx. The rest of the text, with much struck out, is in Marx's writing. That the draft was written on 21 June 1856 can be seen from Marx's letter to his wife written on the same day. Ironside answered the letter on 23 June 1856.—57

[74] This refers to the publication of Marx's *Revelations of the Diplomatic History of the 18th Century* in *The Sheffield Free Press* (see Note 61). Further on Marx speaks of Ironside's intention to publish this work in the Urquhartites' *Free Press Serials,* an intention which failed to materialise.—57

[75] This letter was written in reply to one from William Cyples, a member of the *Sheffield Free Press* staff, which Marx reproduced, together with his reply, in a letter to Engels on 28 July 1856. Marx's relations with the newspaper had been complicated by the arbitrary changes made by the editors in his *Revelations of the Diplomatic History of the 18th Century,* which soon led him to stop publication of the work in this paper (see Note 61).

The letter was first published in English as part of Marx's letter to Engels of 28 July 1856 in *Der Briefwechsel zwischen F. Engels und K. Marx. 1844 bis 1883.* Herausgegeben von A. Bebel und Ed. Bernstein. Verlag von J. H. W. Dietz, Bd. II, Stuttgart, 1913.—58, 62

[76] The *Friendly Societies* were workers' organisations whose main purpose was to provide material aid to their members in the event of disability and old age, pay funeral expenses and the like. This was done out of membership dues.—59

[77] This refers to Marx's conflict with *The Sheffield Free Press* over the publication of his *Revelations of the Diplomatic History of the 18th Century* (see Note 61). The following draft of a letter by Wilhelm Pieper to William Cyples has survived:

'28 Dean Street, Soho
London, 17 July 1856

'Sir,

'I am directed by Dr. Marx to inform you that he cannot congratulate you on the emendations you have thought fit to introduce in the copy destined for Saturday's publication.

'Passages that might safely have been omitted—for the sake of space—have been carefully preserved, while the most characteristic portions analyzing the policy of Peter I have been suppressed. This explains why he has interpolated about three lines of absolute importance for the understanding of the reader, in substitution for the same number of lines suppressed in another place, out of consideration for the pressure of space you allege in your letter to Dr. Marx.'—60

[78] Marx means the concluding events of the fourth bourgeois revolution in Spain (1854-56): the resignation of Espartero's liberal government on 14 July 1856, the coming to power of the counter-revolutionary General O'Donnell, and the popular uprising, led by the ex-toreador Pucheta, against the new government in Madrid and a number of other cities. Espartero's refusal to support the insurgents and the weakness of their leaders contributed to the defeat of the movement. On 17 July the uprising was suppressed in Madrid and soon after in the other cities too. Marx described these events in his articles 'The Revolution in Spain' (see present edition, Vol. 15).—61

[79] The *Grand Cophta* was the name of an omnipotent and omniscient priest who headed the non-existent Masonic 'Egyptian Lodge' which the famous eighteenth-century impostor 'Count' Cagliostro (Giuseppe Balsamo) claimed to have founded.—61

[80] Contrary to Urquhart's intention to reserve the new publication of Marx's *Revelations of the Diplomatic History of the 18th Century* for his projected journal, the five chapters of the Introduction that had been written were republished in *The Free Press,* the Urquhartites' London paper (see Note 61).—62

81 *Crapauds* (literally: toads) was the nickname of a group of opportunist deputies (the 'Bog') in the French Convention (1793-95) who vacillated between the Right and the Left wing. Marx and Engels in their letters often used the name in reference to French philistines, in particular French petty-bourgeois refugees, some of whom lived in Jersey until 1855 and later in Guernsey.—65, 225, 229, 249, 264, 268, 309

82 This letter was first published in English in *The Letters of Karl Marx,* selected and translated with explanatory notes and an introduction by Saul K. Padover, Prentice-Hall, Inc., Englewood Cliff, New Jersey, 1979.—66, 97, 122, 143, 225, 315, 321, 328, 369, 378, 429

83 In the second half of August Engels went to London to meet his mother, who was visiting England.—66, 72

84 This refers to the legacy left to Jenny Marx by her mother, Caroline von Westphalen. Part of it consisted in shares which, at the time of the mother's death, were in the hands of her step-son, the Prussian Minister of the Interior Ferdinand von Westphalen.—68

85 Georg Weerth died of jungle fever on 30 July 1856 in Havana while on a tour of West Indian countries as agent of a German commercial firm. Marx and Engels did not learn of their friend's death until much later.—68, 72

86 Marx's information was inaccurate. The book on England, *Englische Freiheit,* was written not by Bruno, but by Edgar Bauer. Marx referred to it later in his letters to Engels of 18 March and 21 April 1857 (see this volume, pp. 106 and 122).—68, 122

87 The *Old Lady of Threadneedle Street*—a name for the Bank of England situated in Threadneedle Street, London.

By the Paris concern Marx means the Banque de France.—71

88 An allusion to the French bankers Isaac and Emile Péreire, who in the 1820s and 1830s adhered to the Saint-Simonist school. In 1852 they set up the joint-stock bank, Crédit mobilier (see Note 45), which they falsely claimed gave effect to the Saint-Simonist idea of overcoming class contradictions and achieving prosperity for all by introducing a new, rational system of public credit. The practical application of the scheme, which had the support of Napoleon III and was called ironically 'Bonapartist socialism' by Marx, led to an orgy of stock-exchange speculation and corruption in France.

Marx uses the term 'imperialism' further on in the sense of 'Bonapartism'.—72

89 The *Crystal Palace*—a structure of metal and glass in London's Hyde Park built for the 1851 Great Exhibition and used for various displays and shows later.—72

90 Marx used the data on the state of the European money market cited in this letter in a number of articles on the approaching economic crisis in Europe which he wrote for the *New-York Daily Tribune* in late September and the first half of October 1856 (see present edition, Vol. 15). These articles opened the long series of his contributions on the 1857 world crisis.—72

91 This refers to Marx's private library which he had built up in the 1840s and left in Cologne in May 1849 in the care of his friend Roland Daniels, a member of the Communist League, when Marx was expelled by the Prussian authorities. Shortly before his arrest in 1851, Daniels hid the books in the storehouse of his brother, a

wine merchant. Acquitted at the Cologne Communist trial at the end of 1852, Roland Daniels came out of prison a sick man and died of tuberculosis in August 1855. In early 1856 his widow undertook to send the books to Marx but, owing to the high carriage costs and other difficulties, Marx did not receive his library until December 1860 after some books had got lost.—72

92 The beginning of this letter has been torn off, the manuscript is damaged in a number of places (indicated by three dots in square brackets). Written in an unknown hand in the upper left corner is the date '27/28 Sept. 1856'. Being a reply to Marx's letters of 22 September and 26 September, the letter could not have been written before 27 September 1856.—72

93 An allusion to Ewerbeck's inordinate literary vanity, on which Engels also commented in a letter to Marx of 15 October 1851 in connection with the publication of Ewerbeck's book *L'Allemagne et les Allemands,* Paris, 1851 (cf. present edition, Vol. 38, p. 478).

The *Père-Lachaise* is a cemetery in Paris where many famous writers and artists are buried.—73

94 Engels means the regular reviews of the Crimean war which he wrote for the *New-York Daily Tribune* in 1855 and 1856 (see present edition, Vols. 12-14). Since Engels was not an official correspondent of the *Tribune,* the reviews were sent to New York by Marx. Most of them were published as leaders. Engels made no copies of the manuscripts he sent to Marx, while issues of the *Tribune* carrying his articles could not always be obtained in Manchester.—73

95 In the period immediately preceding the 1848 revolution in France the *Constitutionnel* newspaper announced almost daily: 'L'horizon politique s'obscurcit' ('The political horizon is darkening'). Marx cited this cliché in his article 'Bonaparte's Present Position', published in the *New-York Daily Tribune* on 1 April 1858 (see present edition, Vol. 15).—73, 290

96 The Marx family moved to 9 Grafton Terrace, London, about 1 October 1856.—74

97 An allusion to Mieroslawski's theory that the Poles had a special mission of liberation and were called upon to serve as an instrument of universal social change (Marx plays on Archimedes' famous words: 'Give me a fulcrum and I will move the earth').—75

98 Marx means the republication in the London *Free Press* of the part of the *Revelations of the Diplomatic History of the 18th Century* which had earlier been published with abridgments and numerous misprints in *The Sheffield Free Press,* and in the same form in *The Free Press* (see Note 61).—75

99 This refers to the continued publication of Marx's *Revelations of the Diplomatic History of the 18th Century* in *The Free Press* (see Note 61). From 16 August 1856 the paper was increased from four pages to eight. Marx and Engels called the enlarged edition the new *Free Press* (see, e.g., Engels' letter to Marx of 31 March 1857, this volume, p. 117).—76, 117

100 Part of this letter was first published in English in Marx and Engels, *Selected Correspondence,* Foreign Languages Publishing House, Moscow, 1955.—80, 380

101 The *ordre équestre* (literally: the order of horsemen)—the social estate of the knights. In medieval Poland peasants who turned up for military service with a warhorse and arms of their own were enlisted in the cavalry, which entitled them to be elevated to knightly status.—80

102 In November 1847 Switzerland was plunged into a civil war unleashed by the *Sonderbund,* a separatist union of seven economically backward Catholic cantons which resisted progressive bourgeois reforms. The Guizot government of France, supported by the governments of Austria and Russia, came out in support of the Sonderbund and the Catholic Church. However, Lord Palmerston, the British Foreign Secretary, seeking to weaken France, prevented her direct intervention in Swiss affairs and thereby contributed to her further rapprochement with Russia. The rout of the Sonderbund army by the Federal forces on 23 November deprived the European powers of a pretext for further diplomatic moves in the Swiss conflict.—81

103 In October 1856 France and Britain, fearing that the reign of reaction and terror in the Kingdom of Naples (the Kingdom of the Two Sicilies) might set off a revolutionary explosion, demanded that Ferdinand II, the Neapolitan King, should pursue a more flexible policy. Ferdinand II, confident of Austria's backing, refused to comply, whereupon France and Britain put their naval squadrons in the Mediterranean on the alert. However, the planned expedition against Naples did not take place owing to differences caused by Napoleon III's intention to instal a prince of the Bonaparte dynasty on the Neapolitan throne.

By the autumn of 1856, the struggle had intensified for the union of the Danubian Principalities of Wallachia and Moldavia and for an end to their dependence on the Ottoman Empire. The British government, apprehensive of France's intention to instal a member of the Bonaparte dynasty as head of the united state, and fearing the growth of Russian influence in the principalities, actively supported Austria's and Turkey's opposition to the movement for unification (this is what Marx had in mind speaking about Palmerston's alliance with Austria on the Turkish issue). However, despite the diplomatic complications and the resistance of the reactionary aristocrats, the principalities merged in 1862 to form the single state of Romania.—81, 107, 243

104 This refers to the Crystal Palace in London (see Note 89).—81

105 The symptoms of economic crisis, the rise in unemployment and in the cost of living, the shortage of housing and food, and the increased taxation led to more frequent manifestations of the workers' discontent in Paris and other French cities, to which the government responded with mass arrests. Those arrested were accused of putting up posters in the streets threatening property owners, landlords, usurers and even Emperor Napoleon III.

The article in the *Moniteur* mentioned by Engels (it appeared on 24 October 1856) protested against attacks in English newspapers on the French government and some of Napoleon III's entourage. It had broad repercussions in the British press.—82

106 Banks patterned on the French Crédit mobilier (see Note 45) were established with the latter's participation in a number of Central European countries.—83

107 Marx used the data contained in Engels' letter and in *The Manchester Guardian* of 17 November 1856, also sent by Engels, in his article 'The Crisis in Europe' published in the *New-York Daily Tribune* on 6 December 1856 (see present edition, Vol. 15).—83

108 Engels means the wars Britain waged almost incessantly as a member of various anti-French coalitions against revolutionary and Napoleonic France in the late eighteenth and early nineteenth centuries (from 1793, when the French Republic officially declared war on it, up to the final fall of Napoleon's empire in 1815). Spain, which originally fought against France and suffered a number

of defeats, concluded a separate peace with the French in 1795 and, under pressure from the French Directory, and later from Napoleon, twice sided with France in the war against Britain (1796-1802 and 1804-08).—84

109 *Le Comité du salut public* (the Committee of Public Safety)—the central body of revolutionary government in France during the Jacobin dictatorship (2 June 1793-27 July 1794).—85

110 In September 1856 there was a royalist uprising in Neuchâtel. Many of the insurgents were arrested by the Swiss authorities. The King of Prussia insisted on their release. In reply, Switzerland demanded that he should relinquish his title to Neuchâtel. Under the pressure of France, on whose initiative a European conference on the issue was held in March 1857, Prussia was forced to renounce her claims.

In the eighteenth century the principality of Neuchâtel and Valangin (in German: Neuenburg and Vallendis) was under Prussian rule. It was ceded to France in 1806, during the Napoleonic wars. In 1815, by a decision of the Vienna Congress, it was incorporated into the Swiss Confederation as its 21st canton, while remaining a vassal of Prussia. On 29 February 1848 a bourgeois revolution in Neuchâtel put an end to Prussian rule and a republic was proclaimed. Prussia, however, laid constant claims to Neuchâtel up to 1857, thus causing an acute conflict with the Swiss Republic.—86, 88, 89

111 Marx presumably alludes to the fact that under the Final Act of the Congress of Vienna (1815) Prussia received what was known as Swedish Pomerania from Denmark. Denmark received in compensation the duchy of Lauenburg from Prussia.—86

112 The Polish region of Silesia, part of the Austrian Empire from 1526, was seized by Prussia during the War of the Austrian Succession (1740-48) caused by the claims of several European powers, above all King Frederick II of Prussia, to the Habsburg domains, which, in default of a male heir at the death of Emperor Charles VI, went to his daughter, Maria Theresa.—86

113 *Pietism* was a trend in the Lutheran Church that emerged in Germany in the seventeenth century. Distinguished by extreme mysticism, it rejected rites and attached special importance to personal religious experience.—86, 575

114 Marx developed these ideas on Prussia's history in his article 'The Right Divine of the Hohenzollerns' (see present edition, Vol. 15).—87

115 An allusion to the fact that in 1848 Valdenaire was a deputy to the Prussian National Assembly, in which the liberal majority favoured a constitution 'by agreement *(Vereinbarung)* with the Crown'. Marx and Engels ironically called the members of the Berlin Assembly 'agreers'.—87

116 Marx means the Imperial Constitution adopted by the Frankfurt National Assembly on 28 March 1849, but rejected by most of the German governments and in the first place by the King of Prussia. In May 1849 uprisings in defence of the Constitution flared up in Saxony, Rhenish Prussia and the South German states of Baden and Palatinate. In the last two a united insurgent army was formed, in which Frederick Engels fought. The movement was led by petty-bourgeois democrats, whose vacillation and passive defence tactics doomed it to defeat. The movement was finally suppressed in July 1849. Engels described it in *The Campaign for the German Imperial Constitution* and *Revolution and Counter-Revolution in Germany* (see present edition, Vols. 10 and 11).—90

117 On the eve of and during the Crimean war Bruno Bauer published the following pamphlets: *Rußland und das Germanenthum,* Charlottenburg, 1853; *Rußland und das Germanenthum.* Zweite Abtheilung. *Die deutsche und die orientalische Frage,* Charlottenburg, 1853; *Deutschland und das Russenthum,* Charlottenburg, 1854; *Die jetzige Stellung Rußlands,* Charlottenburg, 1854; *Rußland und England,* Charlottenburg, 1854 (French edition: *La Russie et l'Angleterre,* Charlottenburg, 1854). These works, particularly the last two, were criticised in Marx's unfinished draft 'Pamphlets über die russische Kollision von B. Bauer', written in January 1857 (see present edition, Vol. 15).—90

118 This study by Bauer was first published in Berlin in 1874 under the title *Philo, Strauss und Renan und das Urchristenthum.*—91

119 In the spring of 1856 floods occurred in the valleys of the Rhône and the Loire. Feigning concern for the victims, Napoleon III visited a number of the affected towns and villages in a boat and personally handed out money. He also directed a message to the Minister of Public Works recommending measures to prevent such calamities.—92

120 The Marx family lived in Dean Street, Soho, an overcrowded and unhealthy London district where poorer refugees lived, from December 1850 to the autumn of 1856.—94

121 Marx means the concessions made by Switzerland to Prussia in the conflict over Neuchâtel (see Note 110).

Initially, the Swiss government had flatly refused to comply with Prussia's demand for the release of the arrested royalists who had rebelled in Neuchâtel in September 1856, and declared it was prepared to resist the threatened Prussian invasion. However, under pressure from Napoleon III, who did not want a war near the French frontier, the Swiss government released those arrested on 16 January 1857. The King of Prussia replied by rescinding the mobilisation order. The conflict was settled through diplomatic channels.—94

122 Marx presumably means the Swiss government's official report to the Federal Diet on the Prusso-Swiss conflict over Neuchâtel (see Note 110) published in the *Neue Preussische Zeitung* on 1 January 1857. It maintained, in particular, that contrary to the assurances of the French government, the King of Prussia had assumed no commitments vis-à-vis the Emperor of France concerning renunciation of his claims to Neuchâtel and Valangin.—94

123 The *Corps législatif* was established, alongside the State Council and the Senate, under the Constitution of 14 February 1852, following the Bonapartist coup d'état of 1851. The members of the State Council and the Senate were appointed by the head of state, while the Corps législatif was an elected body, the elections being supervised by state officials and the police, so that a docile majority was always ensured. As its powers were confined to endorsing bills drawn up by the State Council, the Corps législatif was, in effect, a screen for Napoleon III's unlimited rule.—94, 109

124 The *Orleanists* were supporters of the Orleans dynasty which held power in France during the July monarchy (1830-48). They upheld the interests of the financial aristocracy and the big industrial bourgeoisie.—95, 291, 552

125 Marx means the second of Engels' articles entitled 'Mountain Warfare in the Past and Present' (see present edition, Vol. 15). The *New-York Daily Tribune* did not publish it. A copy of the article, written in Marx's hand, has reached us. Engels discusses the possibility of hostilities breaking out in the Swiss Alps,

particularly in the area between the city of Constance, near the Lake Constance, and Basle, in the event of the Prusso-Swiss conflict over Neuchâtel (see Note 121) growing into war.—95

126 The letter is undated. But since it is Engels' reply to a letter from Marx of 20 January 1857 and was answered by Marx on 23 January, it was presumably written on 21 or 22 January.—96

127 Marx alludes to the influence exerted on the *New-York Daily Tribune* editors by Count Gurowski, a Polish pan-Slavist journalist, of which he had been informed by Olmsted, an agent of *Putnam's Monthly.* Marx attributed to his influence the *Tribune* editors' rejection of some of his own and Engels' articles, and the delay in publishing others (see this volume, p. 81).—98

128 The *New-York Daily Tribune* did not publish the article.—98

129 This refers to the colonial war Britain was waging against Persia (Iran) in 1856-57. In October 1856 Persian troops seized the city of Herat, the centre of the principality of Herat, claimed by Persia and Afghanistan. Britain took advantage of this to declare war on Persia with a view to further expansion in the Middle East, directed against both Persia and Afghanistan. In November a British naval force captured several Persian strong points on the coast of the Persian Gulf. However, growing popular discontent in India compelled the British to hasten the conclusion of a peace treaty in March 1857, under which Persia relinquished her claims to Herat (later annexed to Afghanistan), while Britain withdrew her forces from the area.—98, 107, 134

130 Marx probably means the formation, in 1854, of the US Republican Party, which put forward a programme to limit Negro slavery in the Southern states, and the considerable success it scored in the 1856 Presidential election, its candidate getting over 300,000 votes, one-third of the total. Howard Greeley, the publisher of the *New-York Daily Tribune,* was one of the party's leaders.—98

131 A reference to the article 'Saint-Arnaud', which Engels wrote on the basis of C. L. Bazancourt's book *L'expédition de Crimée* (see Note 60).—100

132 Marx means the supporters of the *currency principle,* one of the schools of the quantity theory of money widely subscribed to in Britain in the first half of the nineteenth century. According to this theory, the value and price of commodities are determined by the quantity of money in circulation, and economic crises are caused mainly by violations of the laws of money circulation. The proponents of the quantity theory sought to maintain the stability of money circulation by means of obligatory gold backing of bank notes. The theory provided the economic justification for Peel's Bank Acts (introduced in England in 1844, and in Scotland in 1845). Under the 1844 Act, the Bank of England was divided into a Banking Department and an Issue Department and fixed proportions were laid down between the amount of bank notes issued and the bullion required to back them. However, the actual demand for currency forced the government to suspend the Act in 1847 and 1857 and to issue paper money in excess of the fixed limit.

Marx showed the untenability of the currency principle in *A Contribution to the Critique of Political Economy* (present edition, Vol. 30). He discussed the 1844 Bank Act in a number of articles (present edition, Vols. 12, 15 and 16).—102, 126, 135, 202, 208, 215

133 The original of the letter has not been found. Only an excerpt reproduced in Freiligrath's letter of 26 February 1857 to Karl Weerth, a high school teacher

in Detmold and brother of Georg Weerth, who died in Havana in July 1856, has reached us. Engels' letter was written in reply to Freiligrath's request of 11 February for enquiries to be made about Georg Weerth's papers, including his diaries, which his relatives wanted to publish in Germany. In a letter to Engels on 16 February Marx also mentioned Freiligrath's request (see this volume, pp. 100-01). On receipt of Engels' reply, Freiligrath, as he said in his letter to Karl Weerth, at once wrote to Detmold. It may therefore be assumed that Engels' letter was posted shortly before, probably about 25 February.—103

134 Engels means the vote of no confidence in Palmerston's government after a debate on the Anglo-Chinese conflict in the House of Commons lasting from 26 February to 3 March 1857. The conflict has been provoked by the bombardment of Canton in October 1856 in retaliation for the Chinese authorities' arrest of a contraband vessel sailing under the British flag. The bombardment was the prelude to another colonial war by Britain—later in alliance with France—against China, the Second Opium War (1856-60). After the vote Palmerston dissolved Parliament, and in the new election his candidates, who supported the aggression against China, beat the Opposition even in their stronghold, Manchester, securing a majority for Palmerston in the House of Commons. Marx dealt with these events in several articles published in the *New-York Daily Tribune* in March and April 1857 (see present edition, Vol. 15).

The *Free Traders* advocated non-interference of the state in the economy. Their stronghold was Manchester (hence the Manchester School and the Manchester Party). In the 1840s and 1850s the Free Traders were an independent political group which later formed the Left wing of the Liberal Party.

The *Peelites* were moderate Tories advocating concessions to the commercial and industrial bourgeoisie. The repeal of the Corn Laws in 1846 by their leader, Robert Peel, caused a split in the Tory party, with the Peelites forming an independent group that allied itself with the Whigs. In the late 1850s they joined the Liberal Party.—104, 107, 109, 111, 113, 115

135 *Aldermen*—members of local government in Britain chosen by borough and county councils.—104

136 The facts connected with the election campaign in Manchester and some data concerning Robert Lowe, John Potter and other candidates for Parliament related by Engels in this letter and those of 11, 20 and 31 March were used by Marx in his article 'The Defeat of Cobden, Bright and Gibson' (present edition, Vol. 15).—104, 110, 117

137 The fraudulent machinations of the *Docks Napoléon* joint-stock company and the breach by Napoleon III's government of its promise to keep young Arthur Berryer, who was implicated in the machinations, out of trouble if his father, the well-known lawyer Pierre Antoine Berryer, refrained from denunciations embarrassing to the ruling quarters, were later discussed by Marx in his article 'Portents of the Day' (present edition, Vol. 15).—105

138 The *Société du dix Décembre* (Society of December 10) was a secret Bonapartist society consisting mainly of *déclassé* elements and political adventurists. Set up in 1849, it owed its name to the election of Louis Napoleon to the Presidency of the French Republic on 10 December 1848. Marx gives a detailed description of the Society in *The Eighteenth Brumaire of Louis Bonaparte* (see present edition, Vol. 11, pp. 149-51, 180-82, 186, 193-96).—107, 157, 436

139 The secret treaty guaranteeing Turkey's frontiers was signed by Britain, France and Austria in Paris on 15 April 1856.—107

140 From 1806 to 1808 the King of Naples was Joseph Bonaparte, elder brother of Napoleon I, and from 1808 to 1815 Joachim Murat, one of Napoleon's marshals.—107

141 "Truly British Minister"—an allusion to Lord Russell's description of Palmerston as a champion of British interests in his House of Commons speech of 20 June 1850, in which he sought to justify Palmerston's military and diplomatic moves against Greece in connection with the burning in Athens in 1847 of the house of the merchant Pacifico, a Portuguese Jew and British subject. Lord Russell argued that Palmerston was motivated by the need to uphold the prestige of British citizens. The actual aim of Palmerston's moves was to make Greece surrender several strategic islands in the Aegean.—107, 116, 276, 431

142 Marx means the policy of Britain's ruling quarters towards Persia, Afghanistan, China and other Asian countries during Palmerston's first term as Foreign Secretary (1830-41). Thus the British government declared the siege of Herat in November 1837 by Persian troops an act of hostility towards Britain and took advantage of it to send a naval squadron to the Persian Gulf. The Shah of Persia was forced to lift the siege in August 1838 and later to conclude a trade agreement with Britain advantageous to the latter.

Palmerston was also Foreign Secretary when Britain unleashed what came to be known as the First Opium War (1840-42), which marked the first stage in turning China into a semi-colony of West European capitalist states.—107

143 The Aberdeen coalition ministry (1852-55) consisted mainly of Peelites (break-away group of Tories) and Whigs. Junior posts were held by Radicals and leaders of the Irish faction in the House of Commons. Marx and Engels described the bankruptcy of this government of 'All the Talents' in the article 'The Late British Government' (present edition, Vol. 13, pp. 620-26).—108

144 Marx means the massacre by government troops of participants in a mass meeting for electoral reform in St. Peter's Field near Manchester on 16 August 1819. By analogy with the battle of Waterloo it was called Peterloo.

The *6 gagging acts*—the six exceptional laws passed by the British Parliament in 1819 after the massacre in St. Peter's Field. Introduced by the Tory ministry, of which Palmerston was a member, they virtually abolished habeas corpus and freedom of the press and of assembly.—108

145 An allusion to the power struggle in France that preceded the Bonapartist coup d'état of 2 December 1851. Louis Bonaparte, President of the Second Republic, was in conflict with the party of Order, the bloc of the two monarchist factions—the Legitimists, supporters of the Bourbons overthrown in 1830, and the Orleanists (see Note 124), who supported the junior (Orleans) branch of the Bourbon dynasty. The party of Order was the strongest force in the French Legislative Assembly which was disbanded by Bonaparte's supporters on 2 December 1851.—108

146 Engels ironically compares the Polish émigrés in the Turkish service who fought on the side of the North Caucasian mountaineers against Russia to the 300 Spartans who, headed by King Leonidas, defended the Pass of Thermopylae against the army of the Persian King Xerxes I in 480 B.C.—109

147 Engels means *Tucker's Political Fly-Sheets,* a series of 12 issues published by the Urquhartite Tucker in London in 1853 and 1854 and republished in 1855.

Issues 1 and 2 contained the pamphlets 'Palmerston and Russia' and 'Palmerston and the Treaty of Unkiar-Skelessy', reproducing the content of articles 3, 4 and 5 of Marx's 8-article series on Palmerston published in *The People's Paper* in 1853 (see present edition, Vol. 12, pp. 341-406). The other issues carried mostly articles by David Urquhart also attacking Palmerston's foreign policy.—110, 111, 115

148 This refers to those articles of Marx's series *Lord Palmerston* which appeared in the *New-York Daily Tribune.* In contrast to *The People's Paper,* which published all eight articles and as a consecutive whole (see present edition, Vol. 12, pp. 341-406), the *Tribune* carried only six articles, in the form of four separate leaders under different titles: 'Palmerston', corresponding to articles 1 and 2 in *The People's Paper* (*NYDT,* 19 October 1853), 'Palmerston and Russia', corresponding to article 3 (*NYDT,* 4 November 1853), 'A Chapter of Modern History', corresponding to articles 4 and 5 (*NYDT,* 21 November 1853), and 'England and Russia', corresponding to article 7 (*NYDT,* 11 January 1854).—111, 115

149 Marx means the seizure by British naval forces of the Iranian port of Bushire in the Persian Gulf during the 1856-57 Anglo-Persian war (see Note 129).—111

150 The *Anti-Corn Law League* was founded in 1838 by the Manchester manufacturers and Free Trade leaders Richard Cobden and John Bright. It advocated the abolition of the high import duties on agricultural produce imposed—in the interests of the landed aristocracy—by a series of Corn Laws to maintain high prices for that produce on the home market. The struggle between the industrial bourgeoisie and the landowners over the Corn Laws ended in their repeal (June 1846), after which the League announced its dissolution. Some of its branches, however, continued in existence for several years.—113, 116, 215, 305

151 Marx means the June 1848 uprising of Paris workers, whose defeat largely predetermined the failure of the 1848-49 revolution and the subsequent period of political reaction in Europe in the 1850s.—113

152 In his letter of 5 March 1857 Charles Dana wrote that of all of Marx's articles only the second instalment of the article on mountain warfare had not been published, and this because interest in the Swiss question had subsided. The two articles on Persia, he wrote, had been merged into one and published, while the second article on Austria's trade had been set and would be published as soon as space permitted. However, it was not until 4 August 1857 that this article entitled, like the first, 'The Maritime Commerce of Austria' actually appeared in print.—114

153 'Geniality leaves off where money matters begin'—this remark was addressed to the King of Prussia by David Hansemann, a leader of the liberal Rhenish bourgeoisie, on 8 June 1847 at a sitting of the First United Diet, from which the government was vainly trying to obtain endorsement of a fresh loan.—114

154 In a speech in the House of Commons on 23 February 1848 Anstey presented the facts relating to the publication in 1835, in Urquhart's series *The Portfolio,* of secret documents from the archives of the Grand Duke Constantine, Viceroy of Poland. The documents had been seized by Polish insurgents in 1830 and were later handed over by Polish refugees to Palmerston. It was only at the insistence of King William IV that Palmerston made them available for publication (for details see present edition, Vol. 12, pp. 386-87).—115

155 The *Peace Party* or the *Peace Society* (*Society for Promoting Permanent and Universal Peace*) was an organisation founded by the Quakers in London in 1816. It was strongly supported by the Free Traders, who held that, given peace, free trade would enable Britain to make full use of her industrial superiority and thus gain economic and political supremacy.—115

156 The *Quakers* (or *Society of Friends*)—a religious sect founded in England during the seventeenth-century revolution and later widespread in North America. The Quakers rejected the Established Church with its rites, and preached peace.—116

157 *Newalls Buildings*—premises in Manchester where the Anti-Corn Law League met from 1838 onwards.—116

158 The information contained in this letter of Engels and in those of 11, 20 and 31 March 1857 was intended for use by Marx in his articles for the *New-York Daily Tribune*.—118

159 The rumour about Schramm's death proved to be false.—119

160 The bombardment of Odessa by an Anglo-French squadron took place on 22 April 1854, soon after Britain and France joined Turkey in the war against Russia (the Crimean war, 1853-56). It was essentially a military demonstration.—119

161 Marx refers to the Vienna Conference of 1855, which was to work out the terms for peace between the participants in the Crimean war (1853-56). It was attended by representatives of Russia, Britain, France, Austria and Turkey and lasted, with intervals, from 15 March to 4 June 1855. The conference was preceded by several rounds of talks between the Ambassadors held in 1853 and 1854 on the initiative of Austrian Foreign Minister Buol, who sought to mediate between the belligerents. The conference produced no results.

Britain was represented by its Special Envoy Lord John Russell.—119

162 The facts mentioned in this paragraph were dealt with in greater detail by Marx in his article 'Result of the Election', published in the *New-York Daily Tribune* on 22 April 1857.—119

163 Marx probably means one of the articles on Pan-Slavism written by Engels for the *New-York Daily Tribune* but not published (see Note 11).—120

164 Engels wrote this letter in reply to Jenny Marx's of 12 April (see this volume, p. 563). The manuscript is not dated. However, the article 'Changes in the Russian Army', which was enclosed in the letter and was published in the *New York Daily Tribune* on 6 May 1857, was presumably sent to New York from London not later than Friday, 17 April, so the letter was probably written on about 16 April.—121

165 A reference to Dana's letter to Marx of 6 April 1857 inviting him to contribute to *The New American Cyclopaedia*, 'a popular dictionary of general knowledge' prepared by a group of progressive bourgeois journalists and publishers on the *New-York Daily Tribune* editorial staff and edited by Charles Dana and George Ripley. It was published in 16 volumes by D. Appleton and Company, New York, in 1858-63 and reprinted in 1868-69. A number of prominent US and European scholars wrote for it. On Engels' advice Marx agreed to contribute a number of articles. But Engels wrote most of them himself so that Marx could complete his economic research. Marx wrote mainly biographical essays on military and political figures with help from Engels in dealing with the military

aspect. Marx and Engels wrote their articles from revolutionary-proletarian, materialist positions notwithstanding the condition laid down by the editors that they should not express their party point of view. Because of this condition Marx limited the range of his subjects mainly to military matters and to studies on different countries, renouncing his initial intention of writing essays on the history of German philosophy, the Napoleonic Code, Chartism, socialism and communism. He held that these subjects could not be dealt with in a spirit of even apparent neutrality. It may have been for this reason also that Marx did not contribute the article 'Aesthetics', as originally planned.

The articles in *The New American Cyclopaedia* were published anonymously, and only volumes II, V and XVI contained lists of the authors of major articles. Marx was mentioned as the author of the articles 'Army', 'Artillery', 'Bernadotte', 'Bolivar', 'Cavalry', 'Fortification', 'Infantry', and 'Navy' (actually these articles, except for 'Bernadotte' and 'Bolivar', were written by Engels). Marx's and Engels' authorship of other articles has been established on the basis of the Marx-Engels correspondence, Charles Dana's letters to Marx, Marx's notebooks, which recorded the despatch of articles to New York, and of other archive material (conspectuses, extracts for articles, etc.). In all, the authorship of 81 articles has been established.

Marx and Engels contributed to *The New American Cyclopaedia* from July 1857 to November 1860, their articles (those we know of) appearing in volumes I-V, VII, IX and XII. They were also included, unchanged, in the 1868-69 edition of the *Cyclopaedia* but were not reprinted any more during the authors' lifetime. They were collected and published in 1933 in the Soviet Union in Marx and Engels, *Works,* First Russian Edition, Vol. XI, Part II. The most complete publications of these articles are to be found in Volumes 14 (1959) and 44 (1977) of the Second Russian Edition of the *Works* of Marx and Engels and in Vol. 18 of the present edition (1982). However, these publications did not include the articles 'Austerlitz', 'Augereau' and 'Badajos', of which Engels was erroneously regarded as the author. When preparing the Russian edition, the editors established the true authors of a number of articles wrongly attributed to Marx and Engels by some bibliographers. Thus the articles 'Abd-el-Kader' and 'Chartism' were written by William Humphrey, 'Austerlitz' by Henry W. Herbert, 'Epicurus' by Hermann Raster, 'Socialism' by Parke Godwin, and 'Hegel' by Henry Smith. The article 'Aesthetics' cannot be by Marx either, for it conflicts with the views on the subject expressed in his works.—122, 134

166 The letter is not dated. Since it was in reply to Marx's letter of 21 April 1857 and Marx answered it on 23 April, Engels must have written it between these dates.—122

167 On 26 February 1857, speaking in the House of Commons about the British government's unlawful actions in the Anglo-Chinese conflict, Cobden tabled a resolution condemning Britain's military operations in China. After a long debate the motion was adopted, resulting in a vote of no confidence in Palmerston's government (see Note 134).—127

168 While working on *Die Philosophie Herakleitos des Dunklen von Ephesos,* Lassalle was also writing a historical drama, *Franz von Sickingen.* In a letter to Marx on 26 April 1857 he said that it would in a sense 'set things alight'.—129

169 Engels arrived in London early in June 1857 and returned to Manchester at the end of the month.—131, 136, 141, 154

170 Marx analysed this report in two articles ('Crédit mobilier') published in

the *New-York Daily Tribune* on 30 May and 1 June 1857 (present edition, Vol. 15).—133

171 *'Social philosophy'* (*'Sozialphilosophie'*) was the term Moses Hess used in his works of the 1840s to denote the teachings of the French Utopian socialists (Saint-Simon, Fourier and others) and the petty-bourgeois social doctrines of Proudhon.—133

172 Most of these articles were soon written and published in *The New American Cyclopaedia* (in the present edition they are in Vol. 18). In addition, Engels undertook to write other 'A' articles ('Alma', 'Ammunition', 'Airey' and 'Army'—all ordered by Dana in his letter to Marx of 8 May 1857). Some articles mentioned in the list ('Axle', 'Approaches', 'Advanced Guard') were not published in the *Cyclopaedia* and probably not written by Engels. The articles 'Abukir', 'Anglesey' and 'Augereau' were in all probability written by other authors.—137

173 On coming to London in early June 1857, Engels had a relapse of the ailment about which he wrote to Marx on 20 May (this volume, pp. 130-31). He probably stayed with his brother-in-law Emil Blank, husband of his sister Marie.

Engels gives only 'Friday morning' as the date of this letter. In earlier editions it was dated 12 June 1857. But since it was written in early June and not later than 10 June (as can be seen from the fact that Marx wrote the draft of his letter to Collet on the back of this letter not later than 10 June—see Note 174), and moreover on a Friday, the letter can only have been written on 5 June.—137

174 The extant draft of the letter (on the back of Engels' letter to Marx of 5 June 1857) is not dated. However, since Collet replied to Marx on 10 June 1857, it may be assumed that the letter was written about 10 June.—138

175 The draft letter is not dated. It was written in reply to Collet's letter to Marx of 10 June, presumably immediately after it was received.—138

176 This letter is written on Dana's letter to Marx of 11 June 1857, which Marx mentions in the first lines. Dana wrote telling Marx that he was returning the manuscript of the article 'Saint-Arnaud' (see Note 60) rejected by *Putnam's Monthly;* Dana did not advise him to write the article 'Ships against Walls' because the editors refused to guarantee its publication. He also wrote that he hoped to be receiving articles for *The New American Cyclopaedia* soon.—140

177 Marx means the list of articles for *The New American Cyclopaedia* which he sent to Dana following the one drawn up by Engels on 28 May 1857 (see this volume, pp. 136-37). This list is not extant.—142

178 Marx refers to the Indian uprising of 1857-59 against British rule. It flared up in May 1857 among the Sepoy units of the Bengal army and spread to large areas of Northern and Central India. (Sepoys were mercenary soldiers recruited from among the Indians and serving under British officers.) Its main strength was provided by the peasants and the poor artisans. Directed by local feudal lords, the uprising was put down owing to the country's disunity, religious and caste differences, and the military and technical superiority of the colonialists.—142, 146, 413, 566

179 Mazzini, who secretly arrived in Genoa at the end of June 1857, and other supporters of revolutionary action, attempted to start an uprising in Italy with a view to liberating and uniting the country. A detachment of revolutionaries led

by Pizacono seized a ship bound for Tunis from Genoa and landed in the Kingdom of Naples. Attempts were also made to start uprisings in Leghorn and Genoa but, like the expedition to the South, they also failed. Pizacono and many of his associates perished in clashes with Neapolitan troops. Mazzini managed to avoid arrest and return to London.—142

180 This refers to excerpts which Marx made from the various sources on the military history of antiquity for Engels, who was working on the article 'Army' for *The New American Cyclopaedia.* The notes from the encyclopaedias of Ersch-Gruber and Pauly mentioned below in the text are extant. Marx also made excerpts, probably later, from Wilkinson's three-volume *Manners and Customs of the Ancient Egyptians,* London, 1837.—147, 565

181 A reference to the second batch of 'A' articles which Engels wrote for *The New American Cyclopaedia* in accordance with his list (see this volume, pp. 136-37). Judging by an entry in Marx's notebook made on 24 July 1857, Marx sent these articles to New York with the first batch of 'A' articles received from Engels on 14 July (see this volume, p. 146).—148, 159

182 The *Loan Societies*—a variety of the Friendly Societies in England (see Note 76)—granted workers low-interest loans repayable in instalments. Their funds, like those of the Friendly Societies, consisted of membership dues. Loans could be made to non-members, provided they had two reliable guarantors.—148, 328

183 From 27 July to 8 November 1857 Engels underwent medical treatment at the seaside: at Waterloo near Liverpool (until the end of August, when he returned to Manchester for a fortnight in view of his father's arrival there), at Ryde on the Isle of Wight (from the 8th to the end of September), and in Jersey (until 8 November), whence he returned to Manchester.—149, 154, 160, 195

184 An excerpt from this letter was first published in English in K. Marx and F. Engels, *The First Indian War of Independence 1857-1859,* Foreign Languages Publishing House, Moscow [1959].—151, 233

185 The letter Engels sent to Jenny Marx from Waterloo, presumably about 11 August 1857, has not been found. It was written in reply to Marx's letter to Engels of 9 August.—151

186 Marx based his assumption of the possible retreat of the British troops from Delhi on the numerical superiority of the insurgents, who had captured this important fortress in the middle of May 1857, soon after the beginning of the Indian uprising (see Note 178). But the insurgents, who adhered to the tactics of passive defence and were demoralised by the treacherous behaviour of the local feudal lords, failed to take advantage of their superiority. This enabled the British to hold out until they received reinforcements. In mid-September they took Delhi.—152

187 The reference is presumably to articles for *The New American Cyclopaedia* or to material for articles which Marx intended to write for it with Engels' help on military questions.—153

188 Conrad Schramm, a member of the Communist League and a close friend of Marx and Engels, was ill with tuberculosis. In 1852 he went to the USA hoping to earn a living and improve his health. In the summer of 1857 he returned to London and, his condition having worsened, he was immediately placed in a hospital for German refugees. On 20 September he moved to Jersey where

Engels too soon came for treatment. Schramm died on 15 January 1858.—158, 171, 312

189 The letter, written presumably on 11 August 1857, when Marx despatched articles for *The New American Cyclopaedia*, has not been found.—159

190 This letter was published in earlier editions without the notes on Bennigsen and Barclay which Engels made for Marx's biographical articles for *The New American Cyclopaedia* (see Note 165). The notes were first published—separately from the letter—in 1977, in Vol. 44 of the Second Russian Edition of the *Works* of Marx and Engels, under the editorial heading 'Bennigsen and Barclay'. In the present edition the letter is published in full with the notes for the first time.—162

191 Here and below Engels describes events during the war of the Fourth Coalition (Britain, Russia, Prussia and Sweden) against Napoleonic France. After the defeat of the Prussian army by Napoleon in the spring of 1806 the main theatre of war shifted to East Prussia, where Napoleon encountered stubborn resistance from the allied army of Russia and Prussia.

The *battle of Preussisch-Eylau* on 7-8 February 1807 between the French army and Russian and Prussian forces was indecisive.—162, 170, 175

192 The French laid siege to Danzig (Gdansk) in March 1807. The garrison, consisting of Prussian troops and a Russian detachment, offered stubborn resistance. The fortress surrendered to superior enemy forces at the end of May 1807.—162

193 The *battle of Smolensk*, during the Patriotic War of Russia against Napoleon, took place on 16-18 August 1812. Units of the First and Second Russian armies (commanded by Barclay de Tolly and Bagration) which had joined up on 3 August rebuffed the attacks of Napoleon's troops to cover the withdrawal of the main forces. At the cost of heavy losses Napoleon captured the city, which was abandoned by the Russian rearguard after the main forces had withdrawn.—163

194 This passage reflects the tendentious presentation of the events of the Patriotic War of Russia, 1812, in Jomini's *Vie politique et militaire de Napoléon* (Vols. 1-4, Paris, 1827) and other books (e.g. Bernhardi's *Denkwürdigkeiten aus dem Leben ... des Grafen von Toll*, Vols. 1-4, Leipzig, 1856), which Engels used as sources. In particular, they contain inaccuracies in explaining why Mikhail Kutuzov, newly appointed commander-in-chief of the Russian army, abandoned the *position at Gzhatsk* (more precisely at Tsarevo-Zaimishche), which it had occupied since 29 August 1812, and withdrew to Borodino. Kutuzov did so because he intended to give decisive battle with a more favourable balance of forces, for which it was necessary to win time and bring up reinforcements. The *battle of Borodino* was fought on 7 September. It brought about a turn in the war in Russia's favour, despite the forced but expedient abandonment of Moscow.—164

195 In the final version of their article 'Barclay de Tolly' Marx and Engels gave a more accurate description of Barclay's role. There the remark concerning the predominance of administrative and diplomatic functions in Barclay's activities during the war of the Sixth Coalition (Russia, Austria, Prussia, Britain, Spain, Sweden and other countries) against Napoleonic France, applied only to the 1814 campaign, and Barclay's role as military commander in a number of battles during the 1813 campaign is noted.—164

196 Published here are three short texts by Engels, probably fragments of a letter to Marx of 11 or 12 September 1857 which has not been preserved in full. Like other letters written at the time, they reflect Engels' help to Marx in writing biographical articles for *The New American Cyclopaedia*.

The first and third fragments (written on separate sheets) were published in the Second Russian Edition of the *Works* of Marx and Engels as the letter in question. The second fragment (written on two sheets) has never been published before. The approximate date of writing has been established on the basis of the previous letter of Engels to Marx, written on 10 September, and Marx's replies written on 15 and 17 September 1857.

The order in which the fragments are presented in this volume is the order in which they are assumed to have been written.—164

197 At the *battle of Grossbeeren* on 23 August and *of Dennewitz* on 6 September 1813, the Prussian corps under Bülow defeated the French. Both battles took place during the war of the Sixth Coalition (Russia, Austria, Prussia, Britain, Spain, Sweden and other countries) against Napoleonic France. In the 1813 campaign Bernadotte commanded the allied Northern Army, which included Bülow's corps.—164, 274

198 At the *battle of Leipzig* (16-19 October 1813) the allied armies of Russia, Austria, Prussia and Sweden defeated Napoleon and his allies. This 'battle of the nations' led to Germany's liberation from Napoleon's rule.—165, 179

199 The *Directory* (consisting of five directors of whom one was re-elected every year) was the leading executive body in France set up under the 1795 Constitution. It governed France until Bonaparte's coup d'état of 1799 and expressed the interests of the big bourgeoisie.—165

200 Engels refers to the military operations in Transylvania (then part of Hungary) of a revolutionary army against the Austrian forces, Romanian detachments, provoked into action against Hungary by the Austrian authorities, and a Russian detachment sent by the Tsarist government to help the Habsburg Empire. Started under Bem's command in December 1848, during the 1848-49 revolution in Hungary, this campaign ended a few months later in the practically complete liberation of Transylvania from the counter-revolutionary forces. However, in the second Transylvanian campaign (mentioned below) called forth by a new concentration of counter-revolutionaries in the summer of 1849 and the arrival of fresh contingents of Tsarist troops, Bem's entire army was routed at the end of July 1849 and he himself had to flee to Turkey.—167

201 Bem's *march into the Banat* (a region in the Serbian Voivodina, then part of Hungary) was undertaken in the spring of 1849 to put down the Serbian movement for autonomy incited by the Austrian authorities and influenced by the Serbian big bourgeoisie, nobility and clergy. As in Transylvania, the struggle in the Banat with its population of Hungarians, Germans and Romanians as well as Serbs, was complicated by clashes between Serbians and non-Serbians, and the erroneous stand adopted by the Hungarian bourgeois and aristocratic revolutionaries on the national question. Only on 28 July 1849, shortly before the fall of the Hungarian Republic, did they officially agree to recognise the equality of all nationalities inhabiting Hungary.—167

202 The last two of these articles, 'Blum' and 'Bourrienne', were not ready for

despatch to New York that day. As is seen from Marx's notebook, they were sent off to Charles Dana on 22 September 1857.—168

203 Here and below Marx writes about Bem's participation in the Polish national liberation uprising of November 1830-October 1831. The majority of its participants were revolutionary gentry (*szlachta*) and its leaders came mostly from the aristocracy. It was suppressed by the Russian army with the support of Prussia and Austria.

At the *battle of Iganin* on 10 May 1831 the Polish insurgents were victorious in a clash with Russian troops.

At the *battle of Ostrolenka* on 26 May 1831 the Polish insurgents were defeated by Russian forces under Dibich. The final blow was delivered when the Russians captured Warsaw (see below) after storming its suburb Vola on 6 September. The remnants of the insurgent army fled to Prussia and Austria.—169, 172

204 The *battle of Austerlitz* (see Note 46) was an important event in the war of the Third Coalition (Austria, Russia, Britain and Sweden) against Napoleonic France (1805).—170, 174

205 On the *battle of Jena* on 14 October 1806 see Note 46. The same day Marshal Davout's army defeated the main Prussian forces at *Auerstädt*. The defeat of Prussia in these two battles led to the quick occupation of the Kingdom of Prussia by the French and to the retreat of the remnants of the Prussian army to the eastern frontier.

These battles occurred during the war of the Fourth Coalition against Napoleonic France (see Note 191).—174, 178

206 At the *battle of Wagram* (Austria) on 5-6 July 1809 during the war of the Fifth Coalition (Austria, Britain), Napoleon's army defeated the Austrians.—170, 175, 176

207 An entry in Marx's notebook shows that he sent Engels' articles 'Algeria' and 'Ammunition' to New York on 18 September 1857.—173

208 A reference to the *Treaty of the Tafna* of 30 May 1837 between Bugeaud and Abd-el-Kader, the leader of the Algerian liberation war which lasted, with short intervals, from 1832 to 1847. The French had resumed operations against Abd-el-Kader in 1835 in violation of the peace treaty concluded a year earlier. Under the treaty of the Tafna France again recognised the independence of Abd-el-Kader's state in Western Algeria, except for a few coastal towns. In 1839 the peace was again violated by the French, and the Algerian liberation struggle was resumed. When working on the article 'Bugeaud', Marx took into account Engels' opinion of this general. In particular, enlarging upon Engels' remark about Bugeaud's venality, Marx wrote: 'A secret article, not reduced to writing, stipulated that 30,000 boojoos (about $12,000) should be paid to Gen. Bugeaud' (present edition, Vol. 18, p. 212).—177

209 The *battle of the Alma* took place on 20 September 1854 between the Russian forces and the numerically superior allied forces of the French, British and Turks. It was the first battle after the Allies' landing in the Crimea (at Eupatoria) on 14 September. The defeat and withdrawal of the Russian forces left the road to Sevastopol open for the Allies.

The *battle of Balaklava* (mentioned below in the text) between the Russian and the allied Anglo-French and Turkish forces took place on 25 October 1854. Units of the Russian army tried to cut off the English and Turkish troops taking part in the siege of Sevastopol from their base in Balaklava. They succeeded in inflicting serious losses on the enemy, especially on the English cavalry, but failed to achieve their main objective.—177, 297

210 A reference to the siege of Sevastopol by the French and British troops during the Crimean War (1853-56) which lasted from September 1854 to August 1855 (349 days).—178

211 This campaign took place during the war of the European coalition (Austria, Prussia, Britain, the Netherlands, Spain, Piedmont, Naples and other monarchies) (1792-97) against the French Republic. Prussia, a member of the coalition from 1792, concluded a separate peace with France in Basle in 1795.—178

212 The *Tugendbund* (Union of Virtue)—one of the patriotic societies founded in Prussia after its defeat by Napoleonic France in 1806-07. It united representatives of the liberal nobility and the bourgeois intelligentsia and aimed at spreading the idea of an anti-Napoleonic liberation war and supporting moderate liberal reforms in Prussia. The Tugendbund was banned on Napoleon's demand on 31 December 1809 by Frederick William III, who also feared its activities. However, it continued to exist secretly until the end of the Napoleonic wars.—178

213 An allusion to the 1848-49 revolutionary movement in Baden. The German petty-bourgeois democrat and journalist Blind took part in it, while the German republican Hecker was a military leader in the Baden uprising in April 1848.—179

214 The *battle of the Katzbach* (Silesia) was fought on 26 August 1813 during the war of the Sixth Coalition (Russia, Prussia, Austria, Britain, Sweden, Spain and Portugal) against Napoleonic France. The Silesian army, commanded by Blücher and consisting of a Prussian corps under York and two Russian corps under Langeron and Sacken, defeated the French army of Marshal Macdonald.—179

215 At the *battle of Dresden* on 26-27 August 1813 Napoleon's army routed the allied forces of Austria, Prussia and Russia (the Bohemian or chief army), commanded by the Austrian Field Marshal Schwarzenberg.—179

216 In a number of battles in the Montmirail region (east of Paris) Napoleon defeated separate units of Blücher's Silesian army in mid-February 1814 by taking advantage of their isolation from one another.—180

217 At the *battle of Waterloo* on 18 June 1815 the Anglo-Dutch and Prussian forces commanded by the Duke of Wellington and Blücher defeated Napoleon's army, thus deciding the allies' final victory over Napoleonic France. The outcome of the battle of Waterloo is credited to Blücher's army which was defeated by Napoleon at Ligny on 16 June but managed to escape French pursuit and join up with the Anglo-Dutch forces.—180, 357

218 Marx's notebook contains an entry of 29 September 1857 about the despatch to New York of his article 'Bessières' and the articles 'Bem' and 'Bosquet' written jointly with Engels.—181

219 As is seen from Marx's notebook, in September and October 1857 he wrote for the *New-York Daily Tribune* a series of five articles on the state of the Second Empire's finances and Napoleon III's financial policy. The articles were not printed. The manuscripts have not been found.—181, 297

220 The letter is written on notepaper bearing a picture of the ruins of a castle and the inscription: 'Carisbrooke Castle, Isle of Wight'.

On the first English publication of this letter see Note 184.—182

221 The *Mahratta principalities* (the Mahrattas or Marathas inhabited a large territory in Western India) were formed on the territory of the Mahratta state, which arose in the latter half of the seventeenth century during the struggle against the Empire of the Great Moguls. Later, particularly in the 1730s and 1740s, it underwent a process of feudal decentralisation. The confederation of the Mahratta principalities thus formed disintegrated in the second half of the eighteenth century. Weakened by the struggle with the Afghans and internal strife the principalities fell prey to the British East India Company which annexed a considerable part of their territories in the three Anglo-Mahratta wars (1775-82, 1803-05 and 1817-18) and made the remaining princes its vassals.—185

222 Marx used the contents of Engels' letter for his two articles, 'The Revolt in India', written on 29 September and 6 October 1857 (see present edition, Vol. 15). The purely military evaluation of possible British operations intended by Engels for Marx's information was supplemented with the political assessment of the aims of the Indian national liberation movement and the efforts of the British colonialists to preserve their rule in India.—185

223 As is seen from entries in Marx's notebook, on 29 September 1857 he sent to New York, besides 'Battery', three articles received from Engels: 'Bivouac', 'Blindage' and 'Bonnet'; on 6 October, he despatched one more batch of 'B' articles: 'Bomb'; 'Bomb-Ketch', 'Bomb-Proof', 'Bomb Vessel', 'Bombardier' and 'Bombardment'.—185

224 An abridged English translation of this letter was first published in Karl Marx and Friedrich Engels, *Correspondence. 1846-1895.* A Selection with Commentary and Notes, Martin Lawrence Ltd., London [1934]. The letter was published in full in *The Letters of Karl Marx*, selected and translated with explanatory notes and an introduction by Saul K. Padover, Prentice-Hall, Inc., Englewood Cliff, New Jersey, 1979.—186

225 *Peculium castrense* (lit. camp property) (Roman law)—property given by fathers to sons during and for military service and which they could dispose of as they liked independently of their fathers' will.

Fabri—craftsmen in the Roman army engaged in building bridges, putting up defence and siege works, making arms, etc. They were formed into special detachments.—186

226 *Condottieri*—leaders of mercenary troops in the service of princes, city republics and Popes in Italy in the fourteenth to sixteenth centuries. Some of them usurped power in individual Italian states and founded new princely dynasties.—187

227 Engels' letter to Marx of 24 September 1857 shows that he proposed to stay in Brighton on 29-30 September, on his way to Jersey to complete his medical treatment (see Note 183). Available sources do not establish with certainty whether Engels and Marx met at the appointed time, but we know from Marx's own words (see present edition, Vol. 17, p. 85) that he and Engels visited their sick friend Conrad Schramm in Jersey, most probably at the beginning of October 1857.—187

228 The letter is written on notepaper bearing a view of the Gulf of St. Catherine in Jersey from the pier.—187

229 Harney, the former leader of revolutionary Chartism, withdrew from the labour movement in the first half of the 1850s, when there was a general decline in the English proletariat's political activity. In the autumn of 1855 he went to St. Hélier, the capital of Jersey, to convey an address of solidarity from British radicals to Victor Hugo on the occasion of the British decision to expel him and other French emigrants from the island (see Note 16). Harney settled there and in mid-1856 became editor of *The Jersey Independent*, whicn he devoted almost entirely to local problems, criticising the local system from bourgeois-radical positions.—188

230 *Hejira* (or *Hegira*)—the flight of Mohammed and his followers from Mecca to Medina in 622, from which the Mohammedan era is dated.

Here Engels alludes to the expulsion of French petty-bourgeois democratic refugees from Jersey in the autumn of 1855 (see Note 16), and calls them *crapauds* (philistines) (see Note 81).—188

231 *Vendée*—a department in the west of France. During the French Revolution it was the centre of a royalist revolt in March 1793 in which the local peasant masses took part. The revolt was suppressed in 1795 but attempts to revive it were made in 1799 and later.—189

232 Engels refers to the list of articles beginning with 'C' for *The New American Cyclopaedia* which Dana sent Marx. Neither the list nor Engels' comments on it have been preserved.—189, 190

233 The letter is written on notepaper bearing a picture of a cave on the Grève au Lançon in Jersey.—190

234 Engels refers to the preliminary draft of the article 'Armada' for *The New American Cyclopaedia* which he wrote on the basis of excerpts made by Marx from various sources. Marx put the finishing touches to Engels' text. The material Engels sent for the *Cyclopaedia* presumably included also the article 'Ayacucho', to which Marx added a final paragraph before sending it and the article 'Armada' to New York on 23 October 1857, as an entry in his notebook shows (for these articles see present edition, Vol. 18).—190

235 This refers to the article 'Artillery', which Charles Dana asked Marx to write for *The New American Cyclopaedia* early in May 1857. Engels undertook to write the article but, busy with 'Army' and smaller articles for the *Cyclopaedia*, he did not begin it till after 19 October. Marx and Engels did not expect that the article could still be included in the current volume with the 'A' articles and thought, as this and the following letters show, that it could be inserted in some other volume, under the title 'Cannon' or as a historical part of the corresponding article ('The History of Cannon'). However, the article was finished by the end of November, despatched to New York on the 27th of that month, and included in Vol. II of the *Cyclopaedia* under the original title 'Artillery'.—190, 195, 198, 199, 200, 207, 251

236 The letter is written on notepaper with a picture of Princes Tower in Jersey.

On the first English publication of this letter see Note 184.—195

237 Many remnants of feudalism still survived in Jersey at the time. Local big landowners, lawyers and bankers (François Godfrey in particular) controlled all administrative institutions and the Royal Court. The radical Reform League

(consisting of local traders, small shipowners and bank clerks), founded by Harney in September 1857, and *The Jersey Independent* edited by him, came out against their arbitrary rule and encroachments on the interests of tenants.—196, 264, 308

238 Further on Engels describes the siege and storming of the insurgent-held fortress of Delhi by British troops during the Indian uprising of 1857-59 (see Note 178). The city fell on 19-20 September 1857. Engels dealt with these events in his article 'The Capture of Delhi' published in the *New-York Daily Tribune* on 5 December 1857 (see present edition, Vol. 15).—197

239 *The New American Cyclopaedia* carried the article 'Blücher' by Marx and Engels without any sub-titles (see present edition, Vol. 18).—198

240 Marx proposed to meet Engels who was returning from Jersey to Manchester via London after his long stay at the seaside (see Note 183). The two friends did not meet, probably because of the 'bad arrangements of the railway Company in Brighton', as Engels wrote to Marx on 15 November 1857 (see p. 200). Marx may also have confused the date of Engels' arrival in London: he was to be there on 9 November (Monday) and not on the 5th (Thursday). So Marx's remark 'a week ago on Thursday' seems to be a mistake. Besides, from the above-mentioned letter of Engels it transpires that it was on the Monday that their meeting was to take place.—199

241 Marx seems to refer to his two articles ('The Revolt in India') published as leaders in the *New-York Daily Tribune* on 13 and 23 October 1857. When Marx wrote them, at the end of September and the beginning of October, he did not have sufficient information on the British siege of Delhi (which was finally captured on 20 September) and assumed that a successful storm of Delhi was hardly possible.—199

242 Engels' information on the rapid increase in exports of English textile goods to India was used by Marx in his article 'The Financial Crisis in Europe', published in the *New-York Daily Tribune* on 22 December 1857 (see present edition, Vol. 15).—202

243 The discovery of gold in California in 1848 and in Australia in 1851 helped to overcome the 1847 economic crisis and its aftermath. The temporary revival of industry and trade after the crisis was also due, to a certain extent, to European and American goods gaining access to the Chinese market as a result of the Anglo-Chinese war of 1840-42 (known as the first Opium War). In 1857, however, this access was hampered by a new military conflict of the European powers with China (see Note 134).—203

244 Ruge's intention to publish a new periodical to succeed to the *Deutsche Jahrbücher für Wissenschaft und Kunst* (published in 1841-43) did not materialise.—209, 227

245 Ernest Jones proposed as early as April 1857 to hold such a conference and to invite bourgeois radicals. In calling for an alliance with the radicals in order to campaign jointly for electoral reform Jones hoped to revive the mass Chartist movement on this basis. However, he made serious political concessions to the radicals when working out a common platform for uniting with them. Of the six points of the People's Charter (universal suffrage, annual Parliaments, vote by secret ballot, equal constituencies, abolition of property qualifications for candidates to Parliament, and payment of M.P.s) he retained only the demand

for universal manhood suffrage. Jones' conciliatory policy caused discontent among the rank-and-file of the National Charter Association. After repeated postponements a joint conference of Chartists and bourgeois radicals was convened in London on 8 February 1858. Marx and Engels regarded Jones' conciliation with the radicals as a manifestation of his political vacillation and broke off their friendly relations with him until a few years later, when Jones again adopted a revolutionary stand.—210, 249, 264, 375

246 George Peabody was a big American financier. From 1851 onwards, he gave annual dinners in London to British aristocrats and American guests to mark the anniversary of US independence (proclaimed on 4 July 1776).—212, 567

247 Engels' information on Hamburg bankruptcies was reproduced almost word for word by Marx in his article 'The Crisis in Europe', published in the *New-York Daily Tribune* on 5 January 1858 (see present edition, Vol. 15).—213

248 Marx dealt in greater detail with the consequences of the repeal of the Corn Laws during the crisis in his article 'The Financial Crisis in Europe', published in the *New-York Daily Tribune* on 22 December 1857 (see present edition, Vol. 15).—215

249 This refers to the *Hamburger Garantie-Diskonto-Verein* founded at the end of November 1857 in connection with the money crisis in Hamburg, to facilitate the circulation of bills and banknotes bearing the stamp of this association.—216

250 In the summer of 1857 Marx began to write a series of economic manuscripts in order to sum up and systematise the results of his extensive economic research started in the 1840s and continued most intensively in the 1850s. (In the first half of the 1850s he filled 24 paginated and several unpaginated notebooks with excerpts from the works of bourgeois economists, books of statistics, documents and periodicals.) These manuscripts were preliminary versions of an extensive economic work in which he intended to investigate the laws governing the development of capitalist production and to criticise bourgeois political economy. Marx outlined the main points of this treatise in an unfinished draft of the 'Introduction' (one of the first manuscripts of the series) and in letters to Engels, Lassalle and Weydemeyer (see pp. 298-304, 269-71, 286-87, 376-78). Further economic study prompted Marx to specify and change his original plan. The central place in the series is occupied by the extensive manuscript, *Critique of Political Economy* (widely known as the *Grundrisse*), on which Marx worked from October 1857 to May 1858. In this preliminary draft of his future *Capital* Marx expounded his theory of surplus value. After the first instalment had been prepared for publication in 1859 under the title *A Contribution to the Critique of Political Economy,* Marx added several more manuscripts to the series in 1861.

The manuscripts of 1857-61 were first published in German by the Institute of Marxism-Leninism of the CC CPSU in 1939 under the editorial heading *Grundrisse der Kritik der politischen Ökonomie (Rohentwurf).* These manuscripts and *A Contribution to the Critique of Political Economy. Part One* are included in Vols. 29 and 30 of the present edition.—217, 224, 226, 238, 244, 249, 256, 270, 287, 307, 499, 566.

251 This is a postscript to Mrs Marx's letter of 8 December 1857 to Conrad Schramm (see pp. 566-68).—217

252 Marx slightly changed the wording of this passage in his article 'The Crisis in

Europe' published in the *New-York Daily Tribune* on 5 January 1858, quoting it as a passage from a private letter from Manchester (see present edition, Vol. 15).—222

253 This idea did not materialise.—224

254 In his letter of 17 December 1857 to Marx, Lassalle enclosed a letter from his cousin Max Friedländer to Marx inviting him to contribute to the Vienna newspaper, *Die Presse.* Friedländer became one of its editors in 1856. Previously he had taken part in publishing the democratic paper *Neue Oder-Zeitung,* to which Marx also contributed throughout 1855. Not knowing the political line of *Die Presse* at the time, Marx did not agree, one of the reasons being probably the condition imposed by Friedländer: to criticise Napoleon III's policy and abstain from attacking Palmerston. In 1859 negotiations with Friedländer were resumed and lasted for a long time. Their success was hampered, on the one hand, by Lassalle's pro-Bonapartist statements during the Italian war of 1859 which evoked dissatisfaction on the part of Friedländer, who for a time thought that Marx approved of these statements, and on the other hand, by the editors' tendency to be duped by the pseudo-constitutional demagogy of the new Austrian government of Schmerling, which put Marx on the alert. Only in October 1861 when *Die Presse* criticised the government did Marx agree to be its London correspondent.—226, 227, 269, 272, 416, 418, 455, 571

255 *Crédit foncier* (Land Credit)—a French joint-stock bank set up in 1852 on the basis of the former Paris Land Bank. It granted short- and long-term loans on the security of immovable property at a definite interest. The Crédit foncier received considerable subsidies from the government.

Comptoir national d'Escompte de Paris (National Discount Bank of Paris) was founded in 1848 by the Provisional Government of the French Republic. Originally it discounted bills and granted credits on the security of goods stored in public warehouses. Under Napoleon III it became a joint-stock society (in 1853) and acquired the privilege of making advances on government bonds and shares of industrial and credit companies.—230

256 The *Zollverein,* a union of German states which established a common customs frontier, was set up in 1834 under the aegis of Prussia. Brought into being by the need to create an all-German market, the Customs Union subsequently embraced all the German states except Austria and a few of the smaller states.—230

257 Some of the thoughts expressed by Marx in this letter were developed in his article 'The Crisis in France', published in the *New-York Daily Tribune* on 12 January 1858 (see present edition, Vol. 15).—232

258 Further Engels refers to an episode in the Indian uprising of 1857-59 (see Note 178). After the fall of Delhi and Cawnpore in the summer of 1857, the centre of resistance to the British shifted to Oudh. A British garrison was besieged in Lucknow, the capital of that state, by the remnants of the Sepoy army and Oudh insurgents. General Havelock's force sent to relieve the garrison reached it in September but was compelled to remain besieged with it. It was not until November 1857 that the garrison was relieved by a force under General Colin Campbell from Cawnpore (Engels describes this episode). However, the insurgents' successful operations in Campbell's rear compelled him to leave Lucknow and return to Cawnpore. Campbell undertook another campaign to Lucknow three months later and captured the city on 19 March 1858.—234

259 According to Marx's notebook, on 27 November 1857 he sent two articles to *The New American Cyclopaedia*: Engels' 'Artillery' and his own 'Bugeaud'.—238

260 Engels' reply to Marx's letter of 22 December 1857 (see this volume, pp. 227-28) has not been found.—239, 242, 250

261 Engels' article 'Army' for *The New American Cyclopaedia* (on Marx's and Engels' contribution to the *Cyclopaedia* see Note 165) was published not in Vol. I but in Vol. II, which appeared in 1858.—239

262 On 7 January 1858 Engels sent Marx three 'C' articles: 'Campaign', 'Cannonade' and 'Captain', which, according to an entry in Marx's notebook, were despatched to New York the next day with Marx's articles 'The Siege and Storm of Lucknow' and 'Bolivar y Ponte'.—241, 244

263 The article 'Caps (Percussion)' was not printed in *The New American Cyclopaedia*.—241, 257, 259

264 Marx refers to statistical data on England's balance of trade and the cost of her imports and exports during the Crimean war, 1854-56. He obtained these figures from a report of the Manchester Foreign Affairs Committee (see Note 57), which was sent to him by the editors of the Urquhartite newspaper *The Free Press* before it was published. *The Free Press* itself did not publish it until 13 January 1858. Marx used these figures in his article 'British Commerce' (see present edition, Vol. 15).—243

265 During the march of General Campbell's troops from Cawnpore to Lucknow in November 1857 to relieve the garrison besieged by the Indian insurgents (see Note 258), General Windham's force, left behind to protect Cawnpore, was defeated by the insurgents on 27 November. This forced Campbell to return hastily to retake Cawnpore instead of consolidating in Lucknow. Later Engels described these events in the article 'Windham's Defeat', published in the *New-York Daily Tribune* on 20 February 1858 (see present edition, Vol. 15).—244

266 The original letter is dated 14 January 1858, which is an obvious slip of the pen. In fact the letter could not have been written earlier than 16 January for in it Marx informed Engels of Conrad Schramm's death on 15 January 1858, acknowledged receipt of Engels' article 'The Relief of Lucknow' despatched from Manchester to London on 14 January, as we see from Engels' letter of that date, and answered questions put to him in that same letter. Besides, in a letter to Engels on 23 January 1858 Marx mentioned this letter, saying it was 'sent off a week ago today', i. e., 16 January.

On the first English publication of this letter (datelined 14 January 1858) see Note 1.—248

267 Marx refers to the Great Redan, Bastion No. 3 of the Sevastopol fortifications, which was attacked by the British at the time of the allies' decisive storm of the fortress on 8 September 1855, during the Crimean war (1853-56) of Britain, France, Turkey and Piedmont against Russia. The storm was repulsed by Sevastopol defenders. On this episode and Windham's role in it see Engels' article 'The Great Event of the War' (present edition, Vol. 14).

On Windham's defeat by the Indian insurgents in November 1857 see Note 265.—249

268 Marx wrote about this in his articles on the Indian national liberation uprising, in particular in those published in the *New-York Daily Tribune*: 'The Revolt in India' (4 August 1857), 'Indian News' (14 August 1857), 'State of the Indian

Insurrection' (18 August 1857), etc. (present edition, Vol. 15).—249

269 On 22 January 1858 Marx made an entry in his notebook about the receipt from Engels and the despatch to New York of the second batch of 'C' articles for *The New American Cyclopaedia*, in particular 'Carabine', 'Carabineers', 'Carcass', 'Carronade', 'Cartouche', 'Cartridge' and 'Case Shot' (see present edition, Vol. 18). The article 'Carabineers' was not published in the *Cyclopaedia* nor has the manuscript been preserved.—251

270 At the end of his article 'Albuera' Engels noted that the siege of the French-held fortress of Badajos (Southwestern Spain) by the allied forces of Britain, Spain and Portugal was raised the day after their victory over the French at Albuera on 16 May 1811 (see present edition, Vol. 18, pp. 10-11). In fact the fortress was besieged by the allies three times during the Peninsular War between Britain and Napoleonic France. The first siege in May 1811 was lifted before the battle of Albuera because of the approaching French reserves. On 25 May, following the victory at Albuera, the allies resumed the siege but they were forced to raise it on 17 June. The allies laid siege to Badajos for the third time in March 1812 and took it on 6 April. As Engels pointed out in his letter to Marx on 18 February 1858 (see this volume, p. 267), the inaccuracy in the article 'Albuera' is accounted for by a mistake in one of the sources he used.—251, 252, 267

271 Marx refers to an attempt on the life of Napoleon III by the Italian revolutionary Felice Orsini on 14 January 1858. Orsini hoped thus to give an impetus to revolutionary actions in Europe and activate the struggle for Italy's unification. The attempt failed and Orsini was executed on 13 March of that year.—251, 255, 256, 257, 266, 271, 289

272 No special article on the 1857 national liberation uprising in India was written for *The New American Cyclopaedia*. Later the description of this uprising was included in the article 'Hindoostan' published in the *Cyclopaedia*.—252

273 Engels' letter to Harney has not been found.—253

274 As can be seen from an entry in Marx's notebook, on 29 January 1858 he sent to New York the following articles received from Engels together with this letter: 'Berme', 'Blenheim' and 'Borodino'. In view of a new request from Dana for 'B' articles, which Marx forwarded to Engels on 23 January (see this volume, p. 251), Engels put off 'C' articles and began fulfilling this request.—254

275 The amnesty of political emigrants who had taken part in the 1848-49 revolution in Germany was not proclaimed by the Prussian government until early 1861.—255, 266

276 Marx refers to the position of Louis Bonaparte as President of the French Republic before the coup d'état of 2 December 1851. His term as president was to expire early in May 1852, and according to the republic's Constitution a person could be elected to the post a second time only after a four-year interval. So Louis Bonaparte was in danger not only of losing his power and salary but also of being prosecuted for numerous debts.—256

277 Marx developed these ideas in his article 'An Attempt on Bonaparte' published in the *New-York Daily Tribune* on 22 February 1858 (see present edition, Vol. 15).—256

278 Lassalle's book on political economy was published in Berlin only in 1864 under

the title *Herr Bastiat-Schulze von Delitzsch, der Ökonomische Julian, oder: Capital und Arbeit.*—261, 355, 396, 542, 547

279 Marx alludes to the peak of the 1857-58 economic crisis experienced by the Manchester businessmen. He calls it the 'Sturm- und Drangperiode' by analogy with the well-known literary movement in Germany in the last three decades of the 18th century, which reflected the discontent of progressive sections of society with the feudal absolutist systems in German states.—263

280 In 1842 bourgeois radical Free Traders made attempts to obtain control of the Chartist movement. To divert the workers from the Chartists' social and political programme they put forward a vague demand for what they called 'complete suffrage'. Joseph Sturge, Edward Miall, Joseph Livesay and other radicals, supported by some conciliatory-minded Chartist leaders (Lovett and others), managed to convoke two conferences of bourgeois radicals and Chartists in Birmingham in 1842 to discuss a joint campaign for electoral reform. However, the Chartist majority at the conferences rejected the proposal to substitute a new 'Bill of Rights' and the 'complete suffrage' demand for the People's Charter, which led to a break between the Chartists and radicals.—264

281 After Orsini's attempt on the life of Napoleon III on 14 January 1858, *Le Moniteur universel* and other official newspapers began publishing chauvinistic addresses of loyalty by higher social and military circles. Many of them accused Britain of granting asylum to terrorists and assassins like Orsini and demanded that they be persecuted in their 'den'. The publication of these addresses was regarded in Britain as an indirect threat and caused an aggravation of Anglo-French relations in 1858.—264

282 When Marx wrote the article 'Bolivar y Ponte', the history of the Latin American countries' war for independence (1810-26) had not yet been adequately studied. Books and memoirs by European adventurers who had taken part in the war out of mercenary motives were widely read at the time (among them Ducoudray Holstein, a Frenchman who had become Bolivar's personal enemy, and the Englishman G. Hippisley). The authors of these books attributed numerous vices to Bolivar (perfidity, arrogance, cowardice) and presented his struggle against federalist and separatist elements for the unification of the Latin American republics as a striving for dictatorship. In reality, Simon Bolivar played an outstanding role in the struggle of several Latin American countries for liberation from the Spanish yoke, the establishment of republican forms of government and for progressive bourgeois reforms.

Marx had only the above-mentioned biassed sources at his disposal. Hence his inevitably one-sided view of Bolivar's personality in his article, in this letter and in *Herr Vogt* written later (see present edition, Vol. 17): His attitude to Bolivar was to a certain extent determined by the fact that the sources he used exaggerated Bolivar's striving for personal power, and over-emphasised the Bonapartist features against which Marx and Engels were then waging a relentless struggle. Nevertheless, Marx pointed out the progressive aspects of Bolivar's activity, such as his emancipation of Negro slaves, and on the whole appreciated the revolutionary anti-colonial struggle for national liberation in Latin America.—266

283 Marx alludes to the rumours about the illegitimate birth of Napoleon III, whose official father was Napoleon I's brother Louis Bonaparte, King of Holland in 1806-10.—266

284 Marx refers to an article in *Cobbett's Annual Register. From July to December, 1802* (Vol. II, London, 1810, columns 128-33) on the aggravation of Anglo-French relations during Napoleon's consulate because of the anti-Napoleonic statements in the press by French political refugees in England. Later Marx used this article and passages quoted in it from *Le Moniteur universel,* No. 320, 9 August 1802, for his article 'The French Trials in London' published in the *New-York Daily Tribune* on 27 April 1858 (see present edition, Vol. 15).—266

285 Engels presumably refers to his articles 'Camp' and 'Catapult' for *The New American Cyclopaedia.* Marx helped Engels to collect material for them (see, for example, Marx's letter to Engels of 1 February 1858). There is no entry in Marx's notebook about their despatch to New York. It is quite possible that Engels sent Marx the article 'Coehorn' with 'Camp' and 'Catapult'.—267

286 An excerpt from this letter was first published in English in Marx and Engels, *Selected Correspondence,* Foreign Languages Publishing House, Moscow, 1955 and in full in *The Letters of Karl Marx,* selected and translated with explanatory notes and an introduction by Saul K. Padover, Prentice-Hall, Inc., Englewood Cliff, New Jersey, 1979.—268

287 After Orsini's attempt on the life of Napoleon III, Count Walewski, Foreign Minister of France, sent the British government a despatch on 20 January 1858 expressing his discontent at Britain's granting asylum to French political refugees. The despatch served as a pretext for Palmerston to introduce a new Aliens Bill, also called Conspiracy to Murder Bill (see Note 16), on 8 February 1858. According to this Bill, anyone living in the United Kingdom, an Englishman or a foreigner, who took part in a conspiracy to murder a person in Britain or any other country, was to be tried by an English court and severely punished. During the second reading of the new Aliens Bill the radicals Milner Gibson and John Bright, who had been defeated at the parliamentary elections in March 1857, when the Whigs, Palmerston's adherents, came to power, but were re-elected in the autumn of that year, moved an amendment censuring Palmerston's government for failing to give a fitting reply to Walewski's despatch. The House of Commons adopted the amendment by a majority vote, rejected the Bill and compelled Palmerston's government to resign.—273, 275

288 Marx analyses the state of France's economy, including agriculture, in early 1858 in his article 'The Economic Crisis in France' published in the *New-York Daily Tribune* on 12 March 1858 (see present edition, Vol. 15).—273

289 A reference to the second Anglo-Burmese war (1852) which resulted in the British capture of the Province of Pegu.—274

290 By '*2 cives romani* [Roman citizens]' Engels means the British Prime Minister Palmerston and Napoleon III. (He alludes here to the Latin expression 'civis Romanus sum'—'I am a Roman citizen' cited by Palmerston in his speech in the House of Commons on 25 June 1850.) Engels has in mind in particular their intention to send an English and a French squadron to the shores of Naples at the end of 1856 under the pretext of bringing pressure to bear on the reactionary regime there (see Note 103), and their repressive measures against democrats in France and Britain after Orsini's attempt on the life of Napoleon III.—276

291 Neither this letter, sent off apparently at the end of February 1858, nor Marx's letter to Collet mentioned below have been found.—277

292 A *cabinet noir* (black bureau)—a secret Post Office institution in France, Prussia, Austria and other states to inspect private correspondence. It existed at the time of absolute monarchies in Europe.—277, 279

293 In their 'Letter to the Parliament and the Press' of 24 February 1858 (an English translation was published in London as a separate booklet), Pyat, Besson and Talandier stated that the crowned personages who usurped political power as Napoleon III had done, deserved to die a violent death and that their assassination would be a justified historical act. The letter caused excitement among British ruling circles and in the British press. Marx sharply criticised such adventurist statements by French petty-bourgeois refugees and their terroristic ideas.—278, 279

294 An allusion to Félix Pyat, who contributed to the French satirical journal *Le Charivari* in the 1830s and 1840s and wrote a number of plays for the Théâtre du Port Saint-Martin (Paris).—278

295 The *Honourable Gentleman opposite*—a form of address used in the British Parliament in respect of an M.P. in the opposition.—278

296 Engels means the German liberals and petty-bourgeois democrats who supported the German Imperial Constitution of 1849 (see Note 116).—279

297 Marx refers to a letter he received from Friedrich Kamm dated 19 December 1857. Kamm, a German refugee in America, wrote that he and his friends had set up a Communist Club in New York and asked Marx to send him information about the communist movement in Europe, certain theoretical works and Communist League documents. He also asked for practical advice in organising the work of a newly founded club. Marx's reply has not been found, but his letter to Joseph Weydemeyer of 1 February 1859 shows that he corresponded with Albrecht Komp, another leader of the New York Communist Club (see this volume, p. 376).—282, 288, 293, 469

298 In 1806, an English expedition under Captain Popam and General Beresford was sent to capture Buenos Aires, which belonged to Spain, then an ally of Napoleonic France. Meeting with no serious resistance from the Spanish colonial authorities, Beresford's force seized Buenos Aires but was surrounded and compelled to surrender by the Argentine patriots.—285

299 This letter is Marx's reply to Lassalle's letter of 3 March 1858, containing a number of questions regarding the publication of Marx's economic work (see this volume, pp. 269-71).

On the first English publication of Marx's letter see Note 82.—286

300 The *Seven Years War* (1756-63)—a war of Britain and Prussia against Austria, France, Russia, Saxony and Sweden. As a result of it France ceded many of its colonies (including Canada and almost all its possessions in the East Indies) to Britain, while Prussia, Austria and Saxony were obliged to recognise in the main its pre-war frontiers.—289, 294, 561

301 Engels refers to the underground gallery connecting the Tuileries Palace with the Seine embankment, where some participants in the June 1848 uprising in Paris were detained after its defeat.—290

302 In his letter to the Editor of *The Times,* published in the newspaper on 17 March 1858 (issue No. 22943), the English poet W. S. Landor refuted the evidence of some witnesses concerning his participation in Orsini's attempt on

the life of Napoleon III, expressed indignation at this, 'the basest of crimes', called the Emperor 'the most legitimate *sovran* in the universe', and declared that he 'detests and abominates democracy'.—290

303 The *Legitimists*—supporters of the Bourbon dynasty overthrown in 1830. They upheld the interests of the big hereditary landowners.

During the Second Republic the Orleanists (see Note 124) and the Legitimists formed the 'party of Order', an influential conservative bloc in the Legislative Assembly (1849-51), which Engels has in mind when he speaks, further on in the text, about the joint rule of these groups under the constitutional-republican system.—291, 552

304 A reference to *La loi relatif à des mesures de sûreté générale* (Law on Public Security Measures) known as *La loi des suspects* (Suspects Law) adopted by the Corps législatif (see Note 123) on 19 February and promulgated on 28 February 1858. It gave the Emperor and his government unlimited power to exile to different parts of France or Algeria or to banish altogether from French territory any person suspected of hostility to the Second Empire.—291

305 Engels refers to the marriage in London on 25 January 1858 of Frederick William, the son of Prince William of Prussia (later King and Emperor William I), and the English Princess Victoria Adelaide Marie Louise, Queen Victoria's eldest daughter.—292

306 In 1848, during the Second Republic, the monarchist Louis Adolphe Thiers actively supported Louis Bonaparte's candidature for the presidency. But later, as a leader of the Orleanist wing of the 'party of Order' plotting the restoration of the Orleans dynasty, he and other members of the party entered into conflict with Louis Bonaparte and his *entourage*. During the Bonapartist coup d'état of 2 December 1851 Thiers was arrested and, after a short detention in the Mazas prison in Paris, was banished from France. Upon his return in August 1852 he became a member of the 'society opposition'.—292

307 Marx refers to a conference of the delegates of the *Italian National Constitutional League*, the liberal-minded big bourgeoisie and nobility, held in London on 1 March 1858. It adopted a number of mainly declarative resolutions, proclaiming the necessity to form a federation of Italian states, introduce a Constitution preserving the monarchic government, and carry out a number of liberal reforms. A special resolution condemned Orsini's attempt on the life of Napoleon III.—294

308 Under Napoleon III's decree of 27 January 1858 the whole of French territory was divided into five military districts, with Paris, Nancy, Lyons, Toulouse and Tours as their centres and Marshals Magnan, Baraguay d'Hilliers, Bosquet, Castellane and Canrobert as their commanders. Marx calls these districts *pashaliks* (a comparison earlier used by the French republican press), to emphasise the similarity of the unlimited powers of the reactionary Marshals and the despotic power of the Turkish pashas.—296

309 *Captain-generalships*—administrative districts set up in Spain and its colonies in the sixteenth century, during the period of absolute monarchy. Civil and military power in these districts was concentrated in the hands of captain-generals, who acted as royal governors.—296

310 Thomas Attwood's views on the ideal unit of money were set forth in the book *The Currency Question. The Gemini Letters*, London, 1844, written anonymously by T. B. Wright and J. Harlow who called themselves 'Gemini'.—301

311 The *Cotton Supply Association*—a Free Trade organisation founded in Manchester in 1857 to promote the import of cotton from India, Africa and other countries.—305

312 *Laissez-faire, laissez-aller*—the formula of economists who advocated Free Trade and non-intervention by the state in economic relations.—305

313 This is the reply to Mrs Marx's letter to Engels of 9 April 1858 (see this volume, pp. 569).—307

314 Surgeon Simon Bernard, a Frenchman living in London, was tried as an accomplice in Felice Orsini's attempt on the life of Napoleon III (manufacture of bombs and so on). The trial took place in London from 12 to 17 April 1858. Bernard was acquitted by the Central Criminal Court on 17 April.—307, 309

315 In April 1858 the Chamber of Representatives of the Kingdom of Piedmont discussed a conspiracy bill. Introduced at the request of Napoleon III's government, it envisaged measures against attempts on the life of foreign monarchs. During the debate on 16 and 17 April, Prime Minister Cavour and General La Marmora recalled the summer 1848 events and exposed the policy of the bourgeois republican general Cavaignac, then head of the executive in France, who refused to support revolutionary Italy in her struggle against Austria.—309

316 Marx refers to the Government Commission on the Workers' Question which met at the Palais du Luxembourg and was presided over by Louis Blanc. The Commission was set up on 28 February 1848 by the Provisional Government of the French Republic under pressure from workers who demanded a Ministry of Labour. It consisted of workers and employers and acted as a mediator in labour conflicts, often taking the side of the employers. On the very next day after the mass actions of 15 May 1848, the government disbanded the Luxembourg Commission.—310

317 Later Marx wrote two articles on this subject: 'A Curious Piece of History' and 'Another Strange Chapter of Modern History', published in the *New-York Daily Tribune* on 16 June and 23 September 1858.—310

318 Marx stayed with Engels in Manchester from 6 to about 24 May. To recover his health he practised sport, riding, etc. While in Manchester Marx continued working on the economic manuscript of 1857-58 (see Note 250), intending to complete his research and begin preparations for publication of the first part of his work, *A Contribution to the Critique of Political Economy*.—312, 315, 368

319 Marx refers to Napoleon III's representation to the Council of State on the introduction of a law on confiscation of landed property of philanthropic institutions and converting it into state interest-bearing securities.

Marx discussed this problem at length in his article 'Bonaparte's Financial Manoeuvres.—Military Despotism' (present edition, Vol. 15).—317

320 Marx received Engels' article 'Cavalry', written for *The New American Cyclopaedia*, by 22 June 1858 and, as seen from an entry in his notebook, sent it off to New York the same day.—323

321 Marx means J. Weydemeyer's letter of 28 February 1858 from Milwaukee and A. Komp's letter of 15 June 1858 from New York, both written to him. Marx did not enclose them in his letter to Engels and they were mislaid among his papers. Some time later, Marx found them and replied to Weydemeyer on 1 February 1859 (see this volume, pp. 374-78). His letter to Komp has not been

found but we may judge of its contents by the above-mentioned letter to Weydemeyer. Komp was a leader of the New York Communist Club, and his letter to Marx contained information and requests similar to those contained in a letter from Friedrich Kamm, another leader of the Club, written on 19 December 1857 (see Note 297). After replying to his American correspondents, Marx forwarded their letters to Engels on 9 February 1859 (see this volume, pp. 384-85).—324, 326, 337, 339, 374, 384

322 *Whitechapel*—a working class district in London's East End.—331, 449

323 The *People's Provident Assurance Society* was founded by John Watts, an English reformer and Owenite, in London in 1853. In 1857 a branch-office was opened in Manchester.—332

324 Marx's letter to his mother has not been found.—334

325 This presumably refers to Engels' article written between 16 and 20 July 1858 and published in the *New-York Daily Tribune* on 13 August. Marx made an entry in his notebook on 27 July about the despatch of the article to New York, giving its heading as 'Transport of Troops to India' (see present edition, Vol. 15). The *Tribune* editors introduced changes into the article and printed it under the heading 'How the Indian War has been Mismanaged'.—334

326 The original letter is dated 4 August 1858, which is presumably a slip of the pen, for in it Marx mentions events about which he could have learned from the newspapers only later: the opening of the Cherbourg naval port after its reconstruction and the actions of Napoleon III's government in connection with this. Engels' reply of 10 August 1858 warrants the assumption that Marx wrote the letter on 8 August.

On the first English publication of the letter see Note 20.—335

327 This seems to refer to Engels' letter in reply to Marx's letter of 25 July 1858 (see this volume, p. 334). The letter has not been found.—335

328 Marx refers to the festivities on the occasion of the opening, on 4 August 1858, of the Cherbourg naval port after its reconstruction.

On the invitation of the French government, Queen Victoria of the United Kingdom and the Prince Consort Albert attended the ceremony. According to Napoleon III's plans, the reception given them was to relax the tension in Anglo-French relations after Orsini's attempt on the life of Napoleon III (see Note 271). However, the demonstration of France's naval strength in Cherbourg aroused new British apprehensions. In this connection Napoleon declared in a Note of 7 August 1858 that the reconstruction of the naval port did not pursue any hostile aims towards Britain.—336, 339, 340

329 Félix Pyat's letter was written on 14 July 1858 and published separately under the title *Lettre au jury. Défence de la lettre au Parlement et à la Presse.* It supplemented the letter of 24 February 1858 by Pyat, Besson and Talandier (see Note 293).—339, 345

330 The article on the slave trade in Cuba written by Marx for the *New-York Daily Tribune* was not published.—340

331 Marx refers to his articles 'The English Bank Act of 1844' and 'Commercial Crises and Currency in Britain', printed in the *New-York Daily Tribune* on 23 and 28 August 1858 as leaders, and 'British Commerce and Finance', published on 4 October.—342

332 Marx refers to the unequal treaties signed in Tientsin in June 1858 by Britain

and France with China during the second Opium War (1856-60). The treaties made new ports available to foreign trade; foreign diplomatic representatives were authorised in Peking; foreigners were allowed to travel freely in the country for commercial or other purposes; Britain and France received economic privileges through the introduction of new commercial rules legalising the opium trade, and were paid indemnities.

Marx discussed these treaties in his articles written in August and early September for the *New-York Daily Tribune:* 'History of the Opium Trade' and 'The Anglo-Chinese Treaty' (see present edition, Vol. 16). However, the article mentioned in this letter was not published in the *Tribune.*—342, 347, 362, 387

333 Engels refers to the official despatches of Lord Canning, Governor General of India, of 17 June and 4 July 1858 to the Secret Committee of the Court of Directors of the British East India Company (they were published in *The Times,* No. 23117, 6 October 1858).

In these despatches Canning defended his proclamation of 3 March 1858 on the confiscation, in favour of Britain, of the lands of Oudh, including the estates of the local feudal lords who had joined the Indian uprising. (Marx assessed this proclamation in his article 'The Annexation of Oudh' published in the *New-York Daily Tribune* on 28 May 1858; see present edition, Vol. 15.) Canning's point of view was not shared by a number of prominent colonial officials and M.P.s who favoured a more flexible policy towards the Indian feudal lords and hoped to win them over with promises to leave their domains intact.

Marx did not write any article about Canning's despatches.—343

334 Engels seems to refer to Jones' speech at a Chartist meeting in Manchester on 4 October 1858, a brief account of which was published in *The Leader,* No. 446, 9 October 1858, in the 'Political Foreshadowings' section.

About Jones' temporary vacillations and his policy of compromise with bourgeois radicals see Note 245.—344, 345

335 Marx writes here about the revolutionary situation in Russia after her defeat in the Crimean war (1853-56). Fearing the growing peasant unrest, Alexander II's government was forced to start preparations for the abolition of serfdom. On 3 January 1857 a Secret Committee consisting of high government officials and headed by the Emperor was formed to discuss the peasant question. In January 1858 the Committee was made public and renamed the Chief Peasant Question Committee.

To discuss the draft peasant reform, it was proposed to hold in St. Petersburg a congress of deputies of the Gubernia Landowners' Committees, called by Marx the 'convocation of notables' by analogy with the convocation of notables in France on the eve of the French Revolution. The congress took place in the autumn of 1859.—346, 349

336 In view of the insanity of Frederick William IV of Prussia the question arose of appointing Regent his brother, Prince William of Prussia (later King and Emperor William I). The Prussian bourgeoisie hoped that the Regency would lead to liberal reforms and remove Manteuffel's reactionary ministry, although the reactionary measures taken by the Prince of Prussia in 1848 gave little ground for such hopes. Nevertheless, similar illusions about the advent of 'a new era' were widespread among liberal monarchist circles. Prince William was appointed Regent on 7 October 1858.—346, 348, 410, 470, 571

337 In his book *Studien über die innern Zustände, das Volksleben und insbesondere die*

ländlichen Einrichtungen Russlands (Th. 1-3, Hannover-Berlin, 1847-52), the Prussian official and writer August Haxthausen who toured Russia in the 1840s, gavc a false idea of the material well-being of the Russian peasantry. He advocated preservation of the peasant commune arguing that this was the only way to save Russia from the revolutionary consequences of its toiling people becoming proletarian. He thought that the abolition of serfdom should be carried out gradually because, he wrote, the necessary conditions for the wage labour system did not exist in Russia.—346

338 This refers to one of the main provisions of the *Nanking Treaty* Britain concluded with China as a result of the Anglo-Chinese war of 1840-42 (known as the first Opium War). It was the first of a series of unequal treaties imposed on China by the Western powers, treaties that reduced it to the status of a semi-colony. Under the Nanking Treaty five Chinese cities—Canton, Shanghai, Amoy, Ninbo and Fuchon—were opened to English trade.—347

339 Under the *Aigun Treaty* of 28(16) May 1858, the left bank of the Amur, from the confluence of the Shilka and the Argun to the sea, was recognised as Russian territory, while the question of the Ussuri Area, from the confluence of the Ussuri and the Amur to the sea, was left open until the final fixing of the frontier between Russia and China. Navigation on the Amur, Sungari and Ussuri was prohibited to all states except Russia and Ching China. The treaty thus returned to Russia the left bank of the Amur developed by the Russians in the seventeenth century and taken from it under the Nerchinsk Treaty of 1689. Besides, it thwarted the British diplomats' attempt to exacerbate Russo-Chinese relations and closed the Amur to West-European shipping. The treaty was ratified by Russia on 8 June 1858.—349

340 This letter is dated only 'Friday'. The exact date of its writing was established on the basis of facts mentioned in it, in particular Marx's reference to an article on rifled cannon published in *The Times* on 22 October 1858.—350

341 Marx seems to refer to his article 'Mr. John Bright' printed in the *New-York Daily Tribune* on 12 November 1858 as a leader, without any heading. It bears signs of the editors' interference (see present edition, Vol. 16).—350

342 A reference to the conflict between France and Portugal caused by the seizure of the French merchant vessel *Charles et Georges* by the Portuguese authorities in Mozambique on 29 November 1857. The vessel had on board a number of East-African Negroes who were to be shipped, allegedly as free emigrants, to the French island of Réunion.

The Franco-Portuguese talks continued for almost a year but brought no results. On 13 October 1858 Napoleon III, whom Marx calls here Quasimodo (a character from Victor Hugo's *Notre-Dame de Paris*), sent a special Note to the Portuguese Government demanding the return of the confiscated vessel and the release of its captain. The demand was backed by the despatch of two French warships to the Portuguese capital. Portugal was compelled to yield.

Marx touches on the subject in his article 'The French Slave Trade' published in the *New-York Daily Tribune* on 1 December 1858 with considerable editorial changes (see present edition, Vol. 16, pp. 621-23).—351, 357

343 This presumably refers to Blind's articles published anonymously in 1858 under the general heading *Flügblätter des Vereins 'Deutsche Einheit und Freiheit' in England.*—351, 353

344 John Bright, a British radical and Free Trade leader, put forward a

programme for electoral reform. Of the six points of the People's Charter (universal suffrage, annual Parliaments, vote by secret ballot, equal constituencies, abolition of property qualifications for candidates to Parliament, and payment of M.P.s), he retained only the demand for vote by secret ballot. The other demands were either omitted altogether or drastically moderated. Thus Bright suggested that suffrage should be granted only to persons paying property tax; in place of equal constituencies he suggested fairer representation for the existing constituencies.—358

345 Marx refers to Freiligrath's letter to him of 6 December 1858 and Freiligrath's poem 'Nach Johanna Kinkels Begräbnis' (written on 20 November 1858 on the occasion of the death of Cottfried Kinkel's wife, Johanna Kinkel, and published in *Die Neue Zeit,* No. 24, 11 December 1859).—359

346 *Cayenne*—a place in French Guiana where political prisoners were sent for penal servitude. The high mortality caused by the hard prison conditions and the unhealthy tropical climate earned it the nickname of the 'Dry Guillotine'.—359

347 Marx is mistaken here. Fitzgerald and Stanley could not have spoken in the House of Commons on Monday, 13 December, for Parliament did not meet from 2 August 1858 to early January 1859. On 14 December *The Times* (No. 23176) reprinted excerpts from Lord Stanley's speech of 13 December 1858 before the young cadets of the Manchester military school, one of the topics being the situation in India. (The speech was reported in greater detail in *The Manchester Guardian.*) Fitzgerald too may have spoken at this meeting. This warrants the assumption that Marx actually meant these speeches.—363

348 Marx means his new article on the Anglo-Chinese Treaty. It was not published by the *New-York Daily Tribune.*—363

349 In his Message to the XXXVth Congress of 6 December 1858, President James Buchanan expressed US aggressive intentions as regards Costa Rica, Nicaragua, Brazil, Paraguay and other countries of Central and South America and US strivings for supremacy on the American continent. In the sphere of home policy, Buchanan asked Congress to increase allocations for the navy and the Postal Department in 1858 and urged the construction of a Pacific railroad.

Marx's article about Buchanan's message was not published by the *New-York Daily Tribune.*—364

350 Marx had asked Engels to write an article for the *New-York Daily Tribune* about the events in the principality of Serbia. On 30 November 1858 the so-called St. Andrew Skupština met after a long interval. At the session, the liberals, who had joined forces with the supporters of the Obrenović dynasty, clashed with the ruling Ustavobranitelji (Defenders of Constitution) group representing the big landowners, traders and the top officialdom. The conflict led to the deposition of Alexander Karageorgiević and the reinstatement of Miloš Obrenović, who agreed to carry out a number of liberal reforms. The St. Andrew Skupština abolished the oligarchic council set up under the 1838 Constitution, restored the Skupština as a permanent legislative body, and declared freedom of the press. Though the liberal reforms were moderate and short-lived, the fall of the Ustavobranitelji regime gave an impulse to Serbia's economic and cultural development.

It is unknown whether Engels wrote the article on Serbia.—364, 366

351 Presumably Engels did not write any article on the proposed changes in the Prussian army. Later, when France and Piedmont were on a collision course with

Austria, he wrote the article 'German Resources for War' (on 10 February 1859) in which he also described the state of Prussia's armed forces (see present edition, Vol. 16).—366, 368

352 Gottfried Kinkel called his weekly after Arminius (Hermann), the leader of the Germanic tribes' struggle against Roman rule in the first century A. D. Marx hints at the coincidence of this title with the name of the hero of Goethe's poem 'Hermann und Dorothea', a simple, patriarchally-minded man striving for peace and a domestic idyll.—366

353 The prospectus for the *Hermann* was an advertisement announcing the forthcoming publication of the weekly, dated 24 December 1858 and signed by Kinkel.

Marx's letter to Freiligrath about 'the Kinkel affair' has not been found.—367

354 The letter is not dated. The approximate time of its writing has been established on the basis of the facts mentioned in it, in particular the reference to Marx's rewriting of Engels' article on Napoleon III's policy, as a result of which the article 'The Money Panic in Europe' virtually written by them both, was sent to New York, its final version having been written on 13 January 1859 (see present edition, Vol. 16). The letter could hardly have been sent off to Manchester later than 15 January because, judging by its opening lines, Marx was expecting a new article for the *New-York Daily Tribune* from Engels by Tuesday, 18 January.—367

355 Marx means the 'Chapter on Capital', which constitutes the bulk of his economic manuscripts of 1857-58 (see Note 250) and was written from October 1857 to May 1858 (see present edition, Vols. 29 and 30).—368, 389

356 In the autumn of 1858, Palmerston, then head of the Whig opposition to the Derby-Disraeli Tory Cabinet, was invited by Napoleon III to Compiègne in order to clarify his position on the impending Franco-Austrian war. At the meeting Palmerston did not object to the Austrians being expelled from Italy, but in his speech at the opening of Parliament on 3 February 1859 he condemned France's action.

On Russia's influence on Napoleon III's policy see Marx's article 'The War Prospect in France' (present edition, Vol. 16).

The *Peace Treaty of Paris* concluded the Crimean war (1853-56). It was signed at the Congress of Paris on 30 March 1856 by Austria, Britain, France, Prussia, Sardinia and Turkey, on the one hand, and Russia, on the other. Under the treaty, Russia ceded the mouth of the Danube and part of Bessarabia, renounced its protectorate over the Danubian principalities and its protection of Christians in Turkey, agreed to the neutralisation of the Black Sea and returned the fortress of Kars to Turkey in exchange for Sevastopol and other Russian towns held by the Allies. By skilfully exploiting the differences between Britain and France the Russian diplomats at the Congress blocked the attempts to impose even more onerous peace terms on Russia.—368, 411, 431

357 This draft of Engels' letter to Freiligrath was enclosed by Engels in his letter to Marx of 27 January 1859 (see this volume, p. 373). As follows from that letter, a three-page fair copy was sent to Freiligrath on 26 January. Neither the fair copy nor the other draft versions which Engels made while writing the letter have been preserved.—370

358 In a letter to Engels that has not reached us Freiligrath probably wrote about

the projected publication of a new revolutionary newspaper which was to be a sequel to the *Neue Rheinische Zeitung,* organ of the proletarian wing of the democratic movement during the 1848-49 revolution in Germany. Freiligrath seems to have given an incorrect interpretation of the trend of the future newspaper as against that of the petty-bourgeois weekly *Hermann* which Gottfried Kinkel began to publish on 1 January 1859.—370, 372

359 Engels paraphrases the dictum 'They have learned nothing and forgotten nothing', which during the restoration of the Bourbons (1815-30) was often applied to their conservative supporters who had failed to draw any lessons from the French Revolution. The dictum was first used, also in referring to the French extreme royalists, by Rear Admiral Chevalier de Panat in a letter to the journalist Mallet du Pan in 1796. In later years it was often attributed to Charles Talleyrand.—370

360 The handwritten weekly *Der Maikäfer, eine Zeitschrift für Nicht-Philister* (May-Bug, a Journal for Non-Philistines) was founded by Gottfried Kinkel and Johanna Mockel in Bonn in 1840, at the time when the literary May-Bug Club was set up. With the outbreak of the revolution in Germany in 1848, both the journal and the club ceased to exist. Marx and Engels gave an ironic characterisation of the periodical and the club in the pamphlet *The Great Men of the Exile* (see present edition, Vol. 11, p. 244).—370

361 The letter is not dated. The approximate time of its writing has been established on the basis of a reply letter from Engels. The article mentioned below was not published by the editors of the *New-York Daily Tribune.*—371, 373

362 Between September 1851 and March 1852 Gottfried Kinkel toured America in an attempt to raise a so-called German-American revolutionary loan. It was to be floated among German refugees and Americans of German extraction and used to begin an immediate revolution in Germany. During the tour Kinkel conducted a slanderous campaign against Marx and Engels. The attempt to distribute the 'revolutionary loan' failed. Marx and Engels in a number of works and letters denounced the undertaking as an adventurist attempt to produce a revolution artificially during a period when the revolutionary movement was on the wane.—372

363 Marx's description of Princess Clotilde, daughter of King Victor Emmanuel of Piedmont (Sardinia), as a 'mild, angelic child' is clearly ironic. When writing about her forthcoming marriage to Napoleon III's cousin, Jerôme Bonaparte (nicknamed Plon-Plon), in his article 'Louis Napoleon's Position' mentioned in this letter, Marx notes that Clotilde, 'despite her young years, is very strong-minded' (Vol. 16, p. 169).—373

364 See Note 45.—374, 567

365 Marx is mistaken here: Georg Weerth died in Havana, Cuba (see Note 85).—374

366 In 1751 J. Ch. Gottsched published in Leipzig an epic poem by Ch. O. von Schönaich devoted to Arminius (Hermann), the leader of the Germanic tribes that had revolted against Roman rule. Gottsched supplied the poem with a laudatory preface, and on his recommendation the Leipzig University crowned Schönaich with the laurels of a poet in 1752.—375

367 The *'great men'* (die 'großen Männer') was the nickname Marx and Engels

applied to German and other refugees, primarily petty-bourgeois democrats, who after the 1848-49 revolution engaged in pseudo-revolutionary activities, organised plots, raised 'revolutionary loans', formed governments in exile, and the like. In their joint work *The Great Men of the Exile* (present edition, Vol. 11) Marx and Engels gave a satirical description of some of them.—376, 500, 502

368 In its issue of 19 October 1711, *The Spectator* propounded the idea that the price of commodities depended on the mass of money in circulation, a view shared by Montesquieu and Hume. In criticising this view in his *A Contribution to the Critique of Political Economy,* Marx referred to this issue of the journal (present edition, Vol. 30).—377

369 In his article 'The French Army' sent to the *New-York Daily Tribune* on 31 January 1859, Engels opposed his calculations concerning the strength of the forces France could field in Italy in case of war to the exaggerated figures contained in Louis Boniface's article datelined Paris, 29 January 1859, which appeared in the *Constitutionnel,* No. 30, on 30 January 1859. Engels pointed out that the *Constitutionnel* data had been furnished by the Emperor himself (see present edition, Vol. 16, p. 171). A report of 31 January from Paris, published in *The Times,* No. 23219, on 2 February 1859, stated outright that Napoleon III, whom Marx calls in this letter Mr Boustrapa (see Note 40), was the author of the article in the *Constitutionnel.*—379

370 This refers to the war preparations of the Kingdom of Sardinia (Piedmont) and France against Austria. The war (29 April to 8 July 1859) was launched by Napoleon III, who under the banner of the 'liberation of Italy' strove for aggrandizement and needed a successful military campaign to shore up the Bonapartist regime in France. Piedmont ruling circles hoped that French support would enable them to unite Italy under the aegis of the Savoy dynasty. The war caused an upsurge of the national liberation movement in Italy. The Austrian army suffered a series of defeats. However Napoleon III, frightened by the scale of the liberation movement in Italy, abruptly ceased hostilities. On 11 July, the French and Austrian emperors concluded a separate preliminary peace in Villafranca. France received Savoy and Nice; Lombardy was annexed to Sardinia; the Venetian Region remained under the Austrians.—380, 399, 401, 405, 462, 537

371 Marx refers here to the *Carbonari,* members of secret political societies in Italy and France in the first half of the nineteenth century. In Italy they fought for national independence, unification of the country and liberal constitutional reforms.

In the latter half of the 1850s a number of attempts were made on the life of Napoleon III, including one by the Italian revolutionary Orsini (see Note 271). Some of these attempts were attributed to the desire to teach Napoleon III a lesson for the breach of his commitments to the Carbonari organisation, of which he was a member in 1831. Part of the questions touched upon in this letter are discussed in the articles 'The Money Panic in Europe' by Marx and Engels, 'Louis Napoleon's Position' by Marx and 'The French Army' by Engels (all three are in Vol. 16 of the present edition).—380

372 The *Rubicon*—the name of a river in Northern Italy, on the boundary between Umbria and Cisalpine Gaul, which Caesar crossed with his army in 49 B.C. thereby starting a civil war with Pompey. *To cross* (or *pass*) *the Rubicon*—to embark on an undertaking from which one cannot turn back.—381

373 Marx refers to the abortive Bonapartist coups in Boulogne on 6 August 1840

and Strasbourg on 30 October 1836, and to the coup d'état in Paris on 2 December 1851 which led to the establishment of Napoleon III's dictatorship and the proclamation of the Second Empire in 1852.—381

374 Marx probably means the tribute to Johanna Mockel, Gottfried Kinkel's wife, published in *The Daily Telegraph* by the German writer Fanny Lewald (Stahr). Marx mentions it in his letter to Lassalle of 3 March 1860 (see present edition, Vol. 41).—383

375 The *New-York Daily Tribune* did not publish this article by Marx.—384

376 On 8 February 1859 Georg Eccarius wrote to Marx saying it had been definitely established that he had consumption. While expressing his readiness to endure his misfortune with fortitude, he wrote about his apprehensions concerning the possible consequences of his disease for his family. In conclusion he asked Marx to send him books for self-education.—386

377 The letter has not been found.—388

378 The letter is not dated. The approximate time of its writing can be deduced from Marx's mentioning that his brother-in-law, Johann Carl Juta, would be travelling to Manchester, and from the fact that on 22 February 1859 Marx wrote a letter of recommendation to Engels for him.—389

379 Engels informed Marx of his intention to write the pamphlet *Po and Phine* (see present edition, Vol. 16) in a letter written in the second half of February 1859 (it has not reached us). In the same letter he obviously outlined the content of the planned work, which Marx then set forth in this letter to Lassalle. Engels finished the pamphlet by 9 March 1859.—391, 393

380 Engels took part in the Baden-Palatinate uprising in June-July 1849 with the detachment of August Willich, whose adjutant he was. He participated in four battles, including the big one at Rastatt.—392

381 Marx refers to the fact that Ferdinand Lassalle was close to the opposition elements of the Prussian liberal bourgeoisie grouped round the Berlin *Volks-Zeitung.* On 31 January 1859 Lassalle, who became disappointed in the newspaper, wrote to Marx as follows: 'The *Volks-Zeitung,* the only halfway democratic newspaper in Berlin, has rushed over to the ministerial camp and plays a role unique for its unworthiness in the history of the democratic press.'—396

382 In this letter, written at the end of February 1859, Lassalle informed Marx that he had reached an agreement with Franz Duncker regarding the publication of Engels' *Po and Rhine.* He stated the terms and suggested that the pamphlet should be published in French translation too.—398

383 In his speech in the Frankfurt National Assembly on 12 August 1848 General Radowitz asserted that Austria's boundary along the Mincio (in other words, continued Austrian rule in Northern Italy) guaranteed Germany against French invasion. This doctrine was refuted in Engels' pamphlet *Po and Rhine* and in Marx's article 'The War Prospect in Prussia' (see present edition, Vol. 16, pp. 216, 235 and 270).—398

384 A reference to the national liberation and anti-feudal uprising in the city of Cracow, which had been under the joint control of Austria, Russia and Prussia from 1815. The insurgents seized power on 22 February 1846 and set up a National Government, which issued a manifesto abolishing feudal services. The

uprising was put down in early March 1846. In November 1846, Austria, Prussia and Russia signed a treaty incorporating Cracow in the Austrian Empire.—401

385 Further events showed that Marx's forecast was true. In April 1859 the British Parliament was dissolved and new elections in June 1859 brought to power a government headed by Palmerston, who had been in opposition until then.

The ideas expressed by Marx in this and other letters of that period concerning the situation in Europe in view of the maturing military crisis, were developed in his article 'The War Prospect in France' written for the *New-York Daily Tribune* (see present edition, Vol. 16).—401, 405, 429

386 Engels means one of the three annual fairs in Leipzig, the spring fair, at which all German publishing houses used to exhibit their books.—402

387 After a long imprisonment, the Italian liberal Carlo Poerio and his associates, participants in the 1848-49 revolution, were expelled by the Neapolitan authorities and placed on a ship bound for America. On the way, the captain set them free at a British port. On 12 March 1859 *The Times* (No. 23252) published a letter to the editor by Lord Shaftesbury hailing Poerio and his friends as 'honest and heroic men'. To support them a committee was set up in London with Lord Shaftesbury as President. Palmerston, too, was a member.—405

388 The letter is not dated. The time of its writing is clear from the enclosed letter of Eccarius to Marx, written on 20 March 1859, and from Marx mentioning his article on the Reform Bill, which was presumably sent to New York on 22 March, Tuesday, one of the two weekdays when articles were despatched to America.—406

389 Besides 'The New British Reform Bill' (see present edition, Vol. 16), Marx wrote two more articles on the 1859 Reform Bill, on 22 March and 1 April 1859, but they were not published in the *New-York Daily Tribune* and have not reached us.—406, 411

390 Marx has in mind cases when the *New-York Daily Tribune* reprinted articles from the London *Times*.—406

391 From 1693 to 1806 Wetzlar was the seat of the *Reichskammergeriecht* (Imperial Court of Justice) which examined disputes between the lands, complaints connected with taxation, and other questions. It was also the highest court of appeal for the lands and cities comprising the Holy Roman Empire of the German Nation. It was notorious for procrastination and red tape.—408

392 Marx means the new proposal Max Friedländer had made to him in the course of negotiations on Marx's work for the Vienna newspaper *Die Presse* (see also Note 254). It was forwarded to him by Lassalle in a letter written at the end of March 1859, and Marx's letter is the reply to it. This time Friedländer did not stipulate that Marx should abstain from criticising Palmerston and proposed that, besides articles, Marx should send telegraphic despatches on current events. In his letter Lassalle also asked Marx for advice concerning his own work for the paper. Marx wrote about the negotiations also in his letter to Engels of 16 April 1859 (see this volume, p. 416).—408

393 On the letter from Lassalle see Note 392.

In his letter of 15 March 1859 Charles Dana informed Marx that it was impossible to find a publisher in America for the English translation of *A*

Contribution to the Critique of Political Economy and offered his help in selling 50-100 copies of the German edition of the book in America. Dana also requested Marx to write articles on 'Fortification' and 'Infantry' for *The New American Cyclopaedia.* Both articles were written by Engels (see present edition, Vol. 18).—410

394 In 1852 the Tory government of Derby was brought down by the Free Traders led by Bright, and Palmerston became Home Secretary in the new coalition government of Aberdeen. The fall of the Aberdeen government in 1855, caused by setbacks in the Crimean War, cost Russell the post of Foreign Secretary, while Palmerston headed the new, Whig government. During the second Derby ministry (1858-59), opposition by Bright and Russell contributed to the government's resignation, clearing the field for Palmerston's second cabinet.—411

395 On 31 March 1859 the House of Commons rejected, after a second reading, the Reform Bill proposed by the Tory government of Derby-Disraeli, which led to the government's fall. In the preceding debate, on 24 March, Bright and Gibson spoke against the Bill. Gibson quoted Bright, who said in one of his earlier speeches that 'there was no Bill so revolutionary as a bad Bill'. While favouring the preservation of some elements of the obsolete system of 'rotten boroughs', Gibson opposed the new distribution of electoral districts proposed by the government.

The ideas expressed in this letter were probably discussed in greater detail in Marx's article on the Reform Bill written on 1 April 1859, which was not published by the *New-York Daily Tribune* editors.—411

396 The letter was first published in an abridged English translation in K. Marx, *On Colonialism and Modernization,* New York, 1969.—412

397 This letter to Charles Dana has not been found.—412

398 While a member of the House of Commons, Thomas Chisholm Anstey, together with David Urquhart, repeatedly criticised Palmerston's foreign policy. As Attorney-General of Hong Kong in 1854-58, he came out against corruption and abuses by the British colonial administration, for which he was virtually removed from office. Upon his return to England in 1859, *The Times* printed, on 9 April, a statement by M.P. Edwin James announcing his intention to publish documents bearing on Anstey's dismissal.—412

399 Marx refers to the *India Loan Bill* introduced in the British House of Commons on 14 February 1859 by Secretary of State for the Affairs of India Stanley. The loan of £7,000,000 was required to cover the extra expenses of the British administration in India. Marx wrote about the Bill and India's financial position in general in his article 'Great Trouble in Indian Finances' (present edition, Vol. 16).—413

400 Marx means the Shanghai Anglo-Chinese trade agreement of 8 November 1858, which supplemented the Tientsin Anglo-Chinese Treaty of 1858. It established general rules of trade and listed goods free from export and import duties (articles of consumption intended for foreigners) and those subject to duties. The import of opium into China was formally allowed only in the form of foreign medicine which, however, was tantamount to the legalisation of the opium trade, though on a restricted scale.—413

401 On 5 April 1859 the *New-York Daily Tribune,* No. 5602, printed a reader's letter signed 'Asbóth' with comments on Engels' article 'Chances of the Impending

War' (see present edition, Vol. 16). The author referred to an earlier letter of his, about Engels' article 'The Austrian Hold on Italy' (see Vol. 16). That other letter, signed 'A', appeared in the *Tribune,* No. 5581, on 11 March 1859 (in Asbóth's second letter the date was given incorrectly as '14th inst'). The later letter largely repeated the first. Asbóth considered the assessment of Austria's possibilities in the impending war given by Engels in his two articles insufficiently thorough and exaggerated.—417

402 In a letter which has not reached us, Engels may have informed Marx of a review of American newspapers published in a supplement to the *Allgemeine Zeitung,* No. 102, on 12 April 1859. Much space in the review was devoted to the *New-York Daily Tribune* which, in the words of the author, had published 'a number of interesting military-scientific articles on the North Italian theatre of war'. The review stressed that the *Tribune* editors were strongly influenced by the ideas of German revolutionaries.—417

403 Marx wrote this letter in reply to one from Lassalle of 8 April 1859. In his letter Lassalle forwarded a postal order to Marx, informed him of the publication of Engels' pamphlet *Po and Rhine* and asked for Marx's opinion on his drama *Franz von Sickingen.* He had sent Marx three copies of his drama (for Marx, Engels and Freiligrath) on 6 March 1859, together with a note explaining the 'tragic idea' of the drama. The aesthetic principles formulated in the note and in the preface to *Sickingen,* and embodied in the drama, were at variance with the demands Marx and Engels made upon realistic art, namely, truthfully to depict in the idiom specific to it the concrete reality of a definite social environment at a given period of history. Lassalle saw the essence of drama in the tragic conflict of the hero—the bearer of a certain abstract idea, in this case a revolutionary one—with the masses, who are incapable of grasping this idea in an adequate form owing to their backwardness and ignorance. This compells the hero to deviate from his ideals in practice and resort to 'cunning' *(Pfiffigkeit),* and ultimately dooms him to defeat.

In his reply Marx gave a critical analysis of *Sickingen* from a dialectical-materialist standpoint and, in effect, argued against Lassalle's principles and the political tendency of the drama.

In English this letter was published, abridged, in Marx and Engels, *Selected Correspondence,* Foreign Languages Publishing House, Moscow, 1955, and in full in *The Letters of Karl Marx,* selected and translated with explanatory notes and an introduction by Saul K. Padover, Prentice-Hall, Inc., Englewood Cliff, New Jersey, 1979.—418

404 This refers to the Polish national liberation uprising of November 1830-October 1831. Its participants belonged mostly to the revolutionary gentry, and its leaders to the aristocracy. The uprising was crushed by Tsarist Russia aided by Prussia and Austria. Lack of support by the peasants, due to the leaders' refusal to abolish serfdom, contributed to its defeat. See also Engels' speech 'On the Polish Question' (present edition, Vol. 6, pp. 549-52), and his *The Peasant War in Germany,* where he writes about the failure of the nobility to win over the peasants in Germany in 1522 and in Poland in 1830 (Vol. 10, p. 444).—420

405 This refers to the withdrawal of the French troops that had occupied Rome during the suppression of the Roman Republic in 1849 and stayed on in subsequent years, as did the Austrians, who in 1849 had occupied the territory of the Legations, Marke and part of Umbria, belonging to the Roman Republic.—425

406 At a reception of the diplomatic corps in the Tuileries on 1 January 1859, Napoleon III said to the Austrian Ambassador J. A. Hübner: 'I regret that our relations with your Government are not as good as formerly.' This statement led to a diplomatic conflict with Austria, war against which had been decided on much earlier: in July 1858, in Plombières, a secret agreement had been reached between France and Piedmont, under which France was promised Savoy and Nice in exchange for participation in the forthcoming war against Austria.—425

407 A reference to the *Final Act* of the Congress of Vienna held by European monarchs in 1814-15. Signed on 9 June 1815, it laid down the frontiers of European states and their regimes—based on the principle of legitimism—as decreed by the victor powers. The Final Act sealed the political fragmentation of Germany and Italy.—426

408 Marx refers to the ultimatum the Austrian government presented to Piedmont on 19 April 1859 in a letter by Count K. Buol-Schauenstein, Austria's Foreign Minister, to Count Cavour, Chairman of the Council of Ministers of Piedmont (published in the *Allgemeine Zeitung*, No. 116, supplement, 26 April 1859). It demanded that Piedmont should disarm within three days and disband the detachments of Italian volunteers. Refusal to comply with these demands would be regarded as a *casus belli*. On 29 April the Austrian army under Field Marshal Gyulay crossed the frontier river Ticino, thus starting the Austro-Italo-French war of 1859.—427

409 Louis Auguste Blanqui was sentenced to ten years' imprisonment for his part in the 1848 revolution. In the spring of 1859, having served his term in Belle-Île and Corsica, he was deported to Algeria. Following the amnesty of 16 August 1859, he returned to Paris.—427

410 Ridiculing Karl Vogt, Marx often puns on his name. *Vogt* or *Landvogt* was the name of provincial governors or other officials in the German Empire in the Middle Ages.

By calling him 'the great imperial Vogt', Marx alludes to the fact that he was one of the five members of the Regency of the Empire *(Reichsregentschaft)* formed in Stuttgart in early June 1849 by the 'Rump' of the Frankfurt National Assembly. The Regency's attempts to enforce the Imperial Constitution (see Note 116) by parliamentary means ended in failure.—428, 434, 436, 450, 460, 488, 521

411 Vogt and his followers intended to publish a weekly, *Die Neue Schweiz*, in Geneva. Later that title was dropped in favour of *Neue Schweizer Zeitung*.

On Vogt's letter to Freiligrath and the 'Programme' appended to it see Marx's exposé *Herr Vogt* (present edition, Vol. 17, p. 115).—428

412 Marx alludes to Blind's call for the union of 'the leaders of all German popular parties' contained in his article published in the *Hermann* on 16 April 1859. According to Blind, this was to put an end to the confusion of opinions on the Italian crisis. Blind himself pronounced against both the pro-Austrian and pro-Bonapartist stand in this article.—428

413 Marx's reply to Friedländer's letter of 12 April 1859 has not been found.—429, 433

414 The *New-York Daily Tribune* did not publish this article by Engels, which presumably dealt with the Austro-Italo-French war, then in its early days.—430

415 The reference is to the secret Paris treaty of 19 February (3 March) 1859 concluded between France and Russia. Russia undertook to adopt a 'political and military stand which most easily proves its favourable neutrality towards France' and not to object to the enlargement of the Kingdom of Sardinia in the event of a war between France and Sardinia on the one hand and Austria on the other. Information about this secret treaty leaked into the press but the Russian Foreign Minister Gorchakov officially denied the existence of any written obligations to France. Marx refers to this treaty in his article 'The Financial Panic' (present edition, Vol. 16).—430, 537

416 The *Holy Alliance*—an association of European monarchs founded in September 1815, on the initiative of the Russian Tsar Alexander I and the Austrian Chancellor Metternich, to suppress revolutionary movements and preserve feudal monarchies in European countries. During the 1848-49 revolution and subsequent years, counter-revolutionary circles in Austria, Prussia and Tsarist Russia attempted to revive the Holy Alliance in a modified form.—430

417 Marx refers to the commercial panic in Vienna started by the bankruptcy on 5 May 1859 of the big firm of Arnstein & Eskeles. Marx deals in detail with this subject in the article 'Highly Important from Vienna' (present edition, Vol. 16).—433

418 A reference to Lassalle's undated letter to Marx written in all probability in mid-May 1859. Marx discusses it in this letter and in one to Engels dated 18 May 1859.—433, 434

419 Marx compares the commercial panic in Vienna in the spring of 1859 (see Note 417) to that in Hamburg during the economic crisis in the autumn of 1857.—434

420 On 9 May 1859 Marx, while attending a public meeting organised by Urquhart in connection with the Italian war, was told by the German democrat Karl Blind that Vogt was in receipt of subsidies from the French government for Bonapartist propaganda and had offered bribes to some writers to induce them to come out in support of Napoleon III (see present edition, Vol. 17, pp. 116-17).—434, 436, 460, 468, 533, 539, 543

421 In his anonymous pamphlet *Der italienische Krieg und die Aufgabe Preußens. Eine Stimme aus der Demokratie,* published in May 1859, Lassalle advocated the dynastic unification of Germany under the aegis of the Prussian monarchy, as against the idea of Germany's unification as a democratic republic put forward by Marx and Engels in 1848. Lassalle also tried to justify the neutrality of Prussia and other German states in the Austro-Italo-French war of 1859, an attitude which, he argued, contributed to the weakening of Austria, Prussia's rival, and the establishment of Prussian hegemony. At the same time he justified the policy of Napoleon III, in particular his demagogy on the nationalities question (the so-called principle of nationalities), and hailed the Bonapartist Second Empire as the potential 'liberator' of Italy.—435

422 Marx uses Lassalle's words here. In a letter to him Lassalle described his work on the pamphlet about the Italian war as follows: 'In the last few days, writing nights through, I have tried to weave from logic and fire something ... which will not be lost on the people in any case..."—436, 458

423 The *Federal Diet*—a representative body of the German Confederation, an ephemeral union of German states, founded in 1815 by decision of the

Congress of Vienna. Though it had no real power, it was nevertheless a vehicle for feudal and monarchical reaction. During the 1848-49 revolution in Germany, reactionary circles made vain attempts to revive the Federal Diet, intending to use it to prevent the democratic unification of Germany. After the defeat of the revolution, the Federal Diet received its former rights in 1850 and survived till 1866.—436

424 The *Peace of Basle* was concluded on 5 April 1795 separately between France and Prussia, the latter being a member of the first anti-French coalition. The treaty was the consequence of the French victories as well as of the differences between the members of the coalition, in particular between Prussia and Austria.—437

425 No manifesto was issued.—437, 447, 449

426 Marx refers to the German Workers' Educational Society in London (see Note 50).—437

427 The International Committee was set up in London on 25 January 1855 on the initiative of Ernest Jones. On 6 May 1856 it was renamed the International Association. It included English Chartists and French, German, Polish, Italian, Hungarian, Spanish and Russian political refugees in London. The Association's political and ideological heterogeneity hampered the performance of its main function, promotion of the international cooperation of democratic forces. The Association ceased to exist in 1859.—437

428 The last two issues of the weekly *Die Neue Zeit*—Nos. 41 and 42 of 10 and 16 April 1859—had only two pages instead of the usual four. It was one of these issues that Marx sent Engels.

The meeting mentioned by Marx was held at the London hotel *Germania* on 1 May 1859 on Liebknecht's initiative. Attended by members of German workers' societies in London, it decided to start publication of *Das Volk,* a weekly representing the views and interests of the German workers in Britain.—437

429 Early in October 1856 the Marx family moved to a London suburb.—438, 464

430 *Das Volk*—a German-language weekly published in London from 7 May to 20 August 1859—was founded as the official organ of the German Workers' Educational Society in London. Its first issue appeared under the editorship of the German journalist and petty-bourgeois democrat Elard Biskamp. Beginning with issue No. 2 Marx took an active part in its publication: he offered advice, edited articles, organised material support, and so on. In issue No. 6 of 11 June, the Editorial Board officially named Karl Marx, Frederick Engels, Ferdinand Freiligrath, Wilhelm Wolff and Heinrich Heise as its contributors (see present edition, Vol. 16).

Marx's first article in the paper—'Spree and Mincio'—was printed on 25 June. Under Marx's influence *Das Volk* began to turn into a militant revolutionary working-class newspaper. In the beginning of July Marx became its virtual editor and manager.

Das Volk carried Marx's preface to his work *A Contribution to the Critique of Political Economy,* six of his articles, seven articles by Engels and his review of Marx's *A Contribution to the Critique of Political Economy.*

Das Volk reflected the elaboration by Marx and Engels of questions concerning the revolutionary theory and tactics of the working-class struggle, described the class struggles of the proletariat, and relentlessly fought the exponents of petty-bourgeois ideology. It analysed from the standpoint of proletarian internationalism the events of the Austro-Italo-French war of 1859 and the questions of German and Italian unification, exposed the foreign policy of Britain, Prussia, France, Russia and other states, and consistently opposed Bonapartism and its overt and covert supporters.

In all, sixteen issues appeared. The newspaper ceased publication for lack of money.—438, 447

431 This refers to a branch of the German Workers' Educational Society in London and to an association, close to it, formed by German refugee workers in London's East End in November 1858.—440

432 In his letter of 24 April 1859 from New York, Albrecht Komp told Marx that there were favourable opportunities for selling copies of the first instalment of his book, *A Contribution to the Critique of Political Economy,* in the USA. Enclosed was a letter from Joseph Weydemeyer of 27 March 1859 confirming Komp's information.—440, 446, 454

433 On 21 March 1859 Lassalle wrote to Engels telling him that he had sent copies of his drama *Franz von Sickingen* to England for him, Marx and Freiligrath. In this connection Lassalle referred to his letter to Marx of 6 March where he had explained his motives for writing the drama, and the aesthetic principles underlying it. He probably meant the note—appended to that letter—in which he elucidated his concept of the 'tragic idea' (see Note 403).

This letter of Engels', with the critical analysis of Lassalle's play, continued the polemic, started by Marx in his letter to Lassalle of 19 April 1859 (see this volume, pp. 418-21), on the evaluation of the historical events and characters presented in the drama, on its political message and on problems of aesthetics and art.

On the first English publication of Engels' letter see Note 100.—441

434 In early 1858 Lassalle published anonymously a stage version of his drama *Franz von Sickingen.* But when the Royal Court Theatre refused to put it on, Lassalle published it as a literary drama (at the beginning of 1859).—442

435 Here and below Engels refers to ideas Lassalle put forward in the preface to his *Franz von Sickingen.* Engels argues against them in one form or another.—442

436 Engels refers to the trial of Lassalle on 3-4 May 1849. He was arrested in Düsseldorf on 22 November 1848 on a charge of inciting people to offer armed resistance to the government in his speech at a popular meeting in Neuss (near Düsseldorf). The proceedings against him were delayed by the legal authorities in every possible way. At Lassalle's request, expressed in his letters to Marx and Engels, the *Neue Rheinische Zeitung* came out in defence of him and of other persecuted Düsseldorf democrats (see present edition, Vol. 8, pp. 344-46, 463-65, 474-76; Vol. 9, pp. 339-41, 377-78, 383-88). Marx and Engels also took part in the efforts of democratic organisations to speed up the investigation. The jury acquitted Lassalle.—442

437 Engels calls the leader of the peasant movement of the early 16th century an "agitator" *(Wühler),* the name moderate constitutionalists in Germany in 1848-49 applied to republican democrats.—444

438 The *Bundschuh* and the *Poor Konrad* were secret peasant associations whose activities prepared the Peasant War in Germany in 1525 (see Engels' *The Peasant*

War in Germany, present edition, Vol. 10, pp. 431-38, 440 and 441).—445

439 A reference to the German Republicans and petty-bourgeois democrats, the names of whose leaders occur in the refrain of a song popular in South Germany during the 1848-49 revolution:

'Hecker, Struve, Blenker, Zitz und Blum,
Bringt die deutschen Fürsten um!'
('Hecker, Struve, Blenker, Zitz and Blum,
Slay the German princes!').

With these lines Engels opens his work *The Campaign for the German Imperial Constitution,* in which he criticises the petty-bourgeois democrats' attitude during the revolution (see present edition, Vol. 10, p. 149).—446

440 *The Free Press,* No. 5, of 27 May 1859 carried Karl Blind's anonymous note 'The Grand Duke Constantine to Be King of Hungary' exposing the plans for giving the Hungarian throne to the Grand Duke Constantine of Russia. Marx mentioned this article in his *Herr Vogt* (see Vol. 17, pp. 122-24). Blind also hinted at the possibility of some refugee German democrats and liberals being bribed by the Bonapartists.

The same issue of the journal carried an excerpt from a private letter comparing Kossuth's tendency to yield to Bonapartist demagogy in the nationalities question with Mazzini's critical attitude to it. Marx may have drawn on the two items for the facts he relates to Engels.—452, 504, 521

441 This refers to the proclamation which Garibaldi addressed to the local population upon the entry of his volunteer corps into Lombardy in May 1859 (see 'Garibaldi's Proclamation to the Lombards', *The Times,* No. 23319, 30 May 1859).—455

442 The reference is probably to the workers' demonstrations for better living conditions held in Berlin on 1 and 4 June 1859. Some of the participants were arrested.—458

443 On 14 May 1859 *Das Volk* (issue No. 2) announced the publication of the pamphlet *Po and Rhine.* On Marx's initiative, the announcement suggested that the author of the pamphlet was a prominent member of the proletarian party. In its issue No. 5 of 4 June *Das Volk* carried an editorial on the publication of Marx's *A Contribution to the Critique of Political Economy.* It contained extracts from the Preface to the book and for the first time named Engels as the author of *Po and Rhine.*—458

444 Marx came to Engels in Manchester approximately on 12 June 1859 to discuss questions connected with the publication of *Das Volk.* From Manchester he went to Scotland to visit former members of the Communist League Peter Imandt and Heinrich Heise, with whom he discussed the financing of the paper. Marx returned to London about 2 July.—459, 462, 470, 472, 497, 520, 538

445 This refers to Lassalle's letter to Marx and Engels of 27 May 1859, in which he replied to the criticism of his drama *Franz von Sickingen* contained in Marx's letter of 19 April and Engels' letter of 18 May 1859 (see this volume, pp. 418-21 and 441-46). In essence Lassalle argued against Marx's and Engels' view of the principles of drama and artistic creation and against their conception of the historical events presented in his drama. Lassalle tried to justify his attempts to glorify the German nobility and play down the historical role of peasant

uprisings, describing the peasantry as class with reactionary tendencies, and Thomas Münzer, the ideologist of the plebeian peasant masses, as a religious fanatic.—460, 461

446 Marx and Engels refrained from openly attacking Lassalle's pamphlet in the press. However, indirect polemic against him could be found in their newspaper articles, in Engels' pamphlet *Savoy, Nice and the Rhine* and in Marx's *Herr Vogt* (see present edition, Vols. 16 and 17). It concerned the appraisal of the Austro-Italo-French war of 1859, the policy of the ruling classes of France and Prussia and the ways of unifying Italy and Germany.—462

447 Marx did not have to issue a public statement because his book, *A Contribution to the Critique of Political Economy* (see present edition, Vol. 30), had appeared, as he soon learned, on 11 June 1859.—463

448 Marx means the first week after his return to London. He came back about 2 July 1859 (see Note 444).—463

449 *Das Volk* regularly published 'Gatherings from the Press', a column with quotations from and critical comments on Kinkel's weekly *Hermann*. Besides Marx, Elard Biskamp took part in writing it (see present edition, Vol. 16, pp. 625-34). Marx's biting 'Gatherings' forced Kinkel to resign from the editorial board of the weekly. He announced his resignation in the *Hermann*, No. 26, 2 July 1859.—463, 468

450 On 8 July 1859 the emperors of France and Austria held a separate meeting—without the King of Piedmont—in Villafranca, at which they reached an agreement on an armistice. The meeting was initiated by Napoleon III, who feared that the protracted war might give a fresh impulse to the revolutionary and national liberation movements in Italy and other European states. On 11 July France and Austria signed a preliminary peace under which Austria was to cede to France its rights to Lombardy and France was to transfer this territory to Piedmont. Venice was to remain under the supreme power of Austria, and the rulers of the states of Central Italy were to be restored to their thrones. It was intended to create a confederation of Italian states under the honorary chairmanship of the Pope.

The Villafranca preliminaries formed the basis of the peace treaty concluded by France, Austria and Piedmont in Zurich on 10 November 1859.—464, 465

451 Presumably an allusion to Lassalle's letter to Marx and Engels of 27 May 1859 (see Note 445), in which he asserted that 'a collision ... that *constantly recurred in all* or almost all the past revolutions, and is bound to recur in future ones, is the tragic collision of the *revolutionary situation* itself'.—465

452 In publishing the 'Memoir on Russia' on 13 July 1859 the editors of *The Free Press* wrote that the document had been discovered during the 'Prussian ministerial crisis'. This put Engels on his guard and made him, like Marx (see his letter to Engels of 19 July 1859, this volume, p. 470), doubt the authenticity of some of the passages.

And indeed, from subsequent issues of *The Free Press* (of 27 and 31 July 1859) it appeared that the publication was based not on the original document but on material published in the German conservative newspaper *Preussisches Wochenblatt zur Besprechung politischer Tagesfragen*, Nos. 23, 24 and 25, June 9, 16 and 23, 1855. This publication quoted neither the source from which the document had been taken nor its title or the full text. Later Bismarck in his memoirs (*Gedanken und Erinnerungen,* Stuttgart, 1898, Bd. 1, S. 111-112) stated outright that the publication had been a forgery.

Though Marx and Engels were sceptical about the document, they did not know that it was completely false. Therefore Marx had it reprinted, from *The Free Press,* in the *New-York Daily Tribune* (early August) and in *Das Volk* (late July-early August 1859) prefacing it with an 'Introductory Note' (see present edition, Vol. 16, p. 415).—468, 470, 476

453 The 'Memoir on Russia, for the Instruction of the Present Emperor', published in *The Free Press,* said that Russia's interests demanded the murder of Prince Alexei (son of Peter I) and Peter of Holstein, i. e., Peter III.—469

454 Marx means his series of articles "Quid pro Quo", which he began publishing in *Das Volk* (see present edition, Vol. 16, pp. 445-64). The series remained unfinished as the newspaper ceased publication. In the published instalments the 'Memoir on Russia' was not dealt with.—470

455 The letter has no date. It was written in reply to Marx's letter of 19 July 1859 (this volume, pp. 469-71) and answered by Marx on 22 July (pp. 472-74). So the letter must have been written between these dates.—471

456 Engels' letter to Duncker has not been found.—474

457 From late June to 20 August 1859 *Das Volk* published a series of articles entitled 'Feierstunden-Arbeit eines Arbeiters' ('Spare-Time Work of a Worker'). The author advocated schools for workers and disparaged the bourgeois phrases about the sanctity of private property, the need for forgiveness and conciliation with one's enemies.

The earlier instalments appeared unsigned but the last three were marked by the letter 'P'. The series was written by the Danish refugee N. Petersen.—476

458 In its 'Feuilleton' column, *Das Volk,* No. 13, 30 July 1859, carried a poem by a Landwehr soldier from Frankfort on the Oder describing the mechanism of the needle gun. The editors supplied it with ironical comments.—477

459 Early in May 1851 Peter Nothjung was sent on a tour of Germany as an emissary of the Cologne Central Committee of the Communist League. On 10 May he was arrested in Leipzig. The documents seized from him enabled the authorities of Prussia and other German states to arrest more League members.—478

460 Crawshay's letter, published in *The Free Press,* No. 8, 27 July 1859, stated that the 'Russian Memoir' had been published in 1855 in a German newspaper (it was the *Preussisches Wochenblatt zur Besprechung politischer Tagesfragen*—see Note 452) and that it had been translated for *The Free Press* by 'a German'. The letter gave no indication as to the identity of that 'German'.—479

461 About the middle of July 1859 Marx talked with Blind, Liebknecht and Hollinger, the owner of the print-shop in which *Das Volk* was printed, about the anti-Vogt anonymous pamphlet *Zur Warnung (A Warning)* which had been reprinted in *Das Volk,* No. 7, 18 June and the Augsburg *Allgemeine Zeitung,* No. 173, 22 June. The pamphlet exposed Vogt as a bribed Bonapartist agent. During the conversation, Marx gave it as his opinion that the pamphlet had been written by Blind as it contained facts which the latter had related to him at a public meeting on 9 May 1859 (see Note 420); Marx also pointed out that the proofs of the pamphlet, discovered by Liebknecht in Hollinger's print-shop

in mid-June and sent by him to the *Allgemeine Zeitung* contained corrections in Blind's handwriting. However, Blind, unwilling openly to attack Vogt, denied his authorship. His attitude was later condemned by Marx in his polemical work *Herr Vogt* (present edition, Vol. 17, pp. 122-32).—479, 486, 498, 503, 539

462 The project to publish the *Union Républicaine* did not materialise. See this volume, p. 484.—480

463 Engels means Duncker's letter of 3 August 1859, which was in reply to Engels' letter, no longer extant, of 25 July. Duncker wrote that he had sent six copies of Engels' pamphlet *Po and Rhine,* and would advertise Marx's *A Contribution to the Critique of Political Economy* in German papers several weeks after its publication because, he maintained, this would make for better sales.—481

464 The Urquhartite *Free Press* had been suggesting that Mazzini was a 'Russian agent'. This idea had been expressed, in particular, in the note 'Kossuth and Mazzini' published in *The Free Press,* No. 5, 27 May 1859.

By Mazzini's 'diplomatic revelations' Engels means his assertions in *The Times* (No. 23381, 10 August 1859) about the existence of a secret agreement between Bonapartist France, Tsarist Russia and the Austrian Empire on combating national liberation movements in Europe.—482

465 Marx means the *Union Républicaine,* which was to be published by Ledru-Rollin and Louis Blanc (see this volume, p. 480).

Napoleon III's amnesty for political offenders (16 August 1859) was to ensure his government the support of liberal circles.—484

466 The letter is not dated. The time of its writing may be established by reference to Marx's mentioning his article about Italy and Hungary. He probably means the article 'Kossuth and Louis Napoleon' published in the *New-York Daily Tribune* on 24 September (No. 5748) and dated 5 September 1859. It is quite possible that Marx sent Engels the letter on the same day.—485

467 The letter is not dated. But since it was in reply to Marx's letter presumably written on 5 September 1859 (see Note 466), the time of its writing can be approximately established by comparing the two letters. Marx asked Engels to send him by Friday (i. e., 9 September) 'a military piece on China' (probably in connection with the resumption of the Western powers' second Opium War against China). Being unable to supply the article by the appointed day, Engels informed Marx of this on the eve, i. e., on 8 September.—486

468 Blind's letter to Liebknecht of 8 September 1859 is quoted in full in Marx's *Herr Vogt* (see present edition, Vol. 17, p. 122).—486

469 Marx means the written declaration given to him on 17 September 1859 by August Vögele, the compositor, testifying that the pamphlet *Zur Warnung* had been set in Fidelio Hollinger's print-shop, that the manuscript was in Blind's hand and that Hollinger had named Blind as the author of the pamphlet (see present edition, Vol. 17, pp. 123, 124-25 and 319).—488, 498

470 On 22 June 1859 the *Allgemeine Zeitung* reprinted the pamphlet *Zur Warnung,* which induced Vogt, in July, to bring an action for libel against the paper. The case was heard on 24 October 1859. In early August the editors of the *Allgemeine Zeitung* had asked Liebknecht for proof of the accusations against Vogt contained in *Zur Warnung.* Liebknecht requested Marx to help him obtain Blind's admission that he, Blind, was the author of the anonymous pamphlet. Marx considered such an admission necessary also because Vogt had declared

Marx to be the author of the pamphlet. Besides, Marx wanted to expose the cowardice of this petty-bourgeois democrat who dared not challenge Bonaparte's agents openly and was, as it were, aiding and abetting Vogt in his dispute with the *Allgemeine Zeitung.* Though Marx emphatically condemned the paper's conservative views, in this case he assisted it in the interests of the common struggle against Bonapartism. The court dismissed Vogt's action (see present edition, Vol. 17, pp. 111-32, also pp. 3 and 8-9).—488, 503, 507, 514, 519, 520

471 Marx refers to the *Friends of the Fatherland Society (Vaterlandsfreundegesellschaft)*—a republican association of German refugees in London that existed in the 1850s and 60s. Karl Blind, Ferdinand Freiligrath and Fidelio Hollinger were among its members.—488

472 The letter has not been found.—489

473 After the publication, in June 1859, of the first instalment of *A Contribution to the Critique of Political Economy* (see present edition, Vol. 30), Marx intended, as previously agreed with the Berlin publisher Duncker, to prepare for the press and publish as the second instalment the 'Chapter on Capital', which constitutes the bulk of his main economic manuscript of 1857-58; and then publish the remaining parts of his economic work (see Notes 250 and 355).

As he proceeded with his plan, however, he realised that he would have to do more research to formulate the basic propositions of his economic theory. But his journalistic activity and other party obligations, above all the need to refute publicly Vogt's slanderous allegations against proletarian revolutionaries, temporarily diverted him from his economic studies. It was not until 1861 that he resumed them in earnest. Later Marx decided to publish his researches not as the second and further instalments of *A Contribution to the Critique of Political Economy* but as a large independent work.—489, 498, 502, 508, 511, 522, 523, 542, 574

474 The letter has not been found.—489

475 Marx means Engels' return to Manchester on 20 September 1859, after accompanying his parents on a short tour of Scotland (see this volume, p. 490).—491

476 Speculation of this kind probably stemmed from the amnesty for political offenders demagogically granted by Napoleon III on 16 August 1859 (see Note 465) and from the expectations of a similar amnesty in Prussia in connection with the forthcoming enthronement of William I.—491

477 The letter is not dated. It was written in reply to Marx's letter of 23 September 1859. Marx answered it, presumably, on 27 September (see Note 480). So this letter seems to have been written between these two dates.—492

478 Marx's letters of 26 September and 8 October 1859 to Bertalan Szemere, the former Prime Minister of the Hungarian revolutionary government, is evidence of his desire to strengthen contacts with refugee Hungarian revolutionary democrats. In these letters Marx criticises Kossuth's attitude in the years of emigration, in particular his tendency to take Napoleon III's demagogy in the nationalities question at face value, and his illusions concerning the possibility of using the French Emperor as an ally in the struggle for Hungary's liberation. This criticism does not extend to Kossuth's activity during the 1848-49 revolution, when he headed the revolutionary forces fighting for Hungary's national independence and, in the words of Engels, was 'a truly

revolutionary figure, a man who in the name of his people dares to accept the challenge of a desperate struggle' (Vol. 8, p. 227).—493, 504

479 On 23 August 1859 the *New-York Daily Tribune* published an anonymous item marked 'From Our Own Correspondent' (written by the Hungarian emigrant Ferenc Pulszky) which was an attempt to justify Kossuth's ties with Napoleon III. Early in September Marx sent two articles to the paper exposing the ties of both Kossuth and his followers, including Pulszky, with Bonapartist circles. The facts testifying to Kossuth's dealings with Napoleon III, which Marx cited in the two articles were given to him by Bertalan Szemere on 1 September 1859 when the latter visited him in London. The *Tribune* published, on 24 September, one article by Marx on the subject, 'Kossuth and Louis Napoleon' (present edition, Vol. 16), possibly combining the two he had sent. Whether Marx's private letter to the *Tribune* editor, Charles Dana, was used in it is not known, for the letter has not been found. On 28 September the London *Free Press* published Marx's article 'Particulars of Kossuth's Transaction with Louis Napoleon', which was a condensed version of the *Tribune* article.—494, 497, 507, 525

480 The letter has no date. The approximate date of its writing has been deduced from Marx's acknowledgment of the money Engels sent him in a letter written between 24 and 26 September (see Note 477), and from the fact that Marx wrote it on an 'article day', i. e., a day when he sent material to the *New-York Daily Tribune*. In this case it was, most likely, Tuesday, 27 September. It has also been taken into account that this letter preceded the one Marx wrote to Engels on 28 September 1859.—495

481 The letter is not dated. It is the reply to Lassalle's letter of 30 September 1859. In sending the latter on to Engels on 5 October 1859, Marx wrote that he had answered it 'by return' (see this volume, p. 502). Taking into account the time letters took to get from Berlin to London, it may be assumed that Marx received Lassalle's not earlier than 2 October.

On the first English publication of Marx's letter see Note 20.—497

482 The article 'The New Portfolio' published in *The Free Press*, No. 9, 31 August 1859 reported the forthcoming publication in Berlin of a collection of diplomatic documents and materials corresponding to the *Portfolio* series published by David Urquhart in London (see Note 18). The German series, edited by Eduard Fischel, appeared in Berlin in 1859-60 under the title *Das Neue Portfolio. Eine Sammlung wichtiger Dokumente und Aktenstücke zur Zeitgeschichte.* The above-mentioned article also said that the 'Memoir on Russia' first appeared, in German, in the *Preussisches Wochenblatt* and that the publication in *The Free Press* was a translation from the German (see Note 452).—500, 547

483 Marx means the lectures on political economy he gave in the German Workers' Educational Society in London in the autumn of 1859, after the publication of his *A Contribution to the Critique of Political Economy.* The draft of one of the lectures has been published in the present edition under the title 'On the Division of Labour' (Vol. 16, pp. 617-18).—502, 520

484 This communication has not been found.—503

485 In a letter to Marx written in October 1859 Lassalle again tried to prove the correctness of the tactics he had advocated in his pamphlet *Der italienische Krieg und die Aufgabe Preußens* (see Note 421). Marx replied to him on 22 November,

supplementing his criticism of Lassalle's anti-proletarian, pro-Bonapartist position on this question with fresh arguments (see this volume, pp. 536-39).—508, 522

486 Marx refers to the festivities to mark the centenary of Schiller's birth on 10 November 1859. The preparations in London were handled by a jubilee committee consisting of petty-bourgeois refugees headed by Gottfried Kinkel, who hoped to use the festival for his own publicity purposes.—508, 511, 514, 525

487 This refers to August Vögele's written declaration (see Note 469), which Marx sent to the editor of the *Allgemeine Zeitung* on 19 October 1859 in connection with Vogt's law-suit against the paper (see Note 470).—508, 513, 515, 521

488 Marx's letter to Ferdinand Freiligrath has not been found.—511

489 Engels seems to refer to the planned march of Romagnese and Tuscan volunteers under Garibaldi to Central and South Italy with a view to reactivating the struggle for Italy's unification. The plan had been put forward by Italy's democrats headed by Mazzini, who were not satisfied with the Villafranca treaty (see Note 370). The march was to take place in late October or early November 1859.

Victor Emmanuel, King of Sardinia, and his liberal following at first sought to exploit Garibaldi for the unification of Italy under the aegis of the Sardinian dynasty, but fearing an outbreak of popular unrest in Central Italy they succeeded in having the expedition cancelled.—515

490 In the summer of 1859 hostilities resumed in the second Opium War in China (1856-60).

In October 1859 Spain declared war on Morocco and invaded the country. This colonial incursion met with stubborn resistance and brought the Spaniards no success. The fighting continued until March 1860. In April a peace treaty was concluded under which Spain received indemnities and insignificant territorial concessions.—515, 523

491 At the time, Engels was studying the Gothic translation of the Bible made by the Visigothic bishop Ulfilas. The extant fragments of Ulfilas' Bible, the main written monument of the Gothic language, were available in a number of editions prepared by different German scholars.—516

492 The Schiller society, founded in Manchester in November 1859 in connection with the centenary of Schiller's birth, was conceived as a cultural and social centre of the city's German colony. At first Engels was critical of the society and kept aloof from it. But after certain amendments were made in the Rules, he became a member of its board, in 1864, and later President of the society, devoting much time to it and exercising a considerable influence on its activities.—517, 531

493 Marx means Lassalle's negotiations with the Berlin publisher Duncker on the publication of the second instalment of *A Contribution to the Critique of Political Economy* (see also Note 473).—518

494 The *Communist League*—the first German and international communist organisation of the proletariat formed under the leadership of Marx and Engels in London early in June 1847, as a result of the reorganisation of the League of the Just (a secret association of workers and artisans that appeared in the 1830s and had communities in Germany, France, Switzerland and

England). The League's members took an active part in the bourgeois-democratic revolution in Germany in 1848-49. In 1849 and 1850, after the defeat of the revolution, it was reorganised and continued its activities. In the summer of 1850 disagreements arose between the supporters of Marx and Engels and the sectarian Willich-Schapper group, which resulted in a split within the League. Owing to police persecutions and arrests of League members in May 1851, the activities of the Communist League as an organisation practically ceased in Germany. On 17 November 1852, on a motion by Marx, the London District announced the dissolution of the League.

The Communist League played an important historical role as the first proletarian party based on the principles of scientific communism, as a school of proletarian revolutionaries, and as the historical forerunner of the International Working Men's Association.—519

495 Marx refers to the war waged by the mountaineers of Daghestan and Chechnya under Shamil against Tsarist Russia. Having defeated Shamil's main forces and taken him prisoner (August 1859), the Russians were breaking the resistance of separate detachments of Shamil's followers.—523

496 During the Italian war of 1859 Kossuth was in Italy where, on his initiative, a Hungarian legion has been formed to fight against Austria on the side of Piedmont and Bonapartist France. He hoped to win independence for Hungary with the help of the latter.

On the Villafranca peace see Note 450.—524, 532

497 On 26 May 1849 Wilhelm Wolff, who shortly before had taken over the seat of a moderate deputy in the Frankfurt National Assembly, spoke in the Assembly against the adoption of an address to the German people drawn up by the poet Uhland in the name of moderate democrats, and proposed declaring the Imperial Regent of Germany, Archduke John of Austria, and his ministers traitors to the people. His speech was sharply criticised by bourgeois deputies, Karl Vogt in particular.—525

498 Marx puns on the phrase *abgerundete Natur* ('an intellectually mature character') used by barrister K. Hermann, who represented Vogt in his lawsuit against the *Allgemeine Zeitung* (see Note 470). The phrase can also mean 'well-rounded character' (in the physical sense), and it is in this sense that Marx later used it in his polemical work *Herr Vogt* (see present edition, Vol. 17, p. 28).—525

499 Marx and Engels ridiculed these attributes of Kinkel in their satire *The Great Men of the Exile* (see present edition, Vol. 11, pp. 252-55).

Black, red and gold symbolise the unity of Germany; petty-bourgeois democrats associated the colours with the idea of a union of autonomous lands in the manner of the Swiss Confederation.—526

500 The letter is not dated. By its contents it is close to Marx's letter to Engels of 16 November 1859. Marx's mentioning that he wanted an article about the war in Morocco 'by tomorrow', and that he was writing an article about the Suez question, 'not having written on Tuesday', suggests that 'tomorrow' means Friday (Tuesday and Friday being the days when Marx sent articles to the *New-York Daily Tribune*), and that this letter was written on Thursday, 17 November.—529

501 Marx's article about the events connected with the building of the Suez Canal, which had aggravated the contradictions between Britain and France, was not published by the *New-York Daily Tribune*.—529

502 The rifle volunteer movement started in Britain at the end of 1850 as a reaction to Napoleon III's aggressive policy, which was seen as holding the threat of a French invasion of the British Isles. Progressive circles believed that the movement could also help reform the extremely conservative British military system.

An article by Engels on the volunteer movement in Britain appeared in the *New-York Daily Tribune* later (see F. Engels, 'The British Volunteer Force', present edition, Vol. 17). Engels also wrote a series of articles on the subject for the Manchester weekly *The Volunteer Journal, for Lancashire and Cheshire* (present edition, Vol. 18).—530, 544, 546

503 On 10 November 1859 the Crystal Palace (see Note 89) was the scene of festivities to mark the centenary of Schiller's birth, with German petty-bourgeois refugees, above all Kinkel, playing the main role.—531, 534

504 The cutting from the *Volksblatt* presumably was a report on Vogt's lawsuit against the *Allgemeine Zeitung* (see Note 470) containing slanderous attacks on Marx and his followers.—532

505 Marx alludes to *Batrachomyomachia* (The Battle of the Frogs and the Mice), an old anonymous Greek parody of Homer's *Iliad*.—532

506 This letter is the reply to two letters by Lassalle, dated mid-November and 20 November 1859. Marx reverts to the disagreements with Lassalle over the assessment of Napoleon III's policy and the tactical line on the question of Italy's and Germany's unification, and answers Lassalle's attempts to prove the correctness of his stand formulated in a letter written in October 1859 (see Note 485).—536

507 In a letter to Marx written in mid-November 1859 Lassalle praised Freiligrath's poem 'Zur Schillerfeier. 10. November 1859. Festlied der Deutschen in London' and at the same time expressed offence at Freiligrath's failing to acknowledge his drama *Franz von Sickingen,* which Lassalle had sent him for comment.—537

508 At the beginning of April 1859 Vogt sent Freiligrath and others his political 'Programme' calling on the states of the German Confederation to maintain neutrality in the war France and Piedmont were preparing against Austria. Vogt urged political leaders to support his 'Programme' in the press (see present edition, Vol. 17, p. 115).—539, 543

509 On 19 August 1851 Marx, accompanied by Ferdinand Freiligrath and Wilhelm Wolff, visited the offices of the London German weekly *How Do You Do?* and demanded satisfaction of the publisher Louis Drucker and the editor Heinrich Beta, who had printed an item containing insulting allusions to Marx's connection with the Prussian Minister of the Interior, Ferdinand von Westphalen (Jenny Marx's stepbrother).—540, 545

510 Marx decided against making his statement (see this volume, p. 535).—541

511 On 15 November 1859 the Augsburg *Allgemeine Zeitung* published Freiligrath's statement (see this volume, p. 533) appending to it a note by Gustav Kolb, the Editor-in-Chief, claiming that in his letter to the newspaper Liebknecht had named Freiligrath among the persons who could come forward with charges against Vogt. Actually, Liebknecht had only written that Freiligrath could, together with Marx, confirm that Blind was the author of the pamphlet *Zur Warnung* (see Note 461).

Cotta was the publisher of the *Allgemeine Zeitung.*—543

512 The long letter mentioned by Marx has probably not been preserved. Another letter containing the *Gartenlaube* and Beta's article was sent, most likely, on 19 November 1859 though that was a Saturday, not a Tuesday (see this volume, pp. 532-36).—542

513 This refers to Lassalle's letter of 20 November 1859, written in reply to Marx's letter of 15 November (see this volume, p. 526). In this letter Lassalle tried to persuade Marx not to publish his declaration against Vogt and Blind in the *Volks-Zeitung* (see present edition, Vol. 17, pp. 8-9).—542

514 This letter to Freiligrath is quoted in full in Marx's letter to Engels of 10 December 1859 (see this volume, pp. 548-49) and has come down to us only in this form. When reproducing the letter Marx did not date it, but he wrote it, as he informed Engels, immediately upon receiving Freiligrath's reply to his letter of 23 November. Freiligrath's reply is also quoted in full in the above-mentioned letter to Engels. Freiligrath, however, had not answered Marx's letter at once but, as Marx wrote, had done so after 'having waited a week', i. e., on 30 November. Marx's letter to Freiligrath quoted in his letter to Engels was written at about this time too.—546

515 The letter is not dated, but it may be assumed from its contents that it was written in reply to Marx's letter of 10 December 1859. Marx answered on 13 December. So Engels must have written his letter between these two dates.—550

516 This letter was first published in English in Karl Marx and Friedrich Engels, *Correspondence. 1846-1895.* A Selection with Commentary and Notes, Martin Lawrence Ltd., London [1934].—551

517 The note mentioned is a letter to Marx from A. Peza, a London bookseller, of 11 December 1859, communicating Hermann Juch's request to appoint the place and time for a meeting. Juch, the proprietor of the London weekly *Hermann,* wished to see Marx in order to get information on the Cologne Communist trial (see Note 71) which he needed because Wilhelm Stieber, the chief of the Prussian political police and the central figure in that trial, had lodged a complaint in a Berlin court against Karl Eichhoff, the Berlin correspondent of the *Hermann,* who had denounced Stieber on its pages (see this volume, p. 536).

In May 1860 Eichhoff was sentenced to 14 months' imprisonment.—552, 554

518 The letter is not dated, but since Marx answered it on 20 December 1859, it may be assumed that it was written the day before. This is confirmed by Engels' mentioning that he had been unable to write the article on Morocco for the day when material was usually despatched from London to New York, in this case Tuesday, 20 December. The last day when an article due to get to London

from Manchester by December 20 ought to have been written was December 19, and that was the day when Engels wrote this letter.—553

519 Engels refers to the events of the Spanish-Moroccan war of 1859-60 (see Note 490). His next article on the subject published in the *New-York Daily Tribune*—'The Moorish War'—was written in mid-January 1860 (see present edition, Vol. 16).—553

520 In a letter published in the *Hermann* on 17 December, Borkheim maintained that Blind enjoyed the same prestige in Baden and Württemberg as Kinkel in Prussia.—555

521 The letter is not dated, but it has much in common in content with Marx's letter to Engels of 25 March 1856. Mrs Marx's mentioning of the report 'from the Berlin correspondent in to-day's *Times*' is evidence that she wrote the letter on 28 March.—561

522 Probably one of Engels' articles on Pan-Slavism for the *New-York Daily Tribune* not published by the editors (see Note 11).—561

523 The letter is not dated. Jenny Marx's asking whether the eye lotion had helped Engels, and the fact that Marx had notified him of the despatch of the lotion in a letter of 9 April 1857 warrant the assumption that Jenny was writing a few days after 9 April. Engels answered her letter about 16 April 1857 (see this volume, p. 121).—563

524 The letter is not dated. Judging by its contents, it was in reply to Engels' letter to Marx of 29 July 1857 and the parcel he had sent the Marx family in London (see this volume, pp. 149-50). Of great help in dating the letter is Jenny's mentioning that Marx was busy 'shaping the Indian news into an article'. Judging by an entry in Marx's notebook, the article was despatched to the *New-York Daily Tribune* on 31 July 1857.—563

525 The letter is not dated. It is the reply to Engels' letter to Mrs Marx of about 11 August 1857, which has not been found. Marx mentions Engels' letter to Jenny in his letter to him of 15 August (see this volume, p. 151). Mrs Marx presumably answered Engels' letter shortly before that date.—565

526 Jenny Marx means Jones' statement in the press in support of the popular uprising in India (see Note 178).—565

527 The letter is not dated. But since Jenny Marx mentions her intention 'to write straight away' to Lassalle, and her letter to him is dated 9 April 1858, there is good reason to believe that her letter to Engels was written on the same day. This assumption is corroborated by Jenny's mentioning the arrival of the *Manchester Guardians* sent by Engels to London on 8 April, of which he informed Marx the next day (see this volume, pp. 304-05).—569

528 This is the reply to Lassalle's letter to Marx of 26 March 1858, in which Lassalle wrote that he had come to terms with the Berlin publisher Duncker on the publication of Marx's *A Contribution to the Critique of Political Economy*.—570

529 The letter is not dated. As can be seen from its contents, it was written during Marx's stay with Engels in Manchester in May 1858 (see Note 318). Jenny probably wrote a few days after Marx's arrival there (6 May), since she mentions the enclosure of Cluss' letter to Marx which she had received after Cluss had visited her. On 11 May Engels communicated to Jenny a request by Marx concerning Cluss which probably had something to do with Cluss' letter which Jenny had forwarded to Marx (see this volume, p. 313).—571

530 The letter is not dated. It was obviously written after 13 August 1859 since Jenny mentions the receipt by Marx of six copies of Engels' pamphlet *Po and Rhine* and Marx's intention to send some of them to Manchester the following week. Marx had promised to send copies of the pamphlet in a letter to Engels of 13 August 1859 (see this volume, p. 483).—572

531 The letter is not dated. It may be assumed that it was written on 4 November 1859, because Engels answered it on 5 November 1859 (see this volume, p. 518) and because Jenny writes about Marx's 'struggling with Friday's article'. 4 November was a Friday, one of the two days when Marx sent articles to the *New-York Daily Tribune*.—573

532 This letter, written in reply to Engels' letter of 22 December 1859, is not dated. As can be seen from its contents, Jenny wrote it a day or two before Christmas, i. e., on 23 or 24 December 1859.—573

533 This article of Marx's for the *New-York Daily Tribune* has not been found.—575

NAME INDEX

A

M.P. (1847-52), Attorney General for Hong Kong (1854-59).—111, 115, 117, 120, 412

Appleton, William Henry (1814-1899)—American publisher, from 1848 head of D. Appleton and Company (New York); published *The New American Cyclopaedia* in 1858-63.—251, 266, 272, 274, 288, 337

Archimedes (c. 287-212 B.C.)—Greek mathematician and engineer.—75

Argout, Antoine Maurice Apollinaire, comte d' (1782-1858)—French statesman and financier, Director-General of the Bank of France (1834-57).—152

Ariosto, Lodovico (1474-1533)—Italian poet of the Renaissance, author of *L'Orlando furioso*.—111, 131

Aristotle (384-322 B.C.)—Greek philosopher.—124, 226, 324, 397

Arminius (Hermann) the Cheruscan (17 B.C.-A.D. 21)—leader of the resistance of Germanic tribes to Roman rule, annihilated a Roman army in the Teutoburg Woods in A.D. 9.—366, 375

Armstrong, William George, Baron of Cragside (1810-1900)—English inventor of rifled cannon.—403

Arndt, Ernst Moritz (1769-1860)—German writer, historian and philologist; took part in the national struggle against Napoleonic rule; deputy to the Frankfurt National Assembly (Right Centre) in 1848-49.—437

Arrighi de Casanova, duchesse de Padoue—wife of the French senator Ernest Louis Henri Hyacinthe Arrighi de Casanova, duc de Padoue (1814-1888).—464

Asbóth, Sándor (Alexander) (1811-1868)—Hungarian colonel, took part in the revolution of 1848-49 in Hungary; emigrated to the USA in 1851; general of the Northern states during the Civil War (1861-64).—417, 494

d'Aspre, Constantin Karl van Hoobreuck, Baron (1761-1809)—Austrian general, took part in the wars against the French Republic and Napoleonic France.—177

Assing, Ludmilla (1821-1880)—German authoress, Lassalle's friend and Marx's acquaintance.—398

Attwood, Thomas (1783-1856)—English banker, economist and radical politician.—301

Augereau, Pierre François Charles, duc de Castiglione (1757-1816)—French general, marshal from 1804; took part in the wars of the French Republic and Napoleonic France.—137

Augustus (Gaius Julius Caesar Octavianus) (63 B.C.-A.D. 14)—Roman Emperor (27 B.C.-A.D. 14).—56

B

Babbage, Charles (1792-1871)—English mathematician, engineer and economist.—278, 279, 281

Bakunin, Mikhail (1814-1876)—Russian democrat, journalist; took part in the 1848-49 revolution in Germany; an ideologist of Narodism and anarchism in later years; opposed Marxism in the First International.—249

Balthasar—see *Slör, Balthasar*

Bamberger, Louis (b. 1821)—German journalist; in the 1850s emigrated to London, where he was engaged in financial operations at his father's bank.—142, 146, 458, 489, 548

Bangya, János (1817-1868)—Hungarian journalist and army officer; took part in the 1848-49 revolution in Hungary; later Kossuth's emissary abroad and at the same time a secret police agent; under the name of Mehemed Bey served in the Turkish army and was a Turkish agent in the Caucasus (1855-58).—108, 109, 112, 113, 310, 318, 319, 324, 342, 365, 436

Napoleon was chief of the Russian General Staff (August-November).—162, 163, 173, 175, 259

Beresford, William Carr, Viscount (1768-1854)—British general and Tory politician; took part in the Peninsular war (1808-14); commander-in-chief of the Portuguese army from 1809 to 1820.—259, 268, 273, 274, 281, 285, 288

Berkeley, George (1685-1753)—Irish subjective idealist philosopher; bishop; in economic works regarded labour as the main source of wealth; exponent of the nominalistic theory of money.—377

Berlichingen, Götz (Gottfried) von (1480-1562)—German knight; took part in the peasant uprising of 1525; elected the leader of the Gay Bright Troop of the Odenwald peasants, he betrayed them at the crucial moment.—419, 420

Bermbach, Adolph (1821-1875)—Cologne lawyer, democrat; member of the Communist League; witness for the defence at the Cologne Communist Trial (1852); liberal in later years.—477

Bernadotte, Jean Baptiste Jules (1763-1844)—Marshal of France, took part in the wars of the French Republic and Napoleonic France; heir to the Swedish throne and regent of Sweden in 1810; fought in the war against Napoleon I in 1813; King of Sweden and Norway as Charles XIV John (1818-44).—91, 164, 165, 166, 169-70, 173-77, 179, 259, 274

Bernard, Martin (1808-1883)—French democrat, a leader of secret societies during the July monarchy; participant in the 1848-49 revolution, was sentenced to exile, fled to England in the early 1850s; returned to France after amnesty in 1859.—255

Bernard, Simon François (Bernard le Clubiste) (1817-1862)—French republican; emigrated to England after the defeat of the 1848 revolution; in 1858 he was accused by the French Government of being an accomplice in Orsini's attempt on the life of Napoleon III but was acquitted by the British Court.—276-78, 307, 309

Berryer, Arthur—agent of the French Government in the joint-stock company, Docks Napoléon; son of lawyer Pierre Antoine Berryer; in March 1857 was sentenced to two-year confinement for participating in the money machinations of the company's governors.—105

Berthier, Louis Alexandre, prince de Neuchâtel, duc de Valengin, prince de Wagram (1753-1815)—Marshal of France, took part in the wars of the French Republic and Napoleonic France; chief of Napoleon I's General Staff.—164, 166, 168, 259

Besser, W.—publisher in Berlin.—376

Bessières, Jean Baptiste, duc d'Istrie (1768-1813)—Marshal of France, took part in the wars of the French Republic and Napoleonic France.—166, 167, 170, 175, 259

Besson, Alexandre—French refugee in London; fitter; joined a group of republicans, supporters of Félix Pyat; later a member of the First International.—277, 278

Beta (pen-name of *Bettziech, Johann Heinrich*) (1813-1876) — German journalist, refugee in London, follower of Gottfried Kinkel.—440, 458, 485, 511, 512, 532, 534, 537, 540, 545, 546, 547, 549-51, 556

Bettziech, Johann Heinrich—see *Beta*

Bibra, L.—owner of a German hotel in London.—477

Birago, Karl, Baron von (1792-1845)—Austrian military engineer, worked out a system of pontoon bridges.—168

Bischoffsheim, Louis Raphaël (1800-1873)—owner of a French joint-stock bank with a branch in London.—535

Biskamp (Biscamp), Elard—German democratic journalist; took part in the 1848-49 revolution in Germany; emigrated after the defeat of the revolution; member of the editorial board of *Das Volk*.—438-39, 450, 452-53, 458, 463, 464, 469, 471, 473, 477, 483, 484, 487, 496, 497, 501, 502, 508, 511, 518, 520-23, 548

Blanc, Jean Joseph Louis (1811-1882)—French petty-bourgeois socialist, historian; member of the Provisional Government and President of the Luxembourg Commission in 1848; pursued a policy of conciliation with the bourgeoisie; a leader of the petty-bourgeois refugees in London from August 1848.—63, 310, 464, 480, 538

Blank, Karl Emil (1817-1893)—German merchant in London, closely connected with socialist circles in the 1840s-50s; husband of Frederick Engels' sister Marie.—65, 422, 424

Blank, Marie (née *Engels*) (1824-1901)—Frederick Engels' sister, Karl Emil Blank's wife from 1845.—422

Blanqui, Louis Auguste (1805-1881)—French revolutionary, utopian communist.—63, 427

Blenker, Ludwig (Louis) (1812-1863)—German democrat, officer; took part in the Baden-Palatinate uprising of 1849; subsequently emigrated to the USA and fought in the Civil War on the side of the Northerners.—446

Blind, Friederike (née *Ettlinger*)—Karl Blind's wife.—356

Blind, Karl (1826-1907)—German democratic journalist; took part in the Baden revolutionary movement in 1848-49; a leader of the German petty-bourgeois refugees in London in the 1850s; national-liberal in the 1860s.—63, 79, 179, 318, 324, 351, 353, 356, 357, 362, 363, 388, 428, 436, 440, 456, 458, 463, 468, 473, 479, 486-87, 488, 498, 502-09, 513, 515, 521, 523, 544

Blücher, Gebhard Leberecht von, Prince von Wahlstatt (1742-1819)—Prussian field-marshal general, took part in the wars against Napoleonic France.—164, 170, 172, 173, 176, 178-80, 198, 247, 259

Blum, Robert (1807-1848)—German democratic journalist; leader of the Left in the Frankfurt National Assembly; took part in the defence of Vienna against counter-revolutionary forces in October 1848; court-martialled and executed after the fall of the city.—158, 168, 173, 259, 358, 446

Böckh, Philipp August (1785-1867)—German philologist and historian of antiquity; professor and for the number of years rector of Berlin University.—336

Boisguillebert, Pierre Le Pesant, sieur de (1646-1714)—French economist, predecessor of Physiocrats, founder of classical political economy in France.—377

Bolivar y Ponte, Simón (1783-1830)—South American politician, one of the chief leaders of the South American Spanish colonies in their war of independence; President of the Republic of Colombia (1819-30).—259, 266

Bona—see *Napoleon III*

Bonaparte—see *Napoleon III*

Bonaparte, Eugène Louis Jean Joseph (1856-1879)—son of Napoleon III, got the title of Imperial Prince at his birth.—306

Bonaparte, Jérôme (1784-1860)—youngest brother of Napoleon I; King of Westphalia (1807-13), Marshal of France from 1850.—170, 293, 381

Bonaparte, Joseph (1768-1844)—eldest brother of Napoleon I; King of Naples (1806-08) and of Spain (1808-13).—170

Bonaparte, Prince Napoléon Joseph Charles Paul (1822-1891)—son of Jérôme Bonaparte, cousin of Napoleon III; adopted the name of Jérôme after the death of his elder brother (1847); commanded a corps in the Italian war of 1859; went by the name of Plon-Plon and the Red Prince.—381, 487, 532

Boniface, Louis (b. 1796)—French journalist, Bonapartist.—381

Borchardt, Louis—German physician, one of Engels' acquaintances in Manchester.—232, 320, 326, 338, 341, 467, 480-82, 484, 516, 517

Borkheim, Sigismund Ludwig (1825-1885)—German democratic journalist; took part in the 1849 Baden-Palatinate uprising; emigrated after its defeat; London merchant from 1851.—555

Bormann—assessor of commissariat in Berlin; took part in Fabrice's attack on Lassalle in May 1858, was prosecuted.—319, 320, 322

Born, David—Stephan Born's brother.—458

Born, Stephan (real name *Buttermilch, Simon*) (1824-1898)—German typesetter, member of the Communist League; leaned towards reformism during the 1848-49 revolution; turned his back on the workers' movement after the revolution.—458

Börne, Karl Ludwig (1786-1837)—German writer and critic; advocated Christian socialism towards the end of his life.—32

Bornstedt, Adalbert von (1808-1851)—German journalist, founder and editor of the *Deutsche-Brüsseler Zeitung* (1847-48); supported the adventurist plan of a revolutionary legion's invasion in Germany; member of the Communist League until his expulsion in March 1848; a secret agent of the Prussian police in the 1840s.—278

Börnstein, Heinrich (1805-1892)—German democratic journalist, founder and editor of *Vorwärts!* in Paris (1844); emigrated to the USA in 1849; publisher of the *Anzeiger des Westens* in the 1850s.—356

Bosquet, Pierre Joseph François (1810-1861)—French general, Marshal of France from 1856; took part in the conquest of Algeria in the 1830s-1850s, commanded a division (1854) and then a corps in the Crimea (1854-55).—170, 173, 177-78, 259, 297

Bötticher, Johann Friedrich Wilhelm (1798—1850) — German philologist and historian.—186

Bourrienne, Louis Antoine Fauvelet de (1769-1834)—French diplomat and politician, personal secretary of Napoleon Bonaparte (1797-1802), chargé d'affaires in Hamburg (1804-13), went over to the Bourbons.—158, 168, 173, 259

Boustrapa—see *Napoleon III*

Braun—see *Lassalle, Ferdinand*

Bray, John Francis (1809-1895)—English economist, utopian socialist, follower of Robert Owen; supporter of the theory of 'labour money'.—301

Bredt, Charlotte—see *Engels, Charlotte*

Bright, John (1811-1889)—English manufacturer and politician, a leader of the Free Traders and founder of the Anti-Corn Law League; M.P. (from 1843).—104, 110, 113, 115, 116-17, 127, 210, 275, 342, 358, 359, 411

Brockhaus, Heinrich (1804-1874)—German publisher, owner of F. A. Brockhaus Publishing House in Leipzig.—17

Bronner, Eduard—German physician, petty-bourgeois democrat; deputy to the Baden Constituent Assembly in 1849; emigrated to England.—357, 362, 363

Brown, Sir George (1790-1865)—British general; took part in the Peninsular war (1808-14) and in the Crimean war (1853-56).—170, 173, 181, 259

Brune, Guillaume Marie Anne (1763-1815)—Marshal of France, Right Dantonist Jacobin during the French Revolution, later Bonapartist; took part in the wars of the French Republic and Napoleonic France.—165, 167, 170, 259

Brüningk, Maria, Baroness von (d. 1853)—wife of Baron A. von Brüningk; helped Gottfried Kinkel to escape from prison in 1850; maintained ties with petty-bourgeois refugees in London from 1851.—359

Brunswick, Karl Wilhelm Ferdinand, Duke of (1735-1806)—ruler of Brunswick (1780-1806), field-marshal general of the Prussian army; participant in the Seven Years War (1756-63) and in the wars against revolutionary and Napoleonic France.—561

Buchanan, James (1791-1868)—American statesman; member of the Democratic Party; President of the United States (1857-61); advocate of slave-owners' interests.—364

Bucher, Lothar (1817-1892)—Prussian official and journalist; deputy to the Prussian National Assembly (Left Centre) in 1848; refugee in London (1850-61); correspondent of the Berlin *National-Zeitung,* shared foreign policy views of David Urquhart in the 1850s; in later years a national-liberal.—5, 18, 62, 75, 428, 440, 458, 479

Buck, Hermann (born. c. 1807)—Prussian official and businessman, Rudolf Schramm's friend.—189, 190, 196

Budberg, Andrei Fyodorovich, Baron (1817-1881) — Russian diplomat; chargé d'affaires in Frankfurt from January 1848, envoy to Berlin (1852-56, 1858-62) and Vienna (1856-58), ambassador to Paris (1862-68).—453

Bugeaud de la Piconnerie, Thomas Robert (1784-1849)—Marshal of France, Orleanist; an organiser of the wars of conquest in Algeria and Morocco, author of works on military questions.—170, 173, 177, 259

Bülow, Friedrich Wilhelm, Count von Dennewitz (1755-1816)—Prussian general, took part in the wars against Napoleonic France.—4, 164, 179, 259, 268, 274, 281, 285, 288, 293, 294

Bunsen, Christian Karl Josias, Baron von (1791-1860)—Prussian diplomat, writer and theologian; envoy to London (1842-54).—525

Buol-Schauenstein, Karl Ferdinand, Count von (1797-1865)—Austrian statesman and diplomat, Prime Minister and Foreign Minister (1852-59).—368

Bürger, Gottfried August (1747-1794)—German poet.—102, 139

Bürgers, Heinrich (1820-1878)—German radical journalist, contributor to the *Rheinische Zeitung* (1842-43); member of the Communist League (1848), an editor of the *Neue Rheinische Zeitung;* member of the Communist League Central Authority from 1850; one of the accused in the Cologne Communist Trial (1852); subsequently a liberal.—27, 209, 337, 385, 388, 452, 477, 479, 554

Burleigh—see *Cecil, William, Baron Burgley*

Busse, von—translator into German of texts included in the book *Fürst Wladimir und dessen Tafelrunde.*—20

Buxhöwden, Fyodor Fyodorovich (Friedrich Wilhelm), Count von (1750-1811)—Russian general; took part in the wars against Napoleonic France in 1805 and 1806.—162

in opposition to Napoleon III's government after the coup d'état of 2 December 1851.—177, 198, 309

Cavanagh—one of Marx's acquaintances in London.—572

Cavour, Camillo Benso, conte di (1810-1861)—Italian statesman, head of the Sardinian government (1852-59, 1860-61); pursued a policy of unifying Italy under the supremacy of the Savoy dynasty relying on the support of Napoleon III; headed the first government of united Italy in 1861.—309

Cecil, William, Baron Burgley (or *Burleigh*) (1520-1598)—British statesman, Chief Secretary of State (1558-72), Lord High Treasurer (1572-98) and Chief Minister of Queen Elisabeth.—195

Chamfort, Sébastien Roch Nicolas, dit de (1741-1794)—French writer.—545

Changarnier, Nicolas Anne Théodule (1793-1877)—French general and politician, monarchist; took part in the conquest of Algeria in the 1830s and 1840s; deputy to the Constituent and Legislative Assemblies (1848-51); expelled from France after the coup d'état of 2 December 1851.—177

Charles I (1600-1649)—King of Great Britain and Ireland (1625-49); beheaded during the English Revolution.—182

Charles II (1630-1685)—King of Great Britain and Ireland (1660-85).—377

Charles V (1500-1558)—Holy Roman Emperor (1519-56) and King of Spain under the name of Charles (Carlos) I (1516-56).—419-21, 443, 445

Charles XII (1682-1718)—King of Sweden (1697-1718).—8, 10, 91

Charles Louis (Karl Ludwig Johann) (1771-1847)—Archduke of Austria, field marshal, took part in the wars against the French Republic and Napoleonic France; War Minister (1805-09).—164

Charras, Jean Baptiste Adolphe (1810-1865)—French military writer, moderate republican; opposed Louis Bonaparte; expelled from France after the coup d'état of 2 December 1851.—258, 285

Cheney, Eliza (born c. 1832)—Felice Orsini's housemaid.—255

Chester (alias *Polly Evans*)—mistress of Potter, Mayor of Manchester.—118

Chojecki, Karol Edmund (pseudonym—*Charles Edmond*) (1822-1899)—Polish journalist, writer and dramatist, lived in France from 1844.—18

Cicero (Marcus Tullius Cicero) (106-43 B.C.)—Roman statesman, orator and philosopher; helped expose Catiline's conspiracy in 63 B.C.—5, 269

Cieszkowski, August, Count (1814-1894)—Polish philosopher and economist, owner of an estate in the Posen district from 1847; deputy to the Prussian National Assembly (Left wing) in 1848; member of the Prussian Provincial Diet (from 1852).—436

Clarendon, George William Frederick Villiers, Earl of, Baron Hyde (1800-1870)—British statesman, Whig, later Liberal; Lord-Lieutenant of Ireland (1847-52); Foreign Secretary (1853-58, 1865-66, 1868-70).—28-30, 119

Clausewitz, Karl von (1780-1831)—Prussian general and military theoretician.—198, 241, 247

Clotilde, princesse de Savoie (1843-1911)—daughter of Victor Emmanuel II of Sardinia; wife of Prince Joseph Napoléon (Plon-Plon) from 1859.—373, 380

Cluss, Adolf (1825-1905)—German engineer; member of the Communist League; emigrated to the USA (1848), where, in the 1850s, he was a member of German-American workers' organisations; one of the first propagandists of scientific communism in America.—96, 313, 317, 363, 366, 374, 375, 571

Cobbett, William (c. 1762-1835)—British politician and radical journalist; published *Cobbett's Annual Register* from 1802.—42, 266

Cobden, Richard (1804-1865)—English manufacturer and politician, a leader of the Free Traders and founder of the Anti-Corn Law League, M.P.—3, 115, 127

Coehorn (Cohorn or *Coehoorn), Menno, Baron van* (1641-1704)—Dutch general and military engineer.—247

Colin—see *Campbell, Sir Colin, Baron Clyde*

**Collet, Collet Dobson*—English radical journalist and public figure, editor and publisher of *The Free Press,* organ of Urquhart's followers (1856-65).—61, 62, 66, 67, 76, 81, 112, 138, 277, 504, 507, 508, 521

Coningham, William (b. 1815)—English radical M.P.; author of the anti-Palmerston pamphlet *The Betrayal of England;* delegated to the Chartist conference in February 1858.—111, 210

Constantine (Konstantin Nikolayevich) (1827-1892)—Grand Duke of Russia, second son of Nicholas I, Admiral-General, head of the Naval Department (1853-81) and commander-in-chief of the Navy (1855-81).—452

Cookes—owners of textile factory in Manchester.—212

Cornelius, Wilhelm—German radical journalist, refugee in London in the 1850s; one of Marx's friends.—92, 94, 119

Cotta, Johann Georg, Baron von Cottendorf (1796-1863) — German publisher, owner of a large publishing house in Augsburg in 1832-63, publisher of the *Allgemeine Zeitung.*—363, 541, 543

Cowley, Henry Richard Charles Wellesley, Earl of (1804-1884)—British diplomat; ambassador to Paris (1852-67).—425-26

Coxe, William (1747-1828)—English historian and traveller, archdeacon in Wiltshire from 1804; collected and published historical documents.—17

Crawshay, George—English journalist, supporter of David Urquhart; an editor of *The Free Press* (1856-60).—479

Cromwell, Oliver (1599-1658)—leader of the English Revolution; Lord Protector of England, Scotland and Ireland from 1653.—182

**Cyples, William* (1831-1882)—English journalist and politician, Urquhartite; contributor to *The Sheffield Free Press* and Secretary of the Sheffield Foreign Committee (1856).—44, 59, 60, 62

D

Dagobert I (born c. 605-639)—Frankish king (629-39).—19

Dähnhardt, Marie Wilhelmine—see *Stirner-Schmidt, Marie Wilhelmine*

Dana, Charles Anderson (1819-1897)—American journalist, an editor and in 1849-62 editor-in-chief of the *New-York Daily Tribune,* an editor of *The New American Cyclopaedia* (1857-63).—68, 81, 93, 97, 101, 114, 119, 122-28, 134, 136, 140, 142, 144-45, 158-60, 168, 170, 173, 177, 190, 195, 197, 223, 238, 239, 241, 250-52, 254, 257, 259, 262, 263-64, 266, 267, 285, 361, 362, 389, 393, 410, 412, 452, 453, 483, 489, 491, 494, 507, 565

Daniells—a man from Manchester who started a lawsuit against Engels in 1859.—490, 491, 500, 510, 524

Daniels, Amalie (née *Müller*) (1820-1895)—Ronald Daniels' wife.—337, 385, 388, 477

* Asterisks are placed before the names of correspondents of Marx and Engels.—*Ed.*

E

G

German historian of literature, a publisher of *Allgemeine Encyclopädie*.—147, 187, 247

Grün, Karl Theodor Ferdinand (pen-name *Ernst von der Haide*) (1817-1887)—German journalist, 'true socialist' in the mid-1840s; petty-bourgeois democrat during the revolution of 1848-49; deputy to the Prussian National Assembly (Left wing).—63

Gumpert, Edouard (d. 1893)—German physician in Manchester, a friend of Marx and Engels.—318, 324, 325, 335, 345, 389, 439, 447, 475, 480

Gurowski, Adam, Count (1805-1866)—Polish journalist; betrayed the national liberation movement; emigrated to the USA in 1849; contributed to the *New-York Daily Tribune* in the 1850s, disseminated pan-Slavist ideas.—81, 94, 101, 123

Gyllenborg, Carl, Count (1679-1746)—Swedish statesman, envoy to London (1715-17), Secretary of State from 1718 and Prime Minister (1739-46).—9, 10

Gyulay, Franz (or *Gyulai, Ferenc*), *Count von Maros-Németh und Nadaska* (1798-1868)—Austrian general, Hungarian by birth; took part in suppressing the 1848-49 revolution in Italy; War Minister (1849-50); during the Italian war of 1859 commanded the Austrian army (April-June 1859).—427, 430

H

Hacquet, Belsazar (Balthasar) (1739-1815)—Austrian scientist and ethnographer.—16

Hájek z Libočan, Václav (c. 1500-1553)—Czech chronicler, priest.—17

Hamelin, François Alphonse (1796-1864)—French admiral, commander-in-chief of the French fleet in the Mediterranean and the Black Sea (1853-54); Minister of the Navy (1855-60).—31

Hamilton, Lord Claud (1813-1884)—British politician, M.P. from 1839.—21

Hanka, Václav (1791-1861) — Czech philologist and historian; held conservative pan-Slavist views.—15, 19, 26

Hannibal (c. 247-183 B.C.)—Carthaginian general.—294

Harney, George Julian (1817-1897)—a leader of the Left-wing Chartists, editor of *The Northern Star* and other Chartist periodicals; was on friendly terms with Marx and Engels; at the end of 1851 temporarily distanced himself from the labour movement and drew closer to democrats.—188, 190, 196, 218, 248, 252-53, 263, 264, 308, 312-13

Harper, James (1795-1869)—American publisher, founder and head of the Harper and Brothers publishing firm.—106

Harring, Harro Paul (1798-1870)—German writer, radical, emigrated in 1828.—264

Hart, Richard—English journalist, Urquhartite, lawyer in Coal Hole.—565

Harvey—English physician.—4

Hatzfeldt, Sophie, Countess von (1805-1881)—German aristocrat who broke with her husband; friend and follower of Lassalle.—23, 24, 27, 227, 257, 260, 478

Hatzfeldt-Wildenburg, Edmund, Count von (1798-1874)—Sophie Hatzfeldt's husband.—23, 27

Haugwitz, Christian August Heinrich Kurt, Count von (1752-1832)—Prussian statesman, Foreign Minister (1792-1804, 1805-06).—537

Havelock, Sir Henry (1795-1857)—British general, took part in several colonial wars and in suppressing the national liberation uprising in India in 1857.—176, 182, 184, 234, 242

I

Inglis, Sir John Eardley Wilmot (1814-1862)—British general; took part in suppressing the national liberation uprising in India in 1857-59.—247

* *Ironside, Isaac*—English journalist, Urquhartite, editor of *The Sheffield Free Press* and an editor of the London *Free Press* (1856-64).—44, 56-62

J

Jacobi, Abraham (1830-1919)—German physician, member of the Communist League, one of the accused in the Cologne Communist Trial (1852), acquitted; later emigrated to the USA.—98

Jacobi, Fritz (d. 1862)—German democrat; took part in the 1848-49 revolution, emigrated to the USA in 1852.—293

Jahn, Friedrich Ludwig (1778-1852)—German writer, organised the sports movement *(Turn- und Sportbewegung)* in Germany, prominent in the German people's liberation struggle against Napoleon's rule; nationalist.—437

Jakob—see *Robinson, Therese Albertine Luise*

James, Edwin John (1812-1882)—English lawyer, M.P.; counsel for the defence at Simon Bernard's trial in April 1858.—309

James Stuart, so-called *James III* (1688-1766)—son of James II; pretender to the English throne.—8-10

James, William (d. 1827)—English military writer.—84

John (Johann) (1782-1859)—Archduke of Austria, field marshal; fought in the wars against Napoleonic France; Imperial Regent of Germany (June 1848-December 1849).—525

Johnson, Samuel (1709-1784)—English lexicographer, compiler of a dictionary of the English language (1755); published an eight-volume edition of Shakespeare's works (1765).—46

Jomini, Antoine Henri, Baron (1779-1869)—Swiss-born general serving in the French and later in the Russian army; military theoretician, author of several works on strategy and military history.—163, 165, 174-75, 177, 289, 293

Jones, Ernest Charles (1819-1869)—English proletarian poet and journalist, Left-wing Chartist leader, editor of the *Notes to the People* and *The People's Paper;* friend of Marx and Engels; in 1858 came to an agreement with bourgeois radicals, which was the cause of Marx's and Engels' temporary break with him (till 1860).—32, 34, 38, 42, 44, 60, 65, 115, 204, 210, 228, 250, 264, 342, 344, 345, 348, 375, 565

Jones, Jane (née *Atherley*) (d. 1857)—Ernest Jones' wife.—147, 565

Jones, John Felix (d. 1878)—English naval officer and military topographer; agent in Bushire (1855-58).—112, 115

Jordan, Johann Christoph—German historian, author of a book on the origin of the Slavs (1745).—16

Joss, Fritz from Untergrombach (died c. 1525)—organiser of secret peasant alliances and conspiracies in South Germany.—444

Joule, James Prescott (1818-1889)—English physicist, experimentally substantiated the law of conservation of energy.—327

Jourdan, Jean Baptiste, comte (1762-1833)—French general, marshal from 1804, fought in the wars of the French Republic and Napoleonic France.—166, 167

Juch, Hermann—German journalist, petty-bourgeois democrat, refugee in London, Kinkel's supporter, editor of the *Hermann* (from July 1859).—404, 438, 473, 512, 552, 554

Jung, Georg Gottlob (1814-1886)—German democratic journalist, Young Hegelian, a manager of the *Rheinische Zeitung;* deputy to the Prussian National Assembly (Left wing) in 1848.—478

Juta, Johann Carl (1824-1886)—Dutch merchant, husband of Karl Marx's sister Luise, bookseller in Cape Town.—363, 387, 389, 390, 394, 418, 489, 494, 506, 572

Juvenal (Decimus Junius Juvenalis) (born c. 60-died after 127)—Roman satirical poet.—391, 469

K

Kamenski, Mikhail Fedotovich, Count (1738-1809)—Russian field-marshal general.—162

Kamm, Friedrich (d. 1867)—German artisan, petty-bourgeois democrat; took part in the 1849 Baden-Palatinate uprising; emigrated first to Switzerland and, in 1852, to the USA; an organiser of the Communist Club in New York (1857).—288, 293, 469

Kant, Immanuel (1724-1804)—German philosopher.—356, 392, 519

Kapper, Siegfried (1821-1879)—Czech writer and poet, translator of Slavic legends and songs into German.—20, 26

Karadžić, Vuk Stefanović (1787-1864)—Serbian philologist, historian and folklore specialist, founder of the modern Serbian literary language.—20, 26

Karl Leopold (1679-1747)—Duke of Mecklenburg (1713-28).—11

Karstens—see *Lessner, Friedrich*

Kerb—owner of a tavern in London.—18

Kinkel, Gottfried (1815-1882)—German poet and democratic journalist; took part in the 1849 Baden-Palatinate uprising; sentenced to life imprisonment by Prussian court; in 1850 escaped and emigrated to London, a leader of the petty-bourgeois refugees; editor of the *Hermann* (1859); opposed Marx and Engels.—203, 293, 340, 345, 351, 356, 359, 361, 363, 366, 367, 369, 370, 371, 372, 375, 376, 383, 385, 386, 388, 399, 404, 408, 415, 438-40, 446, 447-48, 449, 458-60, 463, 468, 477, 482, 508, 511-13, 519, 520, 525-27, 530, 533-36, 537, 541, 545, 547, 551, 553-56, 574

Kinkel, Johanna (née *Mockel*) (1810-1858)—German writer, wife of Gottfried Kinkel.—356, 359, 361, 363, 371, 372, 375, 382, 385, 388, 458, 513, 541, 553

Kiss, Miklós (1820-1902)—Hungarian army officer, democrat, refugee, Kossuth's agent in France and Italy.—532

Klapka, György (1820-1892)—general in the Hungarian revolutionary army (1848-49); emigrated in 1849; maintained contact with Bonapartist circles in the 1850s.—324, 452, 523, 532

Klaproth, Heinrich Julius (1783-1835)—German philologist, orientalist and traveller.—26

Klein, Johann Jacob (c. 1818-c. 1896)—Cologne physician, member of the Communist League, one of the accused in the Cologne Communist Trial (1852), acquitted.—477

Koenigswarter, Maximilien (1815-1878)—French banker, deputy to the Corps législatif (1852-63).—90

Koesteritz von—Chief Public Prosecutor in Düsseldorf, took part in the divorce case of Countess Hatzfeldt.—23

Kolatschek, Adolph (1821-1889)—Austrian journalist and politician; deputy to the Frankfurt National Assembly (1848-49); petty-bourgeois democrat.—106

Kolb, Gustav Eduard (1798-1865)—German journalist, editor-in-chief of the Augsburg *Allgemeine Zeitung* (1837-65).—541, 543, 549

Komp, Albrecht—German refugee in the USA, an organiser of the Communist Club in New York (1857); Joseph Weydemeyer's friend. — 338, 376, 384, 440

Korff, Hermann—Prussian ex-officer, democrat; manager of the *Neue Rheinische Zeitung* (1848-49); later emigrated to the USA.—434

Kościelski, Władisław (1818-1895)—Polish democrat; took part in the Posen national liberation movement (1848), maintained ties with the editors of the *Neue Rheinische Zeitung;* general in the Turkish army (1850s).—109

Kościuszko, Tadeusz Andrzej Bonawentura (1746-1817)—Polish general and leader of the national liberation uprising of 1794; took part in the American War of Independence (1776-83).—85

Kossuth, Lajos (1802-1894)—leader of the Hungarian national liberation movement; head of the revolutionary government (1848-49); after the defeat of the revolution emigrated first to Turkey and later to England and the USA; sought for support in the Bonapartist circles in the 1850s.—258, 318, 324, 342, 382, 452, 456, 458, 465, 476, 494, 497, 505-07, 523, 525, 532, 565, 573

Köster, Heinrich (1807-1881)—German philologist and teacher, an acquaintance of Ferdinand Lassalle and Ferdinand Freiligrath.—353-55

Krosigk, Lisette von (Louise Friederike Ottilie Caroline) (née *von Westphalen*) (1800-1863)—Jenny Marx's stepsister.—562

Krukowiecki, Jan (c. 1770-1850)—Polish general, Governor-General of Warsaw during the 1830-31 Polish insurrection, headed the government (August-September 1831).—169

Kutter, Wilhelm—one of Engels' acquaintances in Bradford.—422

Kutuzov, Mikhail Illarionovich, Prince of Smolensk (1745-1813)—Russian general, field marshal, took part in the wars with Turkey and Napoleonic France, commander-in-chief of the Russian army in 1812.—163

L

La Guéronnière, Louis Étienne Arthur Dubreuil Hélion, vicomte de (1816-1875)—French journalist and politician; Bonapartist in the 1850s.—384

Lallerstedt, Sven Gustaf (1816-1864)—Swedish journalist and historian.—91

La Marmora (Lamarmora), Alfonso Ferrero, marchese de (1804-1878)—Italian general and statesman; War Minister (1848, 1849-55, 1856-59) and Prime Minister (July 1859-January 1860) of Piedmont; commanded a Sardinian corps in the Crimea (1855); Prime Minister of the Kingdom of Italy (1864-66).—309

Lamoricière, Christophe Léon Louis Juchault de (1806-1865)—French general, moderate Republican; took part in the conquest of Algeria in the 1830s-40s and in suppressing the June 1848 uprising in Paris; expelled from France after the coup d'état of 2 December 1851.—89, 177

Landolphe—French socialist, a refugee in London; joined the sectarian Willich-Schapper group in 1850.—357, 363

Landor, Walter Savage (1775-1864)—English poet, writer and critic; was suspected of being an accomplice in Orsini's attempt on the life of Napoleon III in 1858.—290

Lange, F. W. L.—German refugee in London, member of the German Workers' Educational Society in Lon-

tional liberation movement; took part in the 1830-31 Polish insurrection and in the 1848-49 revolution in Germany; later a leader of the moderate Polish democratic émigrés; sought for support among the Bonapartist circles in the 1850s.—75, 80, 85, 91, 105, 106

Miklosich, Franz von (Miklošić, František) (1813-1891)—professor of Slavic philology at Vienna University (1849-86); founder of the comparative grammar of Slavic languages; Slovenian by birth.—403

Mill, James (1773-1836)—English economist and philosopher.—377

Miquel, Johannes von (1828-1901)—German politician, member of the Communist League; later a national-liberal.—31, 42-44, 59, 99, 100, 106, 134, 135, 136

Mirbach, Otto von (born c. 1800)—retired Prussian artillery officer, democrat; commandant of Elberfeld during the May 1849 uprising; emigrated from Germany.—61, 65, 564

Mockel, Johanna—see *Kinkel, Johanna*

Moleschott, Jakob (1822-1893)—Dutch physiologist and philosopher, taught in Germany, Switzerland and Italy.—55, 282, 356

Molière (real name *Jean Baptiste Poquelin*) (1622-1673)—French dramatist.—499

Mommsen, Theodor (1817-1903)—German historian, author of works on the history of Ancient Rome.—127, 294

Montalembert, Charles Forbes René de Tryon, comte de (1810-1870)—French politician and journalist; deputy to the Constituent and Legislative Assemblies (1848-51); Orleanist, leader of the Catholic circles; supported Louis Bonaparte during the coup d'état of 2 December 1851, but soon afterwards joined the opposition.—351, 361

Montesquieu, Charles Louis de Secondat, baron de La Brède et de (1689-1755)—French sociologist, economist and writer.—377, 396

Morell, John Daniel (1816-1891)—English philosopher, theologist and man of letters; a participant in the Schiller festival in Manchester in November 1859.—530

Morny, Charles Auguste Louis Joseph, duc de (1811-1865)—French politician, Bonapartist; an organiser of the coup d'état of 2 December 1851; Minister of the Interior (December 1851-January 1852); President of the Corps législatif (1854-56, 1857-65); ambassador to Russia (1856-57); step-brother of Napoleon III.—7, 34, 83, 94, 105, 291-93

Mortier, Edouard Adolphe Casimir Joseph, duc de Trévise (1768-1835)—Marshal of France, took part in the wars of Napoleonic France.—163, 166, 167

Morton—one of the acquaintances of the Marx family in London.—572

Müffling, Friedrich Karl Ferdinand, Baron von (1775-1851)—Prussian general, later field-marshal general; military writer; took part in the wars against Napoleonic France.—172, 179, 180, 198

Müller, Adam Heinrich, Ritter von Nitterdorf (1779-1829)—German journalist and economist, representative of the so-called Romantic school, which expressed the interests of feudal aristocracy.—4

Münnich (Münich), Khristofor Antonovich (Burkhard Christoph), Count von (1683-1767)—Russian field-marshal general, engineer; commander-in-chief of the Russian forces in the Crimea and Bessarabia during the Russo-Turkish war of 1735-39; German by birth.—3

Muñoz Benavente, José (Pucheta) (1820-1856)—Spanish bull-fighter; active participant in the 1854-56 revolution; a leader of popular masses in Mad-

P

of Trade, Industry and Public Works (April-June 1848), Finance Minister (1858-62).—379

Pauer, Ernst (1826-1905)—Austrian composer and pianist; from 1851 lived in London; professor at the Royal College of Music and director of a German song society.—512

Paul, Sir John Dean (1802-1868)—English banker; went bankrupt in June 1855; was sentenced to penal servitude for financial machinations.—72

Paula-Kröcher (Paulaw) from Breslau (Wrocław).—341, 383

Pauly, August Friedrich von (1796-1845)—German philologist, from 1830 professor of a grammar school in Stuttgart; publisher and editor of *Real-Encyklopädie der classischen Alterthumswissenschaft*.—147, 187

Payne, Annie—English ballet dancer.—118

Peabody, George (1795-1869)—American financier, philanthropist; head of a bank firm in London (from 1837).—212, 567

Peel, Sir Robert (1788-1850)—British statesman, moderate Tory; Home Secretary (1822-27, 1828-30), Prime Minister (1834-35, 1841-46); repealed the Corn Laws in 1846.—102, 104, 107

Pélissier, Aimable Jean Jacques (1794-1864)—Marshal of France, took part in the conquest of Algeria in the 1830s-early 50s; commander-in-chief in the Crimea (May 1855-July 1856); ambassador to London (1858-59); commander of the army of observation at Nancy (1859).—292, 296, 317, 321, 381

Pelletan, Pierre Clément Eugène (1813-1884)—French journalist and politician, moderate republican.—43

Perczel, Mór (1811-1899)—Hungarian general; took part in the 1848-49 revolution in Hungary; after the defeat of the revolution emigrated to Turkey and in 1851 to England.—506

Péreire, Isaac (1806-1880)—French banker, Bonapartist; deputy to the Corps législatif; founded the joint-stock bank Crédit mobilier together with his brother Émile Péreire (1852).—90, 119, 133, 216

Persigny, Jean Gilbert Victor Fialin, comte (1808-1872) — French statesman, Bonapartist; an organiser of the coup d'état of 2 December 1851; Minister of the Interior (1852-54, 1860-63); ambassador to London (1855-58, 1859-60).—278

Peter I (the Great) (1672-1725)—Tsar of Russia (1682-1721), Emperor of Russia (from 1721).—8-11, 58, 91, 120

Petermann, August (1822-1878)—German geographer and cartographer, editor of the periodicals *Mittheilungen aus Justus Perthes' geographischer Anstalt* in Gotha (from 1855).—349

Petersen, Niels Lorenzo (1814-died after 1889)—prominent figure in the Danish and international working-class movement; Communist League member; contributed to *Das Volk* (1859); later member of the First International; a leader of the Left wing of the Social-Democratic Party of Denmark.—476

Peto, Sir Samuel Morton (1809-1889)—English businessman, M.P., liberal.—114

Petty, Sir William (1623-1687)—English economist and statistician, founder of the classical school of political economy in Britain.—298, 377

Pfänder, Karl (c. 1818-1876)—German artist; refugee in London from 1845, member of the German Workers' Educational Society in London, of the Communist League and later of the General Council of the First

International; friend and associate of Marx and Engels.—313, 384, 398, 407, 417, 431, 437, 451

Pfeil, Count von—Prussian Junker, member of the Prussian Provincial Diet.—20, 26

Philips—Dutch relatives of Karl Marx.—332

Philips, Lion (1794-1866)—Dutch merchant, maternal uncle of Karl Marx.—336

Philipson, Grigory Ivanovich (1809-1883)—Russian general; took part in the war against Caucasian mountaineers.—310

Pieper, Wilhelm (born c. 1826-1899)—German philologist and journalist; member of the Communist League; refugee in London; was close to Marx and Engels in 1850-53.—8, 14, 22, 32-33, 35, 41-42, 44, 46, 53, 54, 59-60, 61, 65, 66, 69, 76, 98, 120, 124, 125, 128, 171, 174, 225, 232, 242-43, 255, 350, 351, 384, 412, 451, 561

Pierre—see *Peter I (the Great)*

Pitt, L.K.—cousin of William Pitt the Younger, priest at the English trading station in St. Petersburg.—17

Pitt, William (the Younger) (1759-1806)—British statesman, Tory; Prime Minister (1783-1801, 1804-06).—17

Pius IX (Giovanni Maria Mastai-Ferretti) (1792-1878)—Pope (1846-78).—381, 425

Place, Henri—French financier, a governor of the joint-stock bank Crédit mobilier.—133

Plato (c. 427-c. 347 B. C.)—Greek philosopher.—397

Plon-Plon—see *Bonaparte, Prince Napoléon Joseph Charles Paul*

Plutarch (c. 46-c. 125)—Greek writer, historian and philosopher.—269

Poèrio, Carlo (1803-1867)—Italian liberal, participant in the national liberation movement; Prefect of Police and Minister of Education in Naples (1848); was imprisoned (1849-59); in 1859 was deported to South America but en route fled to England.—405

Pondu, John—businessman in Manchester.—235

Potter, Sir John (d. 1858)—British liberal, M.P., was elected mayor of Manchester three times.—104, 113, 115, 117, 121

Potter, Sir Thomas (1773-1845)—English tradesman and politician, a leader of Manchester liberals and founder of *The Manchester Guardian*, was twice elected mayor of Manchester; John Potter's father.—118

Pozzo di Borgo, Karl Osipovich, Count (1764-1842)—Russian diplomat; Corsican by birth; envoy to Paris (1814-21), ambassador to Paris (1821-35) and to London (1835-39).—9, 468, 470

Prince of Prussia—see *William I*

Procopius (end of 5th cent.-after 562)—Byzantine writer, author of an eight-volume history of Justinian's wars against the Persians, Vandals and Goths, which contained data on the Slavs.—16

Proudhon, Pierre Joseph (1809-1865)—French writer, economist and sociologist; a founder of anarchism.—18, 90, 106, 301, 303, 377, 396, 460, 473, 538

Prutz, Robert Eduard (1816-1872)—German poet, journalist and historian of literature, liberal; associated with Young Hegelians; publisher of the journal *Deutsches Museum* in Leipzig (1851-67).—356, 385

Pucheta—see *Muñoz Benavente, José*

Pulszky, Ferenc (1814-1897)—Hungarian politician, writer and archaeologist; Pole by birth; took part in the 1848-49 revolution in Hungary;

S

chief of the General Staff of the revolutionary army; after the defeat of the revolution emigrated to Turkey where he assumed the name of Ferhad Pasha; fought against Russia in the Caucasus (1857-58).—318

Steinthal—owner of the Manchester trading firm in which Georg Weerth was employed in 1852-56.—72, 100, 103, 484

Stephens (Stevens), John Edward—English banker, a governor of the London and the Eastern Bank, was brought to trial for financial machinations in December 1857.—223

Steuart, Sir James, afterwards *Denham* (1712-1780)—English economist, one of the last representatives of mercantilism.—301, 377

Stewart (afterwards *Vane*), *Charles William, Marquis of Londonderry* (1778-1854)—British general.—164

Stieber, Wilhelm (1818-1882)—Prussian police officer, an organiser of the prosecution at the Cologne Communist Trial (1852), chief of the Prussian political police (1850-60).—31, 41, 56, 378, 379, 536, 552, 554

Stirner, Max (real name *Schmidt, Johann Caspar*) (1806-1856) — German Young Hegelian philosopher, an ideologist of individualism and anarchism.—70

Stirner-Schmidt, Marie Wilhelmine (née *Dähnhardt*) (1818-1902)—Max Stirner's wife.—71

Stockum, Franz August von—merchant in Düsseldorf, Count Hatzfeldt's solicitor in his divorce case, was sentenced to prison for forgery in 1855.—23

Stocqueler, Joachim Hayward (1800-1885)—English journalist, compiler of the military encyclopaedic dictionary.—135

Strahan, William (born c. 1808)—English banker, partner of a firm which went bankrupt in June 1855; was sentenced to penal servitude for financial machinations.—72

Stratford de Redcliffe, Stratford Canning, Viscount (1786-1880)—British diplomat, envoy to Constantinople (1810-12, 1825-28, 1841-58).—28-31

Stritter, Johann Gotthelf (1740-1801)—Russian historian, author of works on the history of Slavs and ancient Russia, German by birth.—16, 17

Strodtmann, Adolf (1829-1879)—German democratic writer; took part in the revolutionary movement in Schleswig-Holstein in 1848; emigrated in 1850; admirer and biographer of Gottfried Kinkel.—359, 553

Strohn, Wilhelm—member of the Communist League, refugee resident in Bradford; an acquaintance of Marx and Engels.—69, 84, 439, 467, 475, 480, 481

Struve, Gustav von (1805-1870)—German democratic journalist; a leader of the Baden uprisings in April and September 1848 and of the Baden-Palatinate uprising of 1849; one of the leaders of the German petty-bourgeois refugees in England; fought in the US Civil War on the side of the Northerners.—359, 446

Sturge, Joseph (1793-1859)—British politician, Free Trader; joined Chartists with the purpose of retaining the working class under the influence of the radical bourgeoisie.—264

Swan—see *Sandwith, Humphry*

Swingwood.—150

Swoboda (Svoboda), Václav Alois (1791-1849)—Czech writer and poet, translated Czech folk songs into German.—19, 26

* *Szemere, Bertalan (Bartholomäus)* (1812-1869)—Hungarian politician and journalist; Minister of the Interior (1848) and head of the revolutionary government (1849); emigrated after the defeat of the revolution.—493-95, 497, 504-05, 523, 525, 532, 573

T

Talandier, Pierre Théodore Alfred (1822-1890)—French democratic journalist; took part in the 1848 revolution; emigrated to London after the coup d'état of 1851.—38, 277, 278

Talleyrand-Périgord, Charles Maurice, prince de (1754-1838)—French diplomat, Foreign Minister (1797-99, 1799-1807, 1814-15); represented France at the Vienna Congress (1814-15).—416

Talvj—see *Robinson, Therese Albertine Luise*

Tassilier—French printer; exiled to Cayenne in June 1848.—31

Taube, Friedrich Wilhelm von (1728-1778)—Austrian lawyer, historian and economist, government official from 1763; made a trip to Southern Slav countries in 1776-77.—15

Tauentzien von Wittenberg, Bogislaw Friedrich Emanuel, Count (1760-1824)—Prussian general, took part in the wars against Napoleonic France in 1813-14.—179

Tausenau, Karl (1808-1873)—Austrian democrat; participant in the 1848 revolution; emigrated to London in 1849.—18, 456

Taylor, Bayard (1825-1878)—American traveller, writer and journalist, correspondent of the *New-York Daily Tribune*.—197, 566

Taylor, Tom (1817-1880)—English dramatist and journalist, in the 1850s contributor to and in 1874-80 editor of the satirical magazine *Punch;* Secretary to the Board of Health from 1854.—113

Tchorzewsky, Stanisław—Polish refugee in London, owner of a bookshop; Alexander Herzen's friend, his agent in publishing and distributing Russian emigrant literature.—349

Teleki, László, Count (1811-1861)—Hungarian politician and writer, represented the Hungarian Republic in France (1848-49); after the defeat of the revolution remained in France.—532

Terence (Publius Terentius Afer) (c. 190-159 B.C.)—Roman author of comedies.—310, 410

Terentianus Maurus (latter half of the 2nd cent.)—Roman grammarian.—441

Thackeray, William Makepeace (1811-1863)—English writer.—441

Theodores—a participant in the Schiller festival in Manchester (November 1859).—530

Theyls, Willem—Dutch diplomat; at the beginning of the 18th century served at Dutch Embassy in Turkey; carried out diplomatic missions for the Russian government.—470

Thiers, Louis Adolphe (1797-1877)—French historian and statesman, Prime Minister (1836, 1840), deputy to the Constituent (1848) and Legislative (1849-51) Assemblies; head of the Orleanists after 1848; organised the suppression of the Paris Commune (1871); President of the Republic (1871-73).—292

Thiersch, Friedrich Wilhelm (1784-1860)—German philologist and teacher; sympathised with the Greek national liberation movement; travelled to Greece in 1831-32.—120

Thimm, Franz—bookseller in Manchester.—447, 467, 473, 492, 496, 500, 511

Tholuck, Friedrich August Gottreu (1799-1877)—German Protestant theologian, pietist.—4

Thurneyssen, Auguste—one of the governors of the Crédit mobilier.—133

Titian (Tiziano Vecellio) (1477-1576)—Italian painter of the Venetian school.—131

Tooke, Thomas (1774-1858)—English economist, adherent of the classical

the Turkish troops on the Kerch Peninsula (1855-56).—28-30

Vögele, August—German refugee, compositor in Hollinger's print-shop in London (1859).—521

Vogt, Karl (1817-1895)—German natural scientist, petty-bourgeois democrat; deputy to the Frankfurt National Assembly (Left wing) in 1848-49; one of the five imperial regents (June 1849); emigrated in 1849; later received subsidies from Napoleon III; slandered proletarian revolutionaries.—428, 434, 436, 458, 460, 465, 468, 477, 479, 486-88, 498, 503, 514, 515, 519, 520, 521-22, 523-25, 533, 537, 539-43, 546, 549, 550

Voigt, Johannes (1786-1863)—German historian, author of a voluminious work on the history of Prussia.—16

Voigt, Mikuláš (Adauctus) (1733-1787)—Czech historian, philologist and numismatist of the Enlightenment; collector of ancient literary texts.—16

Voltaire, François Marie Arouet (1694-1778)—French philosopher, writer and historian of the Enlightenment.—75

Vorontsov (Woronzoff), Mikhail Semyonovich, Prince (1782-1856)—Russian statesman, general, commander-in-chief of the troops in Transcaucasia and Governor-General in the Caucasus; uncle of Sidney Herbert.—119

W

Wachsmuth, Ernst Wilhelm Gottlieb (1784-1866)—German historian, professor in Leipzig.—259

Walewski, Alexandre Florian Joseph Colonna, comte (1810-1868)—French diplomat and statesman, son of Napoleon I and Polish Countess Marie Walewska; Foreign Minister (1855-60).—42

Walpole, Spencer Horatio (Horace) (1806-1898)—British statesman, Tory, Home Secretary (1852, 1858-59, 1866-67).—278

Watts, John (1818-1887)—English utopian socialist, follower of Robert Owen; later a liberal and philanthropist; a founder of the People's Provident Assurance Society in London (1853), in 1857 set up a branch of this society in Manchester.—332

Weerth, Georg Ludwig (1822-1856)—German proletarian poet and journalist, member of the Communist League, an editor of the *Neue Rheinische Zeitung* in 1848-49; friend of Marx and Engels.—68, 72, 100, 103, 226, 374

Weerth, Karl (1812-1889)—German naturalist, teacher of a grammar school in Detmold, brother of Georg Weerth.—100, 103

Weerth, Wilhelmine (1785-1868)—Georg Weerth's mother.—100

Weitling, Wilhelm Christian (1808-1871)—German tailor; one of the early leaders of the working-class movement in Germany; theorist of utopian egalitarian communism; emigrated to the USA in 1849.—358, 440, 451

Weselý, Eugen (1799-1828)—Austrian poet and writer, translated folk songs of Southern Slavs into German.—20

Wesselovsky—see *Veselovsky, Fyodor Pavlovich*

Westphalen, Anna Elisabeth Franziska von (b. 1807)—Jenny Marx's stepsister.—562

Westphalen, Caroline von (née *Heubel*) (1779-1856)—Jenny Marx's mother.—59, 63, 562, 575

Westphalen, Christian Heinrich Philipp von (1724-1792)—secretary and friend of the Duke of Brunswick; took part in the Seven Years War, author of a work on its history; Jenny Marx's grandfather.—561, 562, 575

INDEX OF LITERARY AND MYTHOLOGICAL NAMES

in Lassalle's *Franz von Sickingen*.—419, 420, 443

Benedick (Benedict)—a character in Shakespeare's comedy *Much Ado About Nothing;* a wit and mocker who pretended to be a women-hater but soon fell in love and married.—33

Berlichingen, Götz (Gottfried)—a character in Goethe's play of the same name and in Lassalle's *Franz von Sickingen*.—419, 420

Brey—a character in Goethe's *Ein Fastnachtsspiel auch wohl zu tragieren Ostern, vom Pater Brey, dem falschen Propheten,* a lewd hypocrite.—541

Briseis (Gr. Myth.)—prisoner and beloved of Achilles who caused a quarrel between him and the Greeks' leader Agamemnon in the Trojan War.—512

Caliban—a character in Shakespeare's comedy *The Tempest,* half-a-man, half-a-monster.—81

Capuchin—a character in Schiller's *Wallensteins Lager*.—530

Charles V (Emperor)—a character in Lassalle's *Franz von Sickingen*.—419-21, 443, 445

Crispinus—a character from Juvenal's satire, a courtier of the Roman Emperor Domitian.—391

Don Quixote—the title character in Cervantes' novel.—419

Falstaff, Sir John—a character in Shakespeare's tragedy *King Henry IV* and his comedy *The Merry Wives of Windsor;* a sly fat braggart and jester.—41, 444

Faust—hero of a medieval German legend, the title character in Goethe's tragedy and Marlowe's play *The Tragical History of Doctor Faustus*.—91

Fidelio—fictitious name of Léonore, heroine in Beethoven's opera *Fidelio oder die eheliche Liebe;* a dedicated woman ready to sacrifice herself in the name of love.—503

Fridolin—character in Schiller's ballad *Der Gang nach dem Eisenhammer,* a kindly and modest enamoured youth.—14

Hermann—a character in Goethe's poem *Hermann und Dorothea,* a philistine who sought to keep aloof from the storms of life.—366

Hutten, Ulrich von—a character in Lassalle's *Franz von Sickingen*.—419-21, 442, 445

Jacques le bonhomme (Jack the Simpleton)—ironic nickname of the French peasant; in a broad sense—a mocking name of the French.—216

Jenkins—a name which came to denote a flatterer and toady in England.—278

John, Saint (the Baptist) (Bib.).—370

John Bull—the main character in John Arbuthnot's book *The History of John Bull* (18th cent.); the name is often used to personify England or Englishmen.—73, 113, 116, 215, 275, 276, 297, 413, 431, 457

Jonathan (Brother Jonathan)—the jocular nickname of Americans (from the name of Connecticut's Governor Jonathan Trumbull, whom George Washington called Brother Jonathan).—215-16

Joss, Fritz—a character in Lassalle's *Franz von Sickingen*.—444

Kobes I—the title character in a satirical poem by Heine; the German journalist Jakob Venedey was ridiculed under this name.—32

Legat (Der päpstliche Kardinal-Legat)—a character in Lassalle's *Franz von Sickingen*.—443

Mammon—the idol of wealth among some ancient peoples.—535

Marie—a character in Lassalle's *Franz von Sickingen,* Sickingen's daughter.—421

INDEX OF QUOTED AND MENTIONED LITERATURE

WORKS BY KARL MARX AND FREDERICK ENGELS

Marx, Karl

Affairs in Prussia (present edition, Vol. 16). In: *New-York Daily Tribune,* No. 5471, November 3, 1858.—352, 361, 365

Affairs in Prussia (present edition, Vol. 16). In: *New-York Daily Tribune,* No. 5475, November 8, 1858.—352, 361, 365

Affairs in Prussia (present edition, Vol. 16). In: *New-York Daily Tribune,* No. 5505, December 13, 1858.—355, 365

[*The Anglo-Persian War*] (present edition, Vol. 15). In: *New-York Daily Tribune,* No. 4904, January 7, 1857.—79, 93, 114

Another Strange Chapter of Modern History (present edition, Vol. 16). In: *New-York Daily Tribune,* No. 5436, September 23, 1858.—342

Bernadotte (present edition, Vol. 18). In: *The New American Cyclopaedia,* Vol. III, 1858.—165, 174-77, 259

Berthier (present edition, Vol. 18). In: *The New American Cyclopaedia,* Vol. III, 1858.—161-65, 168, 259

Bessières (present edition, Vol. 18). In: *The New American Cyclopaedia,* Vol. III, 1858.—259

Blum (present edition, Vol. 18). In: *The New American Cyclopaedia,* Vol. III, 1858.—168, 173, 259

Bolivar y Ponte (present edition, Vol. 18). In: *The New American Cyclopaedia,* Vol. III, 1858.—259, 266, 273

[*Bonaparte's Financial Manoeuvres.—Military Despotism*] (present edition, Vol. 15). In: *New-York Daily Tribune,* No. 5348, June 11, 1858.—317

Bonaparte's Present Position (present edition, Vol. 15). In: *New-York Daily Tribune,* No. 5287, April 1, 1858.—294

WORKS BY DIFFERENT AUTHORS

— 1 March 1848. In: *Hansard's Parliamentary Debates.* Third series. Vol. XCVII. London, 1848.—111, 117

Ariosto, L. *L'Orlando furioso.*—111

A[sbóth, A.] *The Austrian Hold on Italy.* To the Editor of *The N. Y. Tribune.* In: *New-York Daily Tribune,* No. 5581, March 11, 1859.—417

Asbóth, [A.] *The Chances of the Impending War.* To the Editor of *The N. Y. Tribune.* In: *New-York Daily Tribune,* No. 5602, April 5, 1859.—417

Asbóth, A. *The Peace of Villafranca and the Hungarian Cause.* In: *New-York Daily Tribune,* No. 5727, August 31, 1859.—494

Babbage, Ch. *On the Economy of Machinery and Manufactures.* London, 1832.—278, 279, 281

Balzac, H. de. *L'Histoire de la grandeur et de la décadence de Cézar Birotteau.*—70

Bastiat, Fr. *Harmonies économiques.* 2-me édition augmentée des manuscrits laissés par l'auteur. Publiée par la Société des amis de Bastiat. Paris, 1851.—249, 303

Batrachomyomachia.—51, 532

Bauer, B. *Deutschland und das Russenthum.* Charlottenburg, 1854.—90
— *Die jetzige Stellung Rußlands.* Charlottenburg, 1854.—90
— *Kritik der Evangelien und Geschichte ihres Ursprungs.* Bände I-IV. Berlin, 1850-1852.—91
— *Kritik der evangelischen Geschichte der Synoptiker.* Bd. 1-2, Leipzig, 1841; Bd. 3, Braunschweig, 1842.—4
— *La Russie et l'Angleterre.* Charlottenburg, 1854.—90
— *Rußland und England.* Charlottenburg, 1854.—90
— *Rußland und das Germanenthum.* Charlottenburg, 1853.—90
— *Rußland und das Germanenthum.* Zweite Abtheilung. *Die deutsche und die orientalische Frage.* Charlottenburg, 1853.—90

Bauer, E. *Englische Freiheit.* Leipzig, 1857.—68, 106, 122
— *Vorträge über die Geschichte der Politik,* gehalten im Arbeiterbildungsverein zu London. Erster Vortrag. In: *Die Neue Zeit,* Nr. 20, 6. November 1858.—353, 358

[Bauer, E.] *Englische Neutralität.* In: *Hermann,* Nr. 18, 7. Mai 1859 ('Politik').—440
— *Das Kloster.* Ein Roman. In: *Die Neue Zeit,* Nr. 38-42, 19., 26. März, 2., 10., 16. April 1859.—415
— *Preussens constitutioneller Imperialismus.* In: *Die Neue Zeit,* Nr. 22, 27. November 1858.—359

Bazancourt, de. *L'expédition de Crimée jusqu'à la prise de Sébastopol. Chroniques de la guerre d'orient.* In 2 parts. Paris, 1856.—5, 51, 71, 73, 80, 93, 124

[Bem, J.] *Ueber die Vertheidigung Warschau's am 6 und 7 Sept. 1831.* In: *Allgemeine Zeitung* (München), Nr. 470-75, 3-6. Dezember, 1831.—169

Berkeley, G. *The Querist Containing Several Queries, Proposed to the Consideration of the Public.* London, 1750.—377

Die Beschwerden und Klagen der Slaven in Ungarn über die gesetzwidrigen Uebergriffe der Magyaren. Vorgetragen von einem ungarischen Slaven. Leipzig, 1843.—20

B[eta, H.] *Ferdinand Freiligrath* (Lebensskizze mit Portrait). In: *Die Gartenlaube. Illustriertes Familienblatt,* Nr. 43, 1859.—532, 534, 537, 540-42, 546, 550, 556

Bray, J. F. *Labour's Wrongs and Labour's Remedy; Or, the Age of Might and the Age of Right.* Leeds, 1839.—301

Bright, J. [Speech at a meeting of Birmingham constituents on October 27, 1858.] In: *The Times,* No. 23136, October 28, 1858.—358
— [Speech in the House of Commons on 24 March 1859.] In: *The Times,* No. 23263, March 25, 1859.—411

Brockhaus' Konversations-Lexikon. Leipzig.—123, 135, 252, 267

B[ucher,] L. *Louis Napoleon's Laufbahn.* In: *Hermann,* Nr. 19, 14. Mai 1859 ('Politik').—440

Bürger, G. A. *Lenore.*—102, 139

Campbell, E. S. N. *A Dictionary of the Military Science: Containing an Explanation of the Principal Terms Used in Mathematics, Artillery, and Fortification, and Comprising the Substance of the Latest Regulations on Courts Martial, Pay, Pensions, Allowances, etc. A Comparative Table of Ancient and Modern Geography; Achievements of the British Army; with an Address to Gentlemen Entering the Army.* London, 1830.—142

Carey, H. Ch. *Essay on the Rate of Wages: with an Examination of the Causes of the Differences in the Condition of the Labouring Population throughout the World.* Philadelphia, 1835.—303

Cathcart, G. *Commentaries on the War in Russia and Germany in 1812 and 1813.* London, 1850.—293

Cavour, C. B. [Speech of 16 April 1858 in the Chamber of Representatives of the Kingdom of Piedmont.] In: *The Times,* No. 22973, April 21, 1858. 'Sardinia'. (From Our Own Correspondent.) Turin, April 17.—309

Chamfort, S. R. N. *Maximes et Pensées.*—545

Charras, J. B. A. *Histoire de la campagne de 1815. Waterloo.* Leipzig, 1857.—258, 285

Clausewitz, C. von. *Der Feldzug von 1812 in Rußland, der Feldzug von 1813 bis zum Waffenstillstand und der Feldzug von 1814 in Frankreich.* In: *Hinterlassene Werke des Generals Carl von Clausewitz über Krieg und Kriegführung.* Bd. 7. Berlin, 1835.—198, 247
— *Der Feldzug von 1815 in Frankreich.* In: *Hinterlassene Werke des Generals Carl von Clausewitz über Krieg und Kriegführung.* Bd. 8. Berlin, 1835.—198, 247
— *Vom Kriege.* In: *Hinterlassene Werke des Generals Carl von Clausewitz über Krieg und Kriegführung.* Bd. 1-3. Berlin, 1832-1834.—242, 243

Cobden, R. *What Next and Next?* London, 1856.—3

Coningham, W. *The Betrayal of England. Addressed to the Working Classes.* London, 1848.—111, 117

Crawshay, G. *The Russian Memoir of 1837.* In: *The Free Press,* No. 8, July 27, 1859.—479

Darimon, A. *De la réforme des banques.* Avec une introduction par M. Émile de Girardin. Paris, 1856.—90

Darwin, Ch. *On the Origin of Species by Means of Natural Selection, or the Preservation of Favoured Races in the Struggle for Life.* London, 1859.—551

Derby, E. G. [Speeches in the House of Lords]
— 1 March 1858. In: *The Times,* No. 22930, March 2, 1858.—278
— 18 April 1859. In: *The Times,* No. 23284, April 19, 1859.—425-27

Desprez, H. *Les peuples de l'Autriche et de la Turquie.* Histoire contemporaine des Illyriens, des Magyars, des Roumains et des Polonais. Tomes 1-2. Paris, 1850.—17, 20

Destrilhes. *Confidences sur la Turquie.* Paris, 1855.—31, 37

Disraeli, B. [Speech in the House of Commons on 18 April 1859]. In: *The Times,* No. 23284, April 19, 1859.—425

[Dobner, J. F.] (Gelasius) *Wenceslai Hagek a Liboczan, Annales Bohemorum e bohemica editione latine redditi, et notis illustrati a P. Victorino a S. Cruce e scholis piis. Nunc plurimis animadversionibus historico-chronologico-criticis, nec non diplomatibus, literis publicis, re genealogica, numaria, variique generis antiquis aeri incisis monumentis aucti a P. Gelasio a S. Catharina ejusdem instituti sacerdote.* Pars I-II. Pragae, 1761-1763.—17

Dobrowsky's Slavin. Bothschaft aus Böhmen an alle slawischen Völker, oder Beiträge zu ihrer Charakteristik, zur Kenntniß ihrer Mythologie, ihrer Geschichte und Alterthümer, ihrer Literatur und ihrer Sprachkunde nach allen Mundarten. Mit einem Anhange: der böhmische Cato, vollständige Ausgabe in vier Büchern. Zweite verbesserte, berichtigte und vermehrte Auflage. Von Wenceslaw Hanka. Prag, 1834.—15-16

Dolch, O. *Geschichte des deutschen Studententhums von der Gründung der deutschen Universitäten bis zu den deutschen Freiheitskriegen.* Leipzig, 1858.—531

Douglas, H. *An Essay on the Principles and Construction of Military Bridges and the Passage of Rivers in Military Operations.* Third Edition. London, 1853.—168

Dupré de Saint-Maure, E. *L'Hermite en Russie, ou Observations sur les moeurs et les usages russes au commencement du XIXe siècle;* Faisant suite à la collection des moeurs françaises, anglaises, italiennes, espagnoles, etc. Tomes 1-3. Paris, 1829.—16

Eichhoff, F. G. *Histoire de la langue et de la littérature des slaves, russes, serbes, bohèmes, polonais et lettons, considérées dans leur origine indienne, leurs anciens monuments, et leur état présent.* Paris-Genève, 1839.—19, 26

[Eichhoff, K. W.] *Berlin, 8. Nov. (Stieber.)* In: *Hermann,* Nr. 45, 12. November 1859 ('Deutschland').—536, 552
— *Stieber.* In: *Hermann,* Nr. 36-38, 40, 42, 43, 10., 17., 24. September, 8., 22., 29. Oktober 1859 ('Schattenbilder der zehnjährigen Corruption in Preußen').—536, 552

Encyclopaedia Britannica, or Dictionary of Arts, Sciences, and General Literature. Eighth edition in 21 volumes. Edinburgh, 1853-1860.—147, 263

Engel, J. Chr. *Geschichte des Ungrischen Reichs und seiner Nebenländer.* In: *Staatskunde und Geschichte von Dalmatien, Croatien, Slawonien, nebst einigen ungedruckten Denkmälern Ungrischer Geschichte.* Zweyter Theil. Halle, 1798.—15

Evans, G. de Lacy. [Speeches in the House of Commons]
— 29 February 1856. In: *The Times,* No. 22304, March 1, 1856.—21
— 3 March 1856. In: *The Times,* No. 22306, March 4, 1856.—22

Expédition d'Igor. In: Eichhoff, F. G. *Histoire de la langue et de la littérature des slaves,*

Congratulate Mr. John Frost, on his Presence in the United States and to Memoralise his Free Return to England'.—42
— *Mr. John Frost to the Secretary of the Chartists of Nottingham.* In: *The People's Paper,* No. 289, November 14, 1857.—210

Fürst Wladimir und dessen Tafelrunde. Alt-Russische Heldenlieder. Leipzig, 1819.—20, 26

Garibaldi, G. *Garibaldi's Proclamation to the Lombards.* In: *The Times,* No. 23319, May 30, 1859.—455

Gatterer, J. Ch. *Einleitung in die synchronistische Universalhistorie zur Erläuterung seiner synchronistischen Tabellen.* Göttingen, 1771.—17

Gebhardi, L. A. *Fortsetzung der Algemeinen Welthistorie durch eine Gesellschaft von Gelehrten in Teutschland und Engeland ausgefertiget.* Ein und fünfzigster Theil. Halle, 1789.—17

Gercken, Ph. W. *Versuch in der ältesten Geschichte der Slaven, besonders in Teutschland.* Aus den besten gleichzeitigen Schriftstellern verfasset. Leipzig, 1771.—17

Gibson, Th. M. [Speech in the House of Commons on 24 March 1859.] In: *The Times,* No. 23263, March 25, 1859.—411

Gladstone, W. E. *Studies on Homer and the Homeric Age.* In Three Volumes. Oxford, 1858.—339

Goethe, J. W. von. *Ein Fastnachtsspiel auch wohl zu tragieren Ostern, vom Pater Brey, dem falschen Propheten.*—541
— *Faust.* Der Tragödie zweiter Teil.—91
— *Götz von Berlichingen mit der eisernen Hand.* Ein Schauspiel.—419, 420
— *Hermann und Dorothea.*—366

Gray, J. *Lectures on the Nature and Use of Money.* Delivered before the Members of the 'Edinburgh Philosophical Institution' during the Months of February and March, 1848. Edinburgh, 1848.—301
— *The Social System: a Treatise on the Principle of Exchange.* Edinburgh, 1831.—301

Griesheim, G. von. *Vorlesungen über die Taktik.* Berlin, 1855.—170, 264

Grimm, J. *Deutsche Grammatik,* Theile I-IV. Göttingen, 1822-1837.—516
— *Geschichte der deutschen Sprache.* Bd. I-II. Leipzig, 1853.—120, 516, 523

[Gyllenborg, C.] *The Northern Crisis. Or, Impartial Reflections on the Policies of the Czar.* Occasioned by Mynheer Von Stocken's Reasons for delaying the Descent upon Schonen. A True Copy of which is prefix'd, verbally Translated, after the Tenour of that in the German Secretary's Office in Copenhagen, October 10, 1716. 2nd ed. London, 1716.—9

Hacquet, B. *Abbildung und Beschreibung der südwest- und östlichen Wenden, Illyrer und Slaven deren geographische Ausbreitung von dem adriatischen Meere bis an den Ponto, deren Sitten, Gebräuche, Handthierung, Gewerbe, Religion u.s.w. nach einer zehnjährigen Reise und vierzigjährigem Aufenthalte in jenen Gegenden dargestellt.* 5 Hefte. Leipzig, 1801-1805.—16
— *Beobachtungen auf einer Reise nach Semlin.* In den Abhandlungen einer Privatgesellschaft in Böhmen. 2 Bd. Prag, 1775.—15

Hamilton, C. [Speech in the House of Commons on 29 February 1856.] In: *The Times*, No. 22304, March 1, 1856.—21

Hansemann, D.J.L. [Speech at a Sitting of the First United Landtag on 8 June 1847.] In: *Preußens Erster Reichstag*. Berlin, 1847. Th. 7.—114

Haxthausen, A. von. *Studien über die innern Zustände, das Volksleben und insbesondere die ländlichen Einrichtungen Russlands*. Th. 1-3. Hannover-Berlin, 1847-1852.—346

Heffter, M. W. *Das Slawenthum*. In: *Unterhaltende Belehrungen zur Förderung allgemeiner Bildung*. Zehntes Bändchen. Leipzig, 1852.—18
— *Der Weltkampf der Deutschen und Slaven seit dem Ende des fünften Jahrhunderts nach christlicher Zeitrechnung, nach seinem Ursprunge, Verlaufe und nach seinen Folgen dargestellt*. Hamburg und Gotha, 1847.—17, 19

Hegel, G. W. F. *Vorlesungen über die Geschichte der Philosophie*.—260
— *Vorlesungen über die Naturphilosophie* als der Encyclopädie der philosophischen Wissenschaften im Grundrisse.—326
— *Die Wissenschaft der Logik*.—249, 259

Heine, H. *Atta Troll. Ein Sommernachtstraum*.—557
— *Deutschland. Ein Wintermärchen*.—42
— 'Die Jahre kommen und gehen...' In: *Buch der Lieder. Die Heimkehr*.—55
— *Kobes I*.—32
— *Den König Wiswamitra*... In: *Buch der Lieder. Die Heimkehr*.—14
— *Ludwig Börne*.—32
— *Testament*.—45
— *Ein Weib*. In: *Romanzen*.—69
— *Zwei Ritter*. In: *Romanzero*—264

Herbert, S. [Speech before the constituents of South Wilts on 19 March 1857.] In: *The Times*, No. 22633, March 20, 1857.—119

Herder, J. G. *Ideen zur Philosophie der Geschichte der Menschheit*. Theil 4, Carlsruhe, 1792.—15

Herrmann, E. *Beiträge zur Geschichte des russischen Reiches*. Leipzig, 1843.—3

Herwegh, G. [*On the occasion of the Federal Marksmen's Festival in Zurich*.] In: *Das Volk*, Nr. 12, 23. Juli 1859 ('Feuilleton').—475, 477

Heß, M. *Naturwissenschaft und Gesellschaftslehre*. Briefe aus Paris, 5. In: *Das Jahrhundert*, Nr. 1, 1857.—106

Hoadley, B. *An Inquiry into the Reasons of the Conduct of Great-Britain, with Relation to the Present State of Affairs in Europe*. London, 1727.—9

[Holleben, H. von] *Militairische Betrachtungen aus den Erfahrungen eines preußischen Offiziers*. Berlin, 1838.—189

Homer. *Iliad*.—512

Horace (Quintus Horatius Flaccus). *Carminum*, III.—9, 271, 546, 549
— *Epistularum*, I.—541
— *Epodos*, II.—353
— *Satirarum*, II, III.—453

Hugo, V. *Napoléon le petit*. Londres, 1852.—266

Humboldt, A. *A Private Letter to Mr. Julius Froebel.* In: *New-York Daily Tribune,* No. 5335, May 27, 1858.—325

James, W. *The Naval History of Great Britain, from the Declaration of War by France in 1793, to the Accession of George IV.* A new edition, with additions and notes, and an account of the Burmese war and the battle of Navarino, by Captain Chamier, R. N. In six volumes. London, 1837.—84

[Jomini, A. H.] *Vie politique et militaire de Napoléon, racontée par lui-même, au tribunal de Cézar, d'Alexandre et de Frédéric.* Tomes 1-4. Paris, 1827.—163, 165-67, 174-77, 289, 293

Jordan, J. Ch. de. *De originibus Slavicis, Opus Chronologico-Geographico-Historicum: Ab antiquitate literis nota, In Seculum usque Christianum decimum: Ex fontibus ipsis antiquis Scriptorum tum Romanorum tum Graecorum, Et ex historiis Variarum aliarum Gentium, Ad res Slavicas illustrandas facientium, deductum.* Tomus 2. Vindobonae, 1745.—16

Juvenal (Decimus Junius Juvenalis). *Satirarum.*—391, 469

Kant, I. *Critik der Urtheilskraft.* Berlin und Libau, 1790.—392

Kapper, S. *Die Gesänge der Serben.* Theile 1-2. Leipzig, 1852.—20
— *Slavische Melodien.* Leipzig, 1844.—20

[Kapper, S.] *Die serbische Bewegung in Südungarn.* Ein Beitrag zur Geschichte der ungarischen Revolution. Berlin, 1851.—20
— *Südslavische Wanderungen im Sommer 1850.* Bände 1-2. Leipzig, 1851.—20
— *A Visit to Belgrade.* London, 1854.—20

Kinkel, G. *An unsere Leser.* In: *Hermann,* Nr. 26, 2. Juli 1859.—468

Kossuth, L. [Letter to J. M' Adam in Glasgow. London, 26 September 1859.] In: *The Times,* No. 23428, October 4, 1859 ('Kossuth and the Hungarians').—505
— *L'Europe, l'Autriche et la Hongrie.* Bruxelles, 1859.—382

Königinhofer Handschrift (Kralodworsky Rukopis). Sammlung altböhmischer lyrisch-epischer Gesänge, nebst andern altböhmischen Gedichten. Aufgefunden und herausgegeben von W. Hanka. Verteutscht und mit einer historisch-kritischen Einleitung versehen von W. A. Swoboda. Prag, 1829.—19, 26

La Guéronnière, A. de. *L'Empereur Napoléon III et l'Italie.* Paris, 1859.—384

Lallerstedt, G. *La Scandinavie, ses craintes et ses espérances.* Paris, 1856.—91

La Marmora, A. F. [Speech of 17 April 1858 in the Chamber of Representatives of the Kingdom of Piedmont.] In: *The Times,* No. 22974, April 22, 1858. 'Sardinia'. (From Our Own Correspondent.) Turin, April 18.—309

Landor, W. S. *To the Editor of 'The Times'.* In: *The Times,* No. 22943, March 17, 1858.—290

Lassalle, F. *Franz von Sickingen.* Eine historische Tragödie. Berlin, 1859.—129, 384, 394, 402, 404, 412, 419-21, 441-46, 449, 460, 461, 477
— *Herr Bastiat-Schulze von Delitzsch, der ökonomische Julian, oder: Capital und Arbeit.* Berlin, 1864.—261, 355, 396, 542
— *Die Philosophie Herakleitos des Dunklen von Ephesos.* Nach einer neuen Sammlung seiner Bruchstücke und der Zeugnisse der Alten dargestellt. Bände I-II. Berlin,

Showing the Transfer to Russia of the Mortgage Held by British Capitalists over its Property and Revenues. London, 1838.—120

Patkul, J. R. von. *Berichte an das Zaarische Cabinet in Moscau, von seinem Gesandtschafts-Posten bey August II. Könige von Polen;* nebst Erklärung der chiffrirten Briefe, erläuternden Anmerkungen, Nachrichten von seinem Leben und andern hieher gehörigen Betrachtungen. Th. I-III. Berlin, 1792-97.—470

Peele, G. *The Turkish Mahomet and Hyrin in the Fair Greek.*—46

[Peter der Große.] *Tagebuch Peters des Großen vom Jahre 1698 bis zum Schlusse des Neustädter Friedens aus dem Russischem Originale übersetzet so nach denen im Archive befindlichen und von Seiner Kayserlichen Majestät eigenhändigen ergänzten Handschriften gedruckt worden.* Berlin und Leipzig, 1773.—9

P[etersen, N.] *Feierstunden-Arbeit eines Arbeiters.* In: *Das Volk,* Nr. 8-10, 12, 16, 25. Juni, 2., 9., 23. Juli, 20. August 1859 ('Arbeiterstimmen').—476

[Petty, W.] *A Treatise of Taxes and Contributions.* London, 1667.—298

P[ieper], W. *The Coup d'Etat in Spain.* In: *The People's Paper,* No. 221, July 26, 1856.—65

Pitt, L. K. *Ueber den russischen Handel* (*Coxe papers.* Manuscript).—17

Prière d'Adalbert. In: Eichhoff, F. G. *Histoire de la langue et de la littérature des slaves, russes, serbes, bohèmes, polonais et lettons, considérées dans leur origine indienne, leurs anciens monuments, et leur état présent.* Paris-Genève, 1839.—19

Proudhon, P. J. *Handbuch des Börsen-Speculanten.* Hannover, 1857.—90
— *Manuel du spéculateur à la bourse.* Paris, 1857.—90, 106
— *Système des contradictions économiques, ou Philosophie de la misère.* Tomes I-II, Paris, 1846.—90

Prutz, R. E. *Literaturgeschichte.* In: *Deutsches Museum,* Nr. 24, 10. Juni 1858 ('Literatur und Kunst').—356

[Pulszky F.] *From Our Own Correspondent. London, April 23, 1858.* In: *New-York Daily Tribune,* No. 5319, May 8, 1858 ('The State of Europe').—318, 324
— *From Our Own Correspondent. Monday, August 7, 1859.* In: *New-York Daily Tribune,* No. 5720, August 23, 1859 ('The State of Europe').—493, 505, 507
— *From Our Own Correspondent. London, Tuesday, Oct. 11, 1859.* In: *New-York Daily Tribune,* No. 5775, October 26, 1859 ('The State of Europe').—523

Pyat, F. *Lettre au jury. Défense de la lettre au Parlement et à la Presse.* Londres, 1858.—339, 345

Pyat, F., Besson, A., Talandier, A. *Letter to the Parliament and the Press. With a Preface by the Publisher.* London, 1858.—277, 278

Pyat, F., Rougée, Jourdain, G. *Lettre à la Reine d'Angleterre.* In: *L'Homme,* No. 45, 10 october 1855.—37

Quételet, A. *Sur l'homme et le développement de ses facultés, ou Essai de physique sociale.* Tomes I-II. Paris, 1835.—286
— *A Treatise on Man and the Development of his Faculties.* Edinburgh, 1842.—286

Quintilian (Marcus Fabius Quintilianus). *De institutione oratoria.*—218

Radowitz, J. M. [Speech in the Frankfurt National Assembly on August 12, 1848.] In: *Neue Rheinische Zeitung,* Nr. 76, 15. August 1848.—398

Schlosser, Fr. Chr. *Zur Beurtheilung Napoleon's und seiner neuesten Tadler und Lobredner, besonders in Beziehung auf die Zeit von 1800-1813.* Frankfurt am Main, 1835.—170

Schlözer, A. L. *Allgemeine Nordische Geschichte.* Aus den neuesten und besten Nordischen Schriftstellern und nach eigenen Untersuchungen beschrieben, und als eine Geographische und Historische Einleitung zur richtigern Kenntniß aller Skandinavischen, Finnischen, Slavischen, Lettischen, und Sibirischen Völker, besonders in alten und mittleren Zeiten. In: *Fortsezung der Algemeinen Welthistorie durch eine Geselschaft von Gelehrten in Teutschland und Engeland ausgefertiget.* Ein und dreyßigster Theil. Verfasset von August Ludwig Schlözer. Halle, 1771.—16

— *Несторъ. Russische Annalen in ihrer Slavonischen Grundsprache verglichen, übersetzt, und erklärt.* Theile 1-5. Göttingen, 1802-09.—16

— [*Vorschlag zu einer allgemeinen vergleichenden slawischen Sprachlehre und Wörterbuch*]. In: *Allgemeine Nordische Geschichte.* Halle, 1771.—16

— *Vorschlag das Russische vollkommen richtig und genau mit Lateinischer Schrift auszudrücken.* In: Schlözer, A. L. *Несторъ. Russische Annalen in ihrer Slavonischen Grundsprache verglichen, übersetzt, und erklärt.* Zweiter Teil. Göttingen, 1802.—16

[Schnurrer, Ch. F.] *Slavischer Bücherdruck in Würtemberg im 16 Jahrhundert.* Ein litterarischer Bericht. Tübingen, 1799.—16

Schönaich, Ch. O. von. *Hermann, oder das befreyte Deutschland, ein Heldengedicht.* Mit einer Vorrede ans Licht gestellet von Joh. Chr. Gottscheden. Leipzig, 1751.—375

[Schramm, R.] [*Correspondence*]. *Ostende, 31 August.* In: *Hermann,* Nr. 36, 10. September 1859 ('Vermischte Nachrichten').—502

[Seiler, F. S.] *Caspar Hauser, der Thronerbe Badens.* Paris, 1847.—13, 22

Senior, N. W. *Letters on the Factory Act, as it affects the Cotton Manufacture, addressed to the Right Honourable the President of the Board of Trade, to which are appended, a Letter to Mr. Senior from Leonard Horner, Esq., and Minutes of a Conversation between Mr. Edmund Ashworth, Mr. Thomson and Mr. Senior.* London, 1837.—283

Serbische Hochzeitslieder, herausgegeben von Dr. Wolf Stephansohn Karadgich. Metrisch in's Deutsche übersetzt und von einer Einleitung begleitet von E. Eugen Wesely. Pest, 1826.—20

Shaftesbury, A. A. C. *To the Editor of 'The Times'.* In: *The Times,* No. 23201, March 12, 1859 ('The Neapolitan Exiles').—455

Shakespeare, W. *Hamlet, Prince of Denmark.*—55

— *King Henry IV.*—46, 127, 444

— *King Henry V.*—127

— *The Merry Wives of Windsor.*—127, 444

— *Much Ado about Nothing.*—33

— *Othello, the Moor of Venice.*—55

— *Plays of W. Shakespeare.* With Notes of Samuel Johnson.—46

— *The Tempest.*—81

Siborne, W. *History of the War in France and Belgium, in 1815.* Containing Minute Details of the Battles of Quatre-Bras, Ligny, Wavre, and Waterloo. Third and revised edition. With remarks upon the Rev. G. R. Gleig's 'Story of Waterloo'. London, 1848.—289

Siebel, C. *Sprüche von Carl Siebel.* Für den *Hermann.* In: *Hermann,* Nr. 33, 20. August 1859 ('Literatur').—485, 500

Simon, L. *Aus dem Exil.* Bände 1-2. Gießen, 1855.—63

[Simon, L., Kolatschek, A., Meyen, E.] *Briefe aus Paris, der Schweiz und London.* In: *Das Jahrhundert,* Nr. 1, 1857.—106

Sire de Franc Boissy (a French song).—6

Slawismus und Pseudomagyarismus. Vom aller Menschen Freunde, nur der Pseudomagyaren Feinde. Leipzig, 1842.—20

Smith, A. *An Inquiry into the Nature and Causes of the Wealth of Nations.* The first edition in two volumes appeared in London in 1776.—284

Sophocles. *Antigone.*—257
— *Oedipus Tyrannus.*—397

Steuart, J. *An Inquiry into the Principals of Political Oeconomy: being an Essay on the Science of Domestic Policy in Free Nations.* Vol. 1-3. Dublin, 1770.—301

Stimmen des russischen Volks in Liedern. Gesammelt und übersetzt von P. von Goetze. Stuttgart, 1828.—20

Stocqueler, J. H. *The Military Encyclopaedia. A Technical, Biographical, and Historical Dictionary, Referring Exclusively to the Military Sciences, the Memoirs of Distinguished Soldiers, and the Narratives of Remarkable Battles.* London, 1853.—135

Stritter, J. G. *Geschichte der Slaven vom J. 495-1222, aus den Byzantinern vollständig beschreiben.* In: *Fortsezung der Algemeinen Welthistorie durch eine Geselschaft von Gelehrten in Teutschland und Engeland ausgefertiget.* Ein und dreyßigster Theil. Verfasset von August Ludwig Schlözer. Halle, 1771.—16
— *Memoriae Populorum, Olim ad Danubium, Pontum Euxinum, Paludem Maeotidem, Caucasum, Mare Caspium, et Inde Magis ad Septemtriones Incolentium, e Scriptoribus Historiae Byzantinae.* Tomus II. Petropoli, 1774.—17

[Struve, G.] *Bildung macht frei!* (Aus der Newyorker *Socialen Republik*). In: *Die Neue Zeit,* Nr. 22, 27. November 1858.—359

[Stur, L.] *Die Beschwerden und Klagen der Slaven in Ungarn über die gesetzwidrigen Uebergriffe der Magyaren.* Vorgetragen von einem ungarischen Slaven. Leipzig, 1843.—20

Talvj (Jakob-Robinson, Th. A. L. von). *Volkslieder der Serben.* Metrisch übersetzt und historisch eingeleitet. Theile 1-2. Leipzig, 1853.—20, 26

Tassilier. *Letter of Citizen Tassilier. To the Minister of Marine.* In: *The People's Paper,* No. 206, April 12, 1856.—31, 37

Taube, F. W. von. *Historische und geographische Beschreibung des Königreiches Slavonien und des Herzogthums Syrmien, sowohl nach ihrer natürlichen Beschaffenheit, als auch nach ihrer ißigen Verfassung und neuen Einrichtung in kirchlichen, bürgerlichen und militärischen Dingen.* I. Buch, Leipzig, 1777.—15

Terence (Publius Terentius Afer). *Andria.*—310, 410

Terentianus Maurus. *De litteris, syllabis et metris* (*Carmen heroicum*).—441

Theyls, W. *Mémoires pour servir à l'histoire de Charles XII, roi de Suède.* Leyde, 1722.—470

Thiersch, Fr. *De l'état actuel de la Grèce et des moyens d'arriver à sa restauration.* En deux volumes. Leipzig, 1833-34.—120

Tooke, Th., Newmarch, W. *A History of Prices, and of the State of the Circulation, during the Nine Years 1848-1856.* In two volumes; forming the fifth and sixth volumes of *The History of Prices from 1792 to the Present Time,* London, 1857.—102, 126

Trübner's Bibliographical Guide to American Literature. A Classed List of Books Published in the United States of America during the Last Forty Years. With Bibliographical Introduction, Notes, and Alphabetical Index. London, 1859.—399

Türr, I. *To the Editor of the 'Presse d'Orient'.* In: *The Free Press,* No. 18, June 30, 1858.—324, 326

Tucker, E. *Political Fly-Sheets,* Nos. I-XII. London, 1853-54, 1855.—110, 111

Unterhaltende Belehrungen zur Förderung allgemeiner Bildung. 1-27 Bändchen. Leipzig, 1851-56.—17

[Urquhart, D.] *Diplomatic Transactions in Central Asia, from 1834 to 1839.* London, 1841.—120

Urquhart, D. *Familiar Words as Affecting England and the English.* London, 1855.—301

Various Papers on the Genius and Character of the Russians (geschriben zu Zeit d. Catherina), 1768. (*Coxe papers,* Vol. 178.)—17

Virgil (Publius Virgilius Maro). *Aeneid.*—9, 315, 399

Vischer, Fr. Th. *Aesthetik oder Wissenschaft des Schönen.* Zum Gebrauche für Vorlesungen. Bd. 1-4. (Theile 1-3.) Reutlingen und Leipzig, Stuttgart, 1846-57.—270

Vogt, K. [Speech in the Frankfurt National Assembly on 26 May 1849.] In: *Stenographischer Bericht über die Verhandlungen der deutschen constituirenden Nationalversammlung zu Frankfurt am Main.* Bd. 9. Frankfurt am Main, 1849.—525
— *Studien zur gegenwärtigen Lage Europas.* Genf und Bern, 1859.—436

[Vogt, K.] *Zur Warnung.* Bern, den 23. Mai. In: *Schweizer Handels-Courier,* Nr. 150 (Ausserordentliche Beilage), 2. Juni 1859.—458, 525, 546, 550

Voigt, J. *Geschichte Preussens,* von den ältesten Zeiten bis zum Untergange der Herrschaft des deutschen Ordens. Bände 1-5. Königsberg, 1827.—16

Wachsmuth, W. *Hellenische Alterthumskunde aus dem Gesichtspunkte des Staats.* The first edition in 2 parts appeared in Halle in 1826-1830.—259

Walewski, A. [Speech at a Plenary Session of the Paris Peace Congress on 8 April 1856.] In: *The Times,* No. 22352, April 26, 1856: 'Count Walewski upon the State of Europe'.—42

Weerth, G. *Humoristische Skizzen aus dem deutschen Handelsleben.* In: *Kölnische Zeitung,* Nr. 318, 14. November 1847; Nr. 337, 3. Dezember 1847; No. 348,

14. Dezember 1847; Nr. 33, 2 Februar 1848; *Neue Rheinische Zeitung,* Nr. 1-4, 16, 18, 28; 1-4., 16., 18., 28. Juni 1848; Nr. 31, 6. Juli 1848.—103

Westphalen, Chr. H. Ph. von. *Geschichte der Feldzüge des Herzogs Ferdinand von Braunschweig-Lüneburg.* Nachgelassenes Manuskript von Christian Heinrich Philipp Edler von Westphalen. Hrsg. von F.O.W.H. v. Westphalen. Bd. 1-2. Berlin, 1859.—574

Wette, W. M. L. de. *Lehrbuch der hebräisch-jüdischen Archäologie nebst einem Grundrisse der hebräisch-jüdischen Geschichte.* Zweite, verbesserte Auflage. Mit zwei lithographirten Tafeln. Leipzig, 1830.—259

Whiteside, J. [Speech in the House of Commons on 25 March 1859.] In: *The Times,* No. 23264, March 26, 1859.—431

Wilks, W. *Palmerston in Three Epochs: a Comparison of Facts with Opinions.* London, 1854.—111, 115

Wuk's Stephanowitsch kleine Serbische Grammatik verdeutscht und mit einer Vorrede von Jacob Grimm. Nebst Bemerkungen über die neueste Auffassung langer Heldenlieder aus dem Munde des Serbischen Volks, und der Uebersicht des merkwürdigsten jener Lieder von Johann Severin Vater. Leipzig und Berlin, 1824.—26

Wurm, Ch. Fr. *Diplomatische Geschichte der Orientalischen Frage.* Leipzig, 1858.—432

Záboj, Slawoj, Ludiek. In: *Königinhofer Handschrift* (*Kralodworsky Rukopis*). Prag, 1829.—19

Ørsted, A. S. Af mit Livs og min Tids Historie. Vol. 1-4. Kjøbenhavn, 1851-57.—132

DOCUMENTS

Accounts Relating to Trade and Navigation for the Seven Months Ended July 31, 1858. In: *The Economist,* No. 783 (supplement), August 28, 1858.—343

An Act for the more effectually preventing Seditious Meetings and Assemblies; to continue in force until the End of the Session of Parliament next after Five Years from the passing of the Act. [24th *December* 1819.] In: *The Statutes of the United Kingdom of Great Britain and Ireland; 60° Geo. III. & 1° Geo. IV.* London, 1822.—108

An Act for the more effectual Prevention and Punishment of blasphemous and seditious Libels. [30th *December* 1819.] In: *The Statutes of the United Kingdom of Great Britain and Ireland; 60° Geo. III. & 1° Geo. IV.* London, 1822.—108

An Act to Amend the Laws Relating to the Importation of Corn, June 26, 1846. In: *The Statutes of the United Kingdom of Great Britain and Ireland, 9 & 10 Victoria, 1846.* London, 1847.—215

An Act to authorize Justices of the Peace, in certain disturbed Countries, to seize and detain Arms collected or kept for purposes dangerous to the Public Peace; to continue in force until the Twenty fifth Day of March One thousand eight hundred and twenty two. [18th *December* 1819.] In: *The Statutes of the United Kingdom of Great Britain and Ireland; 60° Geo. III. & 1° Geo. IV.* London, 1822.—108

An Act to prevent Delay in the Administration of Justice in Cases of Misdemeanor. [23

December 1819.] In: *The Statutes of the United Kingdom of Great Britian and Ireland; 60° Geo. III. & 1° Geo. IV.* London, 1822.—108

An Act to prevent the Training of Persons to the Use of Arms, and to the Practice of Military Evolutions and Exercise. [11th *December* 1819.] In: *The Statutes of the United Kingdom of Great Britain and Ireland; 60° Geo. III. & 1° Geo. IV.* London, 1822.—108

An Act to Regulate the Issue of Bank Notes, and for Giving to the Governor and Company of the Bank of England Certain Privileges for a Limited Period. [19th *July* 1844.] In: *The Statutes of the United Kingdom of Great Britain and Ireland, 7 & 8 Victoria, 1844.* London, 1844.—202, 215, 224

An Act to subject certain Publications to the Duties of Stamps upon Newspapers, and to make other Regulations for restraining the Abuses arising from the Publication of blasphemous and seditious Libels. [30th *December* 1819.] In: *The Statutes of the United Kingdom of Great Britain and Ireland; 60° Geo. III. & 1° Geo. IV.* London, 1822.—108

Bourse du Jeudi 29 octobre 1857. In: *Le Moniteur universel,* No. 303, 30 octobre 1857.—230

Bourse de Jeudi 26 novembre 1857. In: *Le Moniteur universel,* No. 331, 27 novembre 1857.—230

Bourse du Mardi 22 décembre 1857. In: *Le Moniteur universel,* No. 357, 23 décembre 1857.—230

Buchanan, J. [*The President's Message to the XXXVth Congress.*] In: *The Times,* No. 23181, December 20, 1858; *New-York Daily Tribune,* No. 5500, December 7, 1858.—363

[Buol-Schauenstein, K.] *Copie d'une lettre de M. le Comte Buol-Schauenstein à M. le Comte de Cavour en date de Vienne de 19 avril 1859.* In: *Allgemeine Zeitung,* Nr. 116 (Beilage), 26. April 1859.—427

Canning, Ch. J. *Despatch of 17 June 1858 to the Hon. the Secret Committee of the Hon. the Court of Directors.* In: *The Times,* No. 23117, October 6, 1858.—343

— *Despatch of 4 July 1858 to the Hon. the Court of Directors of the East India Company.* In: *The Times,* No. 23117, October 6, 1858.—343

Code Napoléon. Paris und Leipzig, 1808.—23, 124

Copies and Extracts of several letters written by the King of Sweden and his Ministers, relating to the Negotiations of Baron Görtz etc. which letters were found in a ship driven, ashore in Norway by a storm, and published at Copenhagen by order of the King of Denmark. London, 1717.—10

Correspondence 1839-1841, Relative to the Affairs of the East, and the Conflict between Egypt and Turkey. 4 Parts.—120

Correspondence Respecting the Affairs of Italy. From January to June 30, 1848. Presented to both Houses of Parliament by Command of Her Majesty. July 31, 1849. Part II. London, 1849.—431

The Defensive Treaty Concluded in the Year 1700, betwixt His Late Majesty King William of ever Glorious Memory, and His Present Swedish Majesty King Charles the XII.—8

Francis Joseph I. [*Manifesto of 15 July 1859.*] In: *The Times,* No. 23364, July 21, 1859 ('Austria').—473

Gortschakoff, A. M. *Circularschreiben an die russischen Gesandtschaften vom 15(27) Mai 1859.* In: *Allgemeine Zeitung,* Nr. 167, 16. Juni 1859 ('Rußland und Polen').—537

Letters which passed between Count Gyllenborg, the Barons Görtz, Sparre, and others; Relating to the Design of Raising a Rebellion in His Majesty's Dominions, to be Supported by a Force from Sweden. London, 1717.—10

Louis Philippe. *Ordonances du roi* [*of 16 December 1847*]. In: *Le Moniteur universel,* No. 352, 18 décembre 1847 ('Partie officielle').—229

— [*Speech before the Throne on 28 December 1847.*] In: *Le Moniteur universel, No. 363, 29 décembre 1847 ('Partie officielle').—229*

Memoir on Russia, for the Instruction of the Present Emperor. Drawn up by the Cabinet in 1837. In: *The Free Press,* No. 7, July 13, 1859.—465, 468, 470, 476, 500

Memoir on the State and Prospects of Germany. Drawn up under the Direction of a Minister at St. Petersburgh, and Confidently Communicated to Several of the German Governments. In: *The Portfolio,* Vol. I, London, 1836.—468

Napoleon III. *Decret autorisant la fonction des operations des sociétés la Caisse paternelle et la Minerve.* In: *Le Moniteur universel,* No. 75, 15 mars 1856.—133

— [*Decree on grain reserves of 16 November 1858*]. In: *Le Moniteur universel,* No. 322, 18 novembre 1858.—357, 381

— *Discours de S. M. L'Impereur.* Session législative de 1859. In: *Le Moniteur universel,* No. 39. Edition extraordinaire, 7 février 1859.—384

— [*Speech at a reception for members of the State Council, the Senate and the Corps législatif in the Palace of Saint-Cloud on July 19, 1859.*] In: *Le Moniteur universel,* No. 201, 20 juillet 1859.—473

— [*Speech before the diplomatic corps on 21 July 1859.*]. In: *Le Moniteur universel,* No. 203, 22 juillet 1859 ('Partie non officielle').—476

Papers Relative to Military Affairs in Asiatic Turkey, and the Defence and Capitulation of Kars. Presented to both Houses of Parliament by Command of Her Majesty. London, 1856.—28, 31, 34, 37

[Pozzo di Borgo, K. O.] *Copy of a Despatch from Count Pozzo di Borgo, Addressed to Count Nesselrode. Dated Paris, 10th (22nd) December, 1826.* In: *The Portfolio,* Vol. I, London, 1836.—468

— *Copy of a Very Secret Despatch from Count Pozzo di Borgo, dated Paris, the 28th November, 1828.* In: *The Portfolio,* Vol. I, London, 1836.—468

Report from the Select Committee on Bank Acts; Together with the Proceedings of the Committee, Minutes of Evidence, Appendix and Index. Ordered, by the House of Commons, to be Printed, 30 July 1857.—342

Report from the Select Committee on the Bank Acts; Together with the Proceedings of the Committee, Minutes of Evidence and Index. Ordered, by the House of Commons, to be Printed, 1 July 1858.—342

Report from the Select Committee of the House of Commons, on the High Price of Gold Bullion. Ordered to be printed, 8 June 1810.—377

Reports of the Inspectors of Factories to Her Majesty's Principal Secretary of State for the Home Department, for the Half Year ending 31st October 1858. Presented to both Houses of Parliament by Command of Her Majesty. London, 1858.—389

Russisches Memoir zur Belehrung des gegenwärtigen Kaisers. Verfast vom Cabinet im Jahre 1837. In: *Das Volk,* Nr. 12, 13, 14, 15, 16; 23., 30. Juli, 6., 13., 20. August 1859.—476, 479

Schleinitz, A. [*Despatches to the Prussian embassies in Britain, Russia and Germany, Berlin, June-July 1859*]. In: *Neue Preußische Zeitung,* Nr. 170, 24. Juli 'Zu der "Vermittlung" '; Nr. 171, 26. Juli 'Preußische Depeschen'; Nr. 174, 29. Juli 1859. 'Deutschland', and *Allgemeine Zeitung,* Nr. 210 (Beilage), 29. Juli 1859 ('Erlaß des Grafen Rockberg an Frhrn. v. Koller'); Nr. 211, 212 (Beilage), 30., 31. Juli 1859 ('Diplomatische Actenstücke').—520, 538

Situation de la banque de France et de ses succursales. In: *Le Moniteur universel,* Nos. 163, 191, 12 juin, 10 juillet 1857.—152

Situation de la banque de France et de ses succursales. In: *Le Moniteur universel,* Nos. 282, 317, 345, 9 octobre, 13 novembre, 11 décembre 1857.—230

Société générale de Crédit mobilier. Rapport présenté par le conseil d'administration dans l'assemblée générale ordinaire des actionnaires du 28 avril 1857. In: *Le Moniteur universel,* No. 120, 30 avril 1857.—133

Traité de garantie entre l'Autriche, la France et la Grande-Bretagne, signé à Paris, le 15 avril 1856.—107

Traité de limites entre la Russie et la Chine, signé à Aighoun, le 16/28 mai 1858.—349

The Treaty between Her Majesty and the Emperor of China, signed at Tien-sin, June 26. In: *The Times,* No. 23109, 27 September 1858 ('The Treaty with China').—347, 362

[Wesselowsky, F. P.] *Mémoire Présenté à Sa Majesté Britannique, par Monsieur Wesselowsky, Ministre de Sa Majesté Czarienne* (A Memorial Presented to His Britannic Majesty, by Monsieur Wesselowsky, Minister from His Czarish Majesty), London, 1717.—9

ANONYMOUS ARTICLES AND REPORTS PUBLISHED IN PERIODIC EDITIONS

Allgemeine Zeitung (Augsburg), Nr. 169, 16. Juni 1856: [*Report from*] *Hannover.* 'Deutschland'.—56
— Nr. 13, 13. Januar 1857: *Die örtliche Vertheidigung des Bodensees.*—95
— Nr. 63 (Beilage), 4. März 1857: [*Reports from*] *Pera, 20 Febr.; Konstantinopel, 20 Febr.* 'Türkei'.—109
— Nr. 102 (Beilage), 12. April 1859: [*Report from*] *New-York, 19. März.* 'Vereinigte Staaten von Nordamerika'.—417
— Nr. 298, 25. Oktober 1859: [*Report from*] *Augsburg, 24. Okt.* 'Deutschland'.—514, 519

Berlinische Nachrichten von Staats- und gelehrten Sachen. 27. Februar 1856.—21

Cobbett's Annual Register. From July to December, 1802. Vol. II, London, 1810: 'Summary of Politics'.—266

The Economist, No. 744, November 28, 1857: (*From Our Correspondent.*) *Paris, Thursday.* 'Foreign Correspondence'.—216
— No. 745, December 5, 1857: *The Deeper Causes of the Recent Pressure.*—217

INDEX OF PERIODICALS

Advertiser—see *The Morning Advertiser*

Allgemeine Zeitung—a conservative daily founded in 1798; from 1810 to 1882 it was published in Augsburg.—3, 13, 22, 26, 56, 95, 110, 169, 345, 392, 417, 474, 488, 498, 503, 505, 507, 508, 513, 515, 519, 520-27, 532-34, 537, 540, 542, 543, 545, 549, 554

Der Anzeiger des Westens—a German-language newspaper published in Saint-Louis (USA) from 1835; in the 1850s it took a democratic stand; during the Civil War it supported the slave-owning states (from 1863).—356

Augsburger—see *Allgemeine Zeitung*

Berlinische Nachrichten von Staats- und gelehrten Sachen—a German semi-official government newspaper of a constitutional-monarchist trend (from 1848); it appeared in Berlin from 1740 to 1874 six times a week; also called *Spenersche Zeitung* after its publisher.—21

Bremer Tages-Chronik. Organ der Demokratie—a German democratic newspaper published in Bremen from 1849 to 1851 under the title *Tages-Chronik.* It was edited by Rudolph Dulon. From January 1851 it appeared under this very title.—519

Le Charivari—a French republican satirical newspaper published in Paris from 1832 to 1934; during the July monarchy it sharply criticised the government; in 1848 it supported Cavaignac's dictatorship.—278

Cobbett's Annual Register—a radical weekly published in London from 1802 to 1835 under different titles.—266

Le Constitutionnel—a French daily published in Paris from 1815 to 1817 and from 1819 to 1870; during the 1848 revolution it voiced the views of the monarchist bourgeoisie (the Thiers party); after the coup d'état of December 1851 it became a Bonapartist newspaper.—73, 290, 381

Constitutionelles Blatt aus Böhmen—a German-language daily published in Prague in 1848-49.—26

Kölner—see *Kölnische Zeitung*

Kölnische Zeitung—a daily published in Cologne from 1802 to 1945; it took an anti-revolutionary stand and attacked the *Neue Rheinische Zeitung* in 1848-49; in the 1850s it expressed the interests of the Prussian liberal bourgeoisie.—26, 103, 336, 375, 382, 385, 388, 437, 463, 474, 571

Колоколъ (*The Bell*)—a revolutionary-democratic newspaper; it was published by Alexander Herzen and Nikolai Ogaryev from 1857 to 1867 in Russian and in 1868-69 in French *(La Cloche)* with Russian supplements; it was published in London until 1865, then in Geneva.—349, 467

Kreuz-Zeitung—see *Neue Preußische Zeitung*

Londoner Deutsche Zeitung—a daily of the German refugees, supporters of the unification of Germany under Austria's supremacy; it appeared in 1858 and 1859 first under this title, then under the title *Germania;* in 1859 Ermani was its editor.—438

Der Maikäfer, eine Zeitschrift für Nicht-Philister—a handwritten weekly founded by Gottfried Kinkel and Johanna Mockel in Bonn in 1840; it ceased publication in 1848, with the outbreak of the revolution in Germany.—370

Manchester Daily Examiner & Times—a liberal newspaper founded in 1848 by the merger of the *Manchester Times* and *Manchester Examiner;* it supported the Free Traders in the 1840s and in 1850s; the newspaper was published until 1894 under different titles.—5, 6, 11, 113, 203, 233

Manchester Examiner—see *Manchester Daily Examiner & Times*

The Manchester Guardian—a daily founded in Manchester in 1821; organ of the Free Traders and from the mid-nineteenth century of the Liberal Party.—5, 6, 11, 75, 80, 83, 92, 105, 106, 109, 110, 119, 121, 203, 204, 207, 211, 219, 224, 225, 233, 241, 243, 251-52, 258, 262, 265-67, 275-76, 279, 284, 285, 288-89, 295, 296, 305, 308, 310, 569

Mannheimer Abendzeitung—a German radical daily founded by Karl Grün; it was published from 1842 to 1848.—351

Mittheilungen aus Justus Perthes' geographischer Anstalt über wichtige neue Erforschungen auf dem Gesammtgebiete der Geographie—a German geographical monthly published in Gotha under the editorship of August Petermann from 1855.—349

Moniteur—see *Le Moniteur universel*

Le Moniteur universel—a daily published in Paris from 1789 to 1901 (under this title from 1811); official government organ from 1799 to 1869.—82, 94, 133, 193, 266, 273, 290, 336, 357, 381, 384, 473, 476

The Morning Advertiser—a London daily published from 1794 to 1934; organ of the radical bourgeoisie in the 1850s.—42, 99, 112, 114, 119, 243, 318, 362, 363, 431, 533, 534

The Morning Herald—a London conservative daily published from 1780 to 1869.—75

SUBJECT INDEX

A

F

N

S

T

U

V